BIOGRAPHICAL DICTIONARY
OF
HISPANIC LITERATURE
IN THE
UNITED STATES

BIOGRAPHICAL DICTIONARY
OF
HISPANIC LITERATURE
IN THE
UNITED STATES

The Literature of
Puerto Ricans, Cuban Americans,
and other Hispanic Writers

EDITED BY

Nicolás Kanellos

GREENWOOD PRESS
New York • Westport, Connecticut • London

Library of Congress Cataloging-in-Publication Data

Kanellos, Nicolás.
  Biographical dictionary of Hispanic literature in
the United States ; the literature of Puerto Ricans,
Cuban Americans, and other Hispanic writers
    Bibliography: p.
    Includes index.
    1. Puerto Rican literature—Bio-bibliography—
Dictionaries.   2. Puerto Rican literature—History
and criticism—Dictionaries.   3. American literature—
Puerto Rican authors—Bio-bibliography—Dictionaries.
4. American literature—Puerto Rican authors—History
and criticism—Dictionaries.   5. Cuban American literature—Bio-bibliography—Dictionaries.   6. Cuban American
literature—History and criticism—Dictionaries.
7. Spanish literature—United States—Bio-bibliography—
Dictionaries.   8. Spanish literature—United States—
History and criticism—Dictionaries.   I. Title.
PQ7420.2.K3   1989   016.86′09′973   88-37288
ISBN 0-313-24465-0 (lib. bdg. : alk. paper)

British Library Cataloguing in Publication Data is available.

Library of Congress Catalog Card Number: 88-37288
ISBN: 0-313-24465-0

First published in 1989

Greenwood Press, Inc.
88 Post Road West, Westport, Connecticut   06881

Printed in the United States of America

∞

The paper used in this book complies with the
Permanent Paper Standard issued by the National
Information Standards Organization (Z39.48-1984).

10 9 8 7 6 5 4 3 2 1

Contents

Preface

The *Biographical Dictionary of Hispanic Literature in the United States* is designed to make accessible to the English-language reader a literary world that, for the most part, has been articulated only in Spanish. To this end, citations of Spanish-language passages and titles will appear in the original Spanish accompanied by an English translation. In referring to titles of works, the following notation systems will be used:

Enterrado Vivo (1960, Buried Alive)—if there is no English edition.

La carreta (1961, *The Oxcart,* 1969)—providing publication dates of both Spanish and English editions.

Time's Now/Ya es tiempo (1985)—indicating a bilingual edition.

In the following introduction and within the entries, the use of an asterisk (*) preceding the last name of an author indicates that there is an entry on the subject. Please note that in Spanish compound names, the legal surname starts with the subject's father's surname, and generally the name is alphabetized here by that paternal surname: Matías *Montes Huidobro, José *Sánchez-Boudy. Some authors may be known by either of their surnames. In these cases, the alternate forms are entered as cross references and both names appear in the index: for instance: SANCHEZ-BOUDY, José (main entry) and BOUDY, José Sánchez (cross reference); HERNÁNDEZ CRUZ, Victor (main entry) CRUZ, Victor Hernández (cross reference).

Each entry in the dictionary begins with a statement that summarizes the importance of the subject and indicates the literary genres and themes cultivated. This is followed by a brief biography of the author, an analysis of major works and themes, and a survey of the criticism of the author's works. As many of the writers covered in this reference guide are new or have been writing within the context of a minority and marginalized literature, the survey of criticism may at times be lacking or very brief. Each entry is followed by a bibliography of works by and about the writer. The former is organized by genre and then chronologically; the latter alphabetically. A general bibliography on Hispanic literature of the United States is included at the end of the dictionary.

Introduction

The *Bibliographical Dictionary of Hispanic Literature in the United States* is a reference guide to representative figures in Hispanic literature within the geographic, political, and cultural boundaries of the United States. For the most part, the dictionary concentrates on contemporary writers who have made or promise to make a lasting contribution to multiethnic letters in this country. The geographic boundaries of this volume extend to the island of Puerto Rico, as a commonwealth of the United States, in addition to the fifty states of the union. With the major exemption of Mexican American writers, who are featured in another Greenwood Press dictionary, *Chicano Literature: A Reference Guide,* edited by Julio A. Martínez and Francisco A. Lomelí (1985), an attempt has been made to include all Hispanic nationality groups residing within the United States whose authors have been productive and have created impact either here or abroad. However, the demographic, political, and historical importance of the Puerto Rican and Cuban communities and the productivity of their authors have made this overwhelmingly a reference to Puerto Rican and Cuban writers. It should also be noted that this dictionary only includes Cuban writers creating their literature in the United States from 1959, the date of the Cuban Revolution, to the present; a forthcoming Greenwood Press dictionary will cover twentieth-century Cuban literature.

There were, indeed, a number of Cuban writers—as well as Puerto Rican, Spanish, Venezuelan, and others—who were productive in Hispanic communities of the United States prior to 1959. Their works were often referred to or appeared in the Spanish-language newspapers that were published in the latter part of the nineteenth century and during the twentieth century, especially in New York and Tampa, Florida. Most of their works have been lost or exist only on newsprint or microfilm, and they have never been studied by scholars. They represent part of the lost or, for the time being, forgotten heritage of Hispanics in the United States. Such is the case of the Cuban playwright, essayist, and columnist Alberto

O'Farill, editor of New York's weekly newspaper *Gráfico* in the late 1920s and early 1930s; the Puerto Rican playwright and poet Franca de Armiño, whose existing only book, of the three published, is *Los hipócritas* (1937, The Hypocrites); and the Venezuelan Alirio Díaz Guevara, who provided us with an early novel of immigration, *Lucas Guevara* (1917). An interesting bibliography published by Joseph Louis Perrier in 1926, *Bibliografía dramática cubana, incluye a Puerto Rico y Santo Domingo* (Cuban Bibliography of Drama, Including Puerto Rico and Santo Domingo), gives us an idea of the rich literary and theatrical life in the Hispanic community of New York during the early 1920s.

As should be expected, there are included here a number of Cuban writers in the United States who see themselves as exiled. However, no such representation has been accorded other Spanish American exiled writers whose work is still viewed very much as a foreign literature and whose residence in the United States is regarded as temporary. The same is true of Hispanic American writers who are teaching in universities in the United States, but whose works are published, circulated, and commented on in Latin America more so than in the United States.

Of course, these are broad guidelines that may be subject to various interpretations and debate. Essentially, this dictionary attempts to identify a corps of writers who are firmly rooted in substantial Hispanic communities in the United States and whose works are published, distributed, and studied in Spanish, English, or both languages primarily in the United States and Puerto Rico.

Puerto Rican Literature

Puerto Rican culture today is a product of the powerful political, economic, and social forces that descend upon small native populations and attempt to evangelize, assimilate, and otherwise transform them. In the case of Puerto Rico, in 1493 Christopher Columbus initiated the process that forever would make of the island's people a blend of the cultures and races of Europe, Africa, and the Americas. It was this act of "discovery" that also resulted in Puerto Rico becoming a colony in the Spanish Empire until 1898, when it was passed into the possession of the next empire to dominate the hemisphere, the United States. It is therefore as a territory subject to overseas rule—politically, economically, and aesthetically as well—that Puerto Rico has been insinuated into the artistic geography of the Americas.

Despite the vulnerability of its colonial culture, Puerto Rican literature has been rich. From the middle of the nineteenth century, it first assumed a creole, Hispanic American identity in opposition to Spanish hegemony. And later, in the twentieth century, it highlighted its Latin American identity in opposition to the Anglo-American United States. Whereas the reaction of Puerto Rican artists to the Spanish ideal was to create a nationalism based on mestizo and New World values, the reaction to the powerful presence of the United States has been a tenacious forefronting of the Spanish language itself and of the links to the booming Latin American aesthetic. But the forces of politics and money were to turn one last irrevocable trick on the island culture: the dispersal of more than one-third of the Puerto Rican population to points as far apart as Hawaii and New York in the United States, which took on the proportions of a mass migration during World War II and continued in full force into the 1950s.

The Puerto Rican diaspora, as it is presently called, has affected every social class of the society and further complicated the process whereby a native, American population seeks to develop and protect its national identity. The sons and daughters of the diaspora, during the first thirty years, have been as likely to express themselves in English as in Spanish and as likely to affirm nationalistic sentiments about their Edenic island's past as of their Manhattan or Chicago barrio. For, as with the Jews, a point is reached where the people must survive as a people despite material, geographic, or linguistic circumstances.

It is to be understood from the outset that the literature of the Puerto Rican people has triumphed over geographic, social class, and linguistic determinants or definitions. Both the lumpen and professional classes have proclaimed themselves Puerto Rican in print in Spanish and English and even in a mixture of both languages. As New York poet Tato *Laviera has often stated to me, "I am the grandson of slaves transplanted from Africa to the Caribbean, a man of the New World come to dominate and revitalize two Old World tongues."

At the turn of the century, the island's literature was developing fully along the lines of Latin American Modernism, heavily influenced by French, Peninsular Spanish, and Latin American models. As was the case in Cuba, Mexico, Peru, and Argentina, Puerto Rico turned to its indigenous people, its folklore, and its national archetypes in an effort to define its true identity. The mestizo highlander, or *jíbaro*, and the black and mulatto became keys that opened up doors to the other Caribbean cultures and created a space that was identifiable as home while challenging the imposition of the English language and the purported benefits of Yankee customs and economic power.

Although he was a European-educated intellectual, Luis *Llorens Torres adapted the verse forms of the plaintive mountain songs (*décimas*) and affected the folk speech of the jíbaros in poems that exalted rural values and innate sagacity rather than citified education. His jíbaros remained wisely skeptical and unmoved by the boastful testimonies of Americanized Puerto Ricans about the wonders of Yankee ingenuity and progress.

Luis *Palés Matos was the first Puerto Rican literary figure to achieve a lasting impact on the evolution of Latin American literature, principally through the development of a poetic style that was inspired by the rhythms and language of Africa and the black Caribbean. His revolutionary book, *Tun tun de pasa y grifería* (1937), whose onomatopoetic title has no translation, openly claimed a black African heritage and presence for the cultural makeup of Puerto Rico. But the primitivism, vigor, and freedom of his black verses was only a point of departure for his critical stance toward Europe and the United States. In Palés Matos's little-studied master poem "La Plena de Menéalo" (The Dance of Shake Them Hips), Puerto Rico is personified by a seductive *mulata,* who profusely sweats rum as she dances enticingly close to, but just out of reach of, a drooling Uncle Sam.

Two figures are essential in recognition of the transition of Puerto Rican literature from the island to the mainland: Julia de *Burgos and René *Marqués. The former cultivated luxuriant verses, odes to her beloved countryside, only to die tragically on the streets of New York. Her lyricism served the parallel desires for personal as well as national liberation. René Marqués, the most widely known Puerto Rican playwright, was able to capture, in universally understood symbols, the true meaning of the disruption of native populations and their emigration to foreign lands and values. He may have achieved this better than anyone else in the hemisphere; even more moving than Steinbeck's *Grapes of Wrath* is the plight of the family of displaced mountain folk in Marqués's *La carreta* (1961, *The Oxcart*, 1969). First produced in New York in 1953, this drama of the writer's religious, linguistic, and moral conflict ends with an appeal for an end to the diaspora, a return to the island and the values of the countryside.

To a great extent, today's major Puerto Rican writers on the island still draw upon Marqués's spirit, style, and message in their attempt to preserve the integrity of the Puerto Rican culture and their call for the political independence of the island. Prose writers like José Luis *González Coiscou, Pedro Juan *Soto, Luis Rafael *Sánchez, and Jaime *Carrero satirize the complacency of the Americanized, pro-statehood middle class, as well as the cold and efficient North Americans. They also continue to develop the topos of the Edenic past and the jíbaro as the child of nature, with his intense code of honor and decency. González, in voluntary exile in Mexico City and very much a participant in the Latin American boom, is the creator of beautiful, poetic narrative in such works as *Balada de otro tiempo* (1978, The Ballad of Another Time) in which he harkens back to the way things were before the disruptive influence of the Yankees. Most of today's island novelists, while romanticizing the island's past, have, however, also created a one-dimensional image of Puerto Ricans in New York, only focusing on the tragedy of the rootlessness, poverty, and oppression of these second-class citizens lost in the bowels of the monster city. Such is the case in Soto's *Spiks* (1956), José Luis González's *En Nueva York y otras desgracias* (1973, In New York and Other Disgraces), and Carrero's *Pipo Subway no sabe reír* (1973, Pipo Subway Doesn't Know How to Laugh).

Until recently, scholars and writers have insisted upon the use of a standard, international Spanish in literature, partly as a spiritual and political link to Spain and the rest of Spanish America and partly as a defense against the incursions of English. In many cases this has led to a stilted, artificial style not capable of capturing the energy and expansiveness of the speech and actions of ordinary people. Marqués's use of mountain dialects in *The Oxcart* was revolutionary for Puerto Rico in its time (1953), although the literatures of Spanish America had gone far beyond this point in claiming their national and regional dialects by then. In *La guaracha del Macho Camacho* (1976, *Macho Camacho's Beat*, 1980), Luis Rafael Sánchez has finally won acceptance for his use of the true vernacular of Puerto Ricans and incorporating it—Anglicisms and dialectical idiosyncrasies and all—into his style. He has proved to the purists that one can still maintain a critical stance toward the United States while employing the "corrupted" or "bastardized" language of a colonized people in a literary text. But beyond that, the language is beautiful, as are the people.

Puerto Rican writing in New York dates back to the end of the nineteenth century and the Spanish-language newspapers that flourished up until the late 1950s, not only as bearers of news and advertising, but also as the primary source for literary essays, poetry, short stories, and serialized novels. Since the nineteenth century there have also existed scores of small presses that published literature in Spanish. Puerto Rican literature in English dates back to the 1930s when Jesús *Colón began to publish his columns in the *Daily Worker*. This represented a rather appropriate beginning, given that most subsequent English-language writers to this day have taken a working-class stance. Unlike the writers of the island, who largely are members of an elite, educated class and many of whom are employed as university professors, the New York writers are products of parents transplanted to the metropolis to work in the service and manufacturing industries. These writers are predominantly bilingual in their poetry and English-dominant in their prose; they hail from a popular tradition heavily influenced by roving bards, salsa-music composers, Hispanic folklore, and the kaleidoscope of American popular culture as experienced in New York.

The New York Puerto Rican writers reach out in solidarity to black, Third World, and other Hispanic writers in the United States and insist that, together with these other multiethnic writers, they represent the only dynamic force of renewal for American literature. Through their verse and prose, they attempt to force the society to accept its mestizo, mulatto, miscegenated culture as its vital force and to relinquish forever its illusion of Nordic purity and monolingualism. In this the New York Puerto Rican writers are building firmly on the foundation established by Palés Matos and other island writers.

The New York Puerto Rican writers, who are as marginalized in America's literary world as they are in the society at large, are members of the true avant-garde of United States letters. Victor *Hernández Cruz, first published by Random House as a teenage jazz poet, has honed his bilingual aesthetic into so fine a cutting edge that his latest book, *By Lingual Wholes* (1982), is forcing readers and reviewers alike to meander through his labyrinth of sound and sense in wondrous discovery and final recognition. Miguel *Algarín, very much the commander of clean and powerful verse, has nurtured his art in the boiling pot of street life and art (*On Call*, 1980), to emerge as a purified seer into the dehumanized, bionic future in his *Body Bee Calling from the 21st Century* (1982). Tato *Laviera, the inheritor of the Spanish oral tradition, with all of its classical formulas, brings both languages and islands (Puerto Rico and Manhattan) together in *Enclave* (1981), a celebration of the diverse personalities of his pantheon: Palés Matos and salsa composers, the neighborhood gossip and John Lennon, Miriam Makeba and Tito Madera Smith. His first book, *La Carreta*

Made a U-Turn (1979), recalls Marqués's *Oxcart* and redirects it right back to the heart of the New York barrios: Puerto Rico can be found here too. Laviera's latest book, *AmeRícan* (1986), calls for full representation of Puerto Ricans in United States society and art. Sandra María *Esteves's book of poems, *Yerba buena* (1980, Mint), is an open proclamation that being Puerto Rican and black and female and working-class are universalizing and respectable qualities. Along with Esteves, Louis *Reyes Rivera (*Who Pays the Cost?* 1977) celebrates the great influence of Afro-American literature.

And it is in the image of black writing that Puerto Rican literature first made its mark on English prose in the United States. Piri *Thomas's *Down These Mean Streets* (1967) can best be understood in the tradition of Claude Brown's *Manchild in the Promised Land* and Ralph Ellison's *The Invisible Man*. Miguel *Piñero's New York City Drama Critics Award- and Obie-winning play, *Short Eyes* (1975), as well as his collections of plays, *The Sun Always Shines for the Cool* (1984) and *Outrageous One-Act Plays* (1986), also reveal, in style and language, an art forged among black writers in prisons and ghettoes.

The most productive and recognized Puerto Rican novelist, however, is Nicholasa *Mohr, whose works, *Nilda* (1974), *El Bronx Remembered* (1975), *In Nueva York* (1979), *Felita* (1981), and *Rituals of Survival: A Woman's Portfolio* (1985), have garnered such awards as the 1974 Jane Addams Children's Book Award, *The New York Times* Outstanding Book of the Year 1973 Award, and the *School Library Journal* Best Children's Book of the Year 1973. Unlike Edward Rivera's *Family Installments* (1982), which follows autobiographically along the lines of the immigrant novel, Mohr's works take American society for granted as a point of departure and create totally fictionalized characters who are not overly conscious of an "identity crisis," displacement, or cultural conflict.

Ed *Vega, in his introduction to *The Comeback* (1985), proclaims, "I started thinking about publishing a book. Then it hit me. I was going to be expected to write one of those great American immigrant stories like *Studs Lonigan, Call It Sleep,* or *Father,* which was written by Charles Calitri, one of my English teachers at Benjamin Franklin High School. Or maybe I'd have to write something like *Manchild in the Promised Land* or a Piri Thomas *Down These Mean Streets*. . . . I suppose I could do it if forced to, but I can't imagine writing a great autobiographical novel about being an immigrant. In fact, I don't like ethnic literature all that much except when the language is so good that you forget about the immigrant writing it."

In Puerto Rican literature we have always had the epic of an extremely small minority, given the size of the globe's population, trying to grapple with superpowers, not only in defense of self and identity, but also to proclaim a presence and contribute to humanity.

Cuban American and Cuban Exile Literature

Like Puerto Rican culture in the United States, that of the Cubans dates back to the nineteenth century when writer-philosopher José Martí and other patriots plotted from the United States mainland for Cuban independence from Spain. Martí and numerous other Cuban, Dominican, and Puerto Rican intellectuals published essays, stories, poems, and editorials in scores of Spanish-language periodicals, such as *El Mensajero Semanal* (1828–1830), *El Mercurio de Nueva York* (1828–1833), *La Patria* (1892–1898), *La Voz de la América* (1865–1867), and *Las Novedades* (1893–1918), which were being published in New York City. Later, in the twentieth century, Cubans and Spaniards dominated Hispanic arts and media in New York, with such figures as actor-playwright Alberto O'Farrill not only staging his plays and revues at the Apollo and the Teatro Hispano, but also publishing his stories and commentaries in *Gráfico* (1927–1931), the weekly newspaper that he edited. The late 1920s and 1930s was also the period when the *bufos cubanos,* Cuban musical comedy revues, competed heavily with Spanish *zarzuelas* for popular attention from audiences during the greatest heyday of Hispanic theatre in New York.

While Cuban culture was on the ascendancy in New York, its island literature had already joined that of Mexico and Argentina in the leadership of Spanish American letters since the nineteenth century, with such acknowledged masters as Gertrudis Gómez de Avellaneda, José Echeverría, Julián del Casal, and José Martí, and in the twentieth century with such a patriarch as Nicolás Guillén, who has taken Spanish American letters from negrist and mulatto verse to a pan-Hispanist preoccupation and artistic support for socialist revolution. Cuba has also contributed its share to the Latin American boom, with such writers as Alejo Carpentier, José Lezama Lima, and Gabriel Cabrera Infante.

It is no wonder then that the inheritors of such a rich and dynamic tradition would contribute so greatly to Hispanic culture in the United States, beginning so recently as 1959 with the diaspora following the Cuban Revolution. It should be noted that while the Puerto Rican diaspora really began during World War II when the American economy drew heavily on its island territory for labor resources, the Cubans came as refugees from a land that had never been a political colony of the United States, although it had been a protectorate and an economic dependent of the United States since the Spanish American War. Thus, the Cuban literary aesthetic, unlike the Puerto Rican one, had never been so obsessed with protecting the Spanish language and Hispanic culture while defending itself against Anglo-American culture and language. It should also be mentioned that while the Puerto Rican diaspora was primarily a movement of workers forced to abandon their island to survive economically, the Cuban diaspora, because of its political cause (the socialist revolution), was a movement of a large section of the Cuban professional, intellectual, and monied classes, as well as workers. Numerous writers and intellectuals relocated to the North American continent, many of whom were eventually able to adapt to and become part of the U.S. Hispanic and mainstream cultural institutions.

Today, after almost three decades of new Cuban culture in New York, New Jersey, Miami, Florida, and dispersed throughout the United States—in contrast to the older Cuban American communities in New York City and Tampa,

Florida—a Cuban American literary and artistic presence is developing. Younger writers are no longer preoccupied with exile, with eyes cast solely on the island past; instead, they are looking forward to participating in the English-language mainstream or serving the intellectual and cultural needs of the U.S. Cuban and Hispanic communities. Thus, as there has developed a definite rift between Puerto Rican writers on the island and those on the mainland, so too is there a division between the aesthetics and purpose of the younger writers, like Roberto *Fernández, Iván Acosta, and Dolores *Prida, and the writers of exile, like Lydia *Cabrera, Matías *Montes Huidobro, and José *Sánchez-Boudy. Also, there continues to be an influx of exiled writers, like Heberto *Padilla, newly disaffected from Cuban communism, who must be viewed differently from the earlier generation of exiles who have already created for themselves a solid niche within Hispanic and mainstream institutions, such as publishing houses, periodicals, and universities.

What we have seen during the last decades is first a literature that almost exclusively attacked the Cuban Revolution and Marxism. The novel of exile became, as José Sánchez-Boudy puts it in his *Historia de la literatura cubana (en el exilio)* (1975, The History of Cuban Literature [in exile]), "un arma de penetración política y de propaganda del mismo tipo" (a weapon of political penetration and propaganda of the same sort). Following the first anti-revolutionary novel, *Enterrado Vivo* (Buried Alive), published in Mexico in 1960 by Andrés Rivero Collado, were a host of others published in the United States and abroad by minor writers like Emilio Fernández Camus, Orlando Núñez, Manuel Cobo Souza, Raúl A. Fowler, Luis Ricardo Alonso, and many others. When they were not openly propagandistic and rhetorical, they were nostalgic for the homeland to the point of idealization. Poetry and drama followed the same course, for the most part. Later, political verse would come to form a special genre of its own, what Hortensia Ruiz del Viso in "Poesía Cubana del Exilio" (Cuban Exile Poetry) has called "poesía del presidio político" (political prisoner poetry) as in the works of Angel Cuadra and Heberto Padilla and also of Armando Valladares, who resides in Spain but is quite active in the United States.

A key figure in providing a new direction for Cuban literature in the United States has been Celedonio *González who, beginning with his *Los primos* (The Cousins) in 1971, changed his focus to concentrate on Cuban life and culture in the United States. Later, in *Los cuatro embajadores* (1973, The Four Ambassadors) and *El espesor del pellejo de un gato ya cadáver* (1978, The Thickness of the Skin on a Cat and a Corpse), he not only examined culture shock and conflict between Cubans and Americans, but he also turned his pen to a formidable taboo topic: criticism of the economic system of the United States, especially in its exploitation of Cuban workers. González presents us with Cubans who do not yet see themselves as Americans but who are also conscious that Cuba is no longer theirs.

It is in the theater, however, that a truly Cuban American literature has emerged. Iván Acosta's *El Super* (1982, The Super) for the first time examined with humor and pathos the contradictions of Cuban American society and pointed the way to developing Cuban culture here in the United States, in recognition of the impossibility of return to the island, especially for the younger generations born and raised here. While *El Super* fully explores the nuances of a Cuban dialect heavily influenced by English, it is Dolores *Prida who, as many Puerto Rican and Chicano writers have done, has developed on stage a fully bilingual play, her most popular and as yet unpublished, *Coser y cantar* (To Sew and To Sing), in which the older and younger generations, the Cuban and the American cultures, the male and female principals are humorously explored through the contrasting Spanish and English. It is noteworthy that this period of transition is facilitated by the great repositories of Cuban humor, through which the community, previously defined by political upheaval, can at least laugh at itself, its contradictions and idiosyncrasies. Ironically, these works emerged in New York rather than from Little Havana in Miami.

It was up to Roberto *Fernández, in *La vida es un special* (1982, Life Is on Special) and *La montaña rusa* (1985, The Roller Coaster), to achieve similar success through humor and satire of Miami's Cuban community. In these two continuous, open-formed, montage-like novels, Fernández presents a mordant but loving burlesque of a community transformed by the materialism and popular culture of the United States, but somewhat paralyzed by the nostalgia and political obsession with a communist Cuba. The hilarious parade of characters, language styles, Keystone-cop-type counter-revolutionary movements, and diverse social and artistic events depicted in his works are aimed at the community taking stock of its present circumstances and reckoning with a future here in the United States.

A final symbol of Cuban assimilation and the evolution of Cuban American literature is Oscar Hijuelos's *Our House Is the Last World* (1983), a typical ethnic autobiography, a standard genre in American literature's accommodation of ethnics within the parameters of official United States culture. Hopefully, as with Piri *Thomas among Puerto Rican writers, José Antonio Villarreal among the Chicanos, as well as countless black, Jewish, Italian, and other ethnic authors of autobiography, Hijuelos's book will represent an opening of the door to mainstream commercial publishing for the Cuban American, Puerto Rican, and the other Hispanic writers.

Hispanic Writers in the United States

A

AGOSIN, MARJORIE (1955–). Marjorie Agosin is a poet and critic who specializes mostly in feminist literary criticism. Her first book of poems published in the United States, *Conchalí* (1980), dealt with the poet's dual feelings of estrangement: a longing for her home environment and culture of Chile and, at the same time, the severing of ties with those elements from that same culture that are oppressive to women. This duality is what permeates her artistic and critical endeavors to date.

Biography

Marjorie Agosin was born on June 15, 1955 in Bethesda, Maryland. She spent her childhood and early adolescence in Santiago de Chile and in Quisco, a place near Neruda's Isla Negra. This factor will be of significant importance later on in her artistic career as she tries to build up through her work what Virginia Woolf calls "a room of one's own"; in Agosin's case an island that "no es isla, ni es negra. Es Conchalí" (is not an island, nor black. It's Conchalí) (From *Conchalí*). Returning to the United States when she was sixteen years old, she attended the University of Georgia from which she graduated with a bachelor of arts in philosophy in 1976. Later on, she received her master's and doctoral degrees from Indiana University. Attending Indiana University at a time when that institution was creating strong publications by and about the works of women writers was very important for Agosin. She was greatly influenced by critical feminist publications of the late 1970s and early 1980s such as *Madwoman in the Attic* and *Shakespeare's Sisters*. Since 1982, Agosin has been an assistant professor of Latin American literature at Wellesley College. She is an active lecturer and artist who has devoted a great deal of her time and energies to the cause of the "arpilleras" in Chile, an underground movement of women to fight political repression. For this political activism, she has been featured in articles in the *New York Times* and other newspapers and journals. She is married to John Wiggins, a physicist.

Her first book of poems, *Gemidos y cantares* (Groans and Chants), published in Chile in 1977, was written under the influence and guidance of María Luisa Bombal. It is not surprising then that Agosin's doctoral dissertation and her first book of critical essays are devoted to the study of the works of Bombal herself. The influence of Bombal in Agosin is significant, since early on in her life she was able to have a strong female writer figure as both mentor and role model. In 1980 Agosin published in New Jersey what, in our opinion, is her first important poetic work, *Conchalí*. This collection deals with both the life and experiences of the poet in Mid-American soil (Indiana) and with her own cultural *baggage* embodied in the figures of Pablo Neruda and Nicanor Parra. In indirect admission of the influence of the former in her poetic career, Agosin has recently devoted a Twayne book to the literary evolution of Neruda. A believer in visual imagery, Agosin published jointly with Emma Nolan a book of photographs and poems entitled *Silencio que se deja oír* (The Silence that Can Be Heard) in 1982. Her latest collection of poems, *Brujas y algo más/Witches and Other Things* (1984), shows a more mature writer who has decided to rewrite the myths of women by which our societies live. A recipient of a 1985 Fulbright Fellowship, she has traveled to South America to establish further contacts with other women writers.

Major Themes

It is difficult to speak of the major themes in a writer whose work is in the process of gestation. One can, however, try to point out some of the processes in the work of Agosin that continue to be developed. As I have mentioned earlier, Agosin's first collection of poems published in the United States, *Conchalí*, is the poet's struggle to find her place, her physical space, amidst luminaries in the poetry of her country. Coming to grips with such figures as Bombal, Neruda, and Parra, the poet has had to deal with what Harold Bloom calls "the anxiety of influence," both in poetic as well as personal terms. One of the best poems to illustrate this aspect in Agosin's work is the one entitled "País dividido" (Divided Country) from *Conchalí*. In it, the speaker through her confrontation/ridiculization of the patriarchal system, exemplified in the poem by Neruda and Parra, carves a place for herself amidst literary tradition. Not finding a comfortable place in Neruda's Isla Negra nor in the topos of Parra's *Antipoemas*, Agosin's poetry takes over a space for her poetic self, a room removed from the proximity of the aforementioned poets and their tradition. In that same collection, Agosin deals with the topics of outward oppression, the condition of the lower classes and of women, and with her own position in academia and in a hostile cultural environment.

The poems that accompany the collection of photographs in *Silencio que se deja oír* follow the same vein of exposure of the injustices that victimize women in Latin America. Her most recent collection, *Brujas y algo más*, which presents the reader with translations of her poems by Cola Frazen, is a more precise picture of her craft in the construction of her poetic room within Latin American poetry. In this collection, Agosin takes on again major figures of literary influence, women in this case, Rosario *Ferré in particular, still in search of the completion and definition of her "space."

The most piercing poems in *Brujas y algo más* deal with the breaking of myths that relate to women. In "The Billiard Table: New Bedford, Mass," the reader is confronted with the historic rape of a woman at a bar, a gang rape, on top of a billiard table. The men in the poem are unable to see the woman in her uniqueness and perceive her only as a symbol of patriarchal categories—as a hole/whore with which to practice their sport of sex. The poet, although dealing with the actual woman in this historic incident, is also dealing with the metaphors by which our society lives. These metaphors are as foul-smelling as the men/ rapists. Agosin revises the imagery that normally has assigned foul smell and vaginal odors to women and transposes these to the male. In doing so, Agosin is also addressing the issue of sexual violence. The stinking men symbolize their rotten actions and the role of men as victimizers of women, a role they wish to escape from by accusing women of being "bitches," smelly objects of sexual pleasure, who attract "innocent" men with their "heat." The biological stigma is shifted in the poem from the women to the men in an important re-vision of male/female imagery.

This rewriting of imagery is taken up again and exemplified in another poem of this latest collection entitled "To Anne Frank." In this poem the image of Anne Frank is reverted by the speaker to show her as a naive individual who actually thought that all men were good and who secluded herself and her writing in order to avoid a confrontation with patriarchal violence, a fact that may have destroyed her pristine image of manhood. Agosin's most potent salvos are against Frank's apolitical stand vis-à-vis the horrors that surrounded her and her inability to arm herself with words of malice to describe the repression under which people of her cultural heritage were living. Frank is seen as a tool of the patriarchy who has made her believe the whitewash of goodness in the world even when she is split into pieces and destroyed by the "good" men of the Nazi armies.

In summary, Agosin's poetry to date is an attempt to rewrite the myths that our society lives by—be they associated with literary influence or political repression. We expect her poetry to continue developing in this important direction.

Survey of Criticism

Outside of the introductions to her work by such major literary figures as María Luisa Bombal, Fernando *Alegría, and Elena Poniatowska, most of the studies published on Agosin's work have been by way of book reviews. These have tended to be general in nature, stressing the feminist quality of her work.

Luz María Umpierre holds an article on "the anxiety of influence" in the work of Agosin. There is no definitive book or article on her work. M. Pérez-

Erdelyi holds an interview with the poet that will appear published in *Hispania*. All of Agosin's books written in the United States are in print.

Bibliography

WORKS BY AGOSIN

Poetry

Chile: Gemidos y cantares. Chile: Editorial El Observador, 1977.
Silencio que se deja oír. Bloomington, Indiana: Third Woman Press, 1982.
Brujas y algo más/Witches and Other Things. Pittsburgh: Latin American Literary Review Press, 1984. Translation of poems by Cola Frazen.

Literary Criticism

Las desterradas del paraíso: protagonistas en la narrativa de María Luisa Bombal. New York: Senda Nueva de Ediciones, 1983.
Pablo Neruda. Boston: Twayne World Author Series, 1986.

WORKS ABOUT AGOSIN

Cavallari, Mario. Review of *Conchalí* in *Literatura chilena: creación y crítica* (March 1982): 50.
Umpierre, Luz María. Review of *Conchalí* in *Revista de estudios hispánicos* 8 (1981): 209–11.
———. "La ansiedad de la influencia en Sandra María Esteves y Marjorie Agosin," in *Woman of Her Word: Hispanic Women Write*, ed. Evangelina Vigil. Houston: Arte Publico Press, 1983.

LUZ MARÍA UMPIERRE

ALEGRÍA, FERNANDO (1918–   ). Fernando Alegría has accomplished, in fifty years of intense intellectual activity, a solid oeuvre as a writer, poet, researcher of Latin American literature, and scholar. A resident in the United States since 1940, his creative works (thirteen novels and four volumes of short stories) have centered primarily on the historical reality of Chile, his native country, but also on the conflictive reality of North American society. He began his academic career in the United States, first as a professor of Latin American literature at Berkeley (between 1947 and 1967) and he later went to Stanford, where he was recently awarded the Sadie Dernham Patek Professor in the Humanities chair, in recognition of his outstanding professional work.

Biography

Fernando Alegría was born in Santiago, Chile, on September 26, 1918, to Santiago Alegría Toro and Julia Alfaro. One of his brothers, Santiago Alegría, is a well-known Chilean painter, while his brother Julio was prominent in Chilean political life and was appointed ambassador to Bulgaria during the government of Salvador Allende. Fernando grew up in the Maruri barrio, a colorful and populous sector of Santiago, where the famous poet Pablo Neruda lived when he was a student. Both Alegría and Neruda would remember later in their memoirs how rich and influential their experiences were in this barrio.

Alegría attended the Academia de Humanidades and the Instituto Nacional, two secondary schools highly valued in Chile for their rich humanist tradition. Later he entered the Instituto Pedagógico of the University of Chile, where he received a degree in Spanish and philosophy. The Instituto Pedagógico has been one of the most important centers of cultural and literary formation in Chile, and Fernando Alegría had the unique opportunity to study with prominent Latin American scholars such as Luis Alberto Sánchez, Pedro Henríquez Ureña, Mariano Latorre, Yolando Pino Saavedra, Eugenio González, and the Chilean philosopher Pedro León Loyola.

In 1938 he came to the United States for the first time to participate in the second international meeting of the Youth for Peace movement, which took place at Vassar College in Poughkeepsie, New York. He had just published his first book in Chile, *Recabarren*, a biographical novel of the founder of the Chilean worker's movement. In order to gather the bibliographical information for his book, he had traveled to the northern provinces of Chile, where the union leader had spent most of his time working with the Chilean miners organizing labor unions, as well as political and cultural centers. In New York, Fernando Alegría had the opportunity to visit Harlem and saw one of the hidden faces of North American reality. From this experience came his first short story: "The Country of Harlem." His first two literary works are focused on Chile and the United States, respectively, and they reflect his interest to define the unofficial historical life of the two different cultures. This concern for the emerging social world, for its ongoing struggles and dreams, is a constant theme in Alegría's literary work.

In 1940 he returned to the United States to study psychology at the University of Bowling Green, Ohio, but soon he changed to English literature, obtaining his M.A. with a thesis on Thomas Mann, the prominent German writer who came to live in the United States during the Nazi period and whom Alegría was able to meet personally. Later he went to Berkeley, where he got his Ph.D. in 1947 with his thesis *La poesía chilena. Orígenes y desarrollo del siglo XVI al XIX* (Chilean Poetry. Its Origins and Development from the XVI Century to the XIX Century), published as a book in 1954.

In 1943 he married Carmen Letona Meléndez, then a student of medicine at Berkeley. The four children of the Alegría-Letona marriage grew up and are settled in this country. In Berkeley Algería studied with outstanding scholars such as Rudolph Schevill, S.G. Morley, and Arturo Torres Ríoseco. After spending a year in Chile, he was offered a position to teach Spanish American literature at Berkeley, where he started his academic career in 1947. Between 1947 and 1973 he traveled frequently to Chile, which allowed him to be in direct contact with the social and cultural life of his country and to participate in the artistic events and cultural debates there. In 1958 he was invited to participate in the

First Congress of Chilean Writers, which took place at the University of Concepción, and he later directed one of the first writers' workshops organized by a Chilean university, attended by young authors who would later become important voices in the Chilean literary scene.

Fernando Alegría's work has been distributed equally between literary creation and research projects on Spanish American literature. His publications clearly reflect this dual interest. In 1946 he was awarded the Pan-American Prize for his contribution to the study and dissemination of Spanish American literature in the United States.

In 1970, when Salvador Allende won the presidential elections in Chile, Fernando Alegría was appointed cultural attaché in the Chilean embassy in Washington, where he worked with Ambassador Orlando Letelier. Alegría, who had known Salvador Allende since the 1950s, while collaborating with his political campaigns, now was able to see him every time he traveled to Chile. Planning to write a biography of Salvador Allende, Alegría met the president a few days before the 1973 military coup to discuss the literary project. Allende invited him to the presidential palace on September 11 for lunch. But at 5:00 in the morning a journalist from La Moneda (the presidential palace) called to alert him of a possible coup d'état. That afternoon, when the troops had taken control of the country, he heard a European broadcast on short-wave radio that President Allende had died fighting in the presidential palace. A few days later Fernando Alegría was forced to leave Chile and returned to the United States, this time as an exile.

His life after 1973 has been oriented toward new commitment to his country. He has participated in numerous conferences denouncing the suppression of civil liberties and human rights in Chile and has been instrumental in disseminating the most recent Chilean literary works in the United States. In 1977, with David Valjaló he founded *Literatura chilena en el exilio* (Chilean Literature in Exile), a literary magazine that has helped reestablish a cultural link between exiled Chilean writers and those who remained in Chile. In 1982 he edited the anthology *Chilean Writers in Exile* (New York: The Crossing Press). His own literary work took on a new, expanded dimension, focusing now on the reformulation of contemporary social and cultural history and on the effects of the 1973 military coup on Chilean national life.

Major Themes

Fernando Alegría belongs to the Generation of 1938, a group of writers that is associated in Chile with the process of social changes initiated by the government of the Popular Front, a center-left coalition that won the presidential elections that year. The Generation of 1938 substantially modified the literary traditions that had prevailed in Chile up to that time. It formulated a conception of the novel that went beyond traditional realism and "criollismo" by focusing on the dialectic relationship between subjectivity and the social determination of man, thereby defining a literary style that incorporated into the novel the avant-garde explorations of new Spanish American poetry. In general, the Generation of 1938's narrative is motivated by social concerns. But rather than presenting a realistic description of life, their works expand this reality into a poetic exploration of the narrated world.

One of the prominent thematic lines in the work of Fernando Alegría is the poetic evocation of the *national hero's* adventure: historical characters whose struggles have advanced the social dynamism of national history. His books, *Recabarren* (1938), *Lautaro, joven liberator de Arauco* (1934, Lautaro, A Young Liberator), and *El paso de los gansos* (1975, The Passing of Geese), focus on three key figures in the history of Chile: Lautaro, the Indian soldier who started his people's struggle for independence during the Spanish conquest; Recabarren, the founder of the worker's movement at the beginning of this century; and Salvador Allende, the political leader and statesman who led one of the most original projects of social changes in contemporary Latin America. The mode of discourse Alegría adopts to narrate the national hero's story is not the traditional biography, but the "biographical novel," in which the historical account of life and events takes on a poetic form.

The complement of this thematic line is the adventure of the *popular hero*: the anonymous character who represents the dreams and daily struggles of the common people to reach a level of social and human dignity in the world. This unknown hero is the protagonist in novels like *Caballo de copas* (1957, Jack of Clubs), *Los días contados* (1968, Counted Days), *La maratón del Palomo* (1968, The Palomo Marathon), and several short stories. In the series on the *national hero*, the concrete testing ground for the dream of historical changes is the overall Chilean society. In the series on the *popular hero*, however, it is the intimate, day-to-day world of the barrio. Here the confrontation is not seen as a warlike or political struggle, but rather as a modest athletic event. But this sporting adventure (for example, the horse González in the racetracks of San Francisco, the marathon runner Palomo on the streets, and the boxer Victorio in the barrio championships) defines a humanity that questions the rules of society's game in the act of losing or delaying an intimate victory.

In general, Alegría's is a narrative that seeks to give literary representation to the heroes and social groups denied or forgotten by official history, a history that in Latin America (although this phenomenon seems to be universal) traditionally has been written by those in power. For Fernando Alegría, these figures that have neither public monuments nor acknowledgment in official history books are the true "fathers of the country." The dialectic bond between the hero and the people is presented with full, poetic intensity in his lyric work, especially in his book *Instrucciones para desnudar a la raza humana* (1979), recently translated into English under the title *Changing Centuries* (1984).

Another significant theme in the author's narrative is the reevaluation of the historical, social, and cultural experience of the Generation of 1938, his generation. Like Cuban writer Alejo Carpentier, Alegría perceives history not as an unfolding of causes through time, but as the dialogical process in which the past proposes certain directions toward the future and the present modifies the hierarchies of the past. This was Fernando Alegría's perspective when he turned his attention to the experience of 1938 in order to redefine it in terms of the specific circumstances of his present. *Mañana los guerreros* (1964, Tomorrow the Warriors), his first book focusing on 1938 as a metaphor for a historical period, evaluated this experience with the optimistic attitude that prevailed among progressive Chilean intellectuals at the beginning of the 1960s. His second book on this theme, the autobiographical novel *Una especie de memoria* (1983, A Type of Memoir), is an intimate recollection of the Generation of 1938's dreams and a reflection of history from the standpoint of a character who has just experienced the overthrow of the Salvador Allende government and the destruction of the democratic system in Chile.

During the 1950s, several Chilean authors focused on the exploration of contemporary life in their country from an existential point of view, in a narrative style that, fortunately, never really took on a solid development. To a certain extent, Fernando Alegría paid tribute to this fleeting narrative tendency, and his novels *Camaleón* (1950, Chameleon), *Las noches del cazador* (1961, The Nights of the Hunter), the collection of short stories *El Poeta que se volvió gusano* (1956, The Poet Who Turned into a Worm), and *El cataclismo* (1960, The Cataclysm) waver between existential subjectivism and the search for a social basis for his characters.

His works after 1973, *El paso de los gansos* (1975), *Coral de guerra* (1979, Coral of War), and *Una especie de memoria* (1983), written from the problematic perspective of the exiled writer, correspond to a new stage in the formulation of his thematic concerns and aesthetic principles. These works continue redefining his vision of contemporary Chilean history, but this time the recent past, the social and cultural projects of his country, the individual and collective dreams are reordered by a ''poetic memory'' with license to freely mix the real and the historical with the imagined and the dreamed. The theme that unites these novels is the search for an imaginary foundation of Chile. This attention to the creative capacity of language places his latest works within the realm of the renovating parameters of the so-called ''Latin American boom's narrative.'' Fernando Alegría has been associated with important Latin American writers such as Julio Cortázar, Ernesto Roa Bastos, Juan Rulfo, and Gabriel García Márquez, among others, and this relationship over the years has stimulated the outpouring of an increasingly original work.

Finally, another distinctive theme in Fernando Alegría's narrative is the description of the contradictory nature of North American society. In his long period of residence in this country, Alegría has become well acquainted with North American literature and has been in contact with many writers, including the Beat poets of San Francisco. He translated and introduced to Chilean readers poems by Ginsberg and Ferlinghetti. His literary works with North American themes analyze the unofficial side of this country from the perspective of the ethnic minority group or the dissident Latin American intellectual. Short stories such as "El país de Harlem" or "El otro lado de la cortina" describe the black and Chicano reality; *Caballo de copas* (1957) is a picaresque novel about a Chilean horse and its rider trying to survive in San Francisco; *Amerika, Amerikka, Amerikkka* (1970, *The Funhouse*, 1986) is a powerful reflection of the Viet Nam war from a Latin American perspective; and his book of poems, *Changing Centuries* (1984), is a poetic vision of the conflictive relationships between Latin America and the United States as well as a meditation on the meaning of history. A literary autobiography centered on his professional experience in the United States is forthcoming.

Survey of Criticism

The traditional criticism that prevailed before the 1960s usually discussed the narrative of Fernando Alegría in terms of certain thematic nuclei, highlighting the ideological perspective and the "social criticism" of the author. During the 1960s, in which a new generation of literary critics emerged in Chile (critics with a solid basis in the new methods of literary analysis), his work began to be studied with an emphasis on its creative values. At the end of the 1960s the Chilean critics Carlos Opazo and Nelson Osorio published two important articles analyzing the narrative structure of *Caballo de copas*, considered one of the finest novels by the author. Shortly after, Fernando Aínsa, Julio Ortega, Luis Leal, and Augusto Roa Bastos published critical pieces on *Los días contados, Amerika, Amerikka, Amerikkka*, and Alegría's short stories.

In 1972 Helmy F. Giacomán edited a volume compiling the principal essays on the work of Fernando Alegría up to that time, entitled *Homenaje a Fernando Alegría*. In the United States, his work is attracting growing critical attention, with several master's and doctoral theses being written on the author. Up to the present, three monographs on his literary work have been published: *Fernando Alegría: vida y obra* (1979) by René Ruiz; *Figuras y contrafiguras en la poesía de Fernando Alegría* (1981) by Moraima Semprún; and *Fernando Alegría: el escritor y su época* (1985) by Víctor Valenzuela.

Other works by the author that have received important critical attention, in addition to *Caballo de copas*, are his three novels published after the military coup. The best of these critical works include essays by Mario Cavallari (on *El paso de los gansos*) and by Marjorie Agosin and René Jara (on *Coral de guerra*).

I recently compiled a selection of new critical essays on Fernando Alegría which will be published in homage to his fifty years of intellectual work. This book (forthcoming from Latinoamericana Editores—Stanford University) includes two articles (by Walter Hoefler and myself) on his poetry, a creative facet that, in our opinion, requires greater critical attention.

Finally, I should mention the book that Fernando Alegría and I have written in collaboration, entitled *Nos reconoce el tiempo y silba su tonada. Una autobiografía literaria* (Santiago, Chile: Ediciones LAR, 1987). It is an interview centered on the relation between the author's social and cultural experiences and his literary work, which evolved into a literary autobiography. This book will include an up-to-date bibliography on the author.

Bibliography

WORKS BY ALEGRÍA

Recabarren. Santiago, Chile: Editora Antares, 1938.
Ideas estéticas de la poesía moderna. Santiago, Chile: Ediciones Multitud, 1939.
Leyenda de la ciudad perdida. Santiago, Chile: Editorial Zig-Zag, 1942.
Lautaro, joven libertador de Arauco. Santiago, Chile: Editorial Zig-Zag, 1943.
Ensayo sobre cinco temas de Thomas Mann. San Salvador, El Salvador: Editorial Funes, 1949.
Camaleón. México: Edición y Distribuidora Iberoamericana, 1950.
La poesía chilena. Orígenes y desarrollo del siglo XVI al XIX. Berkeley: University of California Press, 1954.
Walt Whitman en Hispanoamérica. México: Ediciones Studium, 1954.
El poeta que se volvió gusano y otras historias verídicas. México: Cuadernos Americanos, 1956.
Caballo de copas. Santiago, Chile: Editorial Zig-Zag, 1957.
Breve historia de la novela hispanoamericana. México: Ediciones de Andrea, 1959.
El cataclismo. Santiago, Chile: Editorial Nascimento, 1960.
Las noches del cazador. Santiago, Chile: Editorial Zig-Zag, 1961.
La literatura chilena del siglo XX. Santiago, Chile: Editorial Zig-Zag, 1962.
Mañana los guerreros. Santiago, Chile: Editorial Zig-Zag, 1964.
Novelistas contemporáneos hispanoamericanos. Boston: D. C. Heath, 1964.
Historia de la novela hispanoamericana. 2a. ed. México: Ediciones de Andrea, 1965; 3a. ed. 1966; 4a. ed. 1974; 5a. ed. 1986.
Viva Chile, M. . . . Santiago, Chile: Editorial Universitaria, 1965.
Genio y figura de Gabriela Mistal. Buenos Aires: Eudeba, 1966.
Como un árbol rojo. Santiago, Chile: Editora Santiago, 1968.
Los días contados. México: Siglo XXI Editores, 1968.
Instructions for Undressing the Human Race. San Francisco: Kayak Press, 1968.
La maratón del Palomo. Buenos Aires: Talleres Gráficos Garamond, 1968.
Los mejores cuentos de Fernando Alegría. Santiago, Chile: Zig-Zag, 1968.
Ten Pastoral Psalms. San Francisco: Kayak Press, 1968.
La literatura chilena contemporánea. Buenos Aires: Centro Editor de América Latina, 1969.
La venganza del general. Caracas: Editorial Monte Avila, 1969.
Amerika, Amerikka, Amerikkka, manifiestos de Viet Nam. Santiago, Chile: Editorial Universitaria, 1970.
Literatura y revolución. México: Fondo de Cultura Económica, 1970.
Changing Times. New York: Che Ediciones, 1972.
La prensa, Latin American Press Reader. Boston: D.C. Heath, 1973.
La ciudad de arena. Buenos Aires: Ediciones de la Flor, 1974.
El paso de los gansos. Long Island, N.Y.: Ediciones Puelche, 1975.
Coral de guerra. México: Nueva Imagen, 1979.
Instrucciones para desnudar a la raza humana. México: Nueva Imagen, 1979.
Retratos contemporáneos. New York: Harcourt Brace Jovanovich, 1979.

Chilean Writers in Exile. Trumansburg, N.Y.: The Crossing Press, 1982.
Una especie de memoria. México: Nueva Imagen, 1983.
Changing Centuries. Selected Poems. Pittsburgh: Latin American Literary Review Press, 1984.
The Funhouse. Houston: Arte Publico Press, 1986.
Nos reconoce el tiempo y silba su tonada. Una autobiografía literaria (in collaboration with Juan Armando Epple). Santiago, Chile: Ediciones LAR, 1987.

WORKS ABOUT ALEGRÍA

Epple, Juan Armando. *Para una fundación imaginaria de Chile. La literatura de Fernando Alegría*. Lima, Peru: Latinoamericana Editores 1987.
Gaicomán, Helmy F. *Homenaje a Fernando Alegría. Variaciones interpretativas en torno a su obra*. New York: Las Americas Publishing Co., 1972.
Ruiz, René. *Fernando Alegría: vida y obra*. Madrid: Playor, 1979.
Semprún de Donahue, Moraima de. *Figuras y contrafiguras en la poesía de Fernando Alegría*. Pittsburgh: Latin American Review Press, 1981.
Valenzuela, Víctor. *Fernando Alegría: el escritor y su época*. Madrid: Artes Gráficas Belzal, 1985.

                                                        JUAN ARMANDO EPPLE

ALGARÍN, MIGUEL (1941–   ). Miguel Algarín is a poet, a playwright, a writer of fiction and prose, a teacher, and proprietor of the Nuyorican Poets Cafe. He is a prominent figure in the New York Puerto Rican community of artists and writers known as the Nuyoricans.

Biography

   Miguel Algarín was born in Santurce, Puerto Rico, on September 11, 1941. He is the second child of three (an older brother, Arturo, and a younger sister, Irma) born to Maria Socorro and Miguel Algarín. During his childhood in Puerto Rico, Miguel's mother operated a catering service and a jewelry store and his father managed a chain of Shell gas stations to support their immediate family and the extended family that became Miguel's father's charge when his own father died. With this there was not a great deal of money to go around, but there were a great many pleasurable moments in gardens and open spaces and on trips to the outlying parts of the island where Miguel's grandmother lived. Algarín has fond recollections of his mother and father when he was young. His was a family with a great deal of love and affection. His father was a quiet, musically gifted person who taught Miguel to play the violin and to love opera and classical music. He also introduced him to the ribald humor of Abbot and Costello and the strange characters those two met up with. His mother taught him the value of language and the importance of using words with great care.
   The Algaríns moved to New York City in the early 1950s along with many other Puerto Ricans looking for a better life after the industrialization of Puerto Rico. They settled in Spanish Harlem for a time during which the older Miguel

and Miguel's uncle went into the parking lot business in Queens, and Miguel's mother began the community work, in which she still is very involved today. Her senior citizens groups entertain for religious holidays, and songs that she has written are sung in cabarets around the city of New York.

The Algarín family settled in Queens and the young Miguel began his college education at City College, transferring later to the University of Wisconsin where he received his bachelor's degree in 1963. He went on to earn a master's degree at Pennsylvania State University in 1965. After teaching English literature at Brooklyn College and New York University for a time, Algarín was offered a teaching assistantship at Rutgers to do his doctorate. At present Algarín is an associate professor of English and chairman of the Puerto Rican Studies Department soon to be renamed the Puerto Rican, Hispanic, Caribbean Studies Department to reflect a growing constituency. Miguel Algarín was securing his education just before the period when the American education system had awakened to the fact that minority students were handicapped from the very beginning of their education and that it was necessary to create special programs and "open admissions" in order for them to take part in programs many Americans took for granted. Luckily his family environment was supportive of education, and he had been put into the academic program in New York City high schools, so that he received scholarships on the basis of grades. He also was just ahead of a time in the late 1960s and early 1970s when there was a flurry of attempts to redress the inadequacies of minority education by establishing departments of black studies, Puerto Rican studies, and other such departments, many of which have been aborted since, victims of an everchanging political atmosphere. Since Algarín was a member of a substantial English Department at Rutgers and since he knew the Puerto Rican community and could draw from its strength, he was in a position to help fashion a Puerto Rican studies program that would have solid ties with the English Department and be out of the path of the prevailing political winds. He has made use of the talents of prominent personalities in Puerto Rican music, theater, and politics to engage students, making that department one of the fastest growing departments on the New Brunswick campus and one that reflects the broader Hispanic community of which its student body is composed.

One of Miguel Algarín's most important contributions to community life and particularly to the community of arts and letters is the Nuyorican Poets Cafe. It is an outgrowth of the informal meetings of writers in Algarín's Lower East Side apartment that had virtually turned into a salon. One day he noticed an empty storefront across the street, and that night he sat there instead of in his apartment; thus was born the Nuyorican Poets Cafe. It was a very informal affair; no announcements of events were made. The writers simply showed up to read their works, and people came, all sorts and conditions of people, but those from the working class made up the bulk of the audience and the writers. If the cafe began as something of a Puerto Rican hangout, it soon involved blacks, Germans, Japanese, Irish, and anyone else who wanted to join in. Anyone could read anything, the only limitation being the patience of the audience—its noise level was the test. The cafe branched out at one point to include radio station BAI over which community and international issues ranging from rape to nuclear warfare were discussed. Today the Nuyorican Poets Cafe is being renovated not only in response to but at the same time as the "gentrification" of the Lower East Side is taking place. Whether the working-class nature of this unique institution will be affected is an open question. Algarín is quick to credit others who worked hard to get the cafe on its feet; nevertheless it is his conception and, to a large extent, his salary that for so long has provided a space for writers to be heard.

Algarín can recall the precise moment when he began writing seriously: April 27, 1967. At first his work was ordered collections of words expressing his feelings and insights about his life and the lives of those around him. Four years later he began to collect what he wrote and was asked to contribute to an anthology, *The New Consciousness*. In 1975 Algarín and Miguel *Piñero compiled *Nuyorican Poetry: An Anthology of Puerto Rican Words and Feelings*. This was a landmark publication in that for the first time the poetry of the first full-fledged generation of Puerto Ricans who had spent their formative years on the mainland was identified. The poets in this anthology (which included Algarín and Piñero) called themselves Nuyoricans (New York Puerto Ricans or even new Puerto Ricans in New York); they derived from the urban working class and they wrote for the community they lived in. The language they used was English, and idiomatic English influenced by Spanish and by black English. It was a language that evolved from the street. In Algarín's "Introduction: Nuyorican Language," he explains how Nuyorican identification is centered in language and the political and social ramifications of such a designation.

Major Themes

One of Algarín's poems in *Nuyorican Poetry* became the title of his first book of poetry, *Mongo Affair*, published in 1978. *Mongo Affair* comes out of the work Algarín was doing in the late 1960s and early 1970s in New York City. The poems in it begin with a recognition of the importance of the Nuyorican presence today as well as the Puerto Rican past on the island. They then stretch into the larger scheme of looking for sources in the Old World, especially as seen through language. *Mongo Affair* is divided into four sections. The first, "Short Circuits," centers thematically on the absence of communication among people, even those seemingly close to one another. Algarín sees our minds flooded by electrical impulses, both intellectual and emotional, which are "short-circuited" because we send and receive unclear messages to and from one another. What results from this, suggests Algarín, is a lack of trust and an inability to get in touch with others. This is particularly clear in the last poem of the first section, "What's My Day Like?" Parts I and II of "El Capitán San Miguelito" make up the second section of *Mongo Affair*. These two poems have been read and recited in many places in New York. They further elaborate on the theme of trust. They are an exploration of a street leader, San Miguelito, who creates confrontations that have no substance, but only serve to further his own aims. In the third section, "Currents Corrientes Courants," four Nuyoricans travel from Amsterdam to Tangiers in order to expand their view of the Old World. "Nuyorican Air," the fourth and last section, is made up of bilingual songs, expressing this second-generation Puerto Rican's strong negative/positive feelings about his home, Manhattan, and the persistent clash between the poet's idea of the sense of community of the barrio dweller and what he sees as the ever-present pressure from mainstream America for a homogeneous culture.

The title of Algarín's second book of poetry, *On Call*, suggests the importance of being alert to the real meaning and intent of language. The poet is interested in word order and structure in *On Call*, as is evident in the title of the first and longest section, "Turning Point Grammar." Thematically there are two tendencies in this book, the primary one being that of celebration. Poets, dancers, musicians, and the common people are celebrated beginning in Manhattan, moving across the continent to the Northwest, down the West Coast through San Francisco, and finally to the land of the Pueblo Indians as the poet explores what he calls "the mental landscape" of North America. Algarín demonstrates through the Latin rhythms and the interweaving of English and Spanish in the poems the liberating qualities of music and language. The second tendency in *On Call* is to give voice to the oppressed people of the nation who have been denied what is free and responsive in human existence.

Body Bee Calling from the 21st Century (1982) concerns the ethical problems of the next century. The language he uses in *Body Bee* is strictly English as opposed to a Spanish/English blend. But there is also a new language, one that is necessary because of the new situation confronting people of the twenty-first century. Geographically *Body Bee* covers Rome, Houston, New York, and finally outer space where a station has been set up for the human mutations who have survived the holocaust of nuclear destruction. These poems pose some basic moral questions. What if humans become mere machines because of endless organ transplants? Will only the cerebral count for something, the body being superfluous? What if sex should be a mere release of tension instead of a means for procreation? What matter of being will humans have in the century to come? What is the result of actions we are taking as a human family today? Algarín deals with all these issues and more, ending with a plea for the human race to think ahead. *Body Bee* has been performed as a ballet, choreographed by Miguel Algarín (his first experience with this particular art form). The spaceship built especially for the production still hangs in the Nuyorican Poets Cafe.

Algarín's most recent publication is *Time's Now/Ya Es Tiempo* which he appropriately presents bilingually since the themes he uses often involve Latin America, an area of great concern to him. In Section I Algarín looks at the lives and feelings of the people of South, Central, and North America and writes some love poems to them. His second section explores the politics of Latin America and the United States' presence there. A third section concentrates on finding the ultimate language to communicate with God or that power that is beyond human power.

Algarín is the translator of Pablo Neruda's *Canción de gesta (A Song of Protest)* and the co-author with Tato *Laviera of *Olú Clemente* which was performed at Delacorte Theater in the summer of 1973. He is on the advisory board of the Association of Hispanic Arts in New York City and of *MELUS (Journal of the Society for the Study of Multi-Ethnic Literature of the United States)* and a contributing editor to *The Americas Review* (formerly *Revista Chicano-Riqueña*). He has directed the Nuyorican Playwrights'/Actors' Workshop, which was formed to develop playwrights and actors simultaneously.

Survey of Criticism

There is very little criticism on Miguel Algarín per se. Treatments of him usually are incorporated with pieces on Nuyorican writers in general, these being scarce as well. The main reasons for this are twofold: 1) this writing is relatively new, the Nuyorican writers being a first generation of Puerto Rican writers on the mainland; 2) it has been very difficult to obtain this literature, a situation that may be changing in the near future. The commentary of Efraín Barradas in his "Introducción" to *Herejes y Mitificadores* is useful for a reader first approaching these writers.

Bibliography

WORKS BY ALAGRÍN

Nuyorican Poetry: An Anthology of Puerto Rican Words and Feelings. New York: William Morrow and Co., 1975. Compiled with Miguel Piñero.
Canción de gesta/A Song of Protest. New York: William Morrow and Co., 1976. Translator.
Mongo Affair. New York: Nuyorican Press Book, 1978.
"Volume and Value of the Breath in Poetry." *Revista Chicano-Riqueña* 6, 3 (1978).
On Call. Houston: Arte Publico Press, 1980.
"Nuyorican Literature." *MELUS* (Summer 1981).
Body Bee Calling from the 21st Century. Houston: Arte Publico Press, 1982.
Time's Now/Ya es tiempo. Houston: Arte Publico Press, 1985.
Contributor to *Here, Box 749, Dodeca, Contact II, Mag City,* and other publications.

WORKS ABOUT ALGARÍN

Daydítolson, S. Review of *Herejes y mitificadores: muestra de poesía puertoriqueña en los Estados Unidos,* ed. Efraín Barradas and Rafael Rodríguez. *Bilingual Review* 10 (1983): 81–86.
Mohr, Eugene V. *The Nuyorican Experience.* Westport, Conn.: Greenwood Press, 1982.
Morton, C. "Nuyoricans (New York and Puerto Ricans)." *Latin American Theatre Review* 10 (1976): 80–89.
Santiago, S. "The Nuyoricans." *Village Voice* (February 1979): 14.

Turner, F. "The Evolution of Mainland Puerto Rican Writers." *World Literature Written in English* (WLWE). (Spring 1980): 74–84.
———. Review of *On Call* by Miguel Algarín. *Melus* (Spring 1981).

Anthologies

A Decade of Hispanic Literature: An Anniversary Anthology, ed. Nicolás Kanellos. Houston: *Revista Chicano-Riqueña*, 1981.
Herejes y mitificadores: muestra de poesía puertorriqueña en los Estados Unidos, ed. Efraín Barradas and Rafael Rodríquez. Río Piedras: Ediciones Huracán, 1980.
Nuyorican Poetry: An Anthology of Puerto Rican Words and Feelings, ed. Miguel Algarín and Miguel Piñero. New York: William Morrow and Co., 1975.

FAYTHE TURNER

ARRIVÍ, FRANCISCO (1915–). Francisco Arriví is noted as a playwright, eassyist, poet, and theater director. His most famous play, *Vejigantes* (1958, Masked Devils), assured his fame as a dramatist in Puerto Rico and abroad. *Vejigantes* has been translated into English, anthologized, performed by professionals and amateurs, and has been the subject of scholarly criticism.

Biography

Francisco Arriví was born in 1915. He attended primary and secondary school in Santurce, Puerto Rico. Arriví graduated from the University of Puerto Rico in 1938 with a degree in Spanish. From 1938 to 1941 he was a member of the faculty of the Ponce High School, where he taught Spanish language and literature.

Between 1941 and 1948 Arriví worked as scriptwriter and director of the Escuela del Aire, sponsored by the Department of Education. He attended Columbia University's School of Drama in 1948. In 1949 he returned to Puerto Rico where he was offered a position at WIPR Radio, the public broadcast station. For the next ten years he worked as director and scriptwriter there.

Arriví became the director of the Festival de Teatro Puertorriqueño in 1960, a position he held for many years. *Vejigantes* had its premiere during the first of these festivals in 1959. In fact, most of his plays have been performed in this yearly theatrical event sponsored by the Instituto de Cultura Puertorriqueña.

Arriví's trajectory as a playwright is quite complex. A number of his plays remain unpublished. Arriví has also rewritten some of his plays and these have been performed and printed under different versions. The list of his unpublished dramas includes: *El diablo se humaniza* (1940, The Devil Is Humanized), *Alumbramiento* (1945, Enlightment), *Cuento de hadas* (1949, Fairy Tale), *Caso del muerto en vida* (1951, The Case of the Dead Man in Life), and several versions of *María Soledad*. His published plays, many of which were first published by *Asomante*, include: *Club de solteros* (1950, Bachelors' Club), *María Soledad* (1961), and all the plays that comprise the trilogy *Máscara puertorriqueña* (1971, Puerto Rican Mask): *Bolero y plena* (Bolero and Plena), *Sirena* (Siren), and *Vejigantes*.

Arriví has published a number of essays over the years. His most important collection is *Areyto mayor* (1966, Major Dance Drama). The main topic of his essays is the Puerto Rican theatre. *Vía poética* (1978, The Poetic Path) contains Arriví's major collections of poems dating from 1958. In 1980 another volume of his poetry was published.

Arriví is retired from public life but continues his writing career. In 1982 he was selected Conferenciante Humanista del Año and for this occasion he read a paper entitled "Voluntad del ser puertorriqueño en mi poesía, teatro y ensayo." Even in his retirement Arriví has maintained his interest in Puerto Rican drama and culture.

Major Themes

The trilogy *Máscara puertorriqueña* (1971) contains the major dramas of Arriví. By studying them chronologically one can see the development of Arriví's main theme: racial prejudice in Puerto Rico. One can also discover another important concern of the author's: the search for identity and authenticity. *Bolero y plena* is made up of two one-act plays. The first one, *El murciélago* (The Bat), takes place in New York City. The second play, *Medusas en la bahía* (Jelly Fish in the Bay), begins the treatment of the racial theme. Augusto, who has spent his life in conflict with his racial heritage, makes a futile attempt to effect a reconciliation with his black cousin and ends up killing himself.

Sirena presents the story of a mulata who undergoes surgery in order to please and conquer her white boss whose child she is expecting. Although Cambucha does not succeed as temptress the play has a happy ending.

The culmination of the theme of racial prejudice is found in *Vejigantes*. The first act opens in Loíza Aldea, a predominantly black town, where Toña is seduced by a white Spaniard. The next two acts take place forty-eight years later in the house of Toña's daughter, Marta. She is ashamed of her African heritage; she wears a turban to hide her hair and makes Toña hide from the Condado neighbors. Clarita, Marta's daughter, is fairer and more aware than her mother, as her name implies. The conflict arises when Bill, a Southerner and Clarita's beau, starts asking questions about miscegenation and about Marta's turban. Marta tries to perpetuate her myth of racial purity but Clarita speaks the truth. The drama ends with the reconciliation of the three women and a celebration of their heritage.

There are common elements that unify these plays besides the theme: the use of music (*bolero, plena, danza, bomba,* respectively) as a leitmotif; the use of lights; and the characters who are unable to come to grips with their particular reality and are at a loss about their true identity. The mask motif also serves as a unifying element: the soap Augusto sells that is supposed to whiten your skin; the white makeup that Cambucha wears. In the last play this motif is more direct. The *vejigantes* are masked figures, typical of the feast of Santiago in Loíza

Aldea, representative of evil. These masked dancers appear at the beginning and at the end of the play.

Arriví must be recognized as the dramatist who dared to bring to the public an unrecognized tension in the Puerto Rican psyche. His other plays have never received the acclaim of *Máscara puertorriqueña* but they reflect Arriví's preoccupation with the search for identity and authentic values.

Arriví has also written essays and poetry. Beyond the scholarly merits of his essays, their value is as a document of the Puerto Rican theater since the late 1930s. His poetry, seldom studied, can be described as modern in its form and hermetic in its content. The beauty of it can be easily detected in its richness of imagery inspired by the Island. His best poetic production can be found in the dialogues of his plays.

Survey of Criticism

Throughout his career as a dramatist Arriví has gained recognition from Island critics and scholars. Reviews of all his plays can be found in the local newspapers and journals.

In her most recent book *Literatura puertorriqueña: su proceso en el tiempo* (1983), Josefina Rivera de Alvarez calls Arriví one of the innovators of the theater in Puerto Rico. Marqués is the other one. Angelina Morfi, *Historia crítica de un siglo de teatro puertorriqueño* (1980), again couples him with Marqués and describes their work as the culmination of the development of drama in Puerto Rico. She calls Arriví "nuestro dramaturgo poeta."

The most detailed analysis of Arriví's dramas can be found in Jordan B. Phillips's book of 1973, *Contemporary Puerto Rican Drama*. His access to Arriví's unpublished works and his consideration of his essays add to the value of his analysis.

Arriví is not without his critics. Aníbal Delgado in his dissertation (1983) criticizes Arriví's treatment of the racial theme. He believes that Arriví perpetuates stereotypes and makes the black characters both responsible for the racism and its victims. Conversely, Erminio G. Neglia (1981) applies the theories of Paulo Freire to *Vejigantes* and concludes that the characters have achieved the highest level of liberation.

Arriví's concern for identity and authenticity is recognized by Julia Ortiz Griffin (1981). She compares Arriví's work with that of Rafael Ríos Rey. The latter is a painter who designed the scenery and sets for many of Arriví's plays. She describes their work as a "joyous reaffirmation of the Puerto Rican spirit."

Arriví himself has often served as his own critic. As an expert in Puerto Rican drama, his critical appraisals of his works cannot be dismissed. Not enough work has been done on Arriví outside Puerto Rico. His dramas and his work on behalf of Puerto Rican theater deserve a more complete examination.

Bibliography

WORKS BY ARRIVÍ

Drama

Coctel de Don Nadie. In *Teatro puertorriqueño*, 7. San Juan: Instituto de Cultura Puertorriqueña, 1965.
Tres piezas de teatro puertorriqueño: Club de solteros, María Soledad, Vejigantes. San Juan: Editorial del Departamento de Instrucción Pública, 1968.
Máscara puertorriqueña: Bolero y plena, Sirena, Vejigantes. Río Piedras: Editorial Cultural, 1971.

Essay

Entrada por las raíces. San Juan: Editorial Tinglado Puertorriqueño, 1964.
Areyto mayor. San Juan: Instituto de Cultura Puertorriqueña, 1966.
Conciencia puertorriqueña del teatro contemporáneo: 1937–1956. San Juan: Instituto de Cultura Puertorriqueña, 1967.

Poetry

Vía poética: Isla y nada (1958), Frontera (1960), Ciclo de lo ausente (1962), Escultor de la sombra (1965), En la tenue geografía (1978). Rio Píedras: Editorial Universitaria, 1978.
Ceiba, Areyto, Cemí, Coquí. San Juan: Instituto de Cultura Puertorriqueña, 1980.

WORKS ABOUT ARRIVÍ

Dauster, Frank. "Francisco Arriví: The Mask and the Garden." *Hispania* 45 (1962): 637–43.
Delgado, Aníbal. "Sociedad e ideología en el teatro contemporáneo puertorriqueño." Ph.D. dissertation, University of Pittsburgh, 1983.
Morfi, Angelina. *Historia crítica de un siglo de teatro puertorriqueño*. San Juan: Instituto de Cultura, 1980.
Neglia, Erminio G. "La 'conscientizaçao' de Paulo Freire y su applicación al teatro." *Revista Canandiense de Estudios Hispánicos* 5 (Winter 1981): 157–66.
Ortiz Griffin, Julia. "Two Artists in Search of a Country: Rafael Ríos Rey and Francisco Arriví." *Minority Voices* 5 (Spring-Fall 1981): 53–58.
Phillips, Jordan B. *Contemporary Puerto Rican Drama*. Madrid: Playor, S.A., 1973.
Rivera de Alvarez, Josefina. *Literatura puertorriqueña: su proceso en el tiempo*. Madrid: Ediciones Partenón, 1983.

LETICIA DÍAZ

B

BALSEIRO, JOSÉ AGUSTÍN (1900–   ). José Agustín Balseiro is well known as an essayist, novelist, poet, literary critic, professor, lecturer, composer, and pianist. His books reveal much about his life: family, education, travels, friendships, innermost thoughts, reminiscences, memoirs, honors bestowed upon him, interests, tastes in reading, research, attachment to Puerto Rico, and affinity for nature. He is truly a writer without a mask. His scholarship aids in explicating his books and articles.

Biography

José A. Balseiro was born in 1900 in Barceloneta, Puerto Rico, studied in the University of Puerto Rico and in universities of the United States and Spain. He is a *licenciado* in law and holds the doctorate in letters. In 1931 he was unanimously elected a corresponding member of the Royal Spanish Academy. Two years later (1933), the Center of Historical Studies of Madrid recommended him as Visiting Professor of Literature to the University of Puerto Rico to succeed Gabriela Mistral, Chilean poetess and winner of the Nobel Prize in Literature. In 1938 the secretary of state of the United States appointed him delegate to the meeting in Mexico City of the First International Congress of Ibero-American Literature; he was elected vice-president of the aforesaid congress and delivered the closing address in behalf of the universities and professors from the United States. Later he was selected by the International Program of Educational Exchange to give lectures in nine Latin American republics; while in Argentina, he was named corresponding member of the Sarmiento Institute of History and Sociology and in Chile he was granted the title of Doctor "honoris causa" in Pedagogical Sciences by Catholic University. Several distinguished authors, including Havelock Ellis, Miguel de Unamuno, Alfonso Reyes, Rufino Blanco Fombona, Concha Zardoya, Tomás Navarro Tomás, Alfonso Hernández Catá, and Alberto Insúa, have praised him for his contribution to creative literature and literary criticism. The Puerto Rican Foundation of the Humanities named Balseiro its lecturer for 1983; the title of his lecture was "Puerto Rico en mi obra" ("Puerto Rico in My Work"). He served as professor or visiting professor in a number of North American universities and Puerto Rico: Illinois, Northwestern, Duke, Miami, and Arizona. He also taught in the National University of Mexico.

Major Themes

Novels

La ruta eterna (1923, The Eternal Route), published in Madrid when Balseiro was only twenty-six years old, is his first book of fiction. It is really a biography of the principal character, a young Puerto Rican, whose Spanish father, out of tune with reality and over the mother's objection, insists on letting him grow up free of parental control, skeptical of moral standards, lazy and untrained. A heartless libertine, contemptuous of women and true love, yet he is willing to be supported by them, even with money earned by a poor prostitute; too, he is a liar and deceiver of females, including his mother. At the end of the narrative, he shows compassion for a girl betrayed by her fiancé, motivated to a degree by the opportunity to live at no cost in her father's home in Paris which he wanted to visit. Finally, reformed after an illness caused by debauchery, he falls in love with his wife and ceases to lead a fruitless existence. All the episodes are concerned with him and the women whose lives he blights. While still residing in Puerto Rico, he makes us aware of the changes in life on the island brought about by the Spanish-American War, United States' influence, and the impact of World War I. He also conveys impressions of Madrid and Spanish culture and at the end he brings in glimpses of Paris. The fragmentary, episodic nature of the novel rules out much development of plot or concentration on characters except in the case of the central figure who is a ruthless user of women, domineering and demanding preeminence like the males in D.H. Lawrence's novels which doubtless exerted influence on Balseiro.

The protagonist of the novel *En vela mientras el mundo duerme* (1953, Awake While the World Sleeps) was born and lived during his youth in the mountainous region of Puerto Rico. There the young jíbaro obtained an appreciation of the peasants and their impoverishment. He had the good fortune to be taught by a Spaniard, an extraordinary *maestro* whom he idealized and from whom he learned much in his classroom, the great outdoors. From the rural priest, not deeply versed in theology but who moved into the stable in order to convert the parochial house into a school and dining room for delinquent children, he learned to recognize man's obligations to mankind. After enrolling in the University of Puerto Rico, he made the acquaintance of several people: a more mature student, who had studied previously in foreign countries and also desired to improve conditions on the island, and his sister, a beautiful, sexually attractive flirt. The protagonist favors independence for the island while his friend, more disposed to compromise, believes that the status quo, an associate state of the United States, has advantages and that young leaders who have studied in countries more advanced technically and politically can contribute a great deal toward resolving the island's problems. An elderly, eccentric millionaire, who is also blindly in love with the aforementioned flirt, proclaims the notion that great philosophers, scholars, and writers are found in the northern zones with rigorous climates, whereas the southern ones with warm weather the year round encourage leisureliness and love while discouraging intellectual activity. The novel ends with the protagonist deciding to return to the mountains and become a rural teacher. The characters are skillfully drawn and develop as the narrative unfolds.

La gratitud humana (1969, Human Gratitude) would have a more precise title if it were broadened to *Human Gratitude and Ingratitude,* both qualities illustrated in Balseiro's third novel. Much of the narrative consists of a series of incidents or short stories or subplots strung together but with scant or no relation to the principal characters. The author indulges on occasions in detailed sensual descriptions of sexual intercourse. The sexy school teacher, conceited with her big bosom and other bodily charms, overwhelmingly desirous of having a man, seduces an ex-policeman and the undersecretary of education. The young bride, obsessed by her sexual impulses, is married to a brilliant lawyer-politician who is unable to function as a husband; she fails in her efforts to persuade the gynecologist to have intercourse with her. She is another example of people in whom the flame of sexual desire burns so lewdly that their lust turns into a grotesque parody of love. Balseiro through meditations, conversations, and letters provides a record of intimate moods and displays his distress over the pitiful state in which the world finds itself. Some of the material becomes a bit repetitious and dull, burdened with topics more suitable for discussions in essays. The novel properly ends on a tragic note with the young composer, a noble character, so depressed and confused upon learning of Martin Luther King's assassination that, pitiful, dismayed, and heartbroken, he is taken to an asylum for the insane. In short, he is the personification of present-day society's pitiful condition in this hell on earth. The narrator is very explicit in his diagnosis of society's ills.

Poetry

Balseiro's first book of poetry, titled *La copa de Anacreonte* (1924, Anacreon's Cup), derives its title and creative impulse from the collection of polished songs of love and wine by Anacreon (572?–488 B.C.), Greek court poet, and his followers of the classical period. Typical of the themes developed in the poems are: life has its ups and downs so take them as they come, don't accept entirely the dogma of one religion but seek the truth ("Escucha, alma," "Listen, Soul"); life is an eternal paradox because upon the realization of a goal its attraction is lost ("No esperes nada," "Don't Hope for Anything"); Alcalá Street in Madrid by night ("La noche," "Night"); noises and sights in La Puerta del Sol, the hub of Madrid ("La Puerta del Sol"). All the poems were composed either in Puerto Rico or Madrid while the author was in his early twenties.

In the dedication and poems of *Música cordial* (1926, Heartfelt Music), Balseiro lavishes affection upon his mother, going so far as to anticipate the pleasure of returning home to be with her after years of absence. The musical influence is noticeable in various subtitles of the book. Some poems are inspired by the contemplation of nature. The eight sonnets in the small volume dedicated to Menéndez Pidal show Balseiro to be a neoclassical poet who follows the traditional conventions and techniques inherited from the past. Additional sonnets in this collection along with others and many poems in *La pureza cautiva* (1946, Captive Purity) disclose that destiny opened to the author many paths of adventure to faraway lands. As captain of his Antillean ship he would like to transport the warmth of the tropical sun and the blue Caribbean to the frozen north. Other poems are about Puerto Rico and its attractions, travels in Spain and Italy and other countries. In fact, the key word in much of the collection is *travel,* for the poet is a tireless wanderer who longs to see thousands of seas, mountains, and skies. *Saudades de Puerto Rico* (1957, Homesickness for Puerto Rico) contains poems saturated with nostalgia that recall the allurements of his fatherland. Some verses paint still lifes, others draw profiles of a few famous Puerto Ricans. The poems, in addition to their poetic merit, are a source for learning more about the author's innermost feelings.

In *Vísperas de sombra y otros poemas* (1959, Eves of Shadow and Other Poems)—the title of the first poem as well as of the collection—Balseiro feels he is being dragged toward the kingdom of the Unknown; he knows not whether it is a flight or the end in the afterlife; whether it is a bridge to the horizon or the wing of a haze reappearing in the light. His suffering longs for respite from pain and the anguish of his memories. The other poems in this part, some worded as interrogations, are also concerned with departure from this life and the hereafter. The second part, titled "Intermezzo: canciones de niñez y adolescencia" ("Intermezzo: Songs of Childhood and Adolescence"), offers, as the title indicates, a marked contrast to the preceding one. The first three poems in the third part, "Este tiempo nuestro . . . " ("This Time of Ours"), are denunciations of modern life; discord everywhere; crisis in everything in this labyrinth; man's anguish. Different themes are treated in the remaining poems: profile of a black trumpeter in New Orleans; the immortality of García Lorca's poetry; Anne Frank's *Diary* about the holocaust; hope for peace in the world; the offense to the moon by man's reaching it and the harm he will do; and the crime of our age with threats to innocent children. This small collection of love poems, *El ala y el beso* (1983, The Wing and the Kiss), is the last to come from Balseiro's pen. For him "volar-crear, vivir-amar" ("to fly-to create, to live-to love"), the motivating forces in Balseiro's being and existence; they give meaning to his life. His beloved is the rose attached to the stem; he is anointed by her, the one who excels all other women. In the last poem of this book, "Poema del grande amor" ("Poem of Sublime Love"), the author becomes a bit sensual as he synthesizes the delights he finds in her adorable body, her velvety eyes, rounded bosom waiting to be caressed, her tenderness, her calming voice, affectionate fondling, and so on.

Essays

A major contribution by Balseiro has been in the field of literary criticism, appraising and illuminating the writings of some of Spain's and Spanish America's greatest authors of the nineteenth and twentieth centuries. This extraordinary undertaking, initiated when he was in his early twenties, was to continue over a period of forty years and result in the publication of six major studies—one in eight editions—and half a dozen articles in journals. He was to emerge as one of the better and more widely read critics in the United States who provided studies of some of the most complex and gifted novelists, poets, thinkers, and essayists of Spain and Spanish America, while drawing on his remarkable knowledge of classical Spanish, Spanish American, French, Italian, English, and American literatures; multifarious learning in music, art, history, and international cultures; and success in writing fiction, poetry, and essays. The material incorporated in his critiques involves a network of relations (political, intellectual, philosophical, religious, social, biographical, artistic), literary trends, and influences exerted on the authors. Obviously, Balseiro's critiques have broad perspectives.

The title *El vigía* (1940, The Lookout) given to Balseiro's first major undertaking in literary criticism—it eventually grew into three volumes—comes from the name of a hill, between Barceloneta and Areciblo, which he as a child had climbed with his father to gaze at the ocean. In this significant work are discussed such subjects as ''Unamuno novelist and *nivolista*,'' Pérez de Ayala's novels, commentary on romanticism, notes on Bécquer, María de Hostos' style, and other topics. Unamuno held a special fascination for Balseiro because he was to write three more articles about this Don Quixote of modern Spain who attempted to promote Quixotism to the level of a national religion. In his book *Novelistas españoles modernos* (1933, Modern Spanish Novelists) he included critiques of nine writers of fiction, the best of the second half of the nineteenth century and first quarter of the twentieth. Written especially for North American university students of Spanish, this useful work even dedicates one chapter to two minor novelists in order to give more complete coverage of the narratives written during this unusually rich era. For each novelist there is an account of his life and an evaluation of his novels. In *Cuatro individualistas de España* (1949, Four Individualists of Spain), Balseiro turns again to Blasco Ibáñez, Valle Inclán, Unamuno, and Baroja about whom he had already written critiques. His commentaries provide a composite of biographical details, literary history, analyses of their works, and reminiscences. This book, together with the three volumes of *El vigía* and *Novelistas españoles modernos*—all have gone through several editions—provides illuminating interpretations, discriminating judgment, and reliable guidance for study of aspects of Spanish literary history of the final decades of the nineteenth century and the first half of the twentieth. The extensive bibliographies are extremely helpful for reference.

In *Seis estudios sobre Rubén Darío* (1967, Six Studies on Rubén Darío) Balseiro repeats, in the preface, part of his essay "Rubén Darío y el porvenir" ("Rubén Darío and the Future") which was included in volume I of *El vigía*. The six studies are concerned with Darío and Spain: Spanish writers' comments and appraisal of the Nicaraguan poet and his comments in turn about Spain and Spanish authors. Darío, being an eclectic, experimenter, and composer, learned from the Primitives, the Romantics, Parnassians, Symbolists, and Modernists; Spanish, French, English, and North American poets, in his quest for perfection in different rhythms and structure, fusion of ideas. His relations with Argentina were extensive. He held mixed feelings with regard to the United States, lashing North Americans in articles and poetry and later on recognizing their talents in the fine arts, "Amongst those millions of Calibans the most marvelous Ariels are born." Darío attached much importance to the English language, citing British authors (Shakespeare, Byron, and others) and Americans (Longfellow, Whitman, Poe, Twain, Hawthorne, and others). In the essays included in the two volumes of *Expresión de Hispanoamérica* (1960 and 1963, Hispanic American Expression)—eleven have been translated into English and incorporated in the book titled *The Americas Look at Each Other* (1969)—Balseiro concerns himself with cultural relationships of this hemisphere through discussions of a variety of subjects. His essays attest his versatility and his understanding of the problems that separate and unite the nations of this hemisphere.

Balseiro divided into three parts his *Recuerdos literarios y reminiscencias personales* (1981, Literary Memories and Personal Reminiscences): the first, sentimental and embellished with recollections of oneiric experiences of his childhood and adolescence in Puerto Rico; the second with portraits of famous authors and distinguished scholars whom he came to know in Madrid, notes about his own works and critiques of them by others; the third of a miscellaneous nature with accounts of his travels and lectures in Latin America, Europe, and the United States, honors conferred upon him, and remembrances of former colleagues and students. This book, a sort of farewell, is absorbing because of its intimate details, intuitive impressions, and sketches of distinguished figures of many countries. The contents of his article "Mis recuerdos de Alfonso Reyes" ("My Remembrances of Alfonso Reyes"), published two decades earlier than *Recuerdos literarios* and elegiac in tone and emotional in the last part, record their acquaintanceship begun when Balseiro was a youngster and ended thirty-five years later with Balseiro's visit to Reyes' home in Mexico City. Incidentally, Reyes died shortly afterward. Balseiro had great respect for the Mexican scholar, poet, author of short stories, thinker, lecturer, diplomat, and friend. He felt highly honored that Reyes wrote the prologue to his book *Pureza cautiva* (1946, Captive Purity) and in spite of being gravely ill welcomed him as a guest to his private library.

Edited Works

In adherence to the practice of university professors of the United States, Balseiro felt the need to edit books for the students' use and enlightenment, so he collaborated with J. Riis Owre in editing Alejandro Casona's three plays *La barca sin pescador* (1955, The Boat without a Fisherman) and *Corona de amor y muerte* (1960, Crown of Love and Death) and with Eliana Suárez-Rivero in the edition of *El caballero de las espuelas de oro* (1968, The Gentleman with Spurs of Gold). The three texts have instructive introductions, adequate vocabularies and exercises so they can be used early in the study of Spanish. Balseiro wrote the prologue for the volume that contains two plays by the contemporary Puerto Rican dramatist Méndez Ballester. In his examination of *El clamor de los surcos* (The Clamor of the Furrows) and *Tiempo muerto* (Dull Times)—both full of local color—he notes marked improvement in characters and plots in the second piece even though only two years separated their premieres.

The mayor of Miami, a Puerto Rican, conceived the idea of publishing a book in celebration of the Bicentennial Independence of the United States and recommended that Balseiro, who had been a resident of Florida for more than a quarter of a century, be charged with the project, which resulted in his writing the introduction about distinguished Hispanics who had come to Florida since the arrival of Ponce de León in 1513. Seven essays are included in this book, *Presencia hispánica en la Florida* (1976), translated in English and published with the title *The Hispanic Presence in Florida* (1976).

Bibliography

WORKS BY BALSEIRO

Novels

La ruta eterna. Madrid: Editorial Mundo Latino, 1923.
En vela mientras el mundo duerme. San Juan de Puerto Rico: Biblioteca de Autores Puertorriqueños, 1953.
La gratitud humana. Miami: Mnemosyne Publishing Co., 1969.

Poetry

La copa de Anacreonte, con un prólogo de Eduardo Marquina y un epílogo de Francisco Villaespesa. Madrid: Editorial Mundo Latino, 1924.
Música cordial, poemas, 1923–1925. Madrid: Imprenta Cervantes, 1926.
Sonetos. San Juan de Puerto Rico, 1933. This small volume of nine pages is dedicated to Don Ramón Menéndez Pidal. "¿Sí? ¿No?" and "Raid" are not included in the collection *La pureza cautiva*.
La pureza cautiva, prólogo de Alfonso Reyes. La Habana: Editorial Lex, 1946.
Saudades de Puerto Rico, prólogo de Manuel García Blanco, y *La pureza cautiva*, prólogo de Alfonso Reyes. Madrid: Aguilar, 1957.
Vísperas de sombra y otros poemas. México, D.F.: Ediciones de Andrea, 1959.
El ala y el beso. San Juan de Puerto Rico: Biblioteca de Autores Puertorriqueños, 1983.

Books of Essays

El vigía, ensayos de crítica literaria y musical, premiados por la Academia Española con el Premio Hispanoamericano correspondiente al año 1925. Madrid: Editorial Mundo Latino, 1925. I.

El vigía, ensayos de crítica literaria. Madrid: Editorial Mundo Latino, 1928. II.

El vigía. San Juan de Puerto Rico: Biblioteca de Autores Españoles, 1940? III.

Novelistas españoles modernos: Estudios de crítica literaria acerca de Valera, Pereda, Alarcón, Pérez Galdós, Pardo Bazán, Coloma, Picón, Clarín y Palacio Valdés. New York: Macmillan, 1933.

El Quijote de la España contemporánea: Miguel de Unamuno. Madrid, Ernesto Giménez, 1935.

Blasco Ibáñez, Unamuno, Valle Inclán, Baroja: Cuatro individualistas de España, con un prefacio del Profesor Nicholson B. Adams. Chapel Hill: University of North Carolina Press, 1949.

Expresión de Hispanoamérica. San Juan de Puerto Rico: Instituto de Cultura Puertorriqueña, 1960. I. 1963. II.

Seis estudios sobre Rubén Darío. Madrid: Editorial Gredos, 1967.

Recuerdos literarios y reminiscencias personales. Madrid: Gredos, 1981.

Articles in Journals

"Valle Inclán, la novela y la política." *Hispania* 15 (1932): 437–64.

"The Quijote of Contemporary Spain: Miguel de Unamuno." *PMLA* 49, 2 (1934): 645–56.

"Vicente Blasco Ibáñez, hombre de acción y de letras," revista *Puerto Rico*, San Juan, 1935.

"Baroja y la popularidad." *Hispania* 21 (1938):10–26.

"Mis recuerdos de Alfonso Reyes." *Asomante* 16, 2 (1960): 83–94.

"Rubén Darío y la lengua inglesa." *Asomante* 23, 2 (1967): 35–43.

Works Edited or with Prologue by Balseiro

Rodríguez Alvarez, Alejandro, and Alejandro Casona [pseud.]. *La barca sin pescador*, ed. José A. Balseiro and J. Riis Owre. New York: Oxford University Press, 1955.

Rodríguez Alvarez, Alejandro, and Alejandro Casona [pseud.]. *Corona de amor y muerte*, ed. José A. Balseiro and J. Riis Owre. New York: Oxford University Press, 1960.

Rodríguez Alvarez, Alejandro, and Alejandro Casona [pseud.]. *El caballero de las espuelas de oro*, ed. José A. Balseiro and Eliana Suárez-Rivero. New York: Oxford University Press, 1968.

Méndez Ballester, Manuel. *El clamor de los surcos* y *Tiempo muerto*, con el prólogo "Méndez Ballester y sus dos obras dramáticas" por José A. Balseiro, no date.

Presencia hispánica en la Florida, ed. José Agustín Balseiro. Miami: Ediciones Universal, 1976.

Lectures

"El Estado Libre Asociado de Puerto Rico," conferencia pronunciada por el Doctor José A. Balseiro en el Salón de Actos del Servicio Cultural e Informativo de los Estados Unidos de América, en Buenos Aires, el 15 de julio de 1954. Fue publicada por el Servicio Cultural e Informativo de los Estados Unidos de América.

"Puerto Rico en mi obra," conferencia pronunciada por José A. Balseiro el 6 de abril de 1984 en la sede de la Fundación, al serle conferido el título de Humanista del Año 1983, por la Fundación Puertorriqueña de las Humanidades. Fue publicada por la Fundación Puertorriqueña de las Humanidades en San Juan, P.R., 1984.

Translations of Balseiro's Work in English

The Americas Look at Each Other, trans. Muna Muñoz Lee. Coral Gables, Fla.: University of Miami Press, 1969.

The Hispanic Presence in Florida, ed. José Agustín Balseiro and trans. Piedad Ferrer Robertson. Miami: E.A. Seemann, 1976.

WORKS ABOUT BALSEIRO

Córdova de Braschi, Julita. *"Blasco Ibáñez, Unamuno, Valle Inclán, Baroja." Asomante.* 6, 1 (1950): 86–87.

Rey, Agapito. *"Presencia hispánica en la Florida: ayer y hoy (1513–1976)." Hispania* 60 (1977): 602.

Shoemaker, William H. *"Blasco Ibáñez, Unamuno, Valle Inclán, Baroja." Hispania* 34 (1951): 397–400.

Zimic, Stanislav. *"Seis estudios sobre Rubén Darío." Hispania* 51 (1968): 932–33.

HARVEY JOHNSON

BOUDY, JOSÉ SÁNCHEZ. *See* SÁNCHEZ-BOUDY, JOSÉ.

BURGOS, JULIA DE (1914–1953). Julia de Burgos was one of Puerto Rico's greatest poets. She was a true patriot of her country and a staunch defender of its culture. Her poems sing of the beauty of her land, of her love of nature, and of freedom.

She experienced the plight of the needy and took up their cause for equality and justice. Julia's poems reflect her sensitivity and express through their imagery her suffering, her love, her hopes, and her desires for her country and for humanity.

During her life she traveled to different lands always in search of harmony between reality and self. Even in her moments of happiness, the anguish of existence was ever present. Julia de Burgos's life was a continual dichotomy: hope accompanied by despair, happiness accompanied by sorrow, companionship accompanied by loneliness. Throughout her works, all the complexity of human emotions is present in a surging desire for an expression of love. This love takes many forms; it is mother, lover, nature, country, humanity.

Biography

Julia de Burgos was born on February 17, 1914 in Carolina, Puerto Rico. Her parents were Francisco Burgos Hans and Paula García. She was the eldest of thirteen children. The family suffered from economic difficulties, and only through family sacrifices and through personal tenacity was Julia able to receive an education.

Her father initiated in her an interest in adventure and in imaginary worlds. He would recite episodes of *El Quijote* and other adventurous readings to his daughter which would spark her inquisitive imagination. From her mother, Julia inherited her deep sensitivity and understanding of others and their suffering.

When Julia finished grade school, her family sold their land and moved to Río Piedras with the hope that there Julia would be able to complete her studies. In 1931 Julia completed her high school education at the Escuela Superior de la Universidad. Her interests then centered on teaching, and in 1933 she received her teaching degree.

During the 1930s there was a surge in nationalist spirit all throughout Puerto Rico and Julia was immersed in its ideals. They would form part of her being from then on and would affect her decisions in life.

In 1934 she worked for PRERA (Puerto Rican Economical Rehabilitation Agency) which closed in 1935. At this time, Julia went to Naranjito as a school teacher and, once again, was in contact with the vivid nature of Puerto Rico. This nature would inspire her throughout her life.

In 1937 Julia published *Poemas exactos a mí misma* (Exact Poems to Myself), one of her first works which, later, she tried to reject.

From 1936 to 1937 Julia de Burgos worked for the Escuela del Aire, an educational radio program, but for political reasons she resigned. During this time, she wrote children's plays: *Un paisaje marino* (An Underwater Landscape), *Llamita quiere ser mariposa* (The Flame Wishes to Be a Butterfly), *La parranda del sábado* (Saturday's Party), and *Coplas jíbaras para ser cantadas* (Jíbaro Couplets to Be Sung).

Also during this time, 1937, she divorced her husband, Rubén Rodríguez Beauchamp. Julia had always desired to have a child and as her marriage was coming to an end her maternal instincts were brought to life in her poem "Poema al hijo que no llega."

In 1938 she published *Poemas en veinte surcos* (Poems in Twenty Rows), a collection of poems that represent her poet's quest for identity and her fellowship with nature.

Canción de la verdad sencilla (The Song of Simple Truth) was published in 1939 and is an introspective view of her life and surroundings. For this work she won the Instituto de Literatura Puertorriqueña's prize for literature in 1939.

In 1940 Julia traveled to New York. Julia saw New York as a cold, inhospitable city. She felt as an exile who had lost forever her homeland but who would cherish it in her soul. Many were the times during the following years that plans were made to return to Puerto Rico but they never materialized. Her desire then was to leave New York and go on to Cuba to be reunited with the man she loved.

In July 1940 she arrived in Cuba. Once there, a revitalization of her patriotic spirit occurred as she saw a nation proud of its freedom and its heritage. She longed for social justice in her homeland and considered independence the only path open to justice.

In Cuba she continued writing and some of her works from this period are: "Soneto a Martí" (Sonnet to Marti), "Campo" (Countryside), "La voz de los muertos" (The Voice of the Death), "Canto a Rusia" (Canto to Russia), and *El mar y tú* (1954, The Sea and You).

Her life continued to be a struggle between two polar forces as is indicated in her book *El mar y tú*. The happiness she felt at being again with the man she loved is interlaced with a foreboding sense of desolation as the end of this relationship approached.

In July 1942 she left Cuba and her love to return to New York. The following eleven years would be a mixture of peace and turbulence, of joys and sorrows, which had always been a part of her existence. This unrest was both physical and spiritual. She changed profession and residence many times. Her jobs ranged from lab technician to saleswoman. She continued to search for justice and freedom for her land and for her spirit.

She married Armando Marin and moved to Washington, D.C., in 1944, returning to New York in 1945. In 1946 she received the prize for journalism of the Instituto de Literatura de Puerto Rico for an editoral in *Pueblos Hispanos* that reflected her sociopolitical ideas.

Julia suffered from alcoholism and its effects. Repeatedly she was hospitalized, and during one of these stays she wrote her poem "Farewell in Welfare Island" which bids a final good-bye to the world and its solitude, despair, and emptiness.

In July 1953 her body was found on a New York street without any type of identification. It was not until a month later that relatives claimed Julia's body. On September 6, 1953, Julia returned to her beloved Carolina, Puerto Rico and was laid to rest near the river that was her inspiration and song. She is now one with her land and her people.

Major Themes

Julia de Burgos has been acclaimed as one of the major poets of her land. Her style is precise in its word choices which are charged with connotative meaning and evoke direct images in the mind of the reader. Her prodigious command of words and their interrelationship unites to form a powerful expression of her emotions.

In her book *Poemas en veinte surcos* Julia presents the recurring themes of self-identity and communion with nature. Julia sees herself as a dual being, as essence and form, as a product of society and as a free spirit. Julia de Burgos was a defender of justice and humantarianism. In spite of material obstacles, her spirit soared high. In her poem "Río Grande de Loíza" we find these elements blending together to form a song of love and an expression of identity.

"Río Grande de Loíza" sings to the river that enchanted her childhood and now is her poetic inspiration. Nature here is vibrant, alive, and in contact with human emotions. The river is personified as Julia calls for understanding and finds an answer to her plea. The river is her past, her present, and her future. It symbolizes love, truth, and country.

The river is the quintessence of her spirit. It is an integral part of her being; so much so that she asked that the first five copies of her book *El mar y tú* be cast to the river in a symbolic act of union. The river flows to the sea and thus her book is fed through the river to the sea and on to the rest of the world.

Julia through her poetry demonstrates her universality and her fellowship with mankind. In her poem "Momentos" from this book she expresses these ideals:

Yo, universal,
bebiéndome la vida
en cada estrella desorbitada,
en cada grito estéril,
en cada sentimiento sin orillas.

This book presents more socially oriented themes than are present in later works. In her poem "Ay ay ay de la grifa negra" she cries out against racial prejudice and advocates the oneness of all people. In another poem from this collection, "Ochenta mil," Julia laments the tragedy of war.

In her last poem, "Yo misma fui mi ruta," she once again proclaims her essence, her identity, and her sincerity. She will break away from the norm and be herself. She will not follow others but be her own guide through life. She is an individual who has respect for her individuality and that of others.

Canción de la verdad sencilla presents a portrait of Julia's intimate world. She expresses love to be the essential motivation of her life. Here her poems are characterized by long lines of verse, with slow moving rhythm, which express an introspective attitude toward love and her own identity.

Nature, once again, will be a reflection of love; the wind, the sea, the river all unite in an exaltation of love. This sentiment of love will be accompanied by a sense of suffering. As in her life, her poetry is an expression of dual emotions: hope and fear, love and sorrow. She carries within her "the sorrow of centuries" and love will quiet this sorrow only for a time, as she expresses in her poem "Poema de mi pena dormida" (Poem about My Sleeping Sorrow).

In her poem "Canción de la verdad sencilla" she reiterates the force of her love and the complexity of two beings—night and day, silver and gold, wave and wind—who will forever be one.

The juxtaposition of antithetical ideas is a device frequently used in this collection of poems. This, once again, points to the dichotomy existent in Julia's life and reflected in her work.

El mar y tú is a book also based on the emotion of love. It begins on an optimistic note and ends on a tragic one.

Love is her inspiration and the sea will symbolize love and eternity. Love mixes with sorrow as Julia expresses her disillusionment with humanity as her loved one represents all people and her loss of his love is projected toward all men.

Julia's anguish has been ever present. She has felt it as her constant companion; it never dies. In "Poema a la íntima agonía" (Poem to Intimate Agony) she portrays her agony as ontological and eternal. It will transcend death to accompany her.

Julia searches for eternity and sees as the only road her beloved river Loíza. Her poem "Tres caminos" (Three Roads) sings to the three loves of her life: her lover, her mother, and the river. Only the river can give her the strength to continue on the road to eternity.

The sea is an intimate part of her being: her soul. In "Letanía del mar," Julia calls to the sea in a litany of desperation. The sea is her resting place, her tomb, her universe.

The poem that closes this book, "Poema para mi muerte" (Poem for My Death), addresses her death as a liberation from the chains that tie her to the physical and limit her spirit. This spirit will be immortal and then, through death, she will be called "poet."

Julia de Burgos is universal in her theme, her feeling, and in her inspiration. She suffered and loved as all humans do and through her sensitivity captured these emotions and gave them life in her poetry. Her perception transcended the momentary and reached the immortal. Her quest for identity was quenched through her oneness with nature and her fellowship with man. Her poetry sings to men of all ages through its pure sincerity and emotion.

Bibliography

WORKS BY DE BURGOS

Poetry

Poemas exactos a mí misma. 1937.
Poemas en veinte surcos. San Juan: Imprenta Venezuela, 1938.
Canción de la verdad sencilla. San Juan: Imprenta Baldrich, 1939.
El mar y tú, otros poemas. San Juan: Puerto Rico Printing and Publishing Co., 1954.
Obra poética. San Juan: Instituto de Cultura Puertorriqueña, 1954.
Antología Poética. San Juan: Editorial Coqui, 1967.

Prose

Un paisaje marino. San Juan: Album literario puertorriqueño, V.V.
La parranda del sábado. San Juan: Escuela del Aire, 1935.
Llamita quiere ser mariposa. San Juan: Escuela del Aire, 1935.

WORKS ABOUT DE BURGOS

Arce de Vázquez, Margot. "Los últimos versos de Julia de Burgos." *Artes y Letras* (November, 1953).
Arroyo, Angel M. "Vida, pasión y muerte de Julia de Burgos." *Artes y Letras* (November, 1953).

Jiménez de Báez, Yvette. *Julia de Burgos, Vida y Poesía.* Río Piedras: Editorial Coquí, 1966.

Quiñones, Samuel R. *Temas y letras.* San Juan: Biblioteca de Autroes Puertorriqueños, 1941.

Rivera Matos, Manuel. "Los motivos del río en la poesía de Julia de Burgos." *Revista Atenco Puertorriqueño* (enero-febrero-marzo 1940): 31–41.

MARÍA T. REDMON

C

CABRERA, LYDIA (1900–). Generally regarded as Cuba's foremost female author of the twentieth century, Lydia Cabrera—along with Fernando Ortiz and Nicolás Guillén—is responsible for bringing to light the rich African heritage in Cuban culture. Her scholarly works on Afro-Cuban folklore are important sources of information for the anthropologist, folklorist, historian, ethnographer, and linguist, while her short stories offer an unrivaled portrayal of the African sub-culture in Latin America.

Biography

Lydia Cabrera was born May 20, 1900 in Havana, Cuba. She was the youngest of the eight children of Raimundo Cabrera Bosch, a noted Cuban jurist who had distinguished himself in Cuba's War for Independence, and Elisa Marcaida y Casanova, the daughter of a Basque immigrant.

Lydia's childhood years were spent at her father's mansion on Galiano Street. The home was the meeting place of the most distinguished members of the Cuban intelligentsia; yet, the young girl was more interested in the stories her parents' black servants would tell each night than in the endless *tertulias* at her father's home.

Since young Cuban women did not attend high school in the early years of the republic, Lydia studied at home with a private tutor. She was fascinated with painting, however, and unknown to her father often attended classes at the San Alejandro Academy of Painting where she drew countless sketches depicting Cuban life.

After her father's death in 1923, she became an antique collector and in 1927 decided to study painting in Paris. Three years later she graduated from the acclaimed Ecole du Louvre.

While Lydia was in Paris, she became interested in the theme of negritude. Those were the years in which artists and writers were searching for new themes and directions for their works. In negritude they found a sympathetic theme. Writers like Langston Hughes of the Harlem Renaissance had succeeded in bringing black themes into American literary mainstream. Federico García Lorca, the great Spanish poet, had successfully introduced the figure of the black man in his *Poeta en Nueva York* (The Poet in New York). Negritude had since become the main theme in Caribbean poetry with the publication of the poems of the Cuban Nicolás Guillén and the Puerto Rican Luis *Palés Matos.

Influenced by Blaise Cendrars's *Antologie negre* (Black Anthology), Paul Morand's *Magie noire* (Black Magic), Andre Gide's *Voyages au Congo* (Voyages to the Congo), and Phillippe Soupault's *Le negre* (The Blacks), Lydia Cabrera turned to writing and began a series of short stories based on the tales she had heard during her childhood. She showed them to a friend, Francis de Miomandre, who was so impressed that he quickly translated each story into French. In 1936, Lydia Cabrera's first volume of short stories was published by the prestigious Gallimard Publishing House under the title *Contes negres de Cuba* (Black Stories from Cuba). The book was an instant success in Europe where the critics regarded it as a masterpiece of black folklore.

In 1938, sensing the ambitions of German dictator Adolf Hitler after the Munich appeasement conference, Lydia Cabrera left Paris and returned to her native Cuba. Twenty-two years later history would repeat itself when Lydia Cabrera saw the ambitions of another dictator, Fidel Castro, and left her homeland for the United States.

While in Cuba, Lydia devoted her time to the study of Afro-Cuban folklore. She busied herself writing, collecting material, and interviewing practically every black in Havana. Her persistence and determination bore fruit in 1940 when she published *Cuentos negros de Cuba* (Black Tales from Cuba), the Spanish edition of her first book, followed by the publication of *Por qué . . . ; cuentos negros de Cuba* (1948, Why . . . Black Tales from Cuba), an important collection of twenty-eight Afro-Cuban short stories.

After traveling to every part of the island collecting information on Afro-Cuban culture, Lydia Cabrera wrote her famous *El monte: notas sobre las religiones, la magia, las supersticiones y el folklore de los negros criollos y del pueblo de Cuba* (1954, The Interior: Notes on the Religions, Magic, Superstitions and the Folklore of the Black Creole and the People of Cuba), considered by ethnographers as the most important contribution in the field of Afro-Cuban culture.

The decade of the 1950s also saw the publication of three more of her scholarly works: *Refranes de negros viejos* (1955, Proverbs by Old Blacks), a collection of six hundred Lucumi proverbs; *Anagó: vocabulario Lucumí* (1957, Anagó: Lucumi Vocabulary), an outstanding linguistic study of the Yoruba-Lucumi language as it is spoken in Cuba; and *La sociedad secreta Abakuá* (1958, The Abakua Secret Society), the first and only successful attempt at unmasking the codes of *ñañiguismo*, the secret African religious society in Cuba.

The first ten years of Lydia's exile were not productive. The author could not concentrate on her art after seeing a lifetime of her work lost. In 1970, however, she seemed to reestablish her career in Miami and published her first work in exile, *Otán Iyebiyé: las piedras preciosas* (Otan Iyebiye: Precious Stones), a study of the different meanings of precious stones in the Yoruba religion which also contains a number of barbs aimed at the Castro regime.

The following year Lydia Cabrera published her first work of fiction in twenty-three years, *Ayapá: cuentos de Jicotea* (1971, Ayapá: Humorous Tales), a collection of nineteen humorous and delightful Afro-Cuban short stories.

After the publication of *Ayapá*, Lydia lived in Spain in order to rebuild the library of her writings which had been lost under the Castro regime. She became gravely ill, however, and was forced to return to Miami for medical treatment.

Following a difficult period of convalescence, the expatriate author began writing once again and a series of scholarly works dealing with Afro-Cuban religious rituals were published. Among these works are *La laguna sagrada de San Joaquín* (1973, The Sacred Lagoon of San Joaquin), *Yemayá y Ochún* (1974), *Anaforuana: ritual y símbolos de la iniciación en la sociedad secreta Abakuá* (1975, Anaforuana: Rituals and Symbols of the Secret Abakua Society), *La Regla Kimbisa del Santo Cristo del Buen Viaje* (1977, The Kimbisa Order of Christ the Voyager), *Trinidad de Cuba* (1977, Cuban Trinity), and *Reglas de Congo, Palo Monte Mayombe* (1979, Orders of Congo, Mayombe and Palo Monte). The works are not a mere collection of data, for the author uses the same direct style seen in her works of fiction, and the result is a number of solid and informative works that can be enjoyed by the average reader.

With this newly found strength, Lydia Cabrera published two more works of fiction: *Francisco y Francisca: chascarrillos de negros viejos* (1976, Francisco and Francisca: Jokes by Old Blacks), a collection of forty-five picaresque vignettes that reveal the true feelings of its authentic Afro-Cuban characters and *Cuentos para grandes, chicos y retrasados mentales* (1983, Stories for the Young, Old and Retarded), a volume of easily readable short stories.

Major Themes

Lydia Cabrera's works have always attempted to inform readers about Afro-Cuban life in a charming and pleasant manner. In a direct yet colorful style, she has always managed to integrate the ceremonies, sacrifices, dances, cults, sounds, words, symbols and rhythms of black culture into a work of its own: the Afro-Cuban world.

The publication of *Contes negres de Cuba* not only began this trend in Cuban literature, but also helped to shatter the myth of the black in Cuba. Prior to this work, the black was portrayed in most Cuban literary works as a colorful childlike figure incapable of having its own personality. *Contes negres de Cuba* changed all that and much more for it portrays the black for what he really is: a man of flesh and blood.

The volume is not merely a transcription of known folk tales, but rather is a marvelous view of the most magnificent world of a proud people who were once transplanted from their native Africa to the largest island in the Caribbean. In her stories Cabrera mixes fantasy and reality, past and present, Spanish and Yoruba and creates a unique setting. Her characters are not stock figures but rather real people who act according to their own instincts and who live in a world that is both real and mystical. *Contes negres de Cuba,* an unrivaled piece of literature, remains one of the most widely read books in literature and one of the most magnificent examples of what today is known as magic realism.

Por qué . . . ; cuentos negros de Cuba, Lydia Cabrera's second volume of short stories, has been overshadowed by *Contes negres de Cuba.* Judging from a stylistic point of view, however, the stories in this volume are much more developed and the narrative descriptions are more vigorous and complex. The author uses a wealth of rhetorical devices such as onomatopoeia, alliteration, similes, and metaphors to create a mysterious and fascinating African world. Dialogue is practically nonexistent. Instead, the characters must reveal themselves through their actions. Although all the stories end with a philosophical explanation, the author remains distant from her characters. She observes them, but refuses to judge them. In the end, it is the reader who renders the final verdict.

Ayapá: cuentos de Jicotea is an entertaining collection of short stories whose main characters are animals. All of the nineteen stories in this volume are connected by one character, a turtle named Jicotea. An ugly, slow-moving animal, Jicotea is able to survive thanks to her superior wit and cunning. In *Ayapá* Cabrera reveals herself as a true master of personification, proving once more that in the Afro-Cuban world anything can happen and often does. As in her two previous volumes of short fiction, *Ayapá* contains its share of fragmentation, distortion of time and space, mixing of fantasy and reality, use of imagination and interior monologues, all of which enhance the narrative quality of the stories.

Francisco y Francisca: chascarrillos de negros viejos is perhaps Lydia's simplest yet most delightful piece of fiction. Through the eyes of Francisco and Francisca, an old black couple, the reader obtains a realistic picture of Cuban society during colonial times. The characters' observations on religion, society, politics, and customs are keen and incisive. The result is a work of high literary achievement and rich information.

Her last collection of short stories, *Cuentos para grandes, chicos y retrasados mentales,* is an anthology of stories Lydia heard during her childhood. The stories are well written and interesting, but structurally not as vigorous as her previous works.

Whether as a scholar or as a short-story writer the name Lydia Cabrera will always be synonymous with "Lo Afrocubano."

Survey of Criticism

Lydia Cabrera is still the great name of Afro-Cuban studies. As expected, there have been a number of studies concerning her scholarly work. As far as criticism of her works of fiction is concerned, she has received nothing but praise.

Most studies tend to place Lydia as the pioneer of Afro-Cuban prose fiction. The foremost Cuban novelist of the twentieth century, the late Alejo Carpentier, classified *Cuentos negros de Cuba* in his article *"Cuentos negros* por Lydia Cabrera"* (1940) as a work of utmost importance to the culture of Latin America. The prominent critic of Cuban literature, Manuel Pedro González, exalted Lydia's thematic approach in his study of "Cuentos y recuentos de Lydia Cabrera" (1959).

Criticism of Lydia's works since her exile has also appeared in both Spain and the United States. Rosa Valdés-Cruz's study, *Lo ancestral africano en la narrativa de Lydia Cabrera* (1974), offers new insights into structure and form of her major short stories. Rosario Hiriart's *Lydia Cabrera: Vida hecha arte* (1978) is an informative account of Lydia Cabrera's life as a writer and researcher. Perhaps the most encompassing book on Lydia Cabrera is the *Homenaje a Lydia Cabrera* (1978). Edited by José Antonio Madrigal and Reynaldo Sánchez, the book is a collection of studies by leading Cuban, American, and foreign scholars.

Lydia Cabrera, prolific author and scholar, will long be remembered for bringing to light the African experience in Latin America.

Bibliography

WORKS BY CABRERA

Contes negres de Cuba. Traduits de l'espagnol par Francis de Miomandre. Paris: Gallimard, 1936.
Cuentos negros de Cuba. La Habana: Imprenta La Verónica, 1940.
Por qué . . . ; *Cuentos negros de Cuba.* La Habana: Ediciones Cabrera y Rojas, 1948.
El monte: Notas sobre las religiones, le magia, las supersticiones y el folklore de los negros criollos y del pueblo de Cuba. La Habana: Ediciones Cabrera y Rojas, 1954.
Refranes de negros viejos. La Habana: Ediciones Cabrera y Rojas, 1955.
Anagó: vocabulario Lucumí. La Habana: Ediciones Cabrera y Rojas, 1957.
La sociedad secreta Abakuá. La Habana: Ediciones Cabrera y Rojas, 1958.
Otán Iyebiyé: Las piedras preciosas. Miami: Ediciones Cabrera y Rojas, 1970.
Ayapá: cuentos de Jicotea. Miami: Ediciones Universal, 1971.
La laguna sagrada de San Joaquín. Madrid: Ediciones R, 1973.
Yemayá y Ochún. Madrid: Ediciones R, 1974.
Anaforuana: ritual y símbolos de la iniciacion en la sociedad secreta Abakuá. Madrid: Ediciones R., 1975.
Francisco y Francisca: chascarrillos de negros viejos. Miami: Peninsular Printing, 1976.
La Regla Kimbisa del Santo Cristo del Buen Viaje. Miami: Peninsular Printing, 1977.

Trinidad de Cuba. Miami: Peninsular Printing, 1977.
Reglas de Congo, Palomonte Mayombe. Miami: Peninsular Printing, 1979.
Cuentos para grandes, chicos y retrasados mentales. Miami: Peninsular Printing, 1983.

WORKS ABOUT CABRERA

Carpentier, Alejo. *"Cuentos negros* por Lydia Cabrera." *Carteles,* 1940.
González, Manuel Pedro. "Cuentos y recuentos de Lydia Cabrera." *Nueva Revista Cubana* 2 (1959): 153–61.
Hiriart, Rosario. *Lydia Cabrera: vida hecha arte.* New York: Eliseo Torres and Sons, 1978.
Madrigal, José Antonio, and Reynaldo Sánchez, eds. *Homenaje a Lydia Cabrera.* Miami: Ediciones Universal, 1978.
Valdés-Cruz, Rosa. *Lo ancestral africano en la narrativa de Lydia Cabrera.* Barcelona: Editorial Vosgos, 1974.

JOSÉ B. FERNÁNDEZ

CARRERO, JAIME (1931–   ). Jaime Carrero is a Puerto Rican playwright, novelist, poet, and painter whose literary work is devoted to the interpretation and critique of contemporary Puerto Rican culture and society, both on the island and in New York City. Despite the diversity of the genres and the technical and linguistic experimentation that characterizes it, Carrero's writing possesses a fundamental unity.

Biography

Carrero was born in Mayagüez, Puerto Rico, in 1931 and spent his formative years both on the island and in New York. He received a B.A. in fine arts from the Polytechnic Institute in San Germán (later the Inter-American University) and an M.A. from the Pratt Institute in New York City, and he studied art in Florence and at Columbia University. Although he is better known in the United States for his writing than for his visual art, Carrero's painting have been exhibited in Puerto Rico, the United States, and Mexico, and some are in the permanent collection of the Puerto Rican Museum of Fine Arts. He has taught art and literature at several institutions on the island, and since 1979 he has chaired the Fine Arts Department at the Inter-American University.

The development of Carrero's literary talents coincided with the emergence of his political awareness, specifically of the social, economic, and cultural problems associated with Puerto Rico's colonial relationship to the United States. Major historical upheavals—the Korean War, the war in Vietnam, and the student revolts of the 1960s—shaped Carrero's writing. In the mid–1950s, he participated in the new Puerto Rican poetry movement, along with Hugo Margenat, José María Lima, and Luis Antonio Rosario Quiles, among others, breaking with established poetic modes in both form and content. In the 1960s and early 1970s, Carrero participated in the movement to create a Nuyorican or Neo-Rican aesthetic consciousness that would express the bicultural experience of many Puerto

Ricans, an element that permeates his writing but is most evident in those poems and plays, in both English and Spanish, that examine the lives of Puerto Ricans in New York. These include *Jet neorriqueño-Neo-Rican Jet Liner Poems* (1964) and the plays *Noo Jork* (1972, New York), *Pipo Subway no sabe reír* (1972, Pipo Subway Doesn't Know How to Laugh), and *La caja de caudales FM* (1978, *The FM Safe*, 1979). In 1974 he organized a Neo-Rican seminar at the Inter-American University, and during the same period he became a contributing editor of the U.S.-based, multicultural, bilingual literary magazine, the *Revista Chicano-Riqueña*.

Carrero's published work includes three novels, six plays, and a number of poems and short stories. Although his writing has received almost no scholarly attention, his theatre and prose fiction have been repeatedly recognized in the literary world. His first novel, *Raquelo tiene un mensaje* (1970, Raquelo Has a Message), was awarded first prize in the 1967 novel competition of the *Ateneo Puertorriqueño*, the island's most prestigious artistic institution which also gave an honorable mention to his second novel, *Los nombres* (1972, The Names). His 1966 play *Flag Inside* was awarded first prize in the *Ateneo's* drama competition, and *La caja de caudales FM* was awarded first prize in 1978 by the literary journal *Sin nombre*. His short stories have also been recognized by the *Ateneo,* and his poem "My Graphological Yo" received an award in 1974 from the Illinois Arts Council.

Major Themes

The problem of Puerto Rico lies at the center of Carrero's dramatic and narrative works and includes 1) the dehumanization and destruction of Puerto Rican family and society created by dependence upon North American mass culture and materialism; 2) the "island" status of Puerto Ricans, regardless of their dwelling place, that is, their individual and collective isolation from one another and from the outside world, evident in their inability to reach a consensus about their shared destiny; and 3) the problem of language and linguistic expression in Puerto Rican life, in particular the relationship of language to both cultural identity and political power.

Carrero's published plays include *Flag Inside* (1966), *Capitán F4C* (1968, Captain F4C), *El caballo de Ward* (1972, Ward's Horse), *Pipo Subway no sabe reír* (1972), *Noo Jork* (1972), and *La caja de caudales FM* (1978). The first four were published in 1973 by Ediciones Puerto in the collection *Teatro,* but both *Flag Inside* and *Pipo Subway* had been previously performed by theatre groups in Puerto Rico and New York. *Noo Jork,* also entitled *Noo Jall,* was performed in New York City by the *Teatro rodante puertorriqueño* and was published in 1972 by the *Revista Chicano-Riqueña*. *La caja de caudales FM* was published in 1978 by *Sin nombre* and first performed in San Juan in 1979.

Flag Inside, written in Spanish, dramatizes one day in the life of an island family, reunited after many years by the arrival from Vietnam of the deceased son Alberto whose coffin carries the label "Flag Inside." Characters include

Ursula, an archetypically strong Puerto Rican mother who has lost control of her family, Augusto, an absent father who abandoned his wife and children for a young mistress and espouses the ideals of the American corporation that employs him, Lucía, a hardened and materialistic daughter obsessed with appearances, Raúl, a rebellious son, living in New York, who rejects his father's values and the war that has claimed his brother, and Ana, a mute, retarded adolescent kept hidden away by her family and whose presence is valued only by Raúl. Alberto's dying wish—that no outward symbols, including flags, crosses, or candles, adorn his coffin—motivates a violent argument among his survivors who disagree not only about the request but also about the war and the moral and political issues it raises. The family's inability to communicate or to reach a meaningful consensus is symbolized in the mute Ana— "forced to silence" —whose pantomimic reactions reflect the emotions of her parents and siblings, and their separation and discord assume a broader dimension when compared by Lucía to the exodus of Puerto Ricans from the island.

Vietnam and its aftermath provide the setting for *El caballo de Ward* and *Capitán F4C,* in which conflicting views of the war underscore the absence of consensus in Puerto Rican life. Similar in certain elements to *Flag Inside, Capitán F4C* dramatizes the return from Vietnam of an uncle haunted by memories of napalmed children he saw while serving as a bomber pilot. His arrival causes generational conflicts, and the ensuing family debate examines the dehumanizing effects of war ideology and the mass culture that sustains it, sharpening the family's radical disagreements on Puerto Rico's relationship to that culture. Here Carrero employs techniques typical of political theatre, including the simultaneous juxtaposition, through slides and film, of auditory and visual images with the dramatic action, the use of anti-realistic sets that represent through symbolic structures the power relationships explored in the play and the Brechtian destruction of theatrical illusion created by direct audience confrontation.

The failure of Puerto Ricans to agree about Vietnam or their relationship to the powers waging the war is also the central theme of *El caballo de Ward,* but here the house divides against itself at the societal level. Three inmates of a separate military hospital ward for Hispanics, including a middle-class islander, a perpetual migrant, and a Nuyorican, represent three dimensions of Puerto Rican experience, and the wooden horse their colonel has given them to ride symbolizes the false nationhood of Puerto Rico's commonwealth status. A military investigation of the inmates' Vietnam activities reveals their divergent views of the war as well as their dependent status, a condition for which the ward confining them serves as an apt metaphor. Employing the techniques of existential and absurdist theatre, Carrero locks his characters into a *huis clos* setting—there are no exists or entrances during this play—in order to dramatize their insular status. The relationship of language to power is an important subtheme developed through the Nuyorican's aggressive bilingualism that gives him a measure of control and independence the others do not have.

The fate of Puerto Ricans in the barrios of New York provides the focus of Carrero's other three plays, but though the surroundings differ, the problems of family violence, of the loss of power and identity, and of the dependence upon U.S. mass culture are consistent with the themes of the Vietnam plays. In *Pipo Subway no sabe reír* a twelve-year-old boy, overwhelmed by the obstacles his growing family's poverty presents to the new bicycle he's been promised, pushes his pregnant mother down the stairs hoping to abort her unborn child. Pipo's situation is exacerbated by his divided family (his father and half-siblings live in other cities), by the mixture of religion and superstition that governs his mother's decisions, and by the irrelevance of official views and solutions to the realities of his world. Linguistic nuance is a fundamental technique in this play whose characters' bilingualism captures the essence of barrio existence. Pipo and his friends act out the violent tension of their lives through swift, spontaneous dialogue, full of playful obscenities, but sharp and direct. With linguistic irony, Carrero juxtaposes the empty platitudes of a professional tourist lecture on the innocent beauty of Puerto Rico's inhabitants with the violent discourse of Pipo's world.

Language is used similarly in the more comical and light *Noo Jork,* a collage of exchanges—mostly in English—among several barrio types—including an idealistic dancer, Gladys, a cynical student, Tino, a traditionally religious mother, and an upwardly mobile petty official—who debate without consensus the problems of Puerto Ricans. Their failure to agree, culminating in the rape of Gladys by four petty gamblers, makes a mockery of the Puerto Rican Day parade organized to celebrate cultural pride and unity. In a play with brief and rapid scenes linked by a thin plot, the texture of the language itself provides the substance of the work. Through the same rapid-fire dialogue of *Pipo Subway,* characters are identified by their accents and speech styles as well as distinguishing background themes on the bongos that announce their entrances on the scene. The relationship of language to the tension between identity and acculturation is made explicit when a blond policeman tries without success to teach the mother how to pronounce "New York."

A similar mix of violence and comedy characterizes the erotically slapstick *La caja de caudales FM,* in which a Brooklyn liquor store owner, Vidal, and his girlfriend Marcelina try to resist the invasion of a local gang while disputing the relative merits of life on the island and in the barrio. In an ironic critique of hyperbolic machismo, the dialogue captures the tension of barrio life through the linguistic diversity characterizing Puerto Rican English and Spanish.

In addition to his plays, Carrero has published three novels: *Raquelo tiene un mensaje* (1970), *Los nombres* (1972), both published by the University of Puerto Rico, and *El hombre que no sudaba* (The Man Who Did Not Sweat), published in 1982 by Arte Público Press in Houston. Exploiting the flexibility of perspective available through the strategies of narrative, Carrero develops themes consistent with the concerns of his dramatic work.

In *Raquelo tiene un mensaje*, the insularity and prejudices of a small Puerto Rican town are seen from the point of view of an idealistic young Nuyorican who returns with an Ivy League education to teach English in the public schools. Born on the island but raised in New York, Wayne Rodríguez clashes with local educators when he refuses to let his students sing "The Star Spangled Banner" by rotely mouthing words they can neither pronounce nor understand. Declaring that correctly learned language must be a tool for liberation, the young teacher is accused of leftist ideas, and although he weathers vicious rumors, he eventually decides to leave. The attack comes from Raquelo, a retarded young boy, comparable in symbolic function to Ana of *Flag Inside*, who serves as the town crier at the manipulation of whoever has a message for him to disseminate and who, like the children singing the U.S. national anthem, repeats whatever he is told without comprehending its meaning. As the community's principal agent of communication, this semi-mute character represents the insularity and impotence of the people whose gossip he circulates. Told primarily from a first-person perspective that underscores the protagonist's detachment from the people of the town, this novel combines traditional narrative with stream of consciousness, flashbacks to recalled dialogues, and diary entries.

Less experimental in form than the other two novels, *Los nombres* is similar to *El caballo de Ward* in its use of a wartime ambience, in this case Korea, as a microcosm of Puerto Rican experience. The novel combines a traditional third-person account of the final days in the maneuvers of a Puerto Rican platoon with individual sketches of its members who come from all levels of Puerto Rican society. The title refers to the U.S. Army practice of divesting Hispanic soldiers of their identity by Anglicizing their names. The failure of a news report on the platoon members' heroic death in battle motivates the narrative's objective: to name correctly and portray accurately the lives of those who have been obliterated, in name and in fact, by the war and by the dominant culture on whose behalf they have waged it.

The impotence of contemporary Puerto Rican culture to generate meaningful human activity, including productive work and authentic creative expression, is the theme of *El hombre que no sudaba*. The psychological retrospective of a forcibly retired college professor, this novel employs flashbacks, stream of consciousness narration, shifting narrative perspectives, and dramatic dialogues in its reconstruction of a powerless and solitary life. With shades of the mute Ana and the semi-mute Raquelo, the protagonist grows from a totally silent child, abused by his classmates, to a stuttering and maladjusted adult whose relationships are arbitrarily manipulated by the whims of others, a recasting of Carrero's language and power theme and an extended metaphor for the culture's inability to express itself coherently.

Carrero's dramatic and narrative works present a moving vision of the upheavals and individual tragedies of Puerto Rican life. Though often quite funny and always incorrigibly human, his characters move in a world of discord, alienation, and violence. Although they often recognize the magnitude of their despair and the solitude of their powerless condition and although some of them, especially the Nuyoricans, are vociferous in their protest, they come to neither resolution nor consensus about how to control their destiny. A master at the creation of vividly authentic dialogue with an ear for linguistic nuance, Carrero is at his best when he allows his characters to speak, laugh, argue, tease, threaten, curse, rejoice, and weep for themselves, in whatever language they know and with whatever voice they can find.

Survey of Criticism

Despite the recognition Carrero's work has received from the Puerto Rican literary establishment and despite the favorable New York and San Juan newspaper reviews that marked the performance of his plays in those cities, there has been little in-depth scholarly attention to his writing. Such critical misfortunes are not uncommon among artists who express the experiences and concerns of groups marginalized within a larger society that sets the norms by which verbal art shall be measured. Although uneven in quality, Carrero's writing attains in some works a level of literary achievement and human impact worthy of careful analysis, particularly in *Flag Inside, Pipo Subway no sabe reír, Noo Jork, Raquelo tiene un mensaje,* and, in some aspects, *El hombre que no sudaba.* The situation is due in part to the problem of limited exposure experienced by writers who are published by literary magazines and small presses. In recent years, however, the Arte Público Press of Houston, specializing in works by Puerto Rican and Chicano writers in the United States as well as island writers who address the bicultural experience, has promoted and distributed Carrero's drama collection *Teatro,* published by Ediciones El Puerto, as well as *El hombre que no sudaba,* put out by the press itself. These efforts will give the reading public and the critical establishment greater exposure to his writing.

A study of Carrero's dramatic work by Asela Rodríguez-Seda was published in 1977 by the *Revista Chicano-Riqueña.* Situating the plays in the context of contemporary Latin American drama, she examines his principal themes and the avant-garde techniques he employs—not always successfully, she feels—in their development. Rodríguez-Seda concludes that the most compelling element in Carrero's theatre is his gripping portrayal of Puerto Rican life. In another piece on the relationship of the contemporary Puerto Rican novel to the Latin American boom, also published in the *Revista Chicano-Riqueña,* the same critic mentions Carrero's novels in passing. In an outline history of contemporary Puerto Rican theatre which appeared in *Conjunto* magazine published by the Casa de las Américas in Havana, Manuel Gallich takes note of *Flag Inside* as a significant document of the new theatre in Latin America, and the play itself is reprinted in the same issue.

Despite the current absence of critical work, a careful reading of Carrero's work suggests topics that are fertile ground for further analysis. A productive study might be undertaken, for example, of his conception of language—both thematic and structural—with close attention to the varieties of discourse his characters employ, from the verbally aggressive and adept Nuyoricans to the often silent, stuttering, and semi-mute inhabitants of his island works. Because literary art is enriched by the multiple readings that interpret it, an analysis of Carrero's writing as an aesthetic position would also be worthwhile, that is, as a statement about the power of verbal art and expression in a culturally alienated world.

Bibliography

WORKS BY CARRERO

Aquí los ángeles/Here the angels. San Germán: n.p. 1960.
Tiranosauro Rey, amén, amén. San Germán: Inter-American University, 1963.
Jet neorriqueño/Neo-Rican Jetliner Poems. San Germán: Inter-American University, 1964.
Raquelo tiene un mensaje. San Juan: 1970.
"Usted" and "Chévere." *Poesía nueva puertorriqueña*, ed. Luis Antonio Rosario Quiles, 117–20. Río Piedras: Producciones Bondo, 1971.
Los nombres. Río Piedras: Editorial Universitaria, 1972.
Teatro: Flag Inside, Capitán F4C, El caballo de Ward, Pipo Subway no sabe reír. Río Piedras: Editorial Puerto, 1973.
"My Graphological Yo." *The Rican* (May 1974): 63–66.
Noo Jork. Revista Chicano-Riqueña 2 (Fall 1972): 3–31.
La caja de caudales FM. Sin nombre 8 (January-March 1978): 63–99.
"Vieques del Caribe." *Revista Chicano-Riqueña* 7 (Summer 1979): 9–13.
"The FM Safe." *Chicano and Puerto Rican Drama*, eds. Nicolás Kanellos and Jorge Huerta. Houston: Arte Publico Press, 1979.
El hombre que no sudaba. Houston: Arte Público, 1982.

WORKS ABOUT CARRERO

Alonso, Alberto. *"Sin Bandera* es Página Triste de la Guerra que se Libra en Viet Nam; Rebeldía y Adiós." *El Diario-La Prensa* January 17, 1973.
"Carrero publica su tercera novela." *El Nuevo Día* February 7, 1983.
Collins, J.A. "Carrero's *Cashbox FM* a Theatrical Firebomb." *The San Juan Star* June 22, 1979: 7.
Márquez, Juan Luis. *"Pipo Subway no sabe reír." El Imparcial* May 12, 1972.
Newton, Edmund. *"Noo Jall* Opens: Set to Tour Parks." *New York Post* August 28, 1973: 20.
"Noo Jall: Otro éxito del Teatro Rodante Puertorriqueño." *El Tiempo* August 26, 1973: 18–19.
"Noo Jall Plays in City Parks." *New York Times* August 29, 1973.
O'Haire, Patricia. *"Noo Jall* Lively Play." *Daily News* August 29, 1973: 60.
Valle, Norma. *"Flag Inside*: Obra Humana y de Gran Valor Teatral." *El Mundo* February 25, 1973.

Critical Studies

Gallich, Manuel. "Boceto puertorriqueño." *Conjunto* (July-September 1978): 3–17.
———— "El teatro puertorriqueño dentro del nuevo teatro latinoamericano." *Conjunto* (July-September 1978): 62–68.

Rodríguez-Seda, Asela. "La trayectoria de la novelística puertorriqueña contemporánea—1950–1975." *Revista Chicano-Riqueña* 4 (Winter 1976): 34–45.
———. "El teatro de Jaime Carrero." *Revista Chicano-Riqueña* 5 (Summer 1977): 26–31.

VICKY UNRUH

CASAL, LOURDES (1938–1981). In her relatively short lifetime, Lourdes Casal was a prominent poet, short-story writer, literary critic, political activist, and intellectual. She devoted herself to social psychology and became a professor in this field. Her literary output is not abundant, but it is so intense and so valuable for its autobiographical elements that it is considered outstanding and of indisputable artistic quality. The impact of exile is evident in much of her writing: Casal expresses the alienation and solitude of her daily life as it evolves in a society that is not her own.

Biography

Lourdes Casal was born in Havana in 1938. Her parents were middle-class professionals: her father was a physician and a dentist and her mother a primary school teacher. Casal attended private primary and secondary schools in her native city. She graduated from high school from Institute Number 2 in "El Vedado," a public institution that she attended starting in her third year. She was always a brilliant student and received a bachelor of science and letters degree in 1954. She began her university studies at Universidad Santo Tomás de Villanueva in Marianao, Havana, the same year. There she studied for seven years, first chemical engineering, then psychology. At the same time, she edited and collaborated in several student publications.

During her years at the university, Casal carried out revolutionary activities against the dictatorship of Fulgencio Batista and, after the victory of Fidel Castro's revolution, joined the Student Revolutionary Directorate. In 1961, because she was critical of the revolutionary ideology, Casal moved to the United States and, in 1962, to New York City, were she lived until 1979.

After taking up residence in New York, Casal completed her graduate studies in social psychology and was awarded a master's degree and Ph.D. in 1962 and 1975, respectively, from the New School for Social Research. She was a professor of psychology in several North American universities, including Dominican College of Blauvelt, New York; Brooklyn College of CUNY, and Rutgers University in Newark, New Jersey.

The 1960s was a crucial decade for Lourdes Casal's ideological development. Her participation in the civil rights movement led her to reconsider her political position toward Cuba. Her interest in everything that concerned the Cuban Revolution and in the preservation of Cuban culture in exile showed itself in several ways. Casal was an active member of such organizations as the Cuban National Planning Board, Institute for Cuban Studies, "Circulo de Cultura Cubana,"

Cuban Studies/Estudios cubanos, and others. In 1974, she was a charter member
of the magazine *Areíto*, an institution that attempted to give a new focus to
Cuban culture in the United States. In 1974–1975 she was awarded the Cintas
Fellowship from the Institute for International Education. Other awards received
by Lourdes were:

1977–1978   Ford Foundation Competition on the Movement of Caribbean Peoples

Summer 1978   Social Science Research Council grant for research in Cuba

1978–1979   Woodrow Wilson Fellow. The Woodrow Wilson International Center
                for Scholars, Smithsonian Institution, Washington, D.C.

Casal wrote, published, and edited numerous books, articles, and monographs,
some on psychology, others principally on political and social subjects relating
to the Cuban revolutionary process and the Cuban community living off the
island. Among the most well known of these are *El caso Padilla: literatura y
revolución en Cuba* (1971, The Padilla Case: Literature and Revolution in Cuba),
*The Cuban Minority in the U.S.: Preliminary Report on Need Identification and
Program Evaluation* (1973), and *Contra viento y marea* (1978, Against the Winds
and Currents).

On the literary side, Lourdes Casal devoted herself to short stories and poetry.
Her book *Los fundadores: Alfonso y otros cuentos* (The Founders: Alfonso and
Other Stories) was published in 1973 by Ediciones Universal of Miami. Many
of her poems were compiled posthumously in *Palabras juntan revolución* (1981,
Words Join Revolution).

In 1973, Casal began traveling to Cuba on different occasions. Her political
ideology became evident in a vehement desire to establish communication between the new Cuban revolutionary society and the exile community in the
United States. She participated in dialogues between Castro and representatives
of the Cuban exodus at the end of 1978, which ended in an agreement between
Cuba and the United States to allow the exiles to visit their relatives on the
island.

In 1979, Lourdes Casal, suffering from a serious illness, returned definitively
to Cuba, knowing her life would soon be over. Casal wanted to die in her own
country, and thus it happened, in early 1981.

Major Themes

A number of stories and poems by Lourdes Casal have appeared in different
literary publications in the United States. Here we will limit ourselves to the
two books that contain a compilation of a large part of her creative output: *Los
fundadores: Alfonso y otros cuentos* and *Palabras juntan revolución*.

Los fundadores contains seven stories. The earliest is "Salvador en cuatro
tiempos" (Salvador at Four Times), from 1968. This title encompasses four
"mini" short stories called "Moisés salvado de las aguas" (Moses Rescued

from the Waters), "La cartera de la obviamente no casta Susana" (The Obviously Unchaste Susana's Mailwoman), "El elevador" (The Elevator), and "Encuentro con el león" (Meeting with the Lion). The themes are varied. "Moisés" alludes to the author's childhood; it is a story full of domestic fragrances, childhood memories. "La cartera," written in the tradition of the literature of the absurd, makes reference to the author's college years as well as a view of contemporary New York. "El elevador" also takes place in the United States and treats contemporary technology ironically. The fourth short narrative, "Encuentro con el león," according to Leonel A. de la Cuesta's prologue to Los fundadores, is "the best of the four in this series, for its accurate usage or, better yet, the right mix of reality and fantasy it contains." This Kafkaesque tale has a tendency toward fable and also includes ironic criticism of certain aspects of North American society of our age. In the story "Rodrigo de Triana," dated 1972, de la Cuesta also states that "a mixture of national history and personal biography is present; of all the stories in this book, it is the only one in which Casal adheres to magical realism; reading it brings us to the foreground of the imagination in the style of Jorge Luis Borges . . . and . . . García Márquez." We should add that the author mentions Kafka by name in the narrative. The technological oppression of the individual by society is clearly felt in paragraphs such as this:

I looked in the telephone book, and, sure enough, under the heading of the city government, I found the number of the Commission for the Preservation of Human Resources. I dialed the number, and a syrupy, seductive voice screeched: "This is a recording. The number you have reached has been temporarily disconnected. I repeat this is a recording."

In Los fundadores there are three stories dated 1971. "Los zapaticos me aprietan" (These Tiny Shoes Are Tight) and "Juegos" (Games) have in common the subject of the author's childhood in the "petit bourgeois cubanensis," as she herself calls it in the book, adding that: "The species has adapted and can now be found in colder climates; but its customs and vices have changed since then." "Los zapaticos" is also a humorous narrative at times bordering on Cuban "choteo" (jeering) at such traditions as breaking the piñata at children's birthday parties. In addition to the element of mockery, there is a Freudian sense of repressed violence:

It would have been great to dig my fingers into the eye sockets and pull out the plastic balloons; to beat the obviously hollow chest and smash to pieces the gears of the clockwork that I could sometimes hear so clearly.

"Juegos" is a more serious, more intimate narrative, with greater emphasis on social injustice and the separation of social classes in the Havana of the 1940s.

"María Valdés o la colina de la Universidad" (1971, María Valdés or the University Kitchen) is a clearly Cuban story, as much for its Havana atmosphere as for its parody of *Cecilia Valdés o la loma del Angel* (Cecilia Valdés or the Angel's Hill), the novel by Cirilo Villaverde, a Cuban author of the nineteenth century. It is a story in the folkloric tradition, with detailed descriptions of the neighborhood around the university. The tale takes place in this century.

"Los fundadores: Alfonso" and *"Love Story* according to Cyrano Prufrock" are both dated 1972. According to de la Cuesta, " 'Los fundadores' is the beginning of a series which was to join the history of Cuba with a fantastic, or better, imaginary version of the story of the author's ancestors (Casal summarized the three Cuban races: white, black and Chinese)." We believe that, of all the stories in the book, this one most certainly brings together very personal autobiography with history at a national level, highlighting a very little studied period in Cuban history and the crossbreeding that took place on the island: the Asian component, specifically the Chinese. Lourdes Casal, through one of her ancestors, narrates the importation of coolies from China, begun in 1847, the Chinese presence in the Cuban wars of independence against Spain, the arrival of the "Californian" Chinese on the island, the establishment of Havana's Chinatown in 1913, and the new wave of oriental immigration. All of this information appears mixed in with notes referring to the author's family tree and her own childhood memories.

Unfortunately, death came early and Casal could not continue her sequence, "Los fundadores," which, judging by "Alfonso," promised to equal the best of her literary work.

"Love Story según Cyrano Prufrock" ends this collection of stories. The major themes are: Cuba of the 1950s and New York of the 1970s. Both settings, that of Havana and that of Manhattan, are superimposed on a foundation of pursuit of sexual love that begins in the Cuban capital, continues in New York, and culminates in the loss of the object of desire in the latter city.

Survey of Criticism

Because Lourdes Casal's career was so brief and, perhaps too, because her academic career and writings are so well known, her literary works have attracted little critical attention. Only her stories have attracted some commentary.

Raquel Chang-Rodríguez has said in "Critica" that Lourdes Casal, through her stories, shows us her roots and "transforms a past which, contrapuntally, she looks at nostalgically at the same time as she rejects it." The same critic points out that Casalian storytelling is, more than anything, autobiographical and that its greatest success is in the ironically humorous tone that Casal maintains even in her most serious narratives.

Palabras juntan revolución is a collection of poems, grouped in four parts: "El barrio regresa en sus sonidos" (The Barrio Returns to Its Sounds), "Tanto más vulnerable que la piedra" (A Little More Vulnerable than Stone), "Tigre con una herida en el costado" (Tiger with a Wounded Side), and "Palabras juntan revolución" (Words Join Revolution). In "El barrio," the poems have a nostalgic tone toward the author's memories of her Cuban past. Casal thinks of her childhood, and her relatives, such as "la tía Adela [que] batía con un palo/montañas de ropa blanca/humeante en sus enormes baetas de aluminio" (Aunt Adele who beat with a stick/mountains of white clothes/steaming in her enormous aluminum wash pans). There are broken tones, full of sadness, in "Y qué se ha hecho, dónde está la que yo era/cuando era mío aquel vestido azul/dónde se ha ido aquel mundo que conozco/en sus huellas" (And what have they done/where is the one I was/when that blue dress was mine/where has it gone, that world I know/in its footprints). The past, almost lost, comes back to the author's present in images of Afro-Cuban deities such as Obbatalá and Yemayá Olokun. In the first part of the book there is also a poem intended for her mother, who, Lourdes tells us, "me limpia/me protege/me retorna la quebrantada salud/se posa levemente sobre mis hombros/y sobre mi cabeza" (washes me/protects me/restores my broken health/rests lightly on my shoulders/and on my head). And, in another poem: "De mi padre recuerdo el viejo Studebaker/Negro/(color conservador como le corresponde/a un médico)" (Of my father I remember the old Studebaker/Black/ (a conservative color as it befits/a doctor). Thus Lourdes continues, evoking relatives, birthday parties, bittersweet memories brought to her readers through magic realism, fantastic images, already fading in the dying light of a past growing remote.

"Tanto más vulnerable que la piedra" is the longest part of the book and includes more allusions to exile and its symptoms: solitude, northern winter, the hostility in the atmosphere, the artificiality of the modern city and its inhabitants. In this part we can also glimpse memories of the past, sometimes in the form of flashbacks, but increasingly scarce and less exact. In "La Habana 1968" Casal tells us: "Que se me amarillea y se me gasta,/perfil de mi ciudad, siempre agitándose/en la memoria/y sin embargo,/siempre perdiendo bordes y letreros,/siempre haciéndose toda un amasijo/de imágenes prensadas por los años" (How it yellows and wastes away/profile of my city, always stirring/in my memory/and even so/continually losing edges and legends/continually becoming all kneaded together/images pressed by the years).

Lourdes gives her definition of exile in three lines: "Exilio/es vivir donde no existe casa alguna/en la que hayamos sido niños" (Exile/is to live where no house exists/in which we were children). This doesn't prevent her new city, New York, from becoming her new place of citizenship: "Poco a poco/recobro/mis documentos de ciudadanía newyorkina:/la tarjeta de la Biblioteca Pública,/la del Museo de Arte Moderno,/un ticket viejo del Waverly a media noche/y este recibo de matrícula/del New School" (Little by little/I recover/my New York citizenship papers:/my library card/my MOMA membership card/an old ticket to the midnight show at the Waverly/and my registration receipt/from the New School). Further along in another poem the author reaches the conclusion that she is "demasiado habanera para ser newyorkina,/demasiado newyorkina para ser,/—aun volver a ser—/cualquier otra cosa" (Too Havanian to be New Yorker/too much of a New Yorker to be/—even to go back to being—/anything else).

Lourdes Casal's participation in the civil rights movement in the 1960s and the worry that it created in her spiritual development translate into verses such as these (after describing different characters who are shoving through the streets of New York): "Para que fuera/aquel niño que fue cada uno de estos/confluyeron lejanas caravanas,/sobrevivieron al látigo y al sol/los negros de la trata,/navegaron los gigantes del Norte" (In order for them to be/the child that each of them was/distant caravans converged/and the negros of the slave trade/navigated by the giants of the north/survived the horsewhip and the sun). The Vietnam War appears indirectly in a poem by Lourdes Casal when she says: "Y el mundo me habla con las voces claramente/antipoéticas de Wall Street a las nueve de la mañana/o con los rugidos monótonos de los bombarderos/que visitan mi cocina gracias a Walter Cronkite/y al Sr. Johnson, por las noches" (And the world speaks to me with the clearly antipoetic voices of Wall Street at nine in the morning/or with the monotonous roar of bombers which visit my kitchen at night thanks to Walter Cronkite and Mr. Johnson).

"Tigre con una herida en el costado" is made up of poems, almost all short, in which there are also strong feelings of solitude and nostalgia. The passing of the years, receding youth, and the evocation of past lovers appear in many of these verses. Some, very powerful as images of the entry into middle age, are these: "Acuérdate de abril/ahora que ya bordeamos octubre/riscoso precipicio" (Remember April/now that we are on the edge of October/risky precipice).

The final group of poems has the same title as the book, "Palabras juntan reolución." Some appear to be unclassifiable poems that have been capriciously placed in this last group. Nevertheless, the major theme seems to be the reconsideration, on the author's part, of her political position toward Cuba. In the last section there are lines like these: "afuera tantas cosas me reclaman:/el cadáver del Che sobre la mesa aquella,/los espejuelos rotos y el cabello ensangrentado/ de Allende,/o simplemente,/la escuela/que todavía no hemos terminado de construir,/allá en la Yaya" (outside so many things/demand my attention: Che's cadaver on that table, the broken glasses and bloody hair of Allende, or simply the school we still haven't finished building over there in La Yaya). And these others, which give us her definition of "La Revolución es ese guajirito de Victoria de las Tunas,/analfabeto en las vísperas/ante el huracán de enero" (The revolution is this country boy of Victoria de las Tunas, illiterate on the eve of the January hurricane).

The impact of her reencounter with Cuba after her return can be felt in these lines: "Vivo en Cuba./Siempre he vivido en Cuba,/aun cuando he creído habitar/ muy lejos del caimán de la agonía/siempre he vivido en Cuba" (I live in Cuba./ I have always lived in Cuba,/even when I thought I resided/very far from the alligator of agony, I have always lived in Cuba). But the author makes clear that she doesn't live in the Cuba that *was,* but the Cuba of the present.

Faced by such a brief literary career, though so intense and of such clear artistic value, we can only imagine what position Lourdes Casal might have attained in contemporary Hispanic letters.

Lourdes Casal represents a group of Cuban authors that, through the years of exile, have changed their perspectives and have expressed this process in their artistic creations.

Bibliography

WORKS BY CASAL

Los fundadores: Alfonso y otros cuentos. Miami: Ediciones Universal, 1973.
Palabras juntan revolución. La Habana: Ediciones Casa de las Américas, 1981.

WORKS ABOUT CASAL

Chang-Rodríguez, Raquel. "Crítica. Nota sobre *Los fundadores: Alfonso y otros cuentos.*" *Areíto* 5, 19–20 (1979): 63–64.
de la Cuesta, Leonel A. "A guisa de prólogo." In Lourdes Casal's *Los fundadores: Alfonso y otros cuentos.* Miami: Ediciones Universal, 1973.
de la Cuesta, Leonel A., and María Cristina Herrera, eds. *itinerario ideológico. Antologia de Lourdes Casal.* Miami: Ediciones Diáspora, 1982.
Matas, Julio. "La nostalgia es absurda." Review of *Los fundadores: Alfonso y otros cuentos.Caribe* 1, 2 (Autumn 1976): 127–29.

SILVIA BURUNAT

CATALÁ, RAFAEL (1942–   ). Most Hispanic authors in the United States have written about the experiences of their own ethnic groups. For some, this means reminiscing about the old country. For others, the sociohistorical condition of Hispanics in the United States provides a focus of interest. Rafael Catalá fits neither of these two groups. Yet, his work, a fusion of literature, sociology, theology, history, science, and activism, exemplifies the true praxis of a Hispanic author in the United States. An analysis of his life and his work quickly reveals why Catalá's work is essential in order to understand Hispanic literature in the United States.

Biography

Rafael Catalá was born in Victoria de las Tunas, Cuba, on September 26, 1942. He left Cuba in 1961 and settled in New York City. He has lived in New York and New Jersey since then.

Catalá is special among Cuban American writers for two reasons. First, his entire college education has taken place in the United States. Second, his interest is neither his Cuban past nor his North American present, but a Hispanic cultural totality that goes beyond time and space.

The education that Catalá received in elementary and secondary schools in Cuba has had profound influence on his work. Latin American, as well as Cuban, authors and philosophers, unknown to most Hispanic authors educated in the United States, appear constantly in Catalá's work. For example, mention of the eighteenth- and early nineteenth-century Cuban pedagogues, Félix Varela and

José de la Luz y Caballero, in connection with Paulo Freire's work, reveals an education with profound roots in Cuban and Latin American ideology.

It is precisely the combination of a strong basic Latin American education with the critical perspective achieved through graduate studies in the United States that makes Catalá a powerful author. Catalá devoted many years as an undergraduate student studying psychology. It was only years later, as a graduate student at New York University, that he pursued a Ph.D. in literature. Catalá's interest in psychology has also left a mark on his literary work. We are in the presence of an author who is not threatened by the sciences or by quantification as an alternative way of seeing human reality. In fact, as he states in *Escobas de millo* (1984, Straw Brooms), Catalá is not one of "the good men of the Humanities/ who do not see a connection with sciences,/ as if there were life without reasoning/ or viceversa."

During his years as a doctoral student at New York University, Catalá was editor of the literary journal *Románica*. He was later involved in the literary workshops conducted by the Writing Division of Columbia University. Between 1975 and 1976 he was a member of the workshops directed by Nicanor Parra and Mario Vargas Llosa. He was also a participant in the workshop directed by Gabriel García Marquez at Columbia University in October 1976.

When he arrived in the United States and before devoting himself to full-time studies, Catalá worked in menial and clerical jobs in factories and offices. His interaction with the Hispanic poor in New York City has had a profound influence on his literary praxis.

One of the antagonistic currents that shapes Catalá's forceful work is precisely the perspective gained from living with the oppressed and also being familiar with the oppressor. It is precisely this strength that has made him a favorite leader of alternative literary workshops. In 1980 Rafael Catalá organized the literary and cultural workshop known as Ometeca. "Ometeca," Catalá tells us, comes from Nahuatl and means two in one, that is, theory and creation at the same time. His purpose was to familiarize the participants with Latin American philosophers and writers such as José Martí, Macedonio Fernández, José Lezama Lima, Alfonso Reyes, Darcy Ribeiro,Gustavo Gutiérrez, Angel Rama, and José de Mariátegui. At the same time, it was expected that the participants would generate other theories based on Latin American thought. Catalá's concern was not only in diffusing ideas of the best-known Latin American thinkers, but also in discovering works that had been totally ignored. Thus, a symposium to study the work of Clemente *Soto Vélez was organized, and, together with James Romano, a study of his work and that of the "atalayistas" of the 1920s and 1930s was conducted.

Because of the success and enthusiasm generated by Ometeca, Catalá was invited, in 1983, to direct the literary workshop Rácata in Hostos Community College of the City University of New York. There, in conjunction with others such as Clemente Soto Vélez and Orlando José Hernández, Catalá worked diligently to familiarize the participants with Latin American philosophers and theorists that would be useful to the writer. In the introduction to *Esta urticante pasión de la pimienta* (1983, This Stinging Passion of Pepper), an anthology produced by Rácata I, Catalá says: "Theory, creation and science are constructions that are not created by only one man or one woman, they are but the product of additions, of destructions, that each one of us builds." Another important aspect of these workshops was to familiarize the participants with the production, dissemination, and distribution of their texts since Catalá feels that "the modes of literary diffusion are not separate from the creative process: they are the same thing."

Catalá's most important work as an educator has taken place within these alternative literary workshops. It has been there that he has been able to put into practice Paulo Freire's problem-posing education. As a collaborator in these workshops, Catalá has partaken in the process of conscientization and has been transformed. This has been a more positive experience than the traditional teaching that he had done prior to the workshops at New York University and Lafayette College in Easton, Pennsylvania.

Since 1978 Catalá has constantly searched to find his roots. He has discovered pre-Columbian and Afro-American literature, as well as important Latin American philosophers. His first three books of poetry, *Caminos/Roads* (1972), *Círculo cuadrado* (1974, Squared Circle), and *Ojo sencillo/Triqui-traque* (1975, Simple Eye/Clickety Clack), were written prior to this date. Since then, he has published two books of poetry, *Copulantes* (1981, Copulators) and *Escobas de millo,* and is preparing another one following scientific principles.

Since 1978 Catalá has also written essays: "La cultura en la práctica de la libertad" (Culture in the Practice of Liberty) and "Síntesis de la cultura latinoamericana: teología de la liberación, y su influencia en la literatura latinoamericana" (Synthesis of Latin American Culture: Liberation Theology and Its Influence in Latin American Literature). Today, Catalá is in the process of writing a theoretical book about the unification of science and poetry and another on Gustavo Gutiérrez, the Peruvian theorist on the theology of liberation. His dedication to research and creative work has been interrupted since 1978 only by a year of full-time teaching at Seton Hall University in 1983.

Rafael Catalá has also made an important contribution to Hispanic literature in the United States as editor of the *Index of American Periodical Verse* published annually by Scarecrow Press of Metuchen, New Jersey. Before Catalá became editor of the index, Hispanic poets in the United States, as well as those in Puerto Rico, had been excluded.

Major Themes

Catalá's entire literary work expresses a dialogical search, in a Freirean sense, of a new Latin American man. He struggles to unearth the roots of the "Kingdom" which he knows is "Here. Now." In *Ojo sencillo/Triqui-traque,* which also contains two sections that repeat the compound title of the book, Catalá includes a last section called, significantly, "Cocla." It is perhaps the Greek etymology of the nonsense word "cocla" (kochlos), meaning a spiral or shell, which summarizes Catalá's poetic praxis. Catalá's work is not repetitive, it is not focused on a circular/nonprogressive sublime point as was that of the surrealists. However, his roads are not linear, his progression is not *in* time and space but *of* time and space. That is why his progression from his first book of poetry, *Caminos/Roads,* to his last book of poetry, *Escobas de millo,* does not signal a shift, or even a transcendence, but rather a dynamic spiral that moves outward without losing its inner force.

Caminos/Roads already contained the thematic universe of Catalá's poetry. His total communion with Latin America's *mestizaje* was already evident here: "I take communion with my mulatto and black and white brothers and sisters. I love them because I have it inside." In another poem he states, "I am the Indian who screams in despair, the abused black, the gray-haired white man and already empty." In *Copulantes,* Catalá's communion is not just with Latin Americans but with the entire universe: "but an impulse forces the daily act/ of communion, and afterwards, this delight starts./ . . . Everything is coitus, even this act." Catalá's literary praxis is no longer one of sorrow, but of total joyous communion with the whole universe.

The pantheism with the whole universe had already been introduced in *Caminos/Roads.* However, in *Caminos/Roads* the pantheism remains a desire that still has not been totally fulfilled. For example, in this first book of poetry Catalá says that "One has to be an ocean/ so as to be able to receive impure currents/ and not be stained." Yet, in *Copulantes,* the poet, now in complete unity with the universe, writes from the ocean's consciousness and says, "With the conscience of the ocean there can be no impure stain and one is fish and water, algae and foam." There is no longer a consciousness of the poet's body, but rather "the ego has been dissolved in the course of life" and one can be "there and here, here and there, for there aren't two." This process has been completely finished by the time of the last book of poetry, *Escobas de millo.* Now, the new mystic can say: "What is on earth that is not I?"

The poet and the word are no longer separate from the world. The last poem in *Copulantes,* entitled "Actodeconciencia" (Act of Conscience), reveals a new man as poet, an awareness of having progressed from "estar" to "ser" and even to "ser más" : "I lived in lies when I thought that I wasn't, I sang to the mountains, to love, to truth, toeverythingoutside. . . . Until one day, the day that I knew myself./ Now I know that I sing./ Now that we know that we are and what we are/ the game becomes good . . . and we all know that we are and we move within the page and/ we have our being. Conquering word!" The "new mystic" does not transcend the text and external reality, but becomes one with it. That is why living in the United States and speaking English do not affect this new being and the poet can say: "One devours English and it doesn't stain/ for I am language."

Rafael Catalá's literary praxis takes on universal Latin American dimensions. We are in the presence of an author who transcends ethnic topics. He has escaped an existentialist view of Hispanics in the United States by focusing on contemporary Latin American theorists such as Father Camilo Torres, Paulo Freire, and Father Gustavo Gutiérrez. His work reflects a literary praxis that leads to the liberation of man. Hispanics in the United States are linked to the universal search for the liberation of all oppressed people of the world.

Survey of Criticism

There have been too few attempts to comment on Catalá's work. Unfortunately, his thematic universe is too universal for Hispanic critics in the United States interested in local ethnic topics. It is significant, however, that one of his poems, titled "Sunrise Neuyorkino," did appear in the *Hispanics in the United States: Anthology of Creative Literature* edited by Jiménez and Keller. Fortunately, Catalá's work has recently attracted the attention of Latin American critics previously interested only in analyzing authors still linked to a Latin American country. It is in this light that James Romano's critical analysis of *Copulantes* becomes a very significant contribution. Catalá's work still awaits an integral critical analysis, reflecting not only literary currents, but also philosophical, religious, social, political, and scientific thought.

Bibliography

WORKS BY CATALÁ

Poetry

Caminos/Roads. New York: Hispanic Press, 1972.
Círculo cuadrado. New York: Anaya-Las Américas, 1974.
Ojo sencillo/Triqui-traque. New York: Cartago, 1975.
Copulantes. Santo Domingo, Dominican Republic: Colección Noviluion, L.C.C., 1981.
Escobas de millo. New York: Prisma Books, 1984.

Poems have appeared in the following periodicals:

Irish Review, Románica, Cuaderno de Norte, El Diario, Victoria de las Tunas, ARE Newsletter, Puerto Norte y Sur, Diálogos, Punto de Contacto, Círculo Poético, Listín Diario, Impacto, Lugar sin límite, Septagon, Chasqui, La Noticia: Aquí Suplemento Cultural, Hoy, Writer's Workshop Magazine, New York Times, El Duende, Letra Grande, Catalyst, Maize, Pliegos de Murmurios, Mairena, Alcance, En secreto, and *Areíto*.

Poems have been published in the following anthologies:

Azor en vuelo. Vol. 5. Barcelona: Ediciones Rondas, 1981.
Hispanics in the United States: An Anthology of Creative Literature, ed. Gary D. Keller and F. Jiménez. Ypsilanti, Mich.: Bilingual Review/Press, 1982.
Esta urticante pasión de la pimienta, ed. A. Sepúlveda. New York: Prisma Books, 1983.
Los paraguas amarillos, ed. Iván Silén. Hanover, N.H.: Ediciones del Norte, 1983.
Soles emellis, ed. Robertoluis Lugo and Rafael Catalá. New York: Prisma Books, 1983.

Essays

"Una lectura de 'Autorretrato' de Pedro Mir.'' *Caribe* (Fall 1976).
"Las muertes de Ernesto Álvarez.'' *En rojo* (November 25–29, 1976). "El existenci-
    alismo en *Sin rumbo* de Eugenio Cambaceres.'' En *Festschrift for Rodrigo Molina.
    Estudios de historia, literatura y arte hispánicos.* Madrid: Ediciones Ínsula, 1977.
"La trascendencia en *Primero sueño:* el incesto y el águila.'' *Revista Iberoamericana*
    44 (July-December 1978).
"A propósito de *Ese sol del mundo moral* de Cintio Vitier.'' *Cuadernos Universitarios*
    no. 5 (November-December 1979).
"Educación vs instrucción.'' *Expresión Latina* (Diciembre 1982).
"La evolución del pensamiento en tres poetas del Caribe: Manuel Navarro Luna, Clemente
    Soto Vélez y Pedro Mir.'' *Literatures in Transition: The Many Voices of the
    Caribbean Area: A Symposium.* Rose Minc, ed. College Park, Md.: Hispamérica,
    1982.
"Solidaridad político-histórica y religiosa en *Canto de la locura* de Matos Paoli.'' *Mairena*
    (Winter 1982).
"Sobre el *Neptuno alegórico* de Sor Juana.'' *El Café Literario* 6 (enero-abril 1983).
"La cultura en la práctica de la libertad.'' *Ideologies and Literature* 4 (May-June 1983):
    197–212.
"El Neptuno alegórico de Sor Juana: Ontogenía de América.'' *Plural* 13–17 (April 1984):
    17–27.

WORKS ABOUT CATALÁ

Barradas, Efraín. "La poesía teórica y la teoría poética de Rafael Catalá.'' *En Rojo,*
    suplemento literario de *Claridad* (enero 22–28, de 1982): 9.
Céspedes, Diógenes. *"Copulantes,* de Rafael Catalá.'' *Estudios sobre literatura, cultura
    e ideologías* 49 (República Dominicana, Universidad Central del Este, 1983):
    105–9.
Gómez Ayet, Jesús. Reseña de *Ojo sencillo/Triqui-trague. La Estafeta literaria* (15 de
    enero de 1978): 3065–66.
Hernández, José Orlando. "Rafael Catalá y el anverso ptolomeico: *Círculo Cuadrado.'*
    El Tiempo Hispano (2 de marzo 1975): 18.
Nieves-Colón, Myrna. "Aproximaciones a la simbología en *Círculo Cuadrado* de Rafael
    Catalá.'' *Románica* 12 (1975): 47–54.
Romano, James. "Ecuación del Caribe: *Copulantes* de Rafael Catalá.'' In *Literatures in
    Transition: The Many Voices of the Caribbean Area: A Symposium,* 107–15. Rose
    S. Minc, ed. College Park, Md.: Hispamérica, 1982.

OFELIA GARCÍA

COFER, JUDITH ORTIZ (1952–   ). Judith Ortiz Cofer is a poet and teacher
now working on her first novel based on her family's gradual immigration to
the United States. It chronicles the years from the Depression to the 1960s. Most
of her work reflects her struggle as a writer to create a history for herself out of
the cultural ambiguity of a childhood spent traveling back and forth between the
United States and Puerto Rico.

Biography

Judith Ortiz Cofer was born in Puerto Rico in 1952 to Jesus Ortiz Lugo and Fanny Morot. Her father, who had joined the army shortly after his marriage, enlisted in the navy after the birth of their second child, Rolando. Stationed in Brooklyn Yard, New York City, he decided to settle the family in Paterson, New Jersey, where he had relatives. Though Paterson became their home base, he did not feel that his young wife (she had been fifteen years old at marriage, sixteen and eighteen when she had the two babies) and children were safe in the crime-ridden environment of Paterson. So, when he went to Europe with the cargo fleet to which he had been assigned, he sent Fanny, Judith, and Rolando to stay with either his mother or Fanny's parents in Puerto Rico for up to six months at a time. In Puerto Rico, Judith and her brother attended La Escuela San Jose in San Germán, a Catholic school run by American nuns. Back in Paterson, they first attended public schools, but, due to racial tensions between blacks and Puerto Ricans that resulted in gang fights and violent behavior on the streets and in the classrooms, they were eventually enrolled at Saint Joseph's Catholic School in Paterson.

Because of the frequent moves, and her father's expectation that she should maintain high grades in school, reading became a very important aspect of Judith's life. The Paterson Public Library, a Greek temple in the midst of slums, provided her with a steady supply of material for her fantasy making. She was also known to her friends as "the Comic Book Kid" since she spent her allowance buying Super Heroes comics, her favorite being Supergirl. One summer she read the entire world's fairy tales section of the library. With her brother, Rolando, she would often act out stories from the books they read.

During the months they spent in Puerto Rico, she learned about the *cuentos,* stories told by her grandmothers that had been told in the family for generations. Many of these cuentos would later become the source for poems such as "The Woman Who Was Left at the Altar," "Las Malas Lenguas," "The Man Who Lost His Handwriting," and many others.

In 1968, her father retired early from the navy due to a nervous breakdown he had suffered during the Cuban missile crisis, which had developed into severe depression. The family moved to Augusta, Georgia, where Jesus' two older brothers were stationed at Fort Gordon with the army. There Judith attended public high school and later Augusta College where she met her husband, John. After graduation in 1974 and the birth of their daughter Tanya, they moved to West Palm Beach, Florida. Judith earned her M.A. degree at Florida Atlantic University, where she was awarded a scholarship for graduate work at Oxford University by the English-Speaking Union of America.

It was not until she began teaching in South Florida area colleges that Judith began writing poetry. With a small child to take care of, and her studies, there had been little time for creative activities. In 1978, she showed some poems to a friend who had had some experience editing literary journals, and she was encouraged to send them out. Her poems were soon accepted by journals such as the *New Mexico Humanities Review, Kansas Quarterly, The Bilingual Review,* and others. A regional arts publication, *The Florida Arts Gazette,* asked her to be the poetry editor. For three years she wrote essays and interviews for this journal. In 1981, the Fine Arts Council of Florida recognized her work by selecting her as a recipient for a fellowship in poetry. From 1982 to 1984 she held a lecturer's position at the University of Miami, moving to Athens, Georgia, in 1984 in order to be closer to John's family and for him to finish his education at the University of Georgia where Judith presently teaches in the English Department.

An important event in Judith's poetry career occurred when she received scholarships to the Bread Loaf Writers' Conference in 1981 and 1982, followed by a position on the administrative staff from 1983 to 1985. Here she met important poets such as Linda Pastan, Mark Strand, Galway Kinnell, and William Matthews, who have helped her develop a thorough knowledge of the craft of poetry while providing her with much-needed encouragement.

Though teaching and family obligations take up a majority of her time, Judith continues to write every day. Her work appears regularly in literary journals and in 1985 her entry, *Peregrina,* placed first in the Riverstone International Poetry Chapbook Competition. Her chapbook was published in May 1986 by the Riverstone Press of the Foothills Art Center in Golden, Colorado. *Reaching for the Mainland,* a collection of her poems, was published as part of a trilogy of Hispanic American poets by the Bilingual Review/Press in Tempe in 1987. A book of her poems, *Terms of Survival,* was published by Arte Publico Press of Houston in 1987.

Major Themes

The emphasis of Judith Ortiz Cofer's work is on the effects of the native culture and language on the individual life. She believes that, whether there is acceptance or rejection of one's heritage, it makes and shapes everything we think, say, and do. *Reaching for the Mainland,* as the title implies, is a chronicle of the displaced person's struggle to find a goal, a home, a language, and a history. The divisions of the book, *The Birthplace, The Crossing,* and *The Habit of Movement,* indicate the pilgrim's progress that the poet traces from Puerto Rico to the United States, back and forth, never really belonging to either culture but acquiring in the process a habit of movement: the instability itself becoming the source for creativity.

In her second collection, *Terms of Survival,* she explores the psychodynamics of the Puerto Rican Spanish dialect. During an extended visit to her mother and her maternal grandmother on the Island in 1983, she collected idioms, sayings, and stories that she then transformed into poems that either narrate, dramatize, or extend the definition of these words and phrases, providing a kind of linguistic map to the culture. An example of this type of poem is "Quinceañera," which is an interior monologue by a fifteen-year-old girl in which she reveals her anxiety over being thrust out of childhood and into the adult world by both her family and her own body: "At night I hear myself growing, and wake/to find my hands drifting of their own/will to soothe skin stretched tight/over my bones. I am wound like the guts/of a clock, waiting for each hour/to release me." In other poems, such as "Muerto" (Dead), she analyzes the semantic relationships of sound, movement, and meaning to the Spanish speaker: *"Muerto* is a welting word . . . /*Muerto* is gummy and limp . . . /The word . . . jerks your jaw/down, forcing your lips to circle a moan: o, o, o. *Muerto."*

In the novel she is currently writing, she delves deeper into the theme of the individual set adrift between two cultures and two languages, attempting to find, if not acceptance or answers, at least a means to express herself in art. The novel begins with the two words, *They Say,* which emphasize the importance of the storytelling tradition to the author.

Bibliography

WORKS BY COFER

The Native Dancer, a chapbook. Bourbonnais, Ill.: Pteranodon Press, 1981.
Peregrina, a chapbook. Golden, Colo.: Riverstone Press, Foothills Art Center, 1986.
Reaching for the Mainland. Tempe: Bilingual Review Press, 1987.
Terms of Survival. Houston: Arte Publico Press, 1987.
Individual poems, essays, and articles by Judith Ortiz Cofer have appeared in many journals across the United States including: *The Bilingual Review/Press, The Florida Arts Gazette, Kansas Quarterly, New Letters, Prairie Schooner, Revista Chicano-Riqueña, Southern Humanities Review, Southern Poetry Review,* and others.

WORKS ABOUT COFER

Sapia, Yvonne. "Different Voices." *Woodrider* 3 (1985–1986): 111–14.

NICOLÁS KANELLOS

COLÓN, JESÚS (1901–1974). Little has been written about Jesús Colón, although his single published volume of essays and reminiscences, *A Puerto Rican in New York and Other Sketches* (1961, 1982), is well known. Unlike other Puerto Rican writers of his period who wrote predominantly in Spanish, Jesús Colón wrote in English. Thematically, this makes it possible for him to express concerns that are not limited to those of only the Puerto Rican community in New York City, but include those of a class of workers with which he, as a Puerto Rican, identified. Many of his essays in *A Puerto Rican in New York and Other Sketches* were previously published in the *Daily Worker,* a publication of the Communist party. His book and essays are considered to be seminal for the development of Puerto Rican literature on the United States mainland, precisely because of his use of English, his class stand, and his interest in the issue of race.

Biography

Much of what we know of Jesús Colón's early life comes from his autobiographical essays in *A Puerto Rican in New York and Other Sketches* and from memorials published in his honor after his death in 1974. Born into a working-class family in Cayey, Puerto Rico—his father was a baker—Colón's early experiences were of poverty and the struggle for physical and spiritual survival.

Colón's house was located behind the town cigar factory. Like Bernardo Vega in his *Memorias de Bernardo Vega,* Colón recalls being struck as a young boy by the readers hired by workers to read to them as they worked in the cigar factories. Eloquent and dramatic performers, these readers not only kept workers abreast of current historical events, but they also exposed them to the ideas of thinkers such as Karl Marx and writers such as Zola and Balzac. Taken in conjunction with the reality that he experienced and astutely observed, these ideas were transformed into the beginning of a personal ideology that in later years Colón would identify as socialist. In his early youth, this exposure to ideas through workers' discussions "on the benches in the public square" and a strong personal sense of justice led to an early interest in the power of the word, both spoken and written, as in "My First Literary Venture" and "The Way to Learn," and in the efficacy of group action, as in "My First Strike."

At the age of sixteen, Colón left Puerto Rico as a stowaway on the SS *Carolina*. After a trip undertaken in "strict war regulations, darkness during the night," Colón left the SS *Carolina* at its Brooklyn dock and did not return to accept an offer of full-time employment there. Instead, he stayed in New York and began a series of difficult, dangerous jobs that would expose the exploitation and abuse of lower-class and unskilled workers. From the "easy job, good wages" of the ironic essay of the same name to the life-threatening jobs of the docks in "On the Docks It Was Cold," Colón managed to survive while he observed and chronicled the daily life of lower-class Puerto Rican workers in New York. Even as he survived on the level of laborer, however, he remained involved and active in literary endeavors, such as the ingenuous launching of a Spanish-language newspaper he writes about in "Name in Latin" and the translation of English poetry into Spanish that he recounts in "Hiawatha into Spanish." Throughout those early years of his life in New York, Colón encounters the inevitable rebuffs stemming from racial discrimination. He is offered a job by an editor impressed with his writing and then is denied it because, as the editor tells Colón, "I thought you were white." Similarly, a young girl demonstrates to him that racial prejudice permeates all ages of society when she tells her mother in a cafeteria that she "won't sit next to no nigger."

Despite these difficulties, Colón becomes active in organized community and political activities and advocates on behalf of others. In sketches like "I Heard a Man Crying" and "The Lady Who Lived Near the Statue of a Man on a Horse," Colón matter-of-factly talks about temporarily taking in others less fortunate than he. In "Soap Box in the Swamps," we learn of his successful advocacy, with others, in favor of construction of an apartment building for low-income families.

Colón's active participation in working-class and Puerto Rican communities and his dedication to writing led him to a fifteen-year association with the *Daily Worker*, the publication of the national office of the Communist party in New York, later renamed the *Daily World*. In 1955, he began writing a regular column for the newspaper and continued doing so until only a few years before his death.

In addition to his work with the *Daily Worker*, Colón was also president of Hispanic Publishers (Editorial Hispánica), which published history books, political information pamphlets in Spanish, and even literary books, including these titles: *La verdad sobre selecciones* (The Truth about Selections), *El poder soviético* (which he translated from *The Soviet Power* by the Dean of Canterbury), *El destino de la Lengua española en Puerto Rico* (The Future of the Spanish Language in Puerto Rico) by Emilio Delgado, and *Las raíces humanas*, translated from the Public Affairs Committee pamphlet published in New York City circa 1942, "The Races of Mankind," written by Ruth Benedict and Gene Weltfish. He published two collections of stories by the famed Puerto Rican writer José Luis *González Coiscou: *En la sombra* (In the Shade) and *Cinco cuentos de sangre* (Five Tales of Blood). The last title won a prize in 1945 from the Instituto de Literatura Puertorriqueña.

Colón's association with the Communist party intensified in his years as a writer for the *Daily Worker*, and in 1952 Colón ran for senator on the American Labor party ticket. Perhaps because of his involvement with the Communist party, his outspoken criticism of perceived injustices in New York, and his repeated advocacy of independence for Puerto Rico, Colón was subpoenaed by the Walter Committee on Un-American Activities. Notwithstanding the Red-scare climate of the McCarthy era, Colón's speech of November 16, 1959 condemned tactics and assumptions of the Walter Committee, labeling *its* activities un-American and calling again for the independence of Puerto Rico as the only safeguard against such tactics.

Colón continued his interest and involvement in politics and in 1969 he ran again for public office, on the Communist party ticket. This time, he sought the office of comptroller of the city of New York, running with Rasheed Storey, candidate for mayor. Among Storey and Colón's demands were the creation of jobs for youth at minimum weekly salaries, free day care for children of working mothers, an end to police brutality through the elimination of prejudiced officers from the police force, and an end to the draft and the Vietnam War.

Colón was married twice in his life: once to his wife Concha, who is mentioned in *A Puerto Rican in New York and Other Sketches*, and, after her death in 1958, to Clara Colón. His second wife was a feminist, social activist, and writer in her own right. He survived both of them, and in accordance with his wishes his body was cremated and his ashes were returned to Puerto Rico and scattered over Cayey, the city of his birth.

Colón's numerous efforts on behalf of Hispanics, minorities, and other workers gained him the respect and admiration of co-workers and colleagues and made his writings one basis for the political and social orientation of the Puerto Rican literature to be produced in New York in the 1960s and 1970s. He is a clear forerunner of such writers as Piri *Thomas, Miguel *Algarín, and Nicholasa *Mohr, as well as Puerto Rican scholars who have become part of American institutions of higher learning. Colón's humanism and real concern for intellectual exchange on behalf of a community he called "the people" also won him the affection of even those who disagreed with his point of view. As Marshall Dubin, a campaign worker for another party, phrased it at a memorial to Jesús Colón in 1974 (said speech is in the Colón archives at Hunter College), Colón was a "gentle but not weak man with whom you could disagree yet retain his friendship, provided he knew you were moving in the right direction—for the people."

Major Themes

The Center for Puerto Rican Studies at Hunter College of the City University of New York is in possession of the Jesús Colón Archives. As yet unstudied, these archives contain many more writings by Colón, including a collection of essays being prepared for publication when he died. In *A Puerto Rican in New York and Other Sketches,* Colón's major themes are 1) the creation and development of ideological consciousness, 2) his own literary development and worth, 3) advocacy for the working-class poor, and 4) the injustices of capitalist society in which racial and class discrimination are all too frequent and individual worth seemingly nonexistent. These themes are dispersed in fifty-five separate essays that are contemplative, historical, and often didactic. As a counterpoint to the negatives of capitalist and colonial societies, Colón frequently juxtaposes what he perceives as the egalitarian principles of working-class socialism.

The collection as a whole is richly expressive of a socially conscious and humanistic point of view. In several essays, Colón allows readers to understand that his ideological perspective did not develop solely from intellectual study, but equally from his personal experiences. In "My First Strike," Colón and his elementary-age friends prevail in a school boycott organized to protest a penalty imposed unfairly on all students for the loss by one of a school textbook. Similarly, in "The Way to Learn," Colón and his school friends watch as a dock-worker protest draws the violence of armed retaliation by police. From these experiences early in life, Colón's later concern for the welfare of workers in New York and his involvement and identification with socialist issues are presented as the continuation and further development of early influences.

Colón presents his development as a writer in a similar light; his literary development is seen as progressing hand-in-hand with his ideological awareness. After the incident with the dock-worker protesters, for example, Colón tells of the fiery article written for the school paper, *Adelante,* which he edited. Although in this instance he is proud of his work and that of his reporters, Colón had already recounted that a letter of sympathy by him, written on the death of another student's grandmother, had been selected to be sent to the student, representing the school. His pride at this is quite evident. On other occasions, literary works speak to him as much as his writing speaks to others. In "Kipling and I" Colón reminisces about an inspirational poem by Kipling, "If," a copy of which was his prize possession for many years, encouraging him in the most desolate times. He finally has to set the poem aflame, however, in order to start a fire in his wood stove. Although the words are beautiful, they are not enough in and of themselves, and he is able to burn the poem for the practical benefits of survival. In "Hiawatha into Spanish," Colón's translation of the famous poem into Spanish seems to open the door to greater opportunity for a job in the literary area, but instead, the poem's translation reminds him of what he already knew: that opportunity is often denied to minorities in the United States, notwithstanding words of documents like the Constitution, which promise otherwise. Hinted to in essays like these, the importance of writing for Colón is given in "Soap Box in the Swamps," where he talks about a silence that speaks in a very significant way. In this essay, Colón remembers speakers advocating vocally for a project in an area of New York where "Hooverville homes" had been erected. The silence *then*, rather than indicating disagreement with the speakers' point of view, signaled quiet acquiescence and interest. That silence was marred only infrequently by solitary hecklers shouting "Communist." In pursuing his literary development and writing, Colón breaks a silence that would indicate acquiescence with the derogatory, stereotypical, and misinformed ideas that North American society has of Puerto Ricans and other minorities. This is overtly one of the purposes of the literary venture in "Name in Latin."

As in "Kipling and I," Colón seems to conclude that his literary ventures are not enough in and of themselves. Without the real action of helping others and his political involvement, his literary pursuits are intellectual irrelevancies. Colón not only writes to improve the condition of life for his community, but he actively advocates for that community. This is a third major theme in Colón's book, and it is often tied to the fourth theme of Colón's work: the unfairness of a capitalist society that undervalues the individual. In "I Heard a Man Crying," Colón recounts the episode of a young Spaniard he found starving to death in an empty room. Although strong and able to work, the young man, not knowing English, had been unable to find work or help. Colón feeds the man and helps him to find a job. In "The Lady Who Lived Near the Statue of a Man on a Horse," Colón helps a lost and helpless woman find the house where she has been staying with friends. Although the only information she has as to the house's location is that it is close to a statue, Colón and the woman are able to locate the house after several Sundays of searching the city.

There are other occasions on which Colón helps others throughout the book. Yet in several essays, Colón takes care to remind himself that although more fortunate, he is not better than his fellow workers. In "It Happened One Winter's Night," Colón is pleased by the flattery of an admirer until he compares his intellectual abilities to the man's mechanical capabilities. In a blinding snow-storm, the car in which the two are riding stalls, and Colón's friend is the one with the knowledge and ability to fix it. In the comparison, Colón is reminded, as he reminds his readers, that men are essentially equal and simply have different things to offer. Colón's faith in this principle of equality prevails notwithstanding a society that, in essays like "The Mother, the Daughter, Myself and All of Us," tries to convince him of the inferiority of his color and, in other essays, the dispensability of his worker community.

Survey of Criticism

Eugene V. Mohr includes a section on Jesús Colón's work in the "Proto-Nuyoricans" chapter of his book, *The Nuyorican Experience: Literature of the Puerto Rican Minority*. In this chapter, he also writes about the *Memoirs of Bernardo Vega* and Pedro Juan Labarthe's *The Son of Two Nations: The Private Life of a Columbia Student*. He considers the Colón book to be similar to Bernardo Vega's in content and even ideological perspective, however not as appealing in that it does not focus primarily on the Puerto Rican community in New York, but on the worker community in general. Although he acknowledges that Colón creates some moving portraits in his essays, Mohr further finds fault with the fact that "he gives the impression of being motivated less by personal commit-ment than by a strong imperative to follow a party line in matters he would be expected to comment on." Much of what can be seen as problematic along these lines, however, may be largely due to the fact that some essays were written for publication in the *Daily Worker* and assumed readers already in agreement with their premises. Nevertheless, Mohr states that Colón's "most important service is to reveal, through the example of his life, truths that one easily loses sight of in the messy collage of slums, violence, drugs, and welfare that satisfied the average New Yorker's curiosity about his Hispanic neighbors. He also serves to remind us that the intellectual forces that produced modern Cuba and modern Puerto Rico have roots that go deeper than Castro and Muñoz Marín."

Apart from Eugene Mohr's brief inclusion of the book in his study, Jesús Colón's work has largely been neglected by critics. Much work still needs to be done. As stated previously, the Jesús Colón Archives at the Center for Puerto Rican Studies at Hunter College are available for study. In addition, the History Committee of the National Communist Party Office in New York City maintains a file with material on this long-time associate and writer for the *Daily Worker*.

Bibliography

WORKS BY COLÓN

A Puerto Rican in New York and Other Sketches. New York: Masses & Mainstream, 1961; New York: International Publishers, 1982.

WORKS ABOUT COLÓN

Flores, Juan. Foreword to *A Puerto Rican in New York and Other Sketches*, ix–xvii. New York: International Publishers, 1982.

Mohr, Eugene V. "Proto-Nuyoricans." In *The Nuyorican Experience: Literature of the Puerto Rican Minority*, 3–23. Westport, Conn.: Greenwood Press, 1982.

                                                                                    MARICELA OLIVA

CORRALES, JOSÉ (1937–   ). José Corrales is a poet, critic, and dramatist of Cuban origin who has participated in theatrical and publishing activities in Cuba and New York. His poetic production has been collected in anthologies published in New York, New Jersey, Madrid, and Barcelona. He also is the author of two books: *Razones y amarguras. Poemas del que llega a los cuarenta* (1978, Reasons and Bitterness. Poems of a Forty-Year-Old) and *Los trabajos de Gerión* (1980, The Works of Gerión). Some of his plays, some original and others written in collaboration, have been performed in New York.

Biography

Corrales was born October 20, 1937 in Guanabacoa, a city close to Havana. He attended elementary school at the Escuelas Pías (Pious Schools) in his hometown. He graduated from high school in 1953 in Havana. He began his university studies at the University of Havana, majoring in social sciences, but he could not continue when the university was closed by order of the government under the dictatorship of Fulgencio Batista. He studied acting and drama at the Academia Municipal de Artes Dramáticas (Municipal Academy of Theatrical Arts) in Havana.

At the same time, he worked as an office boy and cashier for a medical supplies firm. During the revolution he took courses in *apreciación de las artes plásticas* (appreciation of the plastic arts) at the Biblioteca Nacional (National Library) in Havana. Between 1963 and 1964 he worked as an editor of children's books in the section for children's theater of the Consejo Nacional de Cultura (National Council of Culture), and he wrote for the weekly magazine *Bohemia* (Bohemia) and *La gaceta de Cuba* (Cuban Gazette) while he also performed as an actor in Francisco Morín's group, Prometeo.

In December 1964 he left Cuba. For several months he lived in Mexico City. In 1965 he moved to New York where he has resided since. There he once again undertook his studies without ceasing to participate in Hispanic theatrical and poetic groups in that city. From 1969 to 1974 he collaborated with the Dumé Spanish Theater as a literary adviser and actor. In 1971 he opened his piece, *Farramalla*, written with the Cuban theatrical director Herberto Dumé. For three years (1973–1976) he contributed articles on theater criticism and the plastic arts for the newspapers *El tiempo* and *El nuevo mundo*, published in New York. From 1974 to 1976 he was director of the Spanish Drama Club of Mercy College of Dobbs Ferry, New York, where he opened his comedies *El espíritu de Navidad* (1974, Christmas Spirit) and *Spics, spices, gringos y gracejo* (1976, Spics, Spices, Gringos and Wit). That same year he was the editor of the first and only issue of *Dobbs Ferry,* the literary magazine of that educational center, in which his poems appeared. In 1975 he received his B.A. summa cum laude from Mercy College with a major in Spanish and a minor in education. Between 1976 and 1977 he was an actor and member of the literary section of the Centro Cultural Cubano (Cuban Cultural Center) and a contributor to the newspaper *Abdala.* In 1977 the New York State Council of the Arts commissioned him along with Manuel Pereiras, another Cuban dramatist in exile, to write a play for children's theater. This work, *The Butterfly Cazador* (The Butterfly Hunter), as well as *Las hetairas habaneras* (Courtesans from Havana), another work written in collaboration with Manuel Pereiras that same year, remains unedited and unperformed. In 1978 the Dumé Spanish Theater opened his comedy *Juana Machete, la muerte en bicicleta* (Juana Machete, Death on a Bicycle).

In recent years, Corrales has dedicated himself to financial activities without abandoning his cultural undertakings. He is one of the editors of *Palabras y papel* (Words and Paper) from its founding in 1983, and he is a member of the board of directors and secretary of the Cooperativa Literaria Circular (Literary Circle Cooperative) of New York. He has traveled in Canada, Mexico, Puerto Rico, Spain, and France.

Major Themes

Corrales's poetic and dramatic productions are related in a few thematic and stylistic aspects. The two have in common his concern for time and his allusion to the lost homeland, at times direct and on other occasions veiled—but always evoked with tempered emotion. Stylistically, both share his use of colloquial language and of bilingualism. The latter on some occasions produces very humorous effects and on others expresses the lack of communication resulting from the confrontation between the native world and the adopted one.

Nada tenemos en común (1974, We Have Nothing in Common) is a pamphlet-style booklet that contains poems by the author and by Mario Peña, as well as sketches by Eloísa Castellanos and photographs by Edy Sánchez. As Omar Torres has pointed out, it is not a typical book of poetry with illustrations. The work is divided into four equal parts: five poems by each poet, five sketches, and five photographs. But its unity does not result from this quantitative symmetry. The poems written by each are not really the five that they seem but rather are a single one with five strophes that are developed like a Japanese *renga* with which the illustrations and photographs are integrated. Corrales's poems present themes that will persist in later books: the joy of brief love affairs in contrast with the nostalgia of true love, the bitter reflection on time, and consequently the frequent relationship between love and death; the motif of the mirror as evidence of "Otredad" and the fatal passage of time. Stylistically, they are written in free verse with a predominance of nominal sentences and apostrophes, that almost always center on the beloved, and with the rejection of punctuation. In spite of the tone of personal suffering in the first poems, the last, "Venceremos" (We Shall Overcome)—that ironically takes as its title one of the political slogans proclaimed during the Cuban Revolution—is a song of hopeful love that wishes to be a valid testimonial for future generations.

Razones y amarguras. Poemas del que llega a los cuarenta (1978, Reasons and Bitterness. Poems of a Forty-Year-Old) includes a quotation from Garcilaso de la Vega: "Receive the words that the mouth/casts forth from the anguished soul/before the body turns into dust." These verses summarize the dominant themes in the twenty-three poems of the book: the anguish caused by the situation of an exiled person immersed in a foreign land ["A long distance cry," "El frasco de *Clairol* y los recuerdos" (The Bottle of *Clairol* and Memories), "Los canarios, la soprano y el peluquero" (The Canaries, the Soprano and the Beautician)]; the anguish of the frustrated search for an ideal love approaching romantic sensibility ["Venceremos" (We Shall Overcome)]; and the anguish of obsessive preoccupation with the passage of time ["El día de mi cumpleaños" (My Birthday), "Elvis Dies at 42"] , a concern that ends in the theme of death ["La vejez tocando a las puertas" (Old Age Knocking at the Door)]. Only love, conceived as spiritual aspiration ["Creencias y pronósticos" (Beliefs and Predictions)] or as physical consummation ["El alma en los pies" (Soul in the Feet), "Física recreativa" (Recreational Physics), "Mentiras y verdades" (Lies and Truths), "Verdades y mentiras" (Truths and Lies)] and art, especially poetry ["Las abejas" (Bees)] seem to compensate the conflictive world in which the writer is submerged. Octavio de la Suarée, Jr., in the prologue, points out as the main characteristics of this book of poetry: existentialism, religiosity, and resignation, among which appears the recurrent theme of suicide. This theme is introduced as the result and means of escape from the total worldview that the poet must confront in his daily struggle. Mireya Robles observes in the work two structuring elements: on the one hand, suicide in varying degrees that goes from symbol ("Christmastide") to personification ["Prohibido suicidarse punto" (Committing Suicide Is Absolutely Forbidden)] and, on the other, the desire for survival that the poet at times discovers in a world of inanimate beings who acquire an almost human sensibility to stop suicide ("Prohibido suicidarse punto"), and at other times he encounters it as an act of will when the poet surrenders to the hope of living a life of plentitude fulfilled by love ["Todavía" (Still)]. Robles maintains that this book is a profoundly human one that reflects the disillusionment, the boredom, and the resignation of the poet as well as wisdom, illusion, and the need to recover oneself in hope.

Los trabajos de Gerión (The Works of Gerión) also is composed of twenty-three poems centered around the amorous experiences of the poet with a lover who receives the name of a mythological three-headed monster. But, it also contains poems on the memories of the lost homeland, a reflection on the uselessness of art ["A solas con *Las meninas*" (Alone with the Maids in Waiting)], a tribute to Jorge Luis Borges ("Three Cheers Borges"), and a song in which he announces his next book, *La Pelona* (The Bald Woman). In *Los trabajos de Gerión* the nostalgia for the native land is sharpened, but without falling into declamatory patriotic clichés. Cuba is present in scattered memories that crop up in contrast with present reality ["Postigos y ventanas" (Shutters and Windows), "Plaza de Santo Domingo" (Santo Domingo Square)], in the morose mention of flora and landscape ["Consejo y súplica al poeta Juan Alonso que se va de viaje" (Advice and request to the poet Juan Alonso who is going on a trip)], and in tribute to two important figures in Cuban literature ["Dos sombras: José Martí y José Lezama Lima" (Two Shadows: José Martí and José Lezama Lima)]. Maya Islas affirms that in this poem Corrales awakens in us feelings, not the topography of the island but rather its atmosphere, converted into interior landscape. Raphael Catalá considers that although Gerión arises from time to time, it does not end up dominating the book, either as a character or a theme, because psychic states and relationships with the beloved beings, literature and art, are imposed beyond the monster. Maya Islas maintains the theory that Gerión is not identified with one single person but rather represents various human beings that have loved, hated, accompanied, and hurt the poet in a direct manner, for which Corrales has bestowed them with a monstrous character. Gerión appears with many faces, including that of the poet himself. The idea of the monster is not as important as the possibility of its presence, since Gerión arrives at the opportune moment ["Cuando ya me estaba yendo" (When I was already leaving)] and injects life into the artist ["Los verbos ser y estar" (The verbs "to be " and "to be")]. Catalá affirms that a significant element is the effective use of Spanish and English with a coherent thematic, phonetic, and grammatical passage of time ["Gerión 8:17 A.M.," "Instantánea" (Instantaneous), "Brevísima historia de amor invernal con un happy end común y corriente" (A very short winter love story with a common and ordinary happy ending)]. Islas also points out the repetitive function of words such as *sábanas* (sheets), *espejos* (mirrors), and *almohadas* (pillows) to create an active vocabulary in the book of poetry, vestiges of *creacionista* (creationist) elements in imagery ("the roads of hell/are paved with horses and songs"),and the presence of *cuerpo* (body) that ends up in the theme of old age, an important one to this author.

In the anthologies *Azor en vuelo V* (1981, Goshawk in Flight V), *Azor en vuelo VII* (1982, Goshawk in Flight VII), and *Colectivo de poetas Q–21* (1983, Poets' Collective Q–21) have appeared some poems belonging to the unpublished book *La Pelona* (The Bald Woman), whose title is taken from a Cuban expression that alludes to death. Those poems intensify in the thematic aspect the nostalgia for the island ["Cuentos de camino" (Tales of the Road)], impetuous memories of the first days of the Revolution ["Me siento en una silla vieja" (I am sitting in an old chair)], the encounter with New York ["Los pies listos a correr" (Feet Prepared to Run)], and the initial poverty in exile ["Nubes frías" (Cold Clouds)] as well as the poet's loneliness and the passage of time ["Abrazado a una estatua" (Embracing a Statue)]. These themes are now enriched by references to his mother ["Pasatiempo 11" (Hobby 11)], to her death ["Después del silencio" (After Silence)], and the inclusion of new motifs like the canary that represents a couple in love ["Poemas" (Poems)]. The poems tend to be shorter and more thoughtful, and they are impregnated with a popular tone in which the musicality is notable ["Por una calle de Guanabacoa" (Through a Street of Guanabacoa)]. Frequently there are splendid surrealist images ["El pozo se llena de picualas" (The Well Is Filled with *Picualas* [a type of Cuban flower])].

As a dramatist, Corrales stands out for his sense of humor, for his concept of theater as spectacle, his skillful handling of "collage," and his insistence on renovating the structures of Cuban popular theater. With Dumé he opened *Farramalla* (1971), a comedy inspired by *La loca de Chaillot* (The Madwoman of Chaillot) by Jean Giraudoux, with interpolated texts by Tennessee Williams. *Bulto postal* (1976, Mail Pouch) is an unpublished comedy that once again treats the author's preoccupation with the passage of time, embodied here in three women: Ella (a retired actress), Catalina, and Lucía. The three rotate around the eternal male represented by a young actor who successively plays the role of a mailman, a sheltered young man, and a milkman. The text is full of propitious fragments from such disparate authors as García de la Huerta, San Juan de la Cruz, and Calderón de la Barca, and it is rich in ingenious dialogues, daring situations, and some techniques deriving from the theater of the absurd. But, in spite of its brilliant surface, it is a profoundly defeatist work related to his poetry of solitude.

Spics, spices, gringos y gracejo (Spices, Spices, Gringos, and Wit), written to celebrate the United States' bicentennial, opened in 1976 and was called a theatrical party by the author. It is exactly that—a party—owing to its open structure in a Pirandello "commedia da fare" style, to its gaiety created by types that function as characters, to its absence of characters and plot in the style of a well-made play, to the liveliness of its situations that are very similar to a revue, and to its agile wordplays with Spanish and English. With the pretext of a bicentennial party in a bilingual education class, Corrales uses language mistakes and other peculiarities such as the periphrastic wordiness of Spanish in contrast to the synthetic terseness of English. He also resorts to popular, common American and Latin songs to create an essentially theatrical text.

Juana Machete, la muerte en bicicleta (1978, Juana Machete, Death on a Bicycle), whose text has not been conserved, has the purpose of revitalizing elements of the Cuban popular *sainete* with very modern ingredients.

In addition, Corrales has written two significant works with Manuel Pereiras. *Las hetairas habaneras* (1977, Courtesans from Havana) treats in a very special way frequent parodic elements of Cuban popular theater. The text is a re-creation of *The Trojan Women* by Euripides. The plot, developed among prostitutes, pimps, and male chauvinists from Havana, is like a great parable of Cuba before and after the Revolution, with the interplay of mythological Afro-Cuban elements. The work follows the formal structure of Greek tragedy and it incorporates in a chorus picturesque Cuban popular expressions and revolutionary slogans either in the form of verse or in a surprisingly rhythmic prose. By means of Cuban *choteo* (mockery), the writers make fun of the triumphant display resulting from the new political situation, but the farce that they achieve is not void of the emotional memory of a hopelessly lost epoch. *The Butterfly Cazador* (1977,

The Butterfly Hunter) is a musical children's comedy. Its title announces one of its more distinguishing features, the imaginative and witty mixture of Spanish and English, in the dialogues as well as the lyrics of the songs. The text proposes various readings. The most literal is a children's fable in which people, animals, and puppets are combined in the real and dream world, where all ends happily with the affirmation of all creatures' right to life and liberty. A second reading uncovers a parable that criticizes the superstructures that rule the American way of life and a third reading is another parable that denounces the present Cuban regime because of the persecution undertaken against some sectors of its population. Whatever reading one selects, *The Butterfly Cazador* is an important work because of its poetry, its wit, its human values, and its dramatic qualities.

Corrales, an artist devoted to polishing his work obsessively, is currently dedicating most of his interest to his poetic production and he continues to publish in the journals *Círculo poético* (Poetic Circle) and *Palabras y papel* (Words and Paper).

Bibliography

WORKS BY CORRALES

Books

With Mario Peña. *Nada tenemos en común*. Illustrations by Eloísa Castellanos and Edy
    Sánchez. New York: Nuevasangre, 1974.
Razones y amarguras. Hoboken, N.J.: Contra viento y marea, 1978.
Los trabajos de Gerión. Barcelona: Rondas, 1980.
Jurado Morales, José, ed. *Selección de poemas de diecisiete poetas cubanos en el exilio*.
    In *Azor en vuelo V*. Barcelona: Rondas, 1981.
Mario, José, ed. *El Puente. Resumen Literario*. 3. 36–37 (1982).
————. ed. *Selección breve de once poetas*. In *Azor en vuelo VII*. Barcelona: Rondas,
    1982.

Anthologies Containing Poems by Corrales

Nueve poetas cubanos. Madrid: Catoblepas, 1984.
González, Ana H., ed. *Círculo Poético*. Cuaderno 15. Verona,N.J.: Círculo de Cultura
    Panamericano, 1984.
————. ed. *Círculo poético*. Cuaderno 16. Verona, N.J.: Círculo de Cultura Panamer-
    icano, 1985.
Le Riverend, ed. *Colectivo de poetas Q–21*. Newark, N.J.: Q–21, 1983.

Plays

With Herberto Dumé. *Farramalla*. Premiere. 1971.
El espíritu de Navidad. Premiere. 1974.
Bulto postal. 1976. Unedited.
Spics, spices, gringos y gracejo. Premiere. 1976.
With Manuel Pereiras. *Las hetairas habaneras*. 1977. Unedited.
Juana Machete, la muerte en bicicleta. Premiere. 1978.
With Manuel Pereiras. Music by Evan Senrich. *The Butterfly Cazador*. 1978. Unedited.

WORKS ABOUT CORRALES

Baeza Flores, Alberto. "Las razones existenciales de José Corrales." *La Nación* (San José, Costa Rica) Jan. 30, 1981: A15.

Catalá, Rafael. "Para leer el *Gerión* de Corrales." *Impacto* November 17–23, 1982: 18.

de la Suarée, Octavio, Jr. "Con tres palabras . . . (Introducción)." *Razones y amarguras: Poemas del que llega a los cuarenta,* by José Corrales. Hoboken, N.J.: Contra viento y marea, 1978.

———. "Veinte años de poesía cubana: extrañamiento, ruptura y continuidad." Lecture presented to the North East Modern Language Association Convention. Southeastern Massachusetts University, March 1980.

Escarpenter, José A. *"Las hetairas habaneras: una parodia cubana."* Lecture presented to the American Association of Teachers of Spanish and Portuguese Conference. New York, November 1985.

———. "Veinticinco años de teatro cubano en el exilio." *Latin American Theatre Review.* 19/2 (Spring, 1986): 57–66.

Gutiérrez de la Solana, Alberto. *Investigación y crítica literaria y lingüística cubana.* New York: Senda Nueva de Ediciones, 1978.

Islas, Maya. Review of *Los trabajos de Gerión,* by José Corrales. *Cuaderno Literario Azor* (Barcelona) 30 (junio 1981): 35.

———. Review of *Los trabajos de Gerión,* by José Corrales. *Mairena* 19 (1985): 135–39.

Jurado Morales, José. Review of *Razones y amarguras,* by José Corrales. *Cuaderno Literario Azor* (Barcelona) 21 (n.d.): 59.

Pereira, Teresinka. Review of *Razones y amarguras,* by José Corrales. *Poema convidado* (Boulder, Colorado) 58 (August 1978): 4.

———. Review of *Razones y amarguras,* by José Corrales. *Vida Universitaria* (Monterrey) September 11, 1978: 13.

Robles, Mireya. Review of *Razones y amarguras,* by José Corrales. *Poesía de Venezuela* (Caracas) 94 (November-December 1978): 5.

———. Review of *Razones y amarguras,* by José Corrales. *El Diario-La Prensa* (New York) December 19, 1978: 27.

———. Review of *Razones y amarguras,* by José Corrales. *Vida Universitaria* (Monterrey) January 1, 1979: 10.

Torres, Omar. Review of *Nada tenemos en común,* by José Corrales and Mario Peña. *El tiempo universal* (New York) September 8, 1974: 21.

JOSÉ ESCARPENTER

CORRETJER, JUAN ANTONIO (1908–   ). Juan Antonio Corretjer is one of the truly distinguished Puerto Rican poets of the last fifty years, the author of more than twenty books of poetry, nine volumes of political prose, one collection of short stories, and a large number of political articles and reviews in newspapers and magazines. His work is intimately related to his political militancy and his consistent fight for an independent socialist republic of Puerto Rico.

Biography

Juan Antonio Corretjer was born in the small town of Ciales, Puerto Rico, on March 3, 1908. His career as a poet began with the writing of the poem "Canto a Ciales" in 1920. Five years later his first poems were published in the magazine *Puerto Rico Ilustrado*. In 1926 he moved from Ciales to San Juan, where he was for a brief period associated with the avant-grade movement of the *noistas*. On the whole, Corretjer kept aloof from the various literary movements and their circles in the capital. During the same year of 1926 he read *Das Kapital* by Karl Marx in an abbreviated Spanish version, which helped to shape his life-long Marxist convictions. In 1929 Corretjer's career as a journalist began with his work at *La Democracia*. The writer's anti-imperialist stance is on record as early as 1929 when he became a member of the New York-based Anti-Imperialist League of the Americas, an organization that fought against the occupation of Nicaragua and Haiti by the United States. From 1930 on, when Corretjer met Pedro Albizu Campos, the leader of the Puerto Rican Nationalist party, until 1946, when he joined the Communist party for a span of two years, his public life was very much determined by the activities of his political affiliation. Corretjer spent the first years of the 1930s in and around the town of Ponce which was then the center of the Nationalists' efforts. In Ponce he was co-editor of the journal *La Opinión* during 1934. On October 25, 1935, he was elected secretary general of the Nationalist party. From April 2, 1936 until July 4, 1942 he was imprisoned, first in San Juan, then, accused of conspiracy against the United States government, in Atlanta, Georgia. It is astounding to see how much Corretjer was able to write and publish despite his intense and often tumultuous political involvement.

In 1932 appeared his first booklet of poetry, *Agüeibana*, followed in 1933 by *Ulises* and the stories "Wl cumplido" (Man of His Word), "El fin de Lucero" (The End of Lucero), and "La aldea" (The Village), all in *Puerto Rico Ilustrado*.*Cántico de guerra* (Canticle of the War) came out in 1936, *Amor de Puerto Rico* (Love of Puerto Rico) in 1937, and *El leñero* (The Woodchopper) in 1944. His journalistic and critical work, collected under the heading *Laurel negro* (Black Laurel), was honored with the Prize in Journalism by the Institute of Puerto Rican Culture in 1943.

The day following the Nationalist uprising on October 30, 1950, Corretjer was arrested and later in 1952 served a sentence of six months for attempted insurgency. Corretjer continued to write *La revolución de Lares* (The Lares Revolution) and *Nuestra bandera* (Our Flag), both published in 1947, and *La lucha por la independencia de Puerto Rico* (The Struggle for Puerto Rican Independence), published in 1949.

In 1959 Corretjer published one of his most impressive works, *Alabanza en la Torre de Ciales* (Homage to the Ciales Tower), which had been written back in 1950. It represents the culmination of his epic quest for a Puerto Rico that is perceived as both physical and mythical. With *Yerba bruja* (Witch Herb) and

Distancias (Distances) that came out in the same year of 1957, we again have major poetic works. Corretjer's encounter with Che Guevara in 1959 meant a deeply felt confirmation of his radical political and humanistic convictions. He spent 1959 and 1960 for the most part in Latin America promoting the independence of Puerto Rico and the case of the Revolution in Cuba. In 1961 his cycle *Imágenes de Borinquen* (Images of Borinquen), which he had started along with *Los primeros años* (The First Years) eleven years earlier, found its completion with *Genio y figura* (Genius and Stature). The following years brought once more a preponderance in essays: *Futuro sin falla (Mito realidad antillana)* (Future without Error [Carribbean Reality Myth]) appeared in 1963, and *La sangre en huelga* (Blood on Strike) in 1966. *Pausa para el amor* (1967, Pause for Love), a moving book of love poetry, he dedicated to wife, doña Consuelo Lee Tapia, herself a poet and Corretjer's companion in all vicissitudes of life since the early 1940s

In 1964 he founded the radical party called the Socialist League, a decision which meant for Juan Antonio and Consuelo close surveillance and, at various instances, incarceration, for example, in the summer of 1971, for accusations of conspiracy and violation of the law regulating the possession of firearms. On July 17, 1970, both barely escaped an attack on their lives. In spite of all these turbulences the production of political, didactic prose and of poetry from Corretjer continued.

Using the 1868 rebellion of Lares as a base for his argument in favor of an armed battle for an independent Puerto Rico, he finished in 1970 the essay *La historia que gritó en Lares* (The History That Screamed in Lares). And only one year later *Canciones de Consuelo que son canciones de protesta* (Songs of Consolation That Are Songs of Protest) reached its public.

The 1970s initiated an increasing recognition for Corretjer's work by liberal and culture-conscious circles in Puerto Rico. The Ateneo Puertorriqueño honored him in 1973 with an Honor's Prize and declared him Puerto Rico's national poet, a distinction the Departments of Spanish and General Studies of the University of Puerto Rico also conferred on him ten years later. In 1975 Corretjer received the National Prize of the Institute of Puerto Rican Culture. The Association of Puerto Rican Lawyers hosted a public homage for him in 1980 at which many artists and intellectuals of the country were present. In this general climate of a diminishing reluctance by the public and by Puerto Rican organizations to accept Corretjer and his work, the poet kept publishing. His continuing fascination with the figure of Albizu Campos found its way into the essays *El líder de la desesperación* (The Leader of Desperation) and *Semblanza polémica de Pedro Albizu Campos* (Polemic Portrait of Pedro Albizu Campos), printed in 1973. His poetic production in the 1970s and early 1980s remained unflagging. *Construcción del Sur* (1972, Southern Construction), *Aguinaldo escarlata* (1974, Scarlet Christmas Gift), *Para que los pueblos canten* (1976, So the Peoples Sing), *El estado del tiempo* (1983, The Weather Report), and *Los días contados* (1984, Numbered Days) bear witness to his fecundity.

In addition to his political work in the Socialist League, which took him frequently to Mexico, Corretjer tried in 1977 to bring Chicano and Puerto Rican writers and intellectuals together as groups who share a common struggle for liberation. The following year he traveled to Québec where he discussed politics and culture with members of the then openly separatist Parti Québecois and fellow socialists.

The growing recognition of Corretjer as a major literary force in the last fifteen years becomes evident also in the compilations of his poetry and prose in anthologies. In 1973 Ramón Felipe Medina and Corretjer edited a selection of poetry *Día antes* (The Day Before). The Institute of Puerto Rican Culture united in volume 1 of *Obras completas* (1977, Complete Works), Corretjer's poetry up to *Aqüinaldo escarlata*. The poet José Luis Vega was responsible for this edition and an enlightening introductory essay. No second volume of Corretjer's *Obras completas* has as yet appeared. In 1979 twenty-four short prose pieces were selected by Ramón Felipe Medina and collected in *El cumplido*. With *Poesía y revolución* (Poetry and Revolution), José Ramón Meléndez established a highly valuable anthology of part of Corretjer's vast body of critical articles and reviews that had appeared in newspapers and magazines over a period of almost half a century.

Major Themes

Juan Antonio Corretjer's work can be characterized as being of inflexible commitment and patriotism. He does not figure among the bourgeois Hispanophiles whose glance backward into history makes them idealize Spain as the generous mother country. His conception of Puerto Rican history is geared toward emancipatory revolutionary phases and figures. To Corretjer only the Taíno Indians were a free people. With the Spaniards the oppressor arrived, an oppressor who was to be superceded by the United States in 1898. It is important to note that his use of the Taíno is not merely historicizing, he re-creates their existence and re-activates the Indian as an element, mythical or not, that readers in our time should be aware of and look up to. The heroic, exemplary, fighting Taíno is present already in the earliest printed book of poetry, *Aqüebana,* a work he dedicated to Albizu Campos. The rebel as Indian and the patriotic duty to resort to the use of arms remain a constant source of inspiration to the poet: "Ausculta, Puerto Rico, a tu jaguar dormido. A filo de machete es que hay que hacer la patria" (*Aqüeibana,* 75). In *Yerba bruja,* the idea of sacrifice, valor, and love for one's country is intimately woven into an extensive treatment of Taíno mythology. In his introductory "Notas Aclaratorias," Corretjer states his motives for his use of the Indian as opposed to the image of the Indian in works of shallow romanticism: "Es que secretamente nos conmueve el sacrificio de los que fueron los últimos paisanos realmente libres. Nuestra añoranza india es nostalgia de la libertad. . . . No es en lo mío . . . emigración imaginativa, sino punto de referencia."

The Hispanic concept of the poet as soldier (and vice versa) represents another pervasive motif in Corretjer's poetry. In "Elegía épica" (Epic Elegy), from *Amor de Puerto Rico*, which he dedicated to one of the Puerto Rican poets he most admires, Francisco González (Pachín) Marín, he writes: "Pero nosotros, tus hermanos,/—poeta, luchador soldado—/ de pie sobre el destino tragico,/aun en la cadena la resuelta mano" (But we, your brothers,/—poet, fighter, soldiers—/standing before a tragic destiny,/the hand enchained still resolute). It does not come as a surprise, then, to find references to Garcilaso, as in *Pausa para el amor*. The poet as soldier appears in *Genio y figura*, in a more somber mood in *Agüinaldo escarlata*, and is a distinct presence in his recent volume *Los días contados*.

The aborted revolution of Lares, one of the truly emancipatory moments in Puerto Rican history, serves as Corretjer's topic in *El leñero*, a poem he wrote in the prison La Princesa in September of 1936. The heroic figure of Manolo Rosado, "Agitando la bandera,/y murió, como una fiera, batiéndose acorralado" (Waving the flag,/he died like a wild animal, beating the cell bars), functions in typical Corretjer fashion as an example for the living. The poem, which consists of 174 *décimas*, ends with this martyr continuing to feed the passionate fires of the independence movement. Another figure from more recent history and a martyr to Corretjer is Elías Beauchamp, who was shot after the Nationalist revolt in February 1936 and is celebrated by Corretjer in "Cántico de guerra."

One of the proverbial symbols for bravery and unfailing combativeness in Puerto Rico is a common, small, grey bird by the name of *pitirre*, the grey kingbird. It is widely used in Corretjer's poetry, for example, "Vieques" or "Perfil de ser" (Profile of Being). A strand of protest poetry touches most of Corretjer's poetry. In *Canciones de Consuelo que son canciones de protesta*, he makes no bones about the forces that he attacks—the United States, which he reduces to the almighty dollar, the world-wide oppressor. The overtly polemical tone in Corretjer's work surfaces most clearly in his uncompromising political prose, for example, in *La lucha por la independencia de Puerto Rico* or *El líder de la desesperación*. Yet Corretjer is basically a lyrical poet in the tradition of *neocriollismo*, with Virgilio Dávila and Luis *Lloréns Torres as immediate predecessors. Corretjer's work is never hermetic, his work is designed to be accessible, popular. While it is futile to separate his less political poetry from poetry of a more ideological nature, it must be stressed that he is one of the very great Puerto Rican poets who celebrate their island, its natural beauty and charm.

Corretjer knows every corner of his country, sheds a loving glance on each valley, and shares his knowledge with his reader. *Alabanza en la Torre de Ciales*, *Amor de Puerto Rico*, and *Distancias* contain pastoral poems of immense lyrical beauty and emotion. Given the ambiguous status of Puerto Rico, the detailed enumerations of what constitutes a collective home, *la patria*, assume not only poetic and cultural but also political dimensions. Corretjer the poet becomes thus the lover of the land and the teacher. Among his outstanding sensuous nature poems are "Arcadia," "Tarde" (Afternoon), and "Camino" (Road), all in *Amor de Puerto Rico*. Corretjer unswervingly names, creates, imagines—he calls himself one of the "imagineros de Borinquen" (imaginers of Borinquen)— postulates the reality of a nation, as in his moving "Ciales" from *Pausa para el amor*. At all times, however, as he states in *Tierra nativa's* "Credo," he remains the defender of a culture, of his native language and his "enslaved" land.

Corretjer's short stories, all written in the 1930s and early 1940s, share the sociopolitical commitment the writer voiced in his much more widely known poetry. As in his poetry, a general, often dialectical, historical optimism prevails. Of special interest is the title story of the collection, "El cumplido," an account of oppression, rebellion, punishment, and ensuing sharpened political conscious-ness. "El fin de Lucero" is remarkable for its irony in handling class differences, and "La aldea" for the revealing of an idealizing writer who finds himself confronted with the reality of his village. The stories that are situated in New York mirror the loneliness and uprootedness of the Puerto Rican emigrant, topics José Luis *González developed in *En la sombra* (1943) and *Paísa* (1950). With "De las llamas al rocío" (From Flames to Dew), Corretjer resorts to the technique of the interior monologue and figures among the first Puerto Rican short-story writers to do so.

Survey of Criticism

There still exists no biography nor a comprehensive critical analysis of Cor-retjer and his work. That his political activism made many potential critics and established publishing houses shy away from both the person and his work holds true until the late 1960s. *Agüeibana*, his first collection in book form, significantly received more reviews in 1932, before the Nationalist unrest shocked the country, than any other book by the author. In general, his works were reviewed mostly in daily newspapers such as *El Mundo* and *El Imparcial*, rarely in quarterlies or literary magazine. The cultural supplement "En Rojo" of the socialist magazine *Claridad* featured reviews of Corretjer's works by the important critic José Emilio González, who wrote on *Día antes* on January 11, 1975, and by Efraín Barradas, who published general appraisals on October 6, 1974 and March 16, 1979 in the same magazine and in *Sin Nombre* of January/March 1980. Juan Martínez Capó covered *Día antes, Agüinaldo escarlata, Para que los pueblos canten, Obras completas, Laurel negro*, and *El estado del tiempo* in his weekly "Libros de Puerto Rico" in *El Mundo*. On January 10, 1982, Gladys Crescioni could refer in her literary society column of *El Mundo* to Corretjer the man and the poet as having assumed "almost mythical dimensions."

Corretjer's passionate love for the mythical, historical, telluric Puerto Rico is recognized and valued by all reviewers and commentators. José Emilio González discusses Corretjer extensively in the context of his capital study of Puerto Rican poetry, *La poesía contemporánea de Puerto Rico (1930–1960)* (1972), and links much of the poet's use of imagery with the *atalayistas*. González calls *Amor de*

Puerto Rico the writer's best work. Josefina Rivera de Alvarez's valorization of Corretjer in volume 1 of her *Diccionario de la literatura puertorriqueña* relies heavily on J.E. González. She stresses his clear, unobfuscated style and his cultivation of essential patriotic Puerto Rican elements. A step ahead in Corretjer criticism was José Luis Vega's introduction to volume 1 of *Obras completas*. Vega successfully attempts a structuring of Corretjer's themes and ideas. Another important piece of criticism is Ramón Felipe Medina's study of Corretjer's short prose, which serves as a preface to Medina's edition of *El cumplido*. The critic puts the stories into their literary context and justly establishes Corretjer, along with Emilio S. Belaval and José Luis *González, as one of the innovators of that genre within Puerto Rican literature. The same critic discussed Corretjer's work, its myths and ideas in the January/March 1975 issue of *Sin Nombre*. Alfredo Villanueva Collado analyzed questions of myth and identity using *Alabanza en la Torre de Ciales* in the Summer 1981 issue of *Revista Chicano-Riqueña*. In 1980, José Ramón Meléndez prefaced his meritorious selection of Corretjer's critical prose with introductory remarks concentrating on "style" and "literary influences" on the work. His remarks, which are put in a curious phonetic transcription, shed hardly any new light on Corretjer's work. Of interest, however, are the essays on Corretjer published in the Winter 1983 issue of the magazine *Mairena*, where the reader will, in addition, find an extensive bibliography established by Ramón Felipe Medina.

Bibliography

WORKS BY CORRETJER

Agüeibana. Ponce: Tipografía del Llano, 1932.
Ulises. (*Versos al mar de un hombre de tierra adentro*). Ponce: Playas del Sur, 1933.
Amor de Puerto Rico. San Juan: La Palabra, 1937.
Cántico de guerra. San Juan: Imprenta Puerto Rico, 1937.
El leñero (Poems de la Revolución de Lares). New York: n.p., 1944.
El buen borincano. New York: n.p., 1945.
Lloréns: juicio histórico. New York: n.p., 1945.
Nuestra bandera. San Juan: n.p., 1947.
La revolución de Lares. San Juan: n.p., 1947.
La lucha por la independencia de Puerto Rico. San Juan: n.p., 1949; 5th ed., Guaynabo: n.p., 1977.
Los primeros años. San Juan: Imprenta Baldrich, 1950.
Tierra nativa. San Juan: Imprenta Baldrich, 1951.
Alabanza en la Torre de Ciales. San José, Costa Rica: Repertorio Americano, 1952; 2d ed., San Juan: Talleres Gráficos Interamericanos, 1965.
Un recuerdo de Cuba. San Juan: n.p., 1952.
Contestación al miedo. San Juan: n.p., 1954.
Don Diego en El Cariño. San Juan: Ediciones La Escrita, 1956.
Distancias. Santurce: Ediciones Vela, 1957.
Yerba bruja. Guaynabo: Imprenta Venezuela, 1957.
Genio y figura (Rapsodia criolla). Guaynabo: Litografía Guilliani, 1961.

Futuro sin falla (Mito realidad antillana). Guaynabo: n.p., 1963.
La sangre en huelga (Notas de la Resistencia al Servicio Militar Obligatorio). Guaynabo: n.p., 1966.
Pausa para el amor. Guaynabo: Cooperativa de Artes Gráficas "Romualdo Real," 1967.
Canciones de Consuelo que son canciones de protesta. Guaynabo: Liga Socialista, 1971.
Construcción del Sur. San Juan: Ediciones Ciba, 1972.
Día antes, cuarenta años de poesía, 1927–1967. Selection, Notes, and Glossary by Ramón Felipe Medina. Río Piedras: Editorial Antillana, 1973.
El líder de la desesperación. Guaynabo: n.p., 1973.
Semblanza polémica de Pedro Albizu Campos. Guayanbo: n.p., 1973.
Agüinaldo escarlata. Guaynabo: n.p., 1974.
Para que los pueblos canten. Guaynabo: n.p., 1976.
Obras completas. Vol. 1. San Juan: Instituto de Cultura Puertorriqueña, 1977. Preface by José Luis Vega.
Poesía y revolución. Río Piedras: Ediciones qeAse, 1981. Edited and prefaced by José Ramón Meléndez.
El estado del tiempo. Guaynabo: Ediciones Islabón, 1983.
Los días contados. Guaynabo: n.p., 1984.

WORKS ABOUT CORRETJER

Arrigoitia, Luis de. "Cuatro poetas puertorriqueños: José de Diego, Luis Lloréns Torres, Luis Palés Matos y Juan Antonio Corretjer." *Caravelle* 18 (1972): 59–76.
Barradas, Efraín. "Lo que es Corretjer." *Claridad*, "En Rojo," October 6, 1974: 22–23.
———. "Después de 'Día antes." *Claridad*, "En Rojo," March 16, 1979: 10–11.
———. Review of *Obras completas*. *Sin Nombre* 10/4 (Jan.-Mar. 1980): 100–101.
Binder, Wolfgang. "'Una literatura de fronteras'—entrevista a Juan Antonio Corretjer con doña Consuelo." *Imagine* 1 (Fall 1984): 46–60.
González, Eduardo. "Pasado, presente y futuro en la plasmación del elemento taíno en poemas de Juan Antonio Corretjer." *Mairena* 5 (Winter 1983): 119–28.
González, José Emilio. "La poesía puertorriqueña de 1930 a 1954." *Asomante* 11 (January-March 1955): 76–92 passim.
———. "Los poetas puertorriqueños de la década de 1930." *Literatura puertorriqueña. 21 Conferencias*. San Juan: Instituto de Cultura Puertorriqueña, 1960.
———. "La poesia puertorriqueña de 1945 a 1964." *Asomante* (July-August 1964): 55–78 passim.
———. *La poesía contemporánea de Puerto Rico (1930–1960)*. San Juan: Instituto de Cultura Puertorriqueña, 1972.
———. Review of *Día antes*. *Claridad*, "En Rojo," January 11, 1975: 14–15.
———. " 'El Estado del Tiempo' de Juan Antonio Corretjer." *Mairena* 5 (Winter 1983): 57–71.
Hernández Aquino, Luis. *Nuestra aventura literaria*. Santo Domingo: Editora Arte Y Cine, 1964.
Irizarry, Carmen. "La violencia en la poesía de Juan Antonio Corretjer." *Mairena* 5 (Winter 1983): 27–42.
López González, Julio César. "El sentido de la patria en un poemario de Juan Antonio Corretjer." *Pasión de poesía*. San Juan: Ediciones Rumbos, 1959.
Martell Morales, Héctor J. "Tres adelantadores en nuestro cuento (Manuel Zeno García, Gustavo Agrait, Juan Antonio Corretjer)." *Renacimiento* 1 (January-June 1981): 8–14.

Matos Paoli, Francisco. " 'Quieto en mi isla voy.' " *Mairena* 5 (Winter 1983): 15–26.
Medina, Ramón Felipe. "Juan Antonio Corretjer: Homenaje a la figura total." *Sin Nombre* 5 (January-March 1975): 49–61.
―――. "Prólogo para un estudio." Introduction to *El cumplido (narraciones arbitrarias)*. Río Piedras: Editorial Antillana, 1979.
Meléndez, José Luis. "Prólogo" to *Poesía y revolución*. Río Piedras: qeAse, 1981.
―――. "Entrevista a Juan Antonio Corretjer." *Reintegro* 3 (August 1983): 2–15 passim.
Montes Cumming, Carmen. "Juan Antonio Corretjer: poeta nacional puertorriqueño." Ph.D. thesis, University of Tennessee, Knoxville, 1982.
―――. "La poesía de Juan Antonio Corretjer en su desarrollo y significado." *Mairena* 5 (Winter 1983): 5–14.
Pérez Ruiz, José Antonio. "La poesía de Corretjer a través de la plástica." *Mairena* 5 (Winter 1983): 109–17.
de la Puebla, Manuel, and Marcos Reyes Dávila. " 'He tenido que vivir mucho más que escribir.' Entrevista a Juan Antonio Corretjer." *Mairena* 5 (Winter 1983): 49–56.
Rivera de Alvarez, Josefina. *Diccionario de la literatura puertorriqueña*. Vol. I. San Juan: Instituto de Cultura Puertorriqueña, rev. ed., 1974.
―――. *Literatura puertorriqueña: su proceso en el tiempo*. Madrid: Ediciones Partenón, 1983.
Santini, Carmen Hilda. "Lo musical en la poesía de Juan Antonio Corretjer." *Mairena* 5 (Winter 1953): 86–98.
Valentín, Francisco. "La ironía en la poesía de Juan Antonio Corretjer." *Mairena* 5 (Winter 1983): 73–82.
Vega, José Luis. "Prólogo" to *Obras completas*. San Juan: Instituto de Cultura Puertorriqueña, 1977.
Villanueva Collado, Alfredo. "Mito e identidad en *Alabanza en la Torre de Ciales* por Juan Antonio Corretjer." *Revista Chicano-Riqueña* 9 (Summer 1981): 61–68.
Zayas, Luis O. "El mito de la ascensión en *Alabanza en la Torre de Ciales*." *Mito y política en la literatura puertorriqueña*. Madrid: Ediciones Partenón, 1981.

WOLFGANG BINDER

CRUZ, VICTOR HERNÁNDEZ. *See* HERNÁNDEZ CRUZ, VICTOR.

E

ESTEVES, SANDRA MARÍA (1948–   ). Sandra María Esteves is one of the first women to stand out among the New York Puerto Rican poets writing in English. Her poetry collections, *Yerba buena* (1980, Mint) and *Tropical Rains: A Bilingual Downpour* (1984), culminate over a decade of poetry readings and extensive publishing in journals and anthologies. Her thematic and stylistic spectrum shares concerns and outlooks with other U.S.-born Puerto Rican poets, yet, presided over by the awareness of her condition as a woman. She is also a visual and performing artist.

Biography

Sandra María Esteves was born in the Bronx, New York, "in the middle of Spring, sometime around the end of the Second World War—on May 10, 1948– in a community inhabited by immigrants which has since been abandoned," according to her opening statement in *Yerba buena*. Her mother is from the Dominican Republic. An orphan, she lived in St. Thomas and Puerto Rico before settling in New York in 1935 at age nineteen. Her father was a sailor whose family emigrated from San Juan, Puerto Rico, in the early 1940s. They separated before Sandra María, an only child, was born.

Esteves was raised among Spanish-speaking women in the Huntspoint area of the South Bronx. Her mother, a single parent, labored in the same needlework factory for forty years; the factory changed owners, but she came with the equipment. Her paternal aunt, Julia Esteves de Domínguez, a dedicated mother and housewife who raised four children of her own while her husband was away in the merchant marine, cared for the girl while her mother was out working.

Sheltered by her overprotective parent concerned with drugs, violence, and sexual abuse, young Esteves was kept off the streets, becoming an introvert, shy and afraid of the world. At age six, she was interned for seven years in a Catholic boarding school, the Holy Rosary Academy, in the Lower East Side of Manhattan. Thus, Esteves lived a dual existence, spending her weekdays in an English-speaking, secluded, disciplinarian environment and her weekends in the boisterous Spanish-speaking world of her four cousins, Aunt Julia, and her mother. While she profited from such education, school entailed another sort of violence: experiencing the double stigma of coming from a Hispanic single-parent household and being prohibited from speaking Spanish in school. By the age of ten, both tongues were intertwined into confusion to the point of feeling intimidated by language itself. From this situation she developed an initial insecurity about language, yet it also implanted an awareness of the connotations of words.

Esteves completed grammar school in St. Anselm, went on to Cardinal Spellman High School, and in 1966 attended Pratt Institute, in Brooklyn, from which she would drop out twice before completing her B.F.A. in 1978, majoring in fine arts, creative writing, and media communications. In spite of being a competent student, by the end of the freshman year her instructors had convinced her that she did not belong in college and should "go back where she came from" and raise children. An acute identity crisis ensued, compounded with sentimental conflicts, that impelled her to abandon college for the next four years.

A period of soul-searching led her for the first time to Puerto Rico, yet, after two months of seeking a well-paying job, she returned to New York. She developed, however, a newfound receptiveness to her homeland's culture and language which prompted her to recognize her personal search in the collective resurgence of ethnic pride, interest in the people's history, and consciousness-raising that culminated toward the end of the 1960s and early 1970s in her native New York. It was the time of militant civil rights and anti–Vietnam War movements, of Power to the People and Viva La Raza, of Black Is Beautiful and Resurrection City, of the Wounded Knee Massacre and the Attica Uprising, of riots throughout the ghettoes and massive student strikes, of the Puerto Rican Young Lords and the demands for ethnic studies. Latin American culture boomed in the hemisphere and bloomed in New York City. This was the time when Esteves attained maturity.

Early in the 1970s, at a community reading in the National Black Theater, she first encountered a people's poetry that talked about things that were close and meaningful to those who produced and received it. In school she had been exposed to the classical poets: men, long deceased, who spoke of lofty subjects with which she could not relate. But now her gut reaction was to go home and write. She had practiced painting for years and crossed over to poetry, discovering that sounds, senses, and feelings expressed in words were another dimension of what she experienced with color. Through poetry, she was to concurrently acquire and disseminate a newfound understanding of herself as a Hispanic woman and of her people.

There followed a whirlwind awakening. The New York Puerto Rican poet and playwright Jesús Papoleto Meléndez took notice of Esteves's poems, encouraged her, and introduced her to the effervescent circles of Hispanic artists, a vanguard movement of innovative painters, muralists, performers, musicians, and poets committed to their working-class communities. By 1973, she was already reading her work alongside Miguel *Algarín, Tato *Laviera, Américo Casiano, and other poets, sharing the stage at Rutgers University with "Grupo Taone," from Puerto Rico. Poets and musicians joined forces to tour the Eastern seaboard and returned to form "El Grupo," a New York-based touring collective of "protest music" made up of performing artists and poets. It was the cultural wing of the Puerto Rican Socialist party in the United States. It represented Esteves's first contact with a political group of Puerto Ricans and other Latin Americans whose artistic work was truly meaningful to her. As a painter, she came in contact with the "Taller Boricua" collective—Jorge Soto, Marcos Dimas, Fernando Salicrup, Martín Pérez—a cohesive group of Puerto Rican visual artists born and raised in New York who could truly understand what she was going through. Musicians Sunny Paz, Bernardo Palombo, José Valdez Montañez, and others added to her newborn awareness of the broader spectrum of Puerto Rican culture: Latin America. Her participation in the 1973 University of Wisconsin's National Ethnic Writers Conference opened her eyes to the common struggle for survival and the right to self-determination of Native-, Afro-, and Asian-Americans, Chicanos, and Puerto Ricans. There she also met Joseph Bruchac, editor of the *Greenfield Review,* who approached her about publishing her first individual collection of poetry, which he did in 1980.

Fortified by this tour de force, Esteves acquired elements of judgment with which to recognize in her own family, neighborhood, and living experience the cultural values that had been transmitted to her orally, and she developed the capacity to return these to her community, crafted by the artist's sensibility. She was rushed to expose her poetry-in-process partly due to the invisibility of other English-writing Hispanic women at a point in history when feminism mandated otherwise. Along with Lorraine Sutton in Chicago, she became the exceptional female voice among the Puerto Rican poets writing in English. She delivered her poetry at cafes, community centers, schools, universities, and rallies; was part of workshops and symposia; emceed radio programs and participated in others; and her work appeared in an ever-increasing number of journals and anthologies. She has worked as literary artist with the Cultural Council Foundation of the CETA Artistic Project (1978–1980); conducted poetry series for the New Rican Village Cultural Center (1979) and for Galería Moriviví (1980, 1982, 1983); has run poetry and drama workshops for the New York State Poets in the Schools (1981 to the present) and the New York Shakespeare Festival (1985). In 1983 she became the executive artistic director of the African Caribbean Poetry Theater, which in 1984 published her second poetry collection, *Tropical Rains.*

Her awards include a New York State Creative Artists Public Service (CAPS) Fellowship for Poetry, in 1980, and a Poetry Fellowship by the New York

Foundation for the Arts, in 1985. Her first collection, *Yerba buena,* was selected as Best Small Press Publication for 1981.

Although painting and drawing receded into the background, Esteves has exhibited in the Habestray Enrichment Movement gallery, Galería Moriviví, Taller Boricua, and the Nuyorican Poets Cafe. Her first poetry collection was illustrated with her drawings.

In December 1984 she participated in a women's conference in Cuba, her first trip outside the United States, save Puerto Rico.

Esteves is a working woman, a wife, and the mother of three daughters, Ifetayo, Christina, and Yaasmiyn.

She considers herself a growing poet and believes that her best writing is still to come.

Major Themes

Esteves's poetry is characterized by thematic and formal diversity strung together and blended by one poetic voice that is categorically feminine. The search for authenticity and assertion of her identity (as a colonized Hispanic woman raised in the United States, non-Caucasian, from a working-class immigrant family, with roots in the Caribbean) is the axis around which other themes revolve. She describes it as "a poetry of discovery for those who pass through the same doors as I."

As other Hispanics born and raised in the United States, Esteves expresses in her poetry a concern with creatively interpreting and struggling to resolve the conflicts of her community, a people conscribed in a country that negates their culture and language to impose assimilation while simultaneously denying access to the goods of the greater society. It is a poetry initially written to be heard, aware of stemming from a community to which it is returned. Influenced in style, tone, and themes by the militant Afro-American poets, particularly the "Last Poets," with whom she shares the experience of growing up in the ghettoes, hers is a critical outlook toward a society tainted by racism and discrimination, alienation and consumerism.

The rejection of all forms of fragmentation and a yearning for harmony between contradictory factors is a recurrent motif in Esteves's poetry. This search for harmony becomes an urge to delete the separation between the urban habitat and the regenerative forces of life. It manifests a longing for communion with nature and humankind as a whole (as in "All of you"). It speaks of comradery and love between men and women and rejects anything that divides and creates disharmony in the cosmos, be it racism, machismo, or contamination of the ecology. In line with this, freedom and lack of freedom is also a recurrent theme. Poems such as "Visiting," "Bedford Hills Is a Women's Prison," "For Lolita Lebrón," and others decry that human beings should be deprived of their liberty.

Her urge to create an original poetic universe, as Matilla has said of Neo-Rican poets, has its matrix in being simultaneously expelled from both Puerto Rico and the United States. Her poetry is a quest for sources of identity and for a better understanding of the links between her New York Hispanic community, Puerto Rico, and the Caribbean, thus seeking a reconciliation with her national identity as a U.S.-born Puerto Rican: "I think much of my culture/ always searching the pieces/ and more, always arriving/ closer to the woman that I am," she states—in Spanish—in "Pienso en los momentos" (I Think of the Moments). This quest generates a dynamic tension between the affirmation of the culture inherited from her family and community in the form of ideas, ideals, and behavioral patterns and the need to locate her position on earth. In some poems this tension takes form in a dichotomy, as in "Here": "I am two parts/ a person/ boricua/ spic/ past and present/ alive and oppressed/ given a cultural beauty/ . . . and robbed of a cultural identity . . . /I may never overcome/ the theft of my isla heritage" The dichotomy dialectically leads to its own resolution as "that reality now a dream/ teaches me to see, and will/ bring me back to me."

The defense and affirmation of the homeland are in Esteves's poetry elements of political resistance to cultural assimilation and to all forms of domination. Myths and feelings extracted from the root culture function as a palliative to the "mutilated harmony," taking on a new meaning in the context where these are re-created. For instance, in "For Tito," the irrationality of urban life is overcome by summoning the forces of tropical nature to enliven "the grey world around me" ("Manhattan"): "Together/ we reap mystical sugarcane in the ghetto/ where all the palm trees grow ripe/ and rich with coconut milk."

It is in this context that Esteves's recourse to two languages must be perceived, for it is a conscious poetic resource rather than a rendition of the linguistic patterns of her community. As Louis *Reyes Rivera has observed, caught in the crux of being a Puerto Rican deprived by historical and social forces of mastering the national language of her homeland, Spanish, as well as the language of the metropolis, English, she chooses to recreate both languages imposed upon her and her people. The menace of being a linguistic pariah is thus transformed into creative impulse as she converts the resulting bilingualism into an element of self-assertion: "I speak the alien tongue/ in sweet borinqueño thoughts" ("Here"); "I speak two languages broken into each other/ but my heart speaks the language of people/ born in oppression" ("María Christina"). The innovative imagery extracted from two counterpointed languages is rooted into two referential cultures, blending sounds and rhyme from Spanish, and rhythmic elements from popular Latin music, into English verse.

This mode of cultural resistance is not devoid of contradictions. Puerto Rico, as a physical place and as a state of mind, is often a paradise lost or a cage that locks her into a set of values that perhaps became archaic since her family emigrated. To Barradas, this contradiction between the unconditional acceptance of the cultural legacy as a source of identity and the need to change the unworkable aspects of this legacy is precisely the ethic-aesthetic fulcrum of Esteves's poetry. Fernández Olmos concurs, pointing out the conflict between her overwhelming drive to belong to a cultural tradition—understood as internalized myths about women's role as "the nurturer of fire which men burn"—and her confronting its patriarchal values. The need to overcome these conflicts clashes with her unwillingness to further estrange herself from the "quintessence" of Puerto Ricanness. Yet, paradoxically, the revision of patriarchal values brings Esteves's poetry closer to her island-based contemporaries, as Umpierre has suggested.

But Esteves's poetry does not shy away from assuming all the contradictions of her social group. Her poetic persona identifies with the collective conscience of Hispanic women: "In the midst of agony and repression, of starvation and injustice, of transitory illusion and rightful reclamation, rises the voice of the multitude to become the ink which fills my pen" (*The Next World*). The exploration of the self thus becomes an exploration of female roles as mother, daughter, lover, wife, worker, and poet. This exploration is often expressed through conventional imagery such as woman-mother-nature, tree of life, fertile soil, "the organic fruit of my womb," yet new meaning is aroused through Afro-Caribbean imagery, as when this woman-goddess is the Yoruba orisha Obatalá.

Womanhood is to Esteves a unifying force, because "the reality of being women touches all racial and class structures," as is apparent in several poems: "For women who keep waiting/ For women who want life/ to be the existence of living"; "we who live in men's worlds/trying to be our souls/like the free spirit of birds in the sky" ("For Tulani"). But if being a woman is crucial, being a colonized woman is even more so. In her best known poems, the oppression of women allegorically addresses the political domination of Esteves's homeland and people. "My Name Is María Christina" is, in this sense, a first stage in a process in which the poetic voice unconditionally embraces the traditional roles of Latin women so that men can be strong to struggle and Hispanic culture may survive: "I do not complain about cooking for my family/because abuela taught me that woman is the master of fire/I do not complain about nursing my children/because I determine the direction of their values . . . /I am the mother of a new age of warriors . . . /Our men . . . they call me negra because they love me/ and in turn I teach them to be strong." "A Julia y a mi" (To Julia and to Me) is a second phase in this process. Identifying the Puerto Rican poet Julia de *Burgos with her mother and her aunt Julia, she fiercely rejects the victimization of women. The process culminates in "From the Common Wealth" and "Transference," where she rejects male preconceptions of womankind by revealing her identity to conclude: "Y si la patria es una mujer" (And if the homeland is a woman) "Then I am also a rebel and a lover of free people."

While Esteves sees Puerto Rico as a source of identity, to the degree that she assumes an anticolonial stance, her gradual recovery of the homeland's culture and history is selective and critical. Her rejection of the present domination extends to the past, to the dominant culture inherited from Spain, the original colonizer. Puerto Rico and the Caribbean are defined in her poetry as a fusion of cultures where the mythical, musical, and historical legacies of the colonized— the popular elements of pre-Columbian Taino and African origins—prevail.

This selective identification with the non-European origins and culture of Puerto Rico is one of the bases for her exaltation of blackness and "brown mixtures'' in ''Por ti, Bro'' (For You, Bro). But, most important, it bridges to other ethnic and national minorities, to the colonized within the United States, with whom she is kinned inimically and stylistically. It also links with all oppressed cultures and ultimately with its universal representation, humanity.

Esteves's poetry expresses a clear awareness of being an agent in the creation of a distinct culture tailored for survival in U.S. soil. While the need to take control of their existence as ''Neo-Ricans'' in an adverse environment may turn latent certain aspects of the homeland's culture, it transforms others into ''a mixture of something unique/a verbal reflection all edged/ to a center beyond sound'' (''I Am More Than . . . '').

Esteves is a poet determined not to lock her work in any one style or thematic range. She also writes prose, which is unpublished, among these ''Ambivalence or Activism from the Nuyorrican Perspective in Poetry'' and ''The Feminist Viewpoint in Poetry of the Puerto Rican Woman in the United States,'' presented at the conference ''Images and Identities: The Puerto Rican in Literature,'' Rutgers University, 1983. She has authored or co-authored four plays: a one-act play on wife abuse *Niña Mesclá* (1981, Mixed Girl), *Master Builder* (1985), *Cry of Lares* (1985), and *On the Roof* (1985), a musical. She is writing her first novel, about a Puerto Rican woman who is a ''santera'' trainee.

Survey of Criticism

It is a recognized fact that if women writers in the United States have been neglected by critics and their voices silenced by publishers, ethnic women have been doubly neglected. Few studies on Esteves's work have been published. This is partly due to the fact that she has been most divulged as an oral poet. Although her poetry has appeared in numerous journals and has been included in several anthologies, her first individual collection was not published until 1980. But, most important, parameters for the aesthetic analysis of Neo-Rican literature have not yet been fully developed.

Efraín Barradas, Margarite Fernández Olmos, and Luz María Umpierre have pioneered the study of Esteves's poetry, examining selected poems in the context of other Puerto Rican and Hispanic poets.

Barradas, in ''De lejos en sueños verla'' (Seeing Her at a Distance in a Dream) and in his landmark essay on U.S.-Puerto Rican poetry included in *Herejes y mitificadores*, analyzes Esteves's poetic vision in terms of her acceptance and rejection of the cultural myths U.S.-born Puerto Rican poets from a distance identify as the ''essence'' of Puerto Rican culture. He fathoms the conflicts encountered by the artist, on the one hand, as myth-maker of an idealized Puerto Rico and, on the other, as a heretic for anathematizing those myths when they run counter to her New York reality.

Fernández Olmos, in ''From the Metropolis,'' considers the evolution of the role of women in Esteves's poetry together with works by island-born Puerto Rican women poets Julia de *Burgos and Edna Iris Rivera, whose poetry also exhibits "the delicate balance between defending one's culture and traditions, and analyzing it with a critical eye."

Umpierre follows the route of intertextuality. In "La ansiedad de la influencia" she applies Harold Blooms's theory of "the anxiety of influence" to "A Julia y a mi" and "A Noel Rico." She explores how Esteves "swerves away" from her precursors in order to arrive at a better understanding of her own self while inserting her work in the island-Puerto Rican poetical tradition. "De la protesta a la creación" (From Protest to Creation) is a comparative study of "From the Common Wealth" and "Transference" and poems by Puerto Rican authors Julia de *Burgos and Rosario *Ferré, focusing on how the rebellion against domesticity and male preconceptions of women in the three poets progresses toward the assertion of female creativity and social change. Umpierre has also prepared an interview with Esteves for publication.

Nancy Mandlove contributes a new angle to the study of Esteves's work in an unpublished paper presented at the National Women Studies Conference in 1984, "Towards a Common Language: Hispanic Women Writers in the United States." Concentrating on the problems of creating a language common to writer and reader, Mandlove considers the recourse to a "richly complex network of tensions between languages, cultures, female and male worlds which is further enhanced by the simultaneous affirmation and negation of various aspects of that bicultural experience" in terms of what this can contribute to the non-Hispanic woman reader.

Louis *Reyes Rivera provides a more comprehensive approach in his insightful introduction to *Yerba buena.*

Also useful is Wolfgang Binder's perceptive review of the same.

Esteves's work is also mentioned in surveys of Puerto Rican writing in the United States (for example, Nicolás Kanellos, "Puerto Rican Literature from the Diaspora to the Mainstream," in *American Book Review).* Works on Neo-Rican poetry in general are also useful background to the study of Esteves.

Bibliography

WORKS BY ESTEVES

Books

Yerba buena: dibujos y poemas. New York: Greenfield Review Press, 1980.
Tropical Rains: A Bilingual Downpour. New York: African Caribbean Poetry Theater, 1984.

Individual Poems

El Grupo: Canciones y poesía de la lucha de los pueblos latinoamericanos. New York: Disco Libre/Center for Cuban Studies, 1974.
"All of you." *Sunbury* 2 1/2 (October 1974): 18.
"Ode to a Tequila Head," "For Tito," "Blanket Weaver," "I look for peace great graveyard." *Nuyorican Poetry: An Anthology of Puerto Rican Words and Feel-*

ings, Miguel Algarín and Miguel Piñero, eds. New York: William Morrow and Co., 1975.

"Untitled." *Black World* 24/11 (September 1975): 74.

"Manhattan." *The Journal of Contemporary Puerto Rican Thought* 2/4 (1975): 21.

"A Cold Place," "Reaching for the Sunrise." *Sunbury* 4 2/1 (Spring 1976): 32.

"Adamayo y Idemaya," "A Julia y a mí," "For Noel Rico," "Death Love," "We Should Have Waited," "He Is My Lover," "Bedford Hills Is a Women's Prison," "The Child Wept When She Had No Home," "For Ife." *Womanrise,* Louis Reyes Rivera, ed. New York: Shamal Books, 1978.

"For Tulani," "Ahora," "Visiting," "Por Ti, Bro," "A Julia y a mí." *Ordinary Women/Mujeres comunes: An Anthology of Poetry by New York City Women,* F. Chiang, S.M. Esteves, P. Jones, S. Miles, eds. New York: Ordinary Women Books, 1978.

"Untitled I-VIII," "Vanguardia," "Untitled X." *The Next World. Poems by 32 Third World Americans,* Joseph Bruchac, ed. Trumansburg, N.Y.: The Crossing Press, 1978.

"Music Is My Lover," "Bedford Hills Is a Women's Prison." *Conditions: Three* 1/3 (Spring 1978): 93–95.

"Let My Spirit Fly," "For Noel Rico," and "So You Want Me." *Revista Chicano-Riqueña* 7/2 (Spring 1979): 8–9; Reprint. *A Decade of Hispanic Literature: An Anniversary Anthology* 10/1–2 (Winter-Spring 1982): 70–71.

"The Snatch" and "From the Commonwealth." *Vórtice* 2/2–3 (1979): 73–74.

Antología de la poesía de la mujer puertorriqueña. New York: Península, 1981.

"A Julia y a mí." *Third Woman* 1/2 (1982): 14–15.

"A Julia y a mí." *Vórtice* 2 (1982): 14–15.

Leaving the Bough. New York: International Publishers, 1982.

"Amor negro," "A Celebration of Home Birth," "Portraits of Shamsul Alam," and "Transference," accompanied by drawings. *Woman of Her Word,* E. Vigil, ed. *Revista Chicano-Riqueña* 11/3–4 (1983): 28–35.

WORKS ABOUT ESTEVES

Barradas, Efraín. "Introducción." *Herejes y mitificadores: Muestra de poesía puerto-rriqueña en los Estados Unidos,* E. Barradas and R. Rodríguez, eds. Río Piedras, P.R.: Huracán, 1980.

———. "Puerto Rico acá, Puerto Rico allá." *Revista Chicano-Riqueña* 8/2 (Spring 1980): 43–49.

———. "Consciencia femenina, consciencia social: la voz de Sandra María Esteves." *Third Woman* 1/2 (1982): 31–34.

Binder, Wolfgang. Review of *Yerba buena. Explorations in Light and Sound* (1982): 15–17.

"Music Is My Lover." *Heresies* 8 2/4 (1979): 65.

"The IRT Is Hot and Humid on August 9th." *Sunbury* 9 3/3 (Fall 1980): 136.

"A Julia y a mí," "My Name Is Maria Christina"/"Me llamo María Cristina." *Herejes y mitificadores: Muestra de poesía puertorriqueña en los Estados Unidos,* E. Barradas and R. Rodríguez, eds. Río Piedras, P.R.: Huracán, 1980.

Words to Go. New York: Cultural Council Foundation, 1980.

"Ahora" and "The rain that muddles against the tracks." *Chiricú* 1/3 (Spring 1980): 38–39.

"Beginnings: Agua que va a caer," "Candumbe," "El Guaguancó de Martín Tito Pérez," "Imágenes nuevas." *New Rain.* Vol. 1. New York: Blind Beggar Press, 1981.

Fernández Olmos, Margarite. "From the Metropolis: Puerto Rican Women Poets and the Immigration Experience." *Third Woman* 1/2 (1982): 40–51.

Mandlove, Nancy. "Towards a Common Language: Hispanic Women Writers in the United States." Paper presented at the National Women Studies Conference, Rutgers University, 1984.

Reyes Rivera, Louis. "Introduction: By Way of Sharing Perspectives." *Yerba buena.* New York: Greenfield Review Press, 1980.

Rivero, Eliana. "Nota sobre las voces femeninas en *Herejes y mitificadores.*" *Third Woman* 1/2 (1982): 91–3.

Turner, Faythe. Review of Mohr's *The Nuyorican Experience. Melus* (Fall 1983): 87.

Umpierre, Luz María. "La ansiedad de la influencia en Sandra María Esteves y Marjorie Agosin." *Revista Chicano-Riqueña* 11/3–4 (Fall-Winter 1983): 139–47.

———. "La ansiedad de la influencia en Sandra María Esteves." *Nuevas aproximaciones críticas a la literatura puertorriqueña contemporánea.* Río Piedras, P.R.: Editorial Cultural, 1983.

———. "De la protesta a la creación: Una nueva visión de la mujer puertorriqueña en la poesía." *Imagine* 2, 1 (Summer 1985); 134–42.

Whitehead, Fred. "Poetry for Her—A Way of Living." *Daily World* (January 12, 1982): 9.

YANIS GORDILS

F

FERNÁNDEZ, ROBERTO (1951–   ). Roberto Fernández is a prose fiction writer and academician. He belongs to the new generation of Cuban American writers who grew up and were educated in the United States. His two major works are *La vida es un special* (1982, Life Is on Special) and *La montaña rusa* (1985, The Roller Coaster). Both works are satirical novels written in Spanish. They portray the manners, linguistic peculiarities, values, and psychology of the large community of Cuban exiles that settled in Miami during the past quarter of a century.

Biography

Roberto Fernández was born in Sagua la Grande, Cuba, on September 24, 1951 to a family of upper-middle-class professionals. In 1961, two years after the takeover of the Cuban government by communists, Roberto and his family left Cuba for the United States. The struggles for a new beginning in an environment that at the outset seemed hostile to the small boy were painful experiences to be relived years later by characters in Fernández's fictional works.

Roberto's family did not settle in Miami, the hub of the Cuban community in exile, but in nearby areas where Anglo-American culture was dominant. They were to visit Miami often, however, and, consequently, the writer was to grow up with a foot in two cultures, so to speak, quietly observing both with the detachment and objectivity of one who does not quite belong.

Coming from a family of talented musicians and composers, his striving for artistic expression seemed quite natural, and at an early age he chose literature as his metier. By late adolescence a teaching career at the university level seemed a natural adjunct to this calling. Therefore, he went on to graduate school, and by the time he completed his Ph.D. in linguistics at Florida State University in 1978 he had also already published two collections of short stories of an experimental nature, *Cuentos sin rumbo* (1975, Directionless Tales) and *El Jardín de la Luna* (1976, The Garden of the Moon).

His first novel, *La vida es un special,* published in 1982 by Universal, a Cuban American press, brought him recognition from critics and scholars interested in Hispanic literature in the United States. Both this novel and *La montaña rusa,* a sequel of sorts, published in 1985 by Arte Publico Press at the University of Houston, have as their main concern the life of Cuban exiles in Miami and both exhibit experimentation with language and structure that brings to mind two writers whose influence the author recognizes, the Cuban Cabrera Infante and Kurt Vonnegut.

Fernández has chosen to write about the Cuban community in exile because he sees it as a vanishing culture. He points out that the average age of its members is thirty-nine. Like his contemporary, Cuban poet Pura del Prado, he feels that when he dies a bit of Cuba will die with him. He has chosen, therefore, to record a way of life that he sees doomed to extinction and to this fact can be attributed the nostalgia that underlies the humor in his works. Because language so much reflects the life of a people and because it is Fernández's academic field of interest, his works re-create with gusto the whole spectrum of the Cuban American dialect of Miami.

At present the writer resides in Tallahassee, Florida, with his young daughter Tatiana. He is on the faculty of Florida State University. Aside from teaching literature, he does research in social linguistics. Recently he completed a study of the impact that the Russian language and revolutionary ideology have had upon the language of post-revolutionary Cuba. Recently also, and in collaboration with his brother, social historian José Fernández, he has published a bibliography of Cuban literature written in the United States.

Major Themes

For Roberto Fernández the Cuban community in Miami is no more a monolith than any society of comparable size and complexity. As the writer has explained in interviews, there are many Miamis: there is the progressive Miami very much in keeping with the changing times and there is that other Miami composed of exiles who have stagnated and who are still living in the Cuba of the 1950s. And it is of this Cuban community whose outlook, attitudes, and values have remained impervious to the passage of time that the author writes in his two novels.

In *La vida es un special* the exiled Cubans, like shipwrecked persons on a desert island, cut off from all they have known before, re-create their lost island paradise guided by their collective memory and by written history, songs, legends, and traditions. Time, distance, and nostalgia distort reality until myths become reality and the past becomes more relevant than the present. For every Cuban institution that once existed there is a counterpart, however grotesque, in Miami, be it the spiritist shop with age-old cures of herbs, fragrances, and powders, now in aerosol cans, or the elaborate coming-out parties for fifteen-

year-old girls transformed by rampant consumerism into choreographic extrav-
aganzas. As the standard of living improves, whatever moral lessons that might
have been drawn from the disasters of the Revolution and the pain of the dis-
persion are forgotten. Social classes are drawn, as in pre-revolutionary Cuba,
along economic lines. Frivolity is the order of the day. Money becomes the only
real value because everything can be bought, from a university diploma to an
exorcism, and, if possible, it is bought for the lowest price, on special. For life,
as the title of the novel implies, when measured exclusively by materialistic
standards, becomes cheap, of little worth. At the end of the novel, after a comic-
opera invasion reminiscent of the ill-fated Bay of Pigs operation, the will of the
majority is thwarted by an insensitive upper class, assisted by representatives of
the American government.

   La montaña rusa explores some of the themes introduced in *La vida es un
special*. Here we find a static society where all social divisions and categories
have been established and where cultural and ideological stagnation are the
keynote. All standards are now set and there is a right way and a wrong way
for art, sex, political thinking, or combing one's hair. Characters continue to
argue about the things they once supposedly owned in that mythical Cuba that
is still more real than the present-day Florida in which they live. A contest for
political essays, art, and literature sponsored by a patriotic organization reveals
the major preoccupations of the community. Anticommunism is a driving force
that borders on paranoia. Those who dare find anything positive in the Cuba of
today are labeled as traitors. On the other hand, exaggerated patriotism is vaunted
as the greatest of virtues. Needless to say, the winners of the contest are those
who adhered to the most conservative standards. Patriotic poems and anticom-
munist essays, regardless of how ungrammatical, trite, and lacking in orginality,
are the winners. In art the preferred entries are those that depict patriotic allegories
or those that repeat old folkloric themes.

   A colorful political campaign for local elections indicates that, several decades
after the Cuban Revolution, business is as usual as far as politicians are concerned. Political slogans and a variety of dirty tricks are carbon copies of their
counterparts in the Cuba of the 1940s and the 1950s. At the end of the novel
the forces of progress are again defeated, as in the previous novel, by the forces
of injustice and obscurantism.

Survey of Criticism

   Roberto Fernández's early short stories have as yet not been the subject of
literary reviews. *La vida es un special,* in print for less than three years now,
is the first of the author's works to be reviewed. Praise has been drawn by the
author's skillful rendition of the Miami Cuban dialect and for the humor and
irony with which he has depicted his characters and situations. The structural
innovations of the novel have also been of interest. They have reminded one
critic of the devices utilized in film making. The novel has been accepted as an
important social document since it is the first attempt in fiction to record the

ways of this exile community. A critic recommends, however, for the author to do a deeper and more careful analysis of his subject.

Of *La montaña rusa,* Gustavo Pérez-Firmat wrote in *Linden Lane Magazine* (January/March 1986) that the principal merit of this novel, which is made up of vignettes, was its honesty and humorous treatment of the inhabitants of Miami's Cuban ghetto.

However, Fernández's greatest success to date has been the reception by the critics of his third novel, *Raining Backwards*. Having been reviewed from coast to coast in such publications as *The New York Times, USA Today* and the *San Francisco Chronicle,* the novel has been seen as an hilarious, chaotic microcosm of the Cuban community in which Fernández's innovative style and cyclical, non-linear structure succeed in creating an energy that captivates all readers. Concluded André Codrescu, in *The New York Times Book Review,* August 14, 1988, "There is a creative freedom with the materials here that augurs well for Latino writing."

Although Fernández's first book of short stories, *Cuentos sin rumbo,* is now out of print, some of his short stories have appeared in anthologies and in literary journals.

Bibliography

WORKS BY FERNÁNDEZ

Cuentos sin rumbo. Miami: Ediciones Universal, 1975.
El jardín de la luna. Tallahassee, Fl.: Jiffy Press, 1976.
"La Encadenada." *20 cuentistas cubanos,* ed. Leonardo Fernández-Marcane. Miami: Ediciones Universal, 1978.
"Entre Juegos." *Nuevos horizontes,* ed. José Fernández. Boston: D.C. Heath, 1982.
La vida es un special. Miami: Ediciones Universal, 1982.
"Los Quince." *Nuevas voces.* New York: Holt, Rinehart & Winston, 1984.
"Coco Rallado." *Linden Lane Magazine* 4 (January-February 1985): 3.
La montaña rusa. Houston: Arte Publico Press, 1985.

In Collaboration with Another Author

Fernández, José B., and Roberto G. Fernández. *Indice bibliográfico de autores cubanos (Diaspora 1959–1979) / Bibliographical Index of Cuban Authors (Diaspora 1959–1979).* Miami: Ediciones Universal, 1983.
Raining Backwards. Houston: Arte Publico Press, 1988.

WORKS ABOUT FERNÁNDEZ

Allen, Bruce. "Neglected but Noteworthy Fiction of '88." *USA Today.* January 3, 1989.
Aguilar Melantzón, Ricardo. *"Raining Backwards." Vista.* September 4, 1988.
Chase, Alfonso. "La vida no es tan especial." *El Debate* (San Jose, Costa Rica). January 28, 1984.
Codrescu, André. "A Mad, Mad, Mad Mundo." *The New York Times Book Review.* August 14, 1988.
Febles, Jorge. *"La vida es un special." Hispania* 67 (May 1984): 315.

———. "Risa, crisis y coronación paródica: lo carnavalesco en *La vida es un special.*" *Confluencia* 3/1 (Fall 1987): 123–28.

Hintereder, Helen. "*La vida es un special.*" *Lector.* 2/2 (September-October 1983): 41.

Kolokithas, Dawn. "Cuban American's Crazy World." *San Francisco Chronicle.* April 14, 1988.

Pérez-Frimat, Gustavo. "*La montaña rusa.*" *Linden Lane Magazine.* (January/March 1986): 35.

Márquez, Myriam. "A Surrealist Novel about US Cubans." *The Philadelphia Inquirer.* December 6, 1988.

"*Raining Backwards*". *Publishers Weekly.* March 11, 1988.

Ruiz del Vizo, Hortensia. "*La vida es un special.*" *Diario de las Américas.* October 9, 1982.

Ulloa, Justo C. "*20 cuentistas cubanos.*" *Hispanic Journal* 1/2 (Spring 1980): 155–56.

Watkins, Steve. " 'Raining Backwards': It's Easy to Replace History with Myth." *Tallahassee Democrat/Sun.* September 18, 1988.

SILVIA NOVO PENA

FERRÉ, ROSARIO (1942–).

Rosario Ferré is a contemporary short-story writer, lecturer, poet, essayist, newspaper columnist, literary critic, and editor-publisher of *Zona de carga y descarga* (1972–1975, Loading and Unloading Zone). Her noteworthy literary creation, her experimentation with language and with universal literary trends to re-create in her fiction the Puerto Rican historical environment, while projecting a strong Antillean voice, assures Rosario a place at the vanguard of Hispanic American literature.

Biography

Rosario was born in Ponce, Puerto Rico. As daughter of Luis A. Ferré, financier and public figure, she met very early the conflicts of her sociopolitical background. The merging of two cultures, the Puerto Rican and the American, since the Treaty of Paris (1898) ceded Puerto Rico to the United States, the merging of two languages, Spanish and English, and the gradual merging of a decadent oligarchic society into the technological age, without first shedding its colonial codes, created the eclectic cosmovision that Rosario later re-created.

Social eclecticism was already apparent in the wealth of Puerto Rican oral literature discovered through her father's and her black ayah's lips before she had learned to read. From her sixth to her fifteenth year Rosario immersed herself in her private library of fairy tales. The pathos of the childhood worlds of Grimm, Hoffman, Andersen, *Alice in Wonderland,* and *A Thousand and One Nights* exerted great influence in Rosario's writing career. The marvelous realism of past folklores and fairy tales, which she extolled in "Cuentos de hadas" (Fairy Tales), lives today in her children's stories, stories that show great respect for a child's intellectual and social rights.

Unwavering respect for literature persevered with Rosario during her Dana Hall and Manhattanville College days. Tolstoy, Dostoyevsky, José Gautier Benítez, José de Diego, Alejandro Dumas, Edgar Allan Poe, Julia de *Burgos, and Luis *Palés Matos were her constant companions. Particularly revered was Hudson's *Green Mansions,* given to Rosario by her father, who in turn had received it from his wife. Her writing was not forgotten. As a child, she had written always—poems to herself when very young, because she liked the exercise of literature. Free time from academia produced articles and romantic vignettes for publication in *El Día,* a Puerto Rican newspaper. Around this time, when Rosario was in her second year of college, family and political duty demanded priority in her life. Her mother became seriously ill and Rosario became the official hostess at "La Fortaleza," the governor's mansion. Her father, Luis A. Ferré, was then governor of Puerto Rico, under the New Progressive party ticket (1968–1972). Sometime later, Rosario embraced the cause for Puerto Rican independence, attracting criticism from a semi-colonial society that espoused social caution and political breeding.

In 1972 Rosario took a momentous step for her literary career. With Iván *Silén, Olga Nolla, Waldo Lloreda, and Luis César Rivera she founded *Zona de carga y descarga,* a literary magazine seemingly propounding an aesthetic-eclectic premise by which to interrogate political systems, a premise implicit always in Rosario's writings. It was in *Zona de carga y descarga* that her first successful story, "La muñeca menor" (1979, "The Youngest Doll," 1980), was published. The story was included in her first book, *Papeles de Pandora* (1976, Pandora's Papers), and published again in 1979 as an individual book, in both Spanish and English; it was later republished as a translation in *Kenyon Review* in 1980.

The year 1974 brought decisive influences into Rosario's writing career. As candidate for a master's degree in Spanish literature at the University of Puerto Rico, she came under the aegis of four noted Hispanic American scholars. Mario Vargas Llosa, Ángel Rama, and Margot Arce de Vázquez gave her a fresh literary perspective and a sense of vocation. But F. Manrique Cabrera pointed the way to social commitment. Through literature, he unfolded in front of her a cyclical vision of Puerto Rican history and identity. The writings of Manuel Alonso, Ramón Emeterio Betances, Eugenio María de Hostos, José de Diego, Luis *Palés Matos, and Julia de *Burgos confidently assured Rosario that Puerto Ricans had not always been acquiescent beings moulded by the postulates of the bureaucracy and that intellectuals must, at times, assume a nihilist social philosophy in the defense of the oppressed and the depressed.

Looking back, from 1972 onwards Rosario's social and literary posture gained momentum. Stories, poems, essays, book reviews, and lectures have been published in Hispanic literary journals and books. Her short stories earned a 1976 award from the *Ateneo Puertorriqueño,* a cultural institution that since 1864 has stimulated promising writers. From 1976 on, she has written almost one book per year. "Maldito amor," a novel still in writing, newspaper columns, conferences, and literary debates around Washington, D.C., where she lives, Puerto Rico, and neighboring countries continue her literary trajectory. Her writing and her family, three children by a first marriage and husband, Mexican novelist Jorge Aguilar Mora, are the most important interests in her life.

Major Themes

Rosario Ferré's major works—*Papeles de Pandora* (1976), *Sitio a Eros (Eros Besieged)*, *Fábulas de la garza desangrada* (1982) Fables of the Bleeding Crane—are considered feminist. In *Papeles de Pandora* the mythical viewpoint of a wrathful Pandora consistently reviews the cultural plight of woman-doll representations, always furthering the social position of unfeeling men. The sedate faceless belle, who sat as social adornment in "La muñeca menor" (The Youngest Doll), the initial story, suffers a radical transformation. In the final story, "Maquinolandera" (Woman of Machine Land), she is metamorphosed from "Luz" (light) into "Luzferita" (fire). This metaphor of Antillean womanhood, implacable as the fabled Amazonian woman, symbolizes a mulatto Mother Earth giving violent birth to hope and raises social implications. Polifacetic woman, creator of life, shaper and mover of her child's first steps, has to be accepted as an individual.

If *Papeles de Pandora* is a manifesto of woman's rights, *Sitio a Eros* (1980) delineates the rising crescendo of woman's social impotence. Thirteen well-researched biographical essays illustrate the socially defeating yet aesthetically rewarding life of significant women writers of the nineteenth and twentieth centuries. Virginia Woolf, Katherine Mansfield, Mary Godwin Shelley, Aurore Dupin, Flora Tristán, Jean Rhys, Anaïs Nin, Tina Modotti, Alexandra Kollontay, Sylvia Plath, Julia de Burgos, and Lillian Hellman represent universal woman unsuccessfully seeking vindication of her rights. Their social alienation, having shed the traditional garments of marriage for free love, allowed them to flourish artistically, which points out the hermeneutic premise of *Sitio a Eros*. In all conscience, the first two essays analyze the eternal question of verisimilitude from a woman writer's perspective. To create, she has to experience life in all of its facets.

In *Papeles de Pandora* Ferré weaved a literary manifesto of woman's social rights; in *Sitio a Eros* she offered an elegy to woman's ingenuity and perseverance; in *Fábulas de la garza desangrada* the a priori genetic fate of woman's social submissiveness and rebelliousness invariably appears. A mythical and worldly Ferré speaks to all the women she has been and is. Particularly significant is the young Medusa in "La prisionera" (The Prisoner), the short essay that accompanies twenty-eight poems and four love letters. As metaphor of perennial Circe, she symbolically refuses to become the Andromeda who births kings and princes. She prefers to be a mere reflection, but of herself. A fitting closing to this collection is "Oivne," a mirror reflection of its initial "Envío" (Package Sent).

The philosophical proposition of correcting social injustice that structured the feminist trilogy is also consistent in Ferré's three collections of children's stories. In *El medio pollito* (1977, Half Chicken), a collection of seven stories, Ferré personalizes animals and objects to parallel human counterparts. Pretense and deceit keep "El reloj de cuerda" (Winding Clock) and "El gato y los tres perros" (The Cat and Three Dogs) on equal footing with "Los tres jorobados" (The Three Hunchbacks) and "Pedro Animala." In "El medio pollito," which gives title to the collection, "Arroz con leche" (Rice Pudding) and "El sombrero mágico" (The Magic Hat), the power of the social institutions is demoralized by a satirical vein in the archetypical characters. Animalization of humans, personalization of animals and objects, and demoralization of institutions embody strong criticism against society.

Los cuentos de Juan Bobo (1981, The Tales of Juan Bobo), a collection of five children's stories, characterized the traditional country bumpkin of Puerto Rican oral literature. Five anecdotes, transformed by a baroque symbiosis of vernacular and cultured lexicons, advance the upper mobility of Juan Bobo and finally place him in the capital, marrying the governor's daughter. Social egalitarianism is the premise of Ferré's innovative syntaxis.

Ferré's consistent juxtaposition of colloquial and institutionalized metalanguages explores the "marvelous realism" technique throughout the six children's stories that structure *La mona que le pisaron la cola* (1981, The Monkey Whose Tail Got Stepped On). The exploitation of man by man points out sociological implications.

Perhaps a comparison could be made between Ferré's feminist trilogy and her Aesopian trilogy of children's stories—*El medio pollito* (1977), *Los cuentos de Juan Bobo* (1981), *La mona que le pisaron la cola* (1981). The rebellious, almost stepping-out-of-the-page social criticism runs syntagmatically with the grotesque, though sedate, social criticism of a fabled environment that contrives and waits for satisfaction and in which yellowed skeletons possess characteristics that humans lack. Children "estribillos" running throughout the stories do little to mask the seemingly furious social critique.

Survey of Criticism

Ferré's work synthesizes the philosophical hypothesis of a new world in which workable alternatives can be offered to erase oppression wherever it exists. Perhaps this narrative voice of universal woman and child diachronically searching for self-identity has deterred usage of Ferré's work as classroom material, but it certainly has not deterred its functioning as literature.

Selections from her work, since publication of "La muñeca menor," have appeared in literary journals such as *Zona de carga y descarga, Sin Nombre, Vórtice, Novedades, Repertorio Lationoamericano, Escritura, Revista de la Universidad de México*, and *Kenyon Review* and also in various literary anthologies. "Maldito amor" (Cursed Love), a chapter of an unfinished novel, is in Ángel Rama's *Novisimos hispanoamericanos narradores en marcha 1964–*

1980 (1981); Rama's introduction to the anthology, "Contestatarios del poder," reviews comparatively a new generation of writers. Ferré is one of four writers examined in Gabriela Mora's "Crítica feminista: apuntes sobre definiciones y problemas," included in *Theory and Practice of Feminist Literary Criticism* (1982). "When Women Love Men," a translation of Ferré's "Cuando las mujeres quieren a los hombres," and "From a Woman's Perspective: The Short Stories of Rosario Ferré and Ana Lydia Vega," Margarite Fernández Olmos's comparative feminist analysis, appear in *Contemporary Women Authors of Latin America* (1983). Ferré's short story "El regalo" and Efraín Barradas's "Palabras apalabradas: Prólogo para una antología de cuentistas puertorriqueños de hoy," a diachronical analysis of literary techniques synchronizing in today's feminist literary viewpoint, are in *Apalabramiento* (1983, Word Avalanche).

Papers on Ferré's fiction and nonfiction have been read at literary congresses. Both Marjorie *Agosín's "La génesis de 'La bailarina': un poema de Rosario Ferré" and María José Chaves's "Fábulas y 'enxiemplos' de mujeres en los cuentos y ensayos de Rosario Ferré: aproximación a *Papeles de Pandora* y *Sitio a Eros*" were read at a December 1982 *MLA* convention in Los Angeles. Both apply formalist criticism to examine the use of allegory and imagery for social confrontation. Lorraine Rose's "Los tristes trópicos de Rosario Ferré," read at a 1982 Congress for the Association of Cuban Studies in Cuba, identifies a feminist thematic.

Most studies admit to an aesthetic cosmovision in Ferré that promises works of consequence. Ángel Rama's "Luis Rafael *Sánchez y Rosario Ferré: dos narradores puertorriqueños" (1978) diachronically examines past Puerto Rican writers' inability to integrate their art into a collective Hispanic American culture. Ferré and Sánchez are two writers who have broken away from cultural insularism. Luz María Umpierre's "Un manifiesto literario: *Papeles de Pandora* de Rosario Ferré" (1982) is a penetrating examination of Ferré's authorial responsibility as woman and as writer.

Luis Rafael *Sánchez's "Claves iniciales de *Papelas de Pandora*" (1978), José Emilio González's "Relatos de Pandora" (1977), and Lisa E. Davis's "La puertorriqueña dócil y rebelde en los cuentos de Rosario Ferré" (1979) identify authorial intent as a keen nihilist observation of human nature that places an orgiastic, uncensored language at the disposal of her protagonist. Efraín Barradas's "De otra manera más de hablar del aquí y del ahora sin así decirlo" (1979), "Estado de cuentas" (1979), "(C)er(c)os a Eros" (1981), and "Por los ojos de un niño: nuevos cuentos de Rosario Ferré" (1982) question Ferré's responsibility in using folkloric material as basis for children's stories, but at the same time maintain her artistic privilege to sustain her cultural imprint.

Literary critics, colleagues, educators, and students of American universities have applied formalist and traditional criticism to selected pieces of Ferré's works, but a book-length biographical study has yet to appear. More than often her writings are considered feminist. And so they are. But behind the unbridled torrent of ideological imagery comes the realization that it is just camouflage to point out by exemplification that in her eclectic Puerto Rican cosmovision there are alternatives.

Bibliography

WORKS BY FERRÉ

Papeles de Pandora. 1976. México, D.F.: Editorial Joaquín Mortiz, 1979 ed.
El medio pollito. Siete cuentos infantiles. Rio Piedras, Puerto Rico: Ediciones Huracán, 1977.
La caja de cristal. México, D.F.: La Máquina de Escribir, 1978.
"Cuando las mujeres quieren a los hombres." In *Papeles de Pandora.* México, D.F.: Editorial Joaquín Mortiz, 1979 ed.
"When Women Love Men," trans. Cynthia Ventura. In *Contemporary Women Authors of Latin America: Introductory Essays in Translation,* ed. Doris Meyer and Margarite Fernández Olmos. Brooklyn, N.Y.: Brooklyn College Press, 1983.
"La muñeca menor." *Zona de carga y descarga.* San Juan, Puerto Rico: Editor Rosario Ferré. *The Youngest Doll,* trans. Rosario Ferré. Río Piedras, Puerto Rico: Ediciones Huracán, 1979. "The Youngest Doll," trans. Gregory Rabassa. *Kenyon Review* 2:1 (1980): 163–67.
Sitio a Eros. México, D.F.: Editorial Joaquín Mortiz, 1980.
"El cuento de hadas." Conferencia dictada en el Colegio Universitario del Turabo. Caguas, Puerto Rico, 25 abril 1980. San Juan, Puerto Rico: *Sin Nombre* 11,2 (julio-septiembre 1980): 36–40.
Los cuentos de Juan Bobo. Río Piedras, Puerto Rico: Ediciones Huracán, 1981.
La mona que le pisaron la cola. Río Piedras, Puerto Rico: Ediciones Huracán, 1981.
"Maldito amor." Chapter of an unfinished novel. Reprinted in *Novísimos narradores hispanoamericanos en marcha: 1964–1980,* ed. Ángel Rama. México, D.F.: Marcha Editores, 1981.
Fábulas de la garza desangrada. México, D.F.: Editorial Joaquín Mortiz, 1982.
"El regalo." México, D.F.: *La mesa llena* 2(Septiembre 1981). Reprinted in *Apalabramiento: cuentos puertorriqueños de hoy,* ed. Efraín Barradas. Hanover, N.H.: Ediciones del Norte, 1983.

WORKS ABOUT FERRÉ

Agosín, Marjorie. "La génesis de 'La bailarina': un poema de Rosario Ferré." Research paper, Wellesley College. Modern Language Association Congress. Los Angeles, December 1982.
Barradas, Efraín. "Reseña de *Papeles de Pandora.*" San Juan, Puerto Rico: *Sin Nombre* 9,1 (abril-junio 1978): 96–97.
————. "De otra manera más de hablar del aquí y del ahora sin así decirlo." San Juan, Puerto Rico: *Claridad,* Suplemento *En Rojo* (4–10 mayo 1979): 6–7.
————. "Estado de cuentas y el cuento." San Juan, Puerto Rico: *Claridad,* Suplemento *En Rojo* (15–21 junio 1979): 8–10.
————. "(C)er(c)os a Eros." San Juan, Puerto Rico: *Claridad,* Suplemento *En Rojo* (27 febrero–7, marzo 1981): 6–7.
————. "Por los ojos de un niño: nuevos cuentos de Rosario Ferré." San Juan, Puerto Rico: *Claridad,* Suplemento *En Rojo* (25 febrero–5 marzo 1982): 4–5.

————. "Palabras apalabradas. Prólogo para una antología de cuentistas puertorriqueños de hoy." *Apalabramiento,* ed. Efraín Barradas. Hanover, N.H.: Ediciones del Norte, 1983.

Chaves, María José. "Fábulas y 'enxiemplos' de mujeres en los cuentos y ensayos de Rosario Ferré: aproximación a *Papeles de Pandora* y *Sitio a Eros.*" Research paper, Arizona State University. Modern Language Association Congress. Los Angeles, December 1982.

Davis, Lisa E. "La puertorriqueña dócil y rebelde en los cuentos de Rosario Ferré." San Juan, Puerto Rico: *Sin Nombre* 9,4 (1979): 82–88.

Fernández Olmos, Margarite. "From a Woman's Perspective: The Short Stories of Rosario Ferré and Ana Lydia Vega." *Contemporary Women Authors of Latin America: Introductory Essays and New Translations,* ed. Doris Meyer and Margarite Fernández Olmos. Brooklyn, N.Y.: Brooklyn College Press, 1983.

González, José Emilio. "Relatos de Pandora." San Juan, Puerto Rico: *Claridad,* Suplemento *En Rojo* (28 julio–5 agosto 1977): 12–13.

Mora, Gabriela. "Crítica feminista: apuntes sobre definiciones y problemas." *Theory and Practice of Feminist Literary Criticism.* Ypsilante, Mich.: Bilingual Review Press, 1982.

Rama, Ángel. "Luis Rafael Sánchez y Rosario Ferré: dos narradores puertorriqueños." Caracas, Venezuela: *El Universal* (19 febrero 1978): 1–2.

————. "Los contestatarios del poder." Introduction. *Novísimos narradores hispanoamericanos en marcha: 1964–1980.* México, D.F.: Marcha Editores, 1981.

Roses, Lorraine. "Los tristes trópicos de Rosario Ferré." Congreso de Estudios Cubanos. Habana, Cuba, julio 1982.

Sánchez, Luis Rafael. "Claves iniciales de *Papeles de Pandora.*" San Juan, Puerto Rico: *Claridad,* Suplemento *En Rojo* (21–27 abril 1977): 12.

Umpierre, Luz María. "Un manifiesto literario: *Papeles de Pandora* de Rosario Ferré." Research paper, Rutgers University of New Jersey. *Bilingual Review* 10,2 (May 1982): 120–26.

JULIA M. GALLARDO COLÓN

FIGUEROA, JOSÉ-ANGEL (1946–). José-Angel Figueroa, a well-known Puerto Rican poet living in New York City, is the author of two books. He is part of the surge in Nuyorican poetry that occurred in that city in the late 1960s and that keeps producing interesting works.

Biography

José-Angel Figueroa was born on November 24, 1946, in Mayagüez, Puerto Rico. He was one of ten children and arrived on the mainland at the age of six. His parents were migrant workers and for years traveled back and forth between the island and various areas in the United States where they followed the crops according to their respective picking seasons. José-Angel thus at an early age knew poverty, the importance of an extended family, and the harsh realities of culture shocks. He grew up in the barrio, in East Harlem, and in the southeastern Bronx.

After high school he obtained a B.A. at New York University and did graduate work at the State University of New York at Buffalo. His acquaintance with Afro-American writing, Latin American writers like Pablo Neruda and the Spaniard García Lorca, both of whom he admires greatly, can be called basically a college experience. As a student, Figueroa was involved in radical student politics, later in community work and teaching. As one of the results of his successful, sensitive stimulation of disadvantaged Third World children from the Bronx, there exists the slim volume *Unknown Poets from the Full-Time Jungle,* edited by Figueroa. It was published in 1975 by the Board of Education of the City of New York.

In the 1970s, he made photography his favorite pastime, which has had effects on his handling dissociated, dream-like imagery in his poetry. He sees today the Puerto Rican existence on the mainland as filled with contradictions as it was in the 1960s and early 1970s. The problems just moved on to another generation. Up to the late seventies, Figueroa formed a loose group with his colleagues Pedro *Pietri and Jesús Papoleto Meléndez. Some of his poetry got published in *Revista Chicano-Riqueña, The Rican, Black Creation, Nimrod,* and *Sunbury.*

Major Themes

José-Angel Figueroa's first book of poetry, *East 110th Street,* was finished by 1970 and comprised over 150 pages. He saw it published in a severely reduced edition three years later by the black, Detroit-based Broadside Press. Instead of the book he had hoped for, he received a forty-five-page pamphlet, a fact which the writer still feels unhappy about today. Figueroa writes in English, Spanish, a juxtaposition of the two, but rarely uses Spanglish, although his work has echoes of the ethnic protest poetry of the sixties. It is, taken as a whole, a document of a painful transcultural experience. The two most salient poems in this collection are "A Conversation w/ Coca Cola" and the title poem. Both show a blend of commitment to his fellow Puerto Ricans, attacks at an oppressive, alienating dominant society, a search for collective identity, all put in daring, often enough surreal imagery, which is used increasingly as his work progresses. Anglo society and its power structure are closely associated with sterility and chemical products that carry ideological, brainwashing connotations. Opposed to the nightmarish visions of pain, hunger, helplessness, and death in these two long poems we find a romanticized vision of Puerto Rico in "I Saw Puerto Rico Once" and "Puertorriqueña," with allusions to the Taíno Indian heritage. His second volume of poetry has also a rather curious and unsatisfactory publication history. *Noo Jork*—a term he took from his mother's use of phonetics and Jaime *Carrero's *Neo-Rican Jetliner* (1972)—has never been published in its original English version. Instead, in 1981 a carefully executed Spanish translation by the late Puerto Rican scholar and poet Víctor Fernández Fragoso came out in San Juan, Puerto Rico, in the Literatura Hoy series, which is administered by the Puerto Rican Institute of Culture. *Noo Jork* was finished by 1975, then edited by Figueroa on and off until 1978. The poet's surreal mode, already tangible in his first book, is heightened in this text. The lack of rationality, of order and cohesiveness, is intended to convey a state of mind in a confusing world where several value systems simultaneously bombard the newcomer. The restlessness inherent in the migrant experience, which the young Figueroa lived and which the adult Figueroa sees as a highly absurd, ongoing state of things, is dealt with in poems like "Aeropuertos: en espera" (Airport :Waiting) or "Equipaje asesinado" (Assassinated Luggage). A lack of structure and meaning in life, and the high-strung atmosphere resembling nervous breakdown, shape his title poem, "Noo Jork." Figueroa's intense, slightly strained romanticism becomes evident in poems such as "Pablo Neruda," "Una boca en el vientre de Lorca" (A Mouth in Lorca's Womb), "Mama," and "Querida" (Beloved).

Survey of Criticism

Critics have so far virtually ignored Figueroa's work. Efraín Barradas refers to "This Book" and "I Saw Puerto Rico Once" in his discussion of the myth-making found in mainland Puerto Rican literature. In 1979 Wolfgang Binder translated "Conversation w/ Coca Cola" into German and prefaced his selection of Nuyorican poetry with an introduction, "Puertoricanische Lyric aus New York," in *Puerto Ricaner in New York*. Linda Riggins reviewed *East 110th Street* as poetry of protest in *Black World* (1974). A brief review of the same work was printed by the *Daily World* (1974).

Bibliography

WORKS BY FIGUEROA

East 110th Street. Detroit: Broadside Press, 1973.
Ed. *Unknown Poets from the Full-Time Jungle*. New York: Board of Education of the City of New York, 1975.
Noo Jork. San Juan de Puerto Rico: Instituto de Cultura Puertorriqueña, 1981. Translation by Víctor Fernández Fragoso.

WORKS ABOUT FIGUEROA

Barradas, Efráin. " 'De lejos en suenos verla . . . ' Visión mítica de Puerto Rico en la poesía neoyorrican." *Revista Chicano-Riqueña* 7 (Summer 1979): 46–56.
Binder, Wolfgang. "Puertoricanische Lyrik aus New York." *Puerto Ricaner in New York. Volk zwischen zwei Kulturen*. Erlangen: Städtische Galerie Erlangen, 1979. Contains a translation of "East 110th Street" into German.
R. A. "Poems on New York Puerto Ricans." *Daily World*, September 27, 1974: 8.
Riggins, Linda. Review of *East 110th Street*. *Black World* 23 (January 1974): 70–74.

WOLFGANG BINDER

FLORIT, EUGENIO (1903–   ). Eugenio Florit is the famed Spanish Cuban poet, playwright, and literary critic who has made an illustrious career for himself at universities in the United States. At Columbia University in the 1940s and 1950s he became the center of New York Hispanic writing.

Biography

The well-known poet and critic Eugenio Florit was born into a literary family in Madrid, Spain. He now sees a gentle irony in the fact that the municipal judge to whom his father applied for the registration of the baby's birth was also a well-known literary critic whose pseudonym was "Andrenio" after one of the two principal characters in Gracián's *El criticón*. Soon afterward the family moved to the city of Barcelona, and then with another new son, Fernando, to Port-Bou, a town on the French border where Ricardo Florit served as governor of customs. Here another brother and a sister were born amid the increasingly unsettled climate that preceded the outbreak of World War I in Europe. In 1918 the family decided to move to Cuba, the home of Eugenio's mother's family. The move was expensive and required sacrifice on the part of the entire family including the children's nanny, who even did her part for a time to help out. With the aid of his uncle, however, the fifteen-year-old Eugenio was able to enroll in La Salle School, from which he still recalls some outstanding teachers and the beginning of several lifelong friendships.

In the next year or so the youngster began writing poetry, even seeing some verses published locally through the good offices of a family connection. Others appeared in the school paper, and his article on Pirandello came out in the literary supplement of Havana's *Diario de la Marina*. Eugenio was now reading as much poetry as he could, including works of Juan Ramón Jiménez, Antonio and Manuel Machado, Jose Martí, Enrique González Martiínez, Amado Nervo, and Rubén Darío as well as French and English verse. His primer in Cuban poetry was Lizaso and Fernando de Castro's *La poesía moderna en Cuba*. He remembers consciously imitating the styles of those identified with the increasingly popular avant-garde movements.

In 1927 Florit published his own first book, entitled *32 poemas breves* (32 Brief Poems). The famous Cuban journal *Revista de avance* brought out a number of the young man's verses in the years 1928–1930. Florit now sees the endeavor represented by the *Revista* as one of the major influences on his formation as a poet, since it acted to bring together many of Cuba's talented young writers and to attract to the island a wealth of important cultural events. Invited to collaborate in the journal's production, he wrote reviews of the works of Mariano Brull, Carmen Conde, Jorge Luis Borges, and others. In his own poems written during this period Florit sees not only a strong tendency toward avant-garde writing but features of the school of "pure poetry" associated with the French poet Paul Valéry as well. In 1927 the young Cuban intelligentsia felt the impact of the celebration of the 300th anniversary of the birth of Luis de Góngora. Florit succumbed to the temptation to—in his words— "gongorizar" a little.

In 1927, now a law school graduate, Florit worked on the organizing committee of the Second International Conference on Emigration and Immigration, of which his uncle was chair. Once the conference concluded, he stayed on in the Cuban department of state, enjoying a close relationship with the young intellectual

Félix Lizaso. Both culture and cultural contacts were stimulated by two important women's organizations. Under the auspices of one of these, the Sociedad Pro-Arte Musical, the great ballerina Alicia Alonso was trained. In the other, the Lyceum, Florit appeared in at least one play, taking a part as well in several literary presentations. Another important forum was the Hispano-Cuban Institute, which kept Cuban writers abreast of peninsular currents. This institute published an important book entitled *La poesía cubana en 1936*, with a prologue and notes by Juan Ramón Jiménez, who arrived the same year to take up residence on the island.

This period saw the writing of the verses Florit was later to publish in his book *Double acento* (1937, Double Accent) and another poem, the "Martirio de San Sebastián," after whose reading Jiménez asked to be presented to the young Florit. In 1938 Florit's *Reino* (Kingdom) was published in a limited edition, with acknowledged echoes of Juan Ramón that were later suppressed. Nevertheless, the book received reviews in places as far way from Cuba as New York and Santiago de Chile. Florit's last book to be published in Cuba (in 1940) was *Cuatro poemas* (Four poems).

In 1938 Florit had traveled to New York for the first time, there to be honored by the Hispanic Institute, presided over by Federico de Onís and attended by Alfonso Reyes. The *Revista Hispánica Moderna* announced in the same year a forthcoming issue to be dedicated to studies of Florit's verse. The poet had for some years entertained the idea of emigrating to the United States as a professor of Spanish. His inability to speak English, among other factors, had prevented this. In 1940, however, after a broken engagement, he asked for and was granted a transfer to New York by the Cuban state department. As an auxiliary consul he worked to promote Hispanic culture on the radio and in film. Soon afterward, he was invited to teach classes in Columbia University. Until his retirement in 1969 as professor emeritus he continued to teach here and in Barnard College, with a brief period in Vermont's Middlebury College.

Unlike other Hispanic poets in the largest U.S. metropolis, Florit did not suffer profound culture shock upon his arrival there, instead experiencing what he describes as "buenos años de cosecha" (good harvest years). In 1947 Letras de México published a 503-page anthology, *Poema mío* (My Poem), consisting of some new works as well as old ones. In 1948 Florit wrote *Asonante final y otros poemas* (Final Assonance and Other Poems), published in 1950. Also in 1948 Florit completed *Conversación a mi padre* (1949, Conversation to My Father), on the anniversary of his father's death. Residence in New York did not lead to a lessening of ties with the Cuban cultural establishment, and the new Cuban journals *Espuela de plata, Nadie parecía,* and *Orígenes* continued to publish his poems. An anthology entitled *Asonante final y otros poemas* (Final Assonance and Other Poems) was brought out in Cuba in 1955, and the following year saw a new *Antología poética* (Poetic Anthology), published in Mexico, this one including all of Florit's preferred poems as well as a sonnet, "A Eugenio Florit," by Alfonso Reyes. Other brief anthologies followed in later years in Montevideo and Madrid.

Honored as one of the most important Hispanic writers in the United States, Florit now lives in Miami, Florida, but he continues to be active in such professional organizations as the American Association of Teachers of Spanish and Portuguese. In "Eugenio Florit," a special issue of the journal *Exilio* (7/4, 1973) dedicated to Florit's life and works, he offers the following observations about poetry.

Poems must be a form of communication and are thus written to be said aloud.
All poems are circumstantial because they are collections of remembrances.
Poetry needs few words; ten or fifteen basic ones will do.
One must wait for poetry, not look for it.
If we are the stuff dreams are made of, then what the poet must do is to write his dreams.

In addition to poetry, Florit is the author of three *autos* (short religious plays), the first of which, "La Estrella" (1947, The Star), he wrote especially for his students at Barnard. His extensive work in literary analysis includes studies of Jorge Guillén, Alfonso Reyes, Juan Ramón Jiménez, Vicente Aleixandre, Federico García Lorca, Nicolás Guillén, Luis *Palés Matos, Pablo Neruda, and many others. With Enrique Anderson Imbert, he is the author of the immensely popular *Literatura hispanoamericana, antología e introducción histórica* (1960, Spanish American Literature, Anthology and Historical Introduction). He has also edited several other anthologies. Florit translated a selection of contemporary North American poetry into Spanish, publishing it with a preliminary essay in 1955.

Major Themes

Most critics agree that the principal theme of all of Florit's poetry is the struggle for serenity despite a clear awareness of the complexity and mutability of human existence. Much of it strikes a deeply religious note that is elegiac in tone. Poetry continues to be seen as an essential means of subordinating reality to ideality by ordering it within formal limits. The trajectory of Florit's works reveals an unending search for aesthetic purity that passes through postmodernism, avant-garde writing, neogongorism, pure poetry, and traditional verse, with the last poems becoming confessional. Mirella D'Ambrosio Servodidio sees a *via crucis* in which polarity is a seminal force, with a dialectic tension between disequilibrium of the spirit and an effort to mediate and integrate experience into a meaningful whole.

José Olivio Jiménez has observed in some of the poems of *32 poemas breve* (1927) a delicacy not unlike that of postmodernist Enrique González Martínez, while others clearly reveal the fragmentation and free association seen in various "isms" of the avant-garde. Florit himself acknowledges his debt to Luis de

Góngora in *Trópico,* published three years later. In its twelve poems addressed to the land and twelve more to the sea, the exuberance of nature is dominated by the poet's intelligence and given a geometrical order. The poems are written in *décimas,* with consonantal rhythm, a Latinized word order, a pattern of antithesis throughout, and many enjambements. Stylistic restraints seem to subdue emotions by displaying them with proportion and balance.

With *Doble acento* (1937) begins what José Olivio Jiménez defines as Florit's most intense and fertile period. In an article appearing in the *Revista cubana* entitled "Una hora conmigo," Florit had written that within his works could be seen elements of Goethe, of Garcilaso, of Walt Whitman and Alberti, but that all of them were somehow also himself. Two evident directions of these poems are toward surrealism and toward pure poetry. The first of these is exemplified in "Poema cósmico," where free-flowing imagery is to be found in lines that also seem to overflow with syllables. The second can be seen particularly well in a sonnet entitled "Estrofas a una estatua," in which this plastic image becomes the very model of the desired serenity that will later acquire a deep religious significance for the poet. José Olivio Jiménez has suggested that in the poems of *Doble acento* Florit fuses the two classic styles of Spanish poetry.

"El martirio de San Sebastián" is one of the best-known poems, having been recited throughout Latin America by the Argentine Berta Singerman. In a dramatic monologue the dying saint addresses himself to the arrows entering his body, calling them little doves and telling them to come swiftly and thus hasten his union with God.

In *Reino* (1938) the trappings of surrealism disappear for good, and many of the poems display the refined vocabulary and elegant craftsmanship associated with Juan Ramón Jiménez's verse. The anthology *Poema mío* (1947) contains all of Florit's earlier verse as well as some previously unpublished. Among the latter "Momento de cielo" stands out as one of Florit's most representative poems. Servodidio sees here in the images of soaring height the description of a state of ecstasy, yet the poetic voice remains always tied to a consciousness of temporality. The struggle for transcendence is thus ever an existential one in Florit.

A radical stylistic change is noted in the poems of *Asonante final,* and *Conversación a mi padre* as Florit is seen to abandon the highly sculptured language of his earlier work and to turn instead to forms with fewer restrictions and a tone much less formal and even colloquial at times. The poetic voice here becomes less intellectual and more conversational. In "Asonante final" it muses over the familiarity with which "we Spanish Americans" have always addressed God. In lines directed to the Creator, death is seen as simply the returning home of a child who has gone out for a walk and come home to find his father waiting for him. The father greets him by asking, "What has taken you so long?" to which the child replies, "I just felt like walking, picking a flower, and looking at a tree. But I came back because I got tired." A final voice asks "Isn't it right that it's like that? And I'm not just making it up?"

Hábito de esperanza (1965, Accustomed to Hope) contains evidence of all of Florit's previous "styles." Its "New Songs" seem to José Olivio Jiménez to take as their theme the love of which man on earth always feels the need. The poet, essentially alone, seems to be totally conscious of his struggle to achieve serenity as he lives out his human vigil. *De tiempo y agonía (Versos del hombre solo)* (1974, About Time and Agony [Verses of a Man Alone]) continues this existential line, with no attempt to evade life's paradoxes and risks but, on the contrary, seeking truth from every perspective. An important theme here is that of old age, from which the poet gazes upon life as from a balcony, but paradoxically "with my eyes closed and my mind wide open." A tremor before death does not prevent the warm note of humanness that has always rung out in Florit's poetry.

Survey of Criticism

An important early study of Florit's work appears in the *Revista Hispánica Moderna* of 1942. Published by the Hispanic Institute of Columbia University, it contains an article on Florit by Angel del Río, an anthology, a list of unpublished works, and a bibliography up to that year. There are several important thematic studies of Eugenio Florit's verse. Orlando E. Saa has written *La serenidad en las obras de Eugenio Florit*. Another is María Castellanos Collins's *Tierra, mar y cielo en la poesía de Eugenio Florit*. Mario Parajón studies the poet and his works in *Eugenio Florit y su poesía*. The most recent book-length study is Mirella D'Ambrosio Servodidio's *The Quest for Harmony: The Dialectics of Communication in the Poetry of Eugenio Florit*.

Marta Linares Pérez studies Mariano Brull, Emilio Ballagas, and Florit in her *La poesía pura en Cuba*. It is José Olivio Jiménez, however, who has laid the groundwork for commentary on Florit's poetry. One important article of his serves as a preliminary study to *Antología penúltima*; the same article is also available as "Eugenio Florit en tres tiempos" in Alice M. Pollin's *Concordancias de la obra poética de Eugenio Florit*. Another article by Jiménez is "La poesía última de Eugenio Florit: Sobre *De tiempo y agonía*" in a special issue of the journal *Exilio* in honor of Florit. This useful issue also contains an autobiographical article by the poet himself, brief articles by Saa, Parajón, and Collins, and literary messages to Florit by Eduardo Mallea, Pedro Salinas, Vicente Aleixandre, Jorge Guillén, Juana de Ibarbouru, and others.

Bibliography

WORKS BY FLORIT

32 poemas breves. La Habana, n.p., 1927.
Trópico. La Habana: Revista de Avance, 1930.
Doble acento. La Habana: Úcar, García, 1937.
Reino. La Habana: Úcar, García, 1938.

Cuatro poemas (private edition). La Habana: n.p. 1940.

La Estrella (Nativity Play). La Habana: Úcar, García, 1947.

Poema mío (collected poems). México: Letras de México, 1947.

Conversación a mi padre (private edition). La Habana, n.p. 1949.

Asonante final y otros poemas. La Habana: Orígenes, 1955.

Antología de la poesía norteamericana contemporánea (selected, translated, with a preliminary essay). Washington, D.C.: Unión Panamericana, 1955.

Antología poética. México: Studium, 1956.

The Selected Writings of Juan Ramón Jiménez. Edited with a preliminary essay. New York: Farrar, Strauss and Gudany, 1957.

Literatura hispanoamericana, antología e introducción histórica (in collaboration with Enrique Anderson Imbert). New York: Holt, Rinehart and Winston, 1960.

Siete poemas. Montevideo: Cuadernos Julio Herrera y Reissig, 1960.

Tres autos religiosos. Palma de Mallorca: "Papeles de Son Armadans," 1960.

Jose Martí. Versos (edited, selected with a preliminary essay and notes). New York: Las Américas, 1962.

Cien de las mejores poesías españolas (selected, with notes). New York: Las Américas, 1965.

Hábito de esperanza. Madrid: Insula, 1965.

Lorca. Obras escogidas (introduction and notes). New York: Laurel Language Library, 1965.

La poesía hispanoamericana desde el Modernismo (anthology with preliminary essay and critical notes, in collaboration with José Olivio Jiménez). New York: Appleton-Century-Crofts, 1968.

Antología penúltima. Madrid: Editorial Plenitud, 1970.

Antología poética de Juan Ramón Jiménez. Madrid: n.p., 1971.

De tiempo y agonía (Versos del hombre solo). Madrid: Ediciones de la Revista de Occidente, 1974.

Poesía casi siempre (Ensayos literarios). Madrid: Editorial Mensaje, 1978.

Poesía en José Martí, Juan Ramón Jiménez, Alfonso Reyes, Federico García Lorca y Pablo Neruda. Miami: Ediciones Universal, 1978.

Versos pequeños (1938–1975). New York: Senda Nueva de Ediciones, 1977.

Obras completas. Vols. 2 and 3. Lincoln, Nebr.: Society of Spanish and Spanish-American Studies, 1982.

WORKS ABOUT FLORIT

Collins, María Castellanos. *Tierra, mar y cielo en la poesía de Eugenio Florit*. Miami: Ediciones Universal, 1976.

"Eugenio Florit." *Exilio* 7, 4 (1973).

Jiménez, José Olivio. "La poesía última de Eugenio Florit: Sobre *De tiempo y agonía*." In *Exilio* 7, 4 (1973): 57–69.

———. Prologue to *Antología penúltima*. Madrid: Plenitud, 1970. Also in Alice M. Pollin's *Concordancias de la obra poética de Eugenio Florit*.

Linares Pérez, Marta. *La poesía pura en Cuba*. Madrid: Playor, 1975.

Parajón, Mario. *Eugenio Florit y su poesía*. Madrid: Insula, 1977.

Pollin, Alice M. *Concordancias de la obra poética de Eugenio Florit*. New York: New York University Press, 1967.

Saa, Orlando E. *La serenidad en las obras de Eugenio Florit*. Miami: Ediciones Universal, 1973.
Servodidio, Mirella D'Ambrosio. *The Quest for Harmony: The Dialectics of Communication in the Poetry of Eugenio Florit*. Lincoln, Nebr.: The Society of Spanish and Spanish American Studies, 1979.

LEE H. DOWLING

G

GOLDEMBERG, ISAAC (1945–   ). Isaac Goldemberg is the Peruvian Jewish novelist who has for many years organized Hispanic writers who write in Spanish in New York. His literary activism goes back to the New Blood Poets in New York and extends to his organizing the annual Hispanic American book fairs. As a novelist he weds the tradition of South American social activism with the Jewish literary tradition.

Biography

Isaac Goldemberg was born in Chepén, Peru, on November 15, 1945, to a Russian Jewish father and a Peruvian mother whose background includes, on her father's side, English, Italian, and Basque ancestors and Andalusian and Quechuan blood on her mother's side. Until the age of eight, Isaac lived with his Catholic mother and her family, which consisted of her parents and her nine brothers and sisters, in the small northern town of his birth.

In 1953, Isaac's life was radically transformed when he went to live with his father in Lima, where he was immersed in both city life and Judaism. He entered a Jewish elementary school and later was sent to a military high school where he was one of only a few Jewish students.

At the age of seventeen, Isaac went to Israel where he lived on a kibbutz for a year and a half. He had intended to return to Peru, but his father's death during Isaac's absence led him to postpone his return. Instead, he began to study medicine in Barcelona, but he left after a year and returned to Lima. Staying in Peru seemed pointless without his father, and his North American wife and the birth of his first child convinced him to come to New York where he has lived since 1965. He is currently producing prose and poetry while teaching in the Spanish and Portuguese Department of New York University.

Major Themes

The unifying thread of Goldemberg's poetry and prose is the theme of multiple cultures: the Peruvian, which in itself is a combination of the ancient Indian and the colonizing Spanish plus more recent immigrant populations such as those evidenced in the background of Isaac's maternal grandfather, and the Jewish, with its history of a search for a spiritual and physical home. Goldemberg grapples with the question of how these diverse elements might be unified and, failing unification, expresses the inevitable marginality of one who cannot be assimilated into either culture. His works reflect his search for the father who is missing from his earliest childhood and the Jewish community's search for a place within the larger context of Peruvian society.

The poetic voice expresses the ambiguity of his multicultural experience while, at the same time, it demonstrates an awareness that the conflict of his Indian/Catholic/Jewish roots cannot in reality be resolved and must, in the end, be simply accepted. *Hombre de paso/Just Passing Through* (1981), his most widely known book of poetry, is a bilingual edition, with the English translations written by David Unger and Goldemberg himself. It includes many revised poems from an earlier collection, *De Chepén a La Habana* (1973, From Chepén to Havana).

The seven poems entitled "Crónicas/Chronicles" consist of Goldemberg's reflections on his family and contain images of both his and his parents' loneliness: "1945 / is witness / to a mother who was never there / and a gray-haired father / who came into and left / my world at the same time." Each is locked and unreachable in his or her own world of Jewish ritual and ancient Peruvian culture. But the last "Crónicas," the final poem in the volume, acknowledges Goldemberg's discovery that the civilizations that created him are, in fact, one in the same; a reconciliation is possible with the realization that the names of his cultures' heroes are irrelevant to his own history: "Who cared if Wiracocha was born in a Bethlehem manger / or if Jesus was Lake Titicaca's son / we didn't need sperm tests / but rather tests of conscience / . . . and that's why it's better to be called ram than Abraham / lamb instead of Jesus / or llama instead of Manko."

The picture Goldemberg paints of the Jewish community of his youth is one of disintegration, of old men with little vitality, like those portrayed in "Yom Kippur": "The rabbi blows the shofar / The old men grab each other's hands / lowering their heads / they walk in like ghosts." His own Bar Mitzvah, described in a poem by that name, is witnessed by only three old men and demonstrates the confusion of the boy who has come from a Catholic tradition: "The rabbi nods for me to start the prayers / instead I kneel down." The images of his participation in Jewish rites imply that they did little to give him a foundation on which to build his identity. He seems, rather, to have inherited only the torment of the Jew's perpetual wandering without the solace of knowing he's truly part of the community.

Another series of poems entitled "Hombre de paso / Just Passing Through" highlights Goldemberg's search for personal identity without overt reference to his cultural heritage. The first poem in the series expresses his frustration with life, but the poet concludes that it is nevertheless necessary to begin to live even an alienated existence: "It's hopeless: here's where my life begins / and I'm just passing through." Other similarly existential poems focus on confronting death because, as death is the ultimate absence of identity, acceptance of its inevitability can give him the key to life: "It's just that our body knows nothing about / death / till it goes out and risks / its life." Goldemberg, recognizing that alienation is endemic to modern society, recommends a coming-to-terms with death as a way of giving direction to anyone's life. In "Resucitar un muerto/ Bringing a Dead Man Back to Life," he even calls it a "civic duty" to carry out this project.

The themes of the Peruvian Jewish community and a search for identity within a multicultural context are apparent in Goldemberg's novels as well. *La vida a plazos de don Jacobo Lerner* (The Fragmented Life of Don Jacobo Lerner) was published first in English (translated by Robert S. Picciotto) in 1976, then in Spanish in 1978. Jacobo's fragmented life is mirrored by the fragmented structure of the novel with its various narrators: an omniscient narrative voice describing Jacobo's actions and interior monologues by Jacobo's son Efraín, a friend of Jacobo's, Jacobo's sister-in-law, her sister, and Jacobo's lover. Articles from the *Alma Hebrea,* a fictional Jewish newspaper published in Lima, and various "Crónicas" documenting factual and fictional events from 1923 to 1935 are interspersed chronologically throughout the novel. The plot centers on Jacobo's life as, from his deathbed, he reflects on his experiences as a boy in Russia, his immigration to Perú, his relationship with Effraín's mother in Chepén, and his life among the Jewish community in Lima.

The theme of marginality exists on three levels within the novel: Jacobo's life, the Jewish community, and Efraín's life. The absence of Jacobo's voice structurally mirrors his alienation; he is the only major character whose narrations are conducted by a third-person narrator. His dream to build a future in Peru, complete with social prestige and a Jewish family, is never fulfilled. As a young merchant in Chepén, his Jewishness is a constant barrier, even when his financial success makes him welcome as Virginia's suitor. He cannot continue to live in Chepén's stifling atmosphere after learning of Virginia's pregnancy although the only other Jew in the town, his childhood friend León Mitrani, encourages him to stay.

Jacobo continues to feel alienated even living among Lima's large and increasingly influential Jewish community. His brother Moisés is the epitome of the Jewish leader, but Jacobo has to save him financially with the profits from his whorehouse; nevertheless, his ownership of the bordello is what separates him from the respectable Jews in the city. He separates himself further from the community by accepting a Catholic lover for fifteen years.

Jacobo's personal guilt increases his sense of marginality. He rightly feels that he has abandoned his son, whom he has never seen, and his message from his deathbed to have Efraín sent to him comes much too late to save the child.

His relationship with León Mitrani also torments him, and he suffers greatly when Mitrani dies by accidental poisoning. This guilty conscience is finally personified by a dybbuk in the form of León that overcomes Jacobo until the rabbi exorcises it.

The Jewish community as a whole, portrayed through the *Alma Hebrea*, also finds itself in an alienated environment in Lima. The newspaper provides a broad historical context for the novel together with short vignettes of the community's social life in the form of letters and accounts of events. Its articles describe the rise of Nazi Germany and urge its readers to become assimilated into the Peruvian culture while defensively insisting on the Jewish community's grateful patriotism to the country that has given them a home. As the years go on, the articles adopt a more fearful tone, and rumors of oppression against Jews in northern Peru increase the nervousness of those living in Lima.

Efraín's alienation is evidenced in his monologues which begin when he is seven and end when he is nine. The child is raised in his mother's house, with his grandparents, a young uncle, two teenaged aunts, and a fanatically Catholic aunt who lives next door. Efraín's narrations are particularly poignant, the most successful element of the novel. He is caught in a world that rejects his father so completely that no one answers his questions about him except to insist that his only father is Christ. When León Mitrani reveals something of his father's background, he discovers that he is a Jew, but he doesn't know what that means; he searches in his imagination for his father, confusing him with León and with Christ. He wants his father to save him from the increasingly oppressive atmosphere to which he is subjected as his mother ignores him and his aunts reject him. Finally, the physical pressures of malnourishment and the psychological pressures of abandonment drive him insane.

Tiempo al tiempo (1984, Time for Time) carries forward in the character of Marcos (a child who is essentially Efraín as he might have been had his father rescued him from Chepén) the themes of the search for identity, the Jewish community's place in Peruvian society, and the dual culture.

This novel is more overtly autobiographical, as the protagonist is sent from an unnamed northern village at the age of eight to live with his father in Lima. The novel is divided into two large sections, or "tiempos," each of which opens with a third-person narration focusing on Marcos who, at the age of twelve, has just undergone circumcision. A fanatic of soccer, he drifts into a dream of himself as a soccer player on the Peruvian national squad as it faces the Brazilian team. A television announcer describes the "plays" of Marcos's life in the sections of the soccer match. Alternating with the scenes, two groups of adults recount to an invisible interviewer their memories of Marcos in his Jewish elementary school, León Pinelo, and his military high school, Leoncio Prado. The novel focuses on Marcos's youth in Lima, but we learn that Marcos has died in Israel. His classmates assume he was killed in the Six-Day War, but the interviewer informs them that he committed suicide. The interviewer, whom we know only from the reactions of those who respond to him, is apparently searching for the reasons for that suicide as he delves into Marcos's history.

Marcos is a child caught between two cultures and accepted fully by neither. As in *La vida*, his alienation is reflected structurally by his lack of a narrative voice. In a kind of "color commentary," the soccer announcer interviews the school psychologist from León Pinelo, who points out that an abrupt change of environment might cause severe psychological damage; and indeed, it apparently has. Marcos dreams of the Catholic services he attended in the north and, while he seems to accept with some confusion but without complaint his father's insistence on making him a Jew, the soccer match drifts between his Catholic and his Jewish experience, as well as confirming or denying some of the facts presented by the ex-classmates. This narration is impersonal, and Marcos can no more intervene in the events of his life than he could in an actual televised soccer game.

In contrast to Marcos, the group narrators from the two schools are very sure of their identity. The former students from León Pinelo recount the growth of the school as the Jewish community gained wealth and prestige, and the ex-military students suggest that the torments they suffered as freshmen were a natural part of the process of growing up. Both groups see Marcos as an oddity, but his ability in soccer endears him sooner to his León Pinelo classmates. He suffers more psychological and physical abuse in the military school where he is persecuted for his Judaism and finally expelled when he is discovered having sexual relations with another boy. As a defense against his ostracism by his classmates in high school and against his personal lack of identity, he weaves a tissue of lies designed to convince each group that his social life centers around the other group.

A thread of violence underlies all of the narrative sections and is epitomized in the soccer match. The narration is fast paced, with colons instead of periods separating the sentences. The game itself is violent, as the announcer describes Marcos's "injury" (his circumcision), his beatings by his high school classmates, and his rape by the officer who finds him with his friend. A single line of television news headlines, which travels across the bottom of the pages devoted to the classmates' narrations, emphasizes the violence in Marcos's cultural heritage and turbulent present time in history. The "news" mixes Incan and Jewish history from their earliest legends to the conquest and the Six-Day War with events occurring in the fictional world of Marcos's Lima. Marcos's suicide is the ultimate violent act inflicted upon him. Given his history, the reader can assume that his decision to live in Israel was based on a desire to be accepted fully into one part of his culture; his suicide must have been the result of his failure to do so.

In both novels, Goldemberg draws heavily on his own experience as the son of a Russian Jew and a child witnessing the Jewish community from the outside. His characters, whether protagonists or minor players, have not found their home. Goldemberg's novelistic vision of the Jewish experience in Peru and of his own cross-cultural conflict is all the more vivid because it is not resolved. The novels contain a sense of futility and frustration that, in the poetry, seems to have been more fully resolved by the poet's personal acceptance of his situation and desire to participate more fully in life.

Survey of Criticism

Apart from numerous reviews, little work on Goldemberg's production has been published in the United States. However, the four analyses I shall discuss here shed much light on the link between structure and theme in *La vida a plazos de don Jacobo Lerner*.

Edward H. Friedman (1981) centers his analysis on levels of discourse based on Hayden White's tropes of poetic discourse. In his study of the novel's multiple narrative voices, Friedman concludes that the ironic mode, which stresses negation, most greatly informs the novel's structure because Jacobo is defined by his difference from the other characters. The monologues and the documentary entries all reflect back on Jacobo and/or on the Jewish community, producing levels of irony that reinforce the fragmented nature of Jacobo's life.

Lorraine E. Roses (1984) also focuses on the monologue technique which, she asserts, allows the reader to judge the characters' hypocrisy and lack of moral responsibility. Efraín, whose monologues predominate in number and intensity, emerges as protagonist; his fate leaves little doubt as to Goldemberg's view of the future of the Jewish community in Peru.

Fragmentation is the central theme of Jonathan Tittler's chapter (1984) on *La vida*, but he extends the analysis beyond narrative voice to images of fragmentation and the monologues' linguistic heterogeneity. All of these elements point to a sense of loss of meaning in the exile's existence.

Saúl Sosnowski includes a short study of *La vida* in an article surveying various Latin American Jewish writers (1984). Like Roses, Sosnowski concludes that Efraín's narrations reinforce the theme of the Jews' marginality from Peruvian society. Both Efraín and Jacobo are cut off from society because the society presented in the novel has nothing to offer them.

Bibliography

WORKS BY GOLDEMBERG

De Chepén a La Habana (with José Kozer). New York: Editorial Bayú-Menoráh, 1973.
The Fragmented Life of Don Jacobo Lerner, trans. Robert S. Picciotto. New York: Persea Books, 1976.
La vida a plazos de don Jacobo Lerner. 2d ed. Hanover, N.H.: Ediciones del Norte, 1980.
Hombre de paso/Just Passing Through, trans. David Unger and Isaac Goldemberg. Hanover, N.H.: Point of Contact and Ediciones del Norte, 1981.
Tiempo al tiempo. Hanover, N.H.: Ediciones del Norte, 1984.

WORKS ABOUT GOLDEMBERG

Castañeda, Esther. "Primera aproximación a *La vida a plazos de don Jacobo Lerner.*" *Caballo de Fuego*, Huancayo, Peru (febrero 1980).
Friedman, Edward H. "Marginal Narrative: Levels of Discourse in Isaac Goldemberg's *La vida a plazos de don Jacobo Lerner.*" *Chasqui* 11, 1 (1981): 13–20.
Roses, Lorraine E. "El lector como jurado: El monólogo interior en *La vida a plazos de don Jacobo Lerner.*" *Discurso Literario* 2, 1 (1984): 225–32.
Samuels, Jean Ellen. "The Figure of the Jew in Modern Spanish American Literature: Gerchunoff and Goldemberg." Master's thesis, University of Virginia, 1978.
Sosnowski, Saúl. "Latin American Jewish Writers: A Bridge toward History." *Prooftexts* 4 (1984): 71–92.
Tamayo Vargas, Augusto. "Narrativa peruana contemporánea." *Zona Franca*, Caracas, Venezuela, III época, Núm. 19 (julio/agosto 1980): 12–25.
Tittler, Jonathan. "*The Fragmented Life of don Jacobo Lerner:* The Esthetics of Fragmentation," in *Narrative Irony in the Contemporary Spanish American Novel.* ed. Jonathan Tittler, Ithaca and London: Cornell University Press, 1984.
Williams, Raymond L. "Nuevo tradicionalismo de la novela hispanoamericana." *Suplemento cultural, Ultimas noticias*, Caracas, Venezuela (Agosto 23, 1981).

Selected Reviews

The Fragmented Life of Don Jacobo Lerner and *La vida a plazos de don Jacobo Lerner*
Castañeda, Esther. *Revista de crítica literaria latinoamericana* 6, 12 (1980): 295–96.
Luchting, Wolfgang. *World Literature Today* 51, 4 (1977): 599.
Macshane, Frank. "American Indians, Peruvian Indians." *New York Times Book Review* June 12, 1977: 15, 33.
Minc, Rose S. *Hispania* 66, 3 (1984): 445.
Pearson, Lon. *American Hispanist* 3, 19 (1977): 13.
Williams, Raymond L. *Journal of Spanish Studies: Twentieth Century* 7, 2 (1979): 230–32.
Hombre de paso/Just Passing Through
Goldman, Myrna. *Latin American Literary Review* 11, 22 (1983): 114–16.
Lindstrom, Naomi. *Revista Iberoamericana* Núm. 124 (1983): 659–60.
Luchting, Wolfgang. *World Literature Today* 56, 3 (1982): 491.
Miller, Beth. *Hispania* 66, 4 (1983): 646–47.

PATRICIA MOSIER

GONZÁLEZ, CELEDONIO (1923–). Few Cuban American writers have so vividly depicted the realities, aspirations, frustrations, and disappointments of their fellow countrymen living in the United States as Celedonio González. Indeed he has been dubbed in Cuban American literary circles as "El cronista de la diáspora" for all of his works reflect the experiences of this minority group living in a land of alien culture and language.

Biography

The son of a Spanish father and a Cuban Italian mother, Celedonio González was born on September 9, 1923, in the small town of La Esperanza in Central Cuba.

At the age of seven, Celedonio was sent to the nearby city of Santa Clara where he received a traditional Catholic education at the Marist Brothers School. After finishing his elementary education he began his studies at La Progresiva, a private Protestant high school in the city of Cárdenas. His stay at this institution, coupled with his early Catholic education, caused him to become a religious skeptic, for he stated to me in a tape-recorded interview, "I am neither Catholic nor Protestant; I don't know what I am, other than a religious skeptic."

After graduating from high school, Celedonio returned to La Esperanza where he spent his youth working for his father, strolling in the park in the evenings, and going to the only theater in town on Sundays. The bucolic setting of La Esperanza later influenced his writings where the easygoing Cuban rural life contrasts sharply with the fast pace of American society.

Gradually, Celedonio began to administer his family's farming enterprises and became a sympathizer of the Cuban Orthodox party, whose goal was that of transforming Cuban society into a more egalitarian one.

Although Celedonio's quest for social justice was dealt a severe blow by Fulgencio Batista's coup d'état in 1952, he believed his dreams would come true with the triumph of Fidel Castro's Revolution in 1959. These dreams, however, would soon turn to nightmares because of "Fidel Castro's betrayal of the Revolution." In 1960 he was arrested for conspiring against the regime and imprisoned for two months. He often describes his imprisonment as "a combination of the Kafkian world and the Orwellian world," he told me.

After his release from prison, Celedonio with his wife, Elfrida, and their children, Eduardo and Eloína, migrated to the United States in search of freedom.

The family first settled in Miami where Celedonio eked out a precarious existence working at a number of odd jobs. These experiences ironically proved to be most valuable, for most of the characters in his works are based on his Cuban fellow workers. Promise of a better living drove the González family to Chicago in 1965 where the windy city proved to be no panacea and the family barely existed.

It was in Chicago that he tried his hand at writing a novel and a theater piece. In his own words, "They were so bad that they ended in the trash can."

Subsequently the family returned to Miami where Celedonio worked at various jobs. At the age of forty-one he wrote his first serious novel, *Los primos* (The Cousins), in only ten months. Rejected time after time by different publishers, the novel was not to be published until 1971. *Los primos* was an instant success in Miami's Cuban American community. Celedonio attributed this to the fact that "it was a mirror of Cuban life in Miami in the early 60's."

That same year, his collection of short stories, *La soledad es una amiga que vendrá* (1971, Solitude Is a Friend Who Will Come), depicting the perennial solitude of Cuban exiles in the United States, was published in Miami. In spite of its pessimism, the volume received the same accolades as *Los primos* and some of the stories have been included in Hispano literary anthologies.

While his prose brought him recognition, it did not bring much-needed revenue, and the author was forced again to seek supplemental employment in order to support his family. Writing whenever he could find time, Celedonio spent two years on a new novel, *Los cuatro embajadores* (The Four Ambassadors), which was published in 1973. The novel, an indictment of the American capitalist system and the dehumanizing aspect of "The American Way of Life," while structurally superior to *Los primos,* is somewhat marred by excessive pessimism and bitterness.

The next five years were spent writing what he calls his "masterpiece," *El espesor del pellejo de un gato ya cadáver* (The Thickness of Skin of a Dead Cat), which was published in 1978. In spite of its high degree of experimentation, which does not make it easy to read, the novel remains a valuable piece of fiction for it, too, deals with the life of Cubans in the United States.

Since the publication of *El espesor del pellejo de un gato ya cadáver,* Celedonio has been writing in relative obscurity. He has finished a novel, "Qué veinte años no es nada," and four plays. Although the novel will soon be published, the plays have neither been represented nor published. This, however, has not discouraged him, for he said to me, "It is extremely difficult to be a Cuban writer in the United States. First of all, most of us write in Spanish for a limited audience, and then we are faced with adverse circumstances for we neither receive financial support from the government nor are our works disseminated by any organization."

Celedonio continues to live in Miami where he works as a translator for a number of magazines and is a weekly columnist for the local *Diario Las Américas.*

Major Themes

Celedonio's prevalent concern in all of his literary works is the life of his fellow Cubans in the United States. Therefore, his most common themes are the denunciation of Fidel Castro's dictatorship; nostalgia for the lost island; alienation and solitude; the struggle for identity; and the clash between two distinct cultures.

Los primos, which established Celedonio as a serious chronicler of Cuban life in the United States, is an account of the lives of three Cuban cousins: Eduardo, Arturo, and Valentín. Eduardo, the most interesting character in the novel, escapes Cuba with his family and settles in Miami, but after living for almost ten years in the United States he becomes disenchanted with "The American Way of Life" and decides to return to Cuba with his family. The other cousin, Arturo, cannot adapt himself to American society, yet he remains in the United States. Valentín, an ardent follower of the Cuban regime, becomes frustrated with the Revolution and leaves for Miami. The novel ends with Valentín's uncertain return to Cuba.

An important symbolism underscores the title of this novel. The word *primo* means "cousin" in Spanish, and, indeed, the novel deals with the lives of the three Cuban cousins. It has, however, another meaning: in Cuban slang the word also means "one who is easily deceived." In the final analysis, Celedonio tries to portray the Cuban as a human being who has been easily deceived by both the communists and the United States.

From a strictly stylistic point of view, *Los primos* cannot be considered a masterpiece of Cuban American literature. While highly experimental in its constant use of interior monologues, flashbacks, and fragmented narrations, the novel is in need of careful revision, for some of its pages far outshine others. On the other hand, the true value of *Los primos* is that it offers the reader an authentic portrait of Cuban life in Miami in the early 1960s. The characters, narrative voice, and dialogue are undeniably Cuban and even the metaphors and other rhetorical devices are genuinely Cuban. Thus, *Los primos* is probably the most authentic of the Cuban American novels.

La soledad es una amiga que vendrá, Celedonio's first attempt at the short story, concentrates on reflecting the solitude and alienation of Cuban exiles in Miami along with nostalgic recollections of the island. The author's treatment of the theme, however, is comical, almost farcical in nature, yet, paradoxically, through the use of humor he reveals the anguish and desolation of his characters. His direct style, free of rhetorical devices, reveals an author who is in complete control of his material.

In his second novel, *Los cuatro embajadores,* Celedonio continues to stress his theme of Cuban disenchantment with "The American Way of Life." The novel has neither a plot nor a protagonist in the accepted sense and is rather a documentary of how Americans and Cubans perceive each other. The famous Four Ambassadors Hotel in Miami—which was owned by an American firm but largely staffed by Cubans—is personified as a Cuban American who narrates the story in a fragmented manner. A much more developed novel than *Los primos, Los cuatro embajadores*'s strength lies in the spiced Cuban *costumbrismo*. While its excessive pessimism tends to demean its overall literary value, the novel is a most important microcosm of Miami's Cuban community.

El espesor del pellejo de un gato ya cadáver, Celedonio's shortest yet most ambitious novel, is in reality a trilogy. The three principal characters, Yumbo Lata, a young Cuban revolutionary guerrilla fighter; Timba Figueroa, an old Cuban candymaker; and the omniscient teller, all have one common goal: that of reaching an impossible dream.

For Yumbo, his dream is that of bringing revolution to Bolivia. Yet his dream is never realized for he is betrayed and executed by his own men while fighting in Bolivia.

Timba's quest is that of being reunited with his son Ele, who lives in Puerto Rico. After a number of trials and tribulations, Timba is allowed to leave Cuba and goes to live with his son in Puerto Rico. Yet, the dream is short lived for personality conflicts with his daughter-in-law force him to move to Miami where he dies in penniless obscurity.

The unnamed protagonist's quest is that of making love to Isabel, his ideal yet elusive lady. While his quest is never realized, he is the only major character whose life does not end in bitter disillusionment.

Technically, *El espesor del pellejo de un gato ya cadáver* is a complicated but flawless piece of work. The action moves from one place to another, from one character to the other, from past to present to future. In addition, it is further complicated by a host of minor characters. The narrative itself is fragmented and packed with interior monologues, flashbacks, multiple juxtapositions, and intentional grammatical and typographical errors that require the active participation of the reader if the novel is to be understood.

Concerning this novel, Celedonio has stated to me the following: "In this novel, I expect the full cooperation of my reader to decipher what I am trying to say. If the reader is intelligent, he will immediately find the message; if the reader is somewhat slow, he will have to read the work again, but he will find what I am trying to say." His message, of course, is clear: Cuban exiles should give up their dreams of returning to a liberated Cuba and must resign themselves to accept exile as a way of life.

Celedonio's four plays, which have yet to be represented, again deal with the life of Cubans in the United States. "La muerte de un cantante" is the story of a former Cuban pimp who cannot cope with the American reality and his life ends in tragedy; "El velorio" satirizes Cuban American political intransigency; "José Pérez, candidato a la alcaldía" is the story of a Cuban grocery owner who spends his entire fortune trying to be elected mayor of Hialeah, yet this dream is never materialized because on election day the Latin vote is divided among the numerous Latin candidates thus enabling the sole Anglo candidate to achieve victory; and "Quimera" is a most amusing and yet tragic play that presents the adventures of a young Cuban American professional whose quest in obtaining a government grant causes the disintegration of his family life.

The plays are well written and are extremely interesting. While humor is an integral component of these plays, Celedonio's purpose is not simply that of providing entertainment, but rather that of revealing the aspirations and frustrations of his Cuban characters.

Survey of Criticism

Celedonio's works have until recently been largely ignored by the critics. This is not surprising, for Cuban American literature, like the literature of other Hispanic groups in the United States, has been ignored by the American literary mainstream. Fortunately, in the last decade, interest in Cuban American literature has emerged and published criticism of Celedonio's works is appearing. Yara González Montes and Matías *Montes Huidobro's article, "La novela cubana: El sitio de la palabra" (1976), a study of *Los primos* and three other Cuban American novels, examines the experimental aspects of *Los primos*. My own three articles, "Salient Themes in the Cuban-American Narrative" (1977), *"Los primos:* Retrato del cubano en los Estados Unidos" (1981), and "Celedonio González: El cronista de la diáspora" (1984), discuss the major themes and stylistic features of Celedonio's novels. Mayda Watson-Espener's article, "Observaciones sobre el teatro chicano, nuyorriqueño y cubano en los Estados Unidos" (1978), points out the salient aspects of Celedonio's plays. In addition, Roberto *Fernández's doctoral dissertation, "El cuento cubano del exilio" (1977), examines the thematic aspects of *La soledad es una amiga que vendrá.*

While all the cited critics have generally praised Celedonio's works in their studies, perhaps the best commentary regarding his works comes from the author himself. "My countrymen have enjoyed my works because all I've done is to record their lives in this country and they see themselves in my characters. We Cubans cannot escape our fate. The past cannot be changed but it can be recorded and this is precisely what I have done in my works."

Bibliography

WORKS BY GONZÁLEZ

Los primos. Miami: Ediciones Universal, 1971.
La soledad es una amiga que vendrá. Miami: Ediciones Universal, 1971.
Los cuatro embajadores. Miami: Ediciones Universal, 1973.
El espesor del pellejo de un gato ya cadáver. Miami: Ediciones Universal, 1978.

WORKS ABOUT GONZÁLEZ

Fernández, José B. "Salient Themes in the Cuban-American Narrative." *Chasqui* 6 (May 1977): 76–83.
———. *"Los primos:* Retrato del cubano en los Estados Unidos." *Chiricú* 2 (Spring 1981): 69–77.
———. "Celedonio González: El cronista de la diáspora." *Folio* 16 (Spring 1984): 50–57.
Fernández, Roberto. "El cuento cubano del exilio." Ph.D. dissertation, Florida State University, 1977.
González Montes, Yara, and Matías Montes Huidobro. "La novela cubana: El sitio de la palabra." *Caribe* 1 (Primavera 1976): 138–43.
Watson-Espener, Mayda. "Observaciones sobre el teatro chicano, nuyorriqueño y cubano en los Estados Unidos." *Revista Bilingüe/Bilingual Review* 5 (1978): 120–32.

JOSÉ B. FERNÁNDEZ

GONZÁLEZ COISCOU, JOSÉ LUIS (1926–   ). The late Puerto Rican author and critic René *Marqués was indeed correct when he labeled José Luis González as the true pioneer of the famous "Generation of 1940." This group, composed of such outstanding writers as Pedro Juan *Soto, Emilio Díaz Valcárcel, Abelardo Díaz Alfaro, René Marqués, Luis Rafael *Sánchez, and José Luis himself, became the most brilliant group in the history of Puerto Rican literature. Their contributions rescued Puerto Rican letters from decadence and isolation and restored it to its proper place of eminence.

While many accolades have been bestowed on the group as a whole, it was really José Luis González who was particularly responsible for developing the new themes and techniques that were to guide this group in its quest for literary greatness.

Biography

José Luis González Coiscou was born on March 8, 1926, in Santo Domingo, capital of the Dominican Republic. He was the son of José Luis González Toledo, a Puerto Rican from Camuy, and Mignon Coiscou Henríquez, a member of one of the most prestigious families in Dominican letters. The family migrated to Puerto Rico when José Luis was four years old, and he spent most of his childhood living in the rural town of Guaynabo.

González's interest in literature began at an early age. In a tape-recorded interview he told me, "I guess I was destined to become a writer, for in my family, reading was more important than eating. My grandmother practically made me read everything and by the time I was eleven I had read all of Zola's works. When I was twelve, for example, I met Juan Bosch, the great Dominican writer. Bosch not only became my mentor, but also taught me that literature is an art, a true profession."

During his youth José Luis lived in San Juan, where he graduated from the Escuela Superior Central and then went on to receive his bachelor of social science degree from the University of Puerto Rico in 1946. Prior to his graduation from the university, he had already published two books of short stories, *En la sombra* (1943, In the Shade), a volume whose theme is the plight of the Puerto Rican peasant in the countryside, and *Cinco cuentos de sangre* (1945, Five Stories of Blood), winner of the prestigious Instituto de Literatura Puertorriqueña Prize.

His dissatisfaction with "the unjust American occupation of Puerto Rico," he told me, as well as his deep disgust with the living conditions of his fellow Puerto Ricans caused him to become a militant Marxist and an ardent supporter of the Puerto Rican independence movement.

A year after his graduation from the University of Puerto Rico, José Luis went to New York where he did postgraduate work in political science at the New School for Social Research. His stay in New York enabled him to observe the precarious living conditions of the Puerto Rican immigrants in that city, which would later be used as a theme in his future works.

In 1948 González returned to Puerto Rico and was elected president of the Vanguardia Juvenil Puertorriqueña, a political activist group whose goal was that of implementing socialism on that Caribbean island. That same year, he published another collection of short stories, *El hombre en la calle* (Man in the Street), whose theme is the denunciation of the social and economic oppression of the urban poor in Puerto Rico.

The next two years kept the young author busily occupied in the writing of his famous novelette *Paisa* (Compatriate), one of the earliest and most moving portraits of Puerto Rican life in New York City. After the publication of *Paisa,* González turned to journalism and became a correspondent in Eastern Europe. In 1953, he renounced his American citizenship as an "act of protest against American colonialism," he told me, and moved to Mexico. The American government retaliated by barring González from entering the United States and Puerto Rico.

A year after establishing his residency in Mexico, José Luis published what many consider his best collection of short stories, *En este lado* (1954, On This Side). It is in this volume that one encounters such classics as "En el fondo del caño hay un negrito," "Santa Claus visita a Pichirilo Sánchez," "Una caja de plomo que no se podía abrir," and "El pasaje," often included in Latin American literary anthologies. During his self-imposed exile in Mexico, González obtained his master's degree in Latin American literature and became a professor of literature, first at the University of Guanajuato and then at the National University of Mexico where he still teaches.

After an eighteen-year lull, José Luis wrote another novelette, *Mambrú se fue a la guerra* (1972, Mambrú Went to War), an anti-war piece of fiction. "I had to write this novel," he said to me. "War just repulses me; it is man's worst invention." The novel was followed by the publication of two compilations of his best short stories, *La galería* (1972, The Gallery) and *En Nueva York y otras desgracias* (1973, In New York and Other Disgraces). After a lecture tour in various countries, the Puerto Rican author finished two more novels, *Balada de otro tiempo* (1978, Ballad of Another Time), his first full novel, and *La llegada* (1980, The Arrival), a historical novel concerning the American invasion of Puerto Rico in 1898.

While José Luis González has been allowed to enter the United States and Puerto Rico since 1971, he still resides in Mexico where he continues to write about his beloved Puerto Rico. As he says, "I will always continue to write about the Puerto Rican reality. One does not need to live in Puerto Rico to write about Puerto Rico. I write about the Puerto Rican past in order to better explain the present. We cannot know where we are heading if we don't know our roots."

Major Themes

Ever since he wrote *En la sombra* at the age of seventeen, González's principal concern has been the struggle of the Puerto Rican people against foreign domination and economic oppression. His themes, developed throughout his works of fiction, indicate his sympathy for both the exploited peasants and workers; the denunciation of the American occupation of Puerto Rico; the duality of the Puerto Rican identity; his detestation of the social and political realities in Puerto Rico; the struggle for survival of his fellow Puerto Ricans living in the United States; and his repugnancy for war.

While writers who employ politically oriented themes tend to mar their works with excessive emotionalism, sentimentalism, and dogmatism, this is not the case with José Luis González, for he possesses two great qualities: he knows how to tell a story and he knows how to emotionally involve the reader with his characters. *En la sombra,* for instance, is a denunciation of the exploitation of the Puerto Rican peasant, yet González's superb style saves the work from becoming one more political pamphlet.

Cinco cuentos de sangre is also a message of denunciation against injustices. The stories in this volume portray the life of a people in a world of tension and conflict and Gonzalez's style is marked by irony and violent language.

El hombre en la calle, Jose Luis's first attempt at portraying life in an urban setting, is a most effective re-creation of reality in fiction. The stories in this volume are sharp vignettes characterized by a group of nameless protagonists who survive in a hostile environment.

Paisa, one of the earliest accounts of Puerto Rican life in New York City, is a most moving novelette. The novelette is the story of Andrés, a young Puerto Rican who, lured by the magnetism of a better life in the United States, abandons his family and goes to live in New York City. Yet, life in the promised land is nothing more than a nightmare for Andrés. Unable to find a job this victim of racial and economic discrimination becomes desperate and decides to rob a Harlem grocery. The novelette ends when Andrés is shot to death by the police while performing the robbery.

As a novelette, *Paisa* is emotionally and structurally consistent with character delineation. The style is plain and direct and realism seems to be the order of the day. González uses flashbacks, temporal and spatial transitions, and interior monologues to create a most turbulent collage of life in the big city. While some critics have labeled *Paisa* as a forerunner of the Latin American narrative "boom," its author remains indifferent. He explained to me: "I never imagined that *Paisa* would have caused such an impact. All I did in *Paisa* was to describe something that everyone knew: the alienation and suffering of my compatriots in the United States."

González continued to stress the theme of social and economic oppression in both Puerto Rico and New York in *En este lado.* In a precise and concise style similar to that of Hemingway, José Luis created unforgettable characters such as Pichirilo Sánchez in "Santa Claus visita a Pichirilo Sánchez" (Santa Claus Visits Pichirilo Sánchez), Melodía in "En el fondo del caño hay un negrito" (At the Back of the Cane Field There's a Black Man), and Juan and Jesús in "El pasaje" (The Passage). While critics have perceived a greater degree of stylistic superiority and narrative maturity in this particular volume, it is equally important to point out González's use of colloquial Puerto Rican expressions that give the stories a higher sense of realism and authenticity.

In his second novelette, *Mambrú se fue a la guerra,* José Luis sees war as an aberration. The protagonist, a nameless Puerto Rican soldier, narrates his life story in three parts: his adventures in Paris, his battlefield experience in World

War II, and his return to Puerto Rico and subsequent rejection by his countrymen. Characterized by its fragmented narration and the constant use of interior monologue, the novelette manages to get its message across: War is hell, and its heroes are quickly forgotten.

La galería and *En Nueva York y otras desgracias* are both collections of what José Luis considers his best short stories from his previous volumes. The stories, however, are sequentially arranged in order to illustrate the flight of the Puerto Rican peasant from the countryside to San Juan and then to New York City. In all of the stories, the reader soon realizes the life of the poor Puerto Rican *jíbaro* in a hostile environment.

Balada de otro tiempo, Jose Luis's full-length novel, is perhaps his weakest work of fiction. On the surface the theme appears to be that of the loss of a man's honor—a common theme in Spanish and Latin American literature. The plot is simple: Rosendo Arbona's wife, Dominga, abandons him and goes to live with his rival, Fico Santos. Rosendo, faced with the loss of his honor, seeks revenge, yet at the end of the novel he refuses to kill both lovers. Instead, he leaves his land forever. José Luis then uses the honor theme to illustrate that, like Rosendo's honor, the old values and traditions of Puerto Rican society have been crushed by the Americanization of the island, and Puerto Ricans seem unable or unwilling to confront this serious problem. From a stylistic point of view the principal characteristic of the novel appears to be its lack of experimentation. The narrative is linear, without time distortions, and is full of unbearably long sentences. The characters are never fully developed. While the author might have gotten his message across, *Balada de otro tiempo* will never be remembered as González's best piece of fiction.

La llegada, José Luis's first historical novel, is a most amusing yet didactic one. His main purpose in this novel is to present the life of Llano Verde, a small Puerto Rican town, prior to the American occupation of the island. Through the use of flashbacks, José Luis synthesizes four hundred years of Spanish colonialism in a twenty-four-hour period. Each character represents an aspect of Puerto Rican culture and, in the end, when the Americans occupy Llano Verde, life remains the same. González's message in this historical novel is a clear one: Life for the Puerto Ricans will be the same; they have merely changed colonial masters.

José Luis González, fighter for independence, social crusader, exile and writer, will always continue to write for and about his enchanted island, Puerto Rico.

Survey of Criticism

A major writer like José Luis González is always the center of numerous studies. Most of the studies tend to place González as a major contributor to Puerto Rican letters. Perhaps the best work on and about José Luis González is Arcadio Díaz Quiñones's book *Conversación con José Luis González* which reveals the life of José Luis González as a writer. Andrés Avellaneda's "Para leer a José Luis González" is a most valuable contribution, for it covers the works of the Puerto Rican writer prior to 1978. Rene *Marqués thoroughly discusses González's early works in *Cuentos puertorriqueños de hoy* (1959). Isabel María Ruscalleda Bercedóniz's work, *Bibliografía de José Luis González* (1980), is an important source of information concerning González's work and its criticism. Finally, my own article/interview, "Entrevista con José Luis González," offers González's commentaries concerning his works.

All of González's works are still in print and, as he indicated in my interview, "I will continue to write until I die."

Bibliography

WORKS BY GONZÁLEZ COISCOU

En la sombra. San Juan: Imprenta Venezuela, 1943.
Cinco cuentos de sangre. San Juan: Imprenta Venezuela, 1945.
El hombre en la calle. Santurce: Bohique, 1948.
Paisa. México: Fondo de Cultura Popular, 1950.
En este lado. México: Los Presentes, 1954.
La galería. México: Era, 1972.
Mambrú se fue a la guerra. México: Joaquín Mortiz, 1972.
En Nueva York y otras desgracias. México: Siglo XXI, 1973.
Balada de otro tiempo. México: Nueva Imagen, 1978.
La llegada. Río Piedras: Ediciones Huracán, 1980.

WORKS ABOUT GONZÁLEZ COISCOU

Avellaneda, Andrés. "Para leer a José Luis González." *Cuadernos Hispano-Americanos* 19 (Primavera 1976): 156–69.
Díaz Quiñones, Arcadio. *Conversación con José Luis González*. Río Piedras: Ediciones Huracán, 1976.
Fernández, José B. "Entrevista con José Luis González." *Revista Chicano-Riqueña* 9 (Invierno 1981): 47–57.
Marqués, René. *Cuentos puertorriqueños de hoy*. Río Piedras: Editorial Cultural, 1959.
Ruscalleda Bercedóniz, Isabel. *Bibliografía de José Luis González*. Jalapa: Centro de Investigaciones Lingüístico-Literarias de la Universidad Veracruzana, 1980.

JOSÉ B. FERNÁNDEZ

GONZÁLEZ-CRUZ, LUIS F. (1943–). Luis F. González-Cruz has distinguished himself primarily through his critical studies and his poetry, although he has also cultivated the narrative genre. Regarding the former, his studies on Pablo Neruda have been his major critical contribution, for González-Cruz has developed original and detailed interpretations of Neruda's poetry. *Pablo Neruda y el "Memorial de Isla Negra." Integración de la visión poética* (Pablo Neruda and "Memoirs of Black Island." An Integrated Poetic Vision) appeared in 1972, followed by *Neruda. De "Tentativa" a la totalidad* (Neruda. From the Tentative to the Totality) in 1979. Both books are essential to a thorough understanding of the Chilean poet. With respect to González-Cruz's poetic work, to a large extent scattered throughout numerous magazines, two significant volumes must be mentioned, *Tirando al blanco / Shooting Gallery* (1975) and *Disgregaciones* (Disintegrations), unpublished as yet.

Biography

Luis F. González-Cruz was born in Cárdenas, Cuba. He lived in a small town, Coliseo, where his father had his medical practice and his mother was a teacher, until 1953. He received his elementary education in Coliseo's only public school and in the school of the Trinitarian Fathers in Cárdenas. The family moved to Varadero in 1953; from there he commuted regularly to Cárdenas to pursue the course work toward his B.S. degree. Early in 1961 he left Cuba to begin pre-medical studies in Florida, but returned a few months later. Back in Cuba, he completed the required training to become a laboratory and X-Ray technician at the Havana Carlos J. Finlay Institute of Tropical Medicine, in 1963. Meanwhile, he read voraciously, at the same time writing stories and poems. He began working as a chemistry teacher at Manuel Bisbé Secondary School; at night he attended the University of Havana to do graduate work for an instructional degree in chemistry.

By that time, he had completed a lengthy collection of unpublished short stories, which remained in his family's possession when he left Cuba again in 1965. The manuscript was destroyed by a fire that razed a whole block of houses in Coliseo, among which was the home where he had spent his childhood. In the poem "Primera casa," published in the literary magazine *Consenso,* in 1979, that unfortunate event, although not witnessed by González-Cruz, is re-created from pieces of information contained in family letters.

In 1965, after a stay of several months in Madrid, where he had the opportunity to meet a good number of writers and artists, he took residence in Pittsburgh. There, he began advanced studies at the Department of Hispanic Literature at the University of Pittsburgh, receiving his doctoral degree in 1970. Since 1969 he has taught at Pennsylvania State University, New Kensington, where he is now professor of Hispanic language and literature. He has taught also, on several occasions, at the University of Pittsburgh, where he was a visiting professor in 1983.

Immediately after his arrival in the United States, González-Cruz continued with the creative work he had started in Cuba, producing, besides, a considerable body of literary criticism. To these endeavors must be added his founding of the literary magazine *Consenso,* which he edited from 1977 to 1980. The magazine was devoted mainly to publishing the works of Hispanic writers residing in the United States, but it also included texts by well-known figures of Hispanic letters. In this manner, González-Cruz covers a wide academic and creative territory, passing from poetry to narrative prose, and from both of them to the analysis of the creative text, while at the same time performing the important cultural task of bringing Hispanic literary works to public attention by means of *Consenso.*

Major Themes

The poetic work of Luis F. González-Cruz comprises poems published in different literary reviews (see list) and two verse collections, *Tirando al blanco / Shooting Gallery* and *Disgregaciones*. *Tirando al blanco / Shooting Gallery* is a bilingual book containing forty-nine poems in Spanish, with their corresponding English translation. It is divided into four parts— "Sitios / Places," "Corporales / Corporal Poems," "Caballos / Horses," and "Minerales / Mineral Poems." *Disgregaciones*, still unpublished, is his most recent book, having been awarded an honor mention in a poetry contest organized by the magazine *Mairena* of Puerto Rico, in 1981.

The outstanding feature of González-Cruz's poetry is a direct relationship with things in what we may term objective contact with the daily world. In other words, he departs from some exact everyday event to elaborate his poetic substance. This gives his poetry a kind of objective, almost palpable, consistency, which holds within precise limits any possible lyrical overflow. Frequently, faced with the facts, he adopts a rather narrative tone; then he proceeds toward mysterious, somewhat hermetic lyrical zones. Since the time of "The Demolition," one of his early poems, González-Cruz endows his texts with a concrete landscape that gradually experiences a sort of disintegration. The first lines of this poem re-create a normal situation in the simplest possible way. Nothing in them suggests the grotesque with which the poem ends, the beheading of the statue in the middle of the square. This course is characteristic of many poems by González-Cruz, although there is a variation in overtones. The strong presence of the concrete can also be perceived in his poetic discourse. The poet insists on material details so concrete ("erect / on his rusty saddle") that the poem intentionally acquires a certain mineral, stone-like quality. A poetry is thus produced which possesses physical density, not only with respect to its subject matter, but also in the dynamics of its lyrical-descriptive process.

In another poem, "Pittsburgh U.S.A. III," we find that the foundations on which "The Demolition" rests do not disappear, but they have been transformed and have certainly gained in complexity. The poem is made up of everyday fragments: "Daily journey newspaper ablutions coffee / the small car that passes by / the church with the stained glass now being restored." In a certain sense, it is the same square of the poem previously considered, but richer in its composition by means of more constituting elements: "It is time to listen to the latest song"; "I write in the air but the telephone call stops me"; "another song another coffee another small car." All this is part of the "daily landscape," a kind of objective montage of the pieces of information supplied by each line. There is here an anti-emotional distance that will change along the course of the text. In the beginning, the poet places himself in the landscape ("the sun hits me in the face") in an objective manner, but, in the images that follow, a slight emotion starts breaking through—that of the passage of time and the succession of family generations: "I write a letter to my ancestors / who wait for some consoling lines.'' The concrete, external landscape soon becomes internalized in a process of imagery that moves from the visual composition of the surroundings to the mere physical reality of the I (face, fingerprints, kneecaps), to the enigmatic act (''I cover myself with fish scales but my snake destiny slips away'') that signals that a transformation has taken place.

The everyday tranquility of the initial ''landscape'' has disappeared, including the I of the poet; it has become a dramatic reality far removed from the initial ''set'' of the poem. A quasi-physical commotion has occurred, a kind of internal ''demolition,'' a violent tremor, which is nevertheless conveyed by a poetic discourse always in touch, in spite of occasional distortions that may remind us of the surrealistic procedure, with the concrete and objective.

We are faced with a poetic approach to which a certain experience in the poet's life has in no small way contributed. The trace of a scientific training is easily detected in the way the poet perceives reality. It is significant that in his formative years González-Cruz would feel himself attracted to science instead of the humanities. This explains the physical, chemical, or biological consciousness present in many of his poems—the ''demolition'' of the spirit in the guise of material forms. A poem like ''Teorema'' (Theorem), with its geometrical-mathematical pattern, confirms the influence of the author's scientific background on his poetry. Regardless of its lack of a coherent sequence, it is a text of addition and subtraction within a geometrical design, proposing a ''scientific'' hypothesis that leads to a conclusion: ''Puesto que las mitades / siempre se encaminan / hacia el perfecto desencuentro'' (Given that the halves / always go / toward perfectly separate ways) is stated at the beginning, continuing thus, ''encaro el mineral / oculto la mano / cuadro la superficie de la esfera / y desarrollo la solución letra por letra'' (I face the mineral / hide my hand / square the surface of the sphere / and develop the solution letter by letter). The poet proceeds as if he were confronted with an algebra problem, and his ''letter by letter'' can be taken in a literal sense first, to find its poetic meaning afterwards. Its ''corollary,'' rich in numerical allusions, ''múltiplo de sus divisiones,'' ''fracciones sumadas o restadas'' (multiples of its divisions, added or substracted fractions), ends, though, in a personal note, ''mis impúdicos antojos'' (my youthful desires), which seemingly rejects the exact development of the ''teorema.'' The same can be said of the biological or physiological character of other poems: ''Frente al espejo / me reconcilio con mis cicatrices / con los ocultos misterios de mis glándulas / protegido por esta lisa superficie'' (In front of the mirror / I reconcile myself to my scars / with the hidden mysteries of my glands / protected by this smooth surface). One can feel the physical presence of the body before the mirror, even to the smallest skin details, but, at the same time, the poet reveals a psychological reality, a state of mind, in a progressive movement inward: ''Mírate mírate a los ojos / interrumpe este osario de palabras / desenmascara el rostro que yo tan bien conozco'' (Look look at your eyes / interrupt this boneyard of words / unmask that face I know so well).

His typical distanced attitude also encompasses the vicissitudes of history, although several poems in this vein reach a rather vibrant point. In "Atestiguo" (I Testify) (*Tirando al blanco*), the poet appears as an eyewitness of bloodshed. As in the poems of a more personal character, he maintains a nonparticipatory distance, mere objective rendering of information. But as the poem progresses, the poet expresses his sorrow over those "facts" ("I have cried there every morning"), suggesting in turn that the previous emotional distance is the result of a moral awareness that has chosen distance as the most lucid perception of human horror:

> That is why I would not change the existence
> of the man who suffers and grieves
> that is why it is better for him to walk on his arms
> or to lock himself up in a room full of dust
> with chains and anger and hunger

"That is why" represents a moral commitment, a decision, an act by which the poet takes sides. But even so, it is a restrained attitude ("equation of life"). Now, in poems like "Isla" (Island), which appeared in *Palabra Solar* in 1980, or "Albor" (Sunrise), published in *Homenaje a Angel Cuadra* in 1981—both included in *Disgregaciones*—the poet seems to be breaking away from the restrictions he had imposed previously on his lyrical manner.

Here González-Cruz, as if he were predestined by his mature personal experience, cannot avoid the confrontation with his origins and with recent national history. This sounding apocalyptic note appears as a common syndrome among all present-day Cuban writers, trapped without possible escape in a historical dilemma. Underneath the subconscious strain of the "I witness" and the apparent objectivity of the text, there lies a hidden unifying anguish, even when the poet, by a sense of artistic respect, has imposed a strict discipline on his composition. This historical phenomenon of today's Cuban poetry has still to be studied; but such a study will not be possible until sufficient historical perspective can be attained. But even under these circumstances, González-Cruz's poetry does not indulge in the facile, carefully eluding the commonplace.

To sum up, it can be said that Luis F. González-Cruz's poetry has initially clothed his rich lyrical self in the objective, the material, the exact. During its later evolution it points to a greater emotional freedom that, given González-Cruz's earlier training, will probably flow along a carefully controlled course.

González-Cruz has also published short stories, and an unpublished collection of these, under the title *La fuga y otros relatos* (The Escape and Other Portraits), will appear in the near future. His stories "Historia de un amor del mar" (History of a Sea Love), "Lázaro volando" (Flying Lazarus), " Una guerra muy fructífera" (A Fruitful War), and "Ofertorio a mi niño" (Offertory to My Son) are characterized by their realism, although certain absurdist or dream-like traits prevent them from being strictly realistic. In "Una guerra muy fructífera," for example, reminiscent in a way of Cortázar's "Casa tomada," the narrator, by

means of an extremely simple language, manages to provide the text with a
multiplicity of points of view, adding up, in such a manner, to the interpretative
possibilities of the story.

González-Cruz is a Cuban writer whose contribution to the field of narrative
and literary creation is in a process of growth. In addition to what he has already
achieved, other valuable works are to be expected from him in the future.

Bibliography

WORKS BY GONZÁLEZ-CRUZ

Books

Pablo Neruda y el "Memorial de Isla Negra." Integración de la visión poética. Miami:
 Ediciones Universal, 1972.
Pablo Neruda, César Vallejo y Federico García Lorca. Microcosmos poéticos. New
 York: Las Américas Publishing Company, 1975.
Tirando al blanco / Shooting Gallery. Poemas / Poems. Miami: Ediciones Universal,
 1975.
"Una guerra muy fructífera," a short story in *20 Cuentistas cubanos,* ed. Leonardo
 Fernández Marcane. Miami: Ediciones Universal, 1978.
Neruda. De "Tentativa" a la totalidad. New York: ABRA-Las Américas, 1979.

Works in Anthologies

"Lázaro volando," award-winning short story in *Latino Short Fiction,* an anthology of
 Revista Chicano-Riqueña 8 no. 1 (Winter 1980): 25–28. Also included in *A Decade
 of Hispanic Literature. An Anniversary Anthology. Revista Chicano-Riqueña* 10
 (Winter-Spring 1982): 200–203.

Works in Magazines

"Three Days of Suspense." Short story. *The Penn Statement* 3, 1 (Fall 1969): 3.
"Historia de un amor del mar." Short story. *El Tiempo* (New York), March 15, 1970:13.
"París I." "La demolición." Poems. *Exilio. Revista de Humanidades* (Summer 1972):
 87–88.
"Pittsburgh U.S.A. III." Poem. *Mester* 4, 1 (November 1973): 36.
"A Pablo Neruda." Poem. *Mester* 4, 2 (April 1974): 88.
"Veneza II." *Poema Convidado* no. 6 (May 1975): 17.
"Cronica das Indias." Poem. *Poema Convidado* no. 17 (April 1976):8.
"XXX." Poem. *Poema Convidado* no. 23 (August 1976): 3.
"I Witness / Atestiguo." Poem. *Papeles de la Frontera* (February 1977): 2–3.
"Barco sobrio." "Nueva pérdida." "Los gloriosos" Poems. *Consenso* 1, 1 (May 1977):
 49–52.
"Deposición." "Teorema." Poems. *Citybender* 1, 3 (November 1977): 2–3.
"Frente al espejo." "Primera casa." "Retribución." Poems. *Consenso* 3, 5 (1979): 11–
 14.
"En la maleza." Poem. *Albaida. Revista de Literatura* 2, 8 (Spring-Summer 1979):6.
"Mar poblado." Poem. *Palabra Solar* no. 3 (May 1980):2.
"Incitación." Poem. *Cuaderno Literario Azor,* Ediciones Rondas, vol. 32 (October-
 December 1981): 7–8.

"Al regreso." "Nueva pérdida." Award-winning poems. *Mairena* 4, 10 (Summer 1982): 38–39.

"Disoluciones." Poem. *Cuaderno Literario Azor,* Ediciones Rondas (July-August 1983):12.

"Continuación de puertas." *Cuaderno Literario Azor,* Ediciones Rondas, vol. 42 (April-June 1984):11.

WORKS ABOUT GONZÁLEZ-CRUZ

Bermúdez, María Elvira. Review of *Tirando al blanco. Revista Mujeres* (México), November 30, 1976: 35.

Gutiérrez de la Solana, Alberto. Critical evaluation. *Investigación y crítica literaria y lingüística cubana.* New York: Senda Nueva de Ediciones, Inc., 1978.

MATÍAS MONTES HUIDOBRO

H

HERNÁNDEZ CRUZ, VICTOR (1949–). Among the Nuyorican poets, Victor Hernández Cruz is the consummate bilingual poet. His poetry also echoes the strains of the ancient call of the wild, mingled with sea breezes and the aroma emanating from the hillside. And true to his Puerto Rican heritage, he fuses that spirit with the new experience, the "New Yorker," to form the Nuyorican. From this new union, then, a new poetry, the Nuyorican poetry, is born. Cruz is the best and most acclaimed by the mainstream of the New York Puerto Rican poets. His books have been published by mainstream presses and he has even been featured by *Life* magazine as a major American poet.

Biography

Born on February 6, 1949, in Aguas Buenas, Puerto Rico, Cruz had ample opportunity to be invaded by and imbued with the spirit of the place, even though at age five he moved with the family to New York's Spanish Harlem. Aguas Buenas, a small, country town, is situated on Highway 3 that serpentines its way dangerously from San Juan on the north to Ponce on the south. Puerto Rico itself is only one hundred miles long and thirty-three miles wide so that no matter where one lives on the island one is never far from the Caribbean, over whose fierce waters the fiercer Caribs rowed to wrestle with the peace-loving Tainos and in whose warm, serene waters the Tainos played at Luquillo Beach. However, until recently, the roads have been so arduous that a child living in Aguas Buenas might see the Caribbean's blue stretching to meet that of the sky only once or twice a year. Along the coast, tropical weather prevails, but milder, less-humid temperatures are usual in the mountainous interior. No matter, the climate is kind and a child could survive on the vegetation alone—orange trees grow without cultivation; bananas, coconuts, avocados, and mangos may appear anywhere. With a slingshot a boy could manage quite well.

In the mountains where Cruz lived, folks raised coffee which they handpicked and dried in the sun; sugar cane grew tall in the fields. Life moved pleasantly through friendly days and laughing nights. (Children seem blissfully unaware of any hardships.) People spoke to other people, knew intimately the history of the island and the families; history passed from generation to generation in near-oral tradition. Conversation was an art and conversing was not wasting time. Small boys could wander about discovering the world of sight and sound, of plants and animals, absorbing the very essence of Puerto Ricanhood through bare feet treading generational soil, in much the same way any plant or tree draws sustenance from its roots planted deep in the soil in order to stretch skyward. Arroz con habichuelas always simmered on the stove or over the fire, coffee forever ready with bacalao, plátanos, pan de agua, or batatas, and, on special occasions, cerdo asado. With such wonders of the land, who could wish for the ambrosia of the gods? Certainly not a five-year-old boy. This island world was better. And in the evening the native music, salsas perhaps, played on güiro or cuatro or guitar, filled the spaces in between unpretentious wooden houses. Long after the music ceased and people slept, the coquí kept watch, continuing to signal, ''Co quí, co quí''. With reason Babín describes Puerto Rico as the most ''homogeneous, most congenial country in terms of spiritual and emotional communication among its people.'' Regardless of location, in whatever town or farm, the college professor and the jíbaro share common likes and dislikes of flavors, share common gestures, share common attitudes about love, pride, despair, and rage.

To have spent the first five years, the formative years, in such an environment predestined that Victor would be forever Puerto Rican, would forever carry the essence of the island safe in the vial of memory, would forever find his response to life determined by the voices of Agüeybana and all the others resounding still from coast and mountain. The imprinting of those early years had predetermined both the character of the man, Cruz, and his poetry. The move to New York could alter, but it could not change substantially, his poetic outpourings. As Victor Hernández Cruz explained to me in an interview, his mission is:

My life and work is to clear the smoke—to make things clear—America Vespucci is a strange place with some weird concepts about reality—it is very easy to be confused here. I write from an inner view—realizing that one first understands oneself; because I write about myself from myself I write about people because I am. In words I try to make the Universe into the whole that it is—there is only one reality—interpreted many different ways. Many people don't know that they are alive. Words are magic and should not be treated lightly.

The ''I am'' that Cruz articulates here is undergirded with the island *espiritú*. In the simultaneous lightness and somberness of his words, the paradox, those eternal partners that appear in the above comment, Victor reflects the Taíno ancestry. Behind the knowledge of self and confidence expressed in his affirmation of the magic of words lies Agüeybana's famous speech, which revitalized the cowering Borinqueños, Luis *Lloréns Torres's *El Grito de Lares,* and Luis Muñoz Marín's words to the U.S. Congress. Just so, in this generation the *alma,* the *espiritú* of Puerto Rico lives on in the poet striving to reconcile the world to itself. It is as though Cruz accepts as a torch Babín's assessment of Puerto Rico as the most "homogeneous, most congenial country in terms of spiritual and emotional communication," considering it his charge to make this true also of the larger macrocosm.

So in 1954 Victor Hernández Cruz came with his parents to New York where cement and poverty determined his world, exchanging Puerto Rico's warmth for New York's coldness. We can only imagine the struggles of the child as he learned to cope with a new language and strange attitudes, with people who did not offer *abrazos.* From other Puerto Ricans transplanted to New York, we learn much about the prejudice and ugliness that shaped those early years. In her novel *Nilda,* Nicholasa *Mohr captures the experiences of the young girl facing the harsh reality of the American classroom where to utter a single Spanish word was a cardinal sin, punishable by corporal means. And in his novel *Down These Mean Streets,* Piri *Thomas exposes the street life of the child imprisoned in the tenement-lined streets of New York's Spanish Harlem. One became streetwise very early. In his poem "Dudes," Cruz extracts the quintessence of the youth-experience in New York—the awful wilderness.

However, Cruz did attend Benjamin Franklin High School. Later he married and had a son. His association with the Gut Theater on East 104th Street undoubtedly contributed to and developed more fully his own fine sense of the dramatic which found release in his poetry both structurally and rhythmically—structurally in the vignettes he loves to paint and rhythmically in the tension produced by the nearly wrenched quality of the versification. In fact his vignettes often seem mini one-act dramas replete with dialogue, characters, and plot. And occasionally one senses Browning or Frost or Dos Passos standing in the wings, urging him on.

He became editor of *Umbra* in New York City and some of his poetry appeared in that publication, as well as in *Evergreen Review, New York Review of Books, Ramparts, Down Here,* and several small magazines. He has published several collections of poetry: *Papo Got His Gun* (1966), *Snaps* (1969), *Mainland* (1973), *Tropicalization* (1976), *By Lingual Wholes* (1982) *Rhythm, Content, and Flavor* (1989). In addition, together with Herbert Kohl he edited *Stuff: A Collection of Poems, Visions and Imaginative Happenings from Young Writers in Schools—Opened and Closed* (1970). Departing the New York scene in 1973, Cruz moved to San Francisco where he became active in artistic circles. Cruz continues his own involvement in writing. Presently he is working on a novel.

Major Themes

Victor Hernández Cruz believes that poetry is the stuff of daily living, that the sterility of classroom poetry may be attributed in part to the enforced separation of the students from the language of common experience, that children learn fully only as they are permitted to describe their world in their own personal language and order their experience according to their teacher's perceptions and their own. It is important to note his insistence on the impact of both teacher and student in the creative productions. His work with a group called Poets Incorporated attests to his commitment to his convictions about poetry belonging to the masses.

Classifying his poetry as Afro-Latin, Cruz touches universal themes, multicultural and multiracial. His perspective is realized in his poetry: experience must be ordered but not distorted to fit some preconceived mold. That is, beauty lies in the world as it exists, in its totality, not in the world as it should be. As the poet of things as they are, he becomes the emulsifier that receives global input and blends it into poetry— music not of the spheres but of life. In spite of the vastness and variety of his experience, Victor has not assumed the cynic's stance.

If we were to look for literary techniques that distinguish the corpus of Victor Hernández Cruz's poetry, we must certainly note his delight in languages and experimentation. He delights in all the capabilities of language. In his worldview, the barriers between poetry and prose, poetry and music, or poetry and dance are demolished. His art embraces the artistic expression of humans. Perhaps because he is Puerto Rican and, as Babín in *Borinquen* maintains, the essence of the island is forever in the man, a constant motif must be the rhythm of the salsa. Nicolás Kanellos in his *Institute Paper Series* has developed this thesis at length. Certainly as one reads Cruz's poetry the music captures one because the poems *are* music—the rhythm surges and explodes into a myriad of lights and sounds. The sounds of the qüiro pulsate through all, blending all the writings together as the poet's rhythmic response to life's experiences. While irony, even sarcasm, occurs often in the poetry, Juvenalian satire rarely appears. For Cruz, all of life is the substance of poetry—life as it is, not as it should be.

The fusion of languages, cultures, and myths makes his poetry fully universal. Other poets have interspersed English with Spanish, but none with such naturalness as Cruz. Street jargon and elevated language mingle in a strange and delightful syntax that has nothing to do with dead rules in some grammar book but everything to do with the life of language.

Snaps (1969), as an early work, amplifies the rhythms and worldview that permeate and distinguish Victor's poetry. The poetic structure emulates band sounds, rhythms and beats, converting the language, scenes, and sounds of the urban experience into lyrical but fragmented images of the fragmented world of the barrio, as Nicolás Kanellos noted in his *Institute Paper Series* (1979). The most unique accomplishment of the poet in this work is the brilliant dramatic vignettes of life as it is lived in the ghetto and the poetry that exudes from this human experience. At times the dramatic becomes even more powerful than the poetic, or perhaps more poetic because of the drama, as in a dramatic monologue of Robert Browning.

Although *Stuff* features only five of Cruz's poems, the work plays a major role in revealing the poet's fundamental belief and life commitment. His dedication to teaching and to the poetic expression of children is demonstrated, not discussed. The book is essentially a gathering, a melody of young voices, poetry, irregular and fantastic, of children and young people learning to find poetry in experience, their experience, and in language, their language, not the dead language of many sterile classrooms purporting to teach poetry.

Mainland (1973) records poetically the experiences and responses of the Borinquen on the mainland—the continent as opposed to the island. Not by accident does the poet introduce this volume of poetry with a quotation from the Puerto Rican author Luis *Palés Matos in Spanish, translated afterward into English. Memory of the island experience invades and informs the mainland experience as images, languages, and allusions mingle with the reality of the Bronx, the United States, particularly California, and finally Puerto Rico again. The music of the African drums, the Taino throb, the salsa dances through the streets of the continent and onto the plane that will return the traveler to his home on the island.

Surely Cruz has created Puerto Rican "soul" poetry, achieving universality through the specific—his specific heritage in the very citadels of the "other."

For the writing and publishing of *Tropicalization* (1976), Cruz received a grant from the Creative Artists Public Service Program. All basic themes of Cruz's poetry permeate this work with an increasing sense of the ironic as well. Divided into two parts, "New York Potpourri" and "Electricity," the work begins with *"Cada loco con su tema"* (Each to His Own Madness). Capturing moments, almost extended haikus, the poems are significantly entitled simply "Side 1," or "Side 2," or "Side 31."

In "Electricity" the poetry often becomes prose poems embodying much of the Spanish idiom. These poems have titles that ring with the joy of the dance, the folklore, the food, "the breeze sereno from the opened window which made a whole in our memories." The Boricua does not return to the island; he stays to tropicalize the "Potpourri," to bring the god of the salsa to this chaotic coldness, and to make a musical of the mundane.

By Lingual Wholes (1982) was partially funded by grants from the National Endowment for the Arts and the California Arts Council. Cruz offers quotations from Chinua Achebe, Abu Bakr Muhammed ibn Al Arabi, and Allan Kardec to set the stage for this work that moves even closer to destroying language and cultural barriers, as well as the barriers between the lines that create words and the lines that create diagrams. "The price a world language must be prepared to pay is submission to many different kinds of use," wrote Achebe in 1976. In a sense, this collection of poetry, including brief prose poems, seems a culmination of the poet's vision as well as the successful intermingling of the totality of his experience, actual, imagined, vicariously lived, the mature work of a poet in love with words and experimentation. Possessed of a fine Puerto Rican sense of humor, Cruz plays with words, with forms, with ideas, as well as the interchange of customs, history, and traditions, controlling the "whole" with a lightly ironic touch that barely avoids satire but challenges the reader to think new thoughts and experience life afresh.

Thus as a maestro of pun, paradox, and pictorial poetry, Victor Hernández Cruz directs the orchestration of national and international experience, compelling the reader to respond not only on the microscopic but, at last, on the macroscopic level. Utilizing his heritage of myth, folklore, paisanos, and the libretto, he conducts the orchestra of human experience, emphasizing now the sopranos, now the basses, harmonizing the Puerto Rican reality with global realities, combining Spanish with English and street language with the elevated to create a unique tone. Reaching beyond the salsa and la danza to capture primal Taino rhythms, Cruz has succeeded in tying the modern securely to the ancient, finding a common denominator that underlies the totality of human history. Thus his Puerto Rican heritage provides a broader horizon for his vision that reaches across myth and nations and eras to create at last a cosmic consciousness and "global wit."

The poet invites us to share the life of abandon of the waves, the revelry in nature, the "gold" of past glories of those who conquered the earth and oceans, leaving a legacy of joy for all those who were to follow after. He paints a canvas of free people, yet he is never blatantly didactic.

Survey of Criticism

As a poet, Cruz has been praised by fellow authors such as Allen Ginsberg and Denise Levertov. To be praised, highly praised, by one's contemporaries is praise indeed. The April 1981 issue of *Life* magazine, featuring contemporary American poets, distinguished Victor Hernández Cruz as an outstanding poet. A founding board member of the Before Columbus Foundation and the recipient of a creative writing fellowship from the National Foundation for the Arts, Cruz read at the "Dialogue of the Americas," a conference of writers, artists, and intellectuals convening in Mexico City.

In her 1974 *Borinquen: An Anthology of Puerto Rican Literature,* María Teresa Babín lauds Cruz as one of the most outstanding of the "Neo-Rican or self-styled Rican" poets emerging from the New York barrio. No matter the geographical location of the Puerto Rican, Babín regards that place only as an extension of the island heritage. So in the anthology of the Puerto Rican authors, she includes excerpts from Victor's unpublished novel *Rhythm Section/Part One.* Although city life has transformed social and grammatical forms in the novel, she recognizes the excerpts as the literary grandchildren of the folktale tradition of the island. Finding that the novel portrays at once both the realism and the surrealism of the barrio experience, Babín asserts that his style sets the mode for many barrio poets. In short he's in the vanguard; he's setting and upsetting the pace.

Nicolás Kanellos, too, finds Cruz's poetry to be essentially Puerto Rican, but with special emphasis on the Afro-Caribbean strains of salsa whose origins Cruz locates in Africa and the pre-Columbian West Indies. Cruz's poetry is often a "flowering of the African past." Kanellos describes Cruz's poetry as Puerto Rican "soul" music that emanates from "la salsa de dios" (God's salsa). And the poet records, Kanellos maintains, the odyssey of the Rican in the twentieth century.

But when I searched the libraries in San Juan, Puerto Rico, I did not find Victor Hernández Cruz listed as a Puerto Rican author.

In the United States, Corrine E. Bostic, writing of Victor Hernández Cruz in *Contemporary Poets*, believes that it is his "humorous, angry, brilliant imagery" that distinguishes him from the mass of small contemporary poets; she heralds him as one of "America's finest young poets." However, Bostic's evaluation only prefigures future criticism. The truth is that criticism is scarce. *Crowell's Handbook of Contemporary American Poetry* explains that because Puerto Rican poets for whom English is a first language have only recently begun to be published, Puerto Rican writers have had far less impact on current American literature than black authors. Yet even here, Victor Hernández Cruz is cited as one of the first of the Puerto Ricans to reach a broad American audience.

For all that, Cruz exists in a sort of critical limbo, between the continent and the island. Critics who review his work proclaim him as brilliant, his poetry as "pure musical energy." But the critics are few; consequently, the impact has been less intense. Actually his poetry has yet to find its way to the pages of anthologies of mainstream American poetry. The great poetic outpouring of this American cannot, however, continue to be neglected.

Bibliography

WORKS BY HERNÁNDEZ CRUZ

Papo Got His Gun. New York: Calle Once Publications, 1966.
Snaps: Poems. New York: Random House, 1969.
Stuff: A Collection of Poems, Visions and Imaginative Happenings from Young Writers in Schools—Opened and Closed. Eds. Victor Hernández Cruz and Herbert Kohl. Cleveland: World, 1970.
Mainland. New York: Random House, 1973.
Tropicalization. New York: Reed, Cannon & Johnson, 1976.
By Lingual Wholes. San Francisco: Momo's Press, 1982.
Rhythm, Content & Flavor. Houston: Arte Publico Press, 1989.

WORKS ABOUT HERNÁNDEZ CRUZ

Babín, María Teresa. *Borinquen: An Anthology of Puerto Rican Literature*, ed. María Teresa Babín and Stan Steiner. New York: Vintage Books, 1974.
Bostic, Corrine E. "Victor Hernández Cruz." *Contemporary Poets*, ed. James Vinson. (New York: St. Martin's, 1980): 327.

Crowell's Handbook of Contemporary American Poetry, ed. Karl Malkoff. New York: Crowell, 1973.

Kanellos, Nicolás. "Victor Hernández Cruz and La Salsa de Dios," *Institute Paper Series.* Milwaukee: University of Wisconsin, Spanish-Speaking Outreach Institute of the College of Letters and Science, 1979.

LAVERNE GONZÁLEZ

L

LAGUERRE, ENRIQUE A. (1906–). Enrique A. Laguerre is one of Puerto Rico's most prolific novelists, having produced a considerable body of work that has reflected the historical events that have transformed Puerto Rican culture during his long life: the Jones Act of 1917 giving United States citizenship to Puerto Ricans, the various failures of the island's one-crop economies, migration to urban areas and, in turn, the diaspora to the continental United States, the founding of the commonwealth of Puerto Rico. His rich and varied novelistic production spans the transition from modernism and regionalism to a socially engaged realism and finally a Latin American magic realism. Considered by some critics as a somewhat conventional writer, he nevertheless advocated and practiced a political and social commitment in fiction writing. Laguerre has also distinguished himself as an essayist, columnist, playwright, short-story writer, teacher, and professor.

Biography

Enrique A. Laguerre was born to Juan Laguerre, a small sugar cane farmer, and his wife Antonia Vélez in 1906 in Moca, Puerto Rico. He attended a one-room rural school in Isabela and later transferred to a larger school in Aguadilla where his teacher, Carmen Gómez Tejera, recognized his literary abilities and encouraged him to become a writer.

Laguerre was raised among the jíbaros during the period of transition from autonomy under Spain to United States citizenship. His rural environment and its culture, as well as the uncertain period of political transition, would inform his later novelistic and theatrical works. During his younger days he also witnessed the deterioration of the coffee industry in favor of the sugar culture preferred by the United States, which he evoked in his first novel, *La llamarada* (1935, The Blaze) and his second, *Solar Montoya* (1941, Montoya Plantation).

In 1936, the same year that Laguerre became certified as a teacher, *La llamarada* won an award from the Institute of Puerto Rican Literature. The following year he obtained his bachelor's degree in education from the University of Puerto Rico. In 1941 he completed his master's degree in literature there with a thesis on Puerto Rican modernist poets. He later pursued doctoral work at Columbia University, but never finished.

Laguerre's life as an academic spanned more than five decades, beginning with his job in 1925 as a teacher in rural areas of the island, then as a high school teacher in Fajardo (1937–1938), as a university professor in Rio Piedras at the University of Puerto Rico (1941–1970) and later at Queens College in New York (1972) and after that at the Catholic University of Ponce. In 1972 he became president of the board of directors of the Institute of Puerto Rican Culture. In 1980 he was named an Honorary Fellow of the American Association of Teachers of Spanish and Portuguese.

Laguerre's literary career began with the publication of the prize-winning *La llamarada* in 1935, which to date has seen more than twenty editions, and continued with the publication of nine other novels, the last of which, *Los amos benévolos* (*Benevolent Masters,* 1983), was published in 1977, three years after the Institute of Puerto Rican Culture had published volumes of his complete works, *Obras completas* (1974). Laguerre has also published one play, *The Resentful Woman* (1960, *La resentida*), in translation and various short stories, essays, and academic writings. More important than the latter is his work as a teacher-writer for educational radio in Puerto Rico from 1938 to 1941 and his long-running column, "Hojas Libres" (Open Pages), in Puerto Rico's leading newspaper, *El Mundo,* in which he covered a broad range of subjects, from the political to the cultural.

His leadership in Puerto Rican letters also includes his becoming editor of the magazine *Presente* in 1952 and his being one of the founders of the literary review *Paliques* in 1954, his being elected in 1967 to the presidency of the Society of Puerto Rican Authors, and his election to PEN membership in 1968.

Major Themes

Enrique A. Laguerre's most important contribution is made as a novelist. His long career in prose fiction began with his continuing to elaborate the creole-regionalist themes of rural Puerto Rican life, of which he had firsthand experience, in works like *La llamarada* and *Solar Montoya.* In this vein, his jíbaros and their local color, as well as the elaboration of the theme of man in confrontation with nature, followed not only in the tradition of Manuel Alonso's and Manuel Zeno-Gandia's jíbaros, but also in that of the epic novels of Colombia (José Eustacio Rivera's *La vorágine*), Venezuela (Rómulo Gallegos's *Doña Bárbara*), and Argentina (Ricardo Güiraldes's *Don Segundo Sombra*).

While *La llamarada* deals most directly with the changing rural economy from a sugar back to a coffee culture and criticizes the oppression of the workers by absentee landlords, *Solar Montoya* decries the destruction of the coffee industry and is structurally and stylistically reminiscent of the Argentine bildungsroman, *Don Segundo Sombra*. But instead of emulating a gaucho, the protagonist Gonzalo comes to his maturity and identification with the land and the rural way of life by following in the footsteps of the apotheosis of the jíbaro: Don Alonso Montoya. It is also interesting to note that in *Solar Motoya* we have an early elaboration of the Puerto Rican literary topic of New York as the inhuman Metropolis that is inhospitable to Puerto Ricans. Gonzalo, like the family in René *Marqués's *La carreta*, more than a decade later, ultimately returns to the mountains of Puerto Rico to forge a living in his natural surroundings.

Of the novels that followed, Laguerre's turning point in his evolution as a fiction writer occurred with *La resaca* (1949, The Undertow), which is his only historical novel, set in the nineteenth century and focusing on the total island panorama through the framework of the life of a social bandit, Dolorito Montoya; said framework led to the author's subtitle: "Bionovela." Through *La resaca* Laguerre seeks to examine the theme of oppression in the nineteenth century as a root cause of Puerto Rico's social and political problems in the twentieth century. He accomplishes this by reviewing the Spanish conquest of the Indians, the institution of slavery in Puerto Rico, the attitudes of the Spanish government toward education in Puerto Rico, the United States' occupation of the island, and so forth. On a societal level, oppressive patterns are repeated in the relationship of parents to children and men to women.

The title, "The Undertow," obviously refers to Puerto Rico being caught up in the undertow of history. Interwoven with the historical background, however, is the legendary nature of Dolorito's exploits as a social bandit championing the poor and oppressed, and the allusion to the Taíno myths of Yukiyú and Urayoán.

After *La resaca*, Laguerre's fiction followed another course, that of the diaspora. *La ceiba en el tiesto* (1956, The Ceiba Tree in the Flower Pot) and *El laberinto* (1959, *The Labyrinth*, 1960) both follow their protagonists to the United States and abroad, exploring the theme that Estelle Irizarry has called "The Wandering Puerto Rican" in her book, *Enrique A. Laguerre*. *El laberinto*, the more important of the two, develops the classical motif of the labyrinth in various important ways for the evolution of Puerto Rican narrative: New York as a labyrinth of prejudice and poverty, the psyche of the protagonist as an interior labyrinth into which he retreats, and, finally, the labyrinth of the fictional Republic of Santiago, a Latin American version of Hades where resides the *caudillo* Minotaur, Laguerre's version of the traditional dictator—in this case his real-life referent was the Dominican Republic's dictator, Trujillo. While Laguerre's novel takes on aspects of international intrigue with its assassination plot and the attack of the dictatorship, the work is still fundamentally a psychological study of a Puerto Rican who sacrifices himself for a cause common to the republics of the Caribbean.

It seems that Laguerre's trajectory as a novelist, like that of so many other Puerto Rican writers, led him ultimately to the question of identity. And toward the end of his career, he published two very different works that explored precisely that question: *Cause sin río* (1962, River Bed without a River) and *El fuego y su aire* (1970, Fire and Its Air). In the former, the life of the citified bourgeoisie in Puerto Rico is rejected by the protagonist seeking his true self and values. Laguerre concludes here that growth and progress for Puerto Rican culture must come out of continuity with tradition and that, obliquely, commonwealth status of the island—neither statehood nor independence—must be resolved. The later novel is one of self-discovery which expands on the protagonist's individual identity to embrace the collective and unite the past with the future. However positive the ending of the novel may be, the ardently written and technically complex novel about passion—thus, the reference to fire in the title—is one in which Laguerre's social and political commentary is most acerbic, especially as it relates to the government, prejudice, commercialism, exploitation of workers, and the other ills attendant to modern Puerto Rican society as dominated by the United States.

Laguerre's last novel, *Los amos benévolos* (1977, Benevolent Masters), clearly situates the author within the context of modern Latin American narrative and the literature of the fantastic, often called "magic realism." In *Los amos benévolos* Laguerre creates a mythic and magical island in the heart of the modern metropolis, which he allows to co-exist alongside his customarily realistic vision. Again in this, the last of his novels, Laguerre develops the theme of materialism and power versus human values. And as Estelle Irizarry has pointed out, to a great extent Laguerre has come full circle, returning to many of the concerns of his first novel, *La llamarada,* where the rural and the urban environments conflict, masters reduce the workers to slavery, the Puerto Ricans are alienated from their own land and culture.

Survey of Criticism

There is general unanimity among the critics as to the importance of Enrique A. Laguerre's contribution as a novelist. He is clearly the most prolific of the Puerto Rican novelists and the most sensitive interpreter of the evolution of Puerto Rican culture during this century. What he lacked in originality, he made up for as a storyteller: that talent, learned from his nineteenth-century models, for constructing realistic anecdotes that encompassed the breadth and depth of the nationality, its archetypes and myths, its problems and hopes for the future.

Despite it being his first novel, *La llamarada,* through its numerous editions, is still his most studied work. In the prologue to the second edition in 1937, Antonio A. Pedreira hailed it as the best novel written by a young Puerto Rican writer of his days; future critics, (Luis O. Zayas Micheli, for instance), were to consider it the most important novel since Zeno-Gandía's *La charca.* Other critics, among them Cesáreo Rosa-Nieves, have referred to the poetic style of *La llamarada* and subsequent books. And Francisco Manrique Cabrera, because of its poetic narration and its similarity in theme and structure to his two subsequent novels, considers *La llamarada* as part of a trilogy with *Solar Montoya* and *La resaca*. Most critics today also consider all three of these novels to fall within the tradition of Spanish American regionalist and nationalist literature.

The Laguerre novels that followed these three have continued to be praised and studied by the critics with an occasional mention of the overambitiousness of Laguerre's literary projects. Such is the case in Nilita Vientós Gastón's criticism of the breadth of scope in *La ceiba en el tiesto*.

Laguerre's severest critic has been Luz María Umpierre who concedes that Laguerre has been genial in his exposition of Puerto Rico's social and political problems but has been unable to provide solutions to them. While on the individual level his protagonists begin to resolve their alienation and identity crises by searching for their roots and those of their culture, on the social and national levels his novels just criticize the Establishment without really offering alternatives. She further considers Laguerre's true style to be rather conventional and, in opposition to Estelle Irizarry who praises Laguerre's adoption of the new narrative techniques of the Latin American boom authors, Umpierre states that Laguerre is a fish out of water in his later novels when experimenting with the new style. Despite all of these perceived faults, Umpierre concludes that she nevertheless admires Laguerre's passionate obssession in all of his novels with the question of Puerto Rican nationhood and social problems. To his last novel, she states, he has remained hopeful, if somewhat doubtful, for the future of Puerto Rico.

Bibliography

WORKS BY LAGUERRE

Novels

El 30 de febrero. Vida de un hombre interino. San Juan: Biblioteca de Autores Puertorriqueños, 1934.
La llamarada. Aguadilla, P.R.: Tipografía Fidel Ruiz, 1935.
Solar Montoya. San Juan: Imprenta Venezuela, 1941.
La resaca (Bionovela). San Juan: Biblioteca de Autores Puertorriqueños, 1949.
Los dedos de la mano. San Juan: Biblioteca de Autores Puertorriqueños, 1951.
La ceiba en el tiesto. San Juan: Biblioteca de Autores Puertorriqueños, 1956.
El laberinto. New York: Las Américas, 1959.
The Labyrinth. New York: Las Américas, 1960. Translation by William Rose.
Cauce sin río. Madrid: Nuevas Editoriales Unidas, 1962.
El fuego y su aire. Buenos Aires: Losada, 1970.
Los amos benévolos. Río Piedras: Universidad de Puerto Rico, Editorial Universitaria, 1977.

Complete Works (most recent edition)

Obras completas. San Juan: Instituto de Cultura Puertorriqueña, 1974.

Drama

La resentida. Barcelona: Ediciones Rumbos, 1960.

Essay

Pulso de Puerto Rico, 1952–1954. San Juan: Biblioteca de Autores Puertorriqueños, 1956.
El jíbaro de Puerto Rico: Símbolo y figura, with Esther M. Melón. Sharon, Conn.: Troutman Press, 1968.
La poesía modernista en Puerto Rico. San Juan: Editorial Coquí, 1969.
Polos de la cultura iberoamericana. Boston: Florentia Publishers, 1977.

Short Stories

"El Enemigo" and "Naufragio." In Concha Meléndez, *El arte del cuento en Puerto Rico*. New York: Las Américas, 1961.
"Pacholí" and "Raíces." In Laguerre and Melón, *El jíbaro de Puerto Rico*.

WORKS ABOUT LAGUERRE

Books

Beauchamp, José Juan. *Imagen del puertorriqueño en la novela (En Alejandro Tapia y Rivera, Manuel Zeno-Gandía y Enrique A. Laguerre)*. Río Piedras: Editorial Universitaria, Universidad de Puerto Rico, 1976.
Casanova Sánchez, Olga. *La crítica social en la obra novelística de Enrique A. Laguerre*. Río Piedras: Editorial Cultural, 1975.
García Cabrera, Manuel. *Laguerre y sus polos de la cultura iberoamericana*. San Juan: Biblioteca de Autores Puertorriqueños, 1978.
Irizarry, Estelle. *Enrique A. Laguerre*. Boston: Twayne, 1982.
Rosa-Nieves, Cesáreo. *Cañas al sol en "La Llamarada."* Humacao: Tipografía Comercial, 1938.
Umpierre, Luz María. *Ideología y novela en Puerto Rico. Un estudio de la narrativa de Zeno, Laguerre y Soto*. Madrid: Playor, 1983.
Zayas Micheli, Luis O. *Lo universal en Enrique A. Laguerre (Estudio y conjunto de su obra)*. Río Piedras: Editorial Edil, 1974.

Articles

Cabrera, Francisco Manrique. "Notas sobre la novela puertorriqueña de los últimos 55 años." *Asomante* (San Juan) 2 (1955): 24–28.
Campos, Jorge. "Amor a la tierra, y crítica social. Una novela de Enrique A. Laguerre." *Insula* (September 1962): 11.
González, José Emilio. "El laberinto." *Asomante* 16 (1960): 70–76.
———. *"Cauce sin río."* *Asomante* 19 (1963): 63–66.
Martínez Capó, Juan. "La escena literaria; Enrique A. Laguerre: 'El fuego y su aire.' " *Puerto Rico Ilustrado* (supplement of *El Mundo*), August 15, 1961: 18.
Martínez Nadal, Ernesto. "Consideraciones sobre la novela 'Cauce sin río' de Enrique A. Laguerre." *Revista del Instituto de Cultura Puertorriqueña* 7 (January-March 1964): 11–14.
Pedreira, Antonio A. "Prólogo a la segunda edición" of *La Llamarada*. 19th ed. Barcelona: Ediciones Rumbos, 1968.
Rivera de Alvarez, Josefina. *Diccionario de la literatura puertorriqueña* (October-December 1967): 8–10.

Vientós Gastón, Nilita. "La novela de Laguerre *La ceiba en el tiesto.*" *Indice cultural*,
   vol. 50. Río Piedras: Ediciones de la Universidad de Puerto Rico, 1962.
                                                                     NICOLÁS KANELLOS

LAVIERA, TATO (1950–   ). Tato Laviera is a noted New York-based Puerto
Rican poet, dramatist, musician, songwriter, producer, performer, and community worker. He represents a most felicitous example of the "Nuyorican"
school of writing.

Biography

Tato Laviera was born in Santurce, Puerto Rico, on September 5, 1950. His
family migrated to New York where Tato arrived on July 2, 1960. He grew up
in the Lower East Side, a densely populated, severely disadvantaged area that
did, however, like most ghettos, function as a repository of the traditional values
cherished by the respective immigrant group. His serving as an altar boy in the
Catholic church proved an important source of pride and emotional stability to
him at a time when his outlook on life was grim and his English, the language
of the dominant society, was virtually nonexistent.

   Against great odds, Laviera completed high school and received his diploma
in 1968. He has no further academic training. His remarkable practical experience
in the streets of the Lower East Side, where he came into contact with other
ethnic groups, and his highly developed ethic code pushed him into community
work and teaching, activities that he is keeping up to this day and most of which
he does on a voluntary basis.

   From 1970 to 1980 he was assistant director of the Association of Community
Services and for five years he was its executive director. For fourteen years Tato
Laviera held the chairmanship of the board of directors of "Madison Neighbors
in Action" and served as a member on the board of directors for the "Mobili-
zation for Youth, Inc." His gift as a writer was put to work for many cultural
and social agencies and organizations such as the "Jamaica Arts Center," the
"Puerto Rican Family Institute," and "United Bronx Parents, Inc.," the last
two since 1980.

   His activities as a producer include the 16th Annual Puerto Rican Parade of
Chicago, the First and Second Annual Latino Book Fair and Writers Festival
held in Chicago and Houston. He has been interviewed by and has recited for
television stations such as WNBC in New York City and WNBC-KPRC in
Houston, Texas. For Channel 13 in New York City he authored a film on
spiritualism, *Espiritismo,* in 1973. In 1984 he became the director of the Hispanic
Drama Workshop of the Henry Street Settlement New Federal Theater, after
having been named commissioned playwright by the same establishment one
year earlier. For four years he was artistic producer on a voluntary basis for the
Lower East Side's Teatro 4.

Tato Laviera has chaired a host of conferences and club activities. He has lectured and recited his work with consistent success in and outside New York City. President Carter invited Tato Laviera for a reading at the White House on January 3, 1980, as one of the poets honored with his gathering of American poets.

Major Themes

Already in Tato Laviera's first volume of poetry, *La Carreta Made a U-Turn* (1979), surfaces the author's remarkable skill in portraying an exile's existence in the Lower East Side and yet making a home of it. The title refers to René *Marqués's classic play, *La carreta* (1953), which dealt with the collective drama of Puerto Rican migration to the mainland. In Marqués's play, there was a return to the mythified soil of a rural Puerto Rico. Laviera's title ironically points to the large group of New York's Puerto Ricans, who represent one facet of a multicultural, multiracial society within the United States.

Laviera is a bilingual poet who is capable of giving both worlds, as well as the one that is in the making in New York, their due. His work is refreshing and important also in the sense that despite his keen eye for the suffering, for poverty and alienation, he presents us with a people who are on the whole surviving by amalgamating Spanish and Afro-Caribbean traditions with traits of the dominant society. His vision becomes increasingly optimistic, but he is never naive—he has seen and heard too much.

La Carreta Made a U-Turn is subdivided into three sections, "Metropolis Dreams," "Loisaida Streets: Latinas Sing," and "El Arrabal: Nuevo Rumbón" (The Ghetto: New Directions). Scenes from the barrio dominate all three, with occasional deviations to San Juan, Puerto Rico ("something i heard" and "against muñoz pamphleteering") or the area of Loíza ("savorings, from piñones to loíza").

The feeling of having been sent to the mainland unprepared, of having been duped, of living between at least two cultures is vented in "against muñoz pamphleteering" : "inside my ghetto i learned to understand / your short range visions of where you led us, / across the oceans where i talk about myself / in foreign languages, across where i reach / to lament finding myself re-seasoning my / coffee beans. Your sense of / stars landed me in a / north temperate uprooted zone."

He is criticizing alienation that is pacified and fostered by *tele-novelas,* serialized soap operas, for example, with "the song of an oppressor." Laviera addresses the cultural dilemma, of which the language issue is the most obvious, in his much-quoted poem "my graduation speech" : "hablo lo inglés matao / hablo lo español matao / no sé leer ninguno bien / so it is, spanglish to matao / what i digo / !ay, virgen, yo no sé hablar!" (I speak bad English / I speak bad Spanish / I can't read either well / so it is / Bad Spanglish / What I say / Oh, God / I don't know how to talk!). It goes without saying that the lament has to be read with a touch of subversive irony.

One of the consistent traits the reader finds in Laviera's work is that of an affirmation of individual and collective identity. Whereas section two of the volume gave voice to female figures, part three displays Tato Laviera's African and Afro-Caribbean roots as an essential ingredient for Puerto Rican identity. The quasi-magic vitality and healing power of music, of rhythm, of percussion instruments, such as congas, surfaces in poems like "the new rumbón" : "congas congas / tecata's milk gets warmed / broken veins leave misery / hypodermic needles melt / from the voodoo curse / of the conga madness / the congas clean the gasses / in the air, the congas burn out / everything not natural to our people."

African rhythms as an element that links all of the Caribbean islands with each other and with New York City are praised and, along with a racial joke, are seen as proof of the poet's race and the people's indestructible power such as in "the africa in pedro morejón." The importance of music for Laviera the musician and poet is evident in successful poems like "canción para un parrandero" (Song for a Party Lover) and "la música jíbara" (Jíbaro Music). Music and song are also ties that Laviera's works share with oral traditions, oral poetry, in which the performance element is highly relevant. That he knows his *Palés Matos, the author of *Tuntún de pasa y grifería* (1937), and loves *bombas* and *plenas* is clear in poems like "savorings, from piñones to loíza," "el moreno puertorriqueño (a three-way warning poem)," and "tumbao (for eddie conde)." We find Laviera's affinity for the stage, the poem as drama, in his highly effective poem on spiritualism, "santa bárbara," and his somewhat sentimental extended "coreografía" poems of the same book.

Two years after his first volume of poetry he published *Enclave,* a collection in which the tendency of the writer to function as a commentator, as a repository of things Nuyorican, as a teller of anecdotes and stories, and as a dramatist in poetic forms is reinforced. It is only consistent that the long poem "jesús papote," the story of a Lower East Side Puerto Rican Christ child, was turned into a play. Again, the book is structured by its division into three sections, "Feelings of One," "Oro in Gold," and "Prendas." Again, he handles everyday speech, monologue, and dialogue brilliantly, as in his portrait of "juana bochisme" and in "serious dude." His account of the ritual that goes with the bolita game, the illegal numbers game, and of the thwarted hopes of a bolita player in the South Bronx, as given in "bolita folktale," is more revealing than many sociological treatises.

As in *La Carreta Made a U-Turn,* the second section is dominated by poems either addressed to women or poems having a feminine persona. There is a deliciously sensual Afro-Caribbean love poem, "just before the kiss," which ends with the incantatory plea: "bésame, / to taste your / cinnamon / powdered / tongue."

In "penetration," he juxtaposes Julia de *Burgos, Puerto Rico's great female poet who died miserably in the streets of New York City, and the New York Puerto Rican poet Sandra María *Esteves (who included a poem on and for Julia de Burgos, "A Julia y a Mí," in her selection for *Womanrise,* 1978). With

"Prendas," the last section, the poet's gift to hold on to captivating verbal and behavioral essentials (and facades) reigns supreme. In "vaya carnal" he tackles Chicano linguistic patterns that must have amused him greatly. His admiration for the near-blind Cuban ballet dancer Alicia Alonso, for the South African singer Mirima Makeba, and for the slain ex-Beatle John Lennon, all occasioned poems. Glowing tributes to the Puerto Rican musician Rafael Cortijo and the black Puerto Rican actor and recitator Juan Boria take Laviera into the core of collective Puerto Rican identity and familiar territory. *Enclave* contains an unabashed "homenaje a don luis palés matos" (Homage to Luis Palés Matos), which in typical Laviera manner clarifies, tongue in cheek, a point he wants to make: that Palés Matos must have had black blood. With an emphatic, rhythmically catching statement on "bomba, para siempre," *Enclave* ends. The (song-) writer Laviera sees *la bomba* as his cultural musical base, as a permanent part of Puerto Rican identity, as a celebration of Puerto Rican dignity and pride.

Tato Laviera's third volume of poetry, called *AmeRícan,* was published by Arte Publico Press in 1986 and in 1988 Arte Publico published his fourth, *Mainstream Ethics.* Of his dramas, only one, "Olu Clemente," which he coauthored with Miguel *Algarín, is in print; it appeared in the winter issue, 1979 of *Revista Chicano-Riqueña.*

The poems that are collected in *AmeRícan* were acted out and presented as a drama at Teatro 4 on March 4, 1984. "La Chefa" (The Boss) was given at the Henry Street Settlement New Federal Theater at the end of February 1982. His musical "Here We Come," which was included in the New York Shakespeare Festival in the summer of 1982, was also shown at the Public Theater in the same year. "Piñones," another musical, was produced by Miguel Algarín in his Nuyorican Poets Café in May 1979 and later that year saw twelve productions at the Public Theater and in New York City. In 1980 it was taken to Chicago by the Eleventh Street Theater and to Washington, D.C., for productions at the Shoreham Hotel. Laviera's latest drama, "Becoming García," which was commissioned by the New Federal Theater for the winter season of 1984, shows this writer's continued interest in the dramatic form.

Survey of Criticism

Tato Laviera's work has so far received little critical attention. Efraín Barradas discusses him in "Puerto Rico acá, Puerto Rico allá" (1980). There Laviera's poetry serves as part of Barradas's argument that Puerto Rico is an oppressed, colonized Latin American Caribbean country, that the Puerto Rican nation is a divided one, and that despite many efforts from the colonizer, a Puerto Rican national and cultural identity exists and remains a permanent force. Barradas also refers to Laviera in his anthology *Herejes y mitificadores* (1980), again in the context of a defense of the Spanish language and the Caribbean cultural base of Puerto Ricans living in the United States. A similar, if wider, approach to the same issue of ethnic and/or national resistance of mainland Puerto Ricans versus acculturation is used in J. Flores, J. Attinasi, and P. Pedraza, Jr., *"La*

Carreta Made a U-Turn: Puerto Rican Language and Culture in the United States'' (1981). Eugene V. Mohr stresses in a few brief passages the importance of Afro-Caribbean music and bilingualism in Laviera's poetry (1982). Wolfgang Binder discusses Laviera's Afro-Caribbean identity in a survey article on the Puerto Rican cultural presence in the United States (1980).

La Carreta Made a U-Turn is the only work by Laviera that has had reviews in scholarly magazines. All three reviewers, Wolfgang Binder, Gerard R. Clarke, and Raymond Varisco, rendered favorable accounts. The introduction to *La Carreta Made a U- Turn* by Nicolás Kanellos, the then editor of *Revista Chicano-Riqueña,* and Juan Flores's "Keys to Tato Laviera," which serves as a preface to *Enclave,* are brief, concise, and enthusiastic comments that put Laviera in a sociocultural and poetic context. Wolfgang Binder's introductory remarks to *AmeRícan,* "Celebrating Life: The Nuyorican Poet Tato Laviera," currently in print, attempts to do the same.

Bibliography

WORKS BY LAVIERA

La Carreta Made a U-Turn. Gary, Indiana: Arte Publico Press, 1979.
Enclave. Houston: Arte Publico Press, 1981.
AmeRícan. Houston: Arte Publico, 1986.
Mainstream Ethics. Houston: Arte Publico Press, 1988.

WORKS ABOUT LAVIERA

Barradas, Efraín. "Puerto Rico acá, Puerto Rico allá." *Revista Chicano-Riqueña* 7 (Spring 1980): 43–49.
———. Introduction to *Herejes y mitificadores: muestra de poesía puertorriqueña en los Estados Unidos,* eds. Efraín Barradas and Rafeal Rodríguez. Río Piedras, P.R.: Huracán, 1980.
Binder, Wolfgang. Review of *La Carreta Made a U-Turn. Explorations in Ethnic Studies* 3 (July 1980): 60–62.
———. "Die Nordwanderung der Puertoricaner und ihre Literatur." In B. Ostendorf, *Amerika-Gottoliteratur.* Impulse der Forschung Vol. 42. Darmstatt: Wissenschaftliche Buchgesellschaft, 1983.
Clarke, Gerard R. Review of *La Carreta Made a U-Turn. Melus* 8 (Spring 1981): 81–83.
Flores, Juan, John Attinasi, and Pedro Pedraza, Jr. *"La Carreta Made a U-Turn:* Puerto Rican Language and Culture in the United States." *Daedalus* 110 (Spring 1981): 193–218.
Mohr, Eugene V. *The Nuyorican Experience: Literature of the Puerto Rican Minority.* Westport, Conn.: Greenwood Press, 1982.
Varisco, Raymond. Review of *La Carreta Made a U-Turn. Review/Revista Interamericana* 9 (Winter 1978/1980): 639–640.

WOLFGANG BINDER

LLORÉNS TORRES, LUIS (1878–1944). Luis Lloréns Torres, despite his emergence as a poet during the last decade of the nineteenth century, contributed in an outstanding way to Puerto Rico and Latin America as a poet. Although there were a few who attempted to copy his pancalist and panedist aesthetic theories in poetry, his philosophical thinking resulted in the elaboration of a unique style. His works placed him in an important position among those who have re-created the beauty and substance of the Spanish language, a language whose different levels he knew how to explore. Thus, it has been inevitable for the many historians and anthologists of Latin American and Puerto Rican literature to include his name. Lloréns Torres's most important works are *Al pie de la Alhambra, Visiones de mi Musa, Sonetos Sinfónicos,* and the historical essays *América, Decimario Criollo,* and *Alturas de América.* Because of the nativist flavor, Lloréns Torres came to be known as "The Poet of Puerto Rico."

Biography

Born in Juana Díaz, Puerto Rico, in 1878, Luis Lloréns Torres spent part of his youth in Spain where he studied law at the universities of Barcelona and Granada. There he began his career as poet with the collection entitled *Al pie de la Alhambra* (1899, At the Foot of the Alhambra). At that time he became familiar with Karl Christian Krause's philosophy through the works of Sans del Río and Giner de los Ríos. This, according to Hernández Aquino, gave origin to Lloréns Torres's later aesthetic theories of pancalism and panedism.

As an eloquent lawyer-to-be, Lloréns Torres won his first case by a play on words rather than by basing his defense of his client on the Peninsular code. He managed to convince the judge, by twisting the letters of "atacar" (to attack) into "acatar" (to obey), that the accused fellow student who had participated in a revolt intended to obey instead of face the police. The judge, admiring his ability to manipulate the language, advised Lloréns Torres to go and tell his professors that he was "already a lawyer, said and done."

Upon his return to Puerto Rico, he found his country a colony of the United States and, turning to politics, supported the ideals of José de Diego, Luis Muñoz Rivera, and Rosendo Matienzo Cintrón, who all desired independence for Puerto Rico. He served as congressman for some time; however he did not have great ambition for high political positions. Nevertheless, he always defended his nationalist ideals as a great patriot.

Luis Lloréns Torres was a friend of the many young poets who were in search of their affirmation within the new modernist currents. Luis *Palés Matos was one in this generation and in whom Lloréns showed great interest. These were the years of the famous *Revista de las Antillas* (Antilles Journal), one of the most important literary organs not only in Puerto Rico but also in the rest of Latin America. In it Lloréns Torres, founder and director, published works that eventually made him well known as one of the great poets of the Spanish language. Renowned poets such as José Santos Chocano of Perú and Rubén Darío of Nicaragua, among other great literary figures of the Hispanic world, saw their works published in this journal.

Other literary journals of the Island in which Lloréns Torres published and collaborated with articles and poetry include: *Puerto Rico Ilustrado* (Puerto Rico Illustrated), *Revista Bayoán* (Bayoan Magazine), *Semanario Juan Bobo* (The Juan Bobo Weekly), *El idearium* (The Ideaforum), and the newspapers *El Imparcial, La Correspondencia,* and the U.S. *Saturday Evening Post.*

It has been said by some who knew him personally that in the literary circles, or "peñas," his distinctive voice caught the audience's attention while reading his own poetry.

Luis Lloréns Torres died in New York in 1944 at the age of seventy-six. Still, almost half a century after his death, he, the best-known poet of Puerto Rico, lives on in the memory of his people, mainly in the memory of his "jíbaros." As Palés Matos's poem remarks, Lloréns Torres, author of so many popular "décimas," will always enjoy the eternal homage from a peasant. And the peasant referred to by Luis Palés Matos is the "jíbara in love who will sing one of your couplets, without remembering who you were. In so doing, she will sweeten her life, while anonymously honoring your name."

Major Themes

Lloréns Torres's poetry is multicolored, rich in language expressions, combining the popular tradition with the academic styles in poetry. For this poet-writer, the historical, heroic, and the humanistic are very significant topics. Works of this nature are: *América: estudios históricos y filológicos* (1898, America: Historical and Philological Essays); *El Grito de Lares* (1914, The Lares Proclamation), a drama in verse and prose; *La Canción de las Antillas y otros poemas* (1929, The Song of the Antilles and Other Poems); besides other works published widely in literary journals and newspapers until 1940.

Some of his themes made of him a type of minstrel of his Puerto Rican people, an interpreter of different traditional Latin American values, a voice of the people's spiritual values. He was a singer of love as personified by women, mainly the Puerto Rican woman. At times, love for him was expressed in a sensual and erotic manner. The Antilles, for instance, appeared before his eyes as sensual, beautiful women. Even his own inspiration, or "Musa," takes the form of an erotic female in the poet's soul: "And violently I grab you by the hair, and knock you down and . . . under me."

In his *Criollo,* the poet is quite sensual in regard to his love for the "jíbara campesina," or Puerto Rican peasant woman, and among the most beautiful examples are: "Madrugada," "La hija del viejo Pancho," and "¡Ay, qué lindo es mi bohío!" in which he says:

How wonderful is not knowing
of letters, of astronomy,
but more wonderful is when my woman
lets herself be loved . . . !

The strong ideal of independence as a patriotic theme in Lloréns Torres is quite a constant in his poetry. But it is already present in his *El Grito de Lares,* in which he exalted the historical insurrection of 1867 in Lares, Puerto Rico. In this play the characters like Manuel el Leñero are glorified. His poems of deep patriotism and desire of freedom for his country are: "Rapsodia criolla," "El patito feo," and others. In "El patito feo," Puerto Rico is personified by the Danish writer Hans Christian Andersen's *The Ugly Duckling*. However, his poems of political or patriotic theme cannot be considered as the work of a pamphleteer as may be found among other contemporary Latin American poets.

The black theme in Puerto Rico has its predecessors who did not elaborate it to the point that Luis Palés Matos did during the postmodernist movement called Diepalism and in his subsequent works. Nevertheless, Luis Lloréns Torres also cultivated this theme. There are two poems belonging to the collection *Sonetos Sinfónicos* (1914, Symphonic Sonnets) that present the theme so majestically that it makes one place the poet as a real representative of the subject in Puerto Rican literature of the twentieth century.

The poet's attachment to his homeland encouraged him to dedicate some of his most celebrated poems to the Puerto Rican "jibaría," or men of the mountains of the Island. As a nativist poet, he exalted the "jíbaro" theme, keeping in mind that it is the peasant who has most deeply preserved the Spanish heritage of the country's culture. His most representative poems of this theme are "Mayagüez sabe a mangó," "La campesina," and "Valle de Collores," one of his most well known compositions, in which he describes his departure, while riding a mare, from his beloved village of Collores.

The epic and heroic are found in marvelous poems like "Velas épicas" and the magnificent "Soneto a Bolívar." The latter has been the most anthologized work of this poet.

It could be stated that Lloréns Torres's two aesthetic theories, pancalism and panedism, were also constant themes that permeated his creative writing almost from its first stages to the later works of the poet. Pancalism (*pan*, "all" ; *kalos*, "beauty")) and panedism (*pan* and *edus*, "poetry")), both derived from the Greek, signified his poetic ideals that everything in the work of art is beauty and poetry. He supported his two aesthetic theories with a pantheistic principle.

In relation to the meaning of Beauty, in *Voces de la Campana Mayor* Lloréns Torres claimed:

The notion of what is beautiful is the highest notion that caresses the mind. Beauty is the only rational path to reach God. . . . Beauty is the interpenetration between the flesh and spirit of things.

From the atom up, every being is a compound of soul and body, spirit and flesh. Except that the soul of things does not live in them, but in us, in the vision we have of them.

Stressing the true meaning of Poetry, the poet explained:

However, I continue to insist that the poet must not enclose himself in the cages of technicality; he does not need to know anything of rhythms or metric syllables, but instead, he must follow instinctively the concentration on the musicality of ideas, and give to them adequate meter and rhythm. . . .

Regarding words, . . . the most noble and beautiful will no longer be the most classic or used or aristocratic, but rather the one that would represent the idea or sentiment most simply, precisely and energetically; . . . and a word, alone, revealing word . . . sometimes hurts us and tells us more than that most refined and academic expression.

But it was at the time of his *Al pie de la Alhambra* when the poet showed his concern for aesthetic theories at the service of poetry:

This ideal world, or world of the imagination, however you might call it, is equal to the real world. It is the same real but a perfected world embellished by the beauty of poetry. . . . In one word, the ideal is an equal and superior to the real world that exists only in the artist's imagination. Thus, the goal to be reached by the artist and the poet consists of the presentation in a sensitive manner of scenes and landscapes of the ideal world. . . . The ideal world, existing in every poet's imagination, may be more or less beautiful, but is always superior to the real one. It is at this point, then, and in the different ways to make of beauty a sensitive thing, that we know whether poets are more or less good.

The pancalist theory of Lloréns Torres finds affinity with the Harvard professor James Mark Baldwin who said in his *Genetic Theory of Reality:*

In this sense Pancalism is a constructive affectivism. It shows the way by which feelings may be informed, not remaining blind, but seeing all things *sub especie pulchritudinis.*

We reach an interpretation which finds the aesthetic experience, with all its larger connotation as determining the sphere of art and revealing the quality of Beauty, such a reconstitution of the various reals in a synthesis of realization. To this interpretation we have given the name of Pancalism.

Many have suggested that Lloréns Torres's panedism is like Whitman's free verse, but one has to keep in mind that the same Lloréns Torres indicated that both Whitman as well as Darío opened the road to panedism ingeniously, thus affirming that his panedism was not the same thing as the French free verse. For him, the greatest elegance in language is not knowing of prosody and syntax. In *Sonetos Sinfónicos* he said: "Make rhyme of prose, and you will find the creation of the poetry of the future."

Panedism and pancalism, then, served as the artistic vehicle by which Lloréns Torres instilled the spirituality of the ideal beauty that he so avidly searched for in all his writing. These aesthetic theories were defended by the poet in works such as *Visiones de mi Musa* (1913–1915, Visions of My Muse) and *Sonetos Sinfónicos* and still were manifest in his *Alturas de América.*

His works also expose a personal utopia dream as well as a collective desire for the paradisiacal in the past and future. There is in his poetry a yearning for purity, hope, nostalgia, and the dreams with which he expected to solve all of the aesthetic conflicts.

The folklore, geography, and local urban and rural scenes are themes treated with enthusiastic veneration by Lloréns Torres. And finally, his Island, as his native soil and a colony of the United States, recurs constantly as a patriotic subject for many of his poetic compositions. These themes intermingle characters, the "jíbaros" or peasants, for instance, characteristics, and values derived from the Hispanic cultural heritage in his creative writings, all of which have elevated him to the pedestal of an ever-recognized bard of the Puerto Rican people.

Survey of Criticism

Francisco Manrique Cabrera, in *Historia de la literatura puertorriqueña*, explains that Lloréns Torres's *Al pie de la Alhambra* "as a whole does not offer many innovations, however, it is discreetly fresh." Furthermore, he seems to agree with Enrique A. *Laguerre regarding the poet's second stage. Between the years 1911–1913, he had become a complete modernist, in which he exhibits a metaphoric audacity. Max Henriquez Ureña in *Breve historia del modernismo* also refers to Lloréns Torres as a representative of modernism.

Juan García Ducos, in the prologue to *Voces de la Campana Mayor*, commented that this collection "is not the strongest or most definitive work of the poet. . . . In or outside the Antilles, his ethnic poems, philosophical poems and great 'Décimas' of nativist flavor are without a doubt the ones which have earned for him the most glory and admiration."

María Teresa Babín describes Lloréns Torres's poetic contribution as:

poetry elaborated with "the most absolute and valiant sincerity." It represents in the Puerto Rican soil that which has lasting value in art: independence, character, courage and poetic beauty, without stylistic concern regarding literary schools or modalities. . . . There are prosaic intervals as well as lyrical heights, unforgettable images, psychological intuitive captions and observant penetrations praised by all who have known his poetry. After Gautier Benítez, Lloréns has been the other Puerto Rican poet who, without coming down from the pedestal of learned lyricism, knew how to capture his people's love for poetry. The people, in turn, applaud him in gratitude.

Among the most authorized critics of Luis Lloréns Torres, Juan García Ducos has summed up the value of this poet's work: "Above all, Lloréns Torres stands out because of the vigorous way of thinking which permeates all his writing, both prose and poetry. Regarding this matter, there is no other who surpasses him in the Spanish language. Moreover, he is the most individual and original poet of all. His poetry is his own, absolutely his and unique in Hispanic literature."

Bibliography

WORKS BY LLORÉNS TORRES

América: estudios históricos y filológicos. Madrid: 1898.
Al pie de la Alhambra. Granada, España: Tipografía Viuda e Hijos de Sabatel, 1899.
Sonetos sinfónicos. San Juan, Puerto Rico: Compañía Editorial Antillana, 1913–1915.
Visiones de mi musa. Revista de las Antillas. San Juan, Puerto Rico, 1913–1915.
El Grito de Lares. San Juan, Puerto Rico: Editorial Cordillera, 1967.
La canción de las Antillas y otros poemas. San Juan, Puerto Rico: Negociado de Materiales, 1929.
Voces de la Campana Mayor. 1st ed. Río Piedras, Puerto Rico: Editorial Cultural, 1935. Prologue by Juan García Ducos to the first and second editions.
Alturas de América. Río Piedras, Puerto Rico: Editorial Cordillera, 1940.

WORKS ABOUT LLORÉNS TORRES

In passing.
Babín, María Teresa. *Panorama de la cultura puertorriqueña*. New York: Las Américas Publishing Co., 1958.
Cabrera, Francisco Manrique. *Historia de la literatura puertorriqueña*. Río Piedras, Puerto Rico: Editorial Cultural, 1965.
Díaz Quiñones, Arcadio. "La Isla Afortunada: Sueños Libertadores y Utópicos de Luis Lloréns Torres." *Sin Nombre* 6, 1 (julio-septiembre 1975): 5–19.
García Ducos, Juan. Prólogo *Voces de la Campana Mayor*. Río Piedras, Puerto Rico: Editorial Cultural, 19–35.
Hernández Aquino, Luis. *Nuestra aventura literaria*, San Juan, P.R.: Editorial Universitaria, 1976.
Laguerre, Enrique A. *La poesía modernista en Puerto Rico*. San Juan, P.R.: Editorial Coquí, 1969.
Lloréns, Washington. "El Humorismo, El Epigrama y la Sátira en la Literatura Puertorriqueña." *Literatura puertorriqueña: 21 conferencias*, Instituto de Cultura Puertorriqueña, San Juan, Puerto Rico, 1969.
Onís, Federico de. *Antología de la poesía española e hispanoamericana*. New York: Las Americas Publishing Company, 1961.
Ramos Mimoso, Adriana. "El Modernismo en la Lírica Puertorriqueña." *Literatura puertorriqueña: 21 conferencias*, Instituto de Cultura Puertorriqueña, San Juan, Puerto Rico, 1969.
Rosa-Nieves, Cesáreo. *La lámpara del faro*. Vol. 1. San Juan, Puerto Rico: Editorial Club de la Prensa, 1957.
———. *La poesía en Puerto Rico*. 2d ed. San Juan, Puerto Rico: Editorial Campos, 1958.
———. *Aguinaldo lírico de la poesía puertorriqueña*. Vol. 2. 2d ed. Río Piedras, Puerto Rico: Editorial Edil Inc., 1971.
Ureña, Max H. *Breve historia del Modernismo*. 2d ed. México City: Fondo de Cultura Económica, 1962.

LUCY TORRES

M

MARGENAT, HUGO (1933–1957). In spite of his early death at the age of twenty-four, Hugo Margenat is considered as one of the most important contemporary Puerto Rican poets. His main book, *Mundo abierto* (1958, Open World), is one of the key works of contemporary Puerto Rican poetry because it initiates a new style and conception of militant poetry that will be prevalent during the following decades, above all within the very influential "Guajana" group whose social realism dominates the 1960s. But his poetry has also intrinsic values and more varied themes than what may be expected within social realism. It is intensely human and expresses existential and religious concerns that are essential in him. His style is innovative and combines surrealist and expressionist images with direct everyday language. In more ways than one, he is one of the founders of Puerto Rico's new poetry.

Biography

Margenat was born in San Juan, Puerto Rico, in 1933, at a time when the Nationalist party, under the leadership of Pedro Albizu Campos, had decisive influence in the Island. Albizu Campos struggled for full independence from the United States and reserved himself the right to use political violence against what he considered the illegal occupation of national territory by the United States. This resulted in violent confrontations between nationalist and government authorities and political repression increased. The economic crisis during these depression years was also part of the national scene and extreme poverty also resulted in violent confrontations, especially in the sugar cane fields.

In terms of literary history, the 1930s were the years when the new poetry advanced during the 1920s by brief avant-garde movements finally dominated with poets such as Julia de *Burgos, Juan Antonio *Corretjer, Francisco Manrique Cabrera, and Luis *Palés Matos. The search for national identity and a new flexible and daring lyrical expression were the main characteristics of literary production. They would be persistent during the following decades.

Hugo's father, Alfredo Margenat, has distinguished himself as a poet, journalist, and short-story writer. By 1928 he was an active member of the "atalayista" group, the most important and influential avant-garde movement during the 1920s. He was noted for his knowledge of contemporary French poetry, for his innovative verse and prose, and for the playful, but often also philosophical, tone of his writings. Social and patriotic themes are also present in his early lyrics. He must have been an important influence on his son's intellectual formation. His mother, María Cristina Mediavilla, was also very close to Hugo during his short life.

Hugo was raised in the urban milieu of San Juan and contrary to many other poets before him had no close ties with the rural world that dominated Puerto Rican literature up to the fifties. This urban perspective is present in his poetry and shared by many who came after him. He went to elementary school in San Juan and later to high school in Santurce's Escuela Superior Central, where he distinguished himself as a student and as a young writer. He felt the urge to educate himself and read extensively, combining social and political readings with works on literature, religion, and philosophy. According to his personal friend Ramón Felipe Medina, he read Marx when he was seventeen and during those same years was also very interested in oriental religions and became a fervent disciple of esoteric doctrines. He became a member of the Rosicrucian Order and visited frequently a theosofist temple. He was interested in all that went beyond human reason and penetrated within the realm of the mysterious, searching for the ultimate meaning of human existence. This metaphysical dimension is also very present in his poetry.

During the year 1952, while studying in high school, he founded with fellow students a literary society that published a student journal: "El Palacete." The journal appeared only twice, because of lack of funds, but in its second number Hugo published for the first time. His contributions were a love poem and the first part of an essay titled "El poeta y su creación" (The Poet and his Creation). In this essay poets are idealized as superior beings whose mission is to look into the depths of the universe and find the light that others fail to see. They are visionaries who search knowledge of the divine and the ideal and who should live in a spiritual sphere in order to find it. But the poet also identifies himself with all humanity. He feels the joys and sorrows of his fellow men and throughout history these "sublime dreamers" are found very active in times of crisis and renewal, in the middle of rebellions and struggles against injustice. They are guides, teachers, and soldiers in all those efforts that seek justice and progress. Both conceptions of the poet—as a spiritual visionary and as a social force against injustice—are present in all his poetry, although his first lyrics insist more on the personal, metaphysical dimensions and his later poems move toward social and political engagement.

The personal influence of the Nobel prize-winner, Spanish poet Juan Ramón Jiménez, who lived in Puerto Rico at the time seems to be important. Jiménez defended "pure" poetry and developed highly personal and metaphysical themes. Hugo visited the Spanish poet, gave him the manuscript of his first book, *Vibraciones de mar y tierra* (Vibrations from the Sea and the Earth), and asked for his opinion. Jiménez never answered his letters but published many of his poems in *Universidad*, a journal published by the University of Puerto Rico where he worked. *Vibraciones de mar y tierra* was never published, but *Lámpara apagada* (Extinguished Lamp) appeared in 1954. By this time Hugo had established friendship with older poets like José Emilio González and Laura Gallegos and with younger ones who were then university students, like Jorge Luis Morales, Violeta López Suria, and Anagilda Garrastegui.

Hugo looked forward to finishing high school in order to study at the University of Puerto Rico, but in January 1954 he had to interrupt his academic career in order to serve for two years in the U.S. Army. It wasn't a voluntary decision. He was drafted and considered resisting the draft. By that time, and after the Nationalist Revolt of 1950, he was strongly against North American rule in Puerto Rico and in favor of political independence for the Island. Besides, he considered himself a pacifist. But he finally accepted joining the army to please his mother.

But the two years of military life were harder than what he expected. Considering his personal convictions and his total disagreement with the political situation, this was a traumatic experience. He was stationed at two training camps: Tortuguero, in the northern coast, and Losey Field in the southern part of the Island. He frequently escaped without leave, and considered these two years totally wasted. Nevertheless, he decided to continue his studies and passed the high school equivalence test which would permit him to proceed toward university studies. He also started taking some basic courses at the Catholic University of Ponce, but it was very difficult to harmonize his military duties with his studies so he soon had to abandon them. Poetry was a consolation and he became prolific. In 1955 his second book, *Intemperie* (In the Open), appeared.

Finally, in August 1956, after his two long years in the army, Hugo started to study at the University of Puerto Rico in Río Piedras with great enthusiasm. His army years had marked him. Now he was more militant than ever in favor of Puerto Rican independence and more conscious of Puerto Rico's social, political, and economic problems. He was one of the founders of the "Federación Universitaria Pro Independencia" (Pro Independence University Federation), one of the most active and radical student organizations in the Island.

Besides being very active politically, he was also writing more than ever, as though he could foreshadow his near death. He died on April 7, 1957, only months after the doctors discovered his illness: a strange and acute type of meningitis. He left his best book, *Mundo abierto*, ready for publication and it appeared the following year. He also left abundant unpublished manuscripts, classified under various titles and dated as books: *Primeros poemas* (First Poems)

(1950), *Breves palabras de las horas prietas* (Brief Words of Dark Hours) (1952–1953), *Vibraciones de aire y tierra* (Vibrations of the Air and the Earth) (1953–1954). Some of these poems were gathered and published in 1961 with the title *Ventana hacia lo último* (Window toward the ultimate). In 1974 the Institute of Puerto Rican Culture published a volume with his complete works—poetry and prose—and a recording of his poems read by himself.

Major Themes

Although most of Hugo's poems were written during the last four years of his life, we can trace an evolution in his poetry. His first poems are a result of his metaphysical and religious vision of life. Existential anguish dominates these lyrics that are written in often obscure and highly symbolic style. From this type of poetry he moves toward a different vision of the poet as much more involved in everyday life, less introspective and more sensible to the plight of his fellow men. Although his initial concerns are not absent in these lyrics, they are fused into a more collective vision where political liberation from colonialism and social injustice are felt as general and personal themes.

His first book, *Lámpara apagada* (Extinguished Lamp), is really only a small pamphlet with eight poems. God, love, his tormented inner self, and poetry are his main themes. A pessimistic view of life as a painful effort to penetrate the somber condition of human existence is revealed. Surrealist, sometimes grotesque and fractured images are much present, together with obscure references. The poet is searching his way through darkness, suffering, and death. Only love, in his second poem "Eres muñeca a mis ojos" (You Are a Doll to My Eyes), seems to be a possible solution because of the possibility of sharing intimate pains and sorrows. But we can also see this booklet as the final result of a spiritual stage that has been painfully surmounted. His second book, *Intemperie* (In the Open), published only a year after, reveals a poet who has already crossed the dark tunnel to find the light of a more open and less egocentric view of life. Thirty-seven poems are included in this book where themes are more concretely presented with a poetical language that has moved away from the abstractions of his first book.

In *Intemperie,* as the title suggests, he opens himself to others and to God. In this unsheltered existential condition he finds a kind of liberation. The optimistic tone of the first poems reveals that the poet has found his way. In "Poética viva" (Living Poetics) he projects and exalts this new identification with the external world, because his poetry "se aburre de soledad" (is bored of solitude). Solidarity becomes a key word; solidarity with nature, God, women, and fellow men. God is conceived not as a remote being, but as a personal companion. In his second poem he announces joyfully "Yo y Dios, hemos vuelto" (Me and God, we have returned). And they have come back to Lares and Jayuya, scenes of political revolt against colonialism, and to the workers' callused hands, to open the closed circle and recite the last nocturnal verse.

But love is the main theme of *Intemperie* and the poems are organized in such a way that they trace a story: from the joyous celebration of love and woman, to the agony and loneliness of lost love. The loved woman is painfully present in his memory, not only as a spiritual being, but also as a body that still awakes erotic desires. Erotism is expressed, but also veiled by original metaphorical language which gives these poems romantic and surrealistic qualities. Neruda, Vallejo, and Lorca are present as important influences, but Hugo has found a much more mature, personal expression.

Mundo abierto is not only a culmination of his poetry, but also a total and coherent synthesis. It is a carefully structured book where the poet departs from his personal experience of love to expand his view until it embraces the world and ascends to God. The main themes are love, patriotism, and God; but Margenat approaches each one of these traditional themes in Puerto Rican poetry from a new and personal perspective.

Love occupies most of the book, but it appears as a traumatic and frankly erotic experience, a problematic communion of bodies and souls. The most extensive part, "Erosavia" (a neologism created by the poet from the words that mean "Eros" and "sap"), expresses the alternate ups and downs of the intimate experience of love: fulfillment, loneliness, absence, reconciliation, inner struggles, disillusions, erotic impulse.

"La Patria," the native land, is also seen in a different way. The picturesque painting of its natural scenery is totally absent. For Hugo "La Patria" is above all his fellow countrymen and with them he establishes a dramatic dialogue. He denounces painful Puerto Rican realities of misery, social injustice, and exploitation and ascribes them to Puerto Rico's colonial status. He reproaches his fellow countryman for his passive acceptance of this situation. He remembers for him his history, his past heroes, and martyrs, and incites him to rebel. In poems like "El hoy" (The Today) and "Eslabones" (Links) he anticipates the style of new militant poetry: crude language, direct expression, brisk and energetic tone, a focus on concrete reality. Poetry becomes a weapon used to advance revolution.

The third main theme is God and the poet's relation with Him. Hugo's religious faith is vacillating, "agónica," to use Unamuno's term; but it finally prevails against personal doubts. God is for him, above all, love and life, a being who unites opposed elements, who is present in everyday life. He is the God of justice that aligns himself with the poor and the worker, that takes his stand against social and political injustice. He is a proletarian God that "corta sábanas, trae carbón,/ destruye praderas, levanta barricadas,/ y conmueve a la masa de pétalos,/ llama a la revolución mundial" (cuts sheets, brings coal,/ destroys prairies, builds barricades,/ and stirs the mass of petals,/ calls for world revolution). God is also related to poetry; he is inside the poet, making him say his word. In poems like "La mirada certera" (The Well-Aimed Look), where the poet expresses his desire to be united with the mystery of his divine essence, he points toward mystical heights.

In *Mundo abierto* Hugo reaches his peak as a poet, although if he had lived longer he might have produced even better poems. *Ventana hacia lo último,* published in 1961, after his death, is a collection of twenty-two additional poems very similar to the ones in *Intemperie* and *Mundo abierto.* He also wrote some essays and short stories, but they are not as important as his lyrics.

Survey of Criticism

Although Hugo's importance is generally recognized, there is surprisingly very little critical literature concerning him. This can be explained by the fact that his image as a young talented poet who died early became, in a certain way, more important than his poetry. He became a myth and a symbol. During the 1950s and early 1960s what we generally find are brief notes and reviews of his books which appeared mainly in newspapers. One of his first critics was his friend Ramón Felipe Medina, an important poet himself, who wrote a note about *Lámpara apagada* and who has been the most consistent in studying and writing about him. Other notes were written by Wilfredo Braschi, Juan Antonio *Corretjer, Juan Diez de Audino, Adelaida Lugo Suárez, and Gloria M. Paniagua. After his death, there appeared many biographical sketches and lyrical portraits dedicated to him, as well as some poetical homages written in verse. The most complete of these biographical sketches, "Hugo Margenat: recuerdos para una semblanza" (Hugo Margenat: Remembrances for a Portrait), was written by Medina and published in 1974.

Hugo's myth and interest in his poetry grew during the sixties. The group of young poets who gathered around the important journal *Guajana* saw him as an inspiration for their own image of the poet. The fourth number of *Guajana,* which appeared in 1963, was dedicated to Hugo. They praised him for his very human poetry, full of personal and immediate experiences, full of his deep feeling of universal grief, the grief for colonialism and social injustice which developed into a strong sense of solidarity with fellow men. They clearly saw him as the poet who had anticipated their own aggressive poetry and emphasized his social and political themes. But the poets from *Guajana* were more interested in writing their own poetry than in systematic literary criticism. They also overemphasized Hugo's militant lyrics and gave little attention to the rest. Nevertheless, they made a very important contribution to his recognition. One of *Guajana*'s members, José Manuel Torres Santiago, gathered his complete works (not really complete, as usual) and published them in 1974.

As far as more systematic critical writings are concerned, there are two essays that stand out for their important contribution. The first is "Acercamiento a Hugo Margenat en su poesía" (An Approach to Hugo Margenat in His Poetry) which appeared in 1958 as a prologue to *Mundo abierto* and was written by Adelaida Lugo Suárez. Although it concentrates attention on *Mundo abierto,* it is a general view of Hugo's production up to that book. The critic studies the poet's evolution, influences, main themes, innovative style, and *Mundo abierto*'s organization as a book. This last element is Ramón Felipe Medina's central subject in his study

"Calas a expresiones de amor en *Mundo abierto* de Hugo Margenat" (Stages in the Expression of Love in *Mundo abierto* by Hugo Margenat). Medina studies, above all, the book's internal semantic structures. He concludes that the book reveals a very careful organization that responds to the poet's wish to communicate, even though his subjective style may seem to hinder this communication. He also concludes that the book has an ascensional direction where love constitutes a central axis. Thus there are a series of stages that the poet passes through and that go from love as eroticism to love of God and his countrymen in God. But through this process the poet struggles constantly with himself, which accounts for the existential drama present in the book.

So far, this is the best systematic study of Hugo's poetry. At the present time, Medina is working on a book where he will consider the totality of Hugo's production, including unpublished material. When this study appears we will have a fuller and more solid notion of Hugo's worth as a poet.

Bibliography

WORKS BY MARGENAT

Lámpara apagada. San Juan, P.R.: n.p. 1954.
Intemperie. San Juan, P.R.: Casa Baldrich, 1955.
Mundo abierto. San Juan, P.R.: Imprenta Venezuela, 1958.
Ventana hacia lo último. San Juan, P.R.: Imprenta Venezuela, 1961.
Obras completas. San Juan, P.R.: Instituto de Cultura Puertorriqueña, 1974.

WORKS ABOUT MARGENAT

Lugo Suárez, Adelaida. "Acercamiento a Hugo Margenat en su poesía." Prologue to *Mundo abierto* by Hugo Margenat (1958).
Medina, Ramón Felipe. "Hugo Margenat: recuerdos para una semblanza." *Revista del Instituto de Cultura Puertorriqueña* 62 (January-March 1974): 1–6.
———. "Calas a expresiones de amor en *Mundo abierto* de Hugo Margenat." *Revista del Instituto de Cultura Puertorriqueña* 74 (January-March 1977): 21–29.

RAMÓN LUIS ACEVEDO

MARQUÉS, RENÉ (1919–1979). René Marqués was Puerto Rico's foremost writer of plays and short stories for almost thirty years. His essays and novels are also among the best written in mid-twentieth-century Latin America, and his profound love of freedom—personal and political—can readily be seen throughout his many works.

Biography

René Marqués was born on October 4, 1919, in the city of Arecibo on the north coast of Puerto Rico. His parents were also born in Puerto Rico, but his grandparents had originally been from Mallorca and the Canary Islands. This completely insular and agrarian background—his grandparents were farmers—

undoubtedly explains to some degree Marqués's unyielding love of the land, a theme that appears frequently in his writings. His feeling for the land was not, however, merely a sentimental one; for he studied at the College of Agriculture in Mayagüez, Puerto Rico, received a degree in agronomy, and worked for two years with the Department of Agriculture.

Having become increasingly interested in literature, Marqués went to Spain in 1946 to study for a year at the University of Madrid and familiarize himself with the classical and contemporary Spanish theater. On his return to Puerto Rico, Marqués founded and presided over a little theater group in Arecibo patterned after the group known as *Areyto* in San Juan. The latter organization had been founded in 1940 by the playwright Emilio Belaval and the director Leopoldo Santiago Lavandero for the purposes of presenting plays by Puerto Rican authors and of improving the quality of both the acting and the methods of production then prevailing in San Juan.

While in Arecibo, Marqués began writing reviews and literary critiques for the newspaper *El Mundo* and the magazine *Asomante*. In 1948 he was awarded a grant from the Rockefeller Foundation to study playwriting in the United States. He postponed his acceptance of the award until 1949 when he went to study at both Columbia University and Piscator's Dramatic Workshop in New York City. Returning to San Juan in 1950, Marqués began working as a writer of educational materials for the Division of Community Education of the Department of Public Instruction.

In 1951 Marqués helped found the *Teatro Experimental del Ateneo* in San Juan and was its director for the following three years. He received a Guggenheim grant in 1954, but did not make use of it until 1957 when he spent the year in New York working on his first novel. Not limiting himself solely to aiding in the development of theater in Puerto Rico, Marqués was also one of the founders in 1959 of the *Club del Libro de Puerto Rico,* which published novels, essays, and other works by Puerto Rican authors.

In 1956 the Institute of Puerto Rican Culture, an official organ of the commonwealth government, realized the need for fostering native cultural values in all the arts and appointed the Advisory Theater Council to prepare a step-by-step program for the further development of the theater. One of the council's recommendations was an annual theater festival of Puerto Rican plays, which has been presented each year since the first one in 1958.

While earlier plays produced on the island dealt primarily with immediate social problems and conditions, those of the 1958 Theater Festival and subsequent festivals have been more concerned with the basic and broader problem of the nature of Puerto Rico. Also in the last twenty-five years the emphasis in drama has been away from the earlier tendencies of realism and naturalism. The majority of the newer plays rely heavily on the most contemporary techniques of writing and staging, such as the creation of poetic moods through language, music, and lighting; the use of flashbacks and dream sequences; experimentation with time sequence; and a more psychological type of character development. These techniques are not used as tricks or props to cover dramatic weaknesses but as legitimate means for heightening dramatic expression.

After more than two decades of successful festivals of Puerto Rican plays and several more recent seasons of international dramas—in Spanish—plus frequent independent productions in Spanish or English, it is obvious that theater in Puerto Rico has undergone a radical change and has grown considerably. The most important advances have been the complete renovation of staging techniques, the development of a strong nucleus of serious personnel in all phases of theatrical activity—writers, actors, producers, directors, craftsmen, technicians—and, most important, the creation of the ever-expanding repertory of Puerto Rican plays themselves.

As a writer, Marqués's principal interest lay in the theater; however, his body of short stories and novels will also be discussed here.

One all-important theme that recurs frequently in much of Marqués's writing is that of political independence for his homeland. As a staunch believer in liberty on both personal and national levels, Marqués was an avowed exponent of political sovereignty for Puerto Rico. Although not a Nationalist himself, his writings were the first in Puerto Rico to make use of the revolutionary activities of the Nationalist movement as thematic material. The Nationalists advocated armed violence as a means of achieving independence and were behind such acts as the assassination attempts on President Truman and Governor Muñoz Marín of Puerto Rico in 1950 and the shooting in the United States House of Representatives in 1954. They are not to be confused with the legal Independence party founded in 1946 and still campaigning actively and peacefully for political independence from the United States; for a Nationalist party as such has not existed since the elections of 1932 when it won a mere 2 percent of the total votes cast, a far cry from the minimum of 10 percent required to maintain the legal status of a recognized political party. More recently, however, there have come into being such organized groups as the *Movimiento Pro Independencia* and the *Federación Estudiantil Pro Independencia* which are actively and vociferously campaigning for national sovereignty. Meanwhile, the United States-Puerto Rican Status Commission formed in February 1964 to study the legal status of Puerto Rico ended its series of public hearings in San Juan and submitted its findings and recommendations to the then-president, Lyndon Johnson, and the Puerto Rican legislature in September 1966. Its report led to an island-wide plebiscite to determine whether the island should remain a commonwealth, become the fifty-first state of the United States, or be an independent country. Commonwealth status won, but new parties and politicians continue the debate.

In 1969 Marqués left the Department of Public Instruction, where he had been director of the Editorial Division for sixteen years, to teach at the University of Puerto Rico in Río Piedras. He moved in 1973 to a newly built mountaintop estate far from the noise and confusion of the San Juan metropolitan area, where he immersed himself almost completely in reading and writing and became semiretired from the hectic life of university, literary, and theatrical circles.

After writing a second novel, *La mirada* (1976, *The Look,* 1983), and another volume of short stories, *Inmersos en el silencio* (1976, Immersed in the Silence), Marqués was recording and working on new editions of many of his works when he died from a liver ailment on March 22, 1979, having not yet reached his sixtieth birthday.

Major Themes

Otro día nuestro (Another of Our Days), Marqués's first book of short stories, appeared in 1955 and contains several of the themes such as nationalism, guilt, martyrdom, time, love of the land, and loss of personal identity that will later be repeated and developed in much of his writing.

For example, the protagonist of the story that gives its title to the entire collection is an old man who discovers too late that he is living in a time that is not really his. The character is based on Pedro Albizu Campos, former leader of the Nationalist party which had sought independence from the United States by revolutionary means. The old man feels a desire for death as the only solution to his predicament. He is meant to be a Christ figure whose kingdom is not of the world in which he finds himself.

The story "Isla en Manhattan" (Island in Manhattan) presents the problem of the Puerto Rican who moves to the great metropolis and the effect that this migration has upon him. One of the main characters has willfully allowed himself to become assimilated as much and as quickly as possible, but to achieve this Americanization he has had to give up his "Puerto Ricanness," which for Marqués signifies the denial of one's own being and the disavowal of one's very nature or essence.

The story "Pasión y huida de Juan Santos, santero" (The Passion and Escape of Juan Santos, Sculptor of Saints) presents one of the many serious conflicts encountered in present-day Puerto Rico when a new and different way of life imposes itself upon an older and more traditional one: the conflict between Spanish Catholicism and the North American type of Protestant evangelism that is attempting to supplant it on the island.

"El milagrito de San Antonio" (The Little Miracle of San Antonio) is another story with a religious background, but in this case it deals with two aspects of the same religion: the simple, spontaneous Catholicism of a little old lady from the mountains of Puerto Rico and the meaningless, worn-out, dehumanized variety of "modern" Catholicism which has become too objective and impersonal through overexposure to other aspects of modern life. Like the old man in "Otro día nuestro," this woman is also living in an era that is not really hers.

The protagonist in the story "El juramento" can be taken to represent Puerto Rico in its political relationship with the United States. ("Commonwealth" is rendered paradoxically as "Free Associated State" in Spanish.) On the personal level, the charge of guilt by association is enough to give the protagonist a strong feeling of shame and guilt. On the national level it may help to explain the collective, schizophrenic guilt complex that seems to have affected the entire population, and which may in part account for Puerto Rico's abnormally high rate of suicide. It certainly has become one of Marqués's favorite themes in several other stories and plays: "El niño en el árbol" (The Boy in the Tree); "En la popa hay un cuerpo reclinado" (There's a Body Reclined on the Poop Deck); "Purificación en la calle del Cristo" (Purification on Christ Street); *El sol y los MacDonald* (The Sun and the MacDonalds); *La muerte no entrará en palacio* (Death Will Not Enter the Palace); *Los soles truncos* (The Fanlights); *Un niño azul para esa sombra* (A Blue Boy for That Shadow); and *La casa sin reloj* (The House without a Clock).

Written several years before their publication, the stories "El miedo" (The Fear) and "La muerte" (Death) initiated the existentialist trend in the Puerto Rican short story.

Of the several particular themes that recur throughout these stories, many are social or political in nature: Puerto Rican Nationalism in "Otro día nuestro," "El juramento" (The Vow), and "La muerte"; references to the peculiar status of Puerto Rico in "El miedo" and "El juramento"; pejorative remarks with respect to various aspects of American life and culture in "Otro día nuestro," "Pasión y huida de Juan Santos, santero," "Isla en Manhattan," and "El juramento"; and modern man as a robot or machine in "Otro día nuestro," "El juramento," and "La muerte." Underlying most of these themes is the shock, or clash, brought about by the conflict between the two basically different sets of cultural patterns and ways of life encountered in Puerto Rico—the Hispanic, or Latin, and the North American, or Anglo-Saxon. All these themes, as well as others such as hate and the desire for self-destruction, will constantly reappear in Marqués's second volume of short stories and in his theater and novels.

Marqués's second book of short stories, *En una ciudad llamada San Juan* (In a City Called San Juan), was published in November 1960. It contains ten stories, all of which were written after those found in *Otro día nuestro*. Considerable technical development and a greater insistence on psychological and dramatic elements are evident in this later work. With these tales Marqués has matured as a short-story writer who is fully confident of his art and worthy of ranking among its best contemporary exponents.

Many negative themes such as hate, death, pain, anguish, suffering, and desperation will be encountered in these stories as the author avails himself of them in order to express in literary terms his pessimistic attitude toward contemporary social and political situations in his homeland.

The book is divided into two sections entitled "Before the City" and "In the City." The first contains only one story, which deals with an historical episode from the Spanish conquest of Puerto Rico; the second contains the remaining nine, all of which are set in various parts of present-day San Juan, as the title indicates.

Many of the same themes and elements found in the earlier book, *Otro día nuestro*, reappear in this later volume: Nationalism; anti-Americanism; references to the status of Puerto Rico; time; the use of English; anti-Puerto Rican remarks by Americans; symbols of United States' intervention; and the flashback or retrospective technique so important to the psychological development of the characters. With their increased use, all these elements have been highly developed so that their most important reason for being is an artistic one, regardless of whatever other implications they may contain.

After some experimentation as to style and technique in the earlier work *Otro día nuestro,* Marqués has now discovered and perfected a style that best suits his endeavor to express definite, personal feelings and beliefs in a manner that is basically literary. He has decided upon an approach that is subjective and psychological in relation to his protagonists, as is apparent from the stories in *En una ciudad llamada San Juan.* Whereas his earlier technique was more objective and traditional, Marqués now writes from the mind's eye view of the principal characters and thus is better able to involve the reader in the proceedings while satisfying his own needs as a creative artist. Once he had formulated this approach, it was easier to elaborate and make variations upon similar themes and situations while maintaining the organic unity of the book. Thus there is a closer technical and stylistic relationship among the stories in this second volume than among those found in the previous one. Each tale in *En una ciudad llamada San Juan* may stand alone and be judged as an individual story or it may be taken as part of the author's kaleidoscopic view of the many-faceted world that is the Puerto Rican capital.

With regard to thematic development, a greater unity can also be observed in these later stories. Rather than remaining isolated in individual tales, as they were in *Otro día nuestro,* such themes as Puerto Rican Nationalism, anti-Americanism, the destructive power of time, and the more subjective ones such as guilt, hatred, and the desire for self-degradation or death become united as they appear and reappear throughout *En una ciudad llamada San Juan,* thus strengthening the microcosm constructed and described by the author. In this way these themes become an integral part of Marqués's total creation and also serve to express his pessimistic views toward life and the absurd situations he finds in it. As a result of their inability to cope with these illogical and ambiguous circumstances, his characters are plagued by the various neuroses and complexes already alluded to, such as self-hatred, feelings of guilt, and the desire to be the martyr or Christ figure. Their anguish and desperation at being part of an absurd world bereft of any positive moral values are reflected at the very beginning of the book in the quotation from Buddha's "Fire Sermon." Each story thus serves in its own way to illustrate the spiritual and physical holocaust that Marqués sees menacing and destroying the Hispanic roots of Puerto Rican culture and civilization and the apparent lack of ability on the part of the people to do anything constructive to inhibit or prevent this destruction from without. It is precisely their acceptance of it that gives rise to the previously mentioned collective guilt complex.

In 1970 Marqués published a new enlarged edition of *En una ciudad llamada San Juan,* which now included three stories from the out-of-print *Otro día nuestro* and two later stories that had appeared separately in magazines, "La crucifixión de Miss Bunning" (The Crucifixion of Miss Bunning) and "La chiringa azul" (The Blue Kite).

Another new story appeared in 1972: "Ese mosaico fresco sobre aquel mosaico antiguo" (That Fresh Mosaic Atop the Old Mosaic). Based on fact and written in the style of magic realism, it is yet another example of one of Marqués's favorite themes, the deliberate destruction of an older, more refined way of life and its values in the name of progress. A separate edition of this story, complete with photographs and two critical essays, was published in 1975.

A new volume of stories, *Inmersos en el silencio*, came out in 1976. Included are four stories from the original *Otro día nuestro*, three from the further expanded fourth edition of *En una ciudad llamada San Juan*, which had been published in 1974, and five others, including "Ese mosaico fresco . . . ," which had never been previously anthologized.

Theater

Before the publication of *Otro día nuestro*, Marqués had already begun writing for the theater. In 1946, in Puerto Rico, he wrote a one-act play, *El hombre y sus sueños* (Man and His Dreams); later that same year and the following he was in Spain, where he wrote a three-act drama, *El sol y los MacDonald*; in 1949 he was at Columbia University in New York taking a course in playwriting for which he wrote *Palm Sunday*, a play in two acts and primarily in English. All three works are experimental in nature and important from both technical and thematic standpoints since they not only introduce certain themes that recur in several later plays but also various dramatic techniques that Marqués subsequently developed and perfected.

El hombre y sus sueños is an allegory dealing with man's yearning for immortality. *El sol y los MacDonald (Tres cuadros de una familia extraña)*, written in Spain in 1947 and staged for the first time in Puerto Rico in September 1950, is an interesting theatrical experiment, but more from the technical standpoint than from the purely literary and dramatic ones. Such devices as the actor-narrator, flashbacks, and monologues which are actually the characters' spoken thoughts are definite innovations as far as Puerto Rican theater is concerned, but the drama itself suffers from the author's lack of familiarity with the setting and action involved in it. Undoubtedly enthused and stimulated by O'Neill's *Mourning Becomes Electra* and *Strange Interlude* (as he had been a year earlier by the Spanish philosopher Unamuno while writing *El hombre y sus sueños*), Marqués decided also to adapt a classical myth to a modern situation and employ certain newly learned techniques in the process. The legends that he chose are those of Oedipus and Electra; the setting is the contemporary Deep South of the United States, a locale that also gives him the opportunity to begin the anti-Americanism developed later in his short stories. Racial prejudice is certainly important and relevant to the characters and setting, but it serves more to justify the theme of incest perpetuated throughout the several generations of MacDonalds. The title itself suggests the primary importance of the incest theme as symbolized in the myth that gave rise to the classical tragedy of Oedipus: the Sun kills his father, the Night, and marries his mother, the Dawn. Thus *The Sun and the MacDonalds* can be understood as *Oedipus and the MacDonalds* and the inference is quite clear.

Palm Sunday, written in 1949, was produced in Puerto Rico in 1956. The plot is based on an actual historical incident, the violent suppression by the police of a Nationalist march and demonstration on Palm Sunday, 1937, in the city of Ponce. The characters are fictitious: the American police commissioner, his estranged Puerto Rican wife, and their adolescent son. The three are fixed from the start: the stubborn bigot who has come to despise all things Puerto Rican; the docile "native" who pleads for patience and understanding as the only solution to the problems facing both her family and her island; and the young idealist who suddenly becomes the defiant man of action and dies a martyr for a lost cause. The son's desire to die with the demonstrators is an unconscious assumption upon himself of his father's unfelt guilt at having ordered the massacre; and by becoming a victim himself, he thus expiates this guilt and thereby denies any ideological or spiritual kinship to his father (and, by extension, to all things American) while at the same time asserting his Puerto Ricanness.

In these three early plays Marqués laid the groundwork for much of his later development as a playwright. Although far from the best he has done, they are nevertheless to be taken into account primarily for their practical value in allowing the young dramatist to "feel his way around" in his craft and to experiment with various stage techniques and devices that will be of great importance in his later works.

Marqués's dramatic maturity began in 1951 with the writing of his first major theatrical work, *La carreta* (*The Oxcart*, 1969). This play was first presented in New York in May 1953 and in Puerto Rico the following December. In 1957 *La carreta* became the first contemporary Puerto Rican play to be performed in Europe when it was produced by a Spanish company at the Teatro National María Guerrero in Madrid. There, it was as favorably received as it had been in America.

La carreta is the story of one Puerto Rican family's migration from the mountains to San Juan and finally to New York in hope of finding better jobs and better living conditions, first in the island capital and then in the "promised land" to the north. In this way the drama mirrors the movement of many thousands of Puerto Rican country folk who left their plots of land to seek economic advantages in San Juan and then in New York, but, like the family in *La carreta*, found nothing but disillusion, despair, and degradation at each successive step of their pilgrimage.

The old grandfather, Don Chago, who decides to stay in the mountains and manage as best he can, is another of Marqués's many characters who, disenchanted by the materialism and lack of pride and dignity in modern society, voluntarily prefer to live in the less complex world of their past. He states that he once believed in men but now believes only in the land.

To make credible the fact that at the end of the play Juanita, the daughter, is willing to return to her former country life in Puerto Rico, her worldly behavior in New York must be considered more of a temporary rebellion against the discrimination, emptiness, and confusion that she encounters in the huge impersonal city rather than a genuine and lasting change of character. In spite of her outward sophistication, her family ties are still strong enough to heed the call to return to the land. The lesson she has learned is the same one that Marqués feels is applicable to all those who through lack of love for their heritage and their homeland have too readily abandoned them for the false values and false security of a way of life that is basically incompatible with the one they have deserted. Their action is thus a negative one and leads only to unhappiness and disaster. If, however, one's actions stem from an awareness of one's cultural tradition, they will be positive actions, the values sought after will be true, and satisfaction will be found in the knowledge that one is acting in accordance with one's true self and background.

The final words of Doña Gabriela, the long-suffering mother, echo Juanita's resolution to return with her to their native soil where, through hard work stemming from a deep-rooted love of the land, they will find happiness and peace, as the curtain falls on a scene of dignified determination, which is another fine example of Marqués's dramatic and descriptive abilities.

In 1956, five years after writing *La carreta* and one year after his first volume of short stories, Marqués published the libretto for a ballet entitled *Juan Bobo y la Dama de Occidente* (Juan Bobo and the Lady of the West). As a piece of dramatic prose it serves to expose and to ridicule the absurd beliefs of those who, according to Marqués, refuse to recognize Puerto Rico's own cultural heritage and who insist on cultivating there only the supposedly superior "occidental" culture of Europe and the United States. More specifically, he intends it to be a direct satirical attack on this philosophy of the Americanization of Puerto Rico as then expounded by the University of Puerto Rico.

Marqués firmly believed that any real knowledge of and love for Puerto Rico on the part of its people must come from an awareness of their country's past. They have certain definite historical and cultural roots and must use them as a point of departure for knowledge of themselves and of the world. His Juan Bobo, a figure from Puerto Rican folklore, will not blindly accept values thrust upon him from outside by those who insist that they are superior to the ones he already has or is capable of formulating from his own experience and background.

In March 1956, Marqués finished his next play, *La muerte no entrará en palacio*. It received honorable mention in the drama contest sponsored by the Ateneo Puertorriqueño in 1957 but was never produced. This lack of production was due primarily to the fact that the play is a direct attack on the character and policies of the then-governor of Puerto Rico, the late Luis Muñoz Marín, and as such was thematically unacceptable for presentation during any of the theater festivals held while he was in power.

The idea of remaining true to one's chosen destiny and the consequences that befall when one betrays it may be considered both the basic theme of the play and Marqués's indictment of Muñoz Marín for "betraying" himself and the people of Puerto Rico when he reversed his original campaign pledge of political independence and promulgated the commonwealth concept, which became official in 1952.

As Marqués's first full-scale attempt at an original tragedy, *La muerte no entrará en palacio* is a well-conceived and well-written play. Certain dramatic and technical devices such as short scenes occupying only part of the stage, blackouts during which voices and sounds are mechanically reproduced to help further the action, the use of music to create or accent a specific mood, and the male and female choruses are all employed for the first time and to good advantage. The fact that the subject matter is so very contemporary and that several characters are based on real persons does not detract from the play but actually makes it more exciting and controversial.

Marqués always resented the fact that this play was never produced in Puerto Rico during his lifetime. It was not until March 1981, two years after his death, that it was finally presented, but in New York by the Puerto Rican Traveling Theater in both Spanish and English performances.

Marqués's next play, *Los soles truncos,* based on his short story "Purificación en la Calle del Cristo," was finished in February 1958 and first presented in San Juan that year as part of the First Theater Festival. Since then it has become his most-produced play with productions not only throughout Puerto Rico but also in Spain, Mexico, Chicago, and New York. In the latter it has been performed in both Spanish and English.

The play is a very successful one from several standpoints. The author has created an atmosphere that is simultaneously realistic and poetic and in which the central conflict is the clash of two worlds: the real, outside, contemporary world of Old San Juan, and the unreal, subjective world within the ancient house in this part of the capital where the action of the drama occurs and where three spinster sisters reside. Their house is the last stronghold of a more refined and elegant way of life, just as all Puerto Rico was once the last colony of another civilization and culture before it was torn from that dream and made part of another world where everything was, and continues to be, time, action, and present reality. The greatest enemy that these sisters must not allow to enter their house is time, the devourer of all. They refuse to recognize both time and the world as we know it, for over the years neither has been kind to them. Time has robbed them of all they held dear—parents, sweethearts, properties. They therefore try to combat it the only way they know how: by denying its existence.

The final realization that the house—accomplice to their misery and guilt—has been confiscated and that they must be dispossessed heralds the decision to destroy the last link between their world and reality, that of life itself.

In *Los soles truncos* Marqués has masterfully combined all the technical elements with which he had experimented in his previous plays—music, lighting, sound effects, the blackout, concrete objects as symbols—and has integrated them into the work in such a way that they constantly serve to heighten its poetic and dramatic qualities.

Un niño azul para esa sombra, adapted from his stories "El niño en el árbol" and "La sala" (The Living Room), was finished in September 1958, received first prize in the drama contest sponsored by the Ateneo Puertorriqueño that same year, and was presented in April 1960 as the opening work of the Third Theater Festival in San Juan. It is technically superior to all his previous plays and an effective integration of all his playwriting skills exhibited earlier. A new note here is the use for the first time in Puerto Rican theater of a child protagonist as a Christ figure. The play ends, as did *Los soles truncos,* with a suicidal sacrifice when the victim, or victims, could no longer escape from present reality into the comfortable security of a past that was cruelly torn from them. And although it is certainly not their primary function as works of art, both of these plays could serve on a national level as dramatic metaphors symbolizing the entire abnormally high suicide rate of Puerto Rico, a land also torn from a less complex past and forced to become part of a reality with which it was not prepared to cope.

La casa sin reloj, written and staged in 1960, is Marqués's first comedy—serious or dark comedy, but nevertheless comedy—since writing *Juan Bobo y la Dama de Occidente* four years earlier. It is also his first sortie into the so-called Theater of the Absurd, a logical direction, however, for his ideas and talent to take since his stories and plays are full of his "absurd" view of life.

By subtitling his play an anti-poetic comedy, Marqués places it within the framework of reality, albeit a reality that must be understood and accepted in the aforementioned absurd terms. His technique this time is straightforward and realistic without any of the "poetic" devices he had employed in previous plays. There are no blackouts, flashbacks, dream sequences, or special effects of light and sound; on the surface everything—setting, characters, action—seems normal, but one soon becomes aware that something is "out of focus" in this otherwise realistic situation. As in earlier works, time is again the culprit, the unseen villain, but not so much for its presence as for its absence. When, however, it makes itself felt in the "reasonable ending," meaning as reasonable as anything can be in an absurd world, it brings not only the usual disaster that we have come to expect but also a promise of hope and love to Micaela, the leading character, who, until now, has lived without either one because she has lived without guilt and without time in her house without a clock. She is living in an Eden awaiting an act of redemption that will make her a complete person in that she will enter the mainstream of life and come to know both guilt and the implacability of time. In this way she represents the majority of the Puerto Rican people, who, in Marqués's opinion, are merely vegetating under a guilt complex stemming from their docile acceptance of what amounts to colonial status. As in earlier works, expiation and suffering are again equated with redemption and purification, thus making the sufferer a Christ figure.

La casa sin reloj is not so technically complicated or dramatically exciting as Marqués's three preceding tragedies, but it does successfully display his ability for writing comedy and creating comic situations while at the same time maintaining such familiar themes as time, guilt, and nationalism.

In his next two full-length plays following *La casa sin reloj,* Marqués continued to explore the dramatic possibilities of the theater of the absurd. *Carnaval afuera, carnaval adentro* was written in 1960, first performed in Havana in 1962, and not published until 1971. In a flood of lights, sounds, farce, masks, music, and dance, this work likens the circumstances of Puerto Rico and its people to an absurd carnival where the more serious implications and authentic values are hidden by or lost beneath blind, superficial laughter.

El apartamiento premiered in San Juan in April 1964 as part of the Seventh Theater Festival. It is the most absurdist of the three plays, forsaking both the detective-story realism of *La casa sin reloj* and the bombastic farce of *Carnaval afuera, carnaval adentro* for the stark qualities (scenic, dramatic, and linguistic) of the secluded no-man's-land where the "action" occurs.

Clearly influenced by Ionesco, Pinter, and Beckett, *El apartamiento* symbolizes the present predicament of Puerto Rico in its physical isolation and its total dependence upon a foreign government and culture. As in many previous works, Marqués is again couching in new dramatic terms the question of whether or not there is a way out of the absurd situation—economic, political, social, linguistic—in which Puerto Rico finds itself today, and if so, at what cost.

Marqués's next play, *Mariana o el alba* (Mariana or Dawn), was presented in San Juan in May 1965 during the Eighth Theater Festival. His first historical drama, *Mariana o el alba* is based on the true story of Puerto Rican heroine Mariana Bracetti, who, in 1868, embroidered the revolutionary flag to be used during the (unsuccessful) Grito de Lares uprising against Spanish domination. *Mariana* had a much better reception from critics and public alike than the hermetic *El apartamiento* had had the year before. *Mariana's* factual basis, period sets and costumes, and patriotic sentiments were more immediately recognized and accepted than the apparent meaninglessness of the previous work. In *Mariana o el alba* Marqués shows not only his skill at creating drama from historical fact but also his ability to draw analogies between past and present situations affecting his island. Implied throughout the play is the notion that another, or perhaps another and another, uprising will be necessary until Puerto Ricans can shake off their current colonial status and achieve true freedom and independence for future generations.

In 1969 Marqués showed yet another facet of his talent in a drama based on the biblical story of Abraham, Isaac, and Sarah, *Sacrificio en el Monte Moriah* (Sacrifice on Mt. Moriah). Employing a very elaborate staging based on a series of platforms, the play again joins past to present in the theme of a father willing to sacrifice his son to prove his own faith, to placate the "establishment," so to speak. Marqués dedicated the work to his older son, who had been arrested for draft evasion during the Vietnam War, saying that as a father he would never sacrifice his son on the altar of any bloodthirsty or bellicose god.

Marqués continued his exploration of biblical and classical themes in 1970 with *David y Jonatán—Tito y Berenice: Dos dramas de amor, poder y desamor* (David and Jonathan; Tito and Bernice: Two Dramas of Love, Power and Unloving)—his first one-act play since the early experimental *El hombre y sus sueños, Palm Sunday,* and *Juan Bobo.* (*Sacrificio en el Monte Moriah* is really a full-length play even though its fourteen scenes should flow uninterruptedly from first to last according to the playwright's directions.) Although occurring more than a thousand years apart, *David y Jonatán* (1000 B.C.) and *Tito y Berenice* (first century A.D.) are thematically related as their overall title indicates and are intended to be performed on the same program. Each play, although relatively short, is divided into ten scenes that, again, should follow one another as in a film. Both plays have large casts, but the props and scenery have been kept to a minimum to assure this cinematographic flow of scenes. As has been true in most of Marqués's theater, lights and sounds again play major parts in these dramas, and the effect of time is all-important especially in *Tito y Berenice.* Their relevance to the present can be seen not only in the quotation at the beginning of each play— "There is nothing new under the sun"—but also in the struggle between the eternal forces of love and power and how greed for the latter can only bring about a tragic loss of the former.

In 1970 at the request of a group of students from the University of Puerto Rico, Marqués agreed to write—and read—the section corresponding to Station Eleven, Jesus Is Nailed to the Cross, for a *Vía Crucis del Hombre Puertorriqueño* (A Via Crucis of Puerto Rican Man), an oratory to be read on Good Friday that year in Old San Juan in front of La Princesa jail where his son Raúl had been briefly imprisoned for refusing to serve in the army. As noted, this incident had also helped inspire *Sacrificio en el Monte Moriah* and serves here as a point of departure for the Speaker's (Jesus) repeated questioning of his Father's apparent abandonment of him. Like one of today's alienated young people he questions his Father's values and motives, society's treatment of those unfortunates who are merely seeking happiness (the kingdom of Heaven) in their own way and pleads that peace, love, justice, and freedom be granted so that the Promised Land may be here and now on earth.

Novels

In 1957 Marqués accepted a Guggenheim fellowship—an award that had actually been made three years before—and spent most of the year in New York writing his first novel, *La víspera del hombre* (The Eve of Man). Published by the Club del Libro de Puerto Rico in 1959, the work had received first prize as the best novel in the 1958 competition sponsored by the Ateneo Puertorriqueño. Thus in December 1958 Marqués became the only Puerto Rican author to win simultaneously four first prizes from the Ateneo in the categories of novel, theater for *Un niño azul para esa sombra,* short story for "La sala," and essay for "Pesimismo Literario y Optimismo Político: su coexistencia en el Puerto Rico Actual" (Literary Pessimism and Political Optimism: Their Coexistence in Puerto Rico Today).

La víspera del hombre is the first Puerto Rican novel to have a child protagonist; and, as the title implies, the novel deals with the period of his childhood and subsequent emergence into adolescence.

But the novel is also much more than a mere story of a boy's growing up, for not only has Marqués told his tale from the child's viewpoint but he has also included in the book a vast panorama of the sights, sounds, and history of Puerto Rico. Much of the technique is similar to that used in many of his plays and short stories in that it employs the remembrance of past time and events as a means of reliving the past in the present and thereby showing at the same time the relation of the latter to the former. Not once does Marqués mention a specific date or year, for this would then place the action within the restricting confines of man-made measurements of time and thereby hinder the free-flowing backward, as well as forward, movement of time as a life force which he wishes to convey throughout the work.

The novel ends in a way that while inviting a sequel (another picaresque characteristic in addition to that of the child protagonist who has a series of perambulatory adventures, encounters, and disillusions) emphasizes again the cosmic forces which in their eternal return are forever joining past to present to future and uniting man to the other elements of the universe. One cycle of life and of time has been completed but both nature and man are now prepared to face new cycles on their continuing journey into the future.

In August 1973, Marqués completed his second novel, *La mirada,* a masterful blend of all his previous themes, styles, and symbols, and the veritable summit of his artistic creations.

Having been selected as one of the eleven best novels out of 136 submitted to the Ateneo of Seville in 1974, *La mirada*'s publication in Spain was subsequently forbidden by the Department of Popular Culture of the Ministry of Information and Tourism unless the author would be willing to change or delete certain passages deemed obscene. Needless to say, Marqués was unwilling to make any concessions, and the novel was published in Puerto Rico in 1976.

All the elements of his former works converge here—time, politics, guilt, children, colors, the Christ figure, the use of English as a status symbol, Greek mythology, the Bible, death, the absurd—plus a few new ones or a new emphasis on those not really stressed before—sex, drugs, hippies, kidnapping, prison life—and all are combined in a hallucinatory manner against a background of traditional cultural values and ideas that are being eroded by the pressures of contemporary man and society. At the end, the unseen presence of the mysterious Christ figure who appears throughout the book and is perhaps a figment of the nameless protagonist's imagination or another aspect of his own being—of all our beings—is with him as he, a twentieth-century Everyman, sets out alone beneath the heavens in search of his unknown but implacable fate. With its cosmic orientation and multiple interpretations, *La mirada* is Marqués's most universal work.

Survey of Criticism

Until the 1960s Marqués's work was mostly unknown outside of Puerto Rico. *La carreta* had premiered in Spanish in New York in 1953 in a low-budget amateur production even before its appearance in Puerto Rico and thus had at least served to introduce this new playwright to the then-small number of interested aficionados in university and other intellectual circles.

Through the efforts of such professors as María Teresa Babín of New York University and Frank Dauster of Rutgers, interest in Marqués spread rapidly through many American graduate schools, where courses were given and dissertations written about his life and works. His plays have been produced in Mexico, Spain, Cuba, Czechoslovakia, Chicago, and Los Angeles as well as New York; he was the only author from Puerto Rico to be included in a Swedish anthology of Latin American short stories published in 1963; *The Oxcart*, the English version of *La carreta,* ran for almost ninety performances off-Broadway in the 1966–1967 season. Mexican author and critic Carlos Solórzano has called Marqués one of Latin America's exceptional values, while Spanish critic Antonio Espina García has praised him as a writer of international value.

Charles Pilditch's 1976 book, *René Marqués: A Study of His Fiction,* was the first full-length critical analysis to be published of Marqués's theater, stories, and novels from 1948 to 1976 and has served as a basis for much of this entry.

Bibliography

WORKS BY MARQUÉS

Peregrinación (poemas). Arecibo, Puerto Rico, 1944.
El hombre y sus sueños. Asomante no. 2 (1948): 58–72.
Palm Sunday. New York, 1949. (Mimeographed.)
"Mensaje de un Puertorriqueño a los Escritores y Artistas del Perú." *Cuadernos Americanos* no. 6 (1955): 79–86.
Otro día nuestro. San Juan, 1955.
Juan Bobo y la Dama de Occidente. Mexico City: Los Presentes, 1956.
———. Segunda edición. Río Piedras: Editorial Antillana, 1971.
El sol y los MacDonald. Asomante no. 1 (1957): 43–82.
———. Río Piedras: Editorial Cultural, 1971.
"Pesimismo Literario y Optimismo Político: su Coexistencia en el Puerto Rico Actual." *Cuadernos Americanos* no. 3 (1959): 43–74.
Teatro. Mexico City: Arrecife, 1959. Contains *Los soles truncos, Un niño azul para esa sombra, La muerte no entrará en palacio.*
———. Segunda edición. Río Piedras: Editorial Cultural, 1970.
———. Tercera edición. Río Piedras: Editorial Cultural, 1976.
La víspera del hombre. San Juan: Club del Libro de Puerto Rico, 1959.
En una ciudad llamada San Juan. Mexico City: Imprenta Universitaria, 1960.
———. Tercera edición, ampliada. Río Piedras: Editorial Cultural, 1970.

————. Cuarta edición, ampliada. Río Piedras: Editorial Cultural, 1974.

La carreta. Río Piedras: Editorial Cultural, 1961. (As of 1976, twelve editions had been published.)

"Origen y enfoque de un tema puertorriqueño." Program of the Fourth Puerto Rican Theater Festival (San Juan, 1961), p. 6.

La casa sin reloj. Xalapa: Universidad Veracruzana, 1960.

"El puertorriqueño dócil." *Cuadernos Americanos* (enero-febrero 1962): 143–95.

Mariana o el alba. Villa Nevares, Puerto Rico: Private edition, 1965.

————. Río Piedras: Editorial Antillana, 1968.

El apartamiento. Barcelona: Ediciones Rumbos, 1966.

Ensayos (1953–1966). Río Piedras: Editorial Antillana, 1966.

The Oxcart (La carreta). Translated by Charles Pilditch. New York: Charles Scribner's Sons, 1969.

Sacrificio en el Monte Moriah. Río Piedras: Editorial Antillana, 1969.

David y Jonatán—Tito y Berenice: dos dramas de amor, poder y desamor. Río Piedras: Editorial Antillana, 1970.

Carnaval afuera, carnaval adentro. Río Piedras: Editorial Antillana, 1971.

Teatro. Vol. 2. Río Piedras: Editorial Cultural, 1971. Contains *El hombre y sus sueños, El sol y los MacDonald.*

————. Vol. 3. Río Piedras: Editorial Cultural, 1971. Contains *La casa sin reloj, El apartamiento.*

Vía Crucis del Hombre Puertorriqueño (Oratorio). Río Piedras: Editorial Antillana, 1971.

"Ese mosaico fresco sobre mosaico antiguo." *Sin Nombre* (enero-marzo 1972): 7–16.

————. Río Piedras: Editorial Cultural, 1975.

Inmersos en el silencio (Cuentos). Río Piedras: Editorial Antillana, 1976.

La mirada. Río Piedras: Editorial Antillana, 1976.

Un niño azul para esa sombra. Río Piedras: Editorial Cultural, 1976.

Purificación en la Calle del Cristo (Cuento) y Los soles truncos (Teatro). Río Piedras: Editorial Cultural, 1978.

The Look (La mirada). Translated by Charles Pilditch. New York: Senda Nueva de Ediciones, 1983.

WORKS ABOUT MARQUÉS

Arrom, José Juan. Review of *El hombre y sus sueños. Handbook of Latin American Studies* 14 (1948): 234–35.

Babín, María Teresa. "Apuntes sobre *La carreta.*" Sobretiro de *Asomante* no. 4 (1953): 1–17.

————. "De René Marqués: *Juan Bobo y la Dama de Occidente.*" *El Mundo* May 4 1957: 26.

Dauster, Frank. "Cinco años de teatro hispanoamericano." *Asomante* no. 1 (1959): 54–63.

————. Review of *El sol y los MacDonald. Handbook of Latin American Studies* 21 (1959): 228.

————. "The Theater of René Marqués." *Symposium* (Spring 1964): 35–45.

Martínez Capó, Juan. "Un Niño Azul Para Esa Sombra." *El Mundo* April 23, 1960: 31.

Matilla, Alfredo. *"Los soles truncos,* de René Marqués." *El Mundo* June 7, 1958: 25.

Meléndez, Concha. Review of *La víspera del hombre. Asomante* no. 2 (1960): 102–7.

————. "La escena puertorriqueña." *Asomante* no. 2 (1961): 51–58.

————. "Recent Fiction by René Marqués." *Chasqui* (November 1976): 77–79.

————. *René Marqués: A Study of His Fiction.* New York: Plus Ultra, 1976.

————. "Teatro reciente de René Marqués." *Tramoya,* Universidad Veracruzana, Xalapa, Mexico (July-September 1976): 108–10.

————. "*La Carreta.*" *Latin Beat* (April 18, 1977): 4–5.

Pilditch, Charles. "A Brief History of Theater in Puerto Rico." *Revista/Review Interamericana,* Inter American University Press, San Juan (Spring 1979): 5–8.

————. "*La muerte no entrará en palacio:* una obra en busca de un estreno." *Sin Nombre,* San Juan (October-December 1979): 71–83.

CHARLES PILDITCH

MATAS, JULIO (1931–   ). Julio Matas is a Cuban-born poet, fiction writer, playwright, and literary critic. He is the author of several books, creative and critical, and of numerous studies published in scholarly and literary journals in the Hispanic world and the United States. Some of his creative work has appeared in various literary magazines in Cuba and abroad, in Spanish or in translation.

Biography

Julio Matas was born in Havana on May 12, 1931, only child to Julio César Matas and Adolfina Graupera. His father, a lower circuit judge, died when Julio was six years old; and his mother vowed to make her son follow in the footsteps of his father, saving her husband's legal library for the tender lawyer-to-be. Julio, in effect, under his family's pressure, would obtain a law degree (J.D.) from the University of Havana in 1955, although he would never practice as an attorney. He enrolled in the University School for Dramatic Arts at the same time he started his law studies, in 1948; after his graduation from the Drama School, in 1952, driven by his strong vocation, he organized a drama group, "Arena," which staged several plays under his direction.

Julio began writing poetry at an early age. In association with two of his college classmates—Roberto Fernández Retamar and César Leante, who would in time become well-known figures in Cuban letters—he founded a short-lived literary magazine, *Laberinto* (Labyrinth), in 1950, where he published for the first time. Family financial difficulties forced him to find a job before completing his doctoral degree at the university (he held a position with a local bank from 1952 to 1957), a circumstance that would delay his graduation and place a heavy burden on his artistic career; he managed, at great sacrifice, to devote evenings and weekends to his theater work. During this period, Julio also participated with cinematographers Néstor Almendros, Ramón F. Suárez, and Tomás Gutiérrez Alea in some of the early experiments that would lead to the flourishing Cuban film art of the past two decades; he has also been a staff member of the "Cinemateca de Cuba" since its inception in the mid–1950s.

In 1957, Julio applied to the Department of Romance Languages at Harvard University to pursue graduate study in the field of Hispanic literature; he was admitted and granted a teaching fellowship. There he would be able to devote full time to literary research and to writing, an old dream that his precarious situation had so far thwarted. He also found there two eminent mentors and, eventually, generous friends, Stephen Gilman and the late Raimundo Lida, to whom Julio is highly indebted, intellectually as well as personally. He met, during his first year at Harvard, the Spanish poet Jorge Guillén, greatly admired by him since his adolescent years; Guillén read his poetry and gave him a most needed encouragement. His first verse publication, *Homenaje* (1958, Homage), composed of several sonnets dedicated to favorite poets, old and new, appeared in Havana around this time. A second, and in every respect more considerable, volume of poetry, *Retrato de tiempo* (Portrait of Time), was published in 1959.

Julio remained active as a stage director throughout these years, having attained a remarkable success with his mise-en-scène of Ionesco's *The Bald Soprano,* which enjoyed a rather long run in Havana during the 1956–1957 theater season (his production of this play, repeated on several occasions, the last time in 1963, always met with the warmest reception). In the summers of 1957, 1958, and 1959, he staged several Cuban short plays—among them, two by the noted Virgilio Piñera; Ionesco's *The Lesson,* presented in 1958 and again in 1960, would confirm Julio's reputation as a brilliant interpreter of the absurdist master's works.

It was the foundation of the Cuban National Theater, amidst the popular enthusiasm generated by the budding Revolution, that attracted Julio back to Cuba at the beginning of 1960 to become one of the directors of the newly born institution. From 1960 until early 1965, he combined his work in the theater, as director and actor, with other creative activities, having been a contributor to *Lunes* (Monday)—literary supplement of the newspaper *Revolución* (Revolution)—which, under the editorship of Guillermo Cabrera Infante, served as vehicle for the younger generations of writers and artists. In 1961, Julio was appointed dramatic director of the weekly TV program *Lunes* and continued his work for other television projects after the demise of *Lunes* at the end of the same year. He collaborated in some of the productions of the Instituto Cubano del Cine (ICAIC), most notably in the film script of *Las doce sillas* (The Twelve Chairs), directed by Gutiérrez Alea, whom he assisted as well in the capacity of acting coach. Since 1962 he was also stage director of the Teatro Lírico de La Habana.

During this period, two books by Julio were published by Ediciones Revolución, as part of the series "Cuadernos Erre" —the collection of short stories *Catálogo de imprevistos* (1963, Catalog of the Unforeseen) and a play in three acts, *La crónica y el suceso* (1964, The Chronicle and the Event). *Catálogo de imprevistos*—which followed shortly the publication of some of its texts in the magazine *Unión* (organ of the Union of Writers and Artists)—became an instant success; the edition was out of print in a few weeks, and the critic Armando Alvarez Bravo hailed it in the *Gaceta de Cuba* as a refreshing revelation. *La crónica y el suceso* did not find its way to the stage, due to the fact that Julio left the country very soon after it appeared. In May 1965, Julio went to Spain and in September of that year arrived in the United States, where he had been offered a position in the Department of Hispanic Languages and Literatures at the University of Pittsburgh. He is at present full professor in that department.

Julio's writings have been growing ever since he settled in the United States. In 1971, another volume of fiction, *Erinia,* which includes all of the material from *Catálogo,* plus a good number of new stories, was printed by Editions "Alacrán Azul," an outgrowth of the literary magazine of the same name, whose life, like that of many other exile publications, was brief. In 1974 his book on the narrative of the Spanish writer Ramón Pérez de Ayala, *Contra el honor* (Against Honor), appeared in Spain; a volume of essays on Spanish and Latin American literature, *La cuestión del género literario* (On Literary Genres), was published by the prestigious Editorial Gredos of Madrid in its "Biblioteca Románica Hispánica," in 1979. His dramatic piece, *Ladies at Play (Juego de damas),* was included in the anthology *Selected Latin American One-Act Plays,* edited by Julio with a teacher colleague, for the University of Pittsburgh Press in 1973. Many critical studies and reviews, several short narrative works, and another play have also appeared in a variety of journals throughout the past and current decade. He has completed two collections of short stories *Transiciones, migraciones* (Transitions, Migrations) and *El mundo elástico* (The Elastic World) and several plays, all still waiting publication or performance. (Juego de damas has been presented in Spanish and English in various amateur and professional productions).

It is worth noting too that, between 1966 and 1975, Julio served as secretary of the Instituto Internacional de Literatura Iberoamericana and its publication, the *Revista Iberoamericana.*

Major Themes

As a poet, Matas is at his best in the evocative mood, conjuring up in taut imagery the world of his childhood and of familial figures—such poetry constitutes the major part of *Retrato de tiempo* (1959.) Some of his poems, though, transcend the limits of personal evocation, to become metaphors for a wider view of national realities—Cuba, seen in a tragic light, is the subject of a more recent poem, "Es el reino del sol" (*Mundus Artium,* 1970.) In the last analysis, his poetry points to certain human universals—individual joy and anguish, collective concerns, compassion for the other.

The themes of Julio Matas's stories and plays can be summed up as the ironies resulting from the clash between opposite individual aspirations or between the needs of the self and those of the social body. Repressions, obsessions, failures, a vague desire to reach without, an urge to fulfill certain fantasies recur throughout his works; the author's ironic distance is, in every case, mitigated by a pervasive, if subtle, feeling of pity toward his characters. His stories deal with the mysterious or supernatural, as well as with the concrete and immediate, although the same sense of strangeness appears in all of them. The effect achieved by his narrative and his theater is usually grotesque, a feature that does not contradict, but rather merges with the just-mentioned eerie quality.

In his *Prose Fiction of the Cuban Revolution,* Seymour Menton characterizes Matas's narrative literature as "escapist," a label that is, in my view, misleading. Menton seems to miss the point when he classifies Matas's short stories as a "cruel-absurd variety" and states that his other type of narration, "involving abnormal psychology of impotent men and frigid women with a dash of the fantastic," is actually two aspects of the same tragic, albeit humorous vision of mankind, mainly, because the sexual conflicts, which Menton rightfully observes, should be perceived as emblems alluding to deeper frustrations and inadequacies, caused by cruel and sometimes fateful conditions. Such is the case of "Normandía" (Normandy), where the woman in question is left practically a widow, on account of her husband's castration in the war, while the male protagonist's psychological impotency reflects the spiritual castration of his growing up in an East European totalitarian system; or of "Roberta en perspectiva" (Roberta in Perspective), the story of a transsexual who has to adjust to a new existence as a female, fighting against not only the surrounding prejudice, but that of a recently found lover, his/her predicament compounded by the pain of having to leave behind the children fathered during a rather happy marriage. Similar conflictive situations could also bring about acts of aberrant violence, like that of the child protagonist of "Crecimiento," who tries to prove to his father that he has the required *macho* strength by provoking his grandfather's death, or that of the policeman in "Carambola del 57," who, to escape justice, would kill all possible witnesses to a murder of passion he has committed, covered up by the reign of terror of a military dictatorship (specifically Cuban Fulgencio Batista's). Some of Matas's stories are very short parables, poignant and pregnant with meaning, belonging in a genre favored by masters such as Kafka and Borges, and practiced brilliantly in Cuba by Virgilio Piñera.

Matas's most ambitious play to date is the three-act *La crónica y el suceso,* which, within a Pirandellian frame, shows something very different from Pirandello's doomed "authorless" characters—namely, the problematic relationship between the real-life people on which a dramatic work is based and the author of the work; a confrontation that results in the physical destruction of the latter, a sort of victory of chaotic, full-blooded life over the formal constraints of art.

Survey of Criticism

Matas's work has been, so far, the subject of only some short, if keen and thoughtful, critical evaluations.

Erinia has been reviewed by Eduardo Mendicutti in Madrid's *La Estafeta Literaria* (1971), pointing to a common denominator in the stories included in the volume, which for him is the author's desire to take the reader by surprise ("sorprender"); he goes on to indicate their major stylistic and thematic features, detailing the accomplishments (he calls some of the pieces "sharp, pointed, brilliant''); as well as what he sees as their flaws (schematic treatment in the shorter stories, a certain structural looseness in the longer ones). Mendicutti lists "Normandía," "Un gran actor" (A Great Actor), and "Crecimiento" (Growth) as the best narratives in the book, stating that they possess "the right extension and intensity," and also praises, with some reservations, "Sangre de perrros" (Dogs' Blood). A more extensive review by Lourdes *Casal (1972) places Matas's stories in the context of a literary trend that produced a number of remarkable works in Cuba during the decade of the 1960s. She appropriately notes a tendency in *Erinia* toward a more realistic kind of narrative and discusses briefly the situations, technique, and characters of several stories, giving a very sound interpretation of the meaning of the title story, "Erinia" ; the latter is for her a clue to understanding the view and intention of the author throughout them all.

María Elvira Bermúdez, the Mexican writer, has devoted a short article (1974) to the stories contained in *Erinia* and two other stories published later— "Fieles difuntos" (The Faithful Dead) and "La memoria de los pájaros" (The Memory of Birds)—attempting, while considering each one of them, to assess their generic filiation, their narrative procedures, and their particular impact upon the reader. "The Art of Julio Matas" (González-Cruz, 1972) has been the first study to offer not only an overview of Matas's work, but an in-depth exploration of his fictional world through the textual analysis of "Erinia."

La crónica y el suceso has been thoroughly studied by Matías *Montes Huidobro in his *Vida, persona y máscara en el teatro cubano* (1973.)

Bibliography

WORKS BY MATAS

Homenaje. Havana: n.p., 1958.
Retrato de tiempo. Havana: Ucar García Editores, 1959.
Catálogo de imprevistos. Havana: Ediciones "Erre," 1963.
La crónica y el suceso. Havana: Ediciones "Erre," 1964.
Introduction to *Teatro,* by Luigi Pirandello. Havana: Consejo Nacional de Cultura, 1964.
Erinia. Miami-Zaragoza: Colección "Alacrán Azul," Editorial Universal, 1971.
Preface to *Persona, vida y máscara en el teatro cubano,* by Matías Montes Huidobro. Miami: Editorial Universal, 1973.
Selected Latin American One-Act Plays. Selection, translation, introduction, and notes by Julio Matas in collaboration with Francesca Colecchia. Includes an original piece, *Ladies at Play.* Pittsburgh: University of Pittsburgh Press, 1973.
Contra el honor. Las novelas normativas de Ramón Pérez de Ayala. Madrid: Seminarios y Ediciones, 1974.
G. Cabrera Infante (with other authors). Madrid: Colección Espiral/Figuras, Editorial Fundamentos, 1974.
La cuestión del género literario. Casos de las letras hispánicas. Madrid: Editorial Gredos, 1979. Contains studies on Valle-Inclán, García Lorca, Bécquer, Miró, Borges, Bioy Casares, Brull, Cortázar, and Cabrera Infante.

Recent Creative Work Not Included in Books

"It Is the Realm of the Sun . . . " / "Es el reino del sol . . . " Bilingual text. *Mundus Artium* (Winter 1970): 74–77.

"Fieles difuntos." "La memoria de los pájaros." *Exilio. Revista de Humanidades* (Winter-Spring 1972–1973): 27–36.

Translations: "A Bird's Memorandum." *Latin American Literary Review* (Fall 1972): 129–32. "La memoria degli uccelli." *Alla Bottega* (Milan), no. 5 (September-October 1973): 66–67. "Dear Departed." *Pitt Magazine* (May 1975): 28–30.

"Migraciones." *Consenso. Revista de Literatura* 1 (May 1977): 46–48.

Penelope Inside, Out (a play). *Latin American Literary Review* 6 (Fall-Winter 1977): 123–30.

"Apocalíptica." *Punto de Vista. Bilingual Magazine of the Hispanic World* (Kent State University) 1 (Fall 1978): 13–15, 24, 28.

"Carnario." *Consenso* 2 (November 1978): 14–18.

"La memoria de los pájaros." *Linden Lane Magazine* 2 (January-March 1983): 5.

WORKS ABOUT MATAS

Bermúdez, María Elvira. "Cuentos extraños." *Revista de la comunidad latinoamericana de escritores,* no. 15 (1974): 83–84.

Casal, Lourdes. Review of *Erinia. Exilio. Revista de Humanidades* (Fall 1972): 153–55.

González-Cruz, Luis F. "The Art of Julio Matas." *Latin American Literary Review* 1 (Fall 1972): 125–28.

Mendicutti, Eduardo. Review of *Erinia. La Estafeta Literaria* (Madrid), núm. 501 (1971): 1093.

Menton, Seymour. *Prose Fiction of the Cuban Revolution.* Austin: University of Texas Press, 1975.

Montes Huidobro, Matías. *Vida, persona y máscara en el teatro cubano.* Miami: Editorial Universal, 1973.

LUIS F. GONZÁLEZ-CRUZ

MATOS PAOLI, FRANCISCO (1915–　). Francisco Matos Paoli is one of Puerto Rico's most important poets. His work includes some forty books of poetry of which only half have been published. His pristine poetic vision has served him well as he has sought to clarify his relationship to his God, to join in the struggle for Puerto Rican independence, while suffering prison and mental illness as a consequence of it. He has been called the most unique, profound, and original poet of Puerto Rico. His *Canto a Puerto Rico* (1952, Canto to Puerto Rico) won him the poetry prize from the Ateneo Puertorriqueña. In 1944 he won the prize from the Instituto de Literatura Puertorriqueño for his *Habitante del eco* (Inhabitant of the Echo). His richest book is his *Canto de la locura* (1962, Canto to Madness). He stands alone as poet and patriot, madman and mystic in his country.

Biography

Francisco Matos Paoli was born on March 9, 1915, to Juan Matos Vélez and Susana Paoli Goya in the town of Lares, Puerto Rico. He was born on Stone Street, also known as Cuesta del Anón by the townspeople. This is significant because it was up this street that the patriots who proclaimed the Republic in the Grito de Lares in 1868 passed. His mother's mystical demeanor and religious sense of life saw her devoted to charity in all its forms—she particularly favored the poor and the beggars whom she called "God's chosen people." She was also given to speaking with spirits who populated her home where she spent a great deal of her time in a sort of monastic retreat. Her solitude and mysticism are gifts that her son has inherited that have helped him deal with his own demons and ghosts. From his father he received his poetic tendency that enabled him to confront the formidable obstacles of life in a poor colony. His father reputedly composed light verse when jobs were scarce and his satirical poetry helped to ease the pain of adversity.

In Lares he remained through secondary school. There he also pursued one of his mother's interests when he attended the center Luz y Progreso where he studied spiritualism, becoming a sensitive medium. This allowed him in later years to maintain a communication with his mother after her death.

By 1936 we find him at the Universidad de Puerto Rico where he read assiduously. His voracious reading of the classics (Góngora, San Juan de la Cruz, Garcilaso de la Vega, Becquer), poets of Spain's Generation of 1927 (Aleixandre, Alberti, Guillén, Salinas, Cernuda) and of Latin America (Vallejo, Neruda), the contemporary poets such as Miguel Hernández and others like Rilke helped to shape his esthetic sense in the world of poetry.

After he completed his university studies he taught as a professor at the University of Puerto Rico and he became involved in the struggle for Puerto Rican independence. His political life saw him reach the position of secretary of the Partido Nacionalista Puertorriqueño. As such he made two speeches in Lares and in Cabo Rojo inciting the people to join the Revolution of 1950 under the leadership of don Pedro Albizu Campos. These speeches caused his arrest in 1950 shortly after October 30. He was accused of having broken Law 53 of 1948, a law passed during his year in Paris (1947–1948) where he was studying. His letters in that year of absence to his wife, Isabel Freire de Matos, and his two daughters, Susana and Marisal, revealed a deep emotional attachment to the Island much like his nineteenth-century predecessor José Gautier Benítez.

He spent some five years in prison both in La Princesa and in the Presidio Insular. There he was subjected to up to ten months in solitary confinement which caused him to become mentally ill and forced him to go on two separate hunger strikes. The second hunger strike brought him a full pardon from Governor Luis Muñoz Marín on May 26, 1955. After the grant of a full pardon the authorities attempted to revert his status to that of a parolee, but Matos Paoli refused, requesting his return to jail unless the pardon was recognized, since, according to him, he had fought for his country's independence and that was not a crime.

While in prison he had tried to keep his madness at bay by writing verse on the walls and ceiling of his cell, but the guards would come and paint over it, sending him once again into the most solitary of confinements. He left prison and began to sell his poetry in the street until the rector of the University of Puerto Rico, Jaime Benítez, appointed him writer-in-residence, alleviating thus this economic deprivation.

His experience in prison and his mental illness derived from that experience have brought about several periods of internment in the Hospital de Siquiatría since 1955, some seven or eight times.

He remains a resident of San Juan although he has expressed a desire to return to Lares with his family.

His work as a poet begins in 1931 with his youthful collection of poems entitled *Signario de lágrimas* (Singlas of Tears), but most critics agree that his important work begins not at sixteen, but at twenty-two with *Cardo labriego y otros poemas* (1937, Worker's Thorn and Other Poems) followed by *Habitante del eco* (1944), *Teoría del olvido* (1944, Theory of Forgetfulness), *Canto a Puerto Rico* (1952), *Luz de los héroes* (1954, The Light of Heroes), *Criatura del rocío* (1958, Creature of the Dew), *Canto a la locura* (1962), *El viento y la paloma* (1969, The Wind and the Dove), *Cancionero* (1970, Song Book), *La marea sube* (1971, The Rising Tide), *La semilla encendida* (1971, The Enflamed Seed), *El angel con espada* (1971, The Angel with a Sword), *Rostro en la estela* (1973, Stellar Face), *La orilla sitiada* (1974, The Besieged Shore), *El engaño a los ojos* (1974, A Trick to the Eyes), *Ríelo del instante* (1975, Laughing at the Instant), *Unción de la tierra* (1975, Earthly Unction), *Dación y milagro* (1976, Dación and Miracle), *Ya se oye el cenit* (1977, Now You Hear the Zenith), *Loor del espacio* (1977, In Praise of Space), *Cancionero V* (1977, Songbook V), *Los crueles espejos* (1980, The Cruel Mirrors), and *Hacia el hondo vuelo* (1983, Toward Deep Flight). He has also collected his poetry in *Antología poética* (1972, Poetry Anthology) and in *Antología minuto* (1977, Minute Anthology), has written a tome similar to Alberti's *La arboleda perdida* which he entitled *Diario de un poeta* (1973, Diary of a Poet), and has some twenty unpublished works such as "Decimario de la Virgen" and "Testigo de la esperanza" which are reputed to be excellent material by those who have examined them.

Of his seventy years, as of this writing, Matos Paoli has devoted some fifty-four to poetry, from his youthful poems in his native Lares to his mature and complex work. His life and his work remain open to study by serious biographers and scholars.

Major Themes

The work of Francisco Matos Paoli is still incomplete. He has published over twenty books of poetry, but has another twenty-plus books unpublished, not including his poetry published in periodicals, magazines, anthologies, and the like. His early work took much from the masters, both classical and modern, who were the object of his reading, and it is anchored on some of the many issues of his day. His work has been called neoromantic, *neocriollista, vanguardista* (avant-garde), experimental, hermetic, estheticist, religious, philosophical, patriotic, mystical, neobaroque, and *atalayista* (of the group known as *La Atalaya de los Dioses*).

Matos Paoli's poetry fits each and every one of those adjectives. It is a complex body of works which have seen the poet's evolution and his addressing the great preoccupations of his life. His early work, *Cardo labriego y otros poemas* (1937) shares both in the neoromantic and the nativist *neocriollista* movements of the early twentieth century in Puerto Rico. As a neoromantic, Matos Paoli wishes to return to a pure lyric poetry with an esthetic goal in which beauty is raw, alive, and surprising. As a nativist he attempts to reintegrate the emotions of love for the land, for its people, for its freedom—in other words, a lyrical vision of social causes. Many of his later themes are foreshadowed in this refreshing collection of early verse. His religious mysticism, his attraction to sacrifice and martyrdom for his country's freedom, his love of the sea, and his preoccupation with social problems are all there. Also present is his interest in different strophic forms such as the sonnet and the *décima*.

Habitante del eco (1944) initiates one of his major themes that runs throughout a good portion of his work including *Teoría del olvido* (1944), *Criatura del rocío* (1958), *Canto a la locura* (1962), *El viento y la paloma (1961–63)* (1969), and also in *Cancionero* (1970). In these books Matos Paoli examines his anguish before the problem of salvation within a religious-mystical context. The poet's persona seeks a mystical union born of a beatific vision which in its contemplation of ineffable essences of the divine and his desire for purification negates the existence of the world. Matos Paoli employs a technique in these books in which he marries image to symbol in order to penetrate the curtain that separates outward appearance from inner truth.

If *Habitante del eco* reduces the problem of salvation to that of an esthetic plan for literary creation in which the poet attempts to recollect the echo of a message lost in his past, then *Teoría del olvido* carries out the plan in that the abstract nature of the former becomes more human and deeply felt in the latter. *Criatura del rocío*, on the other hand, composed of forty sonnets centered on the *vita-Christi*, intellectualizes the experience of the Christian struggle with the central questions of his faith.

With *Canto a Puerto Rico* (1952) Matos Paoli reaches the zenith of his nativist tendency observable from his early *Cardo labriego y otros poemas* (1937). The *Canto*, written in 1948 while in France, recalls the patriotic fervor of Gautier Benítez's approach to San Juan harbor after his own European tour. The vision of the ineffable presents itself within the context of this world. The poet seeks a political Eden, a freed Puerto Rico in the replay of Gautier's and his own absence from and presence in the island mediated by an evocation of his country. The love of the Caribbean Sea accompanies this nativist vision both in his own work and in that of Gautier and even his contemporary *Corretjer. *Luz de los héroes* (1954) follows the theme of independence. Like the *Canto* it is also dedicated to don Pedro Albizu Campos whom he calls "Beloved of the Fatherland." This book was composed in La Princesa prison. Here he joins the task of national liberation with a mystical and an esthetic enterprise. His tone is less objective than in the *Canto* and the poetic persona becomes less a narrator and more a participant in the struggle. Both books are full of rich imagery and an abundance of metaphors and similes that signal the poet's emotion. They constitute a poetic feast that will be retaken in *La marea sube* (1971) and *La semilla encendida* (1971). These books respond to the social and political circumstances surrounding the poet, whose attitude becomes critical of the status quo.

The *Diario de un poeta* (1973) is a notebook of thoughts, feelings, arguments, descriptions, and evocations that are a repository of ideas, attitudes, and emotions that have not seen the light in his poetry. They serve to illuminate some of the shadows encountered in his poetry books. This is a poetic book also, but one written without the rigor and excruciating discipline of Matos Paoli the poet.

But perhaps his most interesting book is his *Canto a la locura* (1962), written in two days according to his wife. Here the poet's demons all congregate to torment him from every possible angle. He constructs a poem in which the solitude of his madness, of his dreamworld alienates him from others, makes him suffer the estrangement from the world, the incapacity to communicate, and the ridicule of his contemporaries. The poet's search for salvation is inexorable and unswerving. He accepts the world's reality, but rejects its authority and its displacement of a more ephemeral, yet truer, vision of the world from his multiple perspective of poet, madman, and mystic.

Survey of Criticism

The work of Francisco Matos Paoli remains to be studied. There is no reliable bibliography of his production. The secondary bibliography is minuscule and marginal even when major critics have showered the highest of praise on him. But the difficulty of studying his work begins not only with the need to establish a recognized corpus of poetry, but also in the task of critical reading and in the insertion of his own ideosyncratic personality into his works, which provides the reader with few referential anchors in the text. It requires a great deal of relational work by the critic. Likewise, for the literary historian Francisco Matos Paoli is an enigma, because he is so unique a figure in Puerto Rican letters. His work can be associated with many schools, movements, tendencies, and epochs, but he seems to transcend them all regardless of his political and social preoccupations.

His first critic, Margot Arce de Vázquez, called him in 1944 the most profound and original poet in Puerto Rico. She claims that he is head and shoulders above the rest of his generation and of affiliates him with the Spanish poetic Generation of 1927. By 1959 Francisco Manrique Cabrera considered *Criatura del rocío* his most important work because of its lyrical and pure poetic qualities. José

Emilio González has been his most consistent critic, studying the trajectory of his work and the evolution of his style from 1956 until the present.

In 1970 Francisco Matos Paoli was included in the *Biografías puertorriqueñas* by Cesáreo Rosa-Nieves and Esther M. Melón and in the *Diccionario de literatura puertorriqueña* by Josefina Rivera de Alvarez. The treatment in the *Biografías* is surprising since it omits his prison experience, his political life, his mental illness, his mystical and religious experience and hardly tells the story of this remarkable man. The *Diccionario* also omits the salient biographical features, but gives a general account of his work. Both works catalogue his themes and his style. The former practically calls him surrealist without using the term, adding metrical freedom, imagery-laden poetry, baroque syntax, oneiric *creacionismo*, psychic *automatismo*, while the latter more soberly characterizes his work as using all sorts of meters and stanzaic forms, the traditional lyric, and the techniques of the new poetry. They both concur on the thematic content of his poetry.

In addition, Francisco Matos Paoli has been the subject of a number of brief mentions in introductions to anthologies and in newspaper briefs on his books.

With the exception of González Torres's descriptive monograph, Matos Paoli has been the subject of no other major study.

Bibliography

WORKS BY MATOS PAOLI

Signario de lágrimas. Aguadilla, P.R.: Tribuna Libre, 1931.
Cardo labriego y otros poemas. San Juan, P.R.: Imprenta Venezuela, 1937.
Habitante del eco (1937–1941). Santurce, P.R.: Imprenta Soltero, 1944.
Teoría del olvido. San Juan, P.R.: Junta Editora, Universidad de Puerto Rico, 1944.
Canto a Puerto Rico. San Juan, P.R.: n.p., 1952.
Luz de los héroes. San Juan, P.R.: n.p. 1954.
Criatura del rocío. San Juan, P.R.: n.p. 1958.
Canto de la locura. San Juan, P.R.: Ediciones Juan Ponce de León, 1962.
El viento y la paloma, 1961–63. San Juan, P.R.: Ediciones Juan Ponce de León, 1969.
Cancionero. San Juan, P.R.: Ediciones Juan Ponce de León, 1970.
La marea sube. San Juan, P.R.: Ediciones Juan Ponce de León, 1971.
La semilla encendida. San Juan, P.R.: Ediciones Juan Ponce de León, 1971.
Antología poética. Río Piedras, P.R.: Editorial Universitaria, Universidad de Puerto Rico, 1972.
Diario de un poeta. Santurce, P.R.: Ediciones Puerto, 1973.
Rostro en la estela. San Juan, P.R.: Ediciones Juan Ponce de León, 1973.
El engaño a los ojos. San Juan, P.R.: Ediciones Juan Ponce de León, 1974.
La orilla sitiada. San Juan, P.R.: Ediciones Juan Ponce de León, 1974.
Ríelo del instante. San Juan, P.R.: Ediciones Juan Ponce de León, ca. 1975.
Unción de la tierra. San Juan, P.R.: Ediciones Juan Ponce de León, 1975.
Canto de la locura. San Juan, P.R.: Instituto de Cultura Puertorriqueña, 1976.
Dación y milagro. San Juan, P.R.: Ediciones Juan Ponce de León, 1976.
Antología minuto. Mayagüez, P.R.: Colección de Poesía, Jardín de Espejos, 1977.

Cancionero V. (Only available information is date), 1977.
Loor del espacio. Hato Rey, P.R.: Ramallo Bros. Print, 1977.
Ya se oye el cenit. San Juan, P.R.: Ediciones Juan Ponce de León, 1977.
Los crueles espejos. San Juan, P.R., s.d., 1980.
Hacia el hondo vuelo. Río Piedras, P.R.: Editorial Universidad de Puerto Rico, 1983.

WORKS ABOUT MATOS PAOLI

Arce de Vázquez, Margot. "Carta-Prólogo" in *Teoría del olvido.* Río Piedras, P.R.:
    Junta Editora, Universidad de Puerto Rico, 1944.
————. "Prólogo." In Francisco Matos Paoli, *Criatura del rocío.* San Juan, P.R.: Ateneo
    Puertorriqueño, 1958.
Cartañá, Luis. "Prólogo." In Francisco Matos Paoli, *Antología minuto.* 2d ed. Mayagüez,
    P.R.: Jardín de Espejos, 1978.
Dávila, José Antonio. "Cardo labriego de Francisco Matos Paoli." In his *Prosa: ensayos,
    artículos y cartas literarias.* San Juan P.R.: Sociedad de Autores Puertorriqueños,
    1971.
"Francisco Matos Paoli." In *La ciudad de los poetas,* ed. Antonio Coll Vidal. Santurce,
    P.R.: Publicaciones Orsini-Bristto, 1965.
Freire de Matos, Isabel. "Itinerario de un poeta." In Francisco Matos Paoli, *Canto de
    la locura.* 2d ed., rev. and enl. San Juan, P.R.: Instituto de Cultura Puertorriqueña,
    1976.
Gómez Costa, Arturo. "Francisco Matos Paoli." In his *Vendimias en prosa.* Barcelona:
    Vosgos, 1976.
"Canto Nacional a Borinquen" de Francisco Matos Paoli. *El Mundo,* May 26, 1956.
————. "La Luz de los Héroes," de Francisco Matos Paoli. *Alma Latina.* March 24,
    1956.
————. "*Criatura del rocío.*" *Asomante,* 15 4 (1959): 81–83.
González, José Emilio. "*Canto de la locura.*" *Asomante* 20, 1 (1964): 82–85.
————. "Reflexiones sobre la poesía de Francisco Matos Paoli." In Francisco Matos
    Paoli, *Antología poética.* San Juan: Editorial Universitaria, Universidad de Puerto
    Rico, 1972.
González Torres, Rafael A. *La búsqueda de lo absoluto; la poesía de Francisco Matos
    Paoli.* San Juan, P.R.: Biblioteca de Autores Puertorriqueños, 1978.
López, Julio César. "Francisco Matos Paoli y el vanguardismo literario." In his *La patria
    en dos poetas y un paralelo modernista.* Barcelona: Ariel, 1968. Also San Juan,
    1968. Orig. *RICP,* No. 38 (1968): 9–12.
Manrique Cabrera, Francisco. "*Criatura del rocío.*" *Asomante* 15, 4 (1959): 81–83.
————. *Historia de la literatura puertorriqueña.* New York: Las Américas Publishing
    Co., 1956.
Matos Paoli, Francisco. "Mi experiencia como poeta." *BAAC* 11, 1–2 (1975): 88–92.
Pagán Soto, Gladys. "*Criatura del rocío,* de F. Matos Paoli." *El Mundo.* November
    16, 1959.
Puebla, Manuel de la. "El compromiso poético de Francisco Matos Paoli." *Sin Nombre,*
    8, 4 (1978): 10–27.
Rivera de Alvarez, Josefina. *Diccionario de literatura puertorriqueña.* Tomo I. San Juan,
    P.R.: Instituto de Cultura Puertorriqueña, 1970.
Rosa-Nieves, Cesáreo, and Esther M. Melón. *Biografías puertorriqueñas: perfil histórico
    de un pueblo.* Sharon, Conn.: Troutman Press, 1970.

Santos Silva, Loreina. *"Loor del espacio* de Francisco Matos Paoli: una mística mater-
ialista." *CA*, No. 221 (1978): 140–42.
Torre, José R. de la. "Mundo y trasmundo en el *Cancionero* de Matos Paoli." *SinN* 2,
1 (1971): 49–65.

RODOLFO J. CORTINA

MOHR, NICHOLASA (1935–   ). Nicholasa Mohr is a gifted artist, whose
prints and drawings have appeared in numerous exhibitions in New York and
Puerto Rico. She used artistic versatility to author, illustrate, and design the
book jacket for both *Nilda* (1973), an award-winning juvenile novel, and *El
Bronx Remembered* (1975), followed by three other semi-autobiographical books:
In Nueva York (1977), *Felita* (1979), and *Going Home* (1986). An adult-audience
semi-autobiography is her *Rituals of Survival: A Woman's Portfolio* (1985). Each
depicts her early days as the child of Puerto Rican migrants to New York City's
El Barrio (Spanish Harlem). Nicholasa is the first Puerto Rican woman on the
mainland to write in English about her own ethnic origins, and her pictures,
novels, short stories, and essays offer an excellent primary source for interpreting
the private and public tensions of Puerto Rican family and community life in
New York's Lower East Side since World War II.

Biography

Nicholasa was born on November 1, 1935, to Pedro and Nicholasa (Rivera)
Golpi, the father from Vieques and the mother from Ponce, the youngest child
in a family with six older brothers. The young woman admits that she was always
a good story teller, and when she conducted printmaking workshops at Pratt
Institute, her friends would say, "Come on Nicholasa, tell us a story." Her
mother who "kissed the mango tree" entertained the children with folk tales,
and the author says she is blessed with the ability to retain early impressions of
her life.

The heartaches she is more concerned about are those associated with her own
experiences as a first-generation Puerto Rican. However, some background details about the immigrant experience of Puerto Ricans are essential in order to
understand the panoramic vistas of Nicholasa's world. Columbus landed on the
island of Puerto Rico on his second trip to the New World in 1493, but the
Spanish didn't establish settlements until 1508. For more than 400 years Puerto
Rico was part of the Spanish Empire, but as early as the 1860s, political exiles
were working from a base in New York for the independence of the island. As
a result of the Spanish-American War, Puerto Rico was ceded to the United
States and, by 1910, 1,513 Puerto Ricans were living on the mainland, more
than one-third residing in New York City. In 1917 American citizenship was
granted to all Puerto Ricans, making them eligible to migrate to the mainland
without any quota restrictions. Thirty years later, when almost 70,000 Islanders
flew to the mainland, they became America's first airborne immigrants. Instead

of suffering agonizing weeks of shipboard steerage-class travel, facing detention centers at Ellis Island, and waiting five years before applying for citizenship, Puerto Ricans conveniently flew to New York for relatively modest sums. Between 1940 and 1950, the United States Puerto Rican population quadrupled to 301,000. Almost one-third of the Island's population have come to the mainland, with over 1.5 million living in the United States by 1969, and more than 977,000 living in New York City, where they comprised about 11 percent of that city's population. During the 1970s, a trend toward reverse immigration began as many Neoricans (as they are called by their Island-bred relatives) returned to Puerto Rico, and, actually, in 1972 more people returned to the Island than migrated.

As citizens, Puerto Ricans did not face immigration quotas, and so they purchased one-way tickets to the mainland, joining families and friends on Manhattan's Upper East Side, El Barrio, an older Spanish-speaking community. Others moved into congested neighborhoods inhabited by the earlier migrants or their children, while the more recent arrivals formed new neighborhoods in Manhattan's Lower East Side, eventually expanding Spanish Harlem to include the South Bronx, known to Puerto Ricans as "El Bronx."

These migrants and their children, as Nicholasa describes them in her introduction to *El Bronx Remembered,* were "strangers in their own country [having] brought with them a different language, culture, and racial mixture. Like so many before them they hoped for a better life, a new future for their children, and a piece of that good life known as the 'American Dream.' "

Nicholasa's own parents shared this desire for their picture-sketching daughter to have an easier life than they experienced. Trapped by sexist cultural traditions, the young woman remembers how unjust it was for her own mother and other Latin women to conform to the role of wife and mother, always sacrificing themselves for their children. Fortunately her own artistic skills were recognized at an early age, and Nicholasa studied at the Art Students League of New York, 1953–1956, Brooklyn Museum Art School, 1959–1966, and Pratt Center for Contemporary Printmaking, 1966–1969, while supporting herself as a waitress, a clerical factory worker, and a translator. She married Irwin Mohr, a child psychologist, on October 5, 1957, has two sons, David and Jason, and, as a widow living in Brooklyn now, she supports herself by her writing.

Nicholasa's focus in her literature and graphic art is on the first and second generation of those who remained, reflecting her own family's situation. Her parents, with four sons, arrived on the mainland in 1927 and settled in the area of New York that came to be known as El Barrio, Spanish Harlem. Two more sons and Nicholasa, the youngest and only daughter, were born during the Depression decade.

This ambitious girl decided at an early age to become an artist and, after working her way through art schools, she pursued a career as a graphic artist for eighteen years before turning to writing fiction. She never consciously wanted to write, but encouragement from a business acquaintance led her to try. She began with a series of vignettes based upon her experiences in the Spanish-speaking communities in El Barrio where she grew up, and her first book, *Nilda*, won the Jane Addams Children's Book Award and was selected by *School Library Journal* as a Best Book of the Year in 1973. Her book jacket received the Society of Illustrators Citation of Merit, depicting through drawings, symbols, and words the thematic focus of the characters and their interrelationships.

Before embarking upon a writing career, which occupies her entire time at present, Nicholasa's talents as a fine arts painter took her from New York to California, Mexico, and Puerto Rico from 1952 to 1962. She was an instructor at the Art Center of Northern New Jersey from 1971 to 1973 and at the MacDonald Colony in Peterborough, New Hampshire, in 1976. Later she served as a writer-in-residence and an artist-in-residence in the New York City public schools, and in 1977 a lecturer in Puerto Rican Studies at the State University of New York (Stony Brook), a visiting lecturer in creative writing for the University of Illinois Educational Alliance Program (Chicago) also in 1977, the University of Wisconsin (Oshkosh) in 1978, and Bridgeport, Connecticut, public schools in 1978. Her television writing as a consultant on bilingual media with the Young Filmmakers Foundation in 1974 and 1975 produced five half-hour video tapes focusing on the cultural heritage of Caribbean Hispanic Americans entitled "Here and Now." She is recognized as a vibrant new voice among the flourishing group of second-generation Puerto Rican literary leaders in the United States writing in English. She admits that the transition from graphic artist to author, which she considers "another form of creativity," has been rewarding.

Major Themes

Nicholasa's concern about her own Puerto Rican people is evident through the themes developed in her works. A sense of place is evident as she describes what life is like for the 1.3 million Puerto Ricans in the greater New York City area living in the crumbling tenements of Manhattan's Harlem and Lower East Side or in the burned-out wasteland of the South Bronx. For them, life is mostly an unending struggle for survival, as her stories reveal.

She details how and why most unskilled Puerto Ricans are forced to take menial jobs. With one-third of all families on relief, the average family income in 1970 was $49.00 per week. Nicholasa herself describes the feelings of ten-year-old Nilda, actually a thinly disguised semi-autobiographical juvenile story, when the child is forced to miss precious school days because she has to go with her mother to the Welfare Department for food stamps. While waiting, she sees posters of what a person should eat for a well-balanced breakfast as she remains hungry during the long waiting hours before they are given an opportunity to plead their case to be eligible for public assistance before an unfeeling, bureaucratic clerk, who humiliates both work-weary mother and sensitive child with her condescending air.

Nicholasa's depiction of family life in her stories shows that it follows no simple traditional pattern, especially because of the migration of people from the Island to the mainland. Extended families are common, as well as nuclear ones, the latter frequently including children of other unions. Many female-headed households exist with male desertion evident. Consensual unions, relatively stable ones of men and women with no legal or religious sanction, were sometimes common until recently, especially among poorer people in Puerto Rico.

The families in her novels and short stories are described as large and beset with the problems facing a rural people suddenly thrust into an industrial society with the movement of migratory masses. She is particularly bitter about the treatment of her ethnic group after American colonization began, telling about the famine that was rampant throughout the Island of Puerto Rico after nineteen years of American occupation when, in 1917, the Jones Act declared Puerto Ricans citizens so the men could be recruited into the armed forces to fight. In her own words: "This new status legalized an economic dependency, imposed a new language and North American culture, setting Puerto Rico apart from the rest of their Latin American family. A new group of adopted citizens was created, who would become children of a new Diaspora, forced by history to leave their homeland" (Gloria Valencia-Weber, 150–51).

Nicholasa has a missionary zeal to tell what it was like to be born a child of that Diaspora during the Depression years of the 1930s, in what she labels "a small urban village set in the heart of New York City." She realized at an early age that "us Puerto Ricans" were different from other Latinos, because "we were born citizens even in Puerto Rico" (Valencia-Weber, 1980). The subculture of poverty in the slums and the generation gap over the use of vernacular Spanish compared with the significance of English in daily life are explored in her works as well, especially since she knows firsthand what she experienced growing up as a minority child in a power-controlled Anglo culture.

For example, in the classroom the teachers taught from history books that had little respect for those more recent migrants seeking the fulfillment of the American dream. Nicholasa learned, as she said recently, that these same Americans "saved us from the cruel Spaniards, that we had to be grateful, speak only English, and strive toward total assimilation. In essence, to succeed, I would have to reject a culture and history that I actually knew nothing about. My knowledge about myself, the history of the Puerto Rican people, was to come later, when I was able to travel and read books that held the truth" (Valencia-Weber, 151).

And this truth can be found in Nicholasa's four books, too. Her first one, *Nilda* (1973), an anecdotal, semi-autobiographical novel, traces four years of the protagonist's life from 1941 to 1945, her development from a young girl of ten to a señorita completing high school and trying to come to terms with her mother's death. Narrated from the child's viewpoint, the reader is exposed to police brutality, drugs, crime, the influence of the Roman Catholic Church, and a realistic mother-daughter relationship.

Nicholasa's purpose, she told Valencia-Weber, was to make "a strong social statement; the plight and constant struggle of Puerto Ricans on the mainland to receive their basic human rights.'' She depicts her people "with all their variety and complexity through the universal language of humanity.''

Nilda and her family are called "spicks,'' "animals,'' and "you people'' by teachers, social workers, police, and others who control their lives, and the story unfolds like a documentary detailing what it feels like being a despised minority in a family whose daily struggle is to survive. The mother's frustration in trying to take care of six children, a sick husband, a mentally ill aunt, and the pregnant girlfriend of one drug-addicted, prison-bound son is sketched in realistic detail, through a child's vision—questioning, resigned, furious, joyful. Nicholasa's vigorous portrayal of Nilda's large family with the absence of artificial solutions or a contrived ending gives the novel unique strength.

El Barrio serves as the backdrop for the girl's exposure to gang wars, street stabbings, police cruelty, insensitive social workers, the joys of summer camp, a secret garden. Sad episodes such as sadistic teachers, ignorant of diverse ethnic cultures, who shame the Puerto Rican children publicly and her mother's painful death contrast with comic incidents such as an eccentric old woman calling the authorities for help when a numbers den is raided and she can't place her bets there. The story develops in the new tradition of facing life without illusion in juvenile fiction by showing the tragedy of a family broken up after the mother's terminal illness and Nilda, who though rapidly maturing, is experiencing difficult days of sorrow.

She has found that authority figures have no compassion. In *Nilda,* the police are depicted as vicious racists, responding with hostility to children opening a fire hydrant on a sweltering summer day: "God damn you people . . . coming here making trouble. Bunch of animals. . . . The whole God damned bunch of you spicks.'' In another situation, detectives beat two boys so severely that one loses his eyesight.

Nilda's school continues this institutionalized dehumanization. To speak or write in Spanish, she is told, will prevent her from being a "good American.'' One excruciating scene occurs after the grieving girl has been absent for an extended period following her father's death. She explains to the school directors that this lengthy bereavement ritual is "her custom,'' with the following teacher response: "No wonder you don't do anything worthwhile with these kinds of customs. Your mother will have to come in and explain what kind of tribe you belong to.''

The community churches are portrayed as greedy institutions that get rich by taking advantage of parishioners' fears and superstitions. However, Nicholasa's poor in *Nilda,* especially her pious mother, find comfort in holiday celebrations with the entire neighborhood participating in the colorful pageantry of the Mass and sacraments. Folk religious practices continued to flourish on the mainland with spiritualism common. Rooted in the conviction that communication with the dead is possible, séances during Nilda's girlhood were popular. Family solidarity provides support to the bereaved, and the mentally ill such as an elderly aunt are considered troubled by evil spirits, evoking compassionate support from Puerto Ricans, but not from Anglo outsiders.

The security of this ethnic group is threatened further by the changing roles of males and females in the United States. On the Island, the man is the decision-maker, supports his family, and has more freedom than the woman in his sensual behavior. His manhood is defined in part by his power and sexual dominance over women. On the mainland, the availability of employment and education for women and the impact of American culture change the traditional relationship and self-defined roles of the sexes, resulting in a breakdown of family stability. The increasing number of female-headed households in Nicholasa's stories shows that jobs and public welfare ensured the survival of women without men. An intolerable union is terminated with welfare providing an alternative means of survival, but the Puerto Rican children suffer when the family unit is splintered. The teenager's street life, for example, is beyond the ability of the mother to handle, one reason explaining the high drug use, truancy, and delinquency among this ethnic youth group.

Another aspect of the weakening of the immigrant family relationship arises from tensions between the generations. Nicholasa and those depicted in her stories grew up at home in a Puerto Rican culture and became acculturated through school to another. The conflict between family loyalty and individual success occurs when economic opportunities take younger members away from the community forever; at the conclusion of *Nilda,* the mother's death impels the main character to leave her familiar surroundings because work and army careers have scattered the older male family members.

Nicholasa sketches a young girl who becomes aware of the humiliations her people face and of the prejudices within her community. Her people are burdened by violence, poverty, and illness, but her dying mother's message gives Nilda the strength to continue: "You have something all yours. Keep it . . . guard it. Hold on to yourself. . . . A little piece inside has to remain yours. . . . To give it all up . . . you will lose what is real inside you." She has her drawings and her dreams to escape the dehumanizing aspects of daily existence. If the police are verbally abusive, she busies herself by studying the objects carried along the gutter by the water from the fire hydrant—a ghettoized river of life—or she wipes out their presence by thinking about flowers. When her father dies, she studies trees and thinks about the coming of spring. After her mother's death, her brothers leave, and when she is forced to live with an aunt she does not love, Nilda finds consolation in her sketches of a summer camp she attended where there was a special trail in the woods leading to a secret garden. Thus, the story ends optimistically, implying that even a powerless girl has the strength of will, the beauty of nature, and the artistic imagination to cope creatively with inhumanity, sorrow, and death.

Nicholasa not only describes her own background in her stories, she also reveals her personal enthusiasm for life. Despite her protagonists' hardships and struggles, they are enriched through their experiences. Even failure results in a resilient spirit, with characters unwilling to accept ultimate defeat. Good triumphs again and again, especially since many of her works show young girls who personify youthful optimism.

The author's second published volume, a novella and collection of short stories, *El Bronx Remembered* (1975), was a National Book Award Finalist. It features the writer's gripping graphic art on the dust jacket, with other powerful pictures sketched within the volume itself showing the interaction of character, setting, and theme from prints exhibited in New York and Puerto Rican museums. The collection poignantly depicts neighborhood life, telling about some realistic situations such as failed marriages, illegitimacy, and homosexuality. Once again her people suffer, but they endure with resiliency against the entrapment that poverty and despair bring. She never uses slogans or resorts to militant ethnicity, but effectively shows her sympathy through compassionate and comic character delineations. Her Puerto Ricans, not unlike many immigrant groups, seem to be dwelling in an alien rather than a hostile society, and her stories focus upon the universal emotions of pride, nostalgia, hope, love, and fear with Chekovian narrative skill. Nicholasa searches through her memory recalling the late 1940s when her ethnic group arrived en masse, settling in decaying sections of the South Bronx and clinging to the Hispanic culture they brought with them. Her second book continues the story that *Nilda* began, this time describing the postwar decade from 1946 to 1956 and showing that Puerto Rico has become a dreamlike memory for the more settled inhabitants, but the Island customs remain: the changing window displays of the funeral home showing color photographs of the dead, an emigrant mother's attempt to provide eggs for her children by keeping a pet chicken, Joncrofo (Joan Crawford), named after a beloved movie star, and the importance of the neighborhood churches. But the New York environment is never absent, faithfully depicted as well. For example, during a police interrogation, a young girl's testimony saves her from drug charges, and three innocent children playing on a rooftop discover a dead teenage gang member and continue playing, uninvolved and unmoved by the neighborhood violence.

Several stories describe interethnic friendships such as one in which an elderly, lonely Jew is welcomed to join a friendly Puerto Rican family until urban blight forces them to separate with the old man having nothing more to live for. "Wrong Lunch Line" depicts a teacher who does not understand the friendship between two girls, Hispanic and Jewish, trying to share a Passover lunch in the cafeteria. "Shoes for Hector," later produced as a school play in New York City, tells the feelings of a teenager shamed by the forced borrowing of his uncle's orange, pointed-front shoes for a high school graduation where he receives valedictorian honors.

That values and loyalties are changing is evident in *El Bronx Remembered* as Nicholasa tells about Vickie who was born in New York and seldom left the Bronx. At school when she pledges allegiance "to the United States of America, and to the Republic for which it stands," she "never thought of Puerto Rico as

her country." As Nicholasa told Gloria Valencia-Weber, " . . . as a youngster
. . . I wanted to belong. It is not possible to belong when society sees you as an
invisible participant, someone tolerated, rather than accepted as a necessary
member of a group." She feels that her people are treated like adopted children,
"not being wanted, someone doing you a favor . . . " creating a group "who
are near the bottom of the economic scale, . . . discriminated against and rarely
. . . see themselves in positive role models on the media, or anywhere in the
mainstream of American society."

The novella "Herman and Alice" depicts the friendship, marriage of con-
venience, and the inevitable separation of a pitying, middle-aged homosexual
male and a desperate, pregnant unmarried teenager who live in the same apartment building. Alienation, family abandonment, rejection, and fear of aging are
compassionately described in this tale about two people struggling for love and
happiness. Nicholasa admits that the publisher debated whether to include this
story in a collection intended for young adult readers and the publication was
delayed for eight months because of the homosexual references even though
good taste was used.

In Nueva York (1977), Nicholasa's third published volume, won the following
honors: "Best Book for Spring 1977," *School Library Journal*; "Best Books
for Young Adults, 1977," American Library Association; "Notable Trade Book
Award, 1977," National Conference of Social Sciences; "One of Ten Best New
and Noteworthy Paperbacks," the *New York Times*, 1979.

The Nuyorican population, a term coined in the 1970s to describe Puerto
Ricans born or raised in New York, consists of several generations who are well
established but still linked with the homeland, although few arrive from the
Island anymore. Dreamlike segments are sketched by Nicholasa to symbolize
some characters' memories of an idealized Puerto Rican paradise. But her personalities are older, less idealistic, and more realistic. Nilda escapes from tension
by transforming herself into a garden fantasy; the young woman in the vignette,
aptly titled "Coming to Terms," does exactly that. She confronts her problems,
and the people, especially Nicholasa's females, have many. They live in decaying
tenements, frequently separated from husbands, often on welfare as they battle
rats, dirt, junkies, street gangs, ruthless landlords, hostile building inspectors,
greedy politicians, prejudiced teachers, and racist police. They are sustained
through their crises by family and community support, by their religious faith,
and by loving concern for their children. They do more than survive—they fight
back.

This survival theme is personified in *In Nueva York* by an ugly, ancient alley
cat who serves as a symbolic thread. He is introduced in the first story scavenging
for garbage scraps and is served milk and then peacefully falls asleep as the last
tale ends. The characters are survivors, too. Old Mary, coming from San Juan
forty years ago, lured by the promise of higher wages and better opportunities,
purchased a one-way ticket to New York, confident that she could send for her
son. A domestic servant at thirteen, impregnated by her master two years later,

then abandoned and deserted, Mary's life had been difficult on the Island and not better on the mainland. Illegitimate babies, poverty, and alcoholism entrapped her so that her desire to bring this son from Puerto Rico was never fulfilled until the end of her life when she is sick, depressed, and beyond hope. They have a joyful reunion in New York with the entire community involved in the home-coming preparations.

The focal point of this neighborhood in *In Nueva York* is Rudi's lunchroom, where the owner admits that he doesn't miss Puerto Rico because "I been here since I got my discharge in 1946 from the army. I married my first wife here, I love Nueva York . . . it's my home. I go to Puerto Rico and I can't take the slow pace there no more. Nuorquino . . . that's me now."

But those who arrive on the mainland face the shock of color discrimination, a major source of tension and one for which they are not prepared. On the Island, class rather than color is stressed, and among the poor, in particular, an ease of social interaction exists, different from the black experience in the United States. Prejudice exists, but it is less overt and pervasive than in the New York setting. Nicholasa writes about the tensions within the family and community as the result of this discrimination. Being light skinned is favored in the adjustment process, with those who can win acceptance as white assimilating into that community. Hostilities are present between Puerto Ricans and blacks in com-petition for power, jobs, and housing. Street violence often erupts.

Another reason for tension results when Puerto Ricans marry outside their group to non-Hispanics, diminishing ethnic identification and changing the tra-ditional family pattern further. A high rate (20 percent) of intermarriage between Puerto Ricans of different colors is evident in contrast to the low rate of interracial marriage among the total United States population or between Puerto Ricans and American blacks. Nicholasa has concerned herself in recent years, through her writings, with the civil rights and black power movements as they have influenced her own ethnic group. Puerto Ricans have an ambiguous role as a racially mixed group. They are already an integrated population, so their interests focus upon better employment and educational opportunities. Nicholasa's young heroines learn racial and religious understanding from a wise mother or grandmother, so if Puerto Ricans continue to intermingle and intermarry with people of a different color or religion, it could contribute toward easing the racial tensions of mainland American life.

In *In Nueva York*, Nicholasa's realistic interpretation of life for young adult readers is evident in her tasteful tale about a gay couple, sickly Sebastian and army-bound Johnny, and the arranged marriage between the latter and a lesbian nurse to provide Sebastian with health care. The most memorable aspect of the story is the humane acceptance of homosexual liaisons evidenced when the pretty flower girl sings "You've Got a Friend" during the wedding reception. The tragic repercussions of a splintered family for children are obvious in a story aptly entitled "I Never Seen My Father" in which two classroom friends, one college-bound and the other a drug-addicted delinquent, meet to discuss their

futures. The optimistic enthusiasm of the girl whose father has served as a good
role model is compared with the one nervously chain-smoking during the reunion
who has no loving network of support, only a probation officer and anti-poverty
program director as her sole hope for rehabilitation.

Nicholasa's fourth book, *Felita* (1979), written specifically for a juvenile
reader and labeled a "Notable Trade Book" by the National Conference of
Social Studies the same year, traces twelve months in the life of a nine-year-
old girl living in a predominantly Puerto Rican neighborhood section of New
York and explores the impact upon the family when they move to an integrated
neighborhood with cleaner streets, more trees, and better schools. Felita leaves
her community friends reluctantly. The move proves disastrous. They are mer-
cilessly harassed: their mail box is broken, a brother's library books are scattered
in the street, and Felita's dress is torn. The girl in *Felita* is made painfully aware
of what it feels like to be an outsider, despised by other minorities. Non-Hispanic
children taunt her, and their parents are no better: "Your family, what are you?
Niggers? Spicks? Why don't you stay with your own kind? Can't you answer?"
The family, much to Felita's delight, is forced to return to the old neighborhood.
Her grandmother tries to explain why life on the Island was better. "There you
can pick flowers, not like here where they give you a fine." Unlike the racial
prejudices on the mainland, skin pigmentation differences are unimportant. "We
Puerto Ricans are a rainbow of earth colors. Just like the many flowers of one
garden. . . . And when ignoramuses criticize or correct you because you speak
Spanish words, let them know how much better off you are. Look how you and
I can speak in Spanish together. . . . When anyone says, 'Go back to where you
came from' or 'You don't belong here,' tell them Puerto Ricans . . . are citizens."
She urges her discouraged grandchild to develop inner strength in order to face
life's challenges more courageously. The story, intended for young readers, ends
with a plea for universal brotherhood because "everyone can feel sorrow or be
hurt by others. We all share the same basic feelings."

Nicholasa's concern about racial prejudice is described in her short story "An
Awakening . . . Summer 1956" when a dark-skinned young woman is awakened
to the depravity of a segment of America's population when she sees written on
a restaurant wall: "No Coloreds, No Mexicans, No Dogs Will Be Served on
These Premises." She bravely enters the diner on a hot Texas day and demands
a cool drink. When she is treated inhumanely, she smashes a soda bottle on the
diner floor. Later, making friends with other community members, she realizes
that not everyone shares the attitudes of the lunchroom proprietor, and she decides
to dedicate her life to fighting oppression. With the scar from the broken bottle
as a reminder that she must have the courage to never submit to discrimination,
for the first time the Hispanic woman "was proud of all she was, her skin, her
hair and the fact that she was a woman," according to Evangelina Vigil, commenting on "An Awakening . . . Summer 1956" in her introduction to *Woman
of Her Word*.

Nicholasa's most recent works are nostalgic pieces telling about her Christmas memories, "a time of plenty" when Depression hardships and war are temporarily forgotten. "God's plenty" or "just plain luck" enabled her family and community members to prepare traditional festive dishes such as meat pies, seasoned rice, a roasted sow whose aromas permeated the entire street. In "Christmas Was a Time of Plenty," she imagined that her own tenement "would surely elevate to heaven just from the sheer goodness and delight of all those flavors floating around in the atmosphere." Friends and neighbors joined together, some bringing guitars and accordians, others recited poetry, some made speeches, and they danced to the loud music of the latest Latin hits. Three decades later she recalls those girlhood days during "the magical Christmasses . . . in our urban village set in the heart of New York City."

As a teacher, Nicholasa admits in "Their America" that the children attending the public schools in decaying cities, "young people . . . left to grow and survive among the ruins," inspire her most. She delights in gazing upon "a sea of bright dark faces, their eyes shining with an eagerness to learn and a curiosity that is so healthy and natural." She encourages them to "matter to themselves" and have the "strength to achieve the capabilities and the talents they possess." She reminds them of the "sacrifices" made by parents and grandparents, but urges them to remember the "network of Puerto Ricans and other Hispanics, Asian Americans, blacks, Native Americans and the white working class poor."

Nicholasa is optimistic about the future because the more than 1.3 million Puerto Ricans in the New York City area (1980 Census) represent a powerfully vibrant community force of ethnic pride in future decades. In spite of being the largest and most beleaguered group with a high percentage on welfare, representing the city's underclass, contributing to the ghetto plagues of violent crime, drug use, and arson, they have ambivalent feelings about living on the mainland or returning to the Island. Many Puerto Ricans don't vote enough or get involved with the political process because some dream about educating their children and saving enough money to buy a house in Puerto Rico and to retire there. But passivity is on the wane as activists become more involved in education and politics, especially young women identifying with Nicholasa as a successful role model of the American dream fulfilled.

However, New York City's Puerto Ricans are taking a leadership role in the arts. As told to Gloria Valencia-Weber in Nicholasa's own words: "What is amazing . . . is the unique way we have of fusing our own integrated culture with the North American experience . . . music, language, dance, drama, food, religion and now literature. . . . A good example is New York City—once Dutch, later English, Irish, Italian and Jewish, it is now a Latino city. The 'big apple' has become the 'big avocado.' " Nicholasa admits that the struggle for daily survival goes on. Battling against inadequate housing and against low-quality schools where bilingual education is almost nonexistent, Puerto Ricans have "superhuman strength" to survive. She wants her people to achieve "political and social representation" in order to "obtain the power to determine our own destiny and carve a better future for our children . . . not a favor we should ask for, but a right we deserve" (Valencia-Weber, (1980), 154–55).

Survey of Criticism

Nicholasa's attempts to serve as a witness and translator in detailing Puerto Rican experiences in American society during four decades in New York through her books for adults and children, her short stories, essays, and graphic art have won her the many awards already listed. She is at her best when she shows the inner strength that helped her characters survive, sometimes by remembering their beautiful Island, thus escaping the ugliness of inner city squalor. Her sociodocumentary sketches are excellent primary sources for the post–World War II decade when Hispanics hoped for a better future, shaped by two different environmental cultures. As Nicholasa told Gloria Valencia-Weber: "As a child growing up and developing, I did not wake up to a tropical sunrise and retire to the sounds of a tropical island's night breezes. Instead, I lived in a hard grey industrial city and slept to the rhythm of traffic noise. Teachers . . . spoke to me in English. The closest I got to Puerto Rico was listening to the older people's reminiscences and eating the food my mother set on the table. The rest was vague and somewhat of a mystery."

Critics are unanimous in asserting that Nicholasa's creative skill evokes the spirit, the beauty, and the pain of the Puerto Rican American community as a chronicler of life in El Barrio, the South Bronx, and Lower East Side, especially in her realistic depiction of the injustices and struggles her generation faced in their attempts to survive and adapt to a hostile Anglo society. Her work fulfills an important need, especially since the Puerto Rican population is young, with 48 percent of it below the age of twenty. Twenty-three percent of the total school population consists of this ethnic group, and as these children reach marriageable age and begin to raise families, the rapid increase in their numbers will make them by 1990 one of the largest ethnic groups in New York City, so Nicholasa's works are read by an important, impressionable group.

Critics praise the folk religious practices, music, festivals, and family rituals depicted accurately in her stories. She relates well to the streetwise and worldly Nuyoricans and other young adult readers coping more aggressively than their parents with hardships and discrimination, wanting to read about divorce, family stress, unwed mothers, street gangs, and student demonstrations. Critics admire the way in which Nicholasa realistically writes about the Puerto Rican dichotomy, arriving as immigrants but at the same time citizens. Despite this initial advantage, she tells what it has felt like to face poverty and prejudice that leaves them menial jobs, economic exploitation, unemployment, and the handicaps of limited education. They came to New York as the unskilled jobs were disappearing after World War II, and large areas of New York fell into a state of deterioration, making stable residence difficult.

The reception of her literary works in Puerto Rico has been complex. The complicated political situation on the Island is reflected in the attitudes that

Puerto Ricans there have about those in the states. Nicholasa admitted to Gloria Valencia-Weber that some Islanders have said that "since I write in English, I have no right to be called a Puerto Rican writer. The effects of colonization upon Puerto Rico make people worry about language and that is a definite obstacle to the diffusion of my works."

New York Congressman Herman Badillo, in the foreword to *Nilda,* labels the novel "an accurate and colorful account of a Puerto Rican child's daily life . . . and the efforts to cope with the many and varied problems of a simple youth . . . in Spanish Harlem." The *New York Times* praised its personal aspects as seen "through a child's vision . . . " and the "richness of details" makes the story "sad, funny, fascinating and honest." *Newsweek* admired *Nilda* for its literary merit and "psychological veracity" and "the highly realistic aspects" that speak to young people "in their own language without condescending or trying to be superhip." The reviewer appreciated the ethnic diversity instead of the usual fiction tales "populated by cheerful white teenagers whose biggest worries were to get a date for the senior prom or whether the home team would win the Saturday-night game." Nicholasa's themes about parental problems, racial discrimination, a young girl confronting serious illness and death impressed that *Newsweek* critic. A *New York Times Book Review* writer noted that *Nilda* "provides a sharp candid portrayal of what it means to be poor and to be called 'spicks,' 'animals,' 'you people'—and worse—by the teacher, social workers, policemen, nurses, and other white Americans who exercise power." The book is praised for "its important contribution to the spirit of first generation Puerto Ricans in America" and especially its realistic details of New York City's El Barrio of the early 1940s. The review concludes that this story is more than just another "nightmare tale from the ghetto," exposing instead "the burdens of poverty that crush disadvantaged families and destroy individual souls."

Other critics praised Nicholasa's skill as a graphic artist in *Nilda* by the way in which she combines powerful representational sketches, symbols, and words in striking illustrations that capture the interrelationships of the characters and setting in the young girl's environment. The same reaction is given to her original artistic book jackets of both *Nilda* and *El Bronx Remembered.*

According to Marilyn Sachs's review of *Nilda* in *The New York Times,* although several young people's books have attempted to explore the condition of poor minority children, "few have come up to *Nilda* in describing the crushing humiliations of poverty and in peeling off the ethnic wrappings so we can see the human child underneath." Nicholasa's young protagonists are praised for the way in which they learn how to handle racial and religious discrimination by finding inner strength, escaping from intolerable injustices through the beauty of nature. She helps migrant black children understand rejection in the United States, especially Islanders coming from a culture where pigmentation has little meaning to one where it has a great deal, and where family life is affected; lighter-skinned members are favored over darker ones.

Critics praise Nicholasa's accurate depiction of folk practices such as spiritualism based upon the belief that communication with the dead is possible and the practice of séances. The mentally ill in her stories are considered troubled by evil spirits, evoking compassionate understanding, not abusive rejection, from family members.

In *El Bronx Remembered* and *In Nueva York*, both consisting of short-story collections tied together by their setting, reviewer Aileen Pace Nilson, in *English Journal* (1978), admires Nicholasa's ability to move her characters in and out of the episodes providing "an intimate look into the most interesting parts of several people's lives."

However some critics, such as Georgess McHargue and Irma García, conclude that Nicholasa creates contrived and stereotyped personalities. In the *New York Times Book Review*, McHargue believes that *In Nueva York* appears "too obviously intended as slice-of-life fiction with the result that the characters are busier being Puerto Rican-Americans than being people." And García faults *El Bronx Remembered* for the same defect. While she praises the stories for being "well-written and descriptive," containing "some truths and sharp insights, these are not stories of change, struggle or love. Rather they are negative stories which reinforce stereotypes."

Although these shortcomings are noteworthy, the realism and empathy in Nicholasa's stories impress the critics. In a review of *In Nueva York*, a writer for *Kirkus Reviews* admires "the clarity, wry humor, genuine sympathy and considerable success" with which the author "brings the neighborhood to life." Michael A. Ortiz in *The Lion and the Unicorn* faults Nicholasa for not developing the Depression, the brother's prison episode, and the war years without accepting the fact that Nilda's world was sheltered as the youngest child and only daughter of a traditional Hispanic family. As cited above, Marilyn Sachs in *The New York Times* pays an important tribute to Nicholasa's talents, noting that her "people endure because they are people. Some of them suffer, some of them die, a few of them fail, but most of the time they endure."

Thus, because of the large Puerto Rican community in the United States, Nicholasa's work has given readers the opportunity to learn about the internal and external factors important to American cultural history, and her focus upon her people's pride has added a personal touch to Nicholasa's stories and drawings about the Puerto Rican experience in New York during the decades from the 1930s to the 1980s.

Bibliography

WORKS BY MOHR

Published Books

Nilda. Self-illustrated. New York: Harper & Row, 1973; Bantam, 1974.
El Bronx Remembered. Self-illustrated. New York: Harper & Row, 1975; Bantam, 1976.
In Nueva York. New York: Dial, 1977; Dell, 1979.

Felita. New York: Dial, 1979; Dell, 1981.
Rituals of Survival: A Woman's Portfolio. Houston: Arte Publico Press, 1985.
Going Home. New York: Dial, 1986.

Selections from these books have been reprinted in

Blicksilver, Edith, ed. *The Ethnic American Woman: Problems, Protests, Lifestyle*. Dubuque, Iowa: Kendall/Hunt, 1979.
Reinke, Peter, ed. *The Family in Harmony and Conflict*. New York: Bantam, 1980.

Additional reprints appear in textbooks published by Harcourt Brace Jovanovich; Scott, Foresman and Company; McGraw-Hill; J.P. Lippincott; Holt, Rinehart & Winston; Allyn and Bacon; Kendall/Hunt; Harper & Row; Children's Digest; Scholastic Magazine; Nuestro; and the Educational Development Center.

Additional Published Works

"Christmas Was a Time of Plenty" (short story). *Revista Chicano-Riqueña* (1980): 33–34.
"Puerto Ricans in the U.S.: The Adopted Citizen" (essay). *Ethnic Lifestyles and Mental Health*, Gloria Valencia-Weber, ed. Oklahoma State University, Psychology Department (1980): 147–56.
"A Special Gift" (short story). *Revista Chicano-Riqueña* (1981): 91–100.
"Their America" (article). *Perspectives, The Civil Rights Quarterly* 14 (Summer 1982): 23–24.
"An Awakening . . . Summer 1956, for Hilda Hildalgo" (short story). Evangelina Vigil, ed. *Woman of Her Word: Hispanic Women Write*. Houston: Arte Publico Press, 1983.
"Puerto Ricans in New York: Cultural Evolution and Identity" (article). *Images and Identities: The Puerto Rican in Literature*, Asela Rodríguez de Laguna, ed. New Brunswick, N.J.: Transaction Books, 1987.

WORKS ABOUT MOHR

Flores, Juan. "Back Down These Mean Streets: Introducing Nicholasa Mohr and Louis Reyes Rivera." *Revista Chicano-Riqueña* 8/2 (Spring 1980): 51–56.
Miller, John. "The Emigrant and New York City: A Consideration of Four Puerto Rican Writers." *Melus* 5, 3 (Fall 1978): 94–99.
———. "Nicholasa Mohr: Neorican Writings in Progress 'A View of the Other Culture.' " *"Revista Interamericana* vol. 9 (1979–1980): 543–49.
Nilson, Aileen Pace. "Keeping Score on Some Recent Winners." *English Journal*. 67, 2 (February, 1978): 98–101.
Sachs, Marilyn. *"Nilda." The New York Times*. November 4, 1973.
Turner, Faythe. "The Myth of the American Dream in the Works of Nicholasa Mohr." Unpublished paper. Amherst, Mass.: Amherst College.

                                                          EDITH BLICKSILVER

•

MONTES HUIDOBRO, MATÍAS (1931–   ). Matías Montes Huidobro is one of the Cuban American writers who have reached their greatest prominence in the last twenty years. In the field of literary creativity Matías is an author of plays, novels, short stories, and poetry. He has also been a theater producer and written scripts for radio and television. He has, however, also written books and articles on various aspects of Spanish-language literature, both Spanish and Hispano-American, and textbooks for teaching Spanish in the United States. His work as a teacher, his participation in literary and academic events, his efforts as an editor and a critic in various literary reviews have given him a prominent place as an intellectual. Although the themes he writes about are basically Cuban, they extend to embrace universality as far as his focus on the life of human beings is concerned.

Biography

Matías Montes Huidobro was born in 1931 in Sagua la Grande, a town located on the northern coast of what was then known as the Province of Las Villas in the central region of Cuba. There he obtained his primary education and spent the first year of high school. In 1943 his family moved to the capital of the island, and that is where Matías completed the rest of his secondary education, graduating at the Institute No. 1 in Havana in 1948.

Matías has told us that his family belonged to a very modest, nearly poor, economic class. His childhood memories are not idyllic, with the exception of the cinema which has always been his passion. For various reasons, the young Matías had free access to the various movie houses in Sagua la Grande and he used this opportunity to see films frequently, and he preferred to see those made in Hollywood. Later on, this hobby became partly responsible for his intellectual inclinations as well as for his interest in theatrical and film criticism, and also in writing of dramas.

After he had moved to Havana, Matías remained faithful to his passion for the cinema, and although his family had few economic resources, he arranged things so that he could often go to the movie houses in the capital. In 1948 20th Century Fox organized a contest related to the film *Captain from Castile*; Matías received a prize and was admitted to a summer university course entitled "The Cinema: Industry and Art of Our Time."

In that same year, 1948, Matías enrolled in the School of Education of the Universidad de la Habana and in 1952 obtained his doctorate in pedagogy. In 1949 he already began to be active as a writer. We can see in his curriculum vitae that from that year until 1961 Montes Huidobro published numerous articles of literary criticism. On the creative side, he devoted himself principally to the short story and to drama; he was also a poet and wrote plays for the Cuban radio and television. A number of theatrical plays were staged. Between 1959 and 1971 he was also professor of Spanish literature at the National School of Journalism in Havana.

Due to certain discrepancies of political and intellectual nature with the new Cuban regime, Matías moved to the United States in 1961. After two years, which he devoted to teaching high school Spanish at Meadville, Pennsylvania, he became professor of Spanish language and literature at the University of Hawaii, where he has been ever since 1963.

It is difficult to sum up the literary production of Matías Montes Huidobro because it is so abundant. It should be enough to look at the following list of his publications since his arrival in the United States as it appears in his 1984 curriculum vitae:

1. five books of literary criticism
2. two bibliographies
3. eight articles published in books
4. two textbooks for teaching of Spanish
5. twenty-eight major articles on Spanish (peninsular) literature
6. thirty-two major articles on Hispano-American literature
7. eleven minor articles
8. twenty book reviews
9. three prologues
10. fifty-nine papers presented at literary and academic conventions
11. one book of short stories
12. eight novels
13. one drama
14. one book of poetry

And we are practically unable to add up the number of his poems, dramatic works, and short stories included in various anthologies, collections, and literary magazines. When we talk about his subjects, we will mention some of these where relevant.

As we have just seen, it is evident that Matías Montes Huidobro is a prolific writer of high caliber who has reached the pinnacle of his production and shall remain there for many years to come.

Major Themes

This entry will deal only with the literary production of Montes Huidobro: poetry, short story, novel, and theater.

A book of Matías's poems has been published under the title *La vaca de los ojos largos* (1967, The Cow with the Large Eyes). His poems have also appeared in four anthologies published in Argentina, Spain, and the United States. Forty other poems can be found in various reviews and periodicals. There are no important formal innovations to be found in his poetry, but it has a direct, sharp style related to post-modernism.

Poetry is a literary genre that has been least cultivated by Montes Huidobro, who does not consider himself to be a good poet. He believes that it is more important to write, for example, a novel than poetry. According to him, in a novel a world and personalities can be created, an intimate relationship between the author and his creation. Poetry, in his opinion, does not allow for such a relationship. It is more dehumanized and lends itself better to a mere play with the words. Critic Victoriano Cremer does not seem to agree with the ideas of Matías on his work as a poet. He qualifies the poetry of Matías as "simple, direct, deep, and courageous," adding that his theme derives from his contemplation of the world.

Another critic, Stefan Baciu, explains that when Matías maintains that he detests poetry, he thereby "affirms a great and profound truth, since only such things which are loved and represent an intimate part of our own life can be detested."

La vaca de los ojos largos is a collection of poems, the number of which is hard to determine as the majority of them are untitled. They take up twenty-eight pages and their themes vary from philosophy—"Somos islas. / El mar parece rodearnos. / Tiempo llegará / en que entre las olas nos perderemos" (We are islands. The sea seems to encircle us. The time will come when we shall be lost between the waves)—to existence— "Los encuentros son tan simples / que uno no se da cuenta. / Son como el cielo azul / o el sol / o el mar, / siempre el mar" (Meetings are so simple that we do not notice them. They are like the blue sky, or the sun, or the sea; always the sea)—passing through love "Yo creo en la muerte por amor / Morir por amor / ahora en 1966 / es la única muerte decorosa" (I believe in death by love. Today, in 1966, to die by love is the only decent way to die)—and sex— "Ya que no se ha comprobado / la eternidad del amor / el pene / se ha convertido en símbolo fálico / digno de admiración social" (Inasmuch as the eternity of love has not been confirmed, the penis has been converted into a phallic symbol worthy of social admiration), and also through the nostalgia for the past "y por un instante recordamos / . . . / el cielo azul / las palmeras lejanas de una Cuba / vista alguna vez" (and for a moment we remembered . . . the blue sky, the distant palm trees of a Cuba seen once upon a time).————to the exaltation of nature————"Islas hawaianas /¡ oh, islas hawaianas¡ / nunca olvidaré tu Waimea Canyon / y yo ante él" (Hawaiian Isles, oh, Hawaiian Isles, never shall I forget your Waimea Canyon and me in front of it)————and social justice————"¡Oh valiente Estuchenco / culto te rendimos cuando te vemos / arriesgar / vacaciones en Siberia / por un poema!" (Oh, courageous Yevtushenko, we give homage to you when we see you risking a Siberian holiday for a poem!).

According to Stefan Baciu, in this work by Montes Huidobro "Cuba is close to Brazil and Yugoslavia, to Mexico and France. That is because our meridian is called liberty and our common denominator, poetry."

This geographical disarray discerned in poetry by Matías also encompasses the solitude of the poet who is always marching down abstract and indifferent roads: "Caminamos así, juntos y solos, / por los desolados páramos / de nuestra existencia" (That is how we walk, together and alone, along the desolate, bleak plain of our existence).

Loneliness and pain are also occasionally expressed, as in the criticism of the new society of Cuba, as in the "Soneto a la miliciana cubana": "Introduciéndote / el cañón de tu metralleta / reproduces / con semen de plomo / hijos de plomo" (You make love with your machine gun, and after bullet insemination, you give birth to sons of lead).

Matías affirms his individualism and ethical as well as esthetic independence by using occasionally satire and irony. He shows himself to be a lover of liberty, but also of harmony and beauty. Although his themes are universal, the theme of Hispanity, from Spain to Hispano-America, is frequently encountered in his verse. This is seen in "Castilla es ancha" (Castile is Broad), which also contains references to exile: "Me gusta el Cid / porque exiliado se alejaba en su epopeya / y tierras de Castilla / a sus espaldas / al frente divisaba" (I like El Cid because he, exiled, leaving in his epic the lands of Castile behind he was discerning them ahead).

Influences by Pablo Neruda and César Vallejo have been ascribed to his poetry. In fact, Matías maintains a very personal and intimate tone which differentiates him from other contemporary poets.

Montes Huidobro published a book entitled *La anunciación y otros cuentos cubanos* (1967, The Anunciation and Other Cuban Stories). This is the only volume in which are recompiled probably the ten best short stories by this author. It is not an easy work to catalogue or analyze. Although the word "Cuban" does appear in the title, the themes for these short stories are, in fact, far removed from the Cuban, although an examination of their roots would reveal Cuba, its society, its idiosyncrasy, and even its landscape.

The names of the short stories are "Las auras" (The Auras), "La constante distancia" (The Constant Distance), "Leandro" (Leander), "El ofrecimiento" (The Offering), "La vida bajo las alas" (Life Below Wings), "Muerte nueva en Verona" (New Death in Verona), "La anunciación" (The Annunciation), "Los indignados" (The Indignant), "Ratas en la isla" (Rats on the Island), and "Las islas" (The Islands). The tales take up 190 pages; some are quite extensive, but the majority of them are short. The first three stories take place under the sign of socialist Cuba and they contain a very personal criticism of the system that rules the island. Montes Huidobro does not identify himself totally with either extreme, left or right, and places himself in a solitary and difficult position.

The characters express the psychological relations that are being established between them and expose the range of their individual problems, confront them and try to resolve them, in general without success. The female characters are better, more complete. Frustration is the prevailing sentiment of the women of Montes Huidobro and it seems to become a universal feminine characteristic.

Matías strikes us as a rather pessimistic observer of human beings and contemporary societies. In his tales there is not only economic, but also spiritual, poverty. Many of the specific situations narrated by the author symbolize other, more universal, realities.

Other short stories of his have appeared in various anthologies and magazines in the United States and other countries. Matías began his work as a short-story teller at a very early age. Before he was twenty he had already written three stories which were published in magazines in Havana: "El hijo noveno," "Abono para la tierra," and "Los ojos en los espejos," all dated 1950.

In those narratives, where the new regime in Cuba is criticized, symbols and absurdity are used for this purpose. In his hands this approach acquires veracity. The Cubanism of his stories is also revealed by the language and environment, at times, also by certain characteristics of his heroes. Simultaneously, as we have already indicated, the stories are universal with respect to the problems that are addressed in them and the experiences that are presented.

As we have seen, there are negative sentiments in his narratives, principally frustration and the absence of satisfaction. Humor is rarely overpowering in Montes Huidobro; his principal intent seems to be to show a few scenes of life full of tension, anguish, and anxiety.

Nearly all the stories by Matías are also characterized by their short extension, their scarcity of details, considered by him unnecessary, and by their condensation to the real essentials. One of the stories in which these traits can be appreciated is "Sin nada que hacer" which can be found in the anthology by Julio E. Hernández-Miyares, *Narradores cubanos de hoy*. On one page and a half an episode is narrated, it seems to take place during the last days of the dictatorship of Fulgencio Batista in Cuba, mentioned here only as "el General." The principal character is Bernarda, a servant who, if the insinuations are correct, is part of the revolutionary forces fighting Batista.

Bernarda appears as possibly an informer about the activities of the members of a rich family. A death is anticipated, although nothing happens in the story itself: the death of the doctor and friend of the family for which Bernarda works as a servant.

Eroticism is another constant in the narratives, even more patent in his novels. "El regreso de los perros" (Return of the Dogs), also in the same anthology, is a story of Kafkaesque cut, a true nightmare mixing carnal love and death. The landscape melts with the anecdote and complements it in its sexual aggressiveness. Human beings, animals, and landscape, everything merges into a single exuberant narrative, plethoric with sexuality that leads to destruction and death.

Matías Montes Huidobro has written eight novels. *Desterrados al fuego* (1975, Exiled to the Fire) and *Segar a los muertos* (1980, To Blind the Dead), have been published as separate books. *Desterrados al fuego* received an honorable mention in the *Concurso Hispanoamericano de Primera Novela,* sponsored by the Fondo de Cultura de Mexico. *Cartas de cabeza* (Head Letters) appeared in the 1977 Spring issue of the review *Caribe.* A few chapters of *Los tres Villalobos* (The Three Villaloboses) were published in various literary reviews in 1975 and 1982. The same is true of *Afán de Combat* (Desire for Combat) and *Espirales de Celuloide* (Celluloid Spirals); selections of both having been published in reviews in 1978 and 1983, respectively. And, finally, *Lázaro perseguido* (Lazarus Pursued) was mentioned with honor in the 1968 Premio Alfaguara contest, and the *Lamentación en tres estancias* (Lament in Three Stations) won third place in the Planeta de Novelas contest held in Spain in 1970, but neither was published.

The critics have devoted most attention to Montes Huidobro's novel *Desterrados al fuego*. It is a long, 221-page novel, written in a compact form. The framework of the narrative is exile, banishment. The theme, a human being searching for its real identity within this strange environment; the protagonist, presented in first person, certainly has autobiographical elements by which we mean that the writer is hiding behind his fictional counterpart to express his crises of solitude and alienation. The tone is strong, reaching at times the absurd or the repulsive; the language is rich, baroque, handled within a strict style of a rather rigid structure which denotes the absolute control of the writer. There are humorous touches, but it is black, sarcastic humor. As such, it seems on occasions that it turns into craziness, the narrative thread becomes difficult to follow, and we may wish to stop reading. This novel, however, undoubtedly contains a certain fascination from which we cannot easily escape and which attracts us to continue reading it.

There is a simple plot behind the linguistic, psychological, and stylistic complications of this novel: a married couple of exiles is looking for work in the United States and tries to find its place in a new society. While the wife manages to reach these objectives with relative facility, the husband constantly has to struggle to maintain his emotional equilibrium. Unemployed, he spends his time in an autoreflexive process which leads him to be physically and mentally ill. He becomes a taciturn introvert who exists only in an internal world of distorted fantasies.

This process advances slowly but can be anticipated from the very beginning of the narrative. One of the symbols indicating the psychic state that the protagonist is reaching is a secondhand winter overcoat that he obtained before leaving for the north. This article of clothing becomes his security blanket as well as his damnation. It becomes a part of himself until he cannot take it off. It separates him from the rest of the world but also protects him against the hostility of this world and hides him from the eyes of others. Covered with this coat the protagonist is being physically and mentally corrupted and, ultimately, he distorts the surrounding reality and re-creates it.

Desterrados al fuego is not a political novel. It is a very personal and intimate novel. The theme of the loss of sexual desire is connected to the impossibility of communication between the protagonist and other persons, including his wife, and with the process of autodestruction that afflicts this anti-hero. And right at the beginning of the second half of the book the protagonist slowly begins to recover, both in body and in psyche. The language, invented toward the end of the first part and understood only by him, disappears, and in the second part there appear, besides the Spanish, Afro-Cuban languages indicating perhaps that as he is recovering his reason, he is returning to the Cuban roots that he had lost, together with his own identity, during the alienatory stage.

With the psychical recovery comes a sad realization: Amanda, his beloved wife, had left him. At this point a little play is interposed, dramatizing the loss of Amanda. The protagonist decides to leave, to escape from the place where he was, and we see him again at the airport as we did at the beginning of the novel. Then he takes another decisive step, he takes off his coat and gets rid of it. His destination is Honolulu, Hawaii (autobiographical element), and when he arrives there, Amanda is waiting for him. Thus the ending is happy and optimistic.

As was the case with the short stories of Montes Huidobro, also in his novels the critics have discovered a possible influence of Kafka reflected by the multitude of symbols that appear in *Desterrados al fuego*.

There is no doubt that *Desterrados al fuego* is a novel transcending the specific theme of banishment, in the very strict sense, in order to reach universal dimensions: the spiritual isolation of all human beings within the contemporary world. This observation is completed with hope and a certain degree of optimism; the novel ends in Hawaii, a kind of paradise where love triumphs and the writer is reintegrated with his work. The salvation, his salvation, consists of love and encounter with the word itself as the expressive medium that links him to the rest of the humanity represented by the figure of the reader who, obstacles notwithstanding, had come to the end of the narrative.

The other two published novels by Montes Huidobro, *Cartas de cabeza* and *Segar a los muertos*, are considerably shorter and simpler than the previous one, and their literary quality does not reach that of *Desterrados al fuego*. Both fully belong in the literature of the absurd and use symbols and allegories to show us the contemporary societies and the political problems of Cuba and Hispano-America in general. The very personal humor of Matías is felt in these short novels. His individual perception of reality and his own stumblings in exile can be perceived in these works.

As a literary creator, Montes Huidobro has reached fame principally as a writer of one-act plays. His dramatic production is concentrated in a period when he lived in Cuba, between 1950 and 1961. During the twenty-three years that Matías has been outside Cuba, he has published and/or staged five plays. One of them, *La sal de los muertos* (Salt of the Dead), had been already written in 1960 and published in 1961 in Cuba, but the Cuban government seized it before he left the country. This apparent lack of interest in playwriting is due to the difficulty of publishing and, above all, staging of dramas in the Spanish language in the United States, a fact that discourages many Spanish-speaking playwrights residing here.

Las cuatro brujas, (The Four Witches) a play from his first period written when he was nineteen, does not have a Cuban location. As the title suggests, the action of this play contains elements based on predestination, on magic. The influence of Shakespeare on the theme and of Gracía Lorca on the dialogue is noticeable. *Sobre las mismas rocas* (On the Same Rocks) is also a work from the author's youth. Here, the background is not Cuban either. It deals with a personal conflict that, nevertheless, turns into a universal one: life in the modern metropolis suffering under the burden of prejudices, lack of understanding among human beings, indifference to art due to exaggerated mechanization. It is a play loaded with symbols and has surrealistic patterns.

In 1959, *Los acosados* (The Attacked) and *La botija* (The Jug) were published and later staged. The former, *Los acosados,* was also presented on Cuban television. It also transcends the nationalist limits (a middle-class Cuban family before the Castro revolution) to reach universal frontiers. The only dramatis personae of the play, a man and a woman, symbolize the anguish of everyday life, of the most basic human relations; in all of this is emphasized the agonizing monotony impregnating these contacts. There are external factors, mainly of economic nature, contributing to this climate of near desperation. A possible influence of Sartre on this play of *Los acosados* has been suggested.

La botija is a symbolic representation of the new post-revolutionary Cuban society. This jug represents the capital, the welfare of the people. Throughout the play they are debating as to who should keep it. Toward the end an actor, who is sitting among the audience, rises and claims it. In this way the capital goes to its legitimate owner: the people. This work also has satirical elements that can be found in the despair of the powerful social classes who do not wish to relinquish their economic well-being and share it with the members of less-privileged classes. This theme places *La botija* in the category of the Cuban revolutionary theater after 1959.

El tiro por la culata (Doing Things Backward) and *Las vacas* (The Cows) both date from 1960. The first one, besides being staged, was also shown on television. The other won the first prize in a play contest held in Cuba. *El tiro por la culata* has such a typically Cuban setting that it was presented at the Festival Campesino in 1961. Its theme is also *criollo:* a rich landowner desires a young country girl. Here the theme of exploitation of the humble by the mighty is presented through an "entremés" in the style of Cervantes. In the end the young girl manages to escape the advances of the landowner. For reasons that we can only describe as magic, the uneducated country girl expresses herself in such a reasonable way that she succeeds to escape her moral perdition. *Las vacas* is also a revolutionary play based on the theme of conversion or, at least, political and ideological adjustment of a *latifundista* family. As in *La botija,* the cows also represent capital that finally gets into the hands of the peasants: the people. The play has three acts and Ionesco's influence can be noted there.

Finally, *Gas en los poros* (Gas in the Pores), staged and shown on television in Cuba, is an expressionist drama unfolding between two women, a mother and a daughter. Both are symbolic characters incarnating existential conflicts: the anguish of the past and the uncertainty of the future. The interrelations between the mother and the daughter, and the external social and political situation, develop in a parallel manner. What happens at home reflects events in the general society.

Among the plays of Montes Huidobro published outside Cuba, *La sal de los muertos* was written, as already mentioned, before the expatriation of the author. It is a two-act play taking place in Cuba, where various characters, belonging to the same family divided into three generations, enter into dialogues. These characters symbolize aspects of different time periods: the past (the grandparents), the present (the parents), and the future (the grandson). It is about destroying the past using Freudian theories of family hates and complexes. Ironically, the past and the future resemble each other very much, because Lobito, the grandson, is molded like Tigre, his grandfather. Both die in an absurd confrontation, and the patriarch's riches remain at the disposal of the rest of the family. Unfortunately, this only produces confusion and conscience crises among the family members and the play ends in an atmosphere of quasi-lunacy.

La madre y la guillotina and its English version, *The Guillotine,* is the only one of Montes Huidobro's plays staged in the United States. Like those mentioned previously, it is a symbolic work. In the prologue to Montes's *Persona, vida y máscara,* Matas states, "The Revolution has taken over the collective spirit. Fascinated by the enchanting slogans of the leader, it believes that it is on the road towards the realization of the dream of José Martí. Everybody wants to be clean, to appear innocent in the eyes of the others, to be worthy of his role in the construction of the new fatherland."

This is a criticism of the Castro revolution where the mother and her children fall victim to the revolutionary principles. In this play also appears the dramatic recourse to the theater within a theater which we have already observed in *La sal de los muertos.* This theme is considered to have been influenced by Thomas Mann.

Ojos para no ver (1979, Eyes That Don't See) is the only play published as a book. It is divided into three acts and its central theme is the perception of the evolution of Cuban history.

On the level that symbolizes a contemporary Cuba there are dialogues between a series of characters: the dictator Solavaya, the young María whom he is trying to seduce, their son, a living replica of his father who, in the end, replaces his father in power, the fortune-teller Pútrida, representative of the people, the *Santera* Conga, who represents Afro-Cubanism. María herself changes into four persons: María de la Montaña, María la Anunciación, María la Magdalena, and María la Concepción, incarnating the different stages of the repetitive historical process. María is ultimately transformed into Caridad del Cobre (Our Lady of Charity from Cobre), the patron saint of Cuba who spreads out her blue mantle over the island as a symbol of protection. There are also secondary characters and chorists: Manengue, the governor's aide; Mother Superior; Ruperta, the go-between; soldiers; bedraggled women, etc.

In this work Montes Huidobro transcends the parochial to give us a picture of existential anxieties and neurotic hallucinations of a universal order. Influences of Brecht and Freud can be observed in it. The latter's influence is notable in the psychological aspects of some characters, especially the father and his son.

The last two plays of Montes Huidobro, *Funeral en Teruel* (Funeral in Teruel) and *La navaja de Olofé* (Olofé's Blade), were published in 1982 in literary reviews. The first one is based on the legendary love story of Isabel and Marsilla, and their story is interwoven with references to present figures, including Fidel Castro. There is no precise indication of time in this work: some characters appear dressed in contemporary clothes, others in the style of the thirteenth century. The moral and temporal conflicts taking place is this drama are never resolved.

La navaja de Olofé is a short, one-act play taking place in Santiago de Cuba at a carnival, in the first half of the twentieth century. The characters, like those in *Los acosados,* are a man and a woman. In this case they are mother and son, who also appear as lovers. It is a drama with an Afro-Cuban background, with intense sexual contents.

Seen in their totality, the dramas of Matías Montes Huidobro are eclectic. His critics have attributed to him various "-isms": symbolism, expressionism, impressionism, oneirism, surrealism, etc. The theatrical techniques he uses include choral elements, absurd situations and dialogues, depersonalization of the characters, allegories, and others. For him, a play rests on action and dialogue, not scenography. On the whole, his plays have an open ending, lacking conclusion or thesis. Another element that interests Matías, as demonstrated by his plays, is time. He perceives time as infinite and constant, as a backdrop to human actions. Criticism, made always through symbols, of the present political and social situation in Cuba, can be observed in those of his plays published in exile. In the final analysis, his central concern is with the raison d'être of human existence, perceived pessimistically within a sordid framework of anxiety.

Bibliography

WORKS BY MONTES HUIDOBRO

Prose

La anunciación y otros cuentos cubanos. Madrid: Clemares, 1967.
Espirales de celuloide. Third place, concurso *Planeta* de novelas, Spain, 1970.
Desterrados al fuego. Mexico: Fondo de Cultura Económica, 1975.
"El regreso de los perros," "Sin nada que hacer" (short-stories), included in *Narradores cubanos de hoy*. Miami: Ediciones Universal, 1975.
Los tres Villalobos. Published chapters in: "El asesinato Koblansky-Villalobos," *Chasqui* (Fall 1975); "Cuentos de camino," *Románica* (1975); "Matusalén," *Linden Lane Magazine* (October–December 1982).
Cartas de cabeza. Published in *Caribe* (Spring 1977): 97–154.
Afán de combate. A selection was published in *Consenso* (November 1978): 26–31.
Segar a los muertos. Miami: Ediciones Universal, 1980.

Drama Books

"El tiro por la culata," published in *Teatro cubano revolucionario*. Marianao, Cuba: Ediciones del Municipio de Marianao, 1961.

"Gas en los poros," published in *Teatro cubano en un acto*. Havana, Cuba: Ediciones Revolución, 1963.

La vaca de los ojos largos. Honolulu Ha.: Mele, 1967.

"La sal de los muertos," published in *Teatro contemporáneo hispano-americano*. Vol. 3. Madrid: Escelicer, 1971.

"The Guillotine," published in *Selected Latin American One-Act Plays*. Pittsburgh: University of Pittsburgh Press, 1972.

Ojos para no ver. Miami: Ediciones Universal, 1979.

Poetry

"La vaca de los ojos largos," "Oda a los obreros de la Remington" (poetry), included in *Antología de la poesía hispanoamericana*. Mario Marcilese ed. Buenos Aires: Editorial Rioplatense, 1969.

"Hiroshima Girl Got Married," "Where Are They Now?" "Calendar of Times," "El campo del sueño," "Castilla es ancha," included in *La última poesía cubana*. Orlando Rodríguez-Sardiñas, ed. Madrid: Hispanova, 1973.

"El campo del dueño," "El Sil a cada paso," "Castilla es ancha," "Madre," "A mi madre, en largas pausas," "Irme yo de ti para no irme," "En círculo con tinto," "Hambriento estoy como un ladrillo hambriento," "Paleolítico Interior," "Cuerpos abstractos," included in *Poesía compartida*, ed. Roberto Dávila Cazorla. Miami: Ultra Graphic Corporation, 1980.

Plays Published in Journals

"Los acosados" in *Lunes de Revolución*. Havana. May 4, 1959: 10–14.

"La botija" in *Revista Casa de las Américas*. Havana, 1959.

"Gas en los poros" in *Lunes de Revolución*, Havana, March 27, 1961: 40–43.

"Hablando en chino" in *Escolios*, California State University (May-November 1977): 76–82.

"La navaja de Olofé." *Prismal/Cabral*, University of Maryland (Spring 1982): 120–33.

"Funeral en Teruel" in *Verbena* (Summer 1982): 2–29.

Short stories have been published in the following periodicals: *Bohemia, Nueva Generación, Ministerio de Educación, Carteles, Revista de la Universidad de las Villas, The Husk, Kapa, El Undoso, Diario de las Américas*.

Poems have been published in the following periodicals: *Nueva Generación, Mele, Proa, El Día, Carmorany Delfín, Azor, Círculo Poético, Latin American Literary Review, La Prensa, Mairena*, and *En Rojo*.

WORKS ABOUT MONTES HUIDOBRO

Baciu, Stefan. Prologue to *La vaca de los ojos largos*. Honolulu: Mele, 1967.

Baeza Flores, Alberto. Review of *Desterrados al fuego*. *Miami Herald* May 23, 1977: 4.

Colecchia, Francesca, and Julio Matas, eds. Introduction to *The Guillotine*, published in *Selected Latin American One-Act Plays*. Pittsburgh: University of Pittsburgh Press, 1973.

————. "Matías Montes Huidobro: His Theater." *Latin American Theater Review*, supplement (Summer 1980): 77–80.

————. Review of *Ojos para no ver*. *Hispania* 65, 2 (May 1982): 315.

Cremer, Victoriano. Review of *La vaca de los ojos largos*. *Proa*, León, Spain, October 22, 1967: 16.

Dauster, Frank. Review of *Persona: vida y máscara en el teatro cubano*. *Revista Iberoamericana* 41, 91 (April-June 1975): 371–73.

————. *Historia del teatro hispanoamericano*. Mexico: Ediciones Andrea, 1973.

Febles, Jorge. "La desfiguración enajenante en *Ojos para no ver*." *Crítica Hispánica* 4, 2 (1982): 127–36.

Fernández, José B. Review of *Persona: vida y máscara en el teatro cubano*. *Modern Language Journal* 59, 5–6 (September-October 1975): 296.

Ferro, Hellén. Review of *Bibliografía crítica de la poesía cubana*. *Repertorio Latinoamericano*, Buenos Aires-Caracas, no. 1 (April 1975): 8–9.

————. Review of *Desterrados al fuego*. *Repertorio Latinoamericano*, Buenos Aires-Caracas, no. 9 (December 1975): 12–13.

Gainza, Ramón. Review of *Los Acosados*. *El mundo*. Havana, March 19, 1960: A–14.

Gariano, Carmelo. Review of *Segar a los muertos*. *Hispania* 66, 1 (March 1983): 142–43.

González-Cruz, Luis. "Matías Montes Huidobro: The Poet, Selected Poems and Interviews." *Latin American Literary Review* 2, 4 (Spring-Summer 1974): 163–70.

Hernández-Miyares, Julio. Introduction to Montes Huidobro's short stories in *Narradores cubanos de hoy*. Miami: Ediciones Universal, 1975.

Jaimes Freyre, Mireya. Review of *Desterrados al fuego*. *Latin American Literary Review* 4, 9 (Fall-Winter 1976): 96–98.

Leal, Rine. Introduction to *Gas en los poros*, published in *Teatro cubano en un acto: antología*. Havana: Ediciones Revolución, 1963.

Martí de Cid, Dolores. Review of *Persona: vida y máscara en el teatro cubano*. *Inter-American Review of Bibliography* 24, 1 (January-March 1976): 92–94.

Matas, Julio. Prologue of *Persona, vida y máscara en el teatro cubano*. Miami: Ediciones Universal, 1973.

————. Review of *Persona, vida y máscara en el teatro cubano*. *Cuban Studies* 5, 1 (January 1975): 44–45.

Pérez-Montañer, Jaime. Review of *Desterrados al fuego*. *Chasqui* 6, 2 (February 1977): 87–89.

Raggi, Carlos M. Review of *La vaca de los ojos largos*. *Revista Círculo* vol. 2 (Summer 1970): 135–36.

Roberts, Gemma. Review of *Desterrados al fuego*. *Revista Iberoamericana* 42 (July-December, 1976): 96–97, 642–44.

Rodríguez-Sardiñas, Orlando, and Carlos Miguel Sánchez Radillo. Introduction to *La sal de los muertos*, published in *Teatro selecto contemporáneo hispanoamericano*. Madrid: Escelicer, 1971.

Rodríguez-Sardiñas, Orlando. Introduction to Montes Huidobro's poetry in *La última poesía cubana*. Madrid: Hispanova, 1973.

Siemens, William. "Parallel Transformations in *Desterrados al fuego*." *Término* 2, 6 (Winter 1984): 17–18.

Souza, Raymond D. Review of *Desterrados al fuego*. *Explicación de Textos Literarios* 6, 2 (1978): 241.

Torres Fierro, Danubio. Review of *Desterrados al fuego*. *Plural* (Mexico) 5, 6 (March 1976): 55–56.
Valdivieso, Teresa. Review of *Ojos para no ver*. *Chasqui* 10, 2–3 (February-May 1981): 69–70.
Villaverde, Fernando. Review of *Segar a los muertos*. *Miami Herald*, May 10, 1981: 14.

SILVIA BURUNAT

P

PADILLA, HEBERTO (1932–   ). The noted Cuban poet Heberto Padilla has had a major impact on the reevaluation of the Cuban Revolution by the world's intellectual community, mainly in the Western democracies. With the highly publicized ''Padilla Case'' (1968–1971) a cycle of permissiveness and pluralism in Cuba's literary activities comes to a close.

Biography

The eldest of three brothers, Heberto Padilla Lorenzo was born in Puerta del Golpe, Pinar del Río, Cuba, on January 20, 1932. Padilla received his elementary and secondary education at the provincial schools of his native Pinar del Río. For his higher educational training Padilla studied journalism at the University of Havana and humanities at the same university and at other institutions.

Heberto Padilla formed part of the group of Cubans who chose exile during the dictatorship of Fulgencio Batista (1952–1959). He and his parents lived in the United States during this turbulent period in Cuban history. Padilla left Cuba at an early age, a time when his literary talent was beginning to emerge. During his first experience as a political exile in the United States, Padilla worked primarily as a journalist and radio commentator for Miami's WMIL. Later, he moved to New York and earned a living as a language instructor for Berlitz.

Immediately after the installation of the revolutionary government in Cuba on January 1, 1959, Padilla was named New York correspondent to the newly formed Cuban information agency, Prensa Latina. However, Padilla only stayed in New York for a few more months for he wanted to return to his homeland and be a part of the revolutionary process. While in Cuba, Padilla worked in various media-related jobs. He was to become one of the editors of the cultural supplement to the newspaper *Revolución, Lunes de Revolución*. At this time, he helped established the UNEAC (Union Nacional de Escritores y Artistas de Cuba), Cuba's writers' and artists' union. He also became director of the literary division of UNEAC.

In 1962 Padilla served as correspondent in London and Moscow for Prensa Latina. In 1964 he was in charge of Cubartimpex, whose main purpose was to sell books and related articles to the Scandinavian and Eastern European countries. Through his job assignments, Heberto Padilla spent a great deal of time outside of his homeland. This was when he started to question his attitude toward the Cuban revolutionary process. These changes will be reflected in his literary output.

Upon returning to Cuba from his missions abroad in 1966, Padilla found that his previous place of employment, *Lunes de Revolución*, had been scrapped and many of its contributors had been accused of wasting public funds in endeavors far above the intellect of its audience. Padilla tried to justify the writers in question by debating political and cultural issues in *Juventud Rebelde*, the newspaper of Cuba's Communist Youth Organization. In spite of the fact that the political climate was becoming rather turbulent for Padilla, he was yet to become the director of the international section of the National Culture Council. At this time, Padilla wrote a positive review of Cabrera Infante's *Très Tristes Tigres*. Cabrera had denounced the Cuban Revolution in 1964 while serving as Cuba's cultural attaché in Belgium. This favorable critique of Infante's novel was construed as support for a counterrevolutionary, thus endangering Padilla's position with the Revolution. Evidence that his position with the higher revolutionary echelons was eroding came also in 1966, soon after he was offered a position at a French university; Padilla's travel permit was revoked.

In 1968, Padilla submitted *Fuera del juego* (1969, *Sent off the Field*, 1971) for consideration in the Julián del Casal poetry contest sponsored by the UNEAC. The winner of this literary contest would have his entry published and a journey abroad. The panel judging the works was composed of: J.M. Cohen, English; César Calvo, Peruvian; Jose Lezama Lima, Jose Tallet, and Manuel Díaz Martínez, all Cubans. His entry, *Fuera del juego*, was regarded as counterrevolutionary, bourgeois-oriented literature by the Ministry of Culture, which was determined not to grant Padilla the prize. The ministry officials went as far as to dismiss the younger Cuban poets of the jury. José Lezama Lima, one of the most famous Cuban poets and member of the jury, defended Padilla affirming that the book was not an exercise in counterrevolutionary literature.

After a period of commotion and intrigue the prize was finally awarded. The visit abroad was not permitted. The book was published but with a critical introduction by UNEAC's board. It pointed out Padilla's lack of revolutionary vision and militancy, and it further emphasized that the author had lived always outside Cuba during the country's most traumatic moments.

Now the attacks on Padilla were to begin in earnest, starting with a strong condemnation in *Verde Olivo*, (Olive Green), the journal of the Cuban army. In its article "Las Provocaciones de Heberto Padilla" the poet was described as vain, perverse, and incapable of carrying out the duties the Revolution had entrusted him. By this time, the Padilla dilemma had aroused international attention, which to an extent served to insulate the poet from harsher reprisals.

He was given at this time a lectureship at the University of Havana. Padilla continued to write poetry. The year was 1969.

On March 20, 1971, Heberto Padilla and his wife, Cuban poet and writer Belkis Cuza Malé, were arrested. The charge was conspiracy against the Revolution. The evidence was incriminating letters from Padilla to his friends abroad and the reading of his book *Provocaciones* (Provocations) at a poetry recital sponsored by the UNEAC at the University of Havana. At the end of April, the poet and his wife were released. But his release carried a price, a self-criticism which he read before the assembly of the UNEAC. Padilla's self-criticism was widely circulated by the Cuban press agency. This was the year when many of the intellectuals who had supported the Cuban revolutionary process, and had viewed it as an example to be emulated by other struggling nations, broke with or distanced themselves from the Cuban experiment. Such was the case with Jean Paul Sartre, Alberto Moravia, Simone de Beauvoir, Susan Sontag, Mario Vargas Llosa, Carlos Fuentes, Octavio Paz, Juan Goytisolo, and other literary figures who advocated the right of criticism within the revolutionary process. In response to the "Padilla Case" and the turmoil that was following it, Fidel Castro in April 1971 addressed the First National Congress on Education and Culture. In his speech, Castro accused the Padilla advocates of being bourgeois libelists and stated that the writers did not have the privilege of advocating counterrevolutionary postures under the protectetive umbrella of intellectualism.

From 1971 to 1980 Padilla and his wife resided near Havana. His job was to consist mostly of rendering literary translations for El Instituto del Libro, but incommunicado with all foreign contacts. Nonetheless, the plight of Padilla was not forgotten by his friends abroad. In 1978 a general amnesty for political prisoners was decreed by the Cuban Revolution. Padilla appealed to Castro himself to be granted an exit permit. Although it was denied, his wife was allowed to leave the country. The efforts of such notables as Robert B. Silvers, editor of the *New York Review of Books,* and the novelist Bernard Malamud, through the intervention of Senator Edward Kennedy, would finally secure his release. Heberto Padilla was allowed to fly to the United States, via Montreal, on March 16, 1980, where he began his second exile.

Once in the United States, Padilla was invited by the Institute for Humanities and the Woodrow Wilson International Center for Scholars to continue his literary endeavors as a fellow from 1980 to 1982. Presently, Padilla and his wife reside in Princeton, New Jersey, where he teaches and she directs the prestigious literary quarterly dedicated to Cuban literature, *Linden Lane Magazine.*

Major Themes

Heberto Padilla published privately his first volume of poetry at the age of sixteen, *Las rosas audaces* (1948, Audacious Roses). This collection would open the creative cycle of his generation, which was to be called the new Cuban poetry generation. His first collection of importance was published in Havana in 1962. *El justo tiempo humano* (The Age of Human Justice) is a selection of poems written between 1953 and 1961. This book is of importance since it marks Padilla's transition from violent imagery to irony and social responsibility. As Ramiro Lagos points out, it is the "poetry of a man with a sense of history, concerned with metaphysical reality, conceived in terms of historic changes." The major themes of this collection are: a poor and misunderstood childhood, toiling adolescence, poetry as a net to entrap the lost feeling of time, mitigating love, the return to the homeland, and integration with the Revolution. *El justo tiempo humano* concludes with a series of poems in which the author casts away his ironical tones and accepts the Cuban Revolution. In his poem "El justo tiempo" Padilla sees the Cuban Revolution as a prelude to an age of justice, but not in the narrow scope of the Cuban Revolution per se but rather in an ampler revolutionary movement of which the Cuban component is an integral part but not the whole mosaic. In this poem Padilla writes: Look, life has come out in the open again!/ People are back on the old roads,/ their sickness over,/ and last year's wounded are singing now/ Stern-eyed dreamer/ drop your guard, forget suspicions/ and resentment./ For your country's sake, awake!/ The age of human justice is at hand. From the same collection, in the poem "Infancia de William Blake" (William Blake's Childhood), Padilla prophetically wrote of what was to happen to himself. The poet makes allusions to the inspectors of heresies that persecuted Blake at Felpham. Ten years later Padilla would face a similar ordeal.

In his book *Fuera del juego* (1968, Sent off the Field) the process of change in his political perspective can be illustrated. In poems like "Los que se alejan son los niños" Padilla treats the subject of Cuban emigrés and in reference to them laments the sight of the humiliated, whomever they may be. Perhaps the poems that best reflect his developing awareness of humanity are included in the section entitled "El abedul de hierro" (The Iron Birch Tree) and especially in the "Canción de la torre Spaskaya" (Song of Spaskaya Tower). These are the poems inspired during his stay as a correspondent in the Soviet Union, and Padilla clearly becomes skeptical of the perspectives that modern socialism, its theorists, and political system have to offer. In "Canción de la torre Spaskaya" the poet writes: The sentry / of Spaskaya tower / does not know / his tower is air. /He does not know / that on its stones / remain the marks / of executions; / that sometimes tendrils/ burst with blood / and songs resound / of Tsars long dead; / that in the dormers / watchers lurk. / He does not know / that ancient fear / cannot stay hidden in the air.

Since Padilla was allowed to leave the island, his creativity, now unhampered, has flourished. In 1981 he published *El hombre junto al mar* (The Man by the Sea). In this endeavor Padilla veers from political controversy and deals with the themes of love, the sea, self-introspection, infancy, and the true significance of historical figures. There are two outstanding elements that bind this volume of poems conceived in Cuba: the tone and the language.

Controversial as a poet, Padilla has more recently published several works of prose as well. In 1981 his novel *En mi jardín pastan los héroes* (Heroes Graze in my Garden) was published. In this novel the author narrates the life of a writer, Gregorio Suárez, who in turn narrates the desperate ordeal of Julio, a man who is being persecuted. As the novel progresses, Julio becomes the alter ego of both Gregorio and the author. The novel lacks a true hero. The only hero is the lurking threat of persecution.

Survey of Criticism

Padilla's works have received ample recognition, especially after becoming what he said he never wanted to become, a rebel poet in a socialist society. J. M. Cohen in his introduction to *Sent off the Field* makes reference to the influence of Dylan Thomas and W. H. Auden on Padilla's poetry. Cohen emphasizes that Auden has exerted a more prominent role by helping shape Padilla's usage of history and geography as poetic metaphor, though Padilla tends to view the poet as a prophet.

Another influence cited by critics is the connection between some of his poetry and that of Pasternak, especially in reference to his joy at life's unexpected pleasures, as can be observed in the poem "Los enamorados del bosque Izmailovo" (The Lovers from Izmailovo Woods) from the collection *Fuera del juego*. This comparison is one that flatters the Cuban poet, but he might be closer in spirit to Spain's Antonio Machado than to the Russian poet.

Many of the critical works on Padilla emphasize the degree to which his poetry can be regarded as counterrevolutionary, a label branded on his production by Cuba's literary critics. Ramiro Lagos in *Mester de rebeldía de la poesía hispanoamericana* (1973) fails to see Padilla's poetry as counterrevolutionary. In fact, Lagos views his output as that of a writer with a critical conciousness, what Lagos refers to as the true revolutionary poet. Lagos adds that Padilla's literary production was in tune with the Revolution but, since the poet refused to be directed by it, he was sanctioned. The critic cites as a sample Padilla's "Cantan los nuevos césares."

In his article, "Deciphering Codes," Lewis Hyde identifies as one of the poet's "obsessive themes" the complaint about our modern ideologies of history, pointing out that history for Padilla cannot teach everything. He further discusses the poet's view of our environment as so rationalized and politicized that it is inhospitable to the part of our being that creates a work of art. The critic mentions as an illustrative example Padilla's poem on Blake.

Hyde conceives of the Cuban poet as one "who has not been able to mine the richest vein of his sensibility because of the situation of his birth." The critic then adds that if Padilla had lived in London or Mexico City he might have produced poems on childhood, on sexual love, on the voices of the past, on landscape, and the spirit. But Padilla has produced in *El hombre junto al mar* exactly what Hyde sensed as a lack of development in his poetic sensibility.

All indications seem to point to the rapid proliferation of further studies on Padilla's work, since he has been and continues to be translated and read by a wider audience. Up to the present, however, his prose output, as far as criticism is concerned, seems to have attracted much less attention than his poetry.

How Padilla will evolve living in a radically different society remains to be seen, but many hope that he will not become an ex-rebel poet living in a capitalistic society. The poet's political or ideological orientation is best exposed in his poem "Autorretrato del otro": The Right praises me/ (?in no time they will defame me) / The Left has given me a name/ ?(have they not begun to have doubts?) / Don't greet me, I beg you/ Don't speak to me/ If you see me, keep to one side.

As far as his role in U.S. Hispanic literature is concerned, Padilla views himself as a Cuban poet wholly integrated with Cuba's literary process, living outside his homeland due to circumstances. He perceives Hispanic literature in the United States as a realm belonging to those who have developed within this society. These may consider themselves a marginal part of it, but Padilla nevertheless sees them as an integral part of U.S. culture.

Bibliography

WORKS BY PADILLA

Las rosas audaces. Havana: n.p., 1948.
Fuera del juego. Havana: Instituto Cubano del Libro, 1968.
El justo tiempo humano. Barcelona, Spain: Llibres de Sinera, 1970.
Por el momento. Las Palmas, Spain: Inventarios Provisionales, 1970.
Provocaciones. Madrid: Ediciones La Gota de Agua, 1973.
El hombre junto al mar. Barcelona: Seix-Barral, 1981.
En mi jardín pastan los héroes. Barcelona: Argos-Vergara, 1981.

   Translated Works

Fuera del juego. París: DuSeuil Press, 1969.
Sent off the Field. London: Andre Deutsch Press, 1971.
En mi jardín pastan los héroes. Rome: Mondadori, 1982.
Legacies. New York: Farrar, Straus and Giroux, 1982.
Dans mon jardin paissent les héros. Paris: Presses de la Renaissance, 1983.
Héritages. Paris: Belfond, 1983.

WORKS ABOUT PADILLA

Cabrera, Miguel. "Heberto Padilla: El Poeta de la Prosadia." *Nueva Estafeta* 36 (November 1981): 117–19).
Casal, Lourdes. *El caso Padilla*. Miami: Ediciones Universal, 1971.
Cohen, J. M. *Sent off the Field*. London: Andre Deutsch, 1971.
Hyde, Lewis. "Deciphering Codes." *The Nation* 234, 1 (January 1982): 87–88.
Lagos, Ramiro. *Mester de rebeldía de la poesía hispanoamericana*. Madrid: Dos Mundos, 1973.
Ripoll, Carlos. "The Cuban Scene: Censors and Dissenters." *Partisan Review* 48, 4 (1981): 574–87.

Salvador, A. "Literatura Cubana (1959–1975)." *Casa de las Américas* 113 (1979): 14–26.

ROBERTO G. FERNÁNDEZ

PALÉS MATOS, LUIS (1898–1959). Luis Palés Matos was the first Puerto Rican literary figure to achieve a broad and lasting influence on the evolution of Latin American literature, principally through the development of a poetic style that was inspired by the rhythms and the sounds of African language and music of the Caribbean. His revolutionary book, *Tuntún de pasa y grifería* (1937, its onomatopoetic title has no translation), openly proclaimed a black African heritage and presence for the cultural makeup of Puerto Rico and the Caribbean.

Biography

Luis Palés Matos was born in 1898 in the city of Guayama or "La Ciudad de los Brujos," in the southern littoral of Puerto Rico where the Negro and mulatto population is abundant. He died at the age of sixty-one in Santurce in 1959. His parents, Consuelo Matos and Vicente Palés Anés, were both romantic poets of the end of the nineteenth century. His father was a follower of the French liberal ideas and in his home library had some of the French authors with whom his son, Luis, later became acquainted. The young Luis and his two brothers, Vicente and Gustavo, also poets, enjoyed the environment of a home that provided them with books of all sorts—science, psychology, politics, history, and philosophy.

From his "nana," La Negra Lupe, Palés learned stories and songs that recurred later in his poetry, such as in the refrain of "Falsa canción de baquiné": "¿Adombe gangá mondé, adombe?/Candombe del baquiné,/candombe."

Because of the debt incurred by the publication of his first book of poems, *Azaleas,* he could hardly finish high school. In order to pay the debt, he was forced to work, but his thirst for knowledge enabled him to take advantage of all available sources of information, thus becoming a self-educated man.

His first two works, *Azaleas* and *Sonetos del Campo* (Country Sonnets), so saturated with the young poet's experiences, were published in Guayama in 1915. A clear picture of his native city is found later in his unfinished novel, *El Litoral* (The Coast), in which he evokes the years in school, the years spent with his family and friends, the hours spent studying in the municipal library, the librarian, and the adventures of his adolescent years. On one occasion Palés explained that his main teachers, the inspirers of many of his poems, were in the surroundings of his home in Guayama—the rooster, the neighbor's daughter, the town's barber, a horse trotting along the street, Sundays in that provincial village, and the hours, those slow, lazy, empty hours ticked off by the large clock at the plaza. At twenty-three we find the poet established in San Juan where he enjoyed life among his colleagues who were also poets. However, he always remembered Guayama as if his childhood and adolescence were the greatest passages of his life.

The poet traveled from Guayama to Ponce, covering the area of Arroyo and Salinas during his youth. In those coastal villages he observed the Puerto Rican Negroes and mulattos as poor workers of the docks and the sugar cane fields. He never went to the African continent or to any other of the Caribbean islands where he could have seen Negroes. He knew them only on his own island, in that southern region of the country.

The Negroid environment of Palés was one element, but his considerable reading about the Negro race was another. In the fables of *El decamerón negro* (The Black Decameron) by Leo Frobenius he was provided with the zoological ingredients of his works; Más Laglera with his book, *En el país de los bubis* (In the Land of the Boobies), informed him of the inhabitants of distant Fernando Póo. René Maran's *Batouala*; Vandercook's *Black Majesty*; Paul Morand's *Black Magic*, and William Seabrook's *The Magic Island* contributed to the black world that inhabited Palés's imagination.

Most of the critics of Palés Matos' poetry have emphasized the "poesía afroantillana" (Afro-Caribbean poetry) in their analysis, but in his works the Negroidism is not the only important phase. The cycle of his "Black poetry" corresponds only to *Tuntún de pasa y grifería* of 1937. The most complete collection of his works, however, is *Poesía 1915–1956*.

From the years of *Azaleas* to the time of his death, Palés Matos practiced all of the techniques of contemporary poetry. There can be detected in his works symptoms of neo-romanticism and Parnassianism, impressionism, symbolism, modernism, and vanguardism. Vanguardism serves as a means of expression both for his "poesía afroantillana" and "sinfonías nordícas" (nordic symphonies). His last production was the work of an individualistic artist, matured in all the ways of poetic expression. In his poetry, "black" or white, "topografía" (topography) remains something extremely important to him, a constant feeling that tied him to his native soil: Guayama, Puerto Rico, land of Negroes, mulattos and white, land of creoles and Antilleans.

Major Themes

The reader of Palés Matos's poetry in "black" must bear in mind that he did not explore Negroid folklore from the popular, fashionable, society point of view, but the aesthetic one. He has gone deeper into black and Afro-Antillean folklore, so as to recognize the true values of the Negro man and of his African ancestors, so that his "poesía afroantillana" has resulted in an aesthetic work, on one hand, and in a psychological analysis of the dark race on the other.

Palés Matos is not a simple improviser; his powerful and creative imagination has served him as a vehicle to combine the many sources acquired through his intensive studies about that Afro-Antillean who is constantly present in his "black poetry." At times, the imagination of the poet does not make the black man a plain realistic Negro, but rather a visionary creation of his poetic talent. The poetic vision is not like a simple mirror; rather it can be a magnifying glass where the appearance of reality is made more interesting to the spectator.

The Negro of *Tuntún de pasa y griferfa* is the individual who performs his cults and his rites. Many aspects of his life are seen through the magnifying glass of poetic vision, through that creative imagination that is not a mere result of a dreamworld, but rather a heightened perception, nonetheless a very clear perception. The Negro of this ''black poetry'' touches also the ground of reality.

Naturally, it is a question of different realities; different realities before the work of art and within the work of art. Although the first ones only matter in so far as they are transformed into the latter, it is legitimate to pay attention to the first ones, too. In both ''Pueblo de negros'' and ''Esta noche'' is evident the reality experienced by the black man of Palés Matos's own surroundings in Guayama. In another poem, ''Pueblo Negro,'' he evokes an imaginary reality derived, perhaps, from the world of his readings.

Here, not only are the ''sources'' of a different nature—the one a sum of personal memories, the other a sum of possible readings—but the result is curiously different: the more *lived* source yields the lesser poetry, and the more artificial source leads to the more matured poem. Although it must be admitted that the earlier treatments are more realistic, the latter treatment reaches the higher reality.

The cycle of Negroid poetry contained in *Tuntún de pasa y griferfa* is post-modernistic work, but its postmodernism is more Palesiano than generally Spanish American. His ''poesía afroantillana'' reveals traces of the poet's modernistic works. There are in it, at times, echoes of *Azaleas* and *Sonetos del campo*. [Palés Matos and his friend-poet José I. de Diego Padró were the creators of ''Diepalismo'' (1921), one of the Puerto Rican vanguardist movements.]

The poet's native landscape is reproduced on the screen of *El Jardín de Tembandumba* (Tembandumba Garden), an imaginary African paradise. There, the flora and fauna of Puerto Rico are combined with those of the other Antilles and of Africa. In many of his poems in ''black'' the impressionistic tendencies that are present in his modernistic works are also revealed. Poems like ''Preludio en boricua'' (Boricua Prelude), ''Mulata Antilla'' (Mulatto Antilles), ''Náñigo al cielo'' (African Chant to the Skies), and ''Majestad Negra'' (Black Majesty) could be captured in paintings compared to those of Toulouse-Lautrec and Vincent van Gogh for their many brilliant colors.

However, the most striking and conspicuous quality of Palés Matos's poetry in ''black'' is found not in its colorfulness but in its sonority, in its magical and rhythmical resources. The life of the Negro as it offers itself to the sense of sight certainly interested our poet and inspired many a glowing line, but what translated itself most immediately and most abundantly into poetry were the sounds of the Negro rites and the rhythms of Negro dances.

In the poem ''Bombo,'' for instance, the refrain— ''Bombo del Congo, mongo máximo,/Bombo del Congo está contento'' (Bombo of the Congo, Head Chief,/Bombo of the Congo is content)—is an ardent exclamation, an ejaculation of intense black rhythms. ''Bombo'' is a big, round drum that is played with heavy drum sticks. It is an Afro-Cuban instrument, but also the name of a Congo deity, as the poet presents him in several of his Negroid poems. The refrain is two lines of rich assonance in which the persisting "o" gives the sensation of remote sounds of "atabales" or huge drums calling the Negroes from the distances of dark jungles for the celebration of the ritual dance. The vowel "o" is repeated thirteen times in the mentioned two lines.

The presence of "Bombo," the greatest god of the Congo, in the "Nigricia" (Black World), created by the poet, emphasizes the Negro ritual dance. The first line of the poem—"La bomba dice:———Tombuctú!'' (The Drum says Timbuktu)—announces the sounds of the drum. "Tombuctú" is the name of an African country with onomatopoeic sounds in its three syllables which can be reproduced by the drums. The sound "Tombuctú" is the opening call of the talking drum. The drum is sacred and powerful, and the Africans understand its symbolic attributes.

The Negro dances are performed on the stage of "El Jardín de Tembandumba" and the reader can enjoy them as the poet draws open the curtains of that Afro-Antillean garden. The African dances came to the New World with the Negro slaves, and like the Negro they remained in slavery for centuries. They were dances that formed part of the ritualistic cults of the Negro slaves and were not allowed to be performed publicly. Among the dances of African origin present in this type of poetry are found: "balele," "candombe," "macumba," "calenda," and "rumba." Today both the Old and New World perform dances of African origin, and even when the dances have some primitive remnants, they are not considered to be ritualistic.

The first Negro dance written by the author of "tuntunes" was "Danza Negra." This dance reveals already all the rhythmical and onomatopoeic effects of the Negroes' instruments. Some critics have said that Palés Matos was influenced by Vachel Lindsay when he wrote his "Danza negra," but the Puerto Rican published his poem in 1926, and it was not until 1928 that he became an avid reader of literary and folkloric studies of the Negro race written by North Americans. Thus, no influence of Vachel Lindsay's works can be traced in "Danza Negra" (Black Dance) and in "Candombe." However, these poems do reveal a knowledge acquired by the poet from the works of Leo Frobenius and José Más Laglera. But that knowledge, that cognitive content, is by no means the principal thing in these poems.

The first striking thing in Palés Matos's "Danza negra" is the new sound. In all its thirty-six lines the emphatic endings are "agudos," accentuated vowels, each of which rises up to its vocal climax. They combine a maximum of sound with the minimum of sense.

Words such as "tucutú," "tocotó," "prú-prú-prú," and "cro-cro-cró," etc., are almost pure sound, pure onomatopoeia, pure "jitanjáfora."

"Jitanjáfora" has become an almost necessary technical term for the description of a technique of Palés Matos. "Majestad Negra" and "Danza negra" are wonderful examples of "jitanjáfora" technique.

Besides dances, there are other ceremonies in this "black" poetry. In the poem "Falsa canción de baquiné" (False Song of the Child's Wake) are combined the cultural rites of the Afro-Antillean and Puerto Rican tradition of "velorio de niños" (the child's wake). The "baquiné" or "velorio de niños negros" is a popular tradition in Puerto Rico mainly among the Negroes and mulattos. "Changó" is the equivalent of Saint Barbara in Cuban "Santería." In Haitian Voodoo there are terms like "calalú" and "quimbombó," both meaning a kind of stew, in this case made for ritualistic purposes. Also from Voodoo is the term "papaluá," who is the leading voice in the Voodoo ceremony.

In other poems about the Cuban "ñáñigos," the poet introduces the "Ñañiguismo" when he makes allusions to "Ecué"—the Death—and "Abasí"—the crucifix carried by one of the "oficiantes" (officials) or "grandes sacerdotes" (great priests) during the ceremony of the "ñáñigos."

The poem "Ñam-Ñam" (Yum Yum) is a composition of four stanzas. The first three start with the word—an onomatopoeic sound—for masticating jaws. The last stanza is just four lines, which mention Asia, America, and Europe in order to contrast them with Africa who is just grunting "ñam-ñam." This sound is repeated sixteen times in the poem which is only twenty-eight lines. The emphasis of the sound "ñam-ñam" is to create the cannibalistic and wild environment of a primitive race on a distant continent. The poet portrays with humorous irony the facts witnessed by history. It is not strange to read about the consequences suffered by white men, even during this century, when they tried to get acquainted with certain African tribes. "Ñam-Ñam" is, then, a profoundly descriptive sound. "Ñam-Ñam" is primitivism, wildness, savagery, ferocity. "Ñam-ñam" is a deeply black sound, dark-black as the depths of the forests and the jungles, as the night and its sinister darkness.

On the basis of these poems is a rather thorough knowledge of folklore, not only of the native folklore of Palés Matos's Antillean islands, which he knew through observation, but also of the folklore of distant Africa, which he had learned only through books. The folkloric elements are powerfully elevated into an atmosphere of vision, which owes its uniquely central reality to the peculiar mind of the poet.

In John W. Vandercook's *Black Majesty* are found the two nineteenth-century characters who inspired the poems "Lagarto Verde" and "Elegía del Duque de la Marmelada." These two poems portray the Count of Limonade, an educated (aristocratic) mulatto in the court of Henry Christophe of Haiti, whose original name was Prévost; and the Duque Marmelade, whose name was Richard, a general and the governor of Cape Henry in Haiti.

In these two poems the poet is not trying to make a crude mockery of the civilized Negro, but he is emphasizing the fact that many Negroes in the Antilles pretend to forget their origins and insist on whitening themselves by acting ridiculously in a way foreign to their real nature. His intention is to make the Negro man realize that he, as a civilized man, can be more natural, if he remembers the real value of his own race. Palés Matos was a strong defender of the philosophical and psychological ideals of Spengler and Freud, who believed that instinct was more important than intellectualism and rationalism. The satirical joke of these poems is addressed to many Negroes and mulattos in the Antilles who act like "little counts of Lemonade" and "Dukes of Marmalade."

This Puerto Rican poet has grouped together most of the elements of his "black" poetry in one long poem, "Canción festiva para ser llorada" (Festive Song to Be Cried). This is a little monograph in verse on·the geographical, sociological, and mythical characteristics of the Antilles, the many subtropical islands in all their variety. The tone of the poem (written in the romance form) is a strange mixture of elations and dejections, as it is neatly announced in the very title. Many remember the title "Canción festiva" and forget the "para ser llorada," which is the most important message of the poet of the happy "tuntunes," for it is in this phrase that he cries out with certain irony against the psychological status of his own island, Puerto Rico. Strangely, it is just in the references to his own island that the element of dejection is most easily detected. That "para ser llorada" element comes to the fore best in the one line repeated often at the end of the three-line refrain: "Puerto Rico—burundanga."

Puerto Rico is exactly that, "burundanga," the mixture of everything, the mixture that takes away the real identity of the island. He has called his island "una mitad española/y otra mitad africana" (one half Spanish/the other half African). Going deeper in his meditation about his native country, deeper also in his mood, he realizes that Puerto Rico, his "isla ardiente" (burning island), is nothing else but a "burundanga," a hodgepodge.

As it has been illustrated throughout this entry, our attention has been divided between what one can see in Palés Matos's poems in "black" of the realities, the rites, and the traditions of Antillean Negro life, and what one can hear in the tone pictures and tone poems into which this white man has transposed his experiences, his studies, and his musings concerning the black race and its utterances, especially its musical utterances.

Survey of Criticism

Palés Matos's philosophy of civilization is one of disenchantment, according to Gustavo Agrait in "Una Posible Explicaión del Ciclo Negro en la Poesía de Palés" : "La sofistería que lo civilizado representa sobre lo virgen, lo primitivo, lo ancestral, lo pristino animal del ser humano no parecería contar con el endoso del Palés poeta ni del Palés hombre." (The sophistry that civilization had over the virginal, the primitive, the ancestral, the pristine animalism of human beings was seemingly not endorsed by Palés the poet nor Palés the man).

The variety of tones, from satire and irony to dejection and pessimism, have given rise to a diversity of opinions concerning Palés's attitudes. In the special issue of *Asomante* (1959) dedicated to Palés Matos, María Teresa Babín applauds the poem "La Plena de Menéalo" as a patriotic credo and asserts that Palés was preoccupied with the sad fate of Puerto Rico in the twentieth century. A similarly solemn tone is reflected in the pages of the special issue on Palés Matos of *La*

Torre (1960). Even José I. de Diego Padró remarks that, "In the anti-imperialist anthology of Spanish America, his verses will always have a choice place." Ricardo Gullón discusses the matter with finer distinctions and states that Palés through his poetry became a spokesman for his people.

One of the best critics of the poet, Margot Arce de Vázquez, states in regard to Palés Matos's black poetry that there are just a few thematic and stylistic preferences in this cycle that have become art objects with their own canon. There is no doubt, however, that Palés Matos identified very much with the black cycle and with the Afro-Caribbean experience of his native land. In himself he identified the mixed heritage and culture, despite his not having direct black ancestry, and he often spoke of himself in the same tones as we find in his poetry: mixed humor and depreciation.

Bibliography

WORKS BY PALÉS MATOS

Azaleas. Guayama, Puerto Rico: Rodríguez y Co., 1915.
Tuntún de pasa y grifería. Introd. Angel Valbuena Pratt. San Juan: Biblioteca de Autores Puertorriqueños, 1937.
Luis Palés Matos: vida y obra, bibliografía, antología, poesías inéditas, Federico de Onís, ed. San Juan: Ateneo Puertorriqueño, 1960.
Poesía, 1915–1956. 3d ed. Introd. Federico de Onís, ed. San Juan: Universidad de Puerto Rico, 1968.

WORKS ABOUT PALÉS MATOS

Agrait, Gustavo. "Una Posible Explicación del Ciclo Negro en la Poesía de Palés" (Conferencia inédita).
Arana Soto, Salvador. "Refutando a Luis Palés Matos." *El Mundo* May 25, 1959.
Arce de Vázquez, Margot. "Los poemas negros de Luis Palés Matos." *Ateneo Puertorriqueño* 1, 1 (1935): 35–52.
———. "Los adjetivos de la 'Danza Negra' de Palés Matos." *Ateneo Puertorriqueño* 3 (1939): 147–62.
———. *Impresiones. Notas Puertorriqueñas.* San Juan: Editorial Yaurel, 1950.
Barrera, Héctor. "Renovación poética de Luis Palés Matos." *Asomante* 7 (1951).
Benítez, Jaime. "Luis Palés Matos y el pesimismo en Puerto Rico." *Revista Bimestre Cubana* (November 1942).
Blanco, Tomás. "Homenaje a Luis Palés Matos: un vate boricua en los Madriles." *El Imparcial* January 24, 1934.
———. "Refutación y glosa." *Ateneo Puertorriqueño* 1 (1935).
Colorado, Antonio J. "Un libro de Palés Matos: *Tuntún de pasa y grifería.*" *El Imparcial* December 12, 1959.
———. *Luis Palés Matos: el hombre y el poeta.* San Juan, P.R.: Editorial Rodadero, 1964.
Combas Guerra, E. "En torno a la fortaleza." *El Mundo* August 14, 1963.
Davis, William M. "Animals in the Afro-Antillean Poems of Luis Palés Matos." *Annali Instituto Universitario Orientale,* Napoli (Sezione Romanza), 10 (1968): 377–97.

Díaz Quiñones, Arcadio. "Testimonio autobiográfico de Luis Palés Matos." *Revista del Instituto de Cultura Puertorriqueña* 8, 26 (March 1965).
Diego Padró, José I. de. "Antillanismo, criollismo, negroidismo." *El Mundo* November 19, 1932.
Enamorado Cuesta, J. "Luis Palés Matos, genial fatalista." *Puerto Rico Libre* April 9, 1959.
Enguídanos, Miguel. "Lo que Palés Matos añadió a Puerto Rico." *La Torre* 8 (January-June 1960).
————. *La poesía de Luis Palés Matos*. Río Piedras: Universidad de Puerto Rico, 1962.
Florit, Eugenio. *"Los veros de Palés Matos."* *Revista Hispánica Moderna* 24 (1958): 216–17.
Font Saldaña, Jorge. "El negro lírico de Luis Palés Matos." *Puerto Rico Ilustrado* 29, 1471 (1958).
Géigel Polanco, Vicente. "Movimiento literario de los veinte: el diepalismo." *Artes y Letras* (May 1959).
Gullón, Ricardo. "Situación de Palés Matos." *La Torre* 8 (January-June 1960).
Iduarte, Andrés. "Homenaje a Luis Palés Matos." *Instituto Hispánico* 18 (November 29, 1951).
Jesús Castro, Tomás de. "Palés, joglar y yo." *El Mundo* August 1, 1959.
Lloréns, Washington. "La Jitanjáfora en Luis Palés Matos." *Artes y Letras* 2, 10 (April 1954).
Lluch Mora, Francisco. "Cuatro Estados del Sentimiento Religioso en la Poesía de Luis Palés Matos." *El Mundo* September 4, 1961.
Matos Paoli, Francisco. "El Paisaje en la Poesía de Luis Palés Matos." *Alma Latina* February 24, 1945.
Morales Oliver, Luis. "Dos Aspectos en la Poesía de Luis Palés Matos." *Revista del Instituto de Cultura Puertorriqueña* 9, 33 (December 1966).
Vientós Gastón, Nilita. "Indice Cultural. Una Antología de Luis Palés Matos." *El Mundo* June 28, 1958.
Ward, James H. "The Evolution of the Thought and Poetry of Luis Palés Matos as Seen through a Study of Six Themes." Tulane: *Dissertation Abstracts* 28 (1968): 2660A.

LUCY TORRES

PIETRI, PEDRO (1944–   ). Pedro Pietri is a Nuyorican poet and playwright, a self-described "native New Yorker born in Ponce." He writes in English with an occasional admixture of Spanish words. His first collection of poems, *Puerto Rican Obituary* (1973), is a fundamental work for understanding Nuyorican poetry. His plays have been performed in little theaters on both coasts and have the distinction of having been directed on occasion by the great Puerto Rican actor, José Ferrer. His poetry recitals have also been recorded on commercial records, he being somewhat of a stand-up comic.

Biography

Born in Ponce, Puerto Rico, in 1944 and raised in New York City, Pedro is the second child in a family of four children. Its members are Joe, Carmen, and

Pedro, his brother Willie (nicknamed Dr. Willie) having died in a car accident in 1981. Pietri's parents died while Pedro was still a child and he was brought up by Tata, his grandmother. To the present Pietri has assumed the persona of a street urchin, always dressed in black and creating an aura of mystery as to his background and living habits. In his literature and in his personal life, he identifies totally with marginal man, with the downtrodden, with the lumpen. His first book, *Puerto Rican Obituary*, was so popular that it spawned hundreds of young street poets who imitated his style. Other than these few data, very little is known of Pietri's biography.

Major Themes

Pietri's work is quintessentially urban. He grew up in New York's Upper West Side, and through his several transformations from "street poet" to "drunken poet" to "Latin Insomniac," the city has figured importantly as a protagonist in his work. Moreover, Pietri's poems are written to be read aloud, as they depend partly on the joy of word sounds, on rhyming, for their effect. They are performed in the city's cafes, community centers, and colleges, where the implied reader/audience is urban.

The early poetry of *Puerto Rican Obituary* concentrates primarily on aspects of Puerto Rican life in New York and it is constructed from cultural components such as fundamentalist "old-tyme" religion, spiritualism, exploitation of workers and the poor and Spanish-speaking, the numbers game, the scrambling of poorly paid work—"the lowest wages of the ages"—and poor people's cramped living quarters. The best pieces foreshadow the surrealism that will become dominant in Pedro's later writing. "Suicide Note from a Cockroach in a Low Income Housing Project," for example, could comfortably fit into the work of a later period. It is not until *Traffic Violations* (1983), however, that Pietri's work becomes a full-blown revolt against all the constraints placed on the human mind by social convention. In *Puerto Rican Obituary*, the poet denounces social inequality as well as the foolishness of accepting conventional wisdom. The Puerto Ricans in his poems have sacrificed the beauty of their cultural heritage for the madness of superficiality and scrambling for commodities that will never bring them the social status they so desire. As can be seen in the poem, "Puerto Rican Obituary," the one-upmanship is tragic because the rewards are so ephemeral, mere scraps from the rich man's table. The irony of it is that there was never a chance that these Puerto Ricans would "make it" "because it is against company policy/to promote SPICS SPICS SPICS!"

The poem is a eulogy, but it ends on a positive note, as the five dead Puerto Ricans are visualized in Puerto Rico "where the wind is a stranger to miserable weather conditions" and where "to be called negrito/means to be called LOVE." Irony and black humor also play an important part in all the poems of the *Obituary*. Death is a major theme in all of Pedro's work. In the 1970s he would ride the New York City subways and walk the streets dressed entirely in black and carrying a huge oblong black box on which were printed the words "Rent a Coffin'' in block letters. It was a briefcase—he carried his poems in it—and a prop in a satirical routine. Pedro highlighted everyday absurdities, implicitly advocating the anarchic, authentic life so as to avoid stultification, the coffin of semi-existence that our socialization tricks us into believing is all we can expect in life.

Pedro's life and work both have an anarchistic bent. In both, he questions social convention and ritualized behavior. His poetry is beyond the reach of an ossified, realist rationality; it is about the free play of the imagination which, while it offers us no guarantees, is all we have with which to resist the ever-encroaching tendency to conform. His work is a powerful statement about our fear of freedom.

The dream-like sequences of *Traffic Violations* are evidence of the influence of surrealism in Pietri's work: "When fire hydrants wear long dresses/It will take forever to put out a fire" ("Intermission from Tuesday"). There is also a tendency to juxtapose unrelated images and to play with the logical categories inherited from realist notions of human consciousness as a way of freeing us from those categories of thought. Pedro himself would probably deny any programmatic purposes: As he says in "10th Untitled Poem," "Don't expect me to explain anything/All I can truly say about myself/Is that after monday comes tuesday."

Pedro's current work takes as its material the absurdity of everyday life, the mental prisons people build for themselves out of fear of freedom. His work is profoundly subversive.

In recent years, Pietri has turned his attention to prose. In 1981, Ediciones Huracán published his *Lost in the Museum of Natural History* in a bilingual fold-out edition, part of their *de orilla a orilla* series. The narrative is a surrealistic examination of the alienation people endure—and, paradoxically, learn to like—in modern capitalist societies; it is also a playful reverie on the act of writing. A self-referential first-person narrator repeatedly highlights the arbitrary nature of writing—art as "free play" —for it is a construction of relative order out of chaotic raw materials drawn from life. The implicit question is "Isn't life itself just such a construct?" The story is structured around the events in a day when a little girl, lost at a bench frequented by the city's poor and poorer people, "honest hard workers from neighborhoods that are hazardous to your health," struggles to be recognized, "found." Like the child in Luis Buñuel's *The Phantom of Liberty,* she is never really lost; her lostness consists of being repeatedly misapprehended by those around her, incorporated into other people's "texts" for their own purposes. As she finds herself in a text where rebellion is prohibited, where chewing your food is all the joy you're ever allowed, this little girl is beaten to death by her mother—only to be resurrected later in our narrative when she reappears handing out "gypsy business cards" on the subway. The first-person narrative voice is making up a story from the "notes for future reference" he's compiling as he observes the events; the story he is writing is the very story we are reading. The neat division between "inside the text" and "outside the text'' that we're used to as readers of realist texts, as passive readers, is not possible here, for Pietri's narrative fragments are what Roland Barthes calls "the proairetic code," the ability to rationally determine the result of an action. Pietri's narrative thus creates a discomfort in the passive reader, who, if he is to continue reading, must become active for he does not know what to expect. This forces the reader to question perceived notions of rationality and logic. This story may well be Pietri's most radical break with conventionalized writing thus far. As in the theater of the absurd, the absence of common sense logic constitutes a direct attack on the seemingly innocent notions of sequenciality and rationality. These, he seems to be saying, are merely inherited blinders. In Pietri's *Lost in the Museum* . . . the realist tradition is to modern life as a museum of natural history is to our dreams. Just as people demand empty ritualized behavior and thought from each other, readers demand easy reading, logical sequences, believable— and discardable—tales from their authors. To resist that is to force a re-examination of comfortable, though deadly, perceived notions of order, and of literature, as well.

Survey of Criticism

Because of the unconventional nature of Pietri's work, it has not drawn a great deal of commentary. Much of what has been said refers, in fact, to its linguistic, social, and aesthetic break with conventions, as well as to its identifying with the underclass and the underworld. Of *Puerto Rican Obituary, Library Journal* (March, 1974) stated that "the sad irony is that the people whose pain Pietri is exposing are too busy shooting up or breaking their backs for a dollar to look at his words—their lives—with the insight and perspective he offers." On the other hand, Alfredo Matilla in his article "The Broken English Dream" was the first to see Pietri's poetry as a subversive act because he reflects the dark conception of the world of alienated people and uses it to raise their level of consciousness. And, more than anything, he sees Pietri's poetry as something that profoundly explores the illusion and trickery of the world. He states that Pietri's is the first liberated proletariate creation in Puerto Rican poetry.

Bibliography

WORKS BY PIETRI

Books

Puerto Rican Obituary. New York: Monthly Review Press, 1973.
Lost in the Museum of Natural History. Río Piedras: Ediciones Huracán, 1981.
Traffic Violations. Maplewood, N.J.: Waterfront Press, 1983.
The Masses Are Asses. Maplewood, N.J.: Waterfront Press, 1984.
Poems by Pedro Pietri have been published in the following periodicals: *P'alante, Revista del Instituto de Estudios Puertorriqueños de Brooklyn College, The Rican,* and *Unidad Latina.*

Poems in Anthologies

Algarín, Miguel, and Miguel Piñero. *Nuyorican Poetry*. New York: Morrow, 1975.
Matilla, Alfredo, and Iván Silén. *The Puerto Rican Poets/Los poetas puertorriqueños*.
    New York: Bantam, 1972.
Silén, Iván. *Los paraguas amarillos: los poetas latinos en Nueva York*. Hanover, N.H.:
    Ediciones del Norte, 1983.

WORKS ABOUT PIETRI

"*Puerto Rican Obituary.*" *Library Journal*. 99 (March, 1974): 662.
Matilla, Alfredo. "The Broken English Dream: Poesía puertorriqueña en Nueva York."
    Revista del Instituto de Estudios Puertorriqueños del Brooklyn College 1, 1
    (Spring, 1971): 61–67.
Mohr, Eugene V. *The Nuyorican Experience*. Westport, Conn.: Greenwood Press, 1982.

                                                                    DIANA VÉLEZ

PIÑERO, MIGUEL (1946–1988). Although Miguel Pinñero writes in a number
of different genres—poetry, popular cultural screenplays (as in his most recent
work for the much-heralded television series, "Miami Vice"), and street wise
philosophical prose—his major claim to our attention today is for his prison
drama, *Short Eyes,* an extended commentary about prison violence and the
dialectics of power. *Short Eyes* moves toward a riveting climax, with wild,
whirling twists of irony, illustrating the failings of contemporary vigilante justice.
Short Eyes, awarded the Obie Prize and the New York Critics Circle Award for
best American play of the 1973–1974 season, has been succeeded by several
important plays, including *The Sun Always Shines for the Cool, Midnight Moon
at the Greasy Spoon,* and *Eulogy for a Small Time Thief.* In 1980, Piñero
published his first book of poems, *La Bodega Sold Dreams,* a scorching con-
stellation of postmodernist images, thematizing the author's polemical critique
of American society in late capitalism. As I will show in more detail below,
Piñero's work brings each and every one of his readers/viewers into direct contact
with the urban, post-industrial American city. In brief, Piñero's work can best
be seen as a response to our new postmodernist American environment, illustrating new modes of perception and sensibility in the 1980s.

Biography

   Born in Gurabo, Puerto Rico, on December 19, 1946, brought to New York
by his parents, Miguel Angel Piñero and Adelina Gomez, Miguel Antonio Piñero
was raised on the Lower East Side of New York City, the artistic site of his
major work. At the age of eleven, he was picked up by the state authorities for
truancy; at thirteen, he was arrested for shoplifting and other crimes and sentenced
to three years in prison; at fifteen, he was shooting dope; and at twenty-four,
Piñero, a self-educated junior high-school dropout, was sent to Sing Sing prison
for armed robbery. As Miguel *Algarín explained in his introduction to Nuyor-

ican "Outlaw Poetry" in *Nuyorican Poetry* (1975), edited by Algarín and Piñero, "For many reasons Piñero came out fighting. He has fought for his drugs, and he has fought when he's gotten caught ripping off a pad so that he can keep his chemical cool. He has fought just to fight because he's angry or bored or desperate or just not letting time pass by without confronting an authority that indoctrinates and betrays at the same time."

While an inmate of Sing Sing prison, Piñero began writing and acting in Clay Stevenson's theater workshop. As Piñero said in an interview with Norma Alarcón in *Revista Chicano-Riqueña*, 2/1 (1974), "When you're in prison, you're nowhere being nobody. [I write] to survive." As a result of a *New York Times* article on Piñero's contribution to the prison theatrical workshop at Sing Sing prison, the director of theater for the Riverside Church corresponded with Piñero and subsequently learned that Piñero was busy writing in his cell a full-length play, *Short Eyes*. The Family, an acting troupe comprised of former convicts and former drug-addicts, directed by Marvin Felix Camillo, produced *Short Eyes* at the Riverside Church. Joseph Papp and his New York Shakespeare Festival Public theater gave *Short Eyes* its off-Broadway premiere.

Recently, Piñero has continued his acting career with cameo roles (usually as a dope dealer) in television series such as "Kojak," "Baretta," and "Miami Vice," and in major Hollywood movies about cops and robbers such as *The Godfather* and *Fort Apache, The Bronx*. More recently, Piñero has taught creative writing at Rutgers University. In April 1982, Piñero was the recipient of a Guggenheim Fellowship for playwriting.

Major Themes

Miguel Piñero's work is strong in its realistic evocations of domination—violent though it may be for dramatic purposes. Various kinds of dialects—Nuyorican, black, Irish-American, Greek-American—are well reproduced in his plays, and, though the characters may not always be classically well rounded, they are sharply and skillfully sketched through their language and actions. Thus, Piñero's plays have often been justly praised for their startling innovations of ethnopoetic heteroglossia.

His theater is also important for what it has to say about the theory and practice of coercion and normalization in America. Most of Piñero's dramatic work is directed against the comfortable middle-class aesthetics of his viewers. His plays, therefore, are about urban human beings restricted by poverty, disease, and social corruption. The familiar topos of alienation in Third World American literature, moreover, is disengaged from a one-dimensional perspective as in *Short Eyes* and expanded to describe the emergence of the underside of American postmodernist culture: child molestation, racism, sodomy, jail violence, and vigilante-style murder.

Short Eyes is now justly famous, at least in the United States, but is far from completely understood, for it begins in its extraordinary first and second acts a discussion that has been intractable for ages and remains so: the ubiquity of power. Prison life, for Piñero, is always grounded in power relationships. And, like Michel Foucault's penetrating study of coercion and normalization in *Discipline and Punish: The Birth of the Prison* (1975), Piñero's *Short Eyes* dramatized that a single locus of power could not be identified in a prison world. Rather, Piñero's play illustrated what can be best described as a microphysics of power, probing its multiple and diverse manifestations. The domination Piñero studies in *Short Eyes* is that of prisoners in their mutual relations: the multiple forms of subjugation in a highly administered world.

Piñero's interest in the state's techniques of subjugation and his conviction that they are part of a complex network of power no doubt spring from his own personal experiences in prison. Piñero's image of our administered world is admirably captured in his setting of *Short Eyes*: a New York detention center where people are herded together pending trial, bail, or shipment to a maximum security prison. It is a one-dimensional society, peopled by diverse racial and ethnic groups, each group guarding jealously their prison turf.

At the center of *Short Eyes,* a young Puerto Rican prisoner, Juan, tries to comprehend in a humanistic manner Clive Davis's wild narrative about his libidinous need for and experiences with young girls. The other prisoners, however, respond to "short eyes" (prison slang for child molester) in a less sensitive manner: they tease, cajole, kick, ram Davis into the toilet, attempt to sodomize him, and finally slash his throat—all in the name of prison justice, for child molesters, as opposed to other criminals, are at the lowest end of the prisoners' hierarchy.

In a surprise epilogue, Piñero has the captain of the prison guard tell the convicts that their victim, the alleged "short eyes," had in fact not been identified by the child-victim and was arrested by mistake. Like the prisoners themselves, we are left, at the end of the play, to untangle the ironic twists Piñero has spun out. What is distinctly new about Piñero's *Short Eyes* is the inextricable union of shocking exuberance and popular cultural theater.

After the stringent sufferings of *Short Eyes,* Piñero continued to pen several plays in which his characters—convicts, number runners, heisters, pimps, prostitutes, and johns—painfully learn the futility of their fantasies in light of their real conditions in urban America.

The Sun Always Shines for the Cool (1984), an acute melodrama that combines dancing, disco music, and erotic fooling around, is a lively and engaging portrait of an era—the self-centered 1970s. The earthy dialogue captures the lingo of the streets and male jive; the slang has its own particular melody, and the story—revolving around the problematics of male fantasy and male self-esteem—is comfortably situated in a flashy urban setting: Justice's Bar. As in *Short Eyes,* Piñero's world in *Cool* is concerned with a world that fights against normalization, for according to Piñero, in this environment, "Every player is a poet . . . an actor . . . statesman . . . a priest . . . but most of all he's a player, making up rules as he passes the next car on this highway."

The basic conflict in *Cool* is between two of Piñero's "players," a proud hustler appropriately named Viejo and a young Turk named Cat Eyes. Both of these "players" vie for the love and respect of Chile, Viejo's estranged daughter and Cat Eyes' object of desire. Viejo, just out of prison, hopes to appease his guilt by making up with Chile, and Cat Eyes, a pimp, desires to open a bar of his own and marry Chile, thus earning him what Piñero calls a "decent" life. As is exemplary of Piñero's theater, there is the classical showdown between Viejo and Cat Eyes, a classical climax reminiscent of western romance serials. An artifact of popular culture in the 1970s, *Cool* records the illusory values, aspirations, and the setbacks and sins of these street players, for underneath all the flash of the musical lies the hard reality of their failed dreams.

Like *Cool*, *Eulogy for a Small Time Thief* comes wrapped in a basic Piñero package: a racy, slangy melodrama about the 1970s. David Dancer, the "small time thief" announced in the title of the play, is a part-time mugger, pimp, and full-time dreamer living the urban life of druggy degradation. Like many of Piñero's male characters, Dancer is unable to break out of the harsh patterns of poverty and crime. At times violent, romantic, and loving, Dancer's American dream is to buy himself a place in the country, a space free from the inflexible codes of the street. Although he shares his life with Rosemarie Pearls, he is also romantically involved with Nicole, Rosemarie's younger sister. Sidetracked by his drug habit and by his botched attempt to turn his slum apartment into a brothel, Dancer's dream is to be unfulfilled, for he is destined to die at the hands of a hired hit man.

On the stage, aided by the supremely playable characters, the weaknesses of the drama are camouflaged; on the page, unadorned, the rich details of Piñero's milieu are too often cast in the clichés of country music philosophy. Throughout the play, Nicole, for instance, is determined to "stand by [her] man" at any cost.

No such weaknesses mar *Midnight Moon at the Greasy Spoon*, perhaps Piñero's best play. *Midnight Moon* takes place in a luncheonette in New York's Time Square area. It concerns the nostalgic worlds of two aging patriotic and bigoted Americans, Gerry and Joe, who fear their banishment to an old folk's home. As Gerry says to Joe, "They rate me obsolete, that's what it is, Joe."

Piñero wrote *Greasy Spoon* at Joseph Papp's urgings—exhorting the author to "do something different." *Greasy Spoon*, indeed, is new, for it dramatizes the presentness of an immediate past for Gerry and Joe. In their labors at the luncheonette, tradition is an intense parochialism. In all instances, *Greasy Spoon* describes nicely the stability in America purchased by obedience, by the acknowledgment of hierarchy, by restricted opportunities, and curtailed ambitions. It is altogether a wonderful play about middle America's hermetic view of life in the postmodernist American City.

In *La Bodega Sold Dreams*, Piñero's poetic work illustrates a control of rhythm and tone, and his meticulous orchestration of emotion and action create a work of art of considerable power. La bodega, the corner grocery store, is a socially symbolic trope, neatly summing up Piñero's artistic project: to depict an ever advancing post-industrial society. In essence, "bodega" mentality is irrational, though Piñero shows how it disguises itself in an inexorable technological rationality, a rationality of maximization, standardization, and worldwide colonization, relentlessly sucking everything into its maelstrom. Unlocking the cornucopia of "bodega" plenty, Piñero's verse also opens up the Pandora's box of unimaginable reification, the development of which is paranoia, hysteria, and fear.

What is especially useful for the reader interested in American postmodernist art is Piñero's view of the American City: it resembles nothing so much as the coca-colonial city, with the towers of the white rulers and columns militarily set off from the indigenous city, where "the turf is filled with jibaro y salsa music" ("Spring Garden Philadelphia"). Almost all of the poems in this collection are healthy critiques of the logic of postmodernism: the logic of a claustrophobic space colony attempting to miniaturize nature within itself. In contradistinction to utopian skycrappers (our most concrete allegorization of the postmodern), nowadays constructed with enclosed orange trees, and flowering staircases and air-conditioned spaces, Piñero's postmodernist images mirror an outside perspective, complete with smog-poisoned reality, vast surfaces deflecting the misery of the larger city, but also its vibrancy and authenticity, for it is precisely here in the Lower East Side where Piñero wants to spread his ashes:

> I don't want to be buried in Puerto Rico
> I don't wanna rest in long island cemetery
> I wanna be near the stabbing shooting
> gambling fighting & unnatural dying
> & new birth crying
> so please when I die . . .
> don't take me far away
> keep me near by
> take my ashes and scatter them thru out
> the Lower East Side. . . .

Survey of Criticism

Piñero's major work has not been ignored by mainstream critics. *Short Eyes,* as can be expected, was heavily commented on in various forms, including the *Village Voice, The Nation,* and *The New Republic.* Many of these establishment critics, however, dismissed Piñero's work as "amateurish," revealing their East Coast condescension to Third World American literature.

Perry Potac, for instance, in his 1973 review of *Short Eyes,* in *Plays and Players* wrote: "His characters have no originality, no wit and no comic consistency (as opposed to repetitiveness)." Another critic, Richard Eder, snidely commented in the *New York Times* that Piñero's characters in *Eulogy* are "like puppets, having only a trait or two apiece." Stanley Kauffmann sums up the mainstream criticism of Piñero's work by offering the following commentary: Piñero's monologues "are written on a rusty typewriter."

Not all of the mainstream critics, however, have been so cagily belligerent. Jack Knoll, for example, in his review of *Short Eyes* in *Newsweek* said: "*Short Eyes* is an astonishing work, full of electrifying exuberance and instinctive theatricality." Mr. Knoll even compared Piñero's artistic universe in *Short Eyes* with that of the work by Jean Genet. Likewise, Dan Sullivan, in the *Los Angeles Times,* compared Piñero's *The Sun Always Shines for the Cool* with Genet, writing, "Like Genet, Piñero is attracted to the outlaw life, but he can also see the outlaw as a cripple and a loser."

Summing up the most striking contributions of Piñero's work, Nicolás Kanellos said in *Revista Chicano-Riqueña* that: "Piñero's theater is a milestone for its introduction to the stage of characters who previously appeared only as stereotypes, but now assume real lives of their own . . . Piñero is a craftsman and a magician."

Extended critical interpretations of Piñero's work are now appearing in print. For example, Eugene V. Mohr's *The Nuyorican Experience,* which in several penetrating chapters studies Piñero's "irreverent irony," is the best comprehensive study of Piñero's poetry and theater. Other studies are also forthcoming.

In brief, with extraordinary facility for creating unexpected shocks and contrasts, Miguel Piñero's work stalks the logic of a new cultural order in contemporary American culture, criticizing the delusionary depthless present of urban American society.

Bibliography

WORKS BY PIÑERO

Short Eyes. New York: Hill and Wang, 1975.
La Bodega Sold Dreams. Houston: Arte Público Press, 1980.
The Sun Always Shines for the Cool; Midnight Moon at the Greasy Spoon; Eulogy for a Small Time Thief. Houston: Arte Público Press, 1984.
Outrageous One Act Plays. Houston: Arte Publico Press, 1986.

WORKS ABOUT PIÑERO

Clurman, Harold. Review of *Short Eyes,* by Miguel Piñero. *The Nation.* April 6, 1974: 9.
Eder, Richard. Review of *Eulogy for a Small Time Thief,* by Miguel Piñero. *New York Times.* November 28, 1977: 41.
Feingold, Michael. "Wide View from Narrowed Eyes." Review of *Short Eyes,* by Miguel Piñero. *Village Voice.* March 28, 1974: 68.
Gosciak, JG. "Getting the Goods on Things." Review of *La Bodega Sold Dreams,* by Miguel Piñero. *Contact II* (Summer 1982): 35, 43.
Holmes, Ann. "Ensemble Takes a Bold Step with *Short Eyes.*" Review of *Short Eyes,* by Miguel Piñero. *Houston Chronicle.* June 29, 1985 sec. 4: 1 and 7.
Kanellos, Nicolás, and Jorge Huerta, eds. "Nuevos Pasos: Chicano and Puerto Rican Drama." *Revista Chicano-Riqueña* 7, 1 (1979): 173–74.

Kauffmann, Stanley. Review of *Short Eyes*, by Miguel Piñero. *The New Republic* 20 April 1974: 20.

Knoll, Jack. "In the Oven." Review of *Short Eyes*, by Miguel Piñero. *Newsweek.* April 8, 1974: 81.

McKesson, Norma Alarcón. "An Interview with Miguel Piñero." *Revista Chicano-Riqueña* 2, 1 (1974): 55–57.

Melville, Lee. Review of *The Sun Always Shines for the Cool*, by Miguel Piñero. *The Hollywood Drama Logue.* June 24–30, 1982: 1.

Miller, John C. "Hispanic Theater in New York, 1965–1977." *Revista Chicano-Riqueña* 6, 1 (1977): 40–59.

Mohr, Eugene V. *The Nuyorican Experience: Literature of the Puerto Rican Minority.* Westport, Conn.: Greenwood Press, 1982.

Morton, Carlos. "Social Realism on Aston Place: The Latest Piñero Play." *Revista Chicano-Riqueña* 2, 1 (1974): 33–35.

Newton, Edmund. Review of *Eulogy for a Small Time Thief*, by Miguel Piñero. *New York Post.* November 28, 1977: 27B.

Pontac, Perry. Review of *Short Eyes*, by Miguel Piñero. *Plays and Players* (December 1973): 57.

Sainer, Arthur. Review of *Short Eyes*, by Miguel Piñero. *Village Voice.* January 10, 1974: 55.

Sullivan, Dan. "Playing It *Cool* with Low Life." Review of *The Sun Always Shines for the Cool*, by Miguel Piñero. *Los Angeles Times.* June 21, 1982 sec. Calendar: 1 and 5.

Trebay, Guy. "Talking Heads: Miguel Piñero—Promises Die Hard." *Village Voice.* April 15–21, 1981: 63.

JOSÉ DAVID SALDÍVAR

PRIDA, DOLORES (1943–   ). Dolores Prida is a poet, dramatist, journalist, and translator of Cuban origin who has undertaken her activities in New York. She has published two volumes of poetry: *Treinta y un poemas* (1967, Thirty-One Poems) and the booklet *Women of the Hour* (1971). She has opened seven plays, some of which have received international prizes. They have been performed in New York and other American cities as well as in Puerto Rico, Venezuela, and the Dominican Republic.

Biography

Prida was born September 5, 1943, in Caibarién, a city in the province of Las Villas, Cuba. In 1961 she left the island with her family and settled in New York. She studied at Hunter College with a major in Spanish American literature. Between 1960 and 1970 she was an international correspondent for Collier-McMillan International. In 1970 and 1971 she worked as an assistant editor for Simon and Schuster's International Dictionary. From 1971 to 1973 she was director of Information Services for the National Puerto Rican Forum, writing proposals, speeches, and position papers on the Puerto Rican community in New York. From 1973 to 1974 she was editor of the Spanish-language daily newspaper

El tiempo in New York. In 1975 she worked as the arts and sciences editor in London for *Visión*, the Latin American magazine. The following year she was the New York correspondent for the same publication. That same year (1976) she received the Cintas Fellowship Award for Literature. In 1977 her first play, *Beautiful Señoritas* (Beautiful Misses), was produced by Duo Theatre in New York. From 1977 to 1980 she was executive senior editor of *Nuestro Magazine* (Our Magazine), a national monthly magazine in English, geared to Hispanic Americans. In 1978 and 1979 she traveled to Cuba as a member of the group of Cuban residents in the United States that dealt with the liberation of political prisoners and that successfully established regular trips to the island to visit family and close friends. She received the CAPS (Creative Artistic Public Service) Award for Playwriting for 1979–1980. In 1979 she opened *The Beggars Soap Opera*, a musical comedy based on Brecht's *The Three Penny Opera* produced by Duo Theatre, and she translated, adapted, and directed *La señorita Margarita*, the Spanish version of Roberto Athayde's Broadway hit *Miss Margarita's Way*, also presented by Duo Theatre. From 1980 to 1983 she was literary manager of INTAR Hispanic American Theatre. In 1980 she presented *La era latina* (Latin Era), a bilingual musical comedy co-written with Victor Fragoso, produced by the Puerto Rican Travelling Theatre. In 1981 she opened three works: *Coser y cantar* (Sewing and Singing), a bilingual one-act play, with the Duo Theatre; *Crisp!*, a musical comedy based on Jacinto Benavente's *Los intereses creados* (Bonds of Interest), produced by INTAR, and *Juan Bobo* (John the Fool), produced by Duo Theatre. Since 1983 she has been editor of AHA Hispanic Arts News, a publication of the Association of Hispanic Arts. During the spring of 1985, Prida conducted a workshop on playwriting techniques for Hostos Community College. In this same year she opened *Savings*, a musical comedy in English produced by INTAR. In 1986 *Pantallas* (Screens), a "black" comedy in Spanish, was produced by Duo Theatre.

Prida has also written the script for documentary films and has co-written with Hiram Cintrón a full-length screenplay, *The Spring of the Tiger*.

Major Themes

The brief poetic production and the theater of Dolores Prida are related in their desire to present the problem of women in contemporary society and in their use of bilingualism.

Treinta y un poemas (1967, Thirty-One Poems) is a typical book of youth, different from the rest of her work. She collects poems written in Cuba and New York that express, above all, adolescent conflicts, aggravated by the exile experience: the insistence on success in life ["Ya casi" (Almost Now), "He estado creciendo" (I Have Been Growing), "Con las manos desnudas" (With Bare Hands), "La última hora" (The Final Hour), "Dejadme" (Leave Me)]; the excitement ["Los ojos me han amanecido" (My Eyes Have Dawned)] and the depression that the first love affair produces ["Sobra espacio" (Space Is Left Over), "Busco una palabra" (I Am Looking for One Word)]; the encounter with

New York life ["Verano en Nueva York" (Summer in New York), "Estando envuelta" (Being Involved)]; and nostalgia for Cuba ["Poema a una lágrima" (Poem to a Tear)]. There is also a marked individualistic attitude that rejects faith in man and is changed into desperation ["A un joven idealista" (To a Young Idealist), "Qué me importa!" (What Does It Matter to Me!)]. The majority are short poems in which predominate verses of less than eight syllables, and fluid musicality. Nevertheless, at times there are technical discoveries such as some surrealist images ["Poeta burguesa" (Bourgeois Poet)] and a peculiar use of colors ["Canción de locura y sonrisas" (Song of Madness and Smiles)].

Women of the Hour (1971), selections for a book of poetry as yet unpublished, *Eritrina, flor de cobalto* (Erythirite, Cobalt Bloom), makes evident the writer's maturity and presents features that will define her future work. They are bilingual poems without titles, in free verse, that sing of woman's liberation and the urgency of women's solidarity as the only cure to placate the contemporary world convulsed by wars and nuclear threats.

Theater is the most important genre in Prida's work up to the present. Her theatrical production excels for the skillful use of techniques of musical comedy to offer thematic content quite different from that which prevails on Broadway. Her works are related in content to the theater of protest and deal for the most part with the life of Hispanics in the United States. Prida uses humor and farce to express the serious problems of the Hispanic population in a strange environment, without lacking a poetic and hopeful note.

Beautiful Señoritas, a play with music, develops by the motif of a beauty pageant, an apparently bold exposition of the centuries-old repression of Latin women, subjugated to the demands of Spanish American male chauvinism and Catholicism. The play uses effective Spanish sayings and songs, some of traditional Hispanic culture, others written expressly for the play, as well as dances of great scenographic effectiveness to compose a call for women's liberation. This justifies the character of the little girl who appears throughout the text and gives it unity. She is present in all the scenes of humiliation and self-repression imposed by dominant social forces and she concludes the work with a song of hope: "Don't deny us the music." Feinerman holds the opinion that the work's "most powerful weapon is laughter. At times hilarious, exciting and voluptuous, it leaves the tart aftertaste of satire." Besides being presented in New York this play was produced in Los Angeles (1980) and in San José, California (1981) with a special performance at the National Organization for Women (NOW) National Convention in San Antonio in 1980. It has also been performed by the drama students at Mount Holyoke College and by Teatro Latino de Minnesota (Minnesota Latin Theater) in Minneapolis in 1984.

La era latina (Latin Era), co-written by Victor Fragoso, follows the structure of the "commedia da fare" established by Luigi Pirandello. Chago and Manny, two Latins from New York, try to create a play of Hispanic atmosphere that is adaptable to the demands of a powerful Broadway producer. The action is comprised of scenes that the two imagine, which become materialized with the help of some actors and musicians. By means of this technique, which sharpens the plot, an entertaining play is achieved, but one with a strong critical accent since it attacks at the same time the commercial norms of Broadway and its Latin stereotypes as well as New York Hispanics themselves, who feel incapable of expressing themselves authentically in art. "No sabemos ni qué decir de nosotros mismos" (We do not know what to say about ourselves), affirms Chago. However, as is the norm in Prida's theater, the comedy ends with a declaration of hope: Latins should not betray themselves in order to reach the stages of Broadway but rather they should try to be themselves since "Broadway es sólo una calle" (Broadway is only a street), as the title of the final song says. *La era latina* was produced by the Puerto Rican Travelling Theatre in the summer of 1980, touring over thirty city neighborhoods. It received a Special Award at the International Third World Theatre Competition in Caracas in 1981 and was also produced by Teatro Latino de Minneapolis (Latin Theater) that same year.

Coser y cantar (1981, Sewing and Singing) is "A One-Act Bilingual Fantasy for Two Women." In a New York apartment, two women, Ella and She, are telling without communicating—Ella in Spanish, She in English—the trials and tribulations of their lives. At first, both seem to be roommates but, as the action develops, it is discovered that these women personify the two aspects of the split personality of a Cuban immigrant: thus, there exists really only one character, who debates with herself her Hispanic heritage and the surrounding American influence, thereby converting the work into a type of interior monologue with two voices. In the end, it is suggested that the Latin roots seem to be stronger and will be victorious in the character. Downing believes that the play "goes a long way in stating the problems of living within two cultures" and Torchin affirms that "this is presented in a novel way." Conroy believes that *Coser y cantar* "is thoroughly professional and highly marketable. It speaks to a generation of ambitious young Latinas who want to explore themselves and understand their motivations as perhaps few generations prior to them ever have done." Escarpenter points out the use of bilingualism in the work, since it is not merely an incidental aspect to demonstrate the environment as in other works, but rather a structuring principle of the text in service of the central idea. *Coser y cantar,* besides being presented by the Duo Theater in 1981, 1982, and 1985, was performed at the Women of One World Festival in New York City in 1981 and at the Festival Calderón in San Antonio in 1983. The play has also been on tour of U.S. colleges every year and was produced by Artistas Unidos in San Juan, Puerto Rico, in 1985 and in Chicago in 1985. A radioplay was taped for National Public Radio and it has been broadcast by several local and national radio stations throughout the United States.

Crisp! (1981) is an excellent adaptation of a classic text—in this case Spanish, *Los intereses creados* (Bonds of Interest) by Jacinto Benavente—to the musical theater, as has frequently occurred in American theater. Prida closely follows the Spanish comedy, enriching it with the development of situations hardly emphasized in the original and with witty Italian sayings and frequent anachronisms that succeed in drawing to the present time the apparently remote story developed among the masks of the Italian commedia dell'arte. The text of the songs, an absolutely original contribution of Prida, contributes to defining the psychology of the characters and accenting the cynical and satirical spirit of the Spanish original.

Juan Bobo (1981, John the Fool) is a bilingual play with music for children. The author takes as protagonist that popular Puerto Rican figure who throughout the action crosses through diverse calamities in scenographic episodes full of wit and color. Juan Bobo, thanks to his fairy godmother, is transported from his home town to New York. Therefore, it presents a contrast between both worlds, but the play concludes with a positive message: the New York Hispanics should always be ready to know and to learn to appreciate new and different things. The play includes light songs and demands the imagination and participation of the audience, essential techniques in children's theater. *Juan Bobo* toured New York City public schools as part of the Arts Connection Program during May-June 1982 produced by Duo Theater.

Savings (1985), a musical fable in English, deals with the theme of "gentrification." The action takes place in a bank in an imaginary neighborhood but it alludes to the Lower East Side in New York. There each day a group of clients and employees get together to listen to a pianist. The bank suffers, as does the majority of the clients and workers, from the effects of real estate speculators, those who increase rent and demolish old buildings with the desire to get rich under the pretext of progress. The play makes evident a change in the predominant techniques of Prida's theater: plot is situated in a single setting and it is structured in two acts, the first being divided into two scenes. The characters, although they represent types belonging to the ethnic diversity existing in New York, are more developed than in previous works. The action is slow because it searches for the realistic description of an atmosphere without using elements of farce. The result is a play of denouncement in which there is pity for the characters who are victims of circumstance but who, in the end, and very much in harmony with Prida's theater, are conscious of the situation and get ready to fight, guided by a young female lawyer.

Prida continues to be active in theater. Her last play performed, which she calls "a work in progress," *Pantallas* (1986, Screens) was presented at the Duo Theatre and was also staged at the 1986 Festival Latino de New York (New York Latin Festival) at Joseph Papp's Public Theater in August 1986.

Bibliography

WORKS BY PRIDA

Poetry

Treinta y un poemas. Brooklyn, N.Y.: Fancy Press Editors, 1967.
Women of the Hour. New York: Nuevasangre, 1971.
With Roger Cabán. *The IRT Prayer Book*. In *La nueva sangre* (Summer 1974).

Theater

Beautiful Señoritas. An original play with music. Music by Tania León and Victoria Ruiz. Duo Theatre, New York. Premiere: November 1977.

The Beggars Soap Opera. A musical comedy based on Brecht's *The Three Penny Opera*. Music by Paul Radelat. A Duo Theatre production at INTAR Theatre Row, New York, 1979.

With Victor Fragoso. *La era latina*. A bilingual musical comedy. Music by Paul Radelat. Puerto Rican Travelling Theatre. New York, Summer 1980.

Crisp! A musical play based on Jacinto Benavente's *Los intereses creados*. Music by Galt MacDermont. INTAR Theatre Row, New York, Spring 1981.

Coser y cantar. A bilingual one-act play for two women. Duo Theatre, New York, June 1981.

Juan Bobo. A bilingual play with music for children. Music by Eddie Ruperto. Duo Theatre, New York, 1981.

Savings. A musical comedy. Music by Leon Odenz. INTAR, New York, May 1985.

Pantallas. A "black" comedy in Spanish. Duo Theatre, New York, April 1986.

WORKS ABOUT PRIDA

Bloch, Peter. "Arts Close-up: *Coser y cantar*." *Canales* (August 1981).

Brownstein-Santiago, Cheryl. "Hispanic Theater in Miami under the Gun." *Miami News* May 9, 1986.

Bruckner, D.J.R. "Stage: A Musical about Developers, *Savings*." *New York Times* May 24, 1985.

Castillo, Othón. "Candilejas: Dolores Prida." *La Opinión* April 8, 1979.

Conroy, Ed. "Festival Calderón: *Coser y cantar*." *San Antonio Light* March 26, 1983.

Downing, Roger. "Play Examines Hispanic Woman's 2 sides: *Coser y cantar*." *San Antonio Express* March 25, 1983.

Escarpenter, José A. "Veinticinco años de teatro cubano en el exilio." *Latin American Theatre Review* [to appear in 1986]. 19, 2 (Spring 1986) 57–66.

Fariñas, Lázaro. "Libertad vs totalitarismo." *Miami Herald* May 12, 1986.

Feinerman, Lynn. "Absurdity, Satire and Desperation: *Beautiful señoritas*." *Latin American Woman* (May 1979).

Henkel, Gretchen. "Glamor at the Heart of *Señoritas*." *Los Angeles Times* April 20, 1979.

Peña, Amalia. "Altering Ego: *Coser y cantar*." *Village Voice* July 29, 1981.

Pérez, Miguel. "Real Life Theater in the Barrio: *Savings*." *Daily News* June 13, 1985.

Rivas, Josué R. "Dolores Prida: *Savings*, una obra sobre la gentrificación." *El Diario-La Prensa* May 24, 1985.

Stasio, Marilyn. "*Beggars Soap Opera* Clean Fun." *New York Post* July 21, 1979.

Torchin, Mimi. "Sewing and Singing." *Other Stages* July 2, 1981.

Waldman, Gloria F. "Llegó *La era latina*." *El Nuevo Día* July 5, 1980.

"Welcome to Miami's Theater of the Absurd." Editorial. *Miami News* May 6, 1986.

JOSÉ ESCARPENTER AND LINDA S. GLAZE

R

RAMOS OTERO, MANUEL (1948–   ). Manuel Ramos Otero is a Puerto Rican short-story writer, novelist, and poet whose work has appeared in numerous magazines and journals including *Asomante, Caravelle, Vórtice,* and the *Revista Chicano-Riqueña.* From 1973 to 1975 he served as co-editor of *Zona de carga y descarga,* perhaps the most influential literary journal to appear in Puerto Rico during the decade of the 1970s. He has published one novel, two collections of short stories and a book of poetry. Both from a stylistic and thematic perspective, he is in the vanguard of Puerto Rican fiction today. As a writer he seems to seek a renovation of fiction, which consists at times in the deconstruction of situation, character, style, and language.

Biography

Manuel Ramos Otero was born in the small town of Manatí on the northern coast of Puerto Rico. He moved to Río Piedras, a suburb of San Juan, when he was seven where he received his primary education in parochial schools. He began a lifelong interest in writing at fourteen. From the start his favorite form was the short story. He admits the influence of a confluence of factors in the development of his narrative art. These range from the early tales told to him by his mother to the writings of such varied practitioners of fiction as Tennessee Williams, Jorge Luis Borges, Lezama Lima, Edgar Allan Poe (whom he read in Spanish through a translation prepared by Julio Cortázar), and the Puerto Rican author René *Marqués who was the first writer to exert direct influence on him. The fact that Marqués was a homosexual is of particular importance to Ramos Otero who deals with this theme fairly extensively in his fiction. He holds Tennessee Williams in particular revere as the writer who has had the most direct impact on his work. In 1967 his short story, ''Concierto de metal para un recuerdo'' (Metal Concert for a Memory), an Orwellian tale of love among two robots, was awarded first prize in a contest sponsored by the prestigious Ateneo

Puertorriqueño. Subsequent awards by the same organization in 1969 for "Happy Birthday" and in 1970 for "Alrededor del mundo con la Señorita Mambresí" helped launch his career as one of Puerto Rico's most innovative young writers. After graduating from the University of Puerto Rico-Río Piedras in 1968 with a degree in sociology, he moved to New York City to study both film and theater. He studied direction under the tutelage of Lee Strasberg at the Lee Strasberg Theatre Institute. Subsequently in 1970 he formed his own theatre workshop (*Aspasguanza*) which put on experimental Puerto Rican drama. His work with the traveling theatre continued for the next three years.

In 1969 he earned his M.A. in Spanish and Latin American literature from New York University where he is currently studying for a Ph.D. He currently teaches at La Guardia Community College.

In 1976 Ramos Otero founded a small press, Editorial Libro Viaje, with funding from the Instituto de Cultura Puertorriqueña and the New York Foundation for the Arts. The press published several books of poetry and Ramos Otero's strikingly experimental novel, *La novelabingo* (1976, The Bingo Novel). At present Ramos Otero continues to write both fiction and poetry.

Major Themes

The work of Ramos Otero is characterized by great thematic and technical versatility. His work deals, in general terms, with the universal problems of modern man: love, the passage of time, the stultifying forces of modern technology, solitude, national and ethnic consciousness, and the nature of fiction. Unlike the earlier social realists of Puerto Rican fiction, his fiction and poetry present problems from a subtle, lyric perspective. His first collection of stories, *Concierto de metal para un recuerdo y otras orgías de soledad* (1971, Metal Concert for a Memory and Other Orgies of Solitude), contains briefer, less polished tales that, as the title indicates, deal with the theme of solitude and brooding sexuality. "Alrededor del mundo con la Señorita Mambresí" (Around the World with Miss Mambresí), for example, presents the erotic recollections of an aging matron by means of a complicated interior monologue. In "Hollywood Memorabilia," Ramos Otero, in a fashion very similar to that of the Argentine Manuel Puig, reconstructs the fantasy world of a homosexual man, the night projectionist in a movie theatre, who uses the language of film to articulate his fantasies. Stories such as "Bola de fuego" (Fire Ball), "Piel mutada" (Changed Skin), and "La casa clausurada" (The Cloistered House) all bear the strong stamp of Julio Cortázar although they are by no means wholly derivative.

"Funeral," the tale of the rise and fall of a contemporary rock star, is an example of Ramos Otero's use of the techniques of documentary fiction, a genre made famous by Truman Capote's *In Cold Blood* and now very much in vogue in Latin America among writers such as Miguel Barnet and Manuel Puig. The tale is narrated both from the perspective of a third person narrator and a series of pseudo-newspaper reports which project this tale of fame and personal anguish.

With the 1976 publication of *La novelabingo* Ramos Otero shifted to the experimental novel. The book is a fusion of two phenomena in Hispanic letters: the search for national essence seen in the works of such important writers as Jorge Mañach, Samuel Ramos, Ezquiel Martínez Estrada, and Octavio Paz and the experimental novel of the boom generation (Julio Cortázar's *Rayuela* is a good example). The title announces the theme: the novel as a game of bingo, an expedition into the world of chance.

The game of bingo, like the game of hopscotch in Cortázar's *Rayuela,* speaks to the broader issue of order in the rational world and assaults traditional myths about society and the nature of fiction. The text (and here the debt to the Vanguardists is clear) is presented without pagination and the chapter divisions are arranged out of sequence. From the point of view of theme, organization, language, and style, *La novelabingo* is an assault on the tradition of literature as mimesis, of art as representational, and a self-conscious parody of the art of writing. Some critics have noted that the theme of the search, a well-known topos in western literature, confers the text with a sense of artistic wholeness. Others have pointed out the author's attempt to deconstruct two major mythic obsessions, machismo and matriarchy, which underpin Puerto Rican culture.

In *El cuento de la mujer del mar* (Story of the Sea Woman), Ramos Otero demonstrated greater artistic maturity with a collection of six longer, more technically complex tales which deal with sexual obsessions, solitude, love, and the historical past of his island home. Of particular merit are "Romance de Clara Gardenia Otero," a portrait of an aging beauty who receives flowers from an admirer, "La última plena que bailó Luberza," which chronicles the last day in the life of the owner of a brothel (the resemblance to Mario Vargas Llosa's *La casa verde* comes to mind), and above all "El cuento de la mujer del mar," the longest and perhaps finest story in the book. This story is perhaps the best in the collection and the finest example of the thematic concerns displayed by the author. It is a story of two lovers who agree to tell parallel stories of the legend of the mysterious woman of the sea, in an effort, reminiscent of *The Thousand and One Nights,* to perpetuate the present eternally and sustain their relationship. The two tales, one of Vicenza Vitale and the other of Palmira Parés, are delicately intertwined in a complex intertextual web where beginning and end, story and reality, fuse into a comment on the art of story telling and the desperate loneliness of the two protagonists. An important segment of Puerto Rican cultural history is presented here since the story of Palmira Parés, presented with considerable details (including detailed footnotes), is in reality the biography of Julia de *Burgos, one of Puerto Rico's finest poets.

Two published samples of his forthcoming book *Cuentos de vivos y muertos y desaparecidos,* "La otra isla de Puerto Rico" (The Other Island of Puerto Rico) and "La heredera" (The Inheritor), demonstrate a movement in the direction of longer fiction and a developing concern with the history of Puerto Rico. In the first he blends the techniques of documentary fiction with the metaphysical strategies of Borges to recount the history of Puerto Rico. "La heredera'' moves in much the same direction. It is the chronicle of an upper-class Puerto Rican family which is traced through three distinct narrative modes: the family chronicle, the essay, and the letter. Here the author succeeds in penetrating the core of the national consciousness and in effectively parodying the contemporary literary scene in Puerto Rico.

In sum, during the course of his work Ramos Otero has touched upon many themes and settings. His stories take place in cities as varied as New York, Paris, San Juan, and the imaginary Mamutcandungo. His characters are at times poetic re-creations of historic figures (Julia de Burgos is an example) or are abstractions, projections of fantasies or repressed desires. As a whole his fiction tends to be mysterious, complex, and rich in multileveled structured meanings.

Much like his fiction, the poetry of Ramos Otero breaks down traditional generic boundaries. His verse is close to that of writers such as Brenda Alejandro, Orlando José Hernández, and Iván *Silén in its eschewal of traditional form. The important anthology *Herejes y mitificadores* (1980) contains three poems by Ramos Otero, "En la cuarta pagoda," "Aquí somos negros desde el hombro hasta el hambre," and "De pie a cabeza estaba" which all deal with the problem of language and are imbued with a sense of existential despair.

El libro de la muerte (The Book of Death) contains poems of varied theme such as "Fuegos fúnebres" (Funereal Fires) with a theatrical flair while "Epitafios" (Epitaphs) is a sort of dialogue with writers who are now deceased such as Federico García Lorca, Oscar Wilde, Lezama Lima, and René Marqués whose texts are variously celebrated or satirized. "Epílogo" (Epilog) is a monologue in which the poet traces the story of his life. Through his use of violent, often eschatological images, Ramos Otero deliberately challenges the reader's pre-conceived notions of order and social values.

Survey of Criticism

The exciting work of Manuel Ramos Otero has unfortunately been neglected by mainstream critics of Hispanic literature as has been the case with other excellent writers from Puerto Rico and other parts of the Caribbean. In general terms, the work of Ramos Otero has been studied in the context of and in relationship to a group of Puerto Rican writers who followed the so-called "Generation of 1940," comprised of authors such as Luis Rafael *Sánchez, Tomás López Ramírez, Carmelo Rodríguez Torres, Rosario *Ferré, and others. The publication of three important anthologies of Puerto Rican writers has helped to make his work more familiar to the reading public: *Herejes y mitificadores* (1980), *Apalabramiento: Diez cuentistas puertorriqueños de hoy* (1983), and *Reunión de espejos* (1983). While all three books have fairly extensive intro-ductory essays, the most penetrating and positive analysis of the work of Ramos Otero is to be found in José Luis Vega's collection. Interest in Ramos Otero's work is growing. While *Concierto de metal para un recuerdo* was the object of a brief but praiseworthy review by Juan Martínez Capó in 1971, *La novelabingo* became the focus of considerable interest. Rosario Ferré attacked its "madness" in a 1977 review. Asela Rodríguez Laguna's "Balance novelístico del trienio 1976–1978: Conjunción de signos tradicionales y rebeldes en Puerto Rico" (1979) sees in the novel a criticism of machismo and matriarchy. Juan G. Gelpi-Pérez's "Desorden frente a purismo: La nueva narrativa frente a René Marqués" (1982) is yet more enthusiastic and offers a good textual analysis of the book. *El cuento de la mujer del mar* has thus far been very positively received. Oscar Montero presented a long and detailed review of the book in *Sin Nombre* (1980) in which he carefully detailed the narrative strategies used by the author. The brief assessment published in the *Handbook of Latin American Studies* seems to offer a synthesis of the critical reaction to the book: "Stylistically sophisticated short stories by one of Puerto Rico's more accomplished young writers are well-crafted and worth reading, especially 'Romance de Clara Gardenia Otera,' [which] includes stream of consciousness, surreal narrative techniques, and experiments with punctuation." He has also received good coverage in the *Diccionario de Literatura Puertorriqueña* (1983).

In sum, Manuel Ramos Otero is a writer of great promise and one clearly in the vanguard of Hispanic letters. Both in a personal and physical sense he lives and projects a curious sort of inner exile. He is a man between two cultures who has chosen the written word to brilliantly bridge the gap and give the world a memorable view of the "other Puerto Rico."

Bibliography

WORKS BY RAMOS OTERO

Concierto de metal para un recuerdo y otras orgías de soledad. San Juan, P.R.: Editorial Cultural, 1971.
La novelabingo. New York: Editorial Libro Viaje, 1976.
El cuento de la mujer del mar. Río Piedras, P.R.: Ediciones Huracán, 1979.
El libro de la muerte. Río Piedras, P.R.: Editorial Cultural, 1985.

WORKS ABOUT RAMOS OTERO

Barradas, Efraín. *Apalabramiento: Diez cuentistas puertorriqueños de hoy*. Hanover, N.H.: Ediciones del Norte, 1983.
———. Review of *"Concierto de metal para un recuerdo y otras orgías de soledad."* *Sin Nombre* 3 (1972): 108–10.
Barradas, Efraín, and Rafael Rodríguez, eds. *Herejes y mitificadores: Muestra de poesía puertorriqueña en los Estados Unidos*. Río Piedras: Editorial Huracán, 1980.
Boitano, David. "Encuentro de Escritores." *El Mundo*. April 15, 1983: 5.
Ferré, Rosario. "Ramos Otero o la locura versus la libertad." *El Mundo*. July 12, 1977: 16A.
Martínez Capó, Juan. Review of *"Concierto de metal para un recuerdo y otras orgías de soledad."* *Puerto Rico Ilustrado*, 1971.
Montero, Oscar. Review of *"El cuento de la mujer del mar."* *Sin Nombre* 7 (1980): 65–69.
"Review of *El cuento de la mujer del mar."* *Handbook of Latin American Studies*, vol. 44. Austin: Univ. of Texas, 1982.

Review of *"La novelabingo."* *El Mundo*. May 29, 1977: 16A.

Rivera de Alvarez, Josefina. *Diccionario de literatura puertorriqueña*. San Juan: Instituto de Cultura Puertorriqueña, 1983. pp. 756–758 and 786–787.

Rodríguez de Laguna, Asela "Balance novelístico del trienio 1976–1978: Conjunción de signos tradicionales y rebeldes en Puerto Rico." *Hispamérica* 8 (1979): 134–42.

Thomas, Jo. "Puerto Rican Writers Gather." *New York Times* April 11, 1983: C21.

Vega, José Luis. "Manuel Ramos Otero: Entre la realidad y la ilusion" in *Reunión de espejos*. San Juan: Editorial Cultura, 1983.

EDWARD MULLEN

REYES RIVERA, LOUIS (1945–   ). Louis Reyes Rivera is a poet, critic, and editor of Puerto Rican descent who was raised in Brooklyn, New York. He has contributed to magazines such as *New Rain, Areito,* and *The Black Nation* and has published two volumes of verse and edited several other books of verse. Rivera considers himself to be a poet of the people and his work shows a strong identification with the working class. In the "Introduction" to Sandra María *Esteves's book, *Yerba Buena*, Rivera writes, "Searchers have to find themselves, have to recreate worlds out of misery, or remain still standing on line; & the poet, thus given birth, arrives to overcome the complexity of thought or betray the people's gift."

Biography

Louis Reyes Rivera was born on May 19, 1945, in Brooklyn, New York, and raised in the Marcy projects. He writes: "I was born and raised in Brooklyn. Everything that I have known has been here in the United States proper . . . I have been completely alienated from Puerto Rico. As I grow older, though, finding and facing those contradictions that exist here, I come face to face with knowing that I do not know a lot! And that I have to find out that which has been taken from me. I am finding out that a lot has been taken from me." Reyes Rivera is the publisher of Shamal Books which has published the following titles: *Poets in Motion* (edited by Rivera), *Nubiana* by BJ. Ashanti, *Free!* by Sekou Sundiata, *Who Pays the Cost* by Rivera, *Nommo* by Zizwe Ngafu, and *Womanrise,* an anthology of six young women poets.

He received a B.A. in English and sociology in 1974 from CCNY and is a founding member of the Black Writers Union.

Major Themes

His first book of poetry, *Who Pays the Cost* (1977), is a hard-driving collection of poems dealing with aspects of barrio life. It is written in the tradition of books like *Down These Mean Streets* (1967) by Piri *Thomas, which depict the seamy side of urban life. The book is a blend of photography and verse which attempts a re-creation of the feelings and situations of urban American life. The blend of photography and verse at once calls to mind *The Sweet Flypaper of Life* (1955), a small book of text by the poet Langston Hughes and pictures by the photographer Roy Decarava which dealt with life in Harlem and was told with astonishing verisimilitude in the words of an elderly black woman. Here the narrative voice is more strident but no less real. This slim volume contains nine poems which ask, as the poem which gives title to the book, who pays the cost for the problems of drug addiction, prostitution, and urban blight. In "I Should Resolve to Be Like You," the poet takes to task the industrial-economic complex that exploits the urban poor. In "Young Boy Lost," in which he uses a responsorial structure found in African literature, he describes the cyclical, tragic, and ultimately self-destructive aspects of gang life.

The murder of Malcolm X is described in "A Place I Never Been." Here Rivera describes the full horror of the situation, the shock, the sudden sense of loss through a narrative strategy that reminds one of recent documentary fiction. Scenes are narrated simultaneously from multiple perspectives in quick, jagged strokes in an attempt to re-create the past with the sense of the present moment.

"Red Scars Peeling: A Chant and A Monologue" is another example of the use of Neo-African structural patterns. Here they are used to underscore the poet-narrator's questions about his own condition in America and by extension those of all of those who have been culturally marginated and dispossessed.

"Can't Slash This One Out" is an ironic note on how the principles of the Constitution have been violated resulting in the marginalization of sectors of the U.S. population. It is narrated from an ironic perspective in which the original text of the U.S. Constitution is mingled with the words of the poet, which undermine the original meaning of the document.

"Roaches, Flies, Bees, Bugs," which ends this collection, compares the leaders of the industrial complex ("Corporate Chiefs Are Just Alike") to the vermin that infect urban life. The poem is both an indictment of these evil forces and a sort of implicit consciousness-raising.

The strident tone of this book is somewhat attenuated through the mild eroticism of "Symphony with No Regrets" and a self-reflective piece, "No Hole in a Punctured Poem."

This One for You (1983) is a collection of forty-seven titled poems (many of which are further subdivided into numbered stanzas). Rivera continues to deal with the same issues he raised in his first book, namely a preoccupation with the marginated and dispossessed members of society. The historical dimension of man's inhumanity to his fellow man is the subject of "Scripture Clarified" which draws on the Bible as its linguistic model to comment on the historical roots of the abuse of workers.

Rivera's Puerto Rican heritage becomes the focus of a number of poems in this collection such as "Confession," "En las noticias de hoy" (In Today's News), and "Eye falls," where both Spanish and English are used often in juxtaposition to suggest the bilingual/bicultural world in which the poet lives and writes. Social praxis is not the only concern he deals with, but with the problem of language on a more abstract plane. In "Problems in Translation," for example, Rivera underscores the fact that language is an arbitrary system of symbols and cannot at times be translated.

There are a number of poems in this book which deserve special attention from the point of view of both theme and technique. These are "Signs Unread," "Burning Embers," and "From Live Radio: An Interview." These are not poems in the traditional sense of formal verse but experimental works that attempt to re-create a moment or scene with great realism. Here Rivera uses street language to evoke a special mood or feeling. In "Signs Unread" a conversation between two friends about vasectomy contains a subtext about racial genocide. In "Burning Embers" the reader witnesses a shoot-out and funeral through a fast-paced collage of dialogue, whereas in "From Live Radio: An Interview," Rivera satirizes big business through a mock radio interview.

An emerging theme in the work of Rivera is the exploration of his Puerto Rican past which is seen in recent bilingual poems such as "Marianita" and "Grito de Lares" (The Lares Proclamation). The latter poem is perhaps the best example of this trend in his verse. The poem appears in Spanish (a symbolic act to suggest the supremacy of his ancestral tongue in dealing with the history and landscape) with the English translation printed *en face*. The historical allusions made are seminal to an understanding of the development of the island's culture and identity. The question of the colonial domination of Puerto Rico has been the focal point of political struggle on the island. Resistance to Spanish domination began with the resistance of the natives to slavery. This movement culminated on September 23, 1868, in the "Grito de Lares," an uprising which was repressed by the Spanish authorities. Under pressure they were forced to abolish slavery in 1873. Finding that its hold on the island was growing weaker, Spain made further concessions. In 1897, it granted an "autonomous" government to Puerto Rico, which nevertheless remained within the Spanish Empire. At the conclusion of the Spanish-Cuban-American War, on July 25, 1898, the United States invaded Puerto Rico with 16,000 troops. With the signing of the Treaty of Paris, Puerto Rico, Guam, and the Philippines became colonies of the United States. "El Grito de Lares" is a poetic dramatization of this era, powerfully evoked through a gradual accretion of visual and auditory images.

Survey of Criticism

The work of Louis Reyes Rivera has received scant attention from mainstream literary critics to date. This may be explained, in part, because his poetry has appeared in small magazines and his books have been distributed by a small press (Shamal) which has published a limited number of beautifully produced books. The militant tone of his verse, too, has garnered its share of negative reaction. Typical are the comments about *Who Pays the Cost* which appeared in *Booklist* (1977): "The message is despair and helplessness in these intentionally revolutionary poems. Their craft is frequently sacrificed for the power of the political statement. Rivera, who calls himself a 'cultural worker,' assesses blame directly and without qualms. His devotion to Malcolm X projects a strange, disquieting, religious theme into raging secular poetry. This makes sense: who *does* pay the cost for heroin addiction, prostitution, and genocide?''

In spite of these limitations, Rivera has been included in the *International Who's Who in Poetry* (1982) which is also published as part of the *International Authors and Writers Who's Who* (1982). Further attention was focused on his work when he was anthologized in the important anthology *Herejes y mitificadores* (1980) published by the prestigious Editorial Huracán with a long and thoughtful introduction by Efraín Barradas. This same year, Juan Flores presented a brief thematic sketch of Rivera's poetry in his "Back Down These Mean Streets: Introducing Nicholasa *Mohr and Louis Reyes Rivera." The brief "Overview" which appears as an introduction to *This One for You* (1983) written by Zizwe Omowale-Wa-Ngafua is a brief, thoughtful analysis of his dominant themes and is in general very positive.

Bibliography

WORKS BY REYES RIVERA

Poets in Motion (edited by Reyes Rivera). New York: Shamal Books, 1976.
Who Pays the Cost. New York: Shamal Books, 1977.
Womanrise (edited by Reyes Rivera). New York: Shamal Books, 1978.
This One for You. New York: Shamal Books, 1983.
"Introduction: By Way of Sharing Perspective." In: Sandra María Esteves. *Yerba Buena*. New York: Greenfield Review Press, 1980.

WORKS ABOUT REYES RIVERA

Barradas, Efraín, and Rafael Rodríguez, eds. *Herejes y mitificadores: Muestra de poesía puertorriqueña en los Estados Unidos*. Río Piedras: Editorial Huracán, 1980.
Flores, Juan. "Back Down These Mean Streets: Introducing Nicholasa Mohr and Louis Reyes Rivera." *Revista Chicano-Riqueña* 8 (Primavera 1980): 51–56.
"Louis Reyes Rivera." *International Authors and Writers Who's Who*. Cambridge, England: International Biographical Center, 1982.
Omowale-Wa-Ngafua, Zizwe. "Overview" in *This One for You* by Louis Reyes Rivera. New York: Shamal, 1983.
Review of *"Who Pays the Cost." Booklist* 74 (December 15, 1977): 663.

                                                              EDWARD MULLEN

S

SÁNCHEZ, LUIS RAFAEL (1936–   ). Luis Rafael Sánchez is not only Puerto Rico's best-known living playwright, but an author whose novels and short stories have attracted international critical acclaim. The author of over eight plays, a novel, and many short stories and essays, his works deal above all with the themes of Puerto Rican national identity, the quest for both cultural and political independence, racial relations, and the function of language. He is both a traditionalist and a revolutionary. As a writer of conscience he shares the tradition of a long line of writers before him who have been concerned with Puerto Rican topics. As a literary innovator, he imbues his works with aggressive experimentation in the field of language.

Biography

Luis Rafael Sánchez was born on November 17, 1936, in Humacao, Puerto Rico, and when he was twelve years old he moved with his family to Viejo San Juan, Calle Sol. Both of these memories are present in his work: the small-town life serves as a background for many of his short stories and his *Sol 13, Interior* (1962, Sun 13, Interior) takes its very title from the street where he lived. His early years in school theatricals culminated in a visit in 1955 to México where he won a medal from the Instituto Nacional de la Juventud Mexicana as the best young actor of the year. He returned to the University of Puerto Rico in 1956 where he collaborated on various plays with the Commedietta Universitaria. He also began to take a very active part in radio, working with well-known Puerto Rican actresses. His first literary ventures were in the short story genre. His first dramatic work, in 1958, was *La espera* (1960, The Waiting). Since then he has alternated his creative work with his academic work at the University of Puerto Rico, where he is a professor of Spanish in the School of General Studies. He has studied drama at Columbia University and earned a master of arts at New York University and a Ph.D. from the University of Madrid. He has traveled extensively throughout Europe and Latin America, participating in conferences, theatre festivals, and workshops.

Major Themes

Luis Rafael Sánchez's many interests have led him to explore diverse literary genres: theater, the novel, the short story, and the essay. He began his dramatic career in 1960 with "La Espera" written for a course assignment and staged by the student theater of the University of Puerto Rico. Before the publication of his first prose work in 1976, the spectacularly successful *La guaracha del Macho Camacho* (1976, *Macho Camacho's Beat*, 1980), he had published six plays. In addition to "La espera," these works include *Cuento de Cucarachita Viudita* (1961, The Story of the Little Widowed Cockroach), *La farsa del amor compartido* (1960, Farce of the Shared Love), *La hiel nuestra de cada día* (1961, Our Daily Bile), and *O casi el alma* (1964, Or Almost the Soul). After 1966 he published only two plays, which include his best-known work, *La pasión según Antígona Pérez* (1968, The Passion According to Antigony Perez). Even though he is best known as a result of the fame that his plays and *La guaracha del Macho Camacho* have won for him, he has also published an important collection of short stories, *En cuerpo de camisa* (1966, The Shirt Body) and numerous essays.

Within the wide range of forms that his literary productions have taken, Sánchez's work has been characterized by the predominance of a few constant themes: present-day Puerto Rican circumstances and ethnicity, race, and the role of language as an expression of social class and ethnic identity. His plays serve as dramatic metaphors for his conception of the present-day Puerto Rican circumstances: in *Antígona Pérez* he depicts authentic Puerto Rican qualities in the character of Antígona who demonstrates virtue and purity in the face of the decadent society around her; and in *O casi el alma* the prostitute Maggie's sincerity contrasts with the deceit of the "believers" around her.

Sánchez does not limit his exploration of Puerto Rican identity to his dramatic productions. In his numerous essays he develops and clarifies his thoughts, and in his short stories and novels he further expresses them. In "Literatura puertorriquena y realidad colonial" (1974, Puerto Rican Literature and Colonial Reality) he states his belief of what it means to be a Puerto Rican writer. He accepts the accusation that Puerto Rican literature is monothematic and states that the Puerto Rican author has the duty to act as a corrosive agent on middle-class society in order to change it. In a set of essays entitled "Escritos en Puertorriqueño" (Writings in the Puerto Rican Language), published beginning with 1972, he further develops these ideas. These essays include one called "Donde mi pobre gente se morirá de nada" (1972, Where My Poor People Will Die from Nothing) in which he calls upon his fellow countrymen to work together in order to make constructive changes in their country.

Puerto Rican national identity is also an important unifying theme in Luis Rafael Sánchez's novel *La guaracha del Macho Camacho*. In the novel, native

Puerto Rican values are contrasted to the characters' United States–influenced values, which are presented to them by the mass media and its promotion of the consumer society. Sánchez's protagonists are the casualties of Puerto Rico's embracing the North American ethic of progress and industrialization, as well as the moral corruption and false values of the United States.

Race is another important theme in Sánchez's works. When he analyzes James Baldwin's *The Fire Next Time* in one of his literary essays, he expresses his intense dislike of racial prejudice. In another essay he says that racial prejudice is characterized in Puerto Rico by the tendency to avoid the topic and pretend that racial mixture does not exist there. In a short story called "Aleluya negra" Sánchez defines his ideas on blacks and race that will be developed in his plays and novels. He identifies eroticism with blackness without weakening his traditional defense of blacks and uses his attack on racial prejudice as a means to censure the Puerto Rican upper class. In *La guaracha* he finalizes the identification of race with sexuality. There are two female protagonists in the novel. La China Hereje, the politician's mistress, is a dark-skinned woman of the lower classes who is extremely erotic. Her counterpart is the white wife of the politician who dislikes sex and suffers from all kinds of psychosomatic illnesses. Healthy, vibrant eroticism is identified with blackness while whiteness is equated with ill health, lack of sexuality, and neurosis.

Language is not only an innovative tool in Sánchez's writing, but a theme used to express cultural identity and racial relations. Luis Rafael Sánchez believes that the language used in literature should reflect all social classes, especially the proletariat. In his essay "El teatro de Emilio S. Belaval" (1974, The Theater of Emilio S. Belaval) he criticizes the author for his use of a language for his characters that is too academic and not natural for them.

Linguistic fidelity is apparent in all of Sánchez's plays, although his style and language vary from one play to another. In *La hiel* Piramo and Tisbe speak very differently from Doña Ugo but all use colloquial Puerto Rican Spanish. In *Antígona Pérez* the formal style adopted by the characters who represent the Establishment (Creon, Pilar Varga, Monseñor Bernardo) is an effective device to emphasize the lack of communication or comprehension among them.

But it is in *La guaracha* that language takes the most important role, not only in the innovative techniques used to describe the characters but in the main theme. The novel deals with the negative effect of mass-media language on our consumer society and the creation of idealized images through the power of this language. The effect is reached as a result of the contrast between the illusion of reality, created by the song, and the crude reality of the characters' lives. Parody, sarcasm, humor, and jokes are used to achieve this effect.

Survey of Criticism

Critical studies of Luis Rafael Sánchez and his works are somewhat limited, for only since 1976 has his work begun to attract extensive academic attention. Early studies fall into the following categories: monographic studies, critical mention in general anthologies and manuals on Latin American drama, as well as drama reviews in the media. With the exception of the work done by Angelina Morfi, professor at the University of Puerto Rico, and Jordan B. Phillips's section in his *Contemporary Trends in the Puerto Rican Theater* dedicated to Sánchez, early studies tend to be primarily descriptive and laudative. Later accounts endeavor to be more analytical and are generally more useful. Efraín Barradas's collection of essays entitled *Acercamiento a la obra de Luis Rafael Sánchez: Para leer en puertorriqueño* contains useful insights in addition to bibliographies of Sánchez's writings and of writings about him. Gloria Waldman's unpublished dissertation, "Luis Rafael Sánchez and the New Latin American Theater," is a most useful piece of research for the beginning investigator. Nélida Hernández Vargas's "Luis Rafael Sánchez: guía bibliográfica" (1978), though dated, contains valuable bibliographical information.

Though best known as a dramatist, it is Sánchez's novel *La guaracha del Macho Camacho* that has attracted the most scholarly attention. Carmen Vázquez Arce in "Sexo y malatería: dos sones de la misma guaracha" (1982, Sex and mulatto things: two songs from the same guaracha) applies principles of semiotics and sociological analysis to a study of the female characters in the novel. Vázquez Arce concludes that Sánchez's novel attacks sexual and racial oppression in Puerto Rico and places women as the key element in the process of sociopolitical liberation. Elipidio Laguna-Díaz in *"La guaracha del Macho Camacho*, La novela de aquí" (*Macho Camacho's Beat,* the novel of here, 1981) compares the structure of the novel to a film in which the author plays the role of an editor. Efraín Barradas in "Quién canta la guaracha" (Who sings the *guaracha*) in *Para leer en puerrtorriqueño* (1981) analyzes the role of the author in the novel and the use of intertextuality in Sánchez's works. In another essay in this same volume, entitled "La vida es una nena bien guasona que se mima en un fabuloso Cadillac o sexualidad y clase social en *La guaracha del Macho Camacho*" (Life is a Sassy Babe Who Spoils Herself with a Fabulous Cadillac or Sexuality and Social Class in *Macho Camacho's Beat*), Barradas studies the function of eroticism in the novel and its direct relationship to the characters' social class. He comes to the conclusion that the relationship between erotic themes and social class serves to reinforce the structure of the novel. Luis Arrigoitía in "Una novela escrita en puertorriqueño: *La guaracha del Macho Camacho* de Luis Rafael Sánchez" (1978, A novel written in Puerto Rican: Luis Rafael Sánchez's *Macho Camacho's Beat*) studies the novel's relationship to salsa music. Arrigoitía believes that the words of the guaracha song mentioned in the novel serve as a structure for the work and offset the fact that the book has little action, weak psychological development, and fragmentation of time and action.

The popularity of *La guaracha del Macho Camacho* has produced inevitably comparisons with other Latin American works of a similar style. Three essays compare the novel to the works of writers such as Guillermo Cabrera Infante and Julio Cortazar. The coincidence in subject matter between the traffic jam in Cortázar's short story "La autopista del sur" and Sánchez's *La guaracha* inspires

Ramón García Castro to compare *La guaracha* to another one of Cortázar's works in the essay titled *"La guaracha del Macho Camacho de Luis Rafael Sánchez, y que sepa abrir la puerta para ir a jugar de Julio Cortázar"* (1980, *Macho Camacho's Beat* and He Should Know How to Open the Door to Go Play at Being Julio Cortázar). García Castro believes that Sánchez's basic theme is sex which nevertheless does not serve to make his characters happy. Their unhappy lives contradict the novel's guaracha theme song, "La vida es una cosa fenomenal." A second essay, Jaime Giordano's "Función estructural del bilinguismo en algunos téxtos contemporáneos: Cabrera Infante, Luis R. Sánchez" (1982, The Structural Function of the Bilingualism in Some Contemporary Texts: Cabrera Infante, Luis Rafael Sánchez), uses the comparison between Cabrera Infante and Luis Rafael Sánchez to examine general attitudes toward the English language and the world associated with it in the Caribbean. He finds that there are generally two very different attitudes toward the English-speaking world. It is seen either as a marvelous and unreal world or the writer's attitudes toward it express sarcasm and a desire to unravel the myth. Giordano believes that Sánchez's characters express the first attitude which is accompanied in the novel by a disdain on the part of some of the characters for Puerto Rican values. A third essay by Lorraine Elena Ben-Ur also chooses Guillermo Cabrera Infante as the main writer to compare to Luis Rafael Sánchez. In "Hacia la novela del Caribe: Guillermo Cabrera Infante y Luis Rafael Sánchez" (1978, Toward the Caribbean Novel: Guillermo Cabrera Infante and Luis Rafael Sánchez) the critic compares Cabrera Infante's *Tres tristes tigres* to *La guaracha* and suggests that *Tres tristes tigres* functions as a subtext in Sánchez's novel. Ben-Ur gives as evidence of this the numerous coincidences of lexical items, inversions and parallel situations, even though Sánchez does not adopt Cabrera Infante's surrealistic and experimental techniques.

Though Sánchez has written more plays than novels or short stories, his theater has not attracted the amount nor the variety of criticism that *La guaracha del Macho Camacho* has. Gloria Waldman's articles and her unpublished dissertation and Angelina Morfi's articles and her monograph are essential documentation for anyone interested in the subject matter. The most interesting and thought-provoking studies on Sánchez's theater have been written about his best-known play, *La pasión según Antígona Pérez*.

Two essays, Matías Montes Huidobro's "Luis Rafael Sánchez: Lenguaje e indentidad en el teatro puertorriqueño" (1978, Luis Rafael Sánchez: Language and Identity in Puerto Rican Theater) and Angelina Morfi's "El teatro de Luis Rafael Sánchez" (1982, The Theatre of Luis Rafael Sánchez), are both useful works that provide overall views of part or all of Sánchez's theatre. Matías Montes Huidobro examines the two plays that form part of *Sol 13, Interior: La hiel nuestra de cada día* (Sun 13, Interior: Our Daily Bile) and *Los ángeles se han fatigado* (The Angels Have Become Tired) which he considers important antecedents of Sánchez's other plays. Angelina Morfi gives a general overview of Sánchez's seven best-known plays. She believes that his theatre develops into one of greater social commitment with less use of fantasy and reality.

Luis Rafael Sánchez's short stories have attracted critics' attention mainly as antecedents to his novels. Efraín Barradas explores this topic in two essays, "Hacia una obra completa: Ensayo, novela y autointertextualidad" (Toward a Complete Work: Essay, Novel and Autointertextuality) and "Preludio a *La guaracha*" (Prelude to *The Beat*) (1981). In "Preludio a *La guaracha*" he examines the stories in *En cuerpo de camisa* as antecedents of *La guaracha*. In his other essay he applies structuralist theory, especially the study of intertextuality, to the relationship between *La guaracha* and other works of Sánchez such as his essays and the short story "La guaracha del Macho Camacho." Luis Arrigoitía explores this same relationship between the short story and the novel *La guaracha del Macho Camacho* in his previously mentioned essay.

In order to better understand Sánchez's use of the themes of language, Puerto Rican identity, and cultural colonialism, we must first examine his essays. Of all the genres in which he writes, the essays have received the least amount of critical attention. Only one writer, María Inés Rosa in "Los ensayos de Luis Rafael Sánchez" (1978), has analyzed his considerable production of essays in totality. Rosa believes that Sanchez's essays define the tone of his work and that he continues the tendencies of previous Puerto Rican essayists but with a different use of language. He is not interested in art for art's sake but rather in literature as a tool for social reform.

Luis Rafael Sánchez continues to merit study; he is definitely today not only Puerto Rico's leading living playwright but a prose writer of international recognition. Much, however, remains to be done. Many of his plays, overshadowed by *La pasión según Antígona Pérez*, have not received enough in-depth study. His short stories and essays are also areas virtually untouched by serious academic analysis. Much could be written about his treatment of women in his plays from Antígona Pérez to the female characters of *La guaracha*. The last word has not been said on his treatment of Puerto Rican identity and his imaginative use of language. Of his present success, though, there is little doubt. Almost uniquely among Puerto Rican writers, he has won both popular and critical acclaim, national as well as international recognition.

Bibliography

WORKS BY SÁNCHEZ

Theater

La espera (drama en dos actos), *A y Le*, 37–38 (1960).
Los ángeles se han fatigado. Farsa del amor compraditos. San Juan, Puerto Rico: Ediciones Lugar, 1960.
Cuento de Cucarachita Viudita. Ateneo Puertorriqueño Prize in 1960; produced in 1961.
Sol 13, Interior: La hiel nuestra de cada día; Los ángeles se han fatigado). In: *Teatro Puertorriqueño Cuarto Festival).* San Juan, Puerto Rico: Instituto de Cultural Puertorriqueña, 1962.

. . . *O casi el alma* In: *Teatro Puertorriqueño (Séptimo Festival)*. San Juan, Puerto Rico: Instituto de Cultura Puertorriqueña, 1965.

La pasión según Antígona Pérez (Crónica americana en dos actos). Hato Rey, Puerto Rico: Ediciones Lugar, 1968.

Necesitamos a Marlon Brando, undated ms. copy at Institute of Puerto Rican Culture San Juan.

Vietnam, la noche acaba cited in Porrata, Ramón. *La dramaturgia puertorriqueña, MPR*, August 16, 1970: 15 A.

Responso por un bolitero de la 15 (monólogo), produced as part of Segunda Muestra Mundial de Teatro.

La balada de las hogueras, Honorable Mention in Certamen de Teatro del Ateneo Puertorriqueño, 1965.

Short Stories

En cuerpo de camisa. San Juan, Puerto Rico: Ediciones Lugar, 1966. Includes: "Que sabe a Paraíso"; "La Maroma"; "Tiene la noche una raíz" ; "Aleluya Negra"; "Memoria de un eclipse"; "La muerte minúscula," La muerte mayúscula"; "Jum!"; "La recién nacida sangre"; "El ejemplo del muerto que murío sin avisar que se moría"; "La parentela."

Novels

La guaracha del Macho Camacho. Buenos Aires: Ediciones De la Flor, 1976.
Macho Camacho's Beat. New York: Pantheon, 1980.

WORKS ABOUT SÁNCHEZ

Arrigoitía, Luis M. "Una novela escrita en puertorriqueño: *La guaracha del Macho Camacho* de Luis Rafael Sánchez." *Revista de Estudios Hispánicos* [Puerto Rico] 5 (1978): 71–89.

Barradas, Efraín. *Acercamiento a la obra de Luis Rafael Sánchez: Para leer en puertorriqueño*. Río Piedras: Editorial Cultural, 1981.

Ben-Ur, Lorraine Elena. "Hacia la novela del Caribe: Guillermo Cabrera Infante y Luis Rafael Sánchez." *Revista de Estudios Hispánicos* [Puerto Rico] 5 (1978): 129–38.

Colón Zayas, Eliseo Roberto. "Códigos, ideología y lenguaje en el teatro de Luis Rafael Sánchez." *Dissertation Abstracts International*, 43 (1983): 3330.

García Castro, Ramón. "*La guaracha del Macho Camacho* de Luis Rafael Sánchez y 'que sepa abrir la puerta para ir a jugar' de Julio Cortázar." *Chasqui: Revista de Literatura Latinoamericana* (February–May 1980): 71–74.

Giordano, Jaime. "Función estructural del bilingüismo en algunos textos contemporáneos: Cabrera Infante, Luis R. Sánchez." In Rose S. Minc, ed., *Literatures in Transition: The Many Voices of the Caribbean Area: A Symposium*. Hispamérica: Montclair State College, 1982.

Hernández Vargas, Nélida. "Luis Rafael Sánchez: Guía bibliográfica" *Revista de Estudios Hispánicos*. [Puerto Rico] 5 (1978): 167–96.

Laguna-Díaz, Elipidio. "*La guaracha del Macho Camacho*, La novela de aquí." *Revista Chicano-Riqueña* 9, 1 (1981): 68–73.

López-Baralt, Luce. "La prosa de Luis Rafael Sánchez, escrita en puertorriqueño." *Insula: Revista Bibliográfica de Ciencias y Letras* 356–357 (1976): 9.
Montes Huidobro, Matías. "Luis Rafael Sánchez: Lenguaje e identidad en el teatro puertorriqueño." *The American Hispanist* 4 (1978): 22–25.
Rosa, María Inés. "Los ensayos de Luis Rafael Sánchez." *Revista de Estudios Hispánicos* 5 (1978): 149–65.
Vázquez Arce, Carmen. "Sexo y mulatería: Dos sones de la misma guaracha." *Sin Nombre* (July-September 1982): 51–63.
Waldman, Gloria F. "Sánchez, Luis Rafael." *Revista Review Interamericana* 9 (1979): 9–23.

On His Theater

Arriví, Francisco. *Teatro puertorriqueño. Cuarto Festival.* Introducción. San Juan, Puerto Rico: ICP, 1962.
———— *Areyto mayor.* San Juan, Puerto Rico: ICP, 1966.
Babín, María Teresa. "Veinte años de teatro puertorriqueño (1945–1964)." *Asomante* 20, 4 (1964): 7–20.
Belaval, Emilio S. "Luis Rafael Sánchez." *El Mundo* May 23, 1961.
Cardona, Iván. "La pasión del teatro puertorriqueño según Luis Rafael Sánchez." *La hora* August 2, 1973.
Fernández, Piri. "Temas del teatro puertorriqueno de hoy," in *El autor dramático, primer seminario de dramaturgia.* San Juan, Puerto Rico: Instituto de Cultura Puertorriqueña ICP, 1963.
González, José Emilio. *"Sol 13, Interior,"* in the program of the Cuarto Festival de Teatro. San Juan, Puerto Rico: ICP, 1962.
————. *"O casi el alma* de Luis Rafael Sánchez." *El Mundo* June 1, 1964.
Guerrero Zamora, Juan. "El autor dramático y el teatro de vanguardia," in *El autor dramático, primer seminario de dramaturgia.* San Juan, Puerto Rico: Instituto de Cultura Puertorriqueñ, 1963.
Lewis, Robert. "Theatre Review: *The Farce of Love.*" *San Juan Star* October 24, 1961.
Marqués, René. *Cuentos puertorriqueños de hoy.* Prólogo. San Juan, Puerto Rico: Editorial Cultura, 1971.
Meléndez, Concha. "La literatura de ficción en Puerto Rico (1955–1963." *Asomante* 20, 3 (1964): 7–23.
Morfi, Angelina. *Temas del teatro.* Santo Domingo: Editora del Caribe, 1969.
————. "El teatro de Luis Rafael Sánchez." *Revista canadiense de estudios hispánicos* 7,1 (Autumn 1982): 189–204.
Phillips, Jordan B. *Contemporary Trends in the Puerto Rican Theatre.* Madrid: Plaza Mayor, 1972.
Waldman, Gloria. "Luis Rafael Sánchez and the New Latin American Theatre." *Dissertation Abstracts International* 39, 10A (1979): 6154. 1979.

MAIDA WATSON-ESPENER

SÁNCHEZ-BOUDY, JOSÉ (1928–   ). José Sánchez-Boudy is one of the most prolific Cuban American authors. He has published poetry, short stories, novels, theatre, and essays. His work is best known for its portrayal of a pre-Castro Cuba.

Biography

Sánchez-Boudy was born on October 17, 1928, in Havana, Cuba. His father was a Spaniard who immigrated to Cuba and made a fortune in the shoe industry. His mother was the daughter of a French engineer. His childhood in La Vívora, a neighborhood of Havana, put him in touch with the groups that he portrays in his work. It was there that he listened to and played with poor children and blacks who lived in "solares" (tenement houses). At his father's shoe store, El Mundo, located in Old Havana, he became familiar with the Chinese world and deepened his contact with the lower classes.

He studied with the Marist Brothers in a school in La Vívora. He also attended a school in New Hampshire for two years after graduating from high school in Cuba. Although he started college in the University of Detroit, he returned to Cuba to study law. Sánchez-Boudy graduated in 1953 and became a famous criminalist. In criminal court he deepened even more his knowledge of the lower classes. As a criminal lawyer he became an experienced ethnographer of the areas that are later portrayed in his work. Sánchez-Boudy tells us, for example, that on one occasion he was asked to defend a murderer who had committed a crime in Jesus María, a neighborhood in Havana famous for corruption. He had to spend much time in Jesus María interviewing people. His field notes then, and other times, have provided him with many of the characters, the language, and the plots that appear in his work.

In 1961 Sánchez-Boudy left Cuba and went to Miami. He quickly settled in Puerto Rico where he worked first as a journalist for the newspaper, *El Imparcial*, and later as a professor of literature in the University of Puerto Rico. In 1965, together with his wife and three children, Sánchez-Boudy settled in Greensboro, North Carolina. He is a full professor at the University of North Carolina where he teaches mostly Caribbean literature.

Sánchez-Boudy has contributed to Cuban American literature not only through creative works. He wrote the first volume of the *Historia de la literatura cubana (en el exilio)* (1975, History of Cuban Literature in Exile) and is working on future volumes. He also published the *Diccionario de cubanismos más usuales* (1978, Dictionary of Most Common Cubanisms) which will be followed by at least six more volumes. He writes a weekly column for *El Diario las Américas* in Miami and often writes for *Ideal,* a popular magazine published in Miami. He is, together with Eladio Secades, the best folklorist and critic of Cuban customs. His book *El Picúo, el fisto, el barrio y otras estampas cubanas* (1977, The Picuo, the fisto, the barrio and other Cuban sketches) is an excellent example of this folkloric tradition.

It would be important to point out that Sánchez-Boudy's father, José María Sánchez Priede, was also an accomplished folklorist. His son has published two collections of his poetry, *Güiro Limpio* (1974, Clean Gourd) and *Güiro, Clave y Cencerro* (1977, Gourd, Claves and Drum). These two collections show a gift to record and reproduce popular language which is reminiscent of that in some of the son's work.

Among Cuban American writers there are those who remain linked to a past in pre-Castro Cuba and those who create a Cuban American present within the United States. Sánchez-Boudy's work can certainly be classified as belonging to the group that reminisces about the past in Cuba. What makes his work unique, however, is that the North American present is rarely introduced in his work. Sánchez-Boudy has stated that he is a "solitary writer." Although he remains linked to Cubans in Miami through continuous visits, their reality rarely penetrates his literary world. *Lilayando* (1971) and *Lilayando pal tu* (1978, Liliyando for the You), short folkloric novels, are in this respect unique. The English language, for example, which he knows well after having studied in the United States as a young man, rarely enters his literary world. It is as if José Sánchez-Boudy has taken refuge in the hills of North Carolina so as to "freeze" a pre-Castro Cuba. He has said: "My remembrances have not become less clear. On the contrary, they have been reaffirmed. . . . As the years go by Cuba comes to me sharper, clearer" (Personal communication). This, of course, wouldn't have happened if Sánchez-Boudy had stayed in Miami, where a Cuban present constantly influences the Cuban past. It is perhaps in his last book of poetry, *Tiempo congelado* (1979, Frozen Time) where he best expresses the anguish of his solitary existence. "I died a long time ago when the clock stopped," he tells us in one poem. And he defines himself as an exiled man, "a man with frozen time/who dies slowly in his past."

Major Themes

There is no better synthesis of Sánchez-Boudy's work than that expressed in the poem significantly called "Green Remembrances." In order to preserve his remembrances "green" and vivid, Sánchez-Boudy freezes them in the snow and silence of Greensboro. As Greensboro is surrounded by silence, monotony, and ice (see especially *Poemas del silencio* [1969, Poems of Silence]), Cuba screams loudly through street vendors' cries (see, for example, *Pregones* [1975, Street Chants]), laughs (see especially *Alegrías de coco* [1970, Coconut Happiness]), and sometimes cries in anguish (see, for example, *Cuentos de la niñez* [1983, Tales from Childhood]). The reader is left with the impression that there is no reality in Sánchez-Boudy's present, for there is "Always the same landscape of exile;/ long as fangs of a howling dog" (*Poemas del silencio*).

Sánchez-Boudy's extensive literary work can be generally categorized as belonging to one of three modalities: 1) those that portray a pre-Castro Cuba, 2) those that portray the crisis of the Western world, and 3) those that portray Cuban life in the United States.

His poetry falls mainly within the first modality. His first collection of poetry, *Ritmo de solá (Aquí como allá)* (1967, Tenement Rhythms. Here and There), can be classified as Afro-Caribbean poetry. The "solar" (tenement) with its residents and language becomes alive in the poems. *Alegrías de coco* (1970), *Crocante de maní* (1973, Peanut Candy), and *Pregones* (1975) develop this fresco of popular life in pre-Castro Cuba. "This is the Havana of yesteryear/

boisterous throughout/ that is photographed by the street vendor/ with a sweet taste of honey,'' he tells us in "Pregones de mi padre" (My Father's Chants) (*Pregones*). This stanza expresses precisely the techniques used by Sánchez-Boudy. As an experienced ethnographer with a true ear for popular language, Sánchez-Boudy gives voice to the street vendors, to lower classes, to blacks, to Cuban Chinese. Their voices find their way into his work. For example, we hear the Chinese vendor who does canework express in a Spanish transformed by Chinese phonology: "Chinito pone lejilla, alegre sillón e silla/ pol un plecio balatico/ sillone glande e chico" (Chinaman puts rye/ happy chailand locker/ for a smarr plice/ big chail and smarr). We hear continuously Cuban slang and regionalisms which have disappeared in the United States. For example, the last poem of *Pregones,* titled "Mi calle y mi barrio" (My street and neighborhood), is composed of a series of Cuban sayings that have lost all meaning and are no longer used in the United States. It is in this respect that Sánchez-Boudy's portrayal of the language spoken by the lower classes in a pre-Castro Cuba becomes an important contribution. In effect, Sánchez-Boudy's work fills a vacuum that occurred when only the middle class left Cuba in the 1960s. This group of mostly white middle-class professionals were not the everyday users of this linguistic modality. Part of the sadness and anguish felt by this group in the United States came precisely from the fact that they weren't representative of *all* of Cuban culture. For, in fact, Cuban culture was deeply tied to black culture and more popular traditions. Sánchez-Boudy brings alive all this culture that stayed behind and that was transformed with the change in the social and political system.

Sánchez-Boudy's interest in portraying important Cuban traditions that were not necessarily those of Cubans in the United States led him also to write about African religion and traditions. Three of his books of poetry, *Aché, Babalú, Ayé* (1975), *Ekué, Abanakué Ekué (1977), Ritos Náñigos* (1977, Náñigo Rites) and *Leyendas de azúcar prieta* (1977, Black Sugar Legends), portray African religious rites such as that of the "ñáñigos," African deities such as Obatalá and Changó, and many Afro-Cuban legends.

When Sánchez-Boudy writes not about the Cuban past that no longer exists, but about his solitary North American present, his voice mellows. The cries of the street vendors and the African religious rites are silenced. What emerges is always his own solitary voice crying in anguish. This is the voice of the Sánchez-Boudy who writes *Poemas de otoño e invierno* (1967, Autumn and Winter Poems), *Poemas del silencio* (1969), and *Tiempo congelado (Poemario de una isla ausente)* (1979). His extreme anguish becomes apparent when he appears totally isolated, surrounded by "Greensboro's old houses/ Always alone" (*Poemas del silencio*). In *Tiempo congelado* the presence of the Cuban landscape is veiled by his sadness and by the realization that, as he tells us in a poem, "I awaken and I am here;/ cold country./ And everything is a summer dream." It is as if the extreme anguish of living in exile allows the poet to bring to life those who have disappeared through a new social order, but does not permit him to face the physical reality of a country which is still very much present.

José Sánchez-Boudy's novels encompass the three modalities outlined above. *El Corredor Kresto* (1976, Kresto the Runner) and *Ñiquín el cesante* (1978, Ñiquin the Retired) are part of a series which the author has called "novels of the tragedy." They are a contribution to the fresco about life in pre-Castro Cuba. *Lilayando* (1971) and *Lilayando pal tu* (1978) portray Cuban life in the United States. Finally, *Los cruzados de la aurora* (1973, Crossed by the Dawn), *Orbus Terrarum (la ciudad de Humanitas)* (1974, The Globe, The City of Humanity), and *Los sarracenos del ocaso* (1977, Saracens of Dusk) form the trilogy known as "novels of the crisis" of the Western world.

The first two groups of novels, those that portray life in pre-Castro Cuba and those that portray life in the United States, are greatly related to his poetry through the use of the language of the lower classes. In both *Lilayando* and *Lilayando pal tu* the only protagonist is language itself. Both consist of a series of dialogues or disconnected discourses such as telephone conversations, letters, speeches, radio programs, poetry, etc. These two novels give the appearance of portraying a present, since they take place mostly in the United States. However, their main objective is presenting oral discourse of the past. Often, the conversational style is introduced with "Oye, te quiero contar una cosa" (Hey, I want to tell you a story). Sánchez-Boudy presents us not with a literary *text about* the past, but with oral *utterances in* the past. Perhaps this is confirmed by the fact that in *Lilayando* the English language hardly enters the picture. In fact, we are surprised when at the end of *Lilayando* a character says: "Entonces es como esta vida nuestra aquí en los Yunait: de nunca acabar" (Therefore, it's like our life here in the United States: never ending). What is surprising about this utterance is the use of "los Yunait" (United States), an assimilated loan often said back in Cuba, but rarely said by Hispanics in the United States. Although the use of loans is much more apparent in *Lilayando pal tu* there are characteristics that place this novel, as the first, within a context of *utterances in* the past. For example, the use of Cuban slang and regionalisms is much more abundant than the use of English loans. The novel is full of expressions such as: acere, legisla, estás por la goma, la profe, le dio el betive, consorte, tu sangre, darle pirey y fuerza blanca, etc. When English loans appear they are always orthographically assimilated to Spanish. Examples of these are: "So lon beibi" (So long baby), "polai" (polite), "esplash daun" (splash down), "broder" (brother), "leidi" (lady), "beibi" (baby), "chower" (shower), "nersery" (nursery), "vaqium cline" (vacuum cleaner), "dantaun" (downtown). These examples of English loans are characteristic of much Latin American literature written in Spanish-speaking countries. However, Sánchez-Boudy's work does not include the code-switches, the calques, and the unassimilated loans that characterize much Hispanic literature in the United States. We are in the presence of "frozen" utterances from the past.

In the last scene of *Ñiquín el cesante* a character addresses Sánchez-Boudy himself, who appears in all of his novels, and says: "What a rumpus, Pepito! This island is sinking. No one can put up with this." The corruption which is evident in both of his novels about pre-Castro Cuba is extended throughout the Western world in his "novels of the crisis." For example, in *Orbus Terrarum* the decadence extends since "The Main Sewer has overflown. The pestilence is absolute. The air is unbreathable." Even the Catholic Church appears in crisis in *Los sarracenos del ocaso.* What is important is that the trilogy known as "novels of the crisis" merely extends to a universal realm which includes and contains the local realm, that which Sánchez-Boudy has so well done in the novels that are more folkloric.

The trilogy that makes up the "novels of the crisis" merely extends the local decadence of pre-Castro Cuba to all of the Western world. They are also stylistically intertwined with the other novels and do not constitute a unique and different literary modality. All of the techniques used by Sánchez-Boudy in novels such as *Lilayando* are evident here. For example, besides the literary text of the novel, we find poetry, disconnected dialogues, songs, speeches, texts of others such as Calvino, letters, minutes of meetings, texts of posters, etc. The only difference between the other novels and the "novels of the crisis" is that now the characters are universal and common to all, rather than local and personal to only José Sánchez-Boudy (Pepito) and his friends. That is why instead of Ñiquín, Casimiro, Boloña, Salvat, and Celedonio González, we find Juan Calvino, Miguel Servet, Jerónimo Savonarolo, Plinio, Galileo, Fadel, el Supremo, Espinosa, Erasmus, and Santa Teresa.

The literary techniques which have been so acclaimed in these three novels are much better integrated in those where Sánchez-Boudy focuses on the Cuban past. As in *Poemas del silencio,* in the "novels of the crisis" Sánchez-Boudy expresses an anguish that is not as deeply felt, or as powerfully expressed, as was that of the loss of his Cuban past. The universal corruption and the all-encompassing decaying present are no match for the intensity of the Cuban past that Sánchez-Boudy maintains alive in his other work.

Sánchez-Boudy's short stories are also mainly portrayals of his Cuban past. *Cuentos grises* (1966, Grey Stories), *Cuentos del hombre* (1969, Stories about Man), *Cuentos a luna llena* (1971, Stories of the Full Moon), and *Cuentos de la niñez* (1983) are mainly sketches of "all which was dying" in pre-Castro Cuba. All the decadence is portrayed here vividly as live remembrances. In the short story titled "La maestra" (*Cuentos de la niñez*) Sánchez-Boudy starts by telling us: "Many years have gone by, many, many years. And far from forgetting my childhood, in the peaceful neighborhood of la Vívora, I see it with more clarity than ever." What is interesting about the short stories is that the laughter is completely gone. In fact, most stories end with a piercing cry: "The scream was great, piercing. The old ladies say that it was heard to rumble all through the county" (*Cuentos de la niñez*). Even his childhood is portrayed in this fatal atmosphere. "La Playa" expresses the difference between Sánchez-Boudy's folkloric and joyous poetry and novels, and his sad and fatal short stories. The author tells us: "And when night falls and one hears the voice of vendors . . . a multitude of feelings come to me, failures of very sweet pain. And I see, when as a child, with the swimming trunk that covered my entire body, which my aunt had bought for me, I used to cry at the shore upon feeling the coldness of the water. Then, not even those peddlers who go from house to house announcing their merchandise can wake me up from deep reflection" (*Cuentos de la niñez*). Sánchez-Boudy now focuses on pain and anguish, either his own or someone else's. Nothing distracts him, not even the enticing "pregones" (street vendors' cries). The professor, the dead man, the poet, the sick man, the idiot, the vagabond, the boy, the patriot, the ambitious man, the woman, the persecuted man, the lender, the just man, and the novelist are all protagonists of short stories that show man in all his injustice and evil.

What links these short stories to the poems and the novels is precisely the use of oral utterances intertwined within the literary text. In "Los ojos" Sánchez-Boudy tells us: "I am going to tell you about it. Stop smoking, you make me nervous, and listen. It was in that isolated town" (*Cuentos a luna llena*). The narration is never sustained and ends abruptly. Just as he had done in his poetry and his novels, Sánchez-Boudy presents us here with a series of static photographs. Here, however, the picture is always bleak. It is the effect of writing only from pain, from freezing and captivating "that which was dying."

Sánchez-Boudy's theatre remains largely unknown. *Homo Sapiens. Teatro del no absurdo* (1971, Homo Sapiens [Non-Absurd Theatre]), *La soledad de la Playa Larga (Mañana, mariposa)* (1971, The Loneliness of Long Beach, Tomorrow Butterfly), and *La rebelión de los negros* (1980, The Revolt of the Blacks) constitute his contribution to the theatrical genre. The tradition of oral utterance in the theatre links these three works to Sánchez-Boudy's poetry, novels, and short stories. *Homo Sapiens* is composed of four short pieces which link the past (the Puritans in New England in "El hombre de ayer y de hoy," the slaves in the United States in the seventeenth century in "El negro con olor a azufre") with the present (a city like New York in "Los asesions! Los asesinos!," a subway in "Los apestados") and with an encompassing time and space ("La ciudad de Humanitas"). *La soledad de la Playa Larga* represents the Bay of Pigs and expresses the two principles on which Sánchez-Boudy's literary works rest. One, that the gravest error in the Bay of Pigs was to trust the United States. And two, that there will be a return to Cuba. It is perhaps the combination of these two principles that makes Sánchez-Boudy's literary work what it is, a living fresco of Cubanness which remains separate from either the present life in the United States or the present life in Cuba.

Sánchez-Boudy's literary work is important precisely because it does not partake of the North American present and its influence and does not conform to life in Socialist Cuba. Rather he portrays a Cuban past which he projects into a mythical future. He says in a poem of *Tiempo congelado*: "I cannot die, Lord/ if I am already dead." Sánchez-Boudy writes from the perspective of a dead man about things which are forever dying in their eternal corruption. That is why Cuban voices of the past fill his pages. We are not in the presence of characters, but of voices. These voices of ghosts fill the gap which occurred with the exodus of many Cubans to the United States and the change in social and political order. His work is a desperate attempt to "scream back" his remembrances by focusing on pain and anguish on the one hand, and laughter and folklore on the other.

Survey of Criticism

Although Sánchez-Boudy has published over forty titles and his contribution to *El Diario las Américas* has reached almost one thousand articles, few critics have seriously considered his work. Sánchez-Boudy's literary works have been analyzed mostly by other Cuban Americans. In this respect, the most significant contribution is the recent publication of an anthology titled *La narrativa de José Sánchez-Boudy (tragedia y folklore)*. This book, edited by Laurentino Suárez and published by Universal in Miami in 1973, is a collection of eighteen articles about the author's novels and short stories.

Sánchez-Boudy's poetry has had better fortune. As early as 1974 his poetry was translated into English by Woodrow W. Moore. An English translation of his Afro-Cuban poetry was published in 1978 by Claudio Freixas. This same poetry had been analyzed by René León in a book published by Universal in Miami in 1977.

Most studies to date focus on the Cubanness of Sánchez-Boudy's work, without projecting this past into a mythical future. His work awaits studies that will connect him to other Latin American writers such as Alejo Carpentier, Gabriel García-Márquez, and Miguel Angel Asturias, who have also placed the past in a mythical future.

Bibliography

WORKS BY SÁNCHEZ-BOUDY

Cuentos grises. Barcelona: Bosch, 1966.
Poemas de otoño e invierno. Barcelona: Bosch, 1967.
Ritmo de Solá (Aquí como allá). Barcelona: Bosch, 1967.
Apuntes para una teoría del existencialismo. Barcelona: Bosch, 1968.
Las novelas de César Andreu Iglesias y la problemática puertorriqueña actual. Barcelona: Bosch, 1968.
Cuentos del hombre. Barcelona: Bosch, 1969.
Madame Bovary. Un análisis clínico sobre neurosis y psicosis psicógena. Barcelona: Bosch, 1969.
Poemas del silencio. Barcelona: Bosch, 1969.
La temática novelística de Alejo Carpentier. Miami: Ediciones Universal, 1969.
Alegrías de coco. Barcelona: Bosch, 1970.
Baudelaire (Psicoanálisis e impotencia). Miami: Ediciones Universal, 1970.
Modernismo y americanismo. Barcelona: Bosch, 1970.
Cuentos a luna llena. Miami: Ediciones Universal, 1971.

Homo Sapiens. Teatro del no absurdo. Miami: Ediciones Universal, 1971.
Lilayando. Miami: Ediciones Universal, 1971.
La nueva novela hispanoamericana y tres tristes tigres. Miami: Ediciones Universal, 1971.
Los cruzados de la aurora. Miami: Ediciones Universal, 1972.
Crocante de maní. Miami: Ediciones Universal, 1973.
Lezama Lima: Peregrino inmóvil (Paradiso al desnudo). Miami: Ediciones Universal, 1974.
Orbus Terrarum (La ciudad de Humanitas). Miami: Ediciones Universal, 1974.
Aché, Babalú, Ayé (Retablo afrocubano). Miami: Ediciones Universal, 1975.
Historia de la literatura cubana (en el exilio). Miami: Ediciones Universal, 1975.
Pregones. Miami: Ediciones Universal, 1975.
La soledad de la Playa Larga (Mañana, mariposa). Miami: Ediciones Universal, 1975.
El corredor Kresto. Miami: Ediciones Universal, 1976.
Ekué, Abanakué, Ekué (Ritos Ñáñigos). Miami: Ediciones Universal, 1977.
Leyendas de azúcar prieta. Miami: Ediciones Universal, 1977.
El Picúo, el fisto, el barrio y otras estampas cubanas. Miami: Ediciones Universal, 1977.
Los sarracenos del ocaso. Miami: Ediciones Universal, 1977.
Diccionario de cubanismos más usuales (Como habla el cubano). Miami: Ediciones Universal, 1978.
Lilayando pal tu. Miami: Ediciones Universal, 1978.
Ñiquín el cesante. Miami: Ediciones Universal, 1978.
Tiempo congelado (Poemario de una isla ausente). Miami: Ediciones Universal, 1979.
La rebelión de los negros. Miami: Ediciones Universal, 1980.
Cuentos de la niñez. Miami: Ediciones Universal, 1983.

Translations of Works by Sánchez-Boudy

Freixas, Claudio. *Afro-Cuban Poetry de Oshún a Yemayá. The Afro-Cuban Poetry of José Sánchez-Boudy in English Translation.* Miami: Ediciones Universal, 1978.
Moore, Woodrow W. *Cuba and Her Poets: The Poems of José Sánchez-Boudy.* Miami: Ediciones Universal, 1974.

WORKS ABOUT SÁNCHEZ-BOUDY

De Villa, Alvaro. "La bendita chusmería criolla." Prólogo en José Sánchez-Boudy, *Crocante de maní.* Miami: Ediciones Universal, 1973.
Fernández-Vázquez, Antonio. *"Orbus Terrarum:* Análisis de una anatomía apocalíptica," in *Selected Proceedings of the Twenty-Seventh Annual Mountain Interstate Foreign Language Conference,* edited by M. Laurentino Suárez and Eduardo Zayas-Bazán. Miami, Fla., 1978.
Gutiérrez de la Solana, Alberto. Prólogo en José Sánchez-Boudy, *Ekué, Abanakué, Ekué.* Miami: Ediciones Universal, 1977.
León, René. *La poesía negra de José Sánchez-Boudy.* Miami: Ediciones Universal, 1977.
Núñez, Ana Rosa. Prólogo al libro *Cuentos a luna llena.* Miami: Ediciones Universal, 1971.
Ruiz Ramón, Francisco. Prólogo al libro *Cuentos grises.* Barcelona: Bosch, 1966.
Suárez, Laurentino, ed. *La narrativa de José Sánchez-Boudy (Tragedia y folklore).* Miami: Ediciones Universal, 1973.

Van Praag, J.A. Prólogo en José Sánchez-Boudy, *Cuentos del hombre*. Barcelona: Bosch, 1969.

OFELIA GARCÍA

SANTOS SILVA, LOREINA (1933–   ).

Loreina Santos Silva is a Puerto Rican poet, full professor at the University of Puerto Rico (Mayagüez Campus), and a scholar who has published numerous essays in various countries on poetry, theater, and Puerto Rican women. Her poetry, especially that of her books, projects both a materialistic and mystical vision of the world, moved by "the Energy," which she substitutes for our traditional concept of God.

Biography

Loreina Santos Silva was born in Ciales, a small town in central Puerto Rico. When she was five years old, her mother, Montserrate Santos, who wanted her two children to be adopted by their grandparents, died. However, her father, José Piñeiro, flatly refused the adoption. After ten years of problems and tension between the grandparents and her father, he accepted that she, and not her brother, be adopted. After this time she saw her father only once a year, on January 6, for the celebration of the Arrival of the Three Kings. She recaptures this incident in her poem # 25 in the book *Umbral de soledad* (Entrance into Solitude), which is currently being published, although it was written a long time ago. Loreina had a difficult childhood, since her grandfather, on her mother's side of the family, scorned her mother and even threw her out of the house because she was a leftist and nationalist. When Loreina went to live in her grandparents' home, she had to wait until her grandfather was asleep so that she could go to bed behind his back. The terror which her grandfather provoked in her is engraved in her poem # 4 in *Umbral:*"'Palomo's gallops/ scream on the asphalt," poem's first line depicts the anxiety and nightmares that her grandfather on his horse Palomo caused her.

Due to health problems, Loreina was exposed to the Morovis Homestudy Plan during her high school years. Peggy Ann Bliss comments that this plan gave her "excellent habits of solitary work and research." She received a degree in English as a second language at the University of Michigan at Ann Arbor. In 1957 she received a bachelor of arts at the University of Puerto Rico. She then wanted to study law, but was unable to pursue her objective for economic reasons. She obtained her master of arts in 1963 from the University of California at Berkeley. She then went on to obtain a Ph.D. from Brown University at Providence, Rhode Island, with a dissertation *Emilio Prados: Approximation to Surrealism*.

After 1960, and while she pursued her postgraduate studies, she taught in several institutions, both at the high school and university levels in the United States. In 1968 she became a faculty member of the University of Puerto Rico at Mayagüez, where in 1983 she achieved the rank of full professor.

She married Hurry S. Georas, a Greek whom she met in Berkeley when she was preparing her master's. With him she had three daughters: Evanthea Nike, Anna Loreina, and Chloë Sophia. Bliss explains that Loreina's husband "did everything possible to squelch her Puerto Rican spirit." Her marriage, full of pain and humiliation, lasted nineteen years because she stood fast to the tradition of Hispanic women who save a marriage at all costs. At last, she was divorced and never remarried. Poem # 26 in *Umbral*, "Radiografía de un matrimonio" (X-Ray of a Marriage), which begins with "there are things which are not forgotten," captures in crude form her experiences of those matrimonial years.

At a very early age, Loreina began writing, and her ability to express herself was such that her high school teachers accused her of committing plagiarism. On one occasion, at age fifteen, she wrote a paper in English about the outburst of spring, and the teacher, doubting its originality, threw Loreina's composition into the wastebasket. Repeated incidents of this type made Loreina vow never to write again.

In 1960, three significant events occurred that made her pick up her pen. That year, due to health problems, Adelaida Lugo-Guernelli was a guest in Loreina's home. One day, Adelaida told Loreina that she had had a revealing dream in which Juan Ramón Jiménez had told her that Loreina's path in life was the path of poetry, and that she should dedicate herself to her destiny and begin writing. She laughed because she did not believe in this type of revelation. Several months later, a professor at Berkeley asked each of his students to write a poem. After reading Loreina's poem, he asked her if she was a poet, and she told him that she had never written poetry. Amazed at her talent, he replied, "You don't know what a poet you are." Some time later, she experienced the first crisis of her marriage, only two months after she was married. In her desperation, which led her as far as suicidal thoughts, she expressed the intense desire to compensate for her suicidal tendency by using the escape of prayer, which would permit her to survive the conflict she faced. The next day she wrote a poem, significant because it was the first of her literary career, which up to now encompasses six published books, six unpublished, five in progress. In addition, numerous articles and poems are scattered in literary magazines.

From 1960 to 1970 Loreina wrote *Incertidumbre primera* (1973, Uncertainty Number One), *Incertidumbre segunda* (Uncertainty Number Two), and *Incertidumbre tercera* (Uncertainty Number Three). To date, only the first of the three texts has been published. However, since 1968 her poems started appearing in Puerto Rican literary magazines such as *Atenea, La Gotera, Revista Instituto de Cultura Puertorriqueña,* and *Ceiba*. At that time she used the pen name of Loreina Georas because her husband insisted on publishing under his surname.

Puerto Rican scholars place Loreina's poetry in the Generation of the Sixties, but she thinks that because of her works' themes, she fits better in the recent group related with the atomic era, the industrialized world, and the technology. In my interview of her she declared that poetry of the type she has been creating for quite some time only started recently in the island.

Major Themes

Love and erotism are major themes in Loreina Santos Silva's works. Other themes, such as incertitude, pain, the mystery of life, solitude, are closely related to the major ones. In fact, starting with *Incertidumbre,* love is a positive energy that makes death succumb and immortalizes lovers. Lugo-Guernelli considers that love in Loreina's poetry is "a method of knowledge and understanding the world and the cosmos."

A poet reaches the peak of maturity when becoming the master of a deep philosophy which is congruent with his/her lyrical conception of the cosmos. The metaphysical concern that shows sparingly in *Incertidumbre* takes a definite shape in her last books in what Loreina calls mystical materialism. This mystical materialism is the clue to the other main theme in her works, starting with *Del onto* (1978, Of Being), that of the positive energy. According to Loreina, we are energy in eternal evolution. Energy that "proliferates in the cosmos at various physical and metaphysical levels by means of the eros." She conceives nature as a "network of machines, we ourselves are all machines. . . . Man is the most complex machine for he is able to think, to articulate his thought and thus to establish order in his world. Unfortunately, man has not been able to set the world at equilibrium." In order to project energy, "the cosmos has to participate in heterosexual, homosexual, heterogeneous or homogeneous relationships." This philosophical concept gives shape to her last unpublished book, *Motor mutable* (Mutable Motor). In Loreina's own words, it "is a book conceived within our technological world, but a world that has forgotten the essence of humanity, the spiritual and moral values of men. It prophesizes the exodus of men to another planet," a world where humanity will find equilibrium. In her last book in progress, *Astroalba íntima (The Birth of My Planet),* she creates a new world where man "can live in genuine solidarity with his fellow man."

Loreina Santos Silva thinks of poetry as an imperative longing to reach the insurmountable mystery. For her, any writer "wants to survive in the work of art." The act of writing is "like defeating death," she told me.

Loreina does not carry out extreme experiments in her poetry. In general she tends to adhere to a traditional versification, especially the popular short verses. In *Rikelme* (1974, Rich Soul), the avant-garde movement metaphors bring the Puerto Rican poet nearer to the Spanish Generation of the 27 with which she identifies in terms of style, sensitivity, and themes. Loreina also recognizes the impact in her poetry of Puerto Ricans such as Luis *Palés Matos, Julia de *Burgos, Carmen Marrero, and others. However, she reads avidly any good poet, from the classical Spanish poets to the contemporary ones, no matter which country they represent. Among some of her favorites are Juan Ramón Jiménez, Antonio Machado, and Robert Frost.

Existentialist nuances that include anguish, sorrow, solitude, and nothingness may be observed already in *Incertidumbre* but they are intermingled with a romanticism always present in Loreina's poetry. In her last books the existentialist agony becomes a strong presence in most of the verses.

Another general characteristic of her poetry is the neologisms that already appear in her first book. An imperious need to break with the limitations imposed by the existing vocabulary and to create his/her own language is symptomatic of the authentic poets. In Loreina's last books, neologisms have a polyvalent force which shows the supreme intention of the lyrical voice to unify opposed entities in the whole universe. The most representative are *soliluna* (sunmoon), *uniser* (unibeing), *tierrimar* (sealand), *solalba* (sundawn), etc.

Traces of romanticism and modernism are still present in Loreina's first book, *Incertidumbre*. Irregularities in some poems, predominantly in free verse, give away the premature poet. "The title itself gave an idea of not knowing yet in which way . . . her poetical expression would develop. But here begins the theme of love as a means of metaphysical growth. In fact it is love that is the link between the other themes: yearning for plenitude, uncertainty, sorrow, solitude, mystery of life, poetry, anguish before nothingness. The Greek elements, such as symbolic mythology, are not accidental nor do they follow the modernist patterns: Loreina lived in Greece and has a broad knowledge of the Greek culture, literature, and language.

Between *Incertidumbre* and *Rikelme*, her second published book, there are various unpublished texts. Among them, *Huellas*, a collection of short poems in haiku form. The poet gathers in this book her perceptions of her island and the traces that they leave in her intimate world.

Voz para una resonancia, also unpublished, is important because it shows a new direction in Loreina's poetry, that of a committed writer. It represents a protest against the political situation in Puerto Rico which she considers a form of repression and which does not allow for independence, moral or spiritual growth.

Don Terramor (Mr. Earthlove), of the same period, is a book still in progress. Don Terramor is Loreina's grandfather who loved the earth to the point that he could not have foreseen the future nor industrial development. The text deals with the history of her family (of all Puerto Rican families), of the tobacco as well as sugar cane that vanished from the island. Loreina explains that, like *Martín Fierro*, the text represents "the farewell to the *jíbaro*, the culture, and the traditional past in Puerto Rico."

Originally *Rikelme* was called *Ricalma* (Richsoul). The author changed the title because, on account of her first book of poems, the critic classified her as a sapphic poet. As people usually do not understand that, besides the lesbian meaning of the word, "sapphic" is generally associated with a lyric audacity, as this was her case, she became afraid of being misinterpreted and changed the title. *Rikelme* emphasizes the idea that only authentic people (rich souls) "search for real love, for the affinity of the body and the soul" and try to solve the mystery of the human beings.

Until now, the poet has covered a great distance in which the originality of her lyricism takes shape in a rhythmic and musical assonance of octosyllabic lines. The images in *Rikelme* have become more unusual, daring, suggestive, sensuously erotic. Thus, Loreina's poetry follows the path shown by the rich postmodernist movement in which women writers expressed their erotic intimacy without secrecy. The following key words underline the passionate and sensuous love in the text: breasts, sex, body, flesh, desire, Eros, pyre, fire, forge, flame, incandescent, semen, and so on. Most of the text is the unfolding of remembrances by a woman who contemplates the sea. Each one of the short poems ends with a refrain in which the lyric feminine voice repeats: "How many sublime moments / find shelter in the secret / passing of time over and over!" (Cuántos momentos sublimes / se alojan en los arcanos / repasares de los tiempos!). According to my interview of Loreina, *"Rikelme* portrays the frustration of human love encounters, for very seldom do human beings obtain affinity in their relationships." This pessimistic mood only prevails in the last part of the book. In those final poems the lyric voice explains that "it is the existence scythe / tearing eternal sorrow" (es la hoz de la existencia / rasgando el dolor eterno). Love, pleasure, sorrow, anguish, frustration, disillusionment, which gather around the erotic experience, are *Rikelme*'s themes.

The third published book, *Del onto,* has a dedication in which the poet rejects God and recognizes men as the sole givers of themselves. The poet integrates the neologism "actuarism" into her poetical conception. "Actuarism," related to "act" but not to the juridical terms "actuary" or "actuarian," is the key to the being. Loreina explains in the book's "Exordium" that actuarism is not a question of "isms." In fact it is the effort to save mankind by means of a genuine, strong, positive, and individual emotion always in evolution. It is a deliberate act of love which ties the bonds of affection among all human races.

Once more love and sex, motive forces of the actuarism, are the structural axles and themes of *Del onto.* Love and sex are also means of salvation and of grasping reality, affliction, solitude, guilt, death, mankind, creation, and cosmos. Along these lines, one may perceive a conspicuous search for a center that will bring equilibrium to life. Thus, the circle, another key word in this text, operates as a mandala. The "uniser" (unibeing) or Rikelme, the rich soul, becomes the symbolic fulfillment of this search. However, the center is threatened by the fugacity of time and a swift arrival of death. "An anguish without bounds" (Una angustia sin frontera) sets the tone of the book.

Mi ría (1981, My River) is a key book in Loreina Santos Silva's poetry, because it depicts already the poetic vision that culminates in her last two unpublished texts: *Motor mutable* and *Astralba íntima.* The poems follow the popular lyrical tradition of Hispanic heptasyllables. In her other books the poetic motive of water showed itself dispersely in images and/or symbols (río, ría, mar, ola, torrente, etc.) and also suggested the islander landscape in Puerto Rico; in *Mi ría,* on the contrary, "ría" or estuary becomes the transcendental symbol of the "uniser" (unibeing) or the "ría-ricalma" (estuary-richsoul) that searches

Eros's profound roots. The theme of love and the erotic images continue to give sense and unity to this text as to the others. The secondary themes follow the same patterns set in her previous works.

Vocero del mar (1982, Voices from the Sea) differs from the other books. It started during a walk along Punta Cadena beach and a conversation with a fisherman. There a rich world of legend, myth, and tradition related to the Puerto Rican sea that does not change in essence throughout the centuries and places was revealed to her. Since then, Loreina has traveled along the Puerto Rican beaches talking to the fishermen and collecting their stories in order to adapt them to poetry. In so doing, she usually respects the lyric fisherman's language. Loreina told me that in a way these poems relate "to the principle of energy, for they portray the eternal return of the archetypical fisherman."

At present, Loreina explores the world of the novel and has two in progress. The first, *Yo Helena* (I Helen) is the story of a nymphomaniac and an elaboration of the myth of the beautiful Helena who evolves in the novel along the centuries. This text is based on interviews with a real woman. The second novel, *La panteonera* (The Woman Gravedigger), will try to depict certain psychic phenomena experienced by Loreina in her own house which is located on the grounds of an Indian graveyard.

Survey of Criticism

Most of Loreina's book critiques come from Puerto Rico. The first article on her poetry was published in the Puerto Rican literary magazine *Ventana*.

Especially two critical essays are important to consider. The first one, the prologue written by Ivette López to *Incertidumbre primera*, points out the general and essential trends of Loreina's first poems: themes, motifs, the anguish that prevails in tone throughout the verses, the presence of nature, the anaphoric repetitions and refrains. At the end of the prologue the author emphasizes that in this early stage there is already "an assertion of love as breath of life."

The other important essay is "Portrait of the Poet and Her Works," written by Adelaida Lugo-Guernelli as a prologue to *Del onto*. The author carries out a keen analysis of Loreina's work by reviewing some of the characteristics already pointed out by Ivette López. In addition, she observes that there is a consistent unity and relationship among the trends identified in the three books published at that time. She also recognizes the evolution that is taking place in Loreina's poetry.

Other articles or essays that critique Loreina's texts repeat over and over biographical data and well-known statements. They lack a new, deep, and methodical approach to the critical literary analysis of Loreina's poetry.

There is no doubt that Loreina Santos Silva's poetry reached its prime and lyric maturity with *Motor mutable* and with *Astralba íntima* (in press). Both texts deserve a wide and universal attention from the critics and from the most demanding and well informed Hispanic circles.

Bibliography

WORKS BY SANTOS SILVA

Incertidumbre primera. San Juan, P.R.: Ediciones Juan Ponce de León, 1973.
Rikelme. Río Piedras, P.R.: Editorial Edil, Inc., 1974.
Del onto. San Juan, P.R.: Instituto de Cultura Puertorriqueña, 1978.
Mi ría. Lugo, P.R.: Editorial Alvarellos, 1981.
Vocero del mar. Mayagüez, P.R.: Imprenta Vélez, 1982.

WORKS ABOUT SANTOS SILVA

Bliss, Peggy Ann. "Santos Silva and the Crusade for Women in Art." *Portfolio* October
    21, 1980: 8.
"Intelectual puertorriqueña habla sobre el papel de la mujer en la sociedad." *El Nacional
    de !Ahora!* October 6, 1983: 24.
López, Ivette. "Prólogo" to *Incertidumbre primera,* San Juan, P.R.: Institute de Cultura
    Puertorriqueña, 1978.
Lugo-Guernelli, Adelaida. "Semblanza de la poeta y sus obras," prologue to Santos
    Silva, Lorreina. *Del onto.*
Martínez Capó, Juan. Book review on *Vocero del mar. El Mundo* September 19, 1982.
Valenzuela, Atala. "Loreina Santos Silva, poetisa de Puerto Rico." *Prensa Libre* (Gua-
    temala), April 9, 1983: 31.

RIMA DE VALLBONA

SILÉN, IVÁN (1944–   ). Iván Silén is an outstanding figure in Puerto Rican
poetry, both in Puerto Rico and in the continental United States, where he has
resided for many years. His work includes not only poetry, but also narrative
and essays. He has also been active as an editor, publishing two anthologies of
poetry, and as a director of two publishing houses: Lugar sin límites and El libro
viaje.

Biography

Only a few biographical data are available about Silén (he has refused to
collaborate with the present project), mostly gleaned from back covers of his
books, as well as from prologues to them.

He was born in San Juan, Puerto Rico, in 1944 and was raised in a religious
(Protestant) household and even attended seminary. Later on, religious motifs
and vocabulary would play a very important role in his poetry. He has also
pursued university studies.

He has lived in Puerto Rico, New York, and Paris and has worked as a
dishwasher, book seller, social worker, workshop leader, and professor. In New
York, Silén has seen himself in the leadership of Hispanic writers born abroad,
as a leader of the blood poets (La nueva sangre), as an editor of magazines,
anthologies, and a publishing house. He drew early attention to Puerto Rican
literature in the city through his collaboration with Alfredo Matilla Rivas on *The*

Puerto Rican Poets/Los poetas puertorriqueños (1972), but his anthology, *Los paraguas amarillos* (1983, The Yellow Umbrellas), represents clearly his position against the so-called "newyorican" poets, while he broadens the spectrum of his interest by including other than Puerto Rican poets, through criteria more focused on ideological or stylistic positions. Currently, he is also the editor of *Caronte*.

Other artistic activities include painting. As a painter, he uses the pseudonym 'Nelis,' a transposition of his last name. In his painting we find the same subjects and figures as in his poems, as can clearly be seen in the following titles: "Why have you forsaken me?" "Suicide or homage to Chagall," and "La Maga." His style has been called "neoprimitivist" and associated with nihilism. Another interesting feature of his complex personality is his interest in philosophy, which can be readily seen in his poetics as well as in his aesthetics.

But if data about his actual life are rare, there is another biography, the inner one, penetrating and configurating his books, through which the reader can learn about his ever-changing personality: his inner thought wavers from individualistic nihilism to a collectivist anarchism.

Major Themes

Silén's work includes some eight published books, along with others still unpublished, and many poems included in magazines. His is a work of redefinition, re-creation, and reflection on past experiences, ideas, and feelings. Constantly, the same topics and themes repeat themselves from different points of view or attitudes.

Silén's world is not to be understood as a static one, but rather as a permanent questioning of human life and condition. His world is dominated by two main tendencies, never completely separated: one is oriented toward the exterior reality and the other toward the intimate self. Both tendencies frequently intermingle through lyricism, creating poems in which the author is an active observer/interpreter of reality while commenting upon himself.

In relation to formal devices, throughout his work the reader will notice a preference for the surrealistic image, frequently even for the juxtaposition of images not related to each other. Also, the size of the poem increases, tending to be more narrative in quality in the more recent books, although even in the beginning the poem was never short.

In his first book, *Después del suicidio* (1970, After the Suicide), the tendency to intimacy or introspection is still clearly separated from what we could call social poetry. For the latter, Puerto Rican colonial status appears as a schizophrenia in its inhabitants who are divided between the island and the metropolis, between Spanish and English, citizenship and discrimination. The same idea, in the self-exploring mood, deepens by adding the categories of writer and ideologist, schizoid entities in themselves, according to Silén.

Therefore, madness as a topic, as the only possible attitude toward life, becomes a main subject for Silén, together with the concept of suicide, the ultimate culmination of life and somehow the door to another reality, as suggested by the word "después" (after) in the title. Paradoxically, only by living the absurd can man give sense to an already distorted reality. In the personal field, that eventually leads to hallucination; in the social, to revolution, fight, and the violence of sabotage.

Thus, reality is the land of absurdity and falseness, and the poet's task is to denounce it as an inquisitor, because he is the one to propose another reality and language beyond the ORDER (one of his negative leitmotivs) of psychiatrists and of the Establishment. That will also provoke the denial of God's existence from a nihilist agnosticism, 'nihilist' being defined by Iván Silén (in letter to Faythe Turner, July 18, 1984) as a human being who thinks against the prohibition that any kind of order implies.

On the intimate level, this "other reality" becomes apparent in the surrealistic language and images in which the everyday reality is transformed. It is not infrequent, in this book, that the author recalls for this purpose characters or topics from admired writers such as Julio Cortázar (above all), César Vallejo, or Jean-Paul Sartre, filtered through his own personal view. This will become a permanent device in his later work.

The frequency of religious motifs and vocabulary should also be noticed, mainly used as a paraphrase or as an apostrophe to combat or satirize religion, as in the following example: Everything began one afternoon when I was alone / and God arrived drunk / . . . and now I don't have faith / and then you went walking by the word / and by things / and you killed yourself with the window panes. Again, we will find this technique and theme in later books.

Después del suicidio ends with a very symbolic poem entitled "To a being/ that may be dead." The last word of the poem (and therefore of the book) is "Nada" (Nothing), a clear example of his nihilism at that moment.

In 1972 he published *El pájaro loco* (Woody Woodpecker). This work, that contains many of his best poems, opens with a "Small Manifest" in which the author attacks socialist realism while praising lyricism and offering a new alternative denominated "new surrealism," defined as "an automatic creation of violent metaphors in which one tries to express all the socially repressed poetry that exists in the subconscious." Its genuine form would be the monologue and its goal revolution.

The first thing to notice in this book is that the tone has changed and we now find a more defined space, real and concrete, a world of nightmare and marginality: New York City, the poet, active spectator, descends to his underground world as Orpheus (another symbol-leitmotiv) did to Hades.

But again, beyond this reality the poet observes that there is another world, the world of dreams which one can reach through the surreal and oneiric guided by the poet Orpheus.

The poem becomes longer as the distance of our trip progresses. Now "to walk," "to descend," and related concepts are the main clues together with "eyes" and other words expressing vision.

Madness is again an important idea (five poems are entitled "Psicosis") as part of reality, together with the relativity of time and space. Also important is the appearance of references to the Literature of Evil and poets like Rimbaud, Baudelaire, and others. Literary references are frequent, including the previously cited as well as Cortázar and a few others. In the second part of the book, predominantly social and revolutionary, the references are to partisan poets, and Silén includes poems on Vietnam, occupied Puerto Rico, and sabotage.

As for the religious motifs, now they are related to the theme of Oedipus (recurrent later on). According to the author, Christ would have an oedipal complex, determining his will to replace God the Father (later, the poet himself will be willing to replace God, as we shall see). Oedipus reappears again in a short story that closes the book, seeming to announce the future importance of this topic.

Finally, it should be taken into account the way the poet uses his verses to attack other poets or to defend himself from their attacks. That will also be present later in a more subtle way.

In *Edipo Rey o La caperucita* (1974, King Oedipus or: Little Red Riding Hood), Silén somehow reverses the myth of Oedipus. Luisa, Pablo's sister, representing the mother, plays a role more active than the passive Iocasta would traditionally play. Luisa is a castrating force that dominates the other characters, trying to annihilate them one after the other. First is Arturo, a homosexual that ends up committing suicide; then is Linda, Luisa's own reflection and Pablo's girlfriend, whom Luisa induces to leave after making her discover herself through LSD. Then, Luisa will eventually try to have incestuous relations with her brother/son, but Pablo manages to kill his sister/mother, thus liberating himself.

If the psychological meaning becomes evident, the political image derived from it is just as clear. Luisa is the State, the Order, and Imperialism, trying to get hold of the rest of the characters' minds. Hence, there is only one way to destroy or overcome it: the armed struggle that he has been defending before, since the author proposes an anarchism without mother, country, or gods.

This constitutes a clear evolution in the author's thought and would reinforce the idea of Filí-Melé (the persona's loved one presented in a negative way, the subject of his next book of poetry) as the negative image of Puerto Rico.

Back to *Edipo Rey,* madness and intuition are the psychological bases to understanding the action: madness is the ultimate state of clairvoyance reached by carrying individual tensions to the limit or by using drugs. Thus, Arturo realizes through drugs that what he hates in Luisa is that she is like the negative of Pablo, which leads him to fear castration and leads him to sexual deviancy (a change of roles that liberates him from the burden of having to kill the father).

This is an interesting point, as already noticed, because of its recurrence in *Los poemas de Filí-Melé* (1976, The Poems of Filí-Melé), where we find again this idea of inversion of sexual roles between lovers (curiously enough, using in both books the symbols of Dante and Beatrice).

Arturo, then, realizes that his only outlet is suicide (''the last door,'' in the book), i.e., the transit to another reality.

Linda, too, understands her life through drugs, discovering the lie of her mother selling her body to keep her social position. Through a lyric delirium she acquires clairvoyance and realizes her role as castrating woman (hence her function as a reflection of Luisa). Therefore, Luisa, the Establishment, conquers everyone's mind but her own son's, who would have to kill her, something the reader will observe again in a later book, *El llanto de las ninfómanas/The Wail of the Nymphomaniacs* (1981).

Los poemas de Filí-Melé, published in 1976, has deserved the attention of many critics because of its quality as well as its complexity. Up to a certain point, this book was preceded by the poem ''La luna ofendida'' (The Offended Moon), included in *The Puerto Rican Poets,* but the depth of the book is not evident from the poem in the anthology.

The form of *Filí-Melé* is the culmination of Silén's attempt to bring prose and poetry together. That is why previous references to Juan Ramón Jiménez were not gratuitous. Now, some parts of the book are written in verse, while others are in poetic prose.

An obsession in this new book would be overcoming dichotomies: the poet tries to become one with the loved, the distance between prose and poetry is meant to be suppressed, as already noticed, and the same works for life and death, as well as other mutually opposing ideas.

Although divided into different poems, one has the impression of cantos of a long poem rather than separate poems, when reading the book. Again, there is an attempt to reach the ultimate unity through schizoid patterns. For instance, the mirror will not only reflect the poet, creating thus a double reality, but will also constitute the door (important image again) to Filí-Melé's room. (Does this not only imply that Filí-Melé is nothing but the inverted projection of himself, explaining the inversion of roles?)

On the other hand, Filí-Melé represents Puerto Rico; the only possibility of achieving unity is through destruction and death, which in Silén's personal code means regeneration, new reality.

The book has a high lyric quality with moments of intense beauty and very accurate images, although he tends to overuse nonconnected images.

It was not until 1981 that he published his next book, the first in a bilingual presentation contrasting with the Spanish of the previous books.

El llanto de las ninfómanas/The Wail of the Nymphomaniacs is a collection of three essays that, in spite of its brevity, deserves special attention because it is the first published excerpt of his thought.

In the first essay, which gives its name to the book, Silén goes back to the theme of Oedipus, now from the point of view of the reality of writing, making systematic what in previous books was still being gestated. Here ideology is cast as a ''scandalized mother'' in reaction to the possibility of her son (the writer) flirting with her. The text itself, this way, becomes incest and only by destroying itself (suicide) will it eventually destroy the mother. For Iván Silén this is the only way to defeat the bourgeois order. In terms of literature, that means that both prose and essays must be destroyed (he usually refers to his essays as anti-essays) to create a space for poetry.

But the mother, in her repressive role, becomes also the State, establishing censorship. As a result, the poet/child learns disobedience, i.e., rebellion against the violence of the Establishment. This is, then, the same idea we saw earlier in *Edipo Rey*.

The first essay also deals with madness as related to dreams, because in madness, dreams and reality are the same and therefore there is no gap between the two realities but a synthesis free of contradiction.

The second essay, "La novia es un delito" (The Bride Is a Delinquency), starts from the ideas of Jacques Derrida and deals, among other things, with intertextuality, seen as creation, active imagination, rather than as a robbery authorized by the academies.

The language in this essay, as in the whole book, is almost cryptic, due to the abundance of paradoxes and antitheses, and serves the discussion of the cultural and economic domination imposed on Puerto Rico by the United States after its war with Spain in 1898.

Considering this situation, peace is not possible with the oppressor if one wants to keep internal peace with oneself, and thus the literary text should be the violence able to reject the caricature of Puerto Rico that the oppressor is trying to create by using folkloric stereotypes. Then, translating the new text into English would be like spitting in his face.

The reader of the new and revolutionary (both in form and content) essay must get involved in violence and rebel against writing as a prohibition. Reader and translator are the ones to give eventual meaning to the text.

The last essay, "La experiencia irreductible" (The Irreductible Experience), is another attack on ideology in which the author proposes deicide, i.e., ideicide, since the ideology is a god. The means will not be a text addressed to the masses, but rather a secret one, changing hands as forbidden. The text should not offer any ideology (Silén will insist on that in another essay written in the summer of 1986), but be a useless good attacking from the irreductible experience, i.e., the trauma of being, what would preserve the fury of the literary work.

Also in 1981 appears *El miedo del pantócrata* (The Pantocrator's Fear), another book of poems in which the tendency toward a longer poem is confirmed. Images are carried to the limit and so are introspection and egotism, even leading, in the poem "El príncipe" (The Prince), to identification of the poet with God, as earlier mentioned.

After this book, Silén edited an anthology of Hispanic poets in New York: *Los paraguas amarillos: los poetas latinos en Nueva York* (1983), in which, apart from a prologue, he has included nine of his own poems. In these poems there are important recurrent themes of his poetry, like madness and suicide in the field of irreality (now he thinks that men are just passengers of Death in reality), the oedipal motif (in a poem about the persona's mother's death), and sex.

It is also important to point to the increasing influence of César Vallejo, as well as Silén's interest in the poets of evil, like Rimbaud. His philosophical position is still mainly nihilistic, up to the point of confessing his wish of not being, of never having passed through life.

He has recently also published an experimental novel, *La biografía* (1984, The Biography), in which, with eighteen chapters and an epilogue, he poses the dilemma of the narrator creating a new reality that, in its turn, creates the narrator. Again, the problem of the relationship between creator (writer) and his work becomes one of the main preoccupations. Somehow, this novel represents a reflection on his main themes and obsessions from the perspective of a new way of dealing with the structure of the novel. The real author and implicit author are at the same time characters of the narrator, who is, in his turn, a schizoid entity divided into Julio, the autobiographer, and the narrator himself, representing respectively a homosexual and a male heterosexual side. This game of mirrors has as a goal the destruction of the novel, the suicide of this literary form, achieved in the plot by the suicide of Julio, which is the last step in the tradition of the dialectics of author/creation as cultivated by Unamuno and especially as continued by Borges, whose influence on Silén is increasing. Basically, what it poses is the dilemma of the creator realizing at the end of his life that he has somehow been a creation of someone else.

The literary criticism included in this work is also interesting. It seems as if Silén wanted to evaluate the literary panorama of the Hispanic writers in New York.

Finally, the idea of the essay as an intimate diary of its author is something to be added to Silén's theory of the essay.

In 1986, in an unpublished essay sent to Nicolás Kanellos and entitled "Contra el programa político del ser" (Against the Political Program of Being), Silén has slightly changed his ideological position, moving to an open anarchism (something he denied in the cited letter to Faythe Turner in 1984) and elaborating the idea of the need to overcome the dialectics of oppressor/oppressed in order to free oneself and to avoid the failure of revolutions like the Russian Revolution of 1917. This change is the result of an increasing criticism of Hegelian Marxism, but the most important idea to be noticed in this essay is the absolute abandonment of nihilism.

It is still early to predict how this change is going to affect his future work, but it does show a mind in constant evolution (not always free of internal contradictions) and questioning of the basic principles of life.

In 1986 *Nietzsche o la dama de las ratas* (Nietzsche or the Lady of Rats) also appeared. The whole book is a discussion of Nietzsche's philosophy, as well as an explanation of Silén's own works and ideas. The language is easier than in previous essays, and important themes like the non-being, the exile, the suicide, etc., are discussed again.

The most important novelty is the idea of the Pariah, proposed as the man of non-being, insert in absurdity. The Pariah reunites for the first time (according to Silén) the poet and the philosopher, struggling against domination (that is, the spoliation that provokes the non-being) from nihilism and inconscience (surrealism and oxymoron being the "weapons" of nihilism, already noticed in *El llanto de las ninfómanas*). Unlike Nietzsche's creations (Zarathustra), the Pariah is a reality, that of an oppressed people (the Puerto Rican people).

In its aim, this book attempts to overcome Nietzsche's implicit imperialism, and the same way that the German philosopher could say "God is dead," Silén's book ends up stating "Nietzsche is dead."

Survey of Criticism

There are still few articles dealing with Iván Silén's works. However, his poetry has been analyzed in such important magazines as *Revista Chicano-Riqueña, Insula,* and *Revista del Instituto de Estudios Puertorriqueños del Brooklyn College*. Besides these, two interesting prologues have appeared preceding *Después del suicidio* and *Edipo Rey*.

The first of the two prologues, by Alfredo Matilla Rivas, contains a good definition of Silén as a revolutionary poet, along with the analysis of his role as interpreter of reality. This prologue also deals with some of Silén's major themes (madness, suicide, paranoia, religious motives) and aesthetic procedures (new language, images). Finally, Matilla summarizes the poet's nihilistic existential attitude.

Rosario *Ferré's prologue to *Edipo Rey* is a long psychological approach to the book from the oedipal cultural tradition, as well as from recent literary history. For Ferré, two basic points of reference are needed to approach the book: the concept of the poet as a visionary (as in Rilke) and of salvation through madness (as in Rimbaud) and the interpretations of the folk tale "Little Red Riding Hood" by Erich Fromm and Marc Soriano. The poem, then, is a subversion of the myth of Oedipus and Iocasta with a deep eroticism, in which Iocasta is cast as the Puerto Rican mother (who, according to this interpreter, supplants culturally the father's role while keeping her own). Ferré also interprets the book as a piece of baroque music that constantly repeats two basic themes: to kill the mother and to devour the child. Finally, she criticizes the lack of individualization of the characters, but she does not consider that as negative in a book of poetry, not fiction.

Alfredo Matilla Rivas is also the author of an article, "The Broken English Dream," in which Silén's work is placed in the context of Puerto Rican poetry in New York. Although he only dedicates two paragraphs to Silén, he points out interesting ideas about the author. One of them is that of his poetry as narrative (which, even if Matilla does not consider it, would explain the author's tendency toward the fusion of prose and poetry). Matilla also identifies the two basic orientations of Silén: the compromise and the introspection, discovering in Breton and Trotsky two influences of his worldview. He analyzes the language as an echo of the one they speak on the streets, modified by the experimentation of a cultivated poet.

An article by Dionisio Cañas, "La poesía de Iván Silén o el delirio de la realidad," is a review of both published and unpublished works, with a special focus on *Los poemas de Filí-Melé*. Cañas considers Silén as the artist on the path to rediscovery of the American (in a broad sense) lost values through the symbolic and allegorical interpretations of the myth of Oedipus—the critic considers *Edipo Rey* as an allegory of the different colonizations of Puerto Rico— or the cosmic American woman in *Filí-Melé*. Cañas' analysis of this last book is very useful with regard to the symbols of the moon and moon-influenced animals, interpreted from the point of view of Tarot cards. Cañas also considers Silén's style as a nonrefrained one that tries to translate reality into poetry through the brilliant metaphoric images.

Filí-Melé is also the focus of Alfredo Villanueva-Collado, who compares Silén's and *Palés Matos's elaboration of a feminist theme. After a splendid discussion of the connotations of the name Filí-Melé, Villanueva examines the way both poets deal with the image of woman: the conclusion is that both of them, unconciously, use traditional stereotypes somehow derogatory to women, because of their origin in the male-dominated world. In the case of Silén, Villanueva thinks that the political censure of Puerto Rico (Filí-Melé), in its inability to live up to the expectations of its poets, provokes, through the rejection of such a country, this implicit condemnation of woman. Of particular value is also the distinction between Silén's images in the postsymbolism era and Palés Matos's still in the romantic tradition.

In his Ph.D. thesis, Rubén González discusses several important points on Silén's works. Apart from placing him in a tradition (parasurrealism, the poets of evil, certain Puerto Rican poetry) and analyzing several of his artistic techniques (including an interesting remark on the length of the poem), González carefully considers the process that brings Silén from an enthusiastic social poet to a desperate disillusionist with a tendency to hidden violence and a desire to shock the reader as some writers like Georges Bataille did. Also important is the censure of the confusion derived from linguistic excess, sometimes provoked by the extension of the poem.

Finally, *La generación de escritores de 1970 en Puerto Rico*, by Juan Angel Silén, gives the reader an idea of the context in which Iván Silén's poetry is to be placed. At the same time, this book also provides accurate, although brief, ideas on main themes and ideas on the main literary tendencies in Puerto Rico during those years.

Besides these critical approaches, several reviews of his work as editor of anthologies may be consulted by the reader, as shown in the bibliography.

Bibliography

WORKS BY SILÉN

In Books

Después del suicidio. Santo Domingo: El Caribe, 1970.
El pájaro loco. San Juan: Ediciones Librería Internacional, 1972.
Edipo Rey o La caperucita. Poema a cuatro voces. Montevideo: Arca, 1974.
Los poemas de Filí-Melé. New York: El libro viaje, 1976.
El llanto de las ninfómanas/The Wail of the Nymphomaniacs. New York: El libro viaje, 1981.
El miedo del pantócrata. n.p. 1981. (Unavailable).
La biografía. Iztapalapa: Editorial Villicaña, 1984.
Nietzsche o la dama de las ratas. Iztapalapa: Editorial Villicaña, 1986.

In Anthologies

Marzan, Julio, ed. *Inventing a Word: An Anthology of Twentieth-Century Puerto Rican Poetry*. New York: Columbia University Press, The Center for Inter-American Relations, 1980. Poems included: "A Teresa" and "Por qué no puedo escribir un poema sobre Lares."
Matilla, Alfredo Rivas, and Iván Silén, eds. *The Puerto Rican Poets/ Los poetas puertorriqueños*. New York: Bantam Books, 1972. Poems included: "Cristo–1970," "El pájaro loco," "Es la una y cuarto," and "La luna ofendida."
Rosario Quiles, Luis Antonio, ed. *Poesía nueva puertorriqueña*. San Juan: Editorial Edil, 1971. Poems included: "A un ser que tal vez ha muerto," "Por qué no puedo escribir un poema sobre Lares," and "Usted no sabe."
Silén, Iván, ed. *Los paraguas amarillos: Los poetas latinos en Nueva York*. New York: Bilingual Press/Ediciones del Norte, 1983. Poems included: "La araña contra Dios," "La máscara," "No soporto la lucidez," "Prefacio para un encuentro con la muerte," "¿Qué se hace después del grito?" "(*)Qué tarde nos trajeron para nada!" "¿Quién mató a la madre?" "Soy Artaud," and "Tengo deseos."

In Magazines

"El conde de las greñas." *Escolios* 2, 1–2 (May-November 1977): 54–56.
"El mar en ruina y la noche también en ruina." *Sin Nombre* 6,4 (April-June 1976): 71–72.
"El príncipe." *Revista Chicano-Riqueña* 7,2 (Spring 1979): 17–19.
"Extranjera II." *Revista Chicano-Riqueña* 8,2 (Spring 1980): 16–18.
"La canción del exilio." *Casa de las Américas* 16,96 (May-June 1976): 103–11.
"La extranjera." *Sin Nombre* 8,3 (October-December 1977): 66.
"San Miguelito." *Revista del Instituto de Estudios Puertorriqueños del Brooklyn College* 1,1 (Spring 1971): 68–69.
"Un título de ataud." *Palabras y papel* 3,1 (January-March 1983).
"Yo he gritado VIVA PUERTO RICO LIBRE." *La nueva sangre* 2,8 (Fall 1969): 13–14.
He has also published in *Mester, Versiones, Norte, El Rehilete, Zona: Carga y Descarga, Lugar sin límites,* and *Caronte*.

WORKS ABOUT SILÉN

Arrigoitia, Luis de. "La poesía lírica puertorriqueña." *Insula* 31:256–257 (1976): 11–12.

Cañas, Dionisio. "La poesía de Iván Silén o el delirio de la realidad." *Insula* 33:380–381 (1978): 14.

Ferré, Rosario. "Prólogo." *Edipo Rey o La caperucita. Poema de cuatro voces,* by Iván Silén. Montevideo: Arca, 1974.

González, Rubén. "Quince años de poesía puertorriqueña: 1960–1975." Ph.D. thesis, University of Florida, 1981.

Kanellos, Nicolás. Review of *The Puerto Rican Poets/Los poetas puertorriqueños,* Alfredo Matilla Rivas and Iván Silén, eds. *Books Abroad* (January 1974): 107–8.

Matilla Rivas, Alfredo. "Prólogo." *Después del suicidio,* by Iván Silén. Santo Domingo: El Caribe, 1970.

———. "The Broken English Dream: poesía puertorriqueña en Nueva York." *Revista del Instituto de Estudios Puertorriqueños del Brooklyn College* 1,1 (Spring 1971): 61–67.

Mosier, Patricia. Review of *Los paraguas amarillos: los poetas latinos en Nueva York,* Iván Silén, ed. *Chasqui* 14, 2–3 (February 1985): 63–64.

Quackenbush, C. Howard. Review of *Los paraguas amarillos: Los poetas latinos en Nueva York,* Iván Silén, ed. *Chasqui* 14,1 (November 1984): 157–159.

Roses, Lorraine E. Review of *Los paraguas amarillos: Los poetas latinos en Nueva York,* Iván Silén, ed. *The Americas Review* 14,1 (Spring 1986): 87–88.

Silén, Juan Angel. *La generación de escritores de 1970 en Puerto Rico (1950–1976).* Río Piedras: Editorial Cultural, Inc., 1977.

Villanueva-Collado, Alfredo. "Filí-Melé: Símbolo y mujer en la poesía de Luis Palés Matos e Iván Silén." *Revista Chicano-Riqueña* 10,4 (Fall 1982): 47–54.

MANUEL MARTÍN-RODRÍGUEZ

SOTO, PEDRO JUAN (1928–   ). The task of describing the feelings or emotions of a particular group of people by means of literary characterization is a difficult one. The job, however, becomes relatively less complicated when the group described is intimately known by the author. Such is the case of the Puerto Rican writer, Pedro Juan Soto, whose works embody the dramatic and poignant duality of the Puerto Rican people living on the island and on the mainland.

Biography

The son of Juan Soto and Elena Suárez, Pedro Juan Soto was born on July 11, 1928, in Cataño, a Puerto Rican town across from San Juan Bay, within sight of the ancient Spanish fortress of El Morro.

After completing his elementary and secondary education in Cataño and Bayamón, Pedro Juan Soto moved to New York City at the age of eighteen to study medicine. The city, however, became his "laboratory" for observing the life of his fellow Puerto Ricans and he quickly abandoned his medical studies in favor of a literary career. In 1950, Soto received his bachelor of arts degree in English from the University of Long Island.

The aspiring writer's quest was briefly interrupted when he was drafted by the United States Army where he served for one year. After his army discharge, Pedro Juan Soto married Rosiña Arriví and wrote his first novel, "Los perros anónimos," based on the experiences of the Puerto Rican soldiers in the Korean War. Instead of publishing his novel, Soto enrolled at Columbia University, where he obtained his master of arts degree in 1953.

Upon his graduation from Columbia, Pedro Juan continued writing while working as a theater usher, archivist, part-time mailman, busboy, and company courier until he finally obtained a full-time job as a literary correspondent for the popular Spanish-language magazine, *Visión*.

A keen observer, Pedro Juan Soto was aware of the harsh life of his fellow Puerto Rican immigrants in New York City and in late 1953 wrote his first short story "Garabatos," the story of a struggling Puerto Rican artist living with his nagging wife under the most deplorable conditions in a New York City slum. "Garabatos" was followed by another short story, "Los inocentes" (1954), which vividly depicts the life of Pipe, a mentally retarded thirty-year-old Puerto Rican whose only world is the pigeons on the building across the street from his tenement's room. Soto's powerful portrait of Pipe became a contributing factor when the story was awarded Best Prize by the prestigious Ateneo de Puerto Rico in 1954.

The following year, Soto returned to his native Puerto Rico and went to work as an editor for the Division of Publications of the Puerto Rican Department of Education. While his editorial duties were demanding, Soto never abandoned writing, and his obsession with describing Puerto Rican life in New York City led to his first play, *El huésped* (The Boarder). In spite of its excessive realism, the play was the recipient of the Ateneo's prize for best experimental theater production in 1955.

Propelled by his achievements, Soto published *Spiks* (1956), a collection of seven short stories and six one-page vignettes known as *Miniaturas* (Miniatures) depicting the plight of the Puerto Rican immigrants in the hostile environment of New York City. Such was the impact of *Spiks* that it still remains the best collection of short stories ever written about the saga of the Puerto Rican exodus in New York.

Two years after the publication of *Spiks,* there appeared *Usmaíl* (1958), Soto's first novel dealing with the life of Usmaíl, a young Puerto Rican mulatto living in Vieques, an island off the coast of Puerto Rico under occupation by the American navy.

Usmaíl received favorable reviews from Puerto Rican and Latin American critics and that reception inspired Soto to publish another novel dealing with the life of another Puerto Rican adolescent. *Ardiente suelo, fría estación* (1961, Burning Soil, Cold Season) narrates the life of Eduardo, a Puerto Rican teenager from New York City, and his fruitless search for identity.

After eight years of literary inactivity, Pedro Juan Soto published two novels consecutively, *El francotirador* (1969, The Sniper) and *Temporada de duendes*

(1970 Ghosts' Season). *El francotirador,* Soto's most complex novel, offers a portrait of life in Puerto Rico and Cuba through the use of multiple juxtapositions while *Temporada de duendes* narrates the humorous yet tragic story of Baldomero, a Puerto Rican rascal whose main goal in life is that of escaping reality.

Following the publication of these two novels, Pedro Juan Soto devoted himself to the completion of his doctoral studies in literature and in 1976 was awarded a doctoral degree from the University of Toulouse, France.

While Soto was working on a new novel, tragedy struck his family in 1978 when his son, Roberto, a nationalist sympathizer, was ambushed and killed by Puerto Rican police. The author sought justice and after seven years of lengthy struggle the alleged culprits were finally brought to stand trial.

In 1982, Soto published his highly experimental novel, *Un oscuro pueblo sonriente* (A Dark Smiling People), dealing with the frivolous life-style of a group of Americans living in Puerto Rico. The novel was an instant success and was awarded the prestigious Casa de las Americas prize for best novel published by a Latin American writer in 1982.

Pedro Juan Soto continues to live in Puerto Rico, where he teaches literature at the University of Puerto Rico. Currently, he is finishing a novel about his son, Roberto, and is still active in bringing the dream of independence to his beloved Puerto Rico.

Major Themes

As one of the outstanding members of the Generation of 1940, Pedro Juan Soto's principal goal in all of his literary production is the portrayal of the Puerto Rican reality or "duality" as he labels it. Therefore, themes such as the Puerto Rican struggle against American imperialism, the extinction of the Puerto Rican way of life through American economic and cultural domination of the island, and the alienation and misery of his fellow Puerto Ricans living in the hostile environment of New York City are frequently found in his works.

The publication of *Spiks* consecrated Soto as one of the most powerful writers of the Generation of 1940. The characters in this volume of short stories are either adolescents surrounded by a world of segregation, violence, and hate or women trying to fight the forces that dictate their role in society. While the majority of these characters fail in their struggle, they nevertheless earn the reader's sympathy and admiration. Thus, there is Pipe, the pathetically retarded character in "Los inocentes," whose sole ambition in life is to be free like his only friends the pigeons; Altagracia, the abandoned unwed mother in "Ausencia," who desperately turns to spiritualism in an effort to find her lost lover; Puruco, the adolescent protagonist of "Campeones," who discharges his anger on an innocent victim after his machismo is ridiculed in a pool match with barrio gangleader, Gavilán. While a sense of hopelessness prevails in all of the stories, Pedro Juan Soto has managed to create memorable characters whose common denominator is that of surviving in a hostile world.

While characterization is a powerful component of *Spiks,* language is just as important. Seldom has an author been able to convey the language of the downtrodden so effectively as Pedro Juan Soto does in this book. In all of his stories and *Miniaturas,* Soto rejects the linguistic puritanism of other Spanish-speaking writers in favor of four-letter words, street slang, hybrid creations and transcriptions of "Puerto Rican Spanish." Thus, his characters, through the use of language, revolt against prejudice and discrimination as exemplified in the speech of the impoverished street vendor of "Bayaminiña" (Girl from Bayamón). When harassed by a bigoted policeman who threatens to fine him for not having a health permit to sell his pastries, the nameless protagonist, frustrated and humiliated, smashes his cart and cries "Don't gimme no fine, Gimme a job, saramambich, gimme a job." Through the use of similar phrases, Pedro Juan Soto illustrates the plight of the Puerto Ricans living in a cauldron of prejudice and hate. Indeed, language is an important component of *Spiks.*

Usmaíl, Soto's first attempt at the novel, narrates the tragic story of Usmaíl, an illegitimate Puerto Rican mulatto living in the island of Vieques. After years of mistreatment at the hands of American sailors, Usmaíl is sentenced to prison for killing an American sailor in a fight over a prostitute named Meche. The novel finishes with Usmaíl proudly affirming his Puerto Rican identity at the end of his trial.

Usmaíl, as a literary piece of fiction, is much more than a portrait of a troubled adolescent, for it represents the collective struggle and heroic resistance of the poor inhabitants of Vieques who are forcefully compelled to surrender their property in order to accommodate the Mosquito naval base on that island. The inhabitants, like Usmaíl, resist, only to collapse in the face of the overpowering American presence. In the end, however, they become heroes in the eyes of the reader, for they try to defend that which rightfully belongs to them.

As in *Spiks,* the strength of *Usmaíl* rests in its language deployment. The language used by Soto is simple, like his characters, but it is effective, and his short, incisive phrases contribute to arouse the reader's interest in the sociopolitical dimensions of the Puerto Rican duality.

Soto's second novel, *Ardiente suelo, fría estación,* stresses the theme of a Puerto Rican youth searching for identity. In the novel, Eduardo, a Puerto Rican teenager who lives in New York, decides to return to Puerto Rico to find his roots. Once on the island, however, he is rejected by the Puerto Ricans and cannot adapt himself to life on the island. The novel ends with Eduardo's bitter return to New York.

While *Ardiente suelo, fría estación* makes for interesting reading, it is, without a doubt, Soto's weakest piece of fiction. Its linear plot, excessive sentimentalism, and Eduardo's lame characterization detract from the overall quality of the novel.

El francotirador, considered by many as Soto's finest novel, does not deal with a Puerto Rican protagonist but rather with the life of Tomás Saldivia, a Cuban expatriate novelist teaching at the University of Puerto Rico. Saldivia, however, is not capable of coping with the emptiness and loneliness that permeate his life, and he fantasizes his return to Cuba by creating an imaginary novel. In the end, fantasy becomes reality when Saldivia returns to Cuba as a member of an anti-Castro commando group. Saldivia, though, is captured and in an act of desperation takes away a weapon from one of his captors, shoots him, and then commits suicide.

Technically, *El francotirador* is characterized by a strong dose of experimentation and linguistic maneuverings. Time, for example, becomes distorted and there is no dividing line between present and future. In addition, all the chapters are juxtaposed, with the odd-numbered ones taking place in Cuba while the even-numbered ones take place in Puerto Rico.

Although *El francotirador* offers a clear view of the Puerto Rican dilemma, the chapters concerning life in revolutionary Cuba are full of historical inaccuracies and are more reminiscent of revolutionary propaganda than of literary creativity. In spite of this shortcoming, the novel is Soto's most noteworthy contribution to the Latin American novelistic boom of the 1960s and 1970s.

In *Temporada de duendes,* Soto's most humorous novel, a cinematographic technique is used to narrate the life of Baldomero, a twentieth-century Puerto Rican Don Pablos who tries to escape reality by tricking everyone he meets; yet, at the end, reality catches up with him and Baldomero commits suicide. *Temporada de duendes,* though uneven in some aspects, is a magnificent portrait of man's inability to cope with those forces that surround him.

Pedro Juan Soto's latest novel, the award-winning *Un oscuro pueblo sonriente,* introduces something new to his repertoire. The protagonists no longer are Puerto Ricans searching for identity or escaping reality, but rather a group of Americans living in Puerto Rico. In this highly sophisticated, elaborate, and complex novel which lacks a formal plot, a collage technique is employed to illustrate how American influences have corrupted the Puerto Rican way of life in the island. The protagonists' lives are reminiscent of a merry-go-round, and chaos seems to be prevalent throughout the novel. This seemingly "crazy" novel, however, gives way to serious reflections on the part of the reader, for Soto's message is a clear one: life in American-occupied Puerto Rico is an empty one.

Pedro Juan Soto is a powerful writer and all of his works have contributed to a better understanding of the Puerto Rican people in their struggle for identity, dignity, and self-determination.

Survey of Criticism

There is no dearth of literary criticism with a writer of the caliber of Pedro Juan Soto. One of the best works concerning Pedro Juan Soto as a writer is René *Marqués's *Cuentos puertorriqueños de hoy* (1959). Though outdated, the study provides valuable insights into Soto's technique as a writer and an interesting interview with Pedro Juan. Concha Meléndez, *El arte del cuento en Puerto Rico* (1961), and Lilian Quiles de la Luz, *El cuento en la literatura puertorriqueña* (1968), offer valid interpretations of Soto's *Spiks,* while Jorge Febles's "'Campeones,' de Pedro Juan Soto y el ambiente corrosivo del Harlem Hispano''

(1974, Champions, about Pedro Juan Soto and the corrosive environment of Spanish Harlem) is a most interesting study of environmental influences on Pedro Juan Soto.

Soto's role as a major contributor to the Puerto Rican novel is partly examined in Asela Rodríguez Aseda's article "La trayectoria de la novelística puertorriqueña contemporánea" (1976, The trajectory of the contemporary Puerto Rican novel). In addition, Soto's innovative techniques are the subject of two excellent studies by Phyllis Zatlin Boring: "Escape from Reality in the Fiction of Pedro Juan Soto" (1972) and *"Usmaíl:* The Puerto Rican Joe Christmas" (1973). Finally, the two most outstanding studies concerning *El francotirador* are found in José Luis Martín's "La yuxtaposición tempoespacial en *El francotirador* de Pedro Juan Soto" (1972) and in Seymour Menton's classic, *Prose Fiction of the Cuban Revolution* (1975).

Though the above cited critics have made excellent contributions in defining the works of Pedro Juan Soto, one still must bear the Puerto Rican author's definition regarding a literary work, for he once said: "It is impossible to define a literary work, one doesn't define it, one feels it." Those who have read his works indeed agree with his statement.

Bibliography

WORKS BY SOTO

Spiks. México: Los presentes, 1956.
Usmaíl. Río Piedras: Editorial Cultural, 1958.
Ardiente suelo, fría estación. México: Universidad Veracruzana, 1961.
El francotirador. México: Joaquín Mortiz, 1969.
Temporada de duendes. México: Editorial Diógenes, 1970.
Un oscuro pueblo sonriente. La Habana: Casa de las Américas, 1982.

WORKS ABOUT SOTO

Febles, Jorge. "'Campeones' de Pedro Juan Soto y el ambiente corrosivo del Harlem Hispano." *Revista Chicano-Riqueña* 2 (Primavera 1974): 41–49.
Marqués, René. *Cuentos puertorriqueños de hoy* Río Piedras: Editorial Cultural, 1959.
Martín, José Luis. "La yuxtaposición tempoespacial en *El francotirador* de Pedro Juan Soto." *Nueva Narrativa Hispano Americana* 2 (Septiembre 1972): 187–94.
Meléndez, Concha. *El arte del cuento en Puerto Rico*. New York: Las Américas Publishing Co., 1961.
Menton, Seymour. *Prose Fiction of the Cuban Revolution*. Austin: University of Texas Press, 1975.
Quiles de la Luz, Lilian. *El cuento en la literatura puertorriqueña*. Río Piedras: Editorial de la Universidad de Puerto Rico, 1968.
Rodríguez Aseda, Asela. "La trayectoria de la novelística puertorriqueña contemporánea." 1976.
Zatlin Boring, Phyllis. "Escape from Reality in the Fiction of Pedro Juan Soto." *Papers in Languages and Literature* 8 (1972): 287–96.

————. "*Usmaíl:* The Puerto Rican Joe Christmas." *College Language Association Journal* 16 (1973): 324–33.

JOSÉ B. FERNÁNDEZ

SOTO VÉLEZ, CLEMENTE (1905–   ). One of the most significant of contemporary Puerto Rican writers, yet presently little-known outside the Puerto Rican community, is Clemente Soto Vélez. His work has been important as a political statement and he personally has been an important literary organizer in Puerto Rico.

Biography

Born in Lares, Puerto Rico, in 1905, Soto Vélez has embodied the spirit of that town, known for the famous Grito de Lares, the rebellion in 1868 against Spanish colonial power. Though he received a minimum of formal education, he moved to the capital at age twenty-two where he worked as a journalist and editor at the newspaper *El Tiempo*. In 1928 he and Alfredo Margenat formed a literary group, calling it "El Hospital de los Sensitivos" (The Hospital of the Attuned). He continued to publish poems under his name and that of the group until, in 1929, another young poet, Graciany Miranda Archilla, moved to San Juan. These three young poets—Soto Vélez, Margenat, and Miranda Archilla—and others formed the literary group "El Atalaya de los Dioses," the "Watchtower of the Gods." Soto Vélez and the other *atalayistas* went on the poetic offensive and soon were publishing their iconoclastic verses in many of the major newspapers and magazines of the island. They caused considerable controversy, attracting a large number of supporters as well as creating considerable opposition. Their poetry and several *manifiestos* spoke of the burying of the old to make way for the new. But while many of the Atalayistas remained in the area of the intellectual vanguard, some of them, including Soto Vélez, and other young Puerto Ricans such as Juan Antonio *Corretjer and Pedro Albizu Campos, became more radicalized. Their visions of independence, freedom for the Puerto Rican spirit, and a break with the colonial past were translated into political action, and a poetic call to arms soon became a political call to arms. In 1936, Soto Vélez and other Nationalist leaders were indicted by a U.S. grand jury on charges of conspiring to overthrow the government of the United States by force and organizing to incite violence. Soto Vélez and the others were found guilty, and he spent a total of seven years in federal prison. At one point, after five years in prison, Soto Vélez was offered a conditional pardon. He refused to sign the papers, maintaining that he would not recognize the papers or the laws of an "occupying country," that the true prisoners were the prison officials and bureaucrats, and that his path to freedom was through fighting for the independence of Puerto Rico. As a result, Soto Vélez was sentenced to the two additional years that had originally been suspended. He was finally released in 1942.

Because of World War II, Soto Vélez was not permitted to return to Puerto Rico. He moved to New York and joined the Spanish Grocers' Association, a union formed in 1937. He soon became active in local sociopolitical causes and fought to save the Spanish-language newspaper *El Diario*. In 1945 he founded the Puerto Rican Merchants Association, whose purpose was to unite the political, economic, and creative resources of the Puerto Rican community in New York. In 1954, Soto Vélez published his first book of poetry, *Abrazo interno* (Internal Embrace), after years of ''non-literary'' activity. One year later he published *Arboles* (Trees), and in 1959, with the publication of *Caballo de palo* (Wooden Horse), Soto Velez had established himself once again fully in the literary field. While his political activities cannot really be separated from his literary life— one reflects the other—it is true that fifteen years passed (1938–1953) from one period of literary production to another.

In 1976 the Instituto de Cultura Puertorriqueña reprinted *Caballo de palo,* and in 1979 they published *La tierra prometida* (1979, The Promised Land). Though Soto Vélez has returned to Puerto Rico on occasion, he maintains his residence in New York City.

Major Themes

Most of the early work of Soto Vélez was published in newspapers and periodicals during the years 1928–1935 and remains to be definitively compiled. Of the approximately forty poems and short prose pieces presently known, the earliest was published in *El Tiempo* on December 22, 1928. Called ''Horas polícromas'' (Polychrome Hours), it is a sonnet signed ''C. Soto Vélez, Hospital de los Sensitivos—San Juan, P.R.'' Modernistic in its themes, it speaks of the ''drowning of the sun in the red silence of its crystal urn.'' This sonnet is followed by other poems in 1929, but now signed ''Atalaya de los dioses,'' suggesting that in that period the transition from ''Hospital de los Sensitivos'' to ''Atalaya de los Dioses'' occurred. This transition is significant because as Atalayismo evolved, so did the definition and actions of the Atalayistas. Modernist themes and influences gave way to the more pressing issues of individual and collective identity, defining one's self and expressing it in both literary and political terms. Thus, Soto Vélez, using his pseudonym ''Archipámpano de Zíntar,'' defines himself through his spatial context: I am the Archipámpano of Zíntar/ the one who converses with continents/ about things and the one who gives life/ the things it needs. This exploration and deification of the Self (Huidobro: ''El poeta es un pequeño dios.'' The poet is a little god to which Soto Vélez responds ''O somos dioses enteros, o no somos nada.'' We are either complete gods or nothing) reaches its maximum expression in Soto Vélez's first book, *Escalio,* (1937 Escalius). Published in 1937 by friends after Soto Vélez was incarcerated, it is a philosophical essay divided into five parts. Its reasoned, balanced dialectical tone is reminiscent of the polemical tracts of the Valdés brothers of the eighteenth century, but it incorporates the theme of political imperialism into its logic, defining it in terms of the process of evolution of the human psyche, the Self:

"Imperialism is the negation of truth; its antidote is the infinite revolution of consciousness." Thus the earlier "I" or "Self" of the 1928–1935 poems evolves and ultimately takes on a political dimension in *Escalio*. The evolution of the Self is the evolution toward freedom, which, politically, is the obverse of imperialism. Soto Vélez, in federal prison at the time of the publication of *Escalio*, had in fact become a demonstration of the very themes about which he had written.

Between 1937 and 1954, Soto Vélez was not active in the literary arena. But in 1954 he published in New York his first book of poetry, *Abrazo interno*, seven poems with themes not too distant from those of *Escalio*, but with the seeds of what would evolve into his unmistakable stylistic recourse, the *dialectical anaphora*. This structure consists of the repetition of a certain word or phrase, followed by slightly varying modifiers. For example, in his poem "Five-Pointed Star" (from *Abrazo interno*), he describes the human hand by repeating the phrase "Hands that . . ." followed by different modifiers. The result is a description of the hand more complete and subtle than possible by an ordinary modifying structure. One year after *Abrazo interno*, Soto Vélez published *Arboles*, a long poem further developing his dialectical anaphora. In it, he uses the anaphorical structures "Those trees . . ." and "These trees . . ." to describe an archetypal Tree-Self. In 1959 *Caballo de palo* was published. This extended poem of eighty-eight pages marks the culmination of the dialectical anaphora style. Whereas his previous poems emphasized the *anaphora*, in *Caballo de palo* the *dialectical* element is brought to the forefront. The structure "Lo conocí . . ." is employed throughout the poem to develop and amplify the main character of the poem, which is the personage "Clemente Soto Vélez." The act of getting to know Clemente Soto Vélez ("Lo conocí") is in fact the act of getting to know himself, of becoming aware of the Self within him, not unlike the themes encountered in *Arboles* and in his earlier works. Yet in *Caballo de palo* the act takes on a dialectical dimension, where the subject (the "I" of "I met him") and the object (the "him") become one and the same entity by the end of the poem. The dialectical evolution of the activity of "conocer," structured by the use of the anaphoric "Lo conocí," makes *Caballo de palo* one of Soto Vélez's strongest works.

The most recently published book of Soto Vélez is *La tierra prometida*. Like *Caballo de palo*, it is a long single poem separated into individual sections. The primary unifying structure here is the phrase "The promised land is / The promised land is not." The poem describes an ideal, or set of principles, which constitute a primordial or original state of the universe: "The promised / land / is where / virginity / loses / its origin / where the immensity / feels / the fragrance of the universal force." But again, Soto Vélez reminds the reader that he is not speaking in ethereal or nonhistorical terms: indeed, his "tierra prometida" is more of an attitude than a place, an attitude that he expresses in such political terms as "ser lares" (being Lares). As mentioned earlier, Lares was the birthplace of Soto Vélez, as well as the symbolic "birthplace" of the Puerto Rican independence movement via the "Grito de Lares" (The Lares Proclamation) of 1868. Thus, " being Lares" is adopting an attitude toward life that incorporates the freedom—political and spiritual—represented in the "Grito de Lares." Using this structure anaphorically, Soto Vélez writes in *La tierra prometida*: "Ser Lares es no ser coquí de acabamiento acústico." The coquí is a small frog-related animal indigenous to Puerto Rico and associated with the island's national identity. Thus to "be Lares" is not to be a "coquí that stops croaking its song" ("acabamiento acústico"). As can be seen, the political message of Soto Vélez, evident from his earliest writings as an atalayista, is still the same in 1979 in *La tierra prometida*.

Survey of Criticism

Little has been done up to now on the work of Soto Vélez. Although a number of articles have appeared in various publications, only two major pieces of criticism have come out. The first is the book *Para leer a Soto Vélez* by James V. Romano, and the other major contribution is a symposium on Soto Vélez that took place at Seton Hall University (South Orange, N.J.) in 1983, and whose proceedings are being edited by Carlos Rodríguez, a major exponent of the work of Soto Vélez.

Aside from the political dimension of the work of Soto Vélez, many themes in his work remain to be explored. Soto Vélez has modified the Spanish alphabet, replacing the "repetitive" soft "g" with the letter "j," for example. Thus, the word "virginidad" is written as "virjinidad." In Soto Vélez's orthography, the letter "h" is dropped because it has no material, or phonetic, value. "Hombre," then, is "ombre." These undercurrents, as well as many others, make up a fertile body waiting to be mined.

Bibliography

WORKS BY SOTO VÉLEZ

Abrazo interno. New York: Las Américas Publishing, 1954.
Arboles. New York: Las Américas Publishing, 1955.
Caballo de palo. New York: Las Américas Publishing, 1959.
Escalio. San Juan, P.R.: n.p., 1937.
La Tierra prometida. San Juan, P.R.: Institute de Cultura Puertorriqueña, 1979.

WORKS ABOUT SOTO VÉLEZ

Catalá, Rafael. "La evolución del pensamiento en tres poetas del Caribe: Manuel Navarro Luna, Clemente Soto Vélez y Pedro Mir" in *Literature in Transition: The Many Voices of the Caribbean Area*. Proceedings of the Fifth Annual Conference on Latin American Literature at Montclair State College (N.J.), March 19, 1982. Buenos Aires: Hispamérica, 1982.
Rodríguez, Carlos, ed. *Actas del Simposio sobre Clemente Soto Vélez*. South Orange, N.J.: Seton Hall University, 1983. Works by: George Yúdice, Pedro López-Adorno, Leo F. Cabranes-Grant, Rafael Catalá, Juan Manuel Rivera, Anagilda

Garrastegui, Hortensia R. Morell, Alberto Sandoval, Luis Hernández Aquino, Víctor de León Hernández, Juan Antonio Corretjer, Ligia Delgado, et al.

Rodríguez, Rafael, et al. "Clemente Soto Vélez." Issue of *En Rojo* dedicated to Clemente Soto Vélez. February 13–19, 1981.

Romano, James V. *Para leer a Soto Vélez*. New York: Prisma Books, 1985.

Señeriz, Jorge. "Clemente Soto Vélez y la filosofía de Leibniz." *Claridad* August 15, 1971: 22.

Zervigón, Pedro. "El poeta puertorriqueño que Neruda admiró." *El Reportero* March 13, 1981: 23.

JAMES V. ROMANO

T

THOMAS, PIRI (1928–   ). Piri Thomas is a prominent Puerto Rican narrator, short-story writer, playwright, and poet from El Barrio (Spanish Harlem), New York. At 39, he was limelighted by the success of his autobiographical narrative *Down These Mean Streets* (1967), the first account about growing up in a United States ghetto written in native English by a second-generation Puerto Rican to bridge over to a mainstream U.S. audience. As his other major works, *Saviour, Saviour Hold My Hand* (1972), *Seven Long Times* (1974), and *Stories from El Barrio* (1978), it chronicles his experiences with life in the street and in prison from the 1930s to the 1960s. Thomas lectures extensively, dramatizes his poetry to young audiences, conducts creative-writing workshops, and also paints.

Biography

Piri (né John Peter) Thomas was born on September 30, 1928, in New York City. His mother, Dolores Montañez, was from Bayamón, Puerto Rico. His father, Juan (James) Thomas, considered himself Puerto Rican, but was born in Oriente Province, Cuba, from where he emigrated to Puerto Rico. They met and married in New York in 1927.

Thomas grew up during the Depression in the stifling poverty of the streets of El Barrio. His father then worked as a digger for the WPA; his mother, a spiritual woman who had a strong influence on young Piri, worked all of her life in needle industry factories and at home doing piecework.

Like many other Puerto Rican children born and raised in the metropolis, young Thomas grew up in confusion as to his identity. His family asserted its Puerto Ricanness and his mother inculcated in her children a longing for and an emotional identification with their homeland, but society perceived Piri as black. The first born of seven children, he felt rejected by his father, who in his eyes favored his brothers and sisters for being light-skinned like their mother while Piri was dark, like him. Young Piri was also torn between the values instilled at home and the contradictory societal values. School, which did not address his community's concerns and language, was an alienating experience. In his early teens, when his family moved to the Italian sector of East Harlem, Thomas became streetwise in order to survive. Since an early age he worked in odd jobs only to realize that discrimination and low pay barred him from the tantalizing offers of a consumer society. He gradually became involved in petty theft and youth gangs, rising to gang leader, concluding that respect could only be achieved through violence: "Whether you're right or wrong, as long as you're strong, you're right" (*DTMS*).

Shortly after the United States' involvement in World War II, his father was employed in a Long Island airplane factory. "Things were looking up for us, but it had taken a damn war to do it. A lousy rumble had to get called so we could start to live better. I thought, 'How do you figure this crap out?' " (*DTMS*). In 1944, Thomas's father hit the numbers and invested the proceeds and his mother's savings in "a little house" in a white, middle-class community in Babylon, Long Island, in order to provide his children "the opportunities, trees, grass and nice schools" unavailable in El Barrio. There, young Thomas was shaken by his classmates' middle-class brand of racism and gradually became further estranged from his father and from his brothers and sisters, whom he perceived were assimilating into the values of white society. Striving to find where he belonged, he left home at age sixteen and returned by himself to Spanish Harlem, where he courted a recently immigrated young Puerto Rican woman—"Trina" in *DTMS*. He pushed dope for a living.

Obsessed by the question of whether he could persist in considering himself a Puerto Rican because of his language and his national origin, or whether he should accept society's labeling as an Afro-American because of his skin, Thomas traveled to the Deep South with a black friend, where he experienced segregation firsthand. As a merchant marine, he also traveled to the West Indies, South America, and Europe—France, Italy, England—and concluded that blacks were discriminated against everywhere. He returned to his mother's deathbed in New York hating everything white, except for his mother and Trina, and turned to heroin addiction and to selling it to support his habit. After kicking the habit "cold turkey," he practiced armed robbery as an alternative way of making easy money.

In 1950, after a holdup in a Greenwich Village nightclub and a shootout with a policeman, in which both were wounded, he was convicted of attempted armed robbery and felonious assault and sentenced to five to fifteen years of hard labor. He spent six weeks recovering in the prison ward of Bellevue Hospital, was transferred to the Bronx Tombs, to Sing Sing, and to Great Meadows, a maximum security state prison in Comstock, New York, where he completed seven years in prison. Jail was to him a microcosm of life in the streets. He had to resist racism in a controlled environment, the dehumanization of being stripped of his name to become a number, having every decision made for him, and, above all, getting used to the abnormalities of confinement. He survived the experience by drawing on his inner strength and a growing understanding of humankind. Against all odds, in prison he obtained a high school equivalency diploma, trained in brickmasonry, and engaged in reading and writing. For a period, he also adopted the Black Muslim faith, in which he found a quiet sense of dignity and self-respect.

After he was paroled, at age twenty-eight, Thomas returned to his old neighborhood, determined to remain out of prison. He lived with his aunt, a strong working woman who participated in his conversion to the Pentecostal religion. Unable to join the brickmasons' union because of the double stigma of being black and an ex-convict, he worked as an "all-around man" and later joined the bakers' union. In church he met a recently immigrated Puerto Rican woman, Daniela, whom he married. Once again he moved to Long Island, next to his family, where they later lost his home through the concerted bigotry of the neighbors. During this period he began his work with Afro-American, Italian, and Puerto Rican gangs in a church youth center, helping them resist drugs and tone down their rivalries and frustrations.

Subsequently, he would work with Dr. Efrem Ramírez, director of the Hospital of Psychiatry in Río Piedras, Puerto Rico, formulating a rehabilitation program called "Nueva Raza" (The New Breed), where former drug addicts worked with addicts. Thomas was in his early thirties when he first visited Puerto Rico.

In 1961–1962, while working in gang rehabilitation and in the film *Petey and Johnny*, Thomas was led to Angus Cameron, an editor at Alfred A. Knopf. Two months later he received a grant from the Louis M. Rabinowitz Foundation to finish writing his autobiography, on which he spent five years. Thomas had begun writing during his last four years in prison. He dates his interest in writing to his childhood, when he played rhyming games, and credits his Babylon English teacher and her husband for nurturing in him the conviction that he could be a writer someday.

With the publication of *Down These Mean Streets* in 1967, soon to be followed by his other books, Thomas became a prominent spokesperson of the Puerto Rican community. He was featured in major newspapers, magazines, conferences, and in the film *The World of Piri Thomas*. He also appeared on television and in radio: "Today Show," "Joe Franklin Show," "Alan Burke Show," "Midday Live," "Kup Show," "The Christopher Show," "Puerto Rican New York," "MacKinney Show," "Barry Gray," "Malachy McCord," "National Broadcasting Co.," and others.

An inspiring and uplifting public speaker, Thomas dedicates his life to addressing young people in schools, colleges, and community centers on his works and the problems of ethnic minorities in the United States. He brings to them a message of dignity, affirmation, and pride in their culture and capabilities. His is a call to a spiritual unity which transcends religious and political party lines and condemns a system based on greed that turns children into criminals. A strong believer in education, he seeks to transform his search and life experience into a collective learning process.

Thomas has married three times and is the father of five children, Pedro, Ricardo, Sandra, Reyna, and Tanee, plus three from his wife, Betty. He has lived in Brooklyn and the Bronx, New York, Puerto Rico, and San Francisco. He travels extensively together with Betty, who is an international lawyer. He visited Cuba to trace his father's origins and there engaged in a comparative study of the penal system in Cuba and the United States.

He continues to write, read poetry, exhibit his paintings, and lecture.

Major Themes

Piri Thomas's overlapping autobiographical narratives chronicle his life in the streets of Spanish Harlem and in prison, from the Depression to the early 1960s, turning the reflection on his own life experience into a penetrating commentary on U.S. society. These revolve around a stock of themes which he tackles from different angles in an unending search for fuller answers to the burning problems of growing up Hispanic, black, and poor in the slums of a racist, unequal society. The thematic unity is achieved by the powerful presence of his literary personae. Narrating his own growth and maturation, through evocative details he gives testimony to a changing, complex urban environment, the multiple facets of racism and discrimination, life within the penal system, the travails of overcoming identity conflicts, the language barrier and alienation, and finding spiritual direction in life through creativity and self-assertion.

The most striking quality of Thomas's distinctive style is, paradoxically, its fictionalized aspect: the dialogues. He re-creates a stylized and very personal, yet convincing, interpretation of Harlem street argots spiced with Spanish words that function as an internal code within his narrative. Characterizations are rendered almost exclusively through word selection, mimicking the speech patterns of ethnic groups and social classes, from black hipster and Southern drawl to Long Island Wasp and halting transliterations of Spanish-speaking newcomers. The narrative voice generates a tour de force inventively combining street language with lyrical imagery, stream of consciousness with rhetorical devices such as alliteration and internal rhyme.

The first of his autobiographical narratives, *Down These Mean Streets,* is a powerful and impassioned account of the adolescent and early adult years of the author from ages twelve to twenty-eight. The core of his story is the identity problems of a black working-class Puerto Rican growing up in a racist society. Following the classical structure of developmental autobiographies, the character is an outsider who must find his place in a society that refuses him unless he denies what he is and conforms to a norm. The search starts in the inner city, takes him through a journey where he must prove his worth, and returns to the place of departure. It re-creates a vivid picture of the environment as he chronicles his painful search to validate his manhood as well as his racial and national identity and the struggle against seemingly insuperable odds. It is a story of violence, drugs, and street codes but also of camaraderie, hope, and the search for dignity. It involves a troubled father-son relationship, conflicts in school, home relief, sex, gang fights, petty larceny, drug addiction, and the tortured process of "cold turkey," armed robbery, imprisonment, eventual parole, and movement toward a new life. While this testimony could have been caustic, it is surprisingly compassionate and humorous. Garvin has described it as "an account of the victory of innocent values over a dehumanizing environment."

Down These Mean Streets forms part of the testimonial genre upsurge of the 1960s, a decade that rendered such angry classics as *Manchild in the Promised Land*, by Claude Brown, *Soul on Ice*, by Eldridge Cleaver, *The Autobiography of Malcom X*, and *Soledad Brothers*. Along these lines, Thomas focuses on the brutal aspects of East Harlem life as a way to purge himself and return it to its breeders. His exposé stems from his concern "that poverty and denial of dignity warp, embitter and destroy millions of lives." He speaks in the name of the "struggle of the greater part of the ghetto people for our rights to justice, equality, dignity, for our rights to first-class citizenship" (*Sat. Review*, September 23, 1967).

Saviour, Saviour Hold My Hand (1972) is a sequel that chronologically picks up Thomas's autobiography where *Down These Mean Streets* ends. It is a story about salvation, but not necessarily of the religious sort, but of hard-earned self-assertiveness and self-assertiveness and self-actualization. The underlying themes are the strengths of family and community life, liberal and conservative institutional racism, and the hypocritical use of institutionalized religion for opportunistic ends.

He recounts the difficult first months after his release from prison and his return to El Barrio, where he overcomes the social conditions that push ex-convicts into recidivism. It narrates his frustrating search for work with the double stigma of being black and a parolee, his conversion to Pentecostalism, courtship, getting married and having a child, moving to Long Island and back after once again experiencing suburban bigotry, and his work as a counsellor at a youth club with the hypocritical white Christian minister, "John Clause." At the end of the account he is skeptical about institutional religions, concluding that "to us people of the Barrio, the ghetto is our church, and the only way we're gonna make heaven out of this hell is by getting together."

His third autobiographical narrative, *Seven Long Times* (1974), has been called "a handbook on how to survive in prison." Recounting his seven years in the New York penal system, Thomas relays the physical and mental degradation, the experiences and emotions the incarcerated individual goes through. He targets the oppressive nature of the institution itself, turning his testimony into an indictment of so-called "rehabilitation," which he describes as "revenge." Thomas places the ultimate responsibility for criminal behavior on "this country's racial and economic inequalities" that breed the anger and frustration that lead "into deep, dark whirlpools of drugs and crime." He appends an essay suggesting improvements in the penal system.

Thomas's work as a playwright remains unpublished. *The Golden Streets*, a ninety-minute play, continues the call for attention to the problems of slum life.

The title is ironical. It begins with a young Puerto Rican released from prison who returns to the grey streets of El Barrio, where he works in a rehabilitation center, as Thomas did. It was staged in parks throughout New York City by the Puerto Rican Traveling Theater in August 1970 and performed in Puerto Rico in the summer of 1972. *Affinity* is a one-act, two-character love story between a black man and a white woman. *Lay-dies and Mistus,* another one-act play, tells of a young Puerto Rican who works in New York's garment district. *East 104th Street,* a three-act musical drama, elaborates on Thomas's motto, "Walk tall or not at all," in a generational confrontation of young Puerto Ricans who question the kind of life they have inherited. *Chago,* a screenplay, is about a young man who holds on to a mental image of Puerto Rico as a base of identity, even though he has never been there, in an agonizing struggle to retain his rights as a human being. *Ole Ole Oy Vey* is about a Puerto Rican man married to a Jewish woman.

Thomas's credits include collaboration in two documentary films. He both appeared and provided narration in *Petey and Johnny,* about the rehabilitation work in the East Harlem community, produced by Time-Life/Robert Drew Associates (awarded first prize at the Festival Dei Populi, Florence, Italy, 1964), and *The World of Piri Thomas,* a TV documentary concerned with street life in El Barrio, directed by Gordon Parks for WNET, in which Thomas participated as writer and narrator.

Thomas moves away from the painful autobiographical narratives in *Stories from El Barrio* (1978), a collection of eight short stories, two of which are written in blank verse, dedicated "to young people of all ages" with the message "Doubt not your creative beauties and allow no one to doubt you." In this work he delves into eight facets of a larger collective character: the youth which must grow up in the larger New York Hispanic neighborhoods. The stories reflect a mature author not conscripted to his native Spanish Harlem; they reflect the loving vision of a man who moves with equal ease through "Loisaida" (the Lower East Side), the Bronx, and Brooklyn, where the Hispanic community dwells. Humor and tenderness prevail in this book. Supportive and strong families, youthful innocence, and the power of friendship are the foundations on which he spins yarns like a seasoned raconteur: the hilarious adventures of three urban kids in a Boy Scouts' outing to the New Jersey marshes, the lessons of a frustrating hair-straightening episode, the complex fantasy world of a crippled child, the importance of being oneself in adolescent courtship, a story where friendship and solidarity prevail over individual gain. On the other hand, three aspects of this same collective character expound on ways in which the deprivations of poverty can lead to crime, in spite of high family values.

Thomas considers himself primarily a poet of dramatic readings. His poetry, collected under the title *Sounds from the Street,* is written to be heard and performed, rather than read, and remains unpublished.

He is also the author of various articles on current events involving the minorities in the United States and other issues of public concern. As an observer in the 1984 Nicaraguan elections, he published a report.

Survey of Criticism

Piri Thomas was the first and still is one of the few U.S.-born Puerto Rican writers to have broken through the mainstream publishers' lack of responsiveness to literature by minority authors. His four major books are published with the imprimatur of Knopf, Praeger, Vintage, Signet, and Doubleday. Mainstream critics spared no adjectives in praise of *Down These Mean Streets,* which was extensively reviewed throughout major newspapers, journals, and magazines: "a book of the highest literary quality" (*Choice*), "written from the heart and with literary distinction" (*New York Times Book Review*), "magnificent" (*Washington Star*), "provocative" (*English Journal*), "anguished scandal" (*Catholic World*), "devastatingly frank" (*Harper's*), "tough, lyrical" (*New York Times Book Review*), "earthy and realistic" (*English Journal*), "poetic, brutal, and very effective" (*Booklist*). Even critics who considered the literary qualities of the book uneven recognized its power, its effective use of language, and its documental/testimonial value. It soon became a best-selling classic, repeatedly reprinted and anthologized, and staple college-curriculum reading on the Puerto Rican community. His later works were also reviewed in major publications, though less profusely.

The resonance of Thomas's pioneering works can be attributed in part to the timing of his first publication. The political climate of the 1960s and the strength of the civil rights movement opened up avenues to the recognition of his talent. There was a growing market for books that provided clues to the nature of the social unrest and frequent riots in inner-city slums, prisons, and college campuses throughout the United States. Calder implies that the deserved success of *Down These Mean Streets* was boosted by some publisher's understanding that there's money to be made in minority studies, abetted by the guilty conscience of liberals and by the fact that public violence, from the Westerns on, lies close to the American heart.

While Thomas's books were celebrated with scores of reviews, in-depth comprehensive studies are still scarce. Several factors have militated in this direction. Thomas is not exempt from the established categorization of literature by minority authors as works of greater sociological than literary interest. Mainstream critics and scholars tend to pay less attention to his skills as a creative writer than to the "success story" of a "rehabilitated" ex-gangleader, ex-junkie, and ex-convict. Some of these have gravitated to selectively interpreting Thomas's accounts of his own life as an edifying crime thriller, an archetypical rendition of Puerto Ricans in the United States. This analysis comfortably meshes such interpretations with preconceptions and stereotypes established by Anglo portrayals of Puerto Rican communities in *La Vida* and *West Side Story*: the so-called culture of poverty of the unemployed, welfare-dependent, drug- and crime-ridden Hispanic.

In line with this, the book has been manipulated for ideological ends. Shockley, for instance, recommends it for its "redemptive virtue," as "therapeutic" reading for the "disadvantaged ones" who have lost hope in individual solutions, "excellent for proving that men as defiant against society as . . . Piri Thomas *did* finally have the sanity to try to steer themselves in a more meaningful direction" and "that there *can* be a promised land down those mean streets."

Herein lies a clue to the dissident voices that stand out in the generally appreciative criticism that Thomas's subsequent books aroused. While most critics hailed the more mature, politically aware, and seasoned writer, for others he was no longer "authentic enough." Lask, for instance, interprets Thomas's broadened range and greater understanding of the human condition in his short stories as lacking an "organic link to the Barrio," that is, to the preconceptions of a wolfish Hispanic slum.

As the civil rights movement lost the visibility it had in the 1960s, and pressure from minority groups receded, even *Down These Mean Streets* was the subject of controversy. The school board of Queens School District 25, New York, moved to ban it from junior high school libraries on the basis of "obscene language" and "explicit descriptions of homosexual and heterosexual acts" (see: *New York Times,* April 6:47, 8:26, 17:28, 21:42, 22:48, 30:38, May 9:71–82, June 3:43, August 5:30 1971; September 17, 24, November 7:1, 26:146 1972; December 27:21 1975). Other school districts across the nation took a similar stance. The bans, however, were later repealed. This case is cited in discussions of censorship in the United States (e.g., K.A. McLane's article in the *UCLA Law Review* 26 1979: 1410).

Reference to Piri Thomas's works is found in practically all surveys of U.S. Puerto Rican literature. His work is discussed in a number of dissertations, such as Holte's "The Newcomers in America: A Study of Italian and Puerto Rican-American Personal Narratives." Klan's 1977 University of Puerto Rico doctoral dissertation, "The Use of Spanish in the Works of Piri Thomas," contributes to the understanding of this aspect of his style. Of particular interest is Mohr's monographic study, incorporated into *The Nuyorican Experience.*

Bibliography

WORKS BY THOMAS

Books

Down These Mean Streets. New York: Knopf, 1967. Reprint. New York: New American Library-Signet, 1968. Reprint. London: Barrie & Jenkins, 1970. Reprint. New York: Vintage Books, 1974. Reprint. Canada.
Saviour, Saviour Hold My Hand. Garden City, N.Y.: Doubleday, 1972.
Seven Long Times. New York: Praeger, 1974.
Stories from El Barrio. New York: Knopf, 1978. Reprint. New York: Avon, 1980.

Articles

"A Nightmare Night in 'Mi Barrio.' " *New York Times Magazine* (August 13, 1967): 16–17, 70, 75–77.

"From Arson to a Thousand Candles" (review of "From the Ashes"). *Saturday Review* 50 (September 23, 1967): 78.

"Alien Turf," "Home Relief," "Little Red Schoolhouse" (reprint from *DTMS*). *A Gathering of Ghetto Writers: Irish, Italian, Jewish, Black and Puerto Rican.* Wayne Miller, ed. New York: New York University Press, 1972.

"It's the Decent People vs. the Ripoffs, in and out of Uniform." *New York Times Magazine* (September 24, 1972): 92–94.

"Bicentennial without a Puerto Rican Colony." *Crisis* 82 (December 1975): 407–10.

Report on the 1984 Elections. *Democracy in Nicaragua.* San Francisco: U.S. Out of Central America, 1985.

WORKS ABOUT THOMAS

Acosta Belén, Edna. "The Literature of the Puerto Rican National Minority in the United States." *Bilingual Review* 5 (July-August 1978): 112–13.

Adams, Phoebe. Review of *SLT*. *Atlantic Monthly* 234 (August 1974): 91.

Aldrich, Nelson. Review of *DTMS*. *Book Week* (May 21, 1967): 4.

Anderson, George. Review of *SLT*. *America* 131 (September 14, 1974): 120.

———. Review of *SSHMH*. *America* 127 (December 9, 1972): 500, 502.

Banks, James A. "Evaluating and Selecting Ethnic Studies Materials" (Review of *DTMS*). *Educational Leadership* 31 (April 1974): 594.

Barradas, Efraín. "De lejos en sueños verla . . . : Visión mítica de Puerto Rico en la poesía neoyorrican." *Revista Chicano-Riqueña* 7 (Summer 1979): 46–48.

———. Review of *SFEB*. *Revista Chicano-Riqueña* 7, 4 (Fall 1979): 65.

Beckham, Barry. Review of *SSHMH*. *New York Times Book Review* (September 17, 1972): 5.

Bendiner, Elmer. "Machismo" (review of *DTMS*). *Nation* 205 (September 25, 1967): 283–84.

Binder, Wolfgang. "An Interview with Piri Thomas." *Minority Voices* 4 (Spring 1980): 63–78.

Bondurant, P. Review of *SFEB*. *School Library Journal* 25 (November 1978): 80.

Breslin, John. "A Prospect of Books" (review of *SSHMH*). *America* 127 (October 7, 1972): 267.

Calder, Angus. "Playing the Dozens" (review of *DTMS*). *New Statesman* 80 (August 28, 1970): 242–43.

Clarke, J. J. Review of *DTMS*. *Best Sellers* 27 (June 1, 1967): 95.

Cordasco, Frank. Review of *DTMS*. *Journal of Human Relations* 16, 3 (1968): 451–52.

"Dialogue with Piri Thomas." *Journal of Contemporary Puerto Rican Thought* 2 (Winter 1972): 18–31.

Dybek, Caren. "Black Literature for Adolescents" (review of *SSHMH*). *English Journal* 63 (January 1974): 67.

"El Barrio" (review of *SFEB*). *New York Times Book Review* 85 (August 10, 1980): 31.

Fitzpatrick, Joseph P. "A Review: *DTMS*." *IRCD Bulletin* 4, 1 (1968): 8. Reprint. *The Puerto Ricans.* New York: Arno, 1975.

————. *Puerto Rican Americans*. Englewood Cliffs, N.J.: Prentice-Hall, 1971.

Flannery, M. C. Review of *SFEB*. *Best Sellers* 38 (March 1979): 411.

Flowers, Ann A. Review of *SFEB*. *Horn Book* 55 (April 1979): 196.

Forslund, Morris A. Review of *DTMS*. *Library Journal* 92 (April 15, 1967): 1637.

Fort, Joel. Review of *DTMS*."Available in the Drugstore." *New York Times Book Review* (February 13, 1972): 5, 22.

Garvin, Larry. "The New World of Piri Thomas." *Crisis* 82 (June-July 1975): 196–203.

Goodsell, J. N. Review of *DTMS*. *Christian Science Monitor* 59 (June 15, 1967): 9.

Gould, Jack. "Life in Spanish Harlem: A Cry of Dignity" (review of "The World of Piri Thomas"). *New York Times* (November 20, 1968).

Graham, Gladys P. Review of *SSHMH*. *Voice* (December 22, 1972).

Gregory, Valeria. Review of *DTMS*. *Library Journal* 92 (October 15, 1967): 3877.

Gussow, Mel. "Theater: A New Play by Piri Thomas" (review of *The Golden Streets*). *New York Times* (August 14, 1970): 21.

Handlin, Oscar. "Reader's Choice" (review of *DTMS*). *Atlantic Monthly* 219 (June 1967): 130.

Haro, R. P. Review of *SSHMH*. *Library Journal* 97 (August 1972): 2579.

Hogan, William. Review of *DTMS*. *Chronicle* (San Francisco, December 31, 1967).

Holte, James Craig. "The Newcomers in America: A Study of Italian and Puerto Rican-American Personal Narratives." Ph.D. diss., University of Cincinnati, 1978.

Horwitz, Elinor Lander. Review of *SLT*. *Star* (Washington, D.C., September 15, 1974).

Howard, Thomas L. A. Review of *SLT*. *Bestsellers* 34 (October 15, 1974): 318.

Jackson, Katherine Gauss. Review of *DTMS*. *Harper's* 234 (June 1967): 109.

Kennedy, John S. Review of *DTMS*. *Sunday Visitor* (December 3, 1967).

Kennedy, William. Review of *SLT*. *New Republic* 171 (August 10–17, 1974): 26.

Killens, John O. Review of *DTMS*. *Negro Digest* 17 (January 1968): 94.

Klan, Sue. "The Use of Spanish in the Works of Piri Thomas." Ph.D. diss., University of Puerto Rico, 1977.

Lane, James B. "Beating the Barrio: Piri Thomas and *DTMS*." *English Journal* 61 (September 1972): 814–23.

Lask, Thomas. Review of *SFEB*. *New York Times Book Review* 84 (March 4, 1979): 32.

Lehmann-Haupt, Christopher. "A Talk with Piri Thomas." *New York Times Book Review* 72 (May 21, 1967): 45–47.

Lingo, Cynthia. Review of *SSHMH*. *Library Journal* 97 (November 15, 1972): 3824.

López, Adalberto. "Literature of the Puerto Rican Diaspora: II." *Caribbean Review* 6, 4 (1974): 45–46.

Maddocks, M. "Knuckle-Hard Code of the Barrio" (review of *DTMS*). *Life* 62 (June 9, 1967): 8.

Maloff, S. "In the Arms of Lady Snow" (review of *DTMS*). *Newsweek* 69 (May 29, 1967): 96–97.

Mandel, B. J. "The Past in Autobiography." *Surroundings* 64, 1 (1981): 75–92.

Marr, Warren, II. Review of *SSHMH*. *Crisis* 79 (November 1972): 321.

Miller, John C. "The Emigrant and New York City: Consideration of Four Puerto Rican Writers." *Melus* 5, 3 (1978): 82–99.

Miller, Wayne. "Introduction." *A Gathering of Ghetto Writers: Irish, Italian, Jewish, Black and Puerto Rican*. New York: New York University Press, 1972.

Mohr, Eugene V. "Lives from El Barrio." *Revista Chicano-Riqueña* 8 (1981): 60–79.

————. *The Nuyorican Experience: Literature of the Puerto Rican Minority.* Westport, Conn.: Greenwood Press, 1982.

————. Review of *SLT. Revista/Review Interamericana* 5, 3 (Fall 1983): 478–79.

————. Review of *SSHMH. Revista/Review Interamericana* 3, 1 (Spring 1973): 105–8.

Nieto, Sonia. "Children's Literature on Puerto Rican Themes, Part II" (review of *SFEB*). *Interracial Books for Children* 14/1 (1983): 15.

————. Review of *SFEB. Interracial Books for Children* 12, 6 (1981): 18–19.

O'Hara, J. D. Review of *SSHMH. Saturday Review* 55 (September 30, 1972): 80.

Pacífico, Patricia. "Piri Thomas Talks at Inter American University." *Revista/Review Interamericana* 7 (1978): 666–73.

Peterson, Beverly. "Piri Thomas: High on Life and Sweet Smell of Success." *San Juan Star* (February 3, 1982).

"Poor Puerto Rican" (review of *DTMS*). *Times Literary Supplement* (London, June 11, 1970): 640.

Portillo Orozco, Febe. "A Bibliography of Hispanic Literature" (review of *DTMS*). *English Journal* 71 (November 1982): 61.

Review of *DTMS. Booklist* 64 (September 1, 1967): 27.

Review of *DTMS. Choice* 4 (February 1968): 1450.

Review of *DTMS. Christian Century* 84 (May 24, 1967): 692.

Review of *DTMS. Kirkus* 35 (March 15, 1967): 401.

Review of *DTMS. New Yorker* 43 (July 29,1967): 84.

Review of *DTMS. New York Post* (June 17, 1967).

Review of *DTMS. Publisher's Weekly* 191 (March 13, 1967: 57.

Review of *DTMS. Publisher's Weekly* 193 (May 13, 1968): 62.

Review of *DTMS. Wilson Quarterly* 4 (Spring 1980): 153

Review of *SSHMH. Booklist* 69 (February 1, 1973): 501.

Review of *SSHMH. Book World* 6 (October 1, 1972): 4.

Review of *SSHMH. Choice* 9 (February 1973): 1667.

Review of *SSHMH. Kirkus* 40 (July 1, 1972): 791.

Review of *SSHMH. Library Journal* 97 (June 15, 1972): 2250.

Review of *SSHMH. Publisher's Weekly* 202 (July 3, 1972): 34.

Review of *SLT. Booklist* 71 (September 15, 1974): 60.

Review of *SLT. Book World* (August 11, 1974): 2.

Review of *SLT. Choice* 11 (November 1974): 1393.

Review of *SLT. Christian Century* 91 (August 7–14, 1974): 778.

Review of *SLT. Cultural Information Service* (July-August 1974).

Review of *SLT. Kirkus* 42 (April 15, 1974): 470.

Review of *SLT. Publisher's Weekly* 205 (April 8, 1974): 82.

Review of *SFEB. Book World* (December 3, 1978): E4.

Review of *SFEB. Center for Children's Books: Bulletin* 32 (Jan 1979): 96.

Review of *SFEB. Kirkus* 46 (December 15, 1978): 1364.

Seligson, Tom. Review of *SLT. New York Times Book Review* (September 22, 1974): 10.

Shockley, Ann Allen. "Two Books with Soul: For Defiant Ones" (review of *DTMS*). *English Journal* 58 (March 8, 1969): 396–98.

Sloat, Warren. "Exploration of Color" (review of *DTMS*). *Saturday Review* 50 (August 5, 1967): 33.

Smith, Joan. Review of *SLT. Contemporary Sociology* 5 (May 1976): 303–4.

Sourcebook of Hispanic Culture in the U.S. David William Foster, ed. Chicago: American Library Association, 1982.

Stern, Daniel. "One Who Got Away" (review of *DTMS*). *New York Times Book Review*. 72 (May 21, 1967): 1, 44.

Taylor, Chet. Review of *DTMS*. *Revista/Review Interamericana* 1 (Winter 1972): 156–57.

Towne, Anthony. "In Plain Truth" (review of *DTMS*). *Catholic World* 206 (October 1967): 42–43.

Wilms, D. M. Review of *SFEB*. *Booklist* 75 (December 1, 1978): 620.

YANIS GORDILS

TORRES, OMAR (1945–   ). Omar Torres is known primarily as a poet and playwright. Additionally, he has published a novel, *Apenas un bolero* (1981, Just a *bolero*), written under the auspices of the Cintas Fellowship Program of the Institute for International Education (1978–1979). In his five published volumes of poetry, in his novels (including *Al partir* [1986, On Leaving] and the unpublished *An Exile's Letter* [1983]), and in his six plays which have been produced in New York City, Omar projects the feeling of a Cuban in exile: a divided being in the process of a perpetual search for himself.

Biography

Omar was born in 1945 in Las Tunas, a small town in the eastern region of Cuba. He first attended an American school, Academia Wilmington, and later the Colegio Puerto Padre. In about 1956, his father set out for Havana and, a little later, made his way to Miami, Florida, where, in 1959, he was reunited with Omar and Omar's mother and brother. In Miami, Omar attended Citrus Grove Junior High School and, later, Miami Senior High School, from where he graduated in 1964.

With the idea of starting a life of greater economic prosperity, his father decided to move to New York and there Omar attended Queens College. His program of study shifted back and forth between architecture, fine arts, and Spanish literature. Not finding himself content in the ambience of a New York college, Omar abandoned formal studies and became his own teacher. His principal fields of inquiry were religion, philosophy, history, art, and literature. His manual artistic talent led him to jewelry design, which is his occupation at the present time.

In his free time, away from the jewelry workshops, Omar took acting classes at the New York Theater of the Americas and little by little became an actor. He received several temporary jobs in the local New York theater as well as in radio and television, after having graduated from the International Television Arts School as an announcer.

In 1972, Omar cofounded the Centro Cultural Cubano de Nueva York. Between 1970 and 1975, he published several articles about art in general, painting, theater, and music in several New York Hispanic periodicals. He founded in

1974 *Cubanacán,* a journal of literature and art, and also was the editor in 1980 and 1981 of *Inter/Cambio,* the bulletin of the Committee of Intellectuals for the Freedom of Cuba. Omar was awarded the best actor's prize of 1979 of the Association of Arts Critics of New York for his performance of Reverend Morell in George Bernard Shaw's *Candide,* produced and shown in Spanish in New York's Talía Theater.

Omar has also made a name for himself in music. He has written songs, including both lyrics and music, and is a classical and popular guitarist. Omar Torres currently lives in Manhattan. Aside from his work as a jewelry designer, a position he has had since 1965, he teaches design at the Fashion Institute of Technology. His artistic career also encompasses oil painting of a realist tendency. At the present time, Omar is working on another novel, *Al otro lado de este lado* (On the Other Side of This Side), while continuing with his poetry and songs.

Major Themes

The five published volumes of poetry of Omar Torres are entitled: *Conversación primera* (1975, First Conversation), *Ecos de un laberinto* (1976, Labyrinthian Echoes), which is one long poem, *Tiempo robado* (1978, Stolen Times), *De nunca a siempre* (1981, From Never to Always), and *Línea en diluvio* (1981, Diluvian Line).

Eugenio *Florit, a Spanish Cuban poet and a New York resident for many years, wrote me that, "Omar is a poet, and among the very good ones. One of the best we have from the terrible exile. I knew it from the start, reading his 1975 book of verses *Conversación primera,* although two years before he had sent me a beautiful poem, "Homenaje a Ezra Pound," which later became incorporated into the book I just mentioned which was written between 1972 and 1975."

The exile and its constants, loneliness, the alienation of the individual, ennui, all appear in the poetry of Omar Torres. Another principal theme is ethnicity which is almost always presented in a mockingly ironic tone. According to Florit, Omar also gives us "the other side of the good coin [his poetry]: the serious and discrete meditator . . . Omar has created, like all poets, a world nostalgic at times, other times full of sensuality in front of a woman's name." In this manner, in his long poem, "Ecos de un laberinto," the poet ends on a happy note, "Ser sobre todas las cosas, /Eterno regocijo" (To be above all things, /eternally rejoicing). Florit believes that a very important aspect of Torres's poetry is the way his poems end, "the last verses in all his poems leave us satisfied. Omar knows how to close the door of all his poems in a precise, fitting manner, almost always necessary. He shows there his quality as a good writer."

From Torres's 1978 book, *Tiempo robado,* Eugenio Florit chooses "El hombre de silencio" (Man of Silence) as "a very important example of what our poet can write when thoughts rest in his able mind and succeed in being reduced to

this: 'pero el hombre olvida siempre la palabra necesaria, /la palabra precisa' "
(But man always forgets the necessary word, /the precise word). Also found in
this collection is "Apenas un bolero" (Only a Bolero), a title the author repeats
in his 1981 novel. It has an existential theme and closes with these lines: "Se
emprende el camino sin temor a su final, /nutriéndose unomismo de certezas. /
Por lo demás, no abandonar las pequeñas inquietudes/al capricho del viento"
(The journey is begun without fear of its end/Nourishing oneself with certainties/
otherwise, not abandoning the little worries, /to the caprice of the wind).

Omar Torres also sings about love in encounters with different women, all
molded together, the essence of LA MUJER, the one who goes away, returns,
is one and many. Love for Omar is an always present feeling but is never wrapped
up in a particular figure. It is part of that search for oneself, it is attached to his
loneliness, which that feeling (love) hides for a moment and, when love dissolves,
loneliness becomes more acute.

In 1981, already at the beginning of his maturity, Omar published *De nunca
a siempre*. The poet, as Florit tells us, uses a "cheerful title which encloses
other unhappinesses such as the elegy, the memory, and the constant factor of
the exile." *De nunca a siempre* is a serious work of profound meditation which
presents the suffering of the exile, the anguish of not being able to identify
himself with the geographical and social environment that surrounds him.

The last book by Omar, *Línea en diluvio,* as noted by Florit, possesses a tone
"of melancholy and serene meditation of man facing his destiny. That destiny
which makes him exclaim in the final untitled verses which leave us a little
sadder than we were, 'Me hallarán un día frente al mar/como una isla a la
deriva' " (They'll find me one day in front of the sea/like an island adrift). An
amorous tone is also found in this work, when Omar asks for: "Un poco de
cuerpo/para la mañana;/un poco de ti:/tu decir, tus cosas" (A little bit of body/
for the morning/a little of you:/your words, your things). And further: "Todo
cambia a la orilla/de tus besos. /Pido besos, pido/ventanas de amores:/tango de
ángeles caídos" (All changes at the shore/of your kisses. /I ask for kisses, I ask
for/windows of love:/tango of fallen angels).

Regarding the formal aspects of Omar Torres's poetry, he manipulates free
verse almost always with an accurate internal rhythm with such a form that,
according to Uva Clavijo, "His poetry doesn't resemble anyone else's. Maybe
because he feels his own soul broken, he breaks syntax and recreates it in his
own way (in an order) not capricious, as some would believe, rather reflecting
the internal disjointedness of a person for whom the support and vital links of
the external world have been snatched away."

Omar Torres has written several plays, six of which have been staged, *Abdala-
José Martí* (1972), written in collaboration with Iván Acosta, *Antes del vuelo y
la palabra* (1976, Before the Flight and the Word), *Cumbancha cubiche,* which
was filmed for the WNET network and broadcast nationally (1976), *Yo dejo mi
palabra en el aire sin llaves y sin velos* (1978, I Leave My Word in the Air
without Keys or Veils), *Latinos,* a musical comedy with songs composed by

Omar and his collaborators, Manuel Martín and Lynn Alvarez (1979), and *Dreamland Melody* (1982), written in English and presented in a dramatic reading directed by the Broadway actor and director Kevin Conway (*The Elephant Man*) at the New York Center for Interamerican Relations. *Abdala-José Martí* was presented at the Henry Street Settlement's New Federal Theater in New York and got a favorable review in the *New York Times*. *Yo dejo mi palabra en el aire sin llaves y sin velos* had the privilege of being shown at the New York Shakespeare Festival Public Theater in March 1978. Omar also wrote two plays that have never been staged: *En el tronco de un árbol* (On a Tree Trunk), written in 1978, and *Reino del sueño* (Kingdom of Dreams), written in 1980.

The constant themes in Omar Torres's plays are: a) patriotism, b) life in exile, and c) Latin American women. *Abdala-José Martí* is a pure Martíesque work composed of Martí's poems, letters, and speeches set in theatrical form. Martí wrote the dramatic poem *Abdala* when he was only sixteen. Abdala was an African youngster who, against his mother's will, was going to liberate his country from foreign invaders. This work was a symbol of the young Martí's struggle to liberate Cuba from Spanish domination. *Abdala-José Martí* by Omar Torres has an authentic Cuban theme, it is an example of the patriotism and philosophy of Cuba's apostle.

Antes del vuelo y la palabra is made up of parts of poems by Eugenio Florit. Also, music in this work was composed by Omar himself. The central theme is human solitude, personal uprooting as a consequence of living away from one's country, the melancholy and nostalgia of a person who lives in New York, away from his natural environment.

Cumbancha Cubiche has two dimensions: a realistic vision of a Cuban family in exile and surrealistic elements that can be found in monologues and dialogues. It emphasizes the lack of communication between generations that is intensified by living in a society with different values from those of Cuba.

Yo dejo mi palabra en el aire sin llaves y sin velos is based on a group of poems written by Latin American women writers. It is a celebration of the Latin American woman through her poetry. Among different themes are: women facing earth, women addressing their men and sons, women analyzing themselves. This work also has a musical background composed by Omar Torres.

Latinos shows a group of youngsters, Hispanic residents of Hispanic ghettos in New York. They tell anecdotes about their lives in regard to their family relationships, drugs, life in the ghetto, difficulties learning a new language, etc. As in previous works, Omar included his own music.

Dreamland Melody was written in English. Its theme is diverse: Cuba at the end of 1958 in the middle of Castro's revolution, life in exile in the United States, and mainly a feminine archetype represented by Elena, the central character in this work.

Elena represents a lower-middle-class Cuban woman who supports her family, consisting almost completely of men. By the end of this work, there is an element that is directed toward her liberation, suggesting hope in the future. Elena starts observing her hands, thus expressing her physical and spiritual discovery. Her thinking of cutting her hair symbolizes a change in her life: maybe she can break with everything and start a new life by herself.

Apenas un bolero (1981) is the first novel published by Omar Torres. The author developed the themes according to Greek mythology: separation from a world, rejection of the call, redeeming initiation and return. The main theme of this novel is the life of the Cuban in exile and the effects that it inflicts on the individual: effects of alienation, loneliness, rejection, and indifference. Miguel Saavedra, the main character, lives in a vacuum, is led by fatal forces because he is a being without willpower. The narration shifts between the first and third persons because, as Omar told me, "this is the only way of feeling the Cuban reality, from both inside and outside simultaneously."

The Chilean critic and writer Alberto Baeza Flores, who currently lives in Spain, tells us that Proust and Joyce can be found in *Apenas un bolero,* in its original integration of time and space. The critic notices the influence of *Ulysses,* another novelistic collage. Its author, Joyce, was also a poet and a dramatist. In an unpublished review, Chilean critic Alberto Baeza Flores stated that Omar "has given us a novel structured with pieces, bits, parts, fragments, slices, intense experiences of life in which the different literary genres are mixed together, support each other, harmonize, come in sequence; everything within a personal style that is also intense, tight, experienced with the hurricane of being and existence. Its style grasps you, impassions you, and involves you in this testimonial and existential novel that is difficult to forget."

The novel takes place in Miami, New York, Union City, New Jersey, and Havana. The myth of "going North," with which millions of Hispanics have tried to solve their problems, is in this narrative. The trip starts in Havana and continues in Miami, first stop in the north. Later the main character moves to New York and tells us, "I remembered that in Cuba when things did not work, people used to say, 'Me voy pal norte' . . . I decided that I also had to go North, to continue the journey. I had to depart, escape, find myself, invent myself. I had to start a cosmic trip towards myself. My history had to be the one of both Icarus and Telemachus at the same time." Some lines above, he had told us, "My life was a myth, my past was a myth, my country was a myth." In a recent conversation, Omar told us that André Bréton after a visit to Cuba in the 1940s said that this was the most surrealistic country where you could live. Omar adds that this surrealistic manifestation continues in the exile.

In an ethnic framework, the author bases his narration on several Cuban constants which according to him are: "choteo" (mockery), the quick shift from the sublime to the ridiculous, the chaotic and absurd sense of life in exile, and a feeling of frustration that is present in the Cuban environment since the beginning of the Republic in 1902. This environment is divided in zones: Miami and the surroundings of Eighth Street in the Southwest with its stores, parties, and popular characters; the pseudo-sophisticate from New York, including the underground counterrevolutionary and the low-class element of Fourteenth Street; the one from Union City in New Jersey with his family that belong to the lower-middle working class, small businessmen, and finally the sober ambience of Havana with its uniformed army and the excited crowd full of political and revolutionary ardor.

A character that Omar described admirably to me in an interview is the *cubanazo*: "In New York, we used to call *cubanazos* those Cubans in Miami because they wore 18 carat gold bracelets and Saint Barbara medallions; because they liked big cars, extravagant houses, altars for saints, picnics and boats; because they ate constantly and spoke about old fashioned politics; because they drank coffee all day long and told stories all the time; because they liked to show themselves at the Versailles Restaurant; because they had fossilized Cuba in Eighth Street; because they were always curious about each other's lives."

He also described the Cuban in New York to me with some irony: "We used to hide ourselves in our small rooms in the North, in an environment so unnatural for Caribbeans who love sun. We used to wear trendy St. Laurent clothes. We used to go to Broadway, to the opera, to the Philharmonic concerts. We used to spend vacations in Spain, France and/or in Italy. We used to read best-sellers and the *New York Times* while we were very up-to-date in the inconsequences of the moment."

Miguel Saavedra, and also Omar Torres, feel the imprint that the exile has made on them. *Apenas un bolero* is not a political novel because Miguel is capable neither of experimenting with passions nor of having an ideology. Loneliness and indifference have shaped him this way. At the end, Miguel emotionally explodes under the pressures he experiences from both left and right.

Apenas un bolero is a novel that represents the feelings of a Cuban American writer. Its themes as well as its form express admirably the dilemma of a community: the problem of exiled Cubans who belong to a generation too young to keep old values, but old enough to feel Cuban and experience the impact of the rejection of both an environment and a society that are not always favorable to them.

Survey of Criticism

As yet Omar Torres's work has not attracted a great deal of critical attention. *Al partir* has, however, been reviewed in the Cuban American press favorably, with noted poet Uva A. Clavijo stating that the novel is an important contribution to Cuban letters and a denunciation of tyranny. Lynn Ellen Rice Cortina has praised *Al partir* for its balance in tone and lovely treatment of the heroine in his lyrical prose.

Bibliography

WORKS BY TORRES

Poetry

Conversación primera. New York: Editorial Niurklen, 1975.
Ecos de un laberinto. New York: Private edition, 1976.

Tiempo robado. Hoboken, N.J.: Ediciones Contra Viento y Marea, 1978.
De nunca a siempre. Miami: Ediciones Universal, 1981.
Línea en diluvio. New York: Editorial Niurklen, 1981.

Produced Theatrical Works

Abdala-José Martí, 1972.
Antes del vuelo y la palabra, 1976.
Cumbancha cubiche, 1976.
Yo dejo mi palabra en el aire sin llaves y sin velos, 1978.
Latinos, 1979.
Dreamland Melody, 1982.

Novels

Apenas un bolero. Miami: Ediciones Universal, 1981.
Al partir. Houston: Arte Publico Press, 1986.

WORKS ABOUT TORRES

"*Apenas un bolero*." *Union City (New) The Dispatch* (Union City, New Jersey), September 22, 1981.
Baeza Flores, Alberto. "Una narrativa entre el 'ghetto' y el 'collage.' " Unpublished ms. 1981.
Burunat, Silvia. "Omar Torres. *Al partir*." *Conferencia* 2, 2 (Spring 1987): 123–24.
Clavijo, Uva A. "Omar Torres y un nuevo *Al partir*." *Diario de la Américas*, December 13, 1986.
Durán, Aleida. "Una Noche en la Tormenta." *The Dispatch*, January 18, 1983.
Gussow, Mel. "Poet Revolutionary Inspires a Drama." *New York Times*, August 23, 1972.
Rice Cortina, Lynn Ellen. "The Perils of Evangelina: A Tale Thrice Told." *Cuban Heritage* 1, 1 (Summer 1987): 42–47.

SILVIA BURUNAT

V

VALLBONA, RIMA DE (1931–   ). The acclaimed author of two novels, several collections of short stories, and an ever-increasing volume of literary criticism, Vallbona is a longtime resident of Houston, Texas, though her ties to her native Costa Rica have remained strong. As professor of Spanish at the University of St. Thomas in Houston, Texas, she continues to write seriously and actively. She is a frequent traveler to both Latin America and Spain, maintaining voluminous correspondence with other Hispanic writers, especially women, both established and neophyte. A popular speaker on literary subjects, she is also an active supporter of Houston's Institute of Hispanic Culture and of the arts in general.

Biography

Rima Gretel Rothe de Vallbona—named after the heroine in W. H. Hudson's best-selling *Green Mansions*—was born in San Jose, Costa Rica, though her family moved shortly afterward to the small village of Guadalupe, some twenty minutes away from the capital. As a child she was so painfully shy that on the publication of her first novel a family friend could not resist asking if it was really true that that "retarded girl who used to speak only in monosyllables" had written a book. She felt especially close to her father, a real estate broker who, like Rima herself, loved to draw and paint and also contributed articles to a San Jose newspaper. It was her father who was the first to recognize his youngest daughter's clear spark of precocious intelligence.

For reasons still unclear to her, Rima was sent to Guadalupe's public school rather than to a private academy, which her family could easily have afforded. Most of the other pupils there came from needy families and not a few were barefoot and even hungry. Rima, well fed and dressed, suffered agonies at being conspicuously better off than the others. But all this was soon to change. In her ninth year her father, the son of a German immigrant, died or was possibly murdered in a Costa Rican wartime concentration camp—a story Rima partially tells in *Las sombras que perseguimos* (1983, The Shadows We Pursue). Her mother, though left amply provided with funds to see the family safely through the war, soon developed an obsessive neurosis that made her resist spending even the money that should have gone for her children's education. She insisted that the older ones earn money by taking on odd jobs. Rima, the fifth child of six, realized that her own family was now experiencing many of the same privations she had previously observed from such an altogether different perspective.

Rima had begun to write stories even before her father's death. Following it, writing became an important escape. The books on politics, philosophy, and religion remaining on the shelves of his library stimulated in a somewhat uneven way the minds of Rima and her youngest brother Fernando, who soon became an outspoken religious skeptic. It was partly Fernando's continual jibes at religion that caused Rima to begin a long search for a position from which to defend Christianity—and thus to begin a gradual move toward the Catholicism she still embraces.

During Rima's adolescence her mother adopted ever more stringent measures to hoard money. She now demanded that her youngest daughter, an excellent student, leave high school and enter secretarial training. Rima resolutely opposed such a plan, and help came just in time from a sympathetic relative. In spite of her mother's disapproval she was later able to enroll for classes at the national university. She found her mother somewhat appeased when a friend offered to allow Rima to work part time in his firm earning money for expenses. Then the Alliance Française of San Jose changed her life by awarding Rima a scholarship to the Sorbonne in Paris.

There Rima earned a diploma entitling her to teach French. During her stay she became acquainted with Carlos Vallbona, a young Spanish medical student. The two became engaged, but marriage plans were delayed by Carlos's need to fulfill his residency requirements in the United States. While staying a summer with his parents in Barcelona, Rima worked first doing research and later teaching in an elementary school, in the afternoon auditing courses at the university there. In January she moved on to Salamanca, Spain, where she earned a second diploma in philology. The scholarship having expired, she now returned to the University of Costa Rica. By transferring some of the credits gained abroad and taking a series of examinations, she was able to advance to the senior undergraduate level. To earn her living she taught French at a local school, attending her own classes in the afternoon.

Upon completing her university course with honors, Rima received a certificate that allowed her to teach Spanish at an experimental secondary school in San Jose. She felt a special bond with her students there, since many of them were returning to finish their education after economic pressures had forced them to drop out. In June of this year Carlos, still in the United States, wrote to his fiancée that they could now be married. Although wishing to join him immediately, Rima loyally finished out the terms of her teaching contract. She left Costa Rica just before Christmas to journey alone to Houston. Knowing no one there, she was deeply moved when Carlos's friends feted her with bridal showers and even made all the arrangements for the couple's wedding ceremony.

Although happy to be with Carlos, Rima now began an immediate struggle with a new language, and many new responsibilities inevitably accompanied the birth of a daughter, Rima Nuri. Rima made arrangements to begin studying for a master's degree at a local university, but the births of two more children, Carlos Fernando and María Teresa (Maite), left her with little time for this. She resumed work, whenever she could snatch a few moments of privacy, on a novel begun several years before in Paris. When Carlos discovered the manuscript, he strongly encouraged her to publish it. She did so in 1968, giving it the title *Noche en vela* (Sleepless Night). At Carlos's insistence the couple's last child received the name María Luisa (Marisa) after the narrator/protagonist of her mother's novel.

In an interview with me, Rima told me that she had intended to write her master's thesis on the Costa Rican writer Carmen Lyra, but she allowed herself to be persuaded by a Houston professor that "Latin American literature is unworthy of such detailed investigation." Substituting the Spanish male novelist Camilo José Cela, Rima spent a summer doing research in Spain while Carlos's parents minded their four young grandchildren. In 1962 she was awarded the M.A. degree by the University of Costa Rica. In spite of this success, she found herself entering a period of acute depression in which all the sacrifices made to obtain an education began to appear wasted in the face of increasing domestic responsibilities. Salvation came in the form of a telephone call from the rector of the University of St. Thomas, a small local Catholic institution. With anything but confidence, Rima accepted his offer of a temporary position as instructor in Spanish. At her students' urging she was retained and granted tenure, later organizing and shaping the school's expanding Spanish department. Resumption of teaching duties eased her depression but left Rima even less time for writing novels. She turned instead to shorter forms (she had already written a second novel, *La espina perenne* [The Perennial Thorn], but continues to deem it unworthy of publication). She began to create a series of vignettes depicting her children's early years, encouraging the children themselves to provide illustrations. These were published privately in 1979 under the title *La salamandra rosada* (The Pink Salamander). The volume also includes imaginative recreations of Carlos's childhood in Cataluña as well as illustrations by the four Vallbona children and by Rima herself.

In response to a request for a short story to be included in a Costa Rican anthology, Rima wrote "La Sísmica," basing it on an anecdote recounted by a visiting aunt. She followed with more stories that now comprise *Polvo del camino* (1971, Dust from the Road). A third novel, *Las sombras que perseguimos,* was written but not published until after the second collection of short stories, *Mujeres y agonías* (1982, Women and Agonies), had been brought out in Houston by the Arte Público Press. While continuing to write, Rima completed requirements for a Ph.D. in modern languages from Middlebury College, Vermont. She received the degree in 1982 with a thesis entitled "Realidad histórica y ficción en *Vida y sucesos de la Monja Alférez*" (Historical Reality and Fiction in *The Life and Times of the Nun Alférez*). In addition, Rima began serving as chair, first of the Spanish section and then of the Department of Modern Foreign Languages of St. Thomas. Between 1972 and 1981 she published three scholarly works including pioneering studies of two important Costa Rican women writers, Yolanda Oreamuno and Eunice Odio. During this period she also offered classes in Spanish for Houston's Institute of Hispanic Culture, serving as well in the capacity of visiting professor at both the University of Houston and Rice University.

Continuing as professor of Spanish at St. Thomas, Rima has now given up her long and successful tenure as chair. As her children gradually take up their own lives away from home, she finds herself able to devote more time to the serious pursuit of her preferred activity, creative writing. She does so amid her own growing recognition as a significant voice within the chorus of Latin American writers now being heard from.

Major Themes

Five related themes dominate the fiction of Rima de Vallbona. These are the questioning of established roles and norms, women's demand for freedom in the modern world, the world as seen through the eyes of children and adolescents, the search for religious faith, and the question of the line separating fantasy from reality. A constant in all of her works is the flow of richly expressive language, whether lyric, colloquial, or invective.

Noche en vela is a bildungsroman narrated by a young girl, Luisa, whose mother is recently deceased. Luisa's father calls upon a relative, Aunt Leonor (called "Leo" throughout the story), to help raise his three daughters. The novel begins years afterward during the wake of the aunt, who has brought the children nothing but grief and has even allowed the middle sister, María, to slip from acute nervousness into paranoia by not seeking proper medical treatment for her. It is to María as she was that the story is dedicated. The novel's epigraph cites words of Prometheus urging the reader not to weep but rather to "come and attend" the recounting of woes.

It is ironic that "la tía Leo," whose sinister doings assume Celestinesque proportions in the work, should seem at times too bad to be true, since the author acknowledges that the individual after whom this character is drawn was actually a great deal worse. In both cases—that of author and that of narrator—it is the injustices suffered in childhood that motivate the act of writing. Joining other relatives at the wake, Luisa recalls in numerous flashbacks her own gradual development along physical, intellectual, and spiritual lines. The device of setting off the girl's thoughts from the rest of the text offers the reader an intimate look at the various stages of her growth. In some finely wrought lyric passages the author marks Luisa's transition from childhood into puberty. Raised almost without religious instruction, Luisa stumbles her way toward faith and the Catholic Church—a catalyst being early conversations with a nonreligious friend. By the novel's final page Luisa's search has yielded sufficient grace on her part to forgive the unkind aunt and look ahead to a new life apart from her. (The reader will note a number of autobiographical elements here.)

The theme of children and growth also informs Rima's second work, *La salamandra rosada*. This unusual volume consists of six stories, eighteen vignettes, and three poems, including as well a short "Autocrítica" (Self-Critique) by the author. It is dedicated to Carlos Vallbona. Each narrative is based upon an actual incident in the life of a Vallbona child—for example, the reaction to an eclipse of the moon, and a short-lived resolution to run away from home. Pathos is kept at a distance by each story's working into a carefully unified bit of verbal art. In "La niña y la luna" (The Little Girl and the Moon), for example, the anecdote appears framed by images of such round objects as the little girl's face and a twinkling ball. Often the glimpse of a child's bare emotion is mediated through the gentle irony of the adult narrator's perception of time's inexorable flow.

Children are also the subject of several of the stories in *Polvo del camino*, but here Rima develops what is probably the major theme of her subsequent writings—the questioning of established social practices. Predominantly feminist in tone, several of these stories depict a girl or a woman with the misfortune to be the victim of scorn or neglect, with settings in both the United States and Costa Rica. In "Cementerio de camiones" (Bus Cemetery), a black woman suffers the results of institutionalized racism in Houston. In "La niña sin amor" (The Loveless Child) a young girl is the victim of both incestuous acts by her own father and unjust blame for these acts at the hands of the local parish priest. In "Con los muertos al cinto" (Girded by the Dead) a young blind girl who is pregnant is persecuted by society, even though her blindness has prevented her from comprehending the rape responsible for her condition. "Caña hueca" (Hollow Cane) is the sensitively told story of a lonely rural schoolteacher who finds consolation in a love affair with another woman, provoking harsh disapproval by all the villagers including, of course, the priest. Other narratives thoughtfully probe the gray area between reality and dream.

All of Vallbona's themes are richly apparent in the collection of short stories entitled *Mujeres y 'agonías*, which includes three selections appearing earlier in *La salamandra rosada*. These—"El árbol del Chumico" (The Chumico Tree), "El arcángel del perdón" (The Pardoning Archangel), and "Día de tinieblas" (Day of Darkness)—comprise a unit of brief fables whose tellability derives from the originality of a child's interpretation of complex events. "El juego de los grandes" (The Adults' Game), whose subject is war, also pursues this line. "Oíd, Adán es sal" (Listen, Adam Is Salt), an anagram of "Dios es la nada" (God Is Nothingness), explores a similar theme with a metaphysical twist. Several other stories deal with protest. "Lo inconfesable" (The Unconfessable) tells of a psychologically disturbed priest who insistently extracts intimate details of masturbatory practices from his young female parishioners. "Beto y Betina" (Robert and Roberta) offers gentle insights into transvestism, and "En el reino de la basura" (In the Garbage Kingdom) is an eloquent lament for a child unable to comprehend either her own indigence or the loudly voiced scorn of those around her. In a different mode altogether "El impostor" (The Impostor) traces the growing madness of a disturbed academic unable to distinguish his own fantasy of revenge from reality. The story is narrated by the madman himself.

The title *Mujeres y agonías* would seem to relate most directly to the work's first two stories, "Penélope en sus bodas de plata" (Penelope's Silver Wedding Anniversary) and "Parábola del Edén imposible" (The Parable of the Impossible Eden). It is these two stories that, along with "Caña hueca" and "El árbol del Chumico," make up *Baraja de soledades* (1983), Deck of Solitude), the collection of Vallbona's stories published recently in Spain. "Penélope" is narrated by the son of a woman whom he sees as, above all, irrevocably dull. While he himself is acutely conscious of his nascent sexuality, he cannot conceive of his mother in any role but that of domestic drudge. At her twenty-fifth anniversary party, however, the mother startles all the guests by climbing upon a stool and scandalously announcing her intention to terminate her frustrating marriage to the boy's father in order to elope immediately with her lover. Resenting his mother previously, the son now dislikes her even more, wishing she would return to normal. "Parábola" presents the other side of the same dilemma: a woman who has run away from a marriage with her lover suddenly finds her "Eden" beginning to pall. She now reflects remorsefully on the role she has left behind.

Mujeres y agonías and her second (published) novel, *Las sombras que perseguimos,* show Rima at her best. In *Sombras* another woman, Cristina, finds herself entrapped within a miserable marriage, in part because she and her husband have never been allowed to communicate freely with one another. Society has decreed instead that the two play out narrow and opposite social roles. Cristina seeks help through the Church but the priest to whom she tells her needs is uncomprehending. This more or less ordinary theme is complicated by the question of Cristina's ontological status: she may be only a character in a book being written by Pedro, an interestingly androgynous narrator/character. Another narrator, most untrustworthy, is Benito, Cristina's husband, with a different version of everything. *Sombras,* with its multiple framings and repeated references to writers and to the act of writing, belongs clearly to the wave of *nueva narrativa* (new narrative) that has recently distinguished Latin American literature. The novel's implied author or authorial voice displays an ideological position clearly in line with that of some of the most important feminist works of the last twenty years. Rima Vallbona's experience of North American culture may constitute one factor in the repeated challenges her work offers to Hispanic women in traditional roles, even though her voice is not the first in Costa Rican literature to embrace such a theme. In any case, she continues to deal with the question in a manner that is as sensitive as it is forthright and highly readable.

Survey of Criticism

Rima de Vallbona's fiction has already won several prizes in literary contests both in Latin America and the United States. Notably, her *Noche en vela* received the National Novel Prize in Costa Rica in 1968, and her stories won the Jorge Luis Borges Short Story Award in Argentina in 1977. In the following year *Las sombras que perseguimos* was awarded the Latin American Novel Prize from Colombia. *Mujeres y agonías* received the prize for literature from SCOLAS, a Latin American studies organization of the southern United States.

All of Rima's books, both literary and scholarly, have been widely reviewed on both of the American continents and in Spain, where *Baraja de soledades* was published. An essay by Juliette Decreus on several of her works appeared in the French journal *Fer de Lance*. *Noche en vela* contains a useful prologue by Jézer González, who discusses the work in terms of its place within modern Costa Rican narrative and then provides a brief analysis of it. Ofelia Durán Cubillo has contributed a master's thesis containing an exhaustive structural analysis of the same novel. There is also a brief discussion of the question of Rima's language in the novel in which the critic chides her for failing to adhere to local linguistic norms.

In *Mujeres y agonías* Vallbona makes the important decision to employ a Costa Rican dialect. Luis Leal, in his prologue, praises her for "knowing how to elevate regional speech to an artistic level that allows her to write cosmopolitan narrative using the most recent techniques." Leal then continues with a brief discussion of her principal themes. Rocío Fernández de Ulibarri and Virginia Zúñiga Tristán have contributed two informative articles that appeared in the San Jose newspaper *La nación*. Fernández presents a general introduction to Rima's writings, stressing especially her use of fantastic motifs and themes. She also provides useful insight into her evolution from traditional structuring to more experimental modes. Zúñiga's article contains a relatively brief but substantive discussion of *Sombras* and its possible significance within Costa Rican culture.

Cida S. Chase provides an analysis of the feminine perspective in several stories of *Polvo del camino* and *Mujeres y agonías,* including "Caña hueca," "Con los muertos al cinto," "La cucaña del deseo," "Balada de un sueño," "El monstruo de las cosas," "Penélope en sus bodas de plata," "Parábola del Edén imposible," and "Alma-en-pena." Chase notes that the women of these works occupy a marginal and traditional position in society and that their concerns are those shared by all women everywhere. Noting that Vallbona prefers questioning to condemnation, she concludes by pointing out that all the stories convey general optimism regarding possible change in the world.

Lee Dowling offers an analytical essay on *Sombras* that probes the structural elements supporting the work's feminist perspective. A longer essay by the same critic is entitled "Rima de Vallbona: desafíos ideológicos y perspectivas de la narración en su obra literaria." Here the writer's development is examined through *Polvo del camino, Mujeres y agonías,* and *Sombras,* in an essay stressing Rima's gradual mastery of discourse as opposed to story. Dowling notes the writer's adept handling of point of view and her use of a ludic metaliterary perspective that combine to make *Sombras* a literary tour de force. As Rima de Vallbona increases her production, and as it becomes more widely known, additional attempts at substantive criticism will undoubtedly be forthcoming.

Bibliography

WORKS BY VALLBONA

Noche en vela (novel). San Jose: Editorial Costa Rica, 1968. 2d ed. San Jose: Editorial Fernández Lobo, 1978. 3d ed. Costa Rica: Editorial Estatal A Distancia, 1982.
Polvo del camino (stories). San Jose: Editorial Autores Unidos, 1971.
Yolanda Oreamuno (literary study). San Jose: Editorial del Ministerio de Cultura, 1972.
La salamandra rosada (short stories). Montevideo, Uruguay: Editorial Géminis, 1979.
La obra en prosa de Eunice Odio (literary study). San Jose: Editorial Costa Rica, 1981.
Mujeres y agonías (short stories). Houston: Arte Público Press, 1982.
Baraja de soledades (short stories). Barcelona: Ediciones Rondas, 1983.
Las sombras que perseguimos (novel). San Jose: Editorial Costa Rica, 1983.

WORKS ABOUT VALLBONA

Chase, Cida S. "El mundo femenino en Rima de Vallbona." *Revista Iberoamericana* Núms. 138–139 (1987): 403–18.
Decreus, Juliette. "Rima R. de Vallbona—Romancier du Costa Rica." *Fer de Lance* (France) 83 (July, August, and September 1973): 14–19.
Dowling, Lee. "Point of View in Rima de Vallbona's Novel *Las sombras que perseguimos.*" *Revista Chicano-Riqueña* 13, 1 (1985): 64–73.
———. "Rima de Vallbona: desafíos ideológicos y perspectivas de la narración en su obra literaria." *Letras* 11–12 (1986): 191–214.
Durán Cubillo, Ofelia. "Rasgos del relato moderno en el tiempo de *Noche en vela* de Rima de Vallbona." Thesis for the degree of *Licenciada* in Hispanic philosophy, University of Costa Rica, 1976.
Fernández de Ulibarri, Rocío. "Vallbona en el límite de lo real." *La nación* (San Jose), August 21, 1983.
González, Jézer. Prologue to *Noche en vela.*
Leal, Luis. Prologue to *Mujeres y agonías.*
Zúñiga Tristán, Virginia. "*Las sombras que perseguimos.*" *La nación* (San Jose), August 21, 1983.

LEE H. DOWLING

VEGA, ED (1936–   ). Ed Vega is a Puerto Rican fiction writer, the author of several books and numerous short stories, all of which have been written in English. The greater part of his works deals with life in the continental United States, most specifically with New York and its Hispanic community, through high satire.

Biography

Edgardo Vega Yunqué was born in Ponce, Puerto Rico, on May 20, 1936, where he lived until his family moved to The Bronx, New York, in 1949. He was raised in a devout Baptist home, his father having been a minister of that faith. In the introduction to his novel, *The Comeback,* Vega states how he felt deprived, because of the strictness of his faith, from being able to dance and to go to the movies, which led him to begin to write and compose his own film strips that he would show to neighborhood children inside of a huge crate in his backyard in Ponce. He also recounts that some of his early readings included Spanish translations of *A Thousand and One Nights, Treasure Island,* and *Swiss Family Robinson,* with beautiful illustrations that enthused him so much that he cut them up to be converted into film strips. All of this led eventually to his father banning his son's incipient cinematic career. This only led, however, to the young Vega beginning to write in earnest, in Spanish of course, and he discovered that writing was what he truly loved.

After moving to New York, his two first and important interests were learning English and learning sports, especially hockey. Here he also became an avid television watcher, after his mother had won a set in a local department store contest. During that time, as well as during the war years, Vega also learned of Hitler's persecution of the Jews and he became obsessed with prejudice and religious persecution. He soon became interested in the opposite sex and sports and no longer wrote, until the age of twenty.

After graduating from high school, he renewed his literary interest while in the Air Force by attempting to write a really pornographic book for his G.I. buddies. He failed miserably, becoming frustrated by his awkwardness as a writer. After being discharged from the service, Vega studied for two years under the G.I. Bill at Santa Monica College. While in California he met and subsequently got married to his wife Patricia, who was to become the mother of his four children. In 1963 Vega almost completed his studies at New York University, having majored in political science; however, he did not complete his last three requisite hours until 1969. His delay in finishing is ironic in that he was about to graduate as a Phi Beta Kappan, with a nomination for a Woodrow Wilson Fellowship. He had already been accepted into several Ph.D. programs. It seems, however, that he became disillusioned after personally experiencing racism from his dean; he thus set aside his plans to pursue a career in college teaching.

After leaving New York University in 1963, Vega worked until 1969 in a number of social services programs: as training director for Black Communities, Inc. (1964–1966); as director of the Addiction Services Agency of the City of New York (1966–1968); and as director of Young Adults University Settlement (1968–1969). In 1969, he returned to academic life as a lecturer for Hunter College and thereafter assumed various other lecturing and assistant professor positions at Hostos Community College, State University of New York at Old

Westbury, and Staten Island Community College until 1977. From 1977 until 1982, he worked with a number of community-based education programs, like Aspira of New Jersey and the After School Program, at times as an administrator and/or counselor, and at other times as a teacher of creative writing and English. Since 1982, with rather brief interruptions, he has been a freelance writer and has devoted himself to producing his literary works.

In 1977, Vega began to publish his short stories in commercial magazines like *Nuestro* and noncommercial literary magazines like *Revista Chicano-Riqueña*. He has also published a book of interrelated short stories, *Mendoza's Dreams* (1987), and a novel, *The Comeback* (1985), and has written or partially written seven as yet unpublished novels, some of which have been repeatedly rejected by the large, commercial publishing houses in New York. Included among these are *Owlsong*, an 800-page generational novel based on his family history; *A Brief History of the Przewalski*, a science fiction love story; *Cartagena*, another generational novel which in its later chapters deals with the Vietnam War and with Puerto Rican revolutionary groups in New York; *Hole*, a sports novel; *Sacrifice*, a baseball novel, baseball being the central metaphor for male aggression against women; *Dhread*, a satire of pornography, with a penis as the central character; and *Shopful of Stars*, which follows two derelicts on an odyssey through New York.

Today, Vega resides in Spanish Harlem with his wife, Patricia, a systems analyst, his children having grown and left home. The whole family has converted to Buddhism of Nichiren Daishonin. In July of 1986 Vega and Patricia became grandparents.

One of Vega's first successful projects, "The Kite," a short story first published in *Revista Chicano-Riqueña* in 1980, was optioned by The American Playhouse of the Corporation for Public Broadcasting and went through several screenplay rewrites by Vega himself, but never made it to final production. Another story idea, "Tony's Kitty," was sold to "Oye, Willie," another C.P.B. series, and met a similar fate. His two published books and several promotional tours were produced by Arte Publico Press of the University of Houston, with support by the National Endowment for the Arts. Although Vega's work is well known within the Puerto Rican communities, to date it has received only one major review, this in *Kirkus*.

Major Themes

Ed Vega is probably the most literary of the New York Puerto Rican writers, consciously and purposefully advancing a literature that draws from both the Spanish- and English-language traditions. At all times Vega establishes a transparent relationship between his narrators and characters that clearly reveals a writer-creator at work. In *Mendoza's Dreams*, in fact, his surrogate narrator, Mendoza, casts himself as the official chronicler of "the people's," i.e., Puerto Ricans', lives and, more than that, he is a type of magician-creator who can make their dreams possible. In *The Comeback*, Vega borrows outright from

Miguel de Unamuno, not only in his highly literary introduction to what he calls his MICKEY—as Unamuno introduced his own *Nivolas* rather than *novelas*—but he also arranges for his protagonist to visit his creator, Ed Vega the novelist, in chapter 32, and strikes a deal with him to ensure the outcome of the book. Add to this, obvious influences from Cervantes in the chapter summaries of *The Comeback*, recasts of tales from Boccaccio and Bernard Malamud in *Mendoza's Dreams*, and *The Comeback*'s direct satire of the genre of ethnic autobiography in American letters, and we have a picture of a writer who has carved out a niche for himself in the evolution of Western literature and is consciously advancing art by making of his works at times a commentary on literature past and present. Within the range of literary themes, styles, and genres, most attractive to Vega are, obviously, (1) ethnic autobiography and the general, ever-present Horatio Alger-American Dream genre; (2) the rambling, linear narrative of at times Byzantine complexity, as found in Cervantes and most certainly in nineteenth-century English, American, and Russian fiction; and (3) high satire.

Of central interest to Vega in his narratives are individual lives, lives as the substance and structure for fiction. Thus many of his stories and novels are biographical in nature, even extending into charting the evolution of families across generations. Vega's works are a virtual portrait gallery, both serious, as in "Felicia Contreras de Manzanet" (an excerpt from *Owlsong*) and "The Kite," and satirized, as in "Mercury Gomez" and "The True Story behind the Writing of the Conquest of Fructifera Soto" from *Mendoza's Dreams*, and, of course, *The Comeback*. Within that broad range of biography, Vega as a Puerto Rican has been bombarded since beginning his writing career with the American ethnic autobiography as cultivated by the children of European immigrants or by black and Hispanic minority writers. And he has been expected to follow that canon as the long-established entry for outsiders to official "American" culture. In the introduction to *The Comeback* he states, "I was going to be expected to write one of those great American immigrant stories, like *Studs Lonigan, Call It Sleep*, or *Father*, which was written by Charles Calitri, one of my English teachers at Benjamin Franklin High School. Or maybe I'd have to write something like *Manchild in the Promised Land*, or a Piri *Thomas *Down These Mean Streets* . . ." But "It is . . . repulsive for me to write an autobiographical novel about being an immigrant. In fact, I don't like ethnic literature, except when the language is so good that you forget about the ethnic writing it."

Vega has become the satirist of the ethnic autobiography, even while obsessed with the Horatio Alger formula that his characters in *Mendoza's Dreams*, like Mayonesa Peralta and Mercury Gomez, seem to illustrate. It is in *The Comeback*, more than anywhere else, that Vega attempts to bury the ethnic autobiography and to satirize the classic identity crisis. He does that by creating a confused protagonist whose background is a fanciful amalgam of central European and Native American lineages and who adopts the disguise of a young Puerto Rican ice hockey player. While the central character suffers a breakdown and is treated by a comic Freudian psychiatrist for his crisis in identity—he is encouraged to be a proud Puerto Rican—this Eskimo Gypsy cum Puerto Rican athlete and revolutionary eventually rises above divisive nationalism and ethnicity.

It is in *Mendoza's Dreams* that Vega's obsession for biography, albeit at times satirized, truly dominates. Of the seven long and tall tales written or "documented" by Mendoza, five of them are biographical in nature, tracing the climb of a black Puerto Rican messenger boy to communications magnate, in " Mercury Gomez"; the tragic tale of a sculptor frustrated in love and art in "Mayonesa Peralta"; the angst of a middle-class, middle-aged Puerto Rican New Yorker who realizes his mixed marriage is a dead end in "Sometimes If You Listen Closely, You Can Hear Crying in the Zoo"; the life of a circus clown and his eventual seduction of a nun in "The True Story behind the Writing of the Conquest of Fructífera Soto"; and the comic misadventures of a Puerto Rican grocer whose escaped goat leads him to love and riches, in "The Pursuit of Happiness."

This and the other stories of *Mendoza's Dreams* are narrated in a humorous and detached manner by the gentlemanly Mendoza, who is sharing with the reader the lives that he has observed in the barrio, the lives that he in part determines and creates. Intense humanity, broad comprehension, and love temper the satire and at times slapstick comedy.

Survey of Criticism

As yet the critics have neither discovered nor commented on Vega's works extensively, with four exceptions. Dave Oliphant, writing about "The Kite" in the *Pawn Review*, found it "sophisticated" and "satisfying." *Kirkus Reviews* stated of *Mendoza's Dreams*, "In all, well written, affecting—despite Vega's clowning—gritty tales of El Barrio life: reality beginning in dreams." David Ballard, while favorably comparing Vega to Gabriel García Márquez and Julio Cortázar, concludes that *Mendoza's Dreams* lacks seriousness, that it "could have been a more complete—and socially responsible—piece of literature if Vega had lifted the thin veil of comedy long enough for us to get a good look at the tragedy lying underneath." Rebecca Bell also compares Vega to the South American magic realists, but found *Mendoza's Dreams* very convincing in narrative technique and content. As Vega's works become better known, perhaps when a major publisher issues them, he is sure to attract the attention that he merits.

Bibliography

WORKS BY VEGA

"Horns." *Nuestro*. 3,6 (August 1979): 31–34.
"Back by Popular Demand." *Maize* 3, 1–2 (Fall-Winter 1979–1980): 16–22.
"The Kite." *Revista Chicano-Riqueña* 8, 1 (Winter 1980): 1–24.
"Spanish Roulette." *Revista Chicano-Riqueña* 7, 2 (Spring 1980): 22–31.

"An Apology to the Moon Furies." *Hispanics in the United States: An Anthology of Creative Literature,* ed. Gary D. Keller and Francisco Jimenez. Ypsilanti, Mich.: The Bilingual Press, 1980.

"Felicia Contreras de Manzanet." *A Decade of Hispanic Literature,* an anthology edited by Nicolás Kanellos. Houston: Arte Publico Press, 1982.

The Comeback. Houston: Arte Publico Press, 1985.

"Mayonesa Peralta." *Americas Review* 14, 3–4 (Summer-Fall 1986): 19–28.

Mendoza's Dreams. Houston: Arte Publico Press, 1987.

WORKS ABOUT VEGA

Ballard, David. "Nonviolent Life in Spanish Harlem. *Mendoza's Dreams.*" *San Francisco Chronicle,* May 17, 1987.

Bell, Rebecca. *"Mendoza's Dreams." Short Story Review* 4, 4 (Fall 1987): 12.

Kanellos, Nicolás. "Puerto Rican Literature from the Diaspora to the Mainstream." *American Book Review* 7, 1 (November-December 1984):16–17.

"Mendoza's Dreams." Kirkus Reviews. February 15, 1987.

Oliphant, Dave. "The Development of U.S. Hispanic Literature." *Pawn Review* 7, 3 (1983): 95–100.

NICOLÁS KANELLOS

VÉLEZ, CLEMENTE SOTO. *See* SOTO VÉLEZ, CLEMENTE.

Bibliography

Abella, Rosa. "Bibliografía de la novela publicada en Cuba y en el extranjero por cubanos desde 1959 hasta 1965." *Revista Iberoamericana* 32, 62 (June-December 1966): 307–18.

Algarín, Miguel. "Volume and Value of the Breath in Poetry." *Revista Chicano-Riqueña* 6, 3 (Summer 1978): 52–69.

Algarín, Miguel, and Miguel Piñero, eds. *Nuyorican Poetry: An Anthology of Puerto Rican Words and Feelings*. New York: William Morrow, 1975.

Armas, José R. de, and Charles W. Steele, eds. *Cuba, Consciousness in Literature*. Miami: Ediciones Universal, 1978.

Babín, María Teresa. *Panorama de la cultura puertorriqueña*. New York: Las Américas Publishing Co., 1958.

———. *The Puerto Ricans' Spirit: Their History, Life, and Culture*. New York: Collier Macmillan, 1971.

Babín, María Teresa, and Stan Steiner, eds. *Borinquen: An Anthology of Puerto Rican Literature*. New York: Vintage Books, 1974.

Barradas, Efraín, and Rafael Rodríguez, eds. *Herejes y mitificadores: Muestra de poesía puertorriqueña en los Estados Unidos*. Río Piedras, P.R.: Ediciones Huracán, 1980.

Cabrera, Francisco Manrique. *Historia de la literatura puertorriqueña*. Río Piedras, P.R.: Editorial Cultural, 1969.

Casal, Lourdes. "The Cuban Novel, 1959–1970: An Annotated Bibliography." *Abraxas* 1, 1 (Fall 1970): 77–92.

———. "A Bibliography of Cuban Creative Literature, 1959–1971." *Cuban Studies Newsletter* 2, 2 (June 1972): 1–29.

Catalog of the Cuban and Caribbean Library. 6 vols. Coral Gables, Fla.: University of Miami Press, 1977.

Delgado, Aníbal. "Sociedad e ideología en el teatro contemporáneo puertorriqueño." Ph.D. diss., University of Pittsburgh, 1983.

Fernández, José B. "Salient Themes in the Cuban-American Narrative." *Chasqui* 6 (May 1977): 76–83.

Fernández, José B., and Roberto G. Fernández. *Bibliographical Index of Cuban Authors (Diaspora 1959–1979).* Miami: Ediciones Universal, 1983.

Fernández, Roberto. *El cuento cubano del exilio.* Ph.D. diss., Florida State University, 1977.

Fernández Vásquez, Antonio. *Novelística cubana de la revolución.* Miami: Ediciones Universal, 1979.

Flores, Juan, John Attinasi, and Pedro Pedraza. *"La Carreta Made a U-Turn*: Puerto Rican Language and Culture in the United States." *Daedalus* 110, 2 (1981): 193–217.

Géigel y Zenón, José, and Abelardo Morales Ferrer. *Bibliografía puertorriqueña.* Barcelona: Editorial Araluce, 1934.

Gutiérrez de la Solana, Alberto. "La novela cubana escrita fuera de Cuba." *Anales de la literatura hispanoamericana* 2–3 (1973–1974): 167–89.

———. *Investigación y crítica literaria y lingüística cubana.* New York: Senda Nueva de Ediciones, 1978.

Hernández Mijares, Julio. "The Cuban Short Story in Exile: A Selected Bibliography." *Hispania* 54, 2 (1971): 384–85.

Hill, Marnesba D., and Harold B. Schleifer. *Puerto Rican Authors: A Bibliographic Handbook.* Metuchen, N.J.: The Scarecrow Press, 1974.

Holte, James Craig. "The Representative Voice: Autobiography and the Ethnic Experience." *Melus* 9 (Summer 1982): 25–46.

Kanellos, Nicolás. "Fifty Years of Theatre in the Latino Communities of Northwest Indiana." *Aztlán* 7, 2 (Summer 1976): 255–65.

Kanellos, Nicolás, ed. *A Decade of Hispanic Literature: An Anniversary Anthology.* Houston: Arte Publico Press, 1982.

Kanellos, Nicolás, ed. *Hispanic Theatre in the United States.* Houston: Arte Publico Press, 1984.

Kanellos, Nicolás, "Puerto Rican Literature from the Diaspora to the Mainstream." *American Book Review* 7, 1 (November-December 1984): 16–17.

Kanellos, Nicolás. "Nuyorican Writing and Beyond: American Academic and Latino Writers." *Contact I* 6, 34–35 (Winter-Spring 1984–1985): 21–23.

Kanellos, Nicolás. "Canto y Declamación en la Poesía Nuyoriqueña." *La Confluencia* 1, 1 (1986): 102–6.

Kanellos, Nicolás. "Towards a History of Hispanic Literature in the United States." *Images and Identities: The Puerto Rican in Literature,* ed. Asela Rodríguez de Laguna. New Brunswick, N.J.: Transaction Books, 1987.

Kanellos, Nicolás, and Jorgue Huerta, eds. *Nuevos Pasos: Chicano and Puerto Rican Drama.* Houston: Arte Publico Press, 1979.

Keller, Gary. "Toward a Stylistic Analysis of Bilingual Texts: From Ernest Hemingway to Contemporary Boricua and Chicano Literature." *The Analysis of Hispanic Texts: Current Trends in Methodology.* Mary Ann Beck, Lisa E. Davis, José Hernández, Gary D. Keller and Isabel C. Taran, eds. New York: Bilingual Press, 1976.

Language Policy Task Force. *Language Policy and the Puerto Rican Community.* New York: Centro de Estudios Puertorriqueños, CUNY, 1979.

López, Adalberto. "Literature for the Puerto Rican Diaspora." *Caribbean Review* 5, 2 (1973): 5–11.

————. "Literature for the Puerto Rican Diaspora II." *Caribbean Review* 6, 4 (1973): 41–46.

Matilla, Alfredo, and Iván Silén, eds. *The Puerto Rican Poets/Los Poetas Puertorriqueños.* New York: Bantam, 1972.

Menton, Seymour. *Prose Fiction of the Cuban Revolution.* Austin: University of Texas Press, 1975.

Mohr, Eugene V. "Fifty Years of Puerto Rican Literature in English—1923–1973: An Annotated Bibliography." *Revista/Review Interamericana* 3, 3 (1973): 290–98.

————. *The Nuyorican Experience: Literature of the Puerto Rican Minority.* Westport, Conn.: Greenwood Press, 1982.

Montes Huidobro, Matías. *Persona, vida y máscara en el teatro cubano.* Madrid: Editorial Playor, 1973.

Montes Huidobro, Matías, and Yara González. *Bibliografía crítica de la poesía cubana* (Exilio: 1959–1971). Madrid: Editorial Playor, 1973.

Mora, Gabriela. "Crítica feminista: apuntes sobre definiciones y problemas." *Theory and Practice of Feminist Literary Criticism.* Ypsilanti, Mich.: Bilingual Press, 1982.

Morfi, Angelina. *Historia crítica de un siglo de teatro puertorriqueño.* San Juan: Instituto de Cultura Puertorriqueña, 1980.

Morton, Carlos. "Nuyoricans (New York and Puerto Ricans)." *Latin American Theatre Review* 10 (1976): 80–89.

Perrier, Joseph Louis. *Bibliografía dramática cubana, incluye a Puerto Rico y Santo Domingo.* New York: The Phos Press, 1926.

Phillips, Jordan B. *Contemporary Trends in the Puerto Rican Theatre.* Madrid: Plaza Mayor, 1972.

Ramírez de Arellano, Diana. *La cultura en el panorama puertorriqueño de Nueva York.* New York: n.p., 1964.

Rivera de Alvarez, Josefina. *Diccionario de la literatura puertorriqueña.* 2 vols. San Juan, P.R.: Instituto de Cultura Puertorriqueña, 1970 and 1974.

————. *Literatura puertorriqueña: su proceso en el tiempo.* Madrid: Ediciones Partenón, 1983.

Rodríguez de Laguna, Asela, ed. *Images and Identities: The Puerto Rican in Literature.* New Brunswick, N.J.: Transaction Books, 1987.

Ruiz del Viso, Hortensia. "Poesía cubana de la rebeldía: Poetas del encierro, poetas del exilio." *Folio* 16 (December 1984): 58–68.

Sánchez, Luis Rafael. "Literatura puertorriqueña y realidad colonial." *Claridad* (Suplemento en Rojo) November 30, 1974: 14–15.

Sánchez-Boudy, José. *Historia de la literatura cubana en el exilio.* Vol. 1. Miami: Ediciones Universal, 1975.

Turner, Faythe. "The Evolution of Mainland Puerto Rican Writers." *World Literature Written in English* (Spring 1980): 74–84.

Vivó, Paquita. *The Puerto Ricans: An Annotated Bibliography.* New York: R. R. Bowker, 1973.

Watson-Espener, Maida. "Observaciones sobre el teatro chicano, nuyorriqueño y cubano en los Estados Unidos." *Revista Bilingüe/Bilingual Review* 5 (1978): 120–32.

Zavala, Iris M., and Rafael Rodríguez, eds. *The Intellectual Roots of Independence: An Anthology of Puerto Rican Political Essays.* New York: Monthly Review Press, 1980.

Index

Italicized page numbers refer to complete entries.

Contributors

RAMÓN LUIS ACEVEDO is professor at the Center for Advanced Studies of Puerto Rico and the Caribbean at the University of Puerto Rico. He is the author of books and articles on Puerto Rican and Central American literature, including *Augusto D'Halmar: novelista* (Río Piedras: Editorial Universitaria, 1976), *La novela centroamericana* (Río Piedras: Editorial Universitaria, 1982), and *Antología general de la poesía puertorriqueña* (Hato Rey, Puerto Rico: Boriken Libros, 1982).

WOLFGANG BINDER is professor of English and American studies at Erlangen, West Germany. He is the author of numerous books and anthologies on Hispanic, black, and Caribbean literatures, including *"Anglos Are Weird People for Me." Interviews with Chicanos and Puerto Ricans* (Berlin, 1979), *Partial Autobiographies. Interviews with Twenty Chicano Poets* (Erlangen, 1985), and *Contemporary Chicano Poetry. An Anthology* (Erlangen, 1986).

EDITH BLICKSILVER is associate professor of literature in the English Department of the Georgia Institute of Technology. She is first vice president of the College English Association and an executive board member of the Society for the Study of the Multi-Ethnic Literature of the United States. She is author of numerous articles in such publications as *The Ethnic American Woman: Problems, Protests and Lifestyles* (Dubuque Iowa: Kendall/Hunt, 1978), *Women's Studies International Forum,* and *The Southwest Review.*

SILVIA BURUNAT is associate professor of Spanish at the City College of New York, CUNY. She is the author of various books and numerous articles on Spanish and Cuban American literature and linguistics, including *Nuevas voces hispanas* (with Julio Burunat. New York: Holt, 1984) and *Veinte años de literatura cubanoamericana* (with Ofelia García. Tempe, Ariz.: Bilingual Review Press, 1987).

RODOLFO J. CORTINA is the director of the Center for Multilingual and Multicultural Studies at Florida International University. He is the author of books on Vicente Blasco Ibáñez, Federico García Lorca, and Hispanic writers in Wisconsin.

LETICIA DÍAZ is assistant professor of Spanish at Illinois State University in Normal.

LEE H. DOWLING is associate professor in the Department of Hispanic and Classical Languages of the University of Houston. She is the author of numerous articles on Spanish American literature in such publications as *Hispania, Language and Style* and *The Americas Review*.

JUAN ARMANDO EPPLE is associate professor of romance languages at the University of Oregon. He is the author of books on Chilean literature, including *Cruzando la cordillera. El cuento chileno 1973–1983* (Mexico: SEP—Casa de Chile, 1986) and *Para una fundación imaginaria de Chile. La literatura de Fernando Alegría* (Lima: Latinoamericana Editores, 1987).

JOSÉ ESCARPENTER is associate professor in the Department of Foreign Languages at Auburn University. He is the author of numerous articles on Cuban theatre and is active in theatre in Miami.

JOSÉ B. FERNÁNDEZ is professor of history and foreign languages at the University of Central Florida. He is the author of books on the Hispanic explorers of North America and on Cuban and Hispanic literature of the United States, including *Alvar Núñez Cabeza de Vaca: The Forgotten Chronicler* (Miami: Ediciones Universal, 1975), *Nuevos horizontes: cuentos chicanos, puertorriqueños y cubanos* (Boston: D. C. Heath and Company, 1982), and *Indice bibliográfico de autores cubanos. Diáspora, 1959–1979* (with Roberto Fernández. Miami: Ediciones Universal, 1983).

ROBERTO G. FERNÁNDEZ is associate professor of Spanish at Florida State University in Tallahasee. He is the author of articles on Spanish linguistics and Hispanic literature and is a prose fiction writer studied in this volume.

JULIA M. GALLARDO COLÓN is a lecturer in the Spanish department at Georgetown University.

OFELIA GARCÍA is assistant professor of education at the City University of New York. She is the author of articles on sociolinguistics, bilingualism, and bilingual education.

LINDA S. GLAZE is Associate Professor of Spanish at Auburn University.

LAVERNE GONZÁLEZ is associate professor of English at San Jose State University and the author of articles on Hispanic writing in New York.

LUIS F. GONZÁLEZ-CRUZ is professor of Spanish at the Pennsylvania State University at New Kensington. He is the author of books on Pablo Neruda, César Vallejo, Federico García Lorca, and Virgilio Piñera. He is also an accomplished poet who is studied in this volume.

YANIS GORDILS is assistant professor in Hispanic studies at the University of Puerto Rico at Cayey. She has published articles on Caribbean literature in such periodicals as *Areito, Cuban Studies,* and *Revista Chicano-Riqueña.*

HARVEY JOHNSON is professor emeritus of the Department of Hispanic and Classical Languages of the University of Houston. He is a pioneer of Hispanic studies in the United States and the author of numerous books on Spanish American literature.

NICOLÁS KANELLOS is professor of Hispanic and classical languages, University of Houston. He is the publisher of Arte Publico Press books and the *Americas Review* (formerly *Revista Chicano-Riqueña*) and also the author of books on U.S. Hispanic theater.

MANUEL MARTÍN-RODRÍGUEZ is a Ph.D. student at the University of California, Santa Barbara. He is the author of articles on U.S. Hispanic literature.

MATÍAS MONTES HUIDOBRO is professor of Spanish at the University of Hawaii and the author of articles on Puerto Rican writing in the United States. He is also an accomplished playwright and poet studied in this volume.

PATRICIA MOSIER is associate professor of Spanish at the University of Houston-Downtown. She is the book review editor for the *Americas Review* and the author of various articles and reviews of Spanish American literature.

EDWARD MULLEN is professor of Spanish at the University of Missouri and the author of books on Carlos Pellicer, Langston Hughes in the Hispanic world, and *The Life and Poems of a Cuban Slave: Juan Francisco Manzano 1797–1854* (Hamden, Conn.: Archon Books, 1981).

MARICELA OLIVA is an instructor at Houston Community College. She holds a master's degree in Spanish from the University of Houston.

SILVIA NOVO PENA is an instructor at the University of St. Thomas in Houston and is an editor of the *Catholic Herald*.

CHARLES PILDITCH is assistant professor of Spanish at Rutgers University-Newark.

MARÍA T. REDMON is assistant professor of Spanish at Central Florida University.

JAMES V. ROMANO is a graduate student in Spanish at the University of Minnesota. He is the author of a thesis on Clemente Soto Vélez and of *Poética de la población marginal: sensibilidades determinantes* (Minneapolis: Institute for the Study of Ideologies and Literature, 1987).

JOSÉ DAVID SALDÍVAR is assistant professor of English at the University of California, Santa Cruz. He is a member of the Commission on the Literatures and Languages of America of the Modern Language Association, author of articles on Chicano literature, and editor of the *Rolando Hinojosa Reader: Essays Historical and Critical* (Houston: Arte Publico Press, 1985).

LUCY TORRES is assistant professor of Spanish at Central Michigan University and author of articles on Puerto Rican literature and folklore. She is also the author of two books of poetry: *Desde estos aposentos míos* (Mexico City: Gráfica Panamericana, 1968) and *Mi libro—My Book* (Barcelona: Editorial Española, 1976).

FAYTHE TURNER is associate professor of humanities at Nichols College and the author of articles on mainland Puerto Rican literature.

LUZ MARÍA UMPIERRE is associate professor of Spanish at Rutgers University. She is the associate editor of *Third Woman* review and the author of *Nuevas aproximaciones críticas a la literatura puertorriqueña* (Río Piedras: Editorial Cultural, 1983). Her books of poetry include *En el país de las maravillas* (Bloomington In.: Third Woman Press, 1983), *. . . y otras desgracias / And Other Misfortunes* (Bloomington In.: Third Woman Press, 1985), and *The Margarita Poems* (Bloomington In.: Third Woman Press, 1987).

VICKY UNRUH is Assistant Professor of Spanish at the University of Kansas. She is the Associate Editor of the *Latin American Theatre Review* and has authored articles on theatre, narrative and the Latin American avant-garde.

RIMA DE VALLBONA is professor of Spanish at the University of St. Thomas, Houston, and is the author of articles and books on Costa Rican and Latin

American literature. She is an accomplished writer of prose fiction who is studied in this volume.

DIANA VÉLEZ is associate professor of Spanish at the University of Iowa. She is the author of articles on Hispanic women's literature.

MAIDA WATSON-ESPENER is associate professor of modern languages at Florida International University. She is the author of articles on Cuban exile theatre and two books: *El cuadro de costumbres en el Perú del siglo decimonónico* (Lima, Peru: Universidad Católica del Perú, 1980) and *Materiales para una historia del teatro en Colombia* (Bogota: Instituto Colombiano de Cultura, 1978).